Behind the Curtain

A Chilling Exposé of the Banking Industry

John Hamer

Behind the Curtain:
A Chilling Exposé of the Banking Industry
Volume 1

John Hamer

Paperback Edition First Published in Great Britain in 2016 by aSys Publishing

eBook Edition First Published in Great Britain in 2016 by aSys Publishing

Copyright © John Hamer 2016

John Hamer has asserted his rights under 'the Copyright Designs and Patents Act 1988' to be identified as the author of this work.

All rights reserved.

No part of this document may be reproduced or transmitted in any form or by any means, electronic, mechanical, photocopying, recording, or otherwise, without prior written permission of the Author.

ISBN: 978-1-910757-22-2
aSys Publishing 2016

This book is dedicated to all the other un-named, un-sung heroes who dedicate their lives to searching for the often elusive truth… sometimes against all odds and defying all attempts to silence them… wherever and whoever you may be.

Table of Contents

Acknowledgements..iii

Foreword..1

Introduction..3

Chapter 1
The Origins of Money and Banking 8

Chapter 2
The Rise of the Banksters 66

Chapter 3
The Bank that Robbed the World 103

Chapter 4
The Elite Money Power..160

Chapter 5
The British Royal Bankster Family 217

Chapter 6
Bankster War Crimes – World War I 264

Chapter 7
The Red, Zionist Menace 299

Chapter 8
The Depths of Depression 331

Chapter 9
World War II – The Problem 369

Chapter 10
World War II – The Reaction 409

Chapter 11
World War II – The (Final) Solution 486

Acknowledgements, Thanks and Dedication

The author would like to acknowledge and express his gratitude to all those dedicated researchers listed below, all of whose works have been an inspiration and in some cases a source for the information contained within this book.

To those of you who have been kind enough to communicate with me in person, I would like to add a special word of thanks. You know who you are!

In alphabetical order…

- Ken Adachi
- Gary Allen
- Markus Allen
- Max Alvarez
- Jon Lee Anderson
- Evan Andrews
- Robert J. Avrech
- Tomas Arbre
- Jonathan Azaziah
- James Bacque
- Russ Baker
- Marilyn Bardsley
- Ann Barnhardt
- David Barrett
- Kevin Barrett
- H. D. Baurmann
- Les Blough
- Shawn Boburg
- Christopher Bollyn

- Kerry Bolton
- Tony Bonn
- Michael Bradley
- Alcuin Bramerton
- Myra Bronstein
- Mae Brussell
- Mark Burdman
- Dan Calabrese
- Dr. Rebecca Carley
- Stephanie Caruana
- David J. Castello
- Anne-Sulvane Chassany
- Bill Christine
- Gregory C. Clark
- Ramsey Clark
- Jeff Cohen
- Dr. John Coleman
- Rupert Colley
- J.C. Collins
- Carol Cooper
- Chris Cooper
- William 'Bill' Cooper
- James Corbett
- Jim Craven
- Scott Creighton
- Sherman Debrosse
- Scott M. Deitche
- James Denver
- Laura Alyssa Devin
- Uri Dowbenko
- Gordon Duff
- Rory Ridley-Duff
- Deborah Dupre

- William Engdahl
- Rob Eshman
- Eliot Estep
- Mimi Eustis
- Chris Everard
- Myron C. Fagan
- Melvin Fairclough
- Ignacio Fernandez
- James Fetzer
- John Friend
- Eric Dubapeter Eyre
- Robert Faurisson
- Trowbridge Ford
- Don Fulsom
- Dean Garrison
- Phil Gasper
- John Taylor Gatto
- Joel Geier
- John Glaser
- Timothy Good
- Carol Anne Grayson
- Percy L. Greaves Jr.
- George Green
- Mackenzie J. Gregory
- G. Edward Griffin
- Laurent Guyenot
- Max Hadden
- Steven Hager
- Nicholas Hagger
- Anthony James Hall
- Greg Hallett
- Dr. David Halpin
- Ron T. Hansig

- Will Harney
- Bryan Harring
- Alan Hart
- John Haydon
- Chris Hedges
- Elisabeth Hellenbroich
- Dean Henderson
- Tom Heneghan
- Anthony John Hill (aka Mu'ad Dib)
- Andrew Carrington Hitchcock
- Dave Hodges
- David Irving
- Mike James
- Larry Jamison
- Nathan Janes
- Matthew D. Jarvie
- Phil Jayhan
- Peter Jukes
- John Kaminski
- Dr. Musahid Kamran
- Neturet Karta
- Bill Kaysing
- Don Keko
- John Kelin
- Mike King
- David M. Klotz
- Laura Knight-Jadczyk
- Judson Knight
- Nick Kollerstrom
- David Krajicek
- Dilip Kumar
- Ken Layne
- Martin A. Lee

- Vivian Lee
- Stephen Lendman
- Adam Letalik
- Clyde Lewis
- David Livingstone
- Grace Livingstone
- Tony Long
- Wayne Madsen
- Dr. Henry Makow
- Harry V. Martin
- Brandon Martinez
- Enver Masud
- Damien McElroy
- Patrick McGilligan
- Ray McGovern
- David McGowan
- Frank McNally
- Joan Mellen
- Thieray Meyssan
- Dr. Donald J. Miller Jr.
- Richard J. Miller
- Greg Mitchell
- Phil Mitchinson
- David Model
- Tracy Monger
- Robert Morrow
- Kathryn Mott
- Daniel P. Murphy
- Jim Naureckas
- John Nolte
- Brendan O'Neill
- Richard J. Ochs
- Judith Ora

- Mark Owen
- Andrew Padyk
- Vince Palamara
- Joseph A. Palermo
- Peter Papaherakles
- Suzi Parker
- Robert Parry
- Kenneth Parsons
- Lisa Pease
- Ben Pimlott
- Michael Collins Piper
- Jason Pipes
- Joe Quinn
- Jesselyn Radach
- Paolo Raimondi
- Justin Raimondo
- Alan Rankin
- Leslie Raphael
- Jon Rappoport
- David Richards
- Mike Ridley
- James Rinnovatore
- David Robb
- Bruce Roberts
- J. M. Roberts
- Paul Craig Roberts
- Walter Rodney
- Andrew Roberts
- Craig Roberts
- James M. Rockefeller
- Jennifer Rosenberg
- Germar Rudolf
- Jon Christian Ryter

- Adrian Salbuchi
- Rowan Scarborough
- Phil Schneider
- Ralph Schoenman
- Patrick Scrivener
- Anne Sebba
- Pat Shannan
- Adrian Shuker
- Lee Siegel
- John Simkin
- Jacqueline Simmons
- Vlada Sindjelic
- Joseph P. Skipper
- Sherman H. Skolnick
- Ashley Smith
- Norman Solomon
- Scott Speidel
- Saundra Spencer
- Deanna Spingola
- Richard Sprague
- T. Stokes (Anthony Thomas Trevor-Stokes)
- Jim Stone
- Kevin Alfred Strom
- Dr. Anthony C. Sutton
- Joan Swirsky
- Nicklaus Thomas-Symonds
- Darren Taylor
- Evan Thomas
- Scott Thompson
- Jim Tittle

- James Tracpierre Tristam
- James P. Tucker Jr.
- Brandon Turbeville
- Ajit Vadakayil
- Ahmad Validat
- Alexandra Valiente
- Joe Vialls
- Les Visible
- Guy Walters
- Harvey Wasserman
- Kristen Watts
- Gary Webb
- Stew Webb
- Mark Weber
- Frank Whalen
- Diana T. Whay
- David White
- John Delane Williams
- Lawrence Wright
- Peter Wright
- Caroline Yeager
- Eric Yosomono
- Peter Yost
- Daniel Zarzeczny
- Tess Zevenbergen

Foreword

"When plunder becomes a way of life for a group of men living together in society, they create for themselves, in the course of time, a legal system that authorises it and a moral code that glorifies it." Frédéric Bastiat

"Some people think the Federal Reserve Banks are US government institutions. They are not... they are private credit monopolies which prey upon the people of the US for the benefit of themselves and their foreign and domestic swindlers, and rich and predatory money lenders. The sack of the United States by the Fed is the greatest crime in history. Every effort has been made by the Fed to conceal its powers, but the truth is the Fed has usurped the government. It controls everything here and it controls all our foreign relations. It makes and breaks governments at will." Congressman Charles McFadden, Chairman, House Banking and Currency Committee, 10th June 1932

So, why *'Behind the Curtain?'*

December 1968 saw a landmark court case in the appropriately named township of Credit River, Minnesota, USA. *First National Bank of Montgomery vs. Daly* was an epic courtroom drama and although unsurprisingly, not widely reported either at the time or subsequently, is actually extremely significant.

Jerome Daly a lawyer by profession, defended himself against the bank's attempted foreclosure on his $14,000 mortgage on the grounds that there was no 'consideration' for the loan. 'Consideration' in legalese, refers to 'the item exchanged' and is an essential element of any legal contract. Daly contended that the bank offered 'no consideration' for his loan on the grounds that they had 'created the money out of thin air' by bookkeeping entry and had therefore not suffered a loss (another relevant point of law) by his refusal or inability to pay back the money.

The proceedings were recorded by Justice William Drexler, who had given no credence whatsoever to the defence, until Mr. Morgan, the bank's president, took to the witness stand. To Drexler's and indeed everyone else present's great surprise, Morgan casually admitted under questioning from Daly's lawyer, that the bank routinely 'created money out of thin air' for all its loans and mortgages and that this indeed was standard practice in all banks. Presiding Justice, Martin Mahoney declared that, *"It sounds exactly like fraud to me,"* accompanied by nods and murmurs of assent from all around the courtroom.

In his summation of the case, Justice Mahoney reported that... *"Plaintiff (the bank) admitted that it, in combination with the Federal Reserve Bank of Minneapolis, did create the entire $14,000.00 in money and credit upon its own books by bookkeeping entry. That this was the consideration used to support the Note dated May 8, 1964 and the Mortgage of the same date. The money and credit first came into existence **when they created it** [my own emphasis—JH.] Morgan admitted that no United States Law or Statute existed which* *gave him the right to do this. A lawful 'consideration'* **must** *exist and be tendered to support the Note."*

So, the court duly rejected the bank's claim for foreclosure and the defendant kept his house. The implications of this case therefore, should have been far-reaching. If bankers are indeed extending credit *without* consideration (which they most definitely are) i.e. without backing their loans with real money they actually have stored in their vaults and were entitled to lend, any judicial decision declaring their loans void, would topple the entire worldwide financial and banking system.

Jerome Daly subsequently wrote in a local news article; *"This decision, which is legally sound, has the effect of declaring all private mortgages on real and personal property, and all US and State bonds held by the Federal Reserve, National and State banks to be null and void. This amounts to an emancipation of this nation from personal, national and state debt purportedly owed to this banking system. Every American owes it to himself to study this decision very carefully . . . for upon it hangs the question of freedom or slavery."*

Perhaps needless to say, the decision utterly failed to change prevailing practice, even though it was never legally challenged or over-ruled. Justice Mahoney actually threatened to prosecute and expose the bank and as a result, somewhat unsurprisingly, he died less than six months after the Daly trial, in an extremely suspicious boating 'accident' and the subsequent autopsy revealed his body to have been full of some unspecified kind of poison. Beware anyone who stands in the way of these people and their nefarious practices.

Since this precedent, many other defendants have attempted to have mortgages and loans nullified using the same defence as Daly, but there has been extremely limited success only. In fact, one judge said, strictly 'off the record,' *"If I let you do that, you and everyone else, it would bring the whole banking system down. I cannot let you go behind the bar of the bank. . . . We are not going behind that curtain!"*

Well suffice to say dear reader, we certainly **are** going on a highly revealing trip **behind the curtain**, so strap-in and be prepared for the ride of your life as we investigate the sordid and murky history of the world of banking and high finance and the people who run it . . . with an iron fist encased in a velvet glove.

John Hamer, 2016.

Introduction

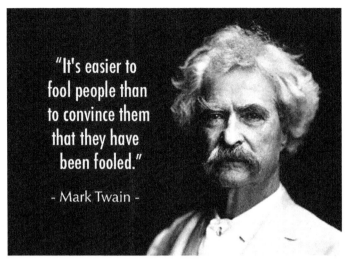

The purpose of this book is to demonstrate beyond all reasonable doubt that the root of all evil in this world is not money itself, as the popular saying would have us believe, but the very small group of people who control our money, credit, government, military, courts, media, industry, agriculture, healthcare, food, education and indeed, anything else of consequence. As incredible and absurd as it all may sound, I will present compelling evidence from the last three hundred years that will demonstrate how this whole diabolical long-term, covert plan has progressed, virtually without interference or detection and with the total co-operation of the highly complicit, mainstream media (TV, radio, and written press,) who are of course ultimately owned by the same entities as all the major banks and corporations.

Many of you, upon reading this book may be shocked by its contents. You may think that you know exactly how the world works and who controls it. If so, please allow me to introduce you to the real truth and make you fully aware of the crimes that the above group has perpetrated over the course of many centuries and even well beyond that, back into the mists of time.

All of us are surely aware by now that there is so much wrong with the world and that life today, for Joe and Josie Public has become more about surviving than living. We seem to constantly lurch from one crisis or major disaster to another; endless wars, rising prices, disappearing jobs and no matter which party is in 'power,' the rich always get richer and the poor get poorer. But more recently it seems, it is the so-called 'middle classes' that are being systematically victimised. The things that we long took for granted; cheap unadulterated and abundant, healthy food, plentiful and affordable food and water for all, social services and proper healthcare, the right to privacy, the right to criticise authority, freedom of speech, and to be presumed innocent until found guilty, are all ever more rapidly becoming distant memories.

Through all the 'civil' and 'world' wars, the endless conflicts, illegal invasions, famines, 'ethnic cleansings,' epidemics, natural disasters, mass-murders and all the unrest and misery, the one single group that has not just prospered from humanity's woes, but has actually done everything humanly possible to cause them and thereby benefit from them... is the 'Central Bankers,' the Elite, the Establishment. Some call them the Illuminati and yet others, the Satanic controllers of the world or the Jewish/Zionist/Freemasonic criminal cabal. Whatever name or label we apply to them, they are certainly the ultimate and most powerful criminal 'gang' the world has ever seen.

There are more than 7 billion people on this planet, but despite the popular myth that states that it is the so-called '1%' that control the remaining '99%,' in reality it is closer to less than one-thousandth of one per cent that firmly control the remaining 99.999% of us.

This book is my humble attempt to connect the dots that link together the crimes, including the wholesale waging of illegal wars that were all committed with a distinct pattern and a clear purpose, despite their outward appearance of having 'random' causes. The indictments against these dark forces are almost literally endless; mass-murder, genocide, high treason, assassination, conspiracy, grand theft, deception, fraud, drug-running, slavery, kidnapping, paedophilia, torture, money-laundering, environmental destruction on a massive scale plus much more. These are all disgraceful crimes against all of humanity and have been committed with impunity and with utter contempt and disregard for their fellow human beings and indeed all living entities, whilst being safe in their certain knowledge that they are immune from prosecution and until lately, even from identification as the ultimate perpetrators.

In order to deceive the world, they rely on the centuries of the instructed 'turning a blind eye' and lying deceptions of their controlled mass-media and of their institutionalised brainwashing and conditioning of us all, together with their deceptive, pervasive advertisements, contributions to charity and the arts and their fake patriotism. They also trust (and with good reason) that the general populace will believe that despite all their sordid dealings and convictions for illegal foreclosures, credit-fixing, massive over-charging, usury, money laundering, fraud and racketeering in the past, they could surely never be either evil or powerful enough to control the whole world and its destiny.

But, these entities loan us and our governments our own currency *at interest* and literally and fraudulently create money 'out of thin air.' They also own and control through their thousands of inter-connecting corporations all the gold, silver, diamonds, other precious metals, minerals, oil, drugs, food-production etc. and also control all the credit and fix all prices including all the financial markets, stocks, shares, bonds, securities, FOREX etc. It is also, maybe surprisingly to some, true to say that no-one can run for political office at ANY level without their endorsement.

"All great truth passes through three stages. First, it is ridiculed. Second, it is violently opposed. Third, it is accepted as being self-evident." Arthur Schopenhauer

This book will surely convince you of the greatest, if not the most vitally important truth of all which is that almost all of what we learned in school, in college and university, our history, economics, science, everything we were and still are 'spoon-fed' by the medical profession, the media and our so-called 'leaders,' indeed almost everything they instilled in us, is a total fantasy, a fairy story to keep us all asleep, unquestioning and obedient citizens. What school ever taught us that the paper money in our wallets and purses was loaned to our governments at interest by private international bankers and not generated by the governments of the countries in which we live—or even backed by any commodity of intrinsic value such as gold? What school ever enlightened us to the fact that these same bankers simultaneously financed the Nazis, the Communists, the left, the right, the centre, the 'Occupy' movement, the 9/11 Truth movement and every terrorist group you ever heard of, down the centuries and decades?

"Need I remind you again that every single dollar in this nation is now brought into existence—not as an honest store of wealth and measure of value for the goods and services created by the people—but as a debt to the bankers, most of whom are enemy aliens, to vacuum-up our wealth while creating nothing of value themselves? Need I remind you that all of our nation's taxes—all of them—now go directly to those bankers to pay them, forever, for money that they created out of thin air, by the stroke of a pen, as a part of the so-called 'National Debt,' and that all national public expenditure is now 'financed' by these same vampire-like alien financiers? No people in the thrall of such slavery could possibly be called free and independent. And no people has been more financially enslaved than the hapless Americans, most of whom don't even have the faintest clue about how their wealth and their future has been stolen from them—and most of whom wave the flag and cheer mindlessly as their own sons are sent to die in the sand to impose this same slavery on others. Americans, realistically viewed, are actually the opposite of a free and independent people." Kevin Alfred Strom, 4th July 2015

Nixon, Reagan, Thatcher, Clinton, Bush, Blair, Cameron, Obama, Churchill, Roosevelt, Stalin, Hitler et al were all financed and/or made electable and manoeuvered into position and controlled by people who profit from death and destruction and who regard the whole world as a 'pie' to be carved up and devoured by their own tiny clique. It was indeed these very same 'banksters' (banker-gangsters) who created many of our greatest so-called institutions of learning and funded and directed exactly what was to be written into our text books and educational curricula. Is it surprising at all then that your mind naturally tends to reject any other premise to the contrary?

"Who amongst us has not been fooled? We believe in our institutions, we love our country and respect our leaders." Mark Twain

We were all raised by our parents to respect and adhere to accepted moral values, to obey the law, work hard and prosper and to do our duty to our country when called upon. Our parents and grandparents, teachers, religious and community leaders, newspapers, radio, film and TV all taught us that 'good always triumphs over evil' and that virtue is its own reward. We were instructed to be good citizens, to respect our government and politicians, love our country, pay all our 'debts' and taxes and never question authority. The baby-boomer generation, of which your author is a member, growing up in the 1950s and 1960s, were instilled with an unshakeable air of pride and optimism for the future. *'You've never had it so good,'* we were told emphatically—yet deceptively.

But it is certainly not by accident that we see all the endless global conflicts and wars, stock market crashes and massive job losses. And it is also no coincidence that the banksters continue to enrich themselves to the detriment of us all, as everything else collapses around us. Think about it...who else could make money out of rising OR falling share prices or could place non-losable bets (with our money) and hope that crops fail and that planes crash and explode into skyscrapers? What research could predict what legislation would pass even before it is introduced or even heard of? And finally, who else could get governments (or more precisely you and I) to bail them out, in effect compensating them for robbing their own customers?

Those at the very top of the pyramid about to be exposed within these pages never go to jail or are ever indicted or even named. They hide in the shadows, protected by countless layers of flunkies, lawyers and ready-made patsies and if that is not enough, they control the legal system by utilising the same 'bribe and blackmail' policy as that with which they control the politicians, corporations, police and military.

When you, as they are, able to create unlimited money purely out of nothing, when you can buy-off or eliminate anyone that gets in your way, nothing that any of us mere mortals could do would be of the slightest consequence to them. They are **the** ultimate masters of deceit and deception in the way that they convince us to dutifully pay taxes that are optional, to fight wars that are illegal, to get away with poisoning our food, our environment and our minds—and if they are able to do this without us realising, then a reasonable question may well be 'what else are they capable of?'

It took the dedication and courage of a great many 'truth-seekers,' to uncover the evidence about to be presented to you no doubt, patriotic, empathetic and caring people from all walks of life and from all parts of the globe. Many of these brave souls are now no longer with us it is sad to say and as you begin to realise and comprehend the full extent and implications of what they have uncovered, the reasons for this should become all too apparent. Those among you who get your news from the free, alternative media will appreciate their efforts more than most, but of course as with the totally bankster-dominated mainstream media, you cannot believe all alternate media sources either as they, in part, have also been infiltrated, corrupted and compromised by the usual suspects too. There are plenty of reliable sources out there, but there is also plenty of 'dis-information' too unfortunately and it is not always easy to tell the difference, immediately.

Certainly, some people you long respected and maybe even regarded as role models will be herein exposed as traitors to their people and totally corrupt and there will be numerous unpleasant surprises and shocks within the pages of this book. You may feel more than just fooled as Mark Twain put it, you may even feel totally betrayed and experience more than just a little cognitive dissonance (see below.) Unfortunately this is nothing more or less than an unavoidable consequence of 'waking-up,' as it is popularly known, to the stark realities of this world.

Finally...the whole purpose of this book is to enlighten people as to what is really going on in the world today, by the examination of the events of the past and relating them to the present day situation. Unfortunately in doing so, there will inevitably be some who will be totally shocked and maybe even offended by some of the evidence presented.

That would be deeply regrettable as my sincere intention is to unite everyone in the search for the truth and not divide. Any 'finger-pointing' at the collective actions of any distinct 'group' racial, political or otherwise, is absolutely not intended to be offensive or disrespectful in any way. It is my sincere belief that all people of ***ALL*** races, colours, creeds and beliefs deserve respect and consideration of their views and should have the right to speak freely, live the lives they wish as long as it does no harm to others and also to believe whatever they wish. I also sincerely believe that 99.99% of people are inherently good, decent, and genuine, caring people but wherever evil abounds, whomsoever the perpetrators, I feel it is my moral obligation to expose it, no matter whom I may upset or offend in the process. The truth is always the truth, whomsoever it may upset.

The dangers of just dismissing all this as some looney 'conspiracy theory,' cannot be over-stated, but, if you prefer to be lied-to or feel a certain comfort in being told that everything is alright, that things are getting better...then without doubt, this book is not for you. However if you are able to judge the information and evidence presented, logically and with an open mind, then maybe, just maybe, between us all we can initiate an unstoppable momentum that will eventually change the world and make it a better place, if not for ourselves, then maybe for our children or perhaps even their children.

To truly understand what is going on in the world, it is vital that we begin to think for ourselves and not simply accept what we are told by the media in all its guises, but in order for this to happen we may well have to suspend our...

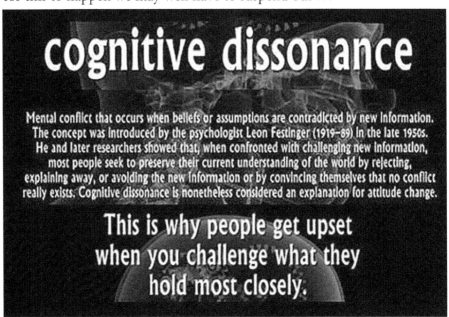

Chapter 1
The Origins of Money and Banking

'Usury' is today defined by the Oxford English Dictionary as... *"The action or practice of lending money at **unreasonably high rates of** interest."*

However, one of the most subtle forms of deception is the Orwellian re-defining of words or concepts to benefit those who rule over us and decide what we should and should not believe. Originally, 'usury' was actually *'The action or practice of lending money at interest,'* but it now appears to be expedient to add the four key, highlighted words above to that definition in order to maintain the desired illusion and to distract anyone seeking the truth from the actual reality.

In the beginning...

The term by which I will refer to those who control our everyday existence, the 'banksters,' is not a new one by any means. Even prior to all the public outrage of 'the too big to fail banks' of recent years, way back in the early 1930s an American immigrant, a Sicilian-born lawyer named Ferdinand Pecora, seems to be the original 'coiner' of the word. At the time he was the chief counsel to the US Senate Committee on Banking, probing the Wall Street Crash of 1929. The name 'banksters' caught on, particularly with 'anti-bankster' economists and combining the definition of a banker with that of a gangster is not only quite inspired, but totally accurate, at least for usage in polite company and for the purposes of this work. Despite the derogatory nickname, the crimes of even the most notorious bank robbers and murderers such as Bonnie and Clyde, John Dillinger, any serial killers you can mention and the infamous New York and Chicago gangsters of the 1920s, compared to those of the banksters are all absolutely trivial.

It is perhaps also important before we go any further to define more precisely who or what is meant by the term, 'bankster.' I do not mean to imply for example, that the lady next door who works as a senior clerk at the local HSBC branch is a 'bankster' and nor even do I mean the legions of middle management who tend to proliferate in great numbers in the banking industry. Similarly, the expensively 'suited and booted,' Aston Martin-driving senior banking executive who earns more in one week than most people earn in a year, but who nevertheless still takes his orders from on high, neither is he a 'bankster.' A 'banker' yes, but a 'bank**st**er'—most definitely not.

No, by this term I mean the usually faceless, major shareholders of the giant banking conglomerates, who often take no active part in the day-to-day running of the business, but remain anonymous, hidden in the shadows, whilst controlling and directing the banks' many insidious policies and taking-part in the ongoing deceptions and evil machinations about to be laid-bare in these pages. The self-styled, hereditary yet secret rulers of us all, who desire to control our every movement and our every thought in order to prevent us discovering their real agendas and despicable intentions for the entire human race, these are the 'banksters.' They control not only the 'strings' of the banks, but also either directly—or by proxy—most other corporations too.

It is a truism to state that the banksters are in a class all of their own. All the evil perpetrated by the so-called underworld, the Jewish Mob, the Sicilian/Italian Mafia, the Mexican/Columbian drug cartels, even the Stalinist, Maoist and Cambodian, Khmer Rouge purges of the twentieth century and various infamous individual mass-murderers or serial killers cannot even come close to matching the multitude of crimes against humanity committed by the banksters.

And it is not just simply financial fraud, foreclosures, artificially induced inflation, booms and depressions and stock-market crashes for their own materialistic ends, of which they stand accused. Amongst their many heinous crimes are also; mass murder, genocide . . . literally hundreds of millions if not billions of deaths. There also happens to be the far from trivial matters such as the brainwashing, deception, bribery and corruption of politicians, judges, law enforcement, military, scientists, educators, medical professionals, the covert 'ownership' of our governments, household-name corporations, the entire popular media and the enslavement of us all through illegally-created debt. These are just *some* of the charges and we should also consider the never-ending wars, conflicts, famines, routine assassinations of opponents, the poisoning of our food, artificially-induced diseases, the too-many-to-mention, deadly pharmaceutical drugs and the destruction of the environment and so on ad nauseum, in any complete list of the charges against the banksters.

Economists and all the financial 'talking heads' on TV and radio and the media in general, continually try and sell the public the idea that recessions or depressions (boom and bust) are a natural part of what they call the 'business, or economic cycle.' However, this is demonstrably NOT the case. Recessions and depressions only occur because the Central Bankers constantly manipulate the money supply upwards and downwards artificially and by design, in order to ensure that more and more ends-up in their hands and less and less in the hands of 'the people.'

Central Banks (the banksters) developed from the ancient 'money changers' and it is with these people that the indictment of modern day banksters begins . . .

In 48BCE (**B**efore the **C**hristian **E**ra) Julius Caesar rescinded the power to create coinage from the money changers and instead minted coins for the benefit of all the citizens of Rome and its burgeoning empire. With this new, now plentiful supply of money, he established many publicly beneficial projects and institutions and built many new houses and public buildings. By making money more plentiful and using it for the benefit of all instead of just a small exclusive clique, he thereby won the love and respect of the ordinary Roman people.

But unfortunately for him, the money changers despised him and swore bloody revenge on him and this eventually culminated in Caesar's assassination, ostensibly by Brutus and his senatorial co-conspirators, but whom in reality, were themselves in thrall to the money-changers. Then, immediately after the assassination the Roman money supply was reduced by 90 per cent, which immediately resulted in increased taxation and eventually in the loss of individuals' savings, lands and homes. Echoes of today in fact.

In the final year of the life of Jesus Christ around 33AD it is recorded in the bible that he utilised actual physical force to eject the 'money changers' from the temple.

When the Jews arrived in Jerusalem to pay their Temple tax, they were only allowed to pay it with a specific coin, a half-shekel and this was a small coin consisting of a half-ounce of pure silver. It was the only coin at that time which was pure silver and of assured weight, without the image of a pagan Emperor and therefore in the logic of the Jews at that time, it was the only coin acceptable to God.

Unfortunately, these coins were very scarce as the money changers had completely 'cornered the market' on them and so they were able to raise the price of them at will, to whatever value they deemed acceptable to themselves. They took advantage of the monopoly that they had on these coins to yield outrageous profits, thus forcing the Jewish populace to pay exorbitant prices for them.

In anger at this practice, Jesus then allegedly bodily ejected the money changers from the Temple as their monopoly on these coins totally violated the sanctity of God's house and its morality. But literally only days later, those money changers used their extreme wealth and thus power to demand the death of Jesus from Pontius Pilate, the Roman governor of Jerusalem at that time. We all know exactly what happened next.

By around 1000 AD, the money changers had gradually acquired control of medieval England's money supply and at this time they had become known, a little more respectably perhaps, as goldsmiths.

But, the story of our modern money really began in Renaissance Europe, around five hundred years ago. At that time the currency consisted mainly of gold and silver coinage, with no paper money. Gold coins of course were very durable and had intrinsic value in themselves (unlike paper currency,) but they were heavy, difficult to transport in large quantities and they were open to theft if not stored securely. As a result of this, the general population therefore deposited their coins with goldsmiths who had strong-rooms and safes in which to store the coins securely and without fear of theft. These goldsmiths issued paper receipts which could be redeemed at any time for the stated amount of gold and eventually these convenient receipts began to be traded themselves instead of the less than convenient, bulky coins they represented.

With the passage of time, the goldsmiths realised that only around 10% of these receipts were ever redeemed in gold at any one time and they could quite comfortably lend the gold in their possession, at interest, time after time as long as they ensured that they retained the 10% of the value of their outstanding loans in actual physical gold to meet any possible demand. By this process, paper money (notes/bills) which were in reality receipts for loans of gold, was born. Notes could now be issued and loans made in amounts that were up to ten times their actual gold holdings. At interest rates of 20%, the same gold could be lent 10 times over yielding a 200% return every year and this was backed by gold that did not even exist! Of course, the goldsmiths were careful not to over-extend themselves and thus became very wealthy at the expense of the rest of the populace without producing anything of intrinsic value.

Since only the principal was lent into the money supply, more money was eventually owed back in principal plus interest than the people as a whole, possessed. They had to continually take-out loans of new paper money to cover the shortfall, causing the wealth of the villages and towns and eventually that of the entire country to be diverted into the vaults of the goldsmiths, whose identity had by this time now become 'bankers,' whilst the country began to systematically drown in debt.

This then was the birth of the insidious system we now know as *'Fractional Reserve Banking'* which then as now, meant that the goldsmiths/banksters were able to make astronomical amounts of money by loaning-out what were essentially fraudulent receipts, as they represented gold that the goldsmiths did not even possess. As they gradually became more confident that their insidious 'game' would never be discovered, they would then loan-out up to ten times the amount they held in their depositories.

The goldsmiths also soon discovered that their control of this fraudulent money supply gave them total control over the economy and the assets of the people. They exacted their control by switching the economy between high and low volumes of 'currency' in circulation at any given time. The way they achieved this was to make money 'easier' to borrow thereby increasing the amount of money in circulation and then suddenly, without warning, limiting the money supply again, removing it from circulation by making loans more difficult to obtain or suspending the issuance of loans altogether.

Why did they do this? Simply because they knew that the result would be that a large percentage of their debtors would be unable to repay their loans and being denied the facility to take out new ones, they would then become 'bankrupt' and be forced to transfer their meagre assets to the goldsmiths for a small fraction of their true worth. Unsurprisingly, this is exactly what is happening in the world economy of today, but is deceptively referred to with such euphemisms as 'the economic cycle,' 'boom and bust,' 'recession,' and 'depression,' in order to bestow respectability upon and attribute pseudo, 'natural causes' to what is nothing more than a complete scam.

In the year 1100, King Henry I succeeded King William II to the throne of England. During his reign he decided to eradicate the power that the goldsmiths had over the people and this he achieved by creating a completely new form of money that took the form of a wooden stick. This stick was referred to as a 'tally stick,' and became the longest-lasting form of currency ever, lasting for more than 700 years until 1826 (even though other currencies came and went in that same period and sat alongside the tally sticks.)

Tally sticks

The tallies were sticks of polished wood around eight inches (20cm) long and had various sizes of notches cut into them, these cuts according to depth, angle and width indicated different currency amounts in pounds, shillings and pence, (£sd) the standard English currency of the day. The tally stick was then split lengthwise, providing each party with an identical transaction record and thus being counterfeit-proof because only the grain from the same stick would match the other half, providing a matched grain 'signature.' The King kept one half to protect against counterfeiting and the other half was introduced into the economy and circulated as money. This 'signature' was accepted as legal proof in courts for several hundred years.

It was also one of the most successful money systems in history as the King demanded that all taxes had to be paid in tally sticks too, so this increased their circulation and acceptance as a legitimate form of money. As a result, for many years, this system would be instrumental in keeping the power away from the 'money changers' in England.

England, from approximately the 13th to the late 17th century was a 'usury-free zone.' This was largely due to the fact that the economic system was based on the tally stick exchanges that ensured, more than anything else during this time period, a relatively prosperous society with full rights to self-determination. Economic prosperity depends very much upon a stable and plentiful supply of currency and what history has demonstrated repeatedly is that usury destroys economies, despite making the usurers themselves, extremely rich in the process. The Magna Carta ('Great Charter' of 1215AD) had its roots in a much older body of law that predates modern history and that body of law, both secular and ecclesiastical in nature, dealt in great detail with the problems, punishments and restrictions on usury.

Although coinage was in circulation during this period, it was totally inadequate as a means of exchange simply because there was simply not enough of it. The basis of the entire economy was the tally sticks that were the principal means of exchange from the 12th century onwards.

It is interesting to note that the tally sticks underwrote part of the stock of the Bank of England in 1694 and they were still in circulation in the early 19th century.

The name 'Guy Fawkes' is still infamous in Britain more than four centuries after the Gunpowder Plot of 1605, even though his alleged attempt to destroy the Houses of Parliament failed. But strange to say, almost no-one now remembers the Irishman Patrick Furlong who DID succeed in destroying the Houses of Parliament, albeit by accident.

There was no gunpowder involved on that occasion and no-one died. The agent of destruction was fire, started deliberately but innocently, in the furnaces beneath the House of Lords. But without intent to do so, Furlong and an accomplice achieved what Fawkes and his companions could not and thus by nightfall on 16th October 1834, the Palace of Westminster was left in ashes.

There were some important historical casualties besides the buildings themselves. Several 'official' measuring units, were completely destroyed including the imperial yard. Yet Furlong, ironically named after an imperial unit of measure himself, somehow escaped lasting opprobrium. Maybe his obscurity stems from the official embarrassment that surrounded the fire's origins as it began after all, during the disposal of a centuries-old accumulation of tally sticks, from the early days of taxation. The tally sticks were taking up space in the cellars of the parliament buildings and although some had already been distributed to the poor for firewood, there was a degree of political sensitivity about their past, when they had, after all, been the *de facto* currency. So the disposal was kept secret and 'in-house' but with palpably disastrous results.

In the 13th century, St. Thomas Aquinas the leading theologian of the Catholic Church argued that the charging of interest was wrong because it applies 'double charging,' i.e. charging for both the money and the *use* of the money. This concept followed the teachings of Aristotle that decreed that the purpose of money was to serve the members of society and to facilitate the exchange of goods needed to lead a virtuous life. Interest was contrary to reason and justice because it put an unnecessary burden on the use of money.

Thus, Christian law in Middle Ages Europe forbade the charging of interest on loans and even made a crime of what it referred to as 'usury.' (Note that this is the correct, original definition of usury and not the distorted, contrived, Orwellian one we use today.)

However this did not last too long as the tyrant, King Henry VIII eventually began to relax the laws regarding usury and true to form, the goldsmiths did not hesitate to re-assert themselves again as the de facto, unofficial controllers of the economy. It is interesting to note that under Henry VIII the Church of England had departed from Rome and Roman Catholicism, whose Church law at that time prevented the charging of interest on money and the goldsmiths soon took advantage of this fact and began taking steps to make their gold and silver coin system dominant once again.

After the death of Henry and his successor, his only son Edward VI who died before attaining the age of majority, the line of succession brought Edward's elder half-sister Mary, the daughter of Henry and Katherine of Aragon to the English throne (apart from a brief nine-day sojourn where Lady Jane Grey had been crowned Queen Jane, largely against her will and then summarily executed for treason.) But throughout all the religious turbulence and persecutions of the 1530s, 1540s and 1550s, Mary had remained a staunch Roman Catholic in the face of great pressure to convert to the new 'Protestant' religion. However, once her reign had become established she began to re-introduce the usury laws again. The money changers of course were not at all impressed and in revenge they tightened the money supply by hoarding gold and silver coins thus causing the economy to plunge into a downward spiral, as was their intent.

Then Mary died childless, leaving her Protestant half—sister Elizabeth, daughter of Anne Boleyn, as Queen. During her reign, Elizabeth decided that in order to maintain control of the money supply, she would have to issue her own gold and silver coins. This she achieved through the public treasury and successfully wrested control of the money supply back from the banksters. This would be a mere short-lived inconvenience for the goldsmiths / banksters however, albeit they had to wait around ninety years after Elizabeth's death to see their long-term scheme come to permanent fruition.

Firstly, in 1609, six years after Elizabeth's death, the banksters, for such they had now most definitely become, established the first central bank in history in Amsterdam in the Netherlands (Holland.) This was the beginning of their world financial takeover and although it began slowly the momentum would soon gather pace until the entire world (with a few small exceptions, as we will see) was completely under their influence.

Before we consider the next phase of the banksters' plot, we firstly need to travel backwards in time once again, to 1290 and the 'Edict of Expulsion' issued by **King Edward I,** which expelled all Jews forever from England and decreed that any who remained after 1st November 1290, were to be executed. Indeed England was far from the first nor by any stretch the last, country to expel the Jews for reasons of their propensity for usury, the lending of money at interest and which at the time was totally contrary to the fundamental tenets of Christianity.

Here is a partial list of all the countries and provinces from which the Jews have been banished, sometimes on multiple occasions, over the last one thousand years.

Expulsions of Jews from European States		
Mainz, 1012	Upper Bavaria, 1442	Naples, 1533
France, 1182	Netherlands, 1444	Italy, 1540
Upper Bavaria, 1276	Brandenburg, 1446	Naples, 1541
England, 1290	Mainz 1462	Prague, 1541
France, 1306	Mainz, 1483	Genoa, 1550
France, 1322	Warsaw, 1483	Bavaria, 1551
Saxony, 1349	Spain, 1492	Prague, 1557
Hungary, 1360	Italy, 1492	Papal States, 1569
Belgium, 1370	Lithuania, 1495	Hungary 1582
Slovakia, 1380	Portugal, 1496	Hamburg, 1649
France, 1394	Naples, 1496	Vienna, 1669
Austria, 1420	Navarre, 1498	Slovakia, 1744
Lyons, 1420	Nuremberg, 1498	Moravia, 1744
Cologne, 1424	Brandenburg, 1510	Bohemia, 1744
Mainz, 1438	Prussia, 1510	Moscow, 1891
Augsburg, 1439	Genoa, 1515	

The banishment of the Jews from England in 1290 remained in force for more than 350 years until a certain Oliver Cromwell appeared on the scene. Unknown to most and certainly not recorded in any mainstream histories, Cromwell was in fact bribed and financed by the Jewish banksters of Amsterdam for the purposes of fomenting a 'revolution' in England, and thus allowing them to take control of the money system in England.

"It was fated that England should be the first of a series of Revolutions, which is not yet finished." Isaac Disraeli, father of Benjamin Disraeli, the future British Prime Minister, speaking in 1851.

In London in the latter years of the decade of the 1630s, immediately prior to the English Revolution now more expediently known as the 'English Civil War,' there were many minor, armed uprisings of the 'people,' usually involving the same ringleaders and *'agents provocateurs,'* as is often the case today. These armed mobs caused panic and fear in the streets wherever they went, including the sometimes violent intimidation they inflicted upon members of both houses of Parliament. This in fact was a very similar modus operandus as that employed by the 'Sacred Bands' and the 'Marseillaise' of the French revolution 150 years later. Indeed, the striking similarities between the two events are most noteworthy.

Within the pages of works such as the '*Jewish Encyclopaedia*' and '*The Jews and Modern Capitalism,*' it is possible to discern that at this time, Oliver Cromwell, the prime-mover behind the English Civil War was in constant contact with and actually being financed by the powerful Jewish/Dutch banksters behind the Bank of Amsterdam scam that in effect usurped the control of currency issuance from the Dutch government in the early seventeenth century. Through such figures as Manasseh ben Israel and Fernandez Carvajal, both prominent Jews of the times, the whole of the English Revolution was funded. Carvajal himself was the paymaster of the entire 'New Model Army' or the 'Roundheads,' as Cromwell's fighting forces were disparagingly named as a direct result of the round metal helmets they wore.

In January 1642, the attempted arrest of five Members of Parliament had led to even more extreme mob violence and subsequently to the King and the royal family leaving their palace at Whitehall for security reasons. The five MPs backed by the mobs returned in triumph to Westminster and thus was the stage now set for the Jews to make their moves using none other than Cromwell himself to front their movement.

"1643 brought a large contingent of Jews to England; their rallying point was the house of the Portuguese Ambassador de Souza, a Marrano Jew. Prominent among them was Fernandez Carvajal, a great financier and army contractor." Excerpt from '*The Jews of England.*'

The actual bloodshed and open warfare between the two factions began in earnest at the Battle of Edgehill, Warwickshire later that year in 1642 where a contingent of Royalist troops commanded by Prince Rupert, a nephew of King Charles, fought against a Parliamentary army commanded by Cromwell. The outcome of this battle was totally inconclusive, both sides subsequently claiming victory and over the course of the next several years, a series of major battles and minor skirmishes took place at such locations as for example, Marston Moor, Oxford, Worcester, Newbury and finally Naseby amidst much bloodshed in an ongoing conflict that often pitted father against son and brother against brother in an attempt to gain ultimate supremacy by each of the respective 'sides.'

Eventually after years of attrition, it was Parliament who emerged as victors following the Battle of Naseby. King Charles I was taken prisoner and remained under house arrest at Holmby House in Oxfordshire awaiting a decision on his fate which at the time was fully expected to be no more serious than foreign exile, a fate befalling many a fallen 'royal' in the past. However in 1647, events were about to take a major turn against King Charles.

On 4th June 1647, Cornet Joyce, acting on secret orders from Cromwell himself and unknown even to General Fairfax, Cromwell's army chief of staff, descended upon Holmby House with 500 hand-picked revolutionary troopers and seized the King.

According to Isaac Disraeli... *"The plan was arranged on May 30th at a secret meeting held at Cromwell's house, though later Cromwell pretended that it was without his concurrence."*

So, remaining in constant collusion with his Jewish benefactors throughout the duration of the war, Cromwell wrote to them again at Mulheim Synagogue in Holland in a letter received by them on the 16th June 1647...

"In return for further financial support will advocate admission of Jews to England: This however impossible while Charles living. Charles cannot be executed without trial on adequate grounds which do not at present exist. Therefore advise that Charles be assassinated, but have nothing to do with arrangements for procuring an assassin, though willing to help in his escape."

To which the following reply was sent to Cromwell on the 12th July 1647...

"Will grant financial aid as soon as Charles removed and Jews admitted. Assassination too dangerous. Charles shall be given opportunity to escape. His recapture will make trial and execution possible. The support will be liberal, but useless to discuss terms until trial commences."

The source of this dialogue was a weekly review, *'Plain English'* published by the *'North British Publishing Co.'* and edited by Lord Alfred Douglas, in 1921.

And so it duly came to pass that on 12th November 1647, Charles was 'allowed' an opportunity to escape in order to bring the plan to fruition and he duly absconded to the Isle of Wight, just off the south coast of England, to where he was followed and quickly recaptured by Cromwell's men.

"Contemporary historians have decided that the King from the day of his deportation from Holmby to his escape to the Isle of Wight was throughout the dupe of Cromwell." Isaac Disraeli.

Now all that remained to bring the plot to fruition was to stage the 'show trial' of Charles and sentence him to death, replace him with Cromwell as head of state and the

Jews would have attained their goal of being allowed to officially set foot on English soil for the first time in almost four hundred years, despite protests by the masses (who were of course ignorant of all the background machinations) and by the sub-committee of the Council of State which declared them to be... *"...a grave menace to the State and the Christian religion."*

"The English Revolution under Charles I was unlike any preceding one...From that time and event we contemplate in our history the phases of revolution." Isaac Disraeli.

In fact this was actually just the beginning. The English revolution was followed by the American, French and Russian versions of the same 'trick' all at the behest of and funded by the same group of people. In 1897, the Protocols of the Learned Elders of Zion surfaced and this document contains this noteworthy sentence... *"Remember the French Revolution, the secrets of its preparation are well known to us for it was entirely the work of our hands."* Protocol No. 3—14. This statement could also have referred to all of the above named events.

However, the **real** objective of the revolution was realised around half a century later with the formation of the Bank of England in 1694 and the instigation of the 'National Debt.' The charter that provided for this, handed-over to an anonymous committee, the previously Royal prerogative of minting money and enabled the international banksters to secure their loans on the taxes of the country rather than simply upon a monarch's personal undertaking, thus enslaving the people of Britain forever.

The Act of Union passed by Parliament shortly afterwards in 1706, was simply an expedient way of tying Scotland into the great scam in addition to England. Of course up until that point in time the two countries were distinctly separate, both politically and economically. This then had the effect of making the Scottish Mint redundant and also served to bring the Scottish economy under the umbrella of the English national debt as a whole. Thus was the grip of the banksters extended over England's neighbours in one swift, decisive move.

To safeguard against a possible negative reaction from Parliament, the party system was then brought into being, frustrating true national reaction and enabling the puppeteers to divide and rule and using their newly-established financial power to ensure that their own placemen and their own policies would predominate.

This was also the beginning of the banksters' highly dubious practice of fractional reserve banking whereby gold became the basis of loans, ten times the size of the amount deposited. In other words, £100 of gold would be legal security for a £1,000 loan. At 3% interest therefore, £100 in gold could earn £30 interest annually with no more trouble or inconvenience to the lender than the keeping of a few ledger entries. The owner of £100 worth of land however, still had to slave relentlessly, often around the clock, in order to make a subsistence living.

Thus the stage had been set for the instigation of the Bank of England in 1666, with the so-called, 'Great Fire of London,' which somewhat 'fortuitously,' cleared the land now occupied by the City of London. Throughout 1665 and early 1666 the 'Black

Death' or the 'Great Plague,' as it was commonly known had taken hold in London and decimated the populace, thousands of whom died in misery but the 'Great Fire' in September 1666 destroyed the multitudes of filthy, rat-infested slums and thus prevented the spread of the disease carried by the fleas that lived upon the rats.

Mainstream history records that the fire which allegedly began in a bakers' shop in Pudding Lane was an accident. This part of London was at the time named 'Cheapside' and was a slum area, of no particular concern to anyone and was certainly without any intrinsic 'value' to the ruling Elite of the day. If it was indeed an accident, then the fire was most convenient in its timing. The fire continued for several days and completely razed most of London to the ground, destroying almost everything in its path.

The Great Fire of London, September 1666

When the shocked populace took stock of the damage, they must have wondered if Armageddon had finally arrived. Fully 80% of the city was destroyed, including over 13,000 houses, 89 churches and 52 Company (Guild) Halls. The spiritual hub of the city, St. Paul's Cathedral, was nothing but rubble and ashes. It was a disaster of unprecedented proportions.

But of course, one person's disaster is always another's opportunity. Within days of the fire being extinguished, the architect Christopher Wren had submitted plans to King Charles II for the complete rebuilding of the city. Wren's grand scheme called for cutting wide avenues through the former warren of alleys and byways that had made up old London, opening up the city to light and air. King Charles approved of the scheme, but he realised that the expense and the necessity of rebuilding as fast as possible made it unfeasible. Instead, he appointed Wren to rebuild the city's churches, including St. Paul's Cathedral, a position the young architect filled with brilliance over the next fifty years.

Then in 1688 the banksters in England, following a series of disagreements with the Stuart Kings, Charles II (1660-1685) and his brother, James II (1685-1688), conspired with their far more 'successful' bankster counterparts in the Netherlands, who had already instigated a central bank there. They decided to finance an invasion by William of Orange of the Netherlands whom they had already approached and had pre-established that he would look more favourably upon their demands than his predecessors. The invasion was of course successful despite a small diversion now known to history as the Monmouth rebellion. James II fled to France to live out his remaining days in exile there and William duly ascended to the throne in England as King William III in 1689.

Now the scene was set to establish the English Central Bank. Following a costly series of wars through the previous 50 years, English Government officials pleaded with the banksters for loans in order to maintain the country's rapidly deteriorating infrastructure and the banksters graciously agreed to resolve the problem in exchange for a government-sanctioned, privately-owned bank which of course would then be authorised to issue money created from nothing.

So, in 1694, the deceptively named, **'Bank of England,'** was founded. I say 'deceptively named' because as with its modern-day American counterpart, the *Federal Reserve Bank,* its name gives the strong impression that it is controlled by the Government when in fact it is a private institution founded by Jewish banksters in order to make their fortunes from the ordinary English (and American) people, both rich and poor.

In his book, *'The Breakdown of Money,'* published in 1934, Christopher **Hollis** explained the formation of the Bank of England as follows:

"In 1694, the Government of William III (who had come in from Holland with the Jews) was in sore straits for money. A company of rich men under the leadership of one William Paterson offered to lend William £1,200,000 at 8 per cent on the condition that, 'the Governor and Company of the Bank of England,' as they called themselves, should have the right to issue notes to the full extent of its capital. That is to say, the Bank got the right to collect £1,200,000 in gold and silver and to turn it into £2,400,000 (that is, double it), lending £1,200,000, the gold and silver to the Government, and using the other £1,200,000, the banknotes, themselves.

Paterson was quite right about it that this privilege which had been given to the Bank was a privilege to make money... In practice they did not keep a cash reserve of nearly two or three hundred thousand pounds. By 1696 (ie. within two years) we find them circulating £1,750,000 worth of notes against a cash reserve of £36,000. That is with a, 'backing,' of only about 2 percent of what they issued and drew interest on."

Despite that, the bank was duly chartered anyway and began loaning out several times the money it supposedly had in reserves, all at interest.

Furthermore the Bank of England would loan government officials as much of the new currency as they wished, as long as they secured the debt by direct taxation of the British people which has directly led to all the onerous taxation imposed upon us all today. (These taxes, of all kinds, do not contribute to the economy or towards maintaining the country's infrastructure as we are deceitfully told, but go straight into the cavernous pockets of the banksters.) The Bank of England amounted to nothing less than the legalised counterfeiting of a national currency for private gain, and thus subsequently any country that would fall under the control of a private bank would amount to nothing more than a plutocracy.

Immediately following the formation of the Bank of England, it began an attack on the tally stick system, as it was currency outside of the control of the banksters, just as King Henry I had originally intended. The names of the controllers of the Bank have never been revealed, as is still the case even today, but one thing is certainly clear and that is that the British Royal family were also involved—as indeed they are also suspected to be to this day. However, whilst the covert controllers' identities were withheld and protected, they may have wished they had chosen a more discreet front-man, after William Paterson stated that, *"The Bank hath benefit of interest on all monies which it creates out of nothing."*

The fact that Paterson chose to speak-out openly in this manner, may explain why he eventually died in poverty, outcast by his associates or maybe this 'shabbez goy,' (a non-Jew who clandestinely chooses to represent the interests of Jews) had merely outlived his usefulness to the Jews behind the scenes.

After four years of the Bank of England, by 1698, the Jewish control of the money supply had increased exponentially. They had flooded the country with so much money that the Government and thus the people's debt to the Bank had grown from the initial £1,250,000, to £16,000,000, in only four years, a staggering increase of 1,280% and that was just the beginning.

Why would they do this? Simple really...

Stage 1. If the money in circulation in a country is say, £5m and a Central Bank is created and prints another £15m, before injecting it into the economy through loans etc., this will then reduce the value of the original £5m in circulation before the bank was formed. This is because the initial £5m now represents only 25% of the economy and it will also give the bank control of 75% of the money in circulation, a percentage which obviously increases with every single new note printed. This is also the principal cause of inflation, which is the reduction in the value of money borne by the people, due to the economy being flooded with additional money. In effect a 'hidden' tax.

Stage 2. As an individual's money is then worth less than previously, he has to request a loan from the banking system to help him survive. Then, when the Central Bank is satisfied that there is enough 'debt' in the economy, the bank will immediately restrict the money supply via the expedient of making loans unavailable.

Stage 3. The Bank will then wait for bankruptcies to commence, as they inevitably will. This enables them to seize the 'real' tangible wealth, businesses and property of both companies and individuals, all for a fraction of their true value. Inflation never affects a Central Bank negatively. In fact it is the only entity that can benefit from it as the more money that there is in circulation, the more interest they accrue in the form of the 'National Debt.'

In 1757 Benjamin Franklin travelled to England from the American colonies and in fact spent the next 18 years of his life there until just before the start of the American Revolution. In 1764 he was asked by officials of the Bank of England to account for the prosperity of the colonies in America (...as if they didn't know.) His reply was succinct...

"That is simple. In the Colonies we issue our own money. It is called Colonial Scrip. We issue it in proper proportion to the demands of trade and industry to make the products pass

easily from the producers to the consumers. In this manner creating for ourselves our own paper money, we control its purchasing power and we have no interest to pay no-one [sic]."

As a result of Franklin's statement, and under pressure from the Bank of England, the British Parliament hurriedly passed the Currency Act of 1764. This prohibited colonial officials from issuing their own money and ordered them to pay all future taxes in gold or silver coins. Referring to the situation after this act was passed, Franklin stated the following in his autobiography...

"In one year, the conditions were so reversed that the era of prosperity ended and a depression set-in, to such an extent that the streets of the colonies were filled with the unemployed... The colonies would gladly have borne the little tax on tea and other matters had it not been that England took away from the colonies their money which created unemployment and dissatisfaction. The viability of the colonists to get power to issue their own money permanently out of the hands of King George III and the international bankers was the prime reason for the revolutionary war."

Just to clarify the above for the avoidance of doubt... A country or state that issues currency under governmental control is far more prosperous than one where a predatory Central Bank holds the purse strings, for obvious reasons. Central banksters lend currency to governments at interest and the only way that this interest can be paid is by the printing of more and more money, which in turn accrues more and more interest... and so the spiral continues on. This then is the sole reason for 'national debts' and NOT government inefficiency or overspending or even import-export imbalances. Those explanations (and indeed any others) of how National Debts arise are all a complete fabrication designed and propagated by the banksters themselves, to deflect any criticism of their despicable methods. Unfortunately most people, even including allegedly competent economists, are either duped or controlled by them.

The 18th Century

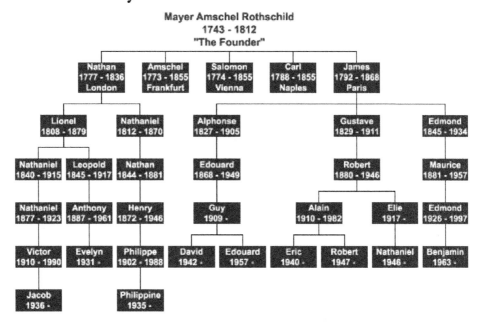

It is no under-statement nor exaggeration to make the claim that the Rothschilds are the richest family in the world, with the possible exception of the British royal family, the Windsors and depending also on exactly how absolute wealth is calculated. Please disregard the much-vaunted 'rich-lists' such as those that appear in Forbes magazine and from time to time, daily newspapers, these lists serve only to deflect us from the real truth of who controls the world's purse=strings. The Rothschilds are without question multi-trillionaires.

As far as the Rothschilds are concerned, there are no such things as ethics, morality or conscience and indeed, acute psychopathy is the norm. They allow nothing and no-one to stand in their way…ever. All that matters to them is that their power and wealth continues to grow exponentially and as of now, they either own or control over 50% of the world's wealth, equivalent to at least $200 trillion.

They are the very top of the pyramid, period. If you are maybe thinking, 'why have I not heard of this before?' or even 'why are their names not on everything, their faces on TV?' etc., it is simply because they deliberately intend it to be that way. They operate in secret, by proxy and by unseen hand. In fact, it is in order to keep their names firmly out of the news, that they began acquiring the media very early in their quest for total world domination. The news services such as Reuters International News Agency, based in London, Havas of France, and Wolf in Germany and latterly Associated Press are all firmly under their control. Considering the fact that it is these news agencies that distribute to ALL the western world's individual news outlets, radio and TV stations etc., then it is not difficult to understand how they are able to easily manipulate and control all the information that reaches the masses, rendering it totally unsurprising that we know only what the Rothschilds want to us to know about their activities.

Carefully feeding us only certain information and plenty of subtle disinformation is one of the factors that has kept the Rothschilds extreme wealth and control a secret, for centuries. They are both the creators and the masters of all our so-called worldwide intelligence and security services. In essence, these entities are the Rothschilds' personal security service as well as their chief assassins. Please do not believe, as we are constantly told, that MI-5/MI-6, the CIA, Mossad, KGB and all the other secret services, operate on behalf of their governments and therefore by default, the people. These entities exist solely to protect the real rulers of the world, the Rothschilds, the Royals and other affiliated bankster families from 'we, the people.'

The Rothschild's power-base from the very beginning was facilitated by use of the octopus-like methodology of slowly but surely spreading their deadly tentacles throughout the financial capitals of the world. Their story began 0n 23rd February 1744, in Frankfurt, Germany with the birth of Mayer Amschel Bauer…

He was the fourth son of Amschel Moses Bauer, a money-lender and counting-house proprietor. By 1760, Bauer was employed by a bank owned by the Oppenheimer family in Hanover, one of many disparate 'German' states at that time and being a bright and shrewd apprentice, he quickly rose through the ranks to become a junior partner. And so in the years following the death of his father, Mayer Amschel Bauer returned to Frankfurt with enough money to take over the family business.

Above the entrance door to the family counting-house was a red shield with a Roman eagle in the centre. There are far deeper, more esoteric aspects to this symbolism, but suffice to say for now, that Rothschild is German for 'Red Shield', 'rot' meaning red and 'schild' meaning shield. Bauer at this point in time then decided to change his name to Mayer Amschel Rothschild and thus an era of unimaginable evil began, an era that would give rise to the House of Rothschild, the root of all the bankster evil to follow.

Mayer Amschel Rothschild wasted no time with his ambitions for personal prominence and profit. He reacquainted himself with someone he met and with whom he had worked back in the days when he was employed by the Oppenheimers, a certain General von Estorff. The General was by this point in time, allied with the court of Prince William IX of Hesse-Hanau (another German state) and Rothschild therefore, began with the help of the General, to conduct business with one of the richest royal houses in Europe, a house made wealthy by the hiring-out of its soldiers as mercenaries to fight in foreign wars. Indeed Britain would later use these troops in the American Revolutionary War, a hugely profitable deal brokered by Mayer Rothschild.

Rothschild immediately ingratiated himself with the Prince by selling him discounted rare coins and jewels, but it wasn't long before he had won Prince William's favour by loaning money to him and his court. By 1769, Rothschild had even become the court agent for Prince William who was the grandson of King George II of England; cousin to George III; nephew to the King of Denmark and brother-in-law to the King of Sweden. Rothschild clearly saw his future lay in associating with and doing business with the rich and powerful and he was even granted permission to use a new 'logo' advertising his services, one that read *'M. A. Rothschild, by appointment court factor to his serene highness, Prince William of Hanau.'*

Rothschild, having now instigated the 'House of Rothschild' and having realised that loaning money to governments and royalty is far more profitable and secure than loaning to individuals, because the loans are much larger and backed by their nations' taxes, then began thinking along even more grandiose lines.

"Let me issue and control a nation's money and I care not who writes the laws." Mayer Amschel Rothschild.

In 1770 Rothschild married Gutle Schnaper, the daughter of a prominent merchant and they produced five daughters and five sons. The first son, Amschel Mayer Rothschild junior was born in 1773 and one year later Salomon Mayer Rothschild entered the world. These two were closely followed in 1777 by Nathan Mayer Rothschild; in 1788 by Kalmann (Karl) Rothschild and finally in 1792, by Jacob (James) Rothschild.

In 1775, the American revolutionary war began in Lexington, Massachusetts. Since Benjamin Franklin's 'discussions' with the British banksters and by this time, the colonies had now been almost totally deprived of silver and gold coins due to onerous

British taxation and as a result of this, the continental government decided that it had no other option but to print their own money in order to finance the war.

At the commencement of the revolution the American money supply stood at $12m and by the end of the war it had reached nearly $500m and as a result the currency was virtually worthless due to the rampant inflation. This also neatly illustrates the inherent dangers of printing an excess of paper money. The reason Colonial Scrip had worked well was because the correct balance had been achieved thus facilitating successful trade. Too much money in the system would have caused runaway inflation and too little would have resulted in a recession.

As a result of the massive devaluation of the value of the currency towards the end of the American Revolution, the Continental Congress were so desperate for money that they allowed Robert Morris, their Financial Superintendent, to establish a privately owned Central Bank in desperation and in the hope that this would 'cure' the financial problem. Morris was a wealthy man who had grown even wealthier during the revolution by trading in war materials.

This, the very first Central Bank in America was known as the 'Bank of North America,' which was created with a four year charter and was closely modelled upon the Bank of England. Significantly, as with all Central Banks, it was allowed to indulge in the highly dubious, if not downright fraudulent practice of fractional reserve banking in order to enable the creation of money from nothing and then charge interest on it.

The bank's charter called for private investors to put up $400,000 of initial capital, which Morris was himself unable to personally raise. Nevertheless he unashamedly used his political influence to arrange for gold to be deposited in the bank which had been loaned to America by France. Morris then acquired the money he needed to buy this bank from this deposit of gold that belonged to the government, or more specifically, the American people.

This 'Bank of North America,' again deceptively named in order that the people would believe it to be under governmental control, was then granted an absolute monopoly on the national currency of the newly formed United States.

However, despite the assurances from Robert Morris that his privately owned Bank of North America would solve the problem of the economy, by 1785, of course the value of the currency had continued to plummet, thereby forcing the Continental Congress into a decision not to renew the bank's charter. The leader of the campaign to kill the Central Bank was William Findlay of Pennsylvania, who stated . . .

"This institution, having no principle but that of avarice, will never be varied in its objective . . . to engross all the wealth, power and influence of the state."

"The rich will strive to establish their dominion and enslave the rest. They always did. They always will . . . They will have the same effect here as elsewhere, if we do not, by the power of government, keep them in their proper spheres." Gouverneur Morris, co-author of the U.S. Constitution in 1787.

James Madison was also vehemently opposed to a privately owned central bank after becoming aware of the exploitation of the people by the Bank of England. He is quoted as saying...

"I believe there are more instances of the abridgement of freedom of the people by gradual and silent encroachments by those in power, than by violent and sudden usurpations."

Thomas Jefferson was also firmly against the Central Bank philosophy and made the following, famous pronouncement...

"If the American people ever allow private banks to control the issue of their currency, first by inflation, then by deflation, the banks and the corporations which grow up around them will deprive the people of all property until their children wake up homeless on the continent their fathers conquered. The issuing power should be taken from the banks and restored to the people, to whom it properly belongs."

Sadly the words of wisdom of Gouverneur Morris and Thomas Jefferson all went unheeded. Alexander Hamilton, Robert Morris and Thomas Willing convinced the bulk of the delegates to the decisive Constitutional convention, not to allow Congress the power to issue paper money and as a result, the Constitution was silent on the issuance of paper money by the Government for the citizens, leaving the door wide open for the banksters in the future.

Jefferson's statement (above) turned out to be a very prophetic statement as within 3 years from the signing of the Constitution in 1790, the newly appointed First Secretary of the Treasury in President George Washington's cabinet, the Rothschild agent Alexander Hamilton, proposed a bill to Congress calling for another new privately owned central bank. Interestingly, Alexander Hamilton's first job subsequent to his graduation from law school in 1782 was as an aide to Robert Morris, a man to whom he had written in 1781 stating, *"...a national debt if it is not excessive will be to us a national blessing."*

So, the three main instigators behind the original Central Bank, the Bank of North America, Robert Morris, Alexander Hamilton and the bank's President, Thomas Willing never gave up their background scheming, despite the demise of the original bank and Alexander Hamilton, now Secretary of the Treasury, a man who described Robert Morris as his 'mentor,' somehow contrived to push the concept for another new, privately-owned central bank through the new Congress.

This new bank, the 'First Bank of the United States,' was founded after a year of intense debate and was granted a 20 year charter. It was also given an absolute monopoly on printing United States currency even though 80% of its stock was held by private investors and was to be run on exactly the same principle as the Bank of North America. Robert Morris controlled it and Thomas Willing was the bank's President, only the name had changed. The other 20% of the stock was purchased by the United States government, but this was not in order to provide the country and its citizens with any form of stake-holding, but to the eternal shame of the US government, simply to provide the capital for the private investors to purchase the remaining 80%.

As was the case with the Bank of England and the now defunct Bank of North America, these private investors never paid the full amount agreed for their shares. In fact, it was through the fraudulent use of the fractional reserve banking methodology that the government's 20% stake which was $2,000,000 in cash, was used to provide the loans to its private investors to purchase the other 80% stake. A total of $8,000,000, for this risk-free investment.

Again the name, 'First Bank of the United States,' was deliberately chosen to hide from the people the fact that it was totally privately owned. And as is always the situation, the names of the investors in this bank were never revealed but it is now widely known that the Rothschilds were instrumental in its foundation.

After the first five years of the First Bank of the United States being in control of the American money supply, the American Government had borrowed $8,200,000 and prices had increased by 72%. In relation to this, Thomas Jefferson, then Secretary of State stated ... *"I wish it were possible to obtain a single amendment to our constitution, taking from the Federal Government their power of borrowing."*

Meanwhile, back in Europe, the Rothschild family was still busy plotting and scheming and in 1798, the now twenty-one year old Nathan Mayer Rothschild had left Frankfurt for England with a sum of money equivalent to £20,000, which he used to found his ubiquitous banking house, *'N M Rothschild & Co.'* He was by far the most able of the five Rothschild brothers.

In 1800 Napoleon Bonaparte, established the 'Bank of France,' which was designed to be a true 'bank of the people' and enable the French government to be responsible for the control of their own economy and the issuance of currency. He declared openly that when a government is dependent on bankers for money, it is the bankers and not the government leaders that are in control.

His opinion of the European banksters was ... *"The hand that gives is among the hand that takes. Money has no motherland. Financiers are without patriotism and without decency. Their sole object is gain."*

A rare but true 'man of the people,' Napoleon established both the Bank of France and the French Bourse (stock exchange) as well as the National and Departmental Tax Boards, to ensure equitable taxation for all. Consequently, the income and standard of living of the French populace soared. He established awards such as the 'Legion d'Honneur' to reward those whose services to the nation merited special recognition. The recipient could be a scientist, composer, legislator, clergyman or writer, or indeed from any sector.

In the arena of public works, over 20,000 miles of imperial and 12,000 miles of regional roads were completed, almost a thousand miles of canals were built, the Great Cornice road was constructed along the Mediterranean coast, mountain roads were constructed across the Alps, for example the Simplon Pass and Mont Cenis and harbours were dredged and expanded at many ports, including Dunkirk and Cherbourg.

In addition, not only was Paris beautified with the construction of many new, wider boulevards, bridges and monuments, but the National Archives received a permanent home. Napoleon also saved the Louvre from closure. Monuments were constructed throughout the Empire and structures such as the Imperial Cathedral of Speyer, made famous by Luther, were preserved while work on the spires of the great cathedral of Cologne were continued on Napoleon's orders. In fact, Napoleon's architectural influences may be found scattered all across Europe, from Rome to Vienna.

Napoleon even ended the schism between the Protestant and Catholic churches and restored the Catholic religion to France via the 'Concordat' in 1801. Despite this, he ensured and guaranteed freedom of religion and equality to the Protestant sects and he even generously declared France the 'homeland of the Jews,' after it became obvious that their national home could not yet be established in Palestine.

The 19th Century

In 1803, President Thomas Jefferson agreed a deal with Napoleon and France. The United States promised Napoleon $3,000,000 of gold in exchange for a large territory to the west of the Mississippi River. This was what came to be known as the 'Louisiana Purchase' and considerably extended the borders of the still fledgling United States.

However, Napoleon used this gold to raise a large army which he immediately engaged in the attempted conquest of most of Europe. But fearing that Napoleon may invade and capture England and thus threaten the Bank of England's money monopoly (or should that be 'monopoly money?') the banksters united in opposition to Napoleon and financed every one of his intended adversaries, in order to protect their own substantial financial interests. Prussia, Austria and then finally Russia all became heavily indebted to the banksters in their attempts to halt Napoleon's military juggernaut.

Then in 1810, the death of powerful banksters Sir Francis Baring and Abraham Goldsmid ensured that Nathan Mayer Rothschild became the senior bankster in England. But during the following year, the charter for the Rothschild-owned First Bank of the United States expired and a bill was immediately set before Congress to renew its charter. The legislatures of both Pennsylvania and Virginia passed resolutions demanding Congress kill the bank altogether and even the national press openly attacked the bank calling it variously . . . *'a great swindle,' 'a vulture,' 'a viper' and 'a cobra.'*

However, in the end, the 'renewal' bill was passed by a single vote in the house but was deadlocked in the Senate. America's fourth President, James Madison was a staunch opponent of the bank and he instructed his Vice-President, George Clinton to break the tie in the Senate which was the final nail in the coffin of the bank.

Upon hearing of all this, Nathan Mayer Rothschild responded curtly and in typical fashion . . . *"Either the application for renewal of the charter is granted, or the United States will find itself involved in a most disastrous war."* But Congress stood by their principles and this incited Rothschild to make good on his threat.

Although history records that the main reasons for the British to go to war with the United States for a second time in three decades, was that American ships were aiding their enemy Napoleon, by running a naval blockade, as well as ongoing disputes with Canada, it fails to mention that N M Rothschild and his vast family wealth and political connections were also a major factor in the British government's decision to declare war on the USA once again.

The main opposition in Britain to the Rothschilds and their 'revenge' war with the Americans was the Prime Minister, Spencer Perceval, a devout Christian but he was soon disposed of at the hands of a 'lone, deranged assassin,' the first and absolutely definitely not the last of those who stand against the banksters to suffer a similar fate. He was recorded by history as the only British Prime Minister to be assassinated whilst in office. His assassin, John Bellingham, who was very quickly and very conveniently, tried, convicted and hanged, was strongly rumoured to be in the employ of the Rothschilds and this would also mark the first time that the Rothschilds would be associated with, or rather conveniently *benefit* from a political assassination. For the record, Perceval was murdered on the 11th May 1812, Bellingham was immediately arrested (he made no attempt to escape, but sat down and waited to be arrested. Where have we heard this story before?) tried on the 15th May and executed on the 18th, a small matter of one week from commission of the crime to execution.

The Rothschilds then assumed that the US would incur so much debt in fighting the British that they would have no choice but to eventually surrender and allow the new central bank charter to be ratified. Unfortunately for them though, the British due to their already ongoing war with Napoleon and France were hampered in their attempts to defeat the Americans although they did manage to burn down the capital city, Washington.

By early 1815 the war had ended in ignominious defeat for the British soon after their loss at the hands of Col. Andrew Jackson in the Battle of New Orleans.

But to backtrack slightly, it was in September of 1812 that the family patriarch Mayer Amschel Rothschild died, leaving a will that left his clear and unequivocal instructions as to how the House of Rothschild should proceed in future without him . . .

1. All key positions in the family business are only ever to be held by family members.
2. Only male members of the family are allowed to participate in the family business.
3. The family is to inter-marry with its first and second cousins to preserve the family fortune.
4. No public inventory of his estate is ever to be published.
5. No legal action is to be taken with regard to the value of the inheritance.

6. The eldest son of the eldest son is to become the head of the family.

So as per instruction no. 6, Nathan Mayer Rothschild succeeded his father, became 'head' of the family and immediately assumed control of their vast undertakings and Jacob (James) Mayer Rothschild instigated the bank, *'de Rothschild Freres,'* (Rothschild Brothers) in Paris, France.

Nathan Rothschild himself, now head of the family, personally assumed control of a plan to smuggle a vital shipment of gold through France to Spain in order to finance an attack by the Duke of Wellington on Napoleon in what was to become the 'Peninsular Wars.' He financed this enterprise through £3 million of gold which was entrusted to his late father by Prince William IX of Hesse-Hanau and subsequently invested with the East India Company. Knowing that the Duke of Wellington would need precious gold in his Peninsula campaign against Napoleon, Nathan used this 'stolen' gold to make large profits for himself on the ensuing transactions.

By 1814, Wellington's victories in Spain and Portugal had eventually forced Napoleon to abdicate and Louis XVIII was crowned King in a temporary restoration of the French monarchy and Napoleon was exiled to the tiny island of Elba, just off the coast of Italy.

However, Napoleon was not held captive for long. He soon escaped his exile and returned to Paris where Royal French troops were sent to re-capture him. But he used his powerful charisma and powers of persuasion to convince these soldiers to rally round him once more, and they subsequently hailed him as their Emperor once again. Then in March 1815, Napoleon assembled a great army in order to fight the Duke of Wellington's forces once again in an attempt to secure one last, decisive victory.

All five of the Rothschild brothers were still very much active in the family business at this point in time and they continued to supply gold to both Wellington's army (through Nathan in England) and to Napoleon's army (through Jacob in France). As Napoleon had stated insightfully some years previously… *"Financiers are without patriotism, without decency…"*

The funding of both sides in a war, was therefore now firmly established as a staple of bankster profiteering, a tradition which continues up to the present day. It is indeed through war that the banksters make their largest and most obscene profits, as war-debt is risk-free, guaranteed by a country's government and backed by the taxes on its population. In addition, the policy of the victor honouring the debts of the losing country makes it even more lucrative.

It is also during this time period that the Rothschilds established their own exclusive courier network, one that also operated as an intelligence network. They utilised both carrier pigeons and fast dispatch riders who were allowed to travel freely between warring nations, unhindered by either side, in order that they may be kept abreast of any developments ahead of time and could thus profit extensively from this 'foreknowledge' of events.

Even though the outcome of a conflict is often predetermined, the banksters are not pre-disposed to any unnecessary risk and so it was therefore, that Nathan Rothschild despatched a trusted courier named Rothworth to the battlefield at Waterloo where he observed the events unfolding from a safe distance. Once the outcome of the battle had been decided, Rothworth immediately set-out for England and brought the news of Wellington's decisive victory to Rothschild a full day ahead of Wellington's own, official courier.

Then Rothschild made his bold move; he immediately gave instructions to his staff to begin selling his stocks and bonds. When the other traders noticed this, being aware of how the Rothschilds always seemed to have foreknowledge of events, they too began selling, panicked into believing that the British had lost the decisive battle. Thus the stock market plummeted and at which point Rothschild and his trustees began surreptitiously buying-up all the bonds they could. Subsequently when the news of the British victory over Napoleon at Waterloo, which effectively ended the ongoing war, eventually arrived and the value of the stock and bonds re-bounded exponentially, Nathan Mayer Rothschild had realised an immense profit of greater than twenty times his original investments.

At this time Nathan Rothschild openly boasted that during his time in England he had increased the initial £20,000 stake given to him by his father, 2500 times over, to £50,000,000. He also said this...

"I care not what puppet is placed upon the throne of England to rule the Empire on which the sun never sets, the man who controls Britain's money supply controls the British Empire... and I control the British money supply."

Interestingly, around 100 years later, the *New York Times* ran a story stating that Nathan Rothschild's grandson had attempted to secure a court order to suppress a book containing this, what we would call today an 'insider trading' story. The Rothschild family claimed that the story was untrue and libellous, but the court denied the Rothschild's request for damages and ordered them to pay all the court costs.

And thus, stock market manipulation became another Rothschild bankster tradition. With their vast majority ownership of bonds, the Rothschilds now had control of not only the British economy, but the financial capital of the world itself, the 'City of London.' Indeed they used this advantageous position to infiltrate the 'Bank of England' and in addition, they advocated the discontinuance of the constant shipping of gold around the world, in favour of using their own five European banks for a system of issuing paper debits and credits. In fact the exact same system we use today, albeit now digitised for the new 'age of information.'

It was also in 1815, during the Congress of Vienna that the Rothschilds attempted to set up a world government, using the debt of the European nations as leverage. The scheme actually failed, but they were at least successful in having Switzerland declared forever a neutral sovereignty in all future wars, in order that the funding of both sides could continue with impunity and unimpeded by the conflict. Even then, they could already visualise the millions of pound and dollar signs representing wars yet to come.

In fact, their ambitious one-world government plan only failed because Tsar Alexander I of Russia refused to be bullied by the Rothschilds. He immediately recognised their machinations as a devious plot to enslave not only his own country, but the world itself. Afterwards in a fit of anger, as is so typical of these people, Nathan Mayer Rothschild vowed that one day either he, or his descendants, would destroy the Tsar's whole family or their descendants. How prophetic. It was in fact, just over a century later in 1917, that Tsar Nicholas II, his wife Alexandra and all their children were indeed brutally murdered by the Rothschild-sponsored Communist, Bolshevik thugs during the so-called Russian Revolution. These people are nothing if not patient in their seemingly never-ending quest for ultimate power.

It was not psychic powers that predicted the abundant wealth that lay in the future for the Rothschilds, it was the sheer confidence of their knowing that they alone held the power and influence to start or end wars, crash a stock market, contract or expand the world money supply and that they could do all this unopposed and with absolute impunity, any time they wished.

Some people may ask, 'why do banksters want war anyway? How do they benefit?' Simple answer; banksters always finance both sides in a war. They do this because war is the greatest debt-generating machine ever devised by man. A nation will borrow huge sums in the desperate hope of securing victory, even though unknown to their puppet politicians, the banksters will have already predetermined the outcome. The ultimate loser is loaned just enough money to be able to maintain a vain hope of victory and the ultimate winner is provided with enough to ensure that he does indeed emerge victorious.

But how do the banksters ensure then that they will always recoup all their loans with interest added? Simply that their loans are granted only on the promise that the victor will also honour the debts of the vanquished. Never a solitary thought is spared for the thousands and even millions of soldiers and civilians that forfeit their lives on the pretext that it is for the ultimate 'good' and / or the honour of their respective nations.

"Of course the people don't want war. But after all, it's the leaders of the country who determine the policy and it's always a simple matter to drag the people along whether it's a democracy, a fascist dictatorship or a parliamentary or a communist dictatorship. Voice or no voice, the people can always be brought to the bidding of the leaders. That is easy. All you have to do is tell them they are being attacked and denounce the pacifists for lack of patriotism and exposing the country to greater danger." Herman Goering, speaking at the Nuremberg trials.

In fact, during the period between the founding of the Bank of England in 1694 and Wellington's victory at Waterloo in 1815, England had, perhaps now unsurprisingly in the light of what we have just learned, been at war for 56 years out the 121 in total, with much of the remaining time spent in intense preparation for conflict. In other words, almost constantly operating under a 'war-based economy.'

Back across the Atlantic, there was even more subterfuge ongoing a year later in 1816 as to no-one's particular surprise, the American Congress passed a bill permitting yet another Rothschild privately-owned central bank. This bank was the 'Second Bank of the United States' and its 20 year charter was an exact copy of that of its predecessor, the 'First Bank of the United States.' The United States government would once again, allegedly 'own 20%' of the shares of the bank.

After their defeat at Waterloo and the extremely costly Napoleonic Wars, the French were by this time now massively in debt to the banksters as the Rothschilds continued to purchase as many government bonds as they could. In almost a repeat of the stock market manipulation that they had engineered in England, the Rothschilds sold all their French government bonds, depressing their value and instigating a huge panic. And then, right on cue when all seemed lost, they stepped manfully into the breach and negotiated the takeover the French economy and money supply.

In fact, the Rothschilds had already planted the seeds of this French economic collapse, when back in 1770 Mayer Amschel Rothschild formulated a cunning plan which was to be carried-out by his agent Adam Weishaupt and his associates. It was in fact the founding of a highly secretive and corrupting organisation known as the Bavarian 'Illuminati,' translated as 'the enlightened ones.'

This group has been covered in extensive detail in many other works, so there is no point focussing here upon their many evil machinations at this juncture. Suffice to say, that one of their first outrages was to foment, provoke and finance the French Revolution and all purely for the benefit of the Rothschilds. Even Sir Walter Scott in volume two of his nine volume work, *'The Life of Napoleon,'* acknowledged this important fact.

Several years later in 1825, the Rothschilds' sworn enemy, Czar Alexander I of Russia, having already survived a kidnapping attempt whilst travelling in Europe, suddenly and mysteriously died from an unspecified illness. So-called 'establishment' historians claimed that he caught a cold that developed into typhus thus conveniently ignoring completely the many death threats made to him over the years by Nathan Mayer Rothschild and his cronies.

And so, after twelve years of its existence and during which period, the 'Second Bank of the United States,' ruthlessly manipulated the American economy to the detriment of the people but to the benefit of their own money-grabbing ends, the American people unsurprisingly were tired of all the deception. Opponents of the bank nominated Senator Andrew Jackson of Tennessee to run for President. He was no friend of the Rothschilds and he had no love of their central bank system either. Immediately upon his election to the highest office, he set about bringing-down the bank and eliminating all Rothschild's many placemen in the government's 'service.' In order to illustrate how deeply this 'cancer' was intertwined within government circles, he dismissed 2,000 of the 11,000 employees of the US Federal Government.

Another immensely lucrative income-stream for the Rothschilds was the drug trade. Their agent was David Sassoon and he controlled the opium-trade monopoly throughout the Far East. The huge Rothschild profits were shared with Queen Victoria and also with her government ministers.

The fact that the Rothschilds and British Royalty were the original drug-lords of this world (and still are) is yet another unpalatable truth that historians and the media alike usually conveniently airbrush from history. They converted China into a land of opium junkies and then spread this insidious epidemic far and wide to almost everywhere else. But in 1839, when Emperor Dao Guang tried to halt the opium trade, the British went to war with China as a result. Those deceitful Chinese eh? How dare they stop buying drugs from us? So just to be clear, Britain sent its army to China to fight them, simply because the Chinese wished to prevent the British Queen and her bankster friends, David Sassoon and the Rothschilds, from poisoning their people with opium. This was what has since become known as the 'Opium Wars.'

What is more, in 1842, when the first Opium War ended with '*The Treaty of Nanking,*' the mighty British bankster Empire managed to have its drug trade thoroughly institutionalised. It forced the Chinese to pay compensation for all the opium they had confiscated and also confirmed the island of Hong Kong as a British colony, before eventually and finally being returned to its rightful owners in 1999. And when the second Opium War ended in 1860, after the British had besieged Peking (now Beijing), the British commander, Lord Elgin ordered all Chinese temples and shrines burned to the ground as a demonstration of Britain's utter contempt for the Chinese and this remember, was all because the Chinese did not want to be drugged by the banksters.

Other factors surrounding the Opium Wars were concerns over trade. China was happy to export its tea, silk and chinaware but it did not need to import the goods of the Europeans, in return. So, in a nutshell, China was becoming rich and the banksters, unacceptably to them, were not getting their share of the spoils. During the period when the Chinese were being forced to buy the opium (an import that saw over 1 million addicts at its height, from lowly workers in the fields to high-ranking government officials), in 1864 alone, the banksters made over £20m from their importation of over 58,000 chests of opium.

How easy it is to make a villain out of a nation, especially when you are in total control of what is and is not reported by the media and the history books.

But back to the USA again, and even after President Jackson's purge of Rothschild's minions, they still managed to gain undue influence with Congress and cajoled them to approve an early renewal of the Second Bank of the United States' charter. Congress, as complicit as ever, sent the bill to President Jackson for signing but he refused their overtures and in his reply to them he stated the following...

"It is not our own citizens only who are to receive the bounty of our Government. More than eight millions of the stock of the Bank are held by foreigners...Is there no danger to our liberty and independence in a bank that in its nature has so little to bind it to our

country? Controlling our currency, receiving our public monies, and holding thousands of our citizens in dependence...would be more formidable and dangerous than a military power of the enemy. If government would confine itself to equal protection, and, as Heaven does its rains, shower the favour alike on the high and the low, the rich and the poor, it would be an unqualified blessing. In the act before me there seems to be wide and unnecessary departure from these just principles."

Congress was of course unable to override President Jackson's veto who then stood for re-election and for the first time in American history he took his argument directly to the people by taking his re-election campaign 'on the road.' His campaign slogan was, *"Jackson and No Bank!"* Even though the banksters poured over $3 million into President Jackson's opponent, the Republican Senator Henry Clay's campaign, Jackson was re-elected by a landslide in November 1832.

President Jackson well knew that the battle was only beginning however and following his victory he stated, *"The hydra of corruption is only scotched, not dead!"*

He appointed Roger B. Taney as Secretary of State for the Treasury with instructions to commence the removal of the government's deposits from the Second Bank of the United States. Jackson's previous two Secretaries of State for the Treasury, William J. Duane and Louis McLane had both refused to comply with the President's request and were dismissed as a result. However the President of the, Second Bank of the United States, Nicholas Biddle, used his massive influence to get the Senate to reject Roger B. Taney's nomination and even threatened to cause a depression if the Bank was not re-chartered.

In retaliation, on 10th September 1833, with an executive order, President Andrew Jackson then removed all Federal funds from the Second Bank of the United States and placed them with various state banks. The Rothschild agent, Nicholas Biddle protested furiously along with all the many 'Rothschild-owned' politicians. Biddle defiantly stated that *"Just because he has scalped Indians and imprisoned judges [does not mean] he is to have his way with the bank. He is mistaken."*

He then threatened Jackson and Congress with this statement...

"Nothing but widespread suffering will produce any effect on Congress... Our only safety is in pursuing a steady course of firm restriction—and I have no doubt that such a course will ultimately lead to restoration of the currency and the re-charter of the bank."

In simple terms he was in effect threatening to instigate a recession by withholding the printing of currency—as was his prerogative of course. After all, the Second Bank of the United States was responsible for the entire economy, totally free from any possible government intervention. This statement alone is proof enough to the world what central banks are really all about. He actually made good on his word and the Second Bank of the United States sharply contracted the money supply by calling in old loans and refusing to issue new ones. Naturally a financial panic ensued, followed by the US being plunged into a deep recession.

Biddle then unashamedly blamed President Jackson for the crash, claiming that it was Jackson's withdrawal of federal funds that had caused it. This crash decimated wages and prices and unemployment soared, along with business bankruptcies. The United States was in uproar and newspaper editors blasted the President in editorials. So, in 1834 Congress assembled what was known as the 'Panic Session,' and on the 28th March, President Jackson was officially censured by Congress for withdrawing funds from the Second Bank of the United States, in a vote which was passed by the Senate by 26 to 20. It was the first time a President had ever been censured by Congress.

Jackson, whose nickname was 'Old Hickory' because of his tough, uncompromising personality, responded to this latest bankster outrage with some powerful words …

"Gentlemen, I have had men watching you for a long time and I am convinced that you have used the funds of the bank to speculate in the breadstuffs of the country. When you won, you divided the profits amongst you, and when you lost, you charged it to the bank. You tell me that if I take the deposits from the bank and annul its charter, I shall ruin ten thousand families. That may be true, gentlemen, but that is your sin! Should I let you go on, you will ruin fifty thousand families, and that would be my sin! You are a den of vipers and thieves. I intend to rout you out, and by the Eternal God, I will rout you out."

But surprisingly and in a complete about-turn on the 4th April, the House of Representatives voted 134 to 82 **against** re-chartering the bank. This was followed by another vote which established a special committee to investigate whether the Bank had caused the crash. Then on 8th January 1835 after Congress had only a few months earlier censured President Andrew Jackson for his so-called 'abuse of power' in relieving the Second Bank of The United States of its Federal deposits, a large assembly of political figures gathered in Washington, a Senator rose to his feet and made a simple, brief announcement … *"Gentlemen … the national debt … is paid!"*

When Jackson took office the national debt of the United States was $58 million, six years of his Presidency later, the debt was zero. Jackson was the only American president to achieve this feat and this was the one and only time that the United States of America was debt-free.

Unfortunately, this debt-free America lasted a mere one year only. On 30th January 1835 President Jackson set another, this time unsought precedent, when he became the first American President to be targeted for assassination. Indeed, the unemployed housepainter Richard Lawrence was also setting a precedent in being the first of a long, long series of so-called 'lone nut' assassins. He approached Jackson outside the House Chamber of the Capitol with two Derringer pistols, taking his first shot at thirteen feet but fortunately for his intended target the percussion cap exploded but there was no discharge.

The outraged 67 year old President raised his cane ready to strike Lawrence as he fired the second pistol close up against Jackson's chest, but it misfired yet again.

The attempted assassination of President Andrew Jackson—30ᵗʰ January 1835

Jackson then beat his would-be assailant with his cane but was interrupted by none other than Senator Davey Crockett of Tennessee, who was to lose his life at the Battle of the Alamo in the following year. It must indeed have been divine intervention that saved the President from death, after ironically attending the funeral of South Carolina congressman Walter R. Davis. Jackson's courage was legendary; he had stared death in the face on many occasions, both in battle and in numerous duels of honour.

Almost one hundred years later in 1930, the two pistols were tested by the Smithsonian Institute and both of them fired normally on the very first attempt. Lawrence was declared insane, as is the general way of things, and later died in an asylum. Jackson sincerely believed, and with good cause, that it was the Rothschilds who made use of this 'useful idiot,' lone-nut assassin.

Before his death in 1845, Jackson left clear instructions for the following inscription to be placed on his tombstone, '*I Killed the Bank.*'

Yet the last word, the last ironic insult, was the banksters' 'honouring' of Jackson by featuring him on their $20 dollar bill many years later, after the creation of their highly criminal enterprise, the Federal Reserve Bank.

The Rothschilds did not take the loss of the charter lightly and so through their ownership of the Bank of England and other allied bankster friends, they contracted the money/credit supply of the United States and caused the infamous 'Panic of 1837.' The Bank of England then refused to accept or discount any bonds, securities or other financial documents from the United States. As a result of this, of the 850 state banks in the US at that time, 342 closed their doors forever and 62 temporarily. Remember, it was the state banks that received the Federal deposits when President Jackson removed them from the Rothschilds' control.

In 1841 William Henry Harrison became the ninth President of the United States and unfortunately he was not at all a welcome appointment as far as the banksters were concerned. In fact, after just thirty-one days in situ, he became the first President to ever die in office. The official cause of death was given as pneumonia, but this was regarded as highly suspicious at the time and upon his death, Vice President John Tyler became the tenth President of the United States. He went on to veto the act to renew the charter for the Bank of the United States and as a result of this, received hundreds of death-threat letters, but of course none signed by a Rothschild. Tyler somehow contrived to complete his term of office but several other subsequent Presidents were not quite so fortunate…

Illegally disenfranchising voters and rigging the Diebold electronic voting machines, as happened in the more recent Bush elections, are just two ways of achieving the ends of the unscrupulous banksters but there is another equally effective strategy that has been regularly employed. However this strategy, assassination, is no 'bloodless coup,' unlike the mere fixing of elections.

Almost from the beginning of the American republic, assassination has been used as an integral tool of control by the banksters and their friends in high office, resulting in the appointment of men who are in effect unelected leaders but who look kindly upon the aims of their 'benefactors,' all at a price of course. It is a sad fact that the banksters' agents poisoned and killed William Henry Harrison on 4th April 1841 and also Zachary Taylor on 9th July 1850. These two Presidents as well as being firmly 'anti-bankster,' had also opposed admitting Texas and California into the Union as slave-owning states and on the 3rd July 1850, Zachary Taylor threatened to hang those 'taken in rebellion against the Union.' The very next day, the President fell ill, vomited a 'blackish' substance and died within one week on the 9th July 1850. In fact Kentucky state authorities recently dug up Taylor's body in a search for evidence of arsenic poisoning, however none was found—or so they said. Perhaps unsurprising after a decomposition period of more than one hundred and fifty years. James Buchanan was also similarly poisoned in 1857, but he fortunately survived against the odds.

"From the time I took office as Chancellor of the Exchequer, I began to learn that the State held, in the face of the Bank and the City, an essentially false position as to finance. The Government itself was not to be a substantive power, but was to leave the Money Power supreme and unquestioned." William Gladstone, future Prime Minister of the United Kingdom, 1852.

Shortly before her death, Gutle, the wife of Mayer Amschel Rothschild made this profound yet chillingly accurate statement…

"If my sons did not want war, there would be none."

And war, perpetual war was what the Rothschilds and indeed the banksters in general were desperate to promulgate. As if there were not already enough wars and conflicts ongoing in the world, the Rothschilds had for some considerable time been cunningly and surreptitiously guiding the still young United States towards its biggest war ever.

Already having lost their latest American central bank in 1836, their exclusive, extortionate scheme to enslave Americans as they already had the Europeans, the Rothschilds were now planning to exact their deadly revenge. Most scholars and historians glibly state that what brought about the American Civil War, was secession and slavery. They certainly never mention the power of the Rothschilds and the fact that the war was deliberately designed and instigated specifically to split the nation, to divide and conquer or to create massive debt on both sides. It was intended that the North would become a British colony annexed to Canada and controlled by Lionel Rothschild, whilst the South was to be given to Napoleon III of France, and controlled by James de Rothschild.

And so in 1857, the seeds for the new Rothschilds' war were sown. Their well-trained lap-dog and banker for the North in New York was August Belmont, assisted by Jay Cooke who would help sell Union bonds in Europe, whilst Belmont would take care of the domestic financing. For the South, the Rothschilds and their other bankster friends, had wealthy slave-owner Judah P. Benjamin of the Louisiana law firm of Slidell, Benjamin and Conrad made Secretary of State for the Confederacy whilst his law partner John Slidell was the Confederate envoy to France. Slidell was the uncle of August Belmont's wife and Slidell's daughter was married to Baron Frederick d'Erlanger in Frankfurt, who was related to the Rothschilds. It was these connections that provided the financing for the Southern Confederacy, indeed Erlanger loaned over $7 million to the Southern States. South Carolina was the first state to secede from the Union on 29th December 1860 but a few weeks later, six other states joined them to form their own, new nation the 'Confederate States of America' with Jefferson Davis as their President. In all there were eventually eleven Confederate states.

In order to instigate the anger of the masses with rumours of secession, the Rothschilds enlisted and financed a secret society, *The Knights of the Golden Circle (KGC)* which they had formed a few years earlier, for the purpose of spreading racial tensions from state to state using slavery as an issue.

The KGC evolved from a Scottish secret society known as *The Society of the Horseman's Word*, otherwise known as the *Horse Whisperers*. This fraternity recited passages from the Bible backwards and practiced folk magic as part of their rituals, in addition to swearing Masonic-style oaths. The KGC was originally conceived as a group to not simply just promote the interests of the South, but to also prepare the way for a 'golden circle' of territories that would include Mexico, Central America and the Caribbean nations, to be included as slave states within the United States.

At its zenith, during the war, the KGC claimed 200,000 members, including all of Lincoln's war cabinet (except Lincoln himself,) the Confederate President Jefferson Davis, actor John Wilkes Booth (Lincoln's assassin) and a teenager later to become the infamous 'outlaw,' Jesse James. As an aside, a very mysterious and controversial figure in the KGC and other secret societies such as the Freemasons, was someone who will attain more prominence as this story further unfolds, a certain Harvard College 'gentleman' by the name of Albert Pike.

So, British agents were despatched in great numbers to all parts of the South, whilst in the Northern states, industrialists and their bankster friends imposed trade tariffs to prevent the Southern states from buying the cheaper European goods. With the same bankster pressure applied in Europe and with Lincoln's naval blockade taking effect, the South was unable to export its cotton to the British cotton mills, which was of course the major part of the South's economy and an equally major element of the economy and livelihoods of hundreds of thousands of cotton mill workers in the British cotton industry heartland of Lancashire in the North West of England.

As a result of this blockade, many British working families were literally at starvation level and the poor-houses and workhouses of major cities such as Manchester and Liverpool and their smaller 'satellite' towns such as Warrington, Wigan, Blackburn, Bolton, Oldham, Rochdale and Bury, were overflowing. Indeed the years 1861-65 saw many thousands of the poor of these areas, actually starve to death, all as a result of course of the banksters' heartless, insatiable quest for power and wealth at whatever cost.

It was the bankster-dominated slave-trade that made the South's cotton business possible. They controlled finance and they controlled the world's shipping. But many so-called 'old-money' families in the North, also made and maintained their fortunes in the lucrative slave trade and by their ownership of slaves themselves, with Rhode Island being the centre of control. Indeed it is an absolute myth that the North was vigorously opposed to slavery, it was merely a convenient expedient for placing the blame for the war on the South and stirring-up sympathy for the North's cause. It is true to say that the issue of slavery only seriously arose, two years into the conflict as a reason for the outbreak of war, following a conversation between Frederick Douglas, a prominent former slave himself, and Abraham Lincoln, following which the President thought it a great idea to 'jump on the bandwagon' of slavery.

Slavery has always been cited as and has been extensively believed to be the one real cause of the war but this was simply not the case. As Lincoln himself stated, *"I have no purpose directly or indirectly to interfere with the institution of slavery in the state where it now exists. I believe I have no lawful right to do so, and I have no inclination to do so…My paramount objective is to save the Union and it is not either to save or destroy slavery. If I could save the Union without freeing any slave, I would do it."*

As French novelist Honore de Balzac said so profoundly, *"Behind every great fortune there lies, a great crime."* The American fortunes of the Baring, Biddle, Brown, Drexel, Dukes, Sturgis and many other high-society families, all derived from the misery and death involved in the slavery and drug trades. Philadelphia, Boston, Baltimore and New York were all centres of trade, finance and institutionalised crime.

The American Civil War 1861-65

One month after Abraham Lincoln was sworn-in as the 16th President of the United States, the American Civil War officially began on the 12th April 1861, when Union troops were attacked by Confederate forces at Fort Sumter, South Carolina, after South Carolina had 'illegally' seceded from the Union.

To demonstrate how the banksters thrive on financing both sides in a war and how they utilise the Hegelian Dialectic (problem, reaction, solution) of opposing forces to advance their agenda for world domination, the Rothschild banksters loaned Napoleon III of France (the Napoleon of the battle of Waterloo fame's nephew), 210 million francs to seize Mexico and then deploy troops along the Southern border of the United States, by taking advantage of the American Civil War to return Mexico to colonial rule.

This was in gross violation of the 'Monroe Doctrine,' which was issued by President James Monroe during his annual 'State of the Union' address to Congress, in 1823. This doctrine proclaimed the United States' opinion that European powers should no longer colonise the Americas or interfere with the affairs of sovereign nations located in the Americas, such as the United States, Mexico, and others. In return for which, the United States agreed to remain neutral in wars between European powers and in wars between a European power and its colonies. However, should the latter type of war occur in the Americas, then the U.S. would be entitled to view such action as being hostile toward itself.

Regardless of this, the banksters encouraged the British government to send 8,000 troops to Canada towards the end of 1861, in complete defiance of the Monroe Doctrine. This was then followed in early 1862, by their sending even more British troops along with those from France and Spain, to Vera Cruz, Mexico, on the pretext of collecting debts from Mexico. This was exactly what the Russian Ambassador to America had warned his government . . . *"England will take advantage of the first opportunity to recognise the seceded states and France will follow her."*

On 1st January 1863, Lincoln issued his Emancipation Proclamation, thus 'freeing' the slaves, at least in principle if not exactly in practice.

Later in 1863, the French army of 30,000 troops was in complete control of Mexico and Czar Alexander II of Russia through his representatives in London and Paris, learned that the Confederacy had offered the states of Louisiana and Texas to Napoleon III of France, on condition that he would deploy his armies against the North. Alexander being no friend of the banksters or their ongoing schemes to establish one of their central banks in Russia, offered his support to President Lincoln and watched keenly for any new developments. He further declared that if Britain and France entered the conflict on the side of the South, then Russia would regard it as an act of war against its interests.

However, as with most actions of those in power, there was an ulterior motive. Lincoln was desperate for recruits for his army and was at this stage even cajoling Irish immigrants into service, directly from the ships. The real truth was that the black slaves were no more valued by the 'North,' than they were by the 'South.'

On the 8th September 1863, at the request of President Lincoln and Secretary of state William H. Seward, Czar Alexander II deployed his Navy to San Francisco and New York and placed it directly under the command of Lincoln. This arrival of the Russians came at a most crucial time for the North and it is no exaggeration to state that it caused the British and French to hesitate and even make a 'U-turn,' on their proposed actions. Entirely contrary to his falsely engendered, saintly, iconic image, Abraham Lincoln certainly had a darker side to his character. He was indeed no friend to the slaves, as documented in detail by researchers and evidenced by personal statements such as quoted above and now repeated here for emphasis . . .

"I have no purpose directly or indirectly to interfere with the institution of slavery in the states where it now exists. I believe I have no lawful right to do so and I have no inclination to do so . . . My paramount objective is to save the Union and it is not either to save or destroy slavery. **If I could save the Union without freeing any slave, I would do it."**

The truth is that Lincoln took the country to war WITHOUT the consent of Congress, completely ignoring the US Constitution, which he had taken an oath to defend. He suspended Habeas Corpus and imprisoned many people without trial. Furthermore he strictly enforced the draft whilst ensuring that his own draft-eligible son remained safe at college.

Was Lincoln doing the banksters' bidding by promoting the war, or was he just anxious to save the Union from them? One thing is certain though and that is that what he did next, proved very costly indeed. Needing money to continue to finance the war, Lincoln travelled to New York with his Secretary of the Treasury, Salomon P. Chase, to borrow money but found the quoted, extremely high 24-36% interest rates that the banksters asked, absolutely out of the question. Of course the banksters knew that fact in advance. Their idea from the very beginning was that the North should lose the war and the country be divided.

So upon returning to Washington, Lincoln sent for his old friend, Colonel Edmund 'Dick' Taylor from Chicago and offered him the position of trying to save the Union's precarious finances with a creative fiscal policy. As a solution, Taylor suggested the very same thing championed by the Rothschilds themselves and that was the creation of money 'out of thin-air.' This then was the birth of the Lincoln debt-free currency, the infamous 'Greenback.' It was in fact the first attempt by a US government to create a national currency in the United States, based upon paper money rather than gold and silver coins. Lincoln obtained the agreement of Congress as it was decreed to be only a 'temporary, emergency measure' and the 'Greenbacks' were duly instigated in July of 1862 with an initial printing of $150 million but this would later total $450 million.

However, Lincoln needed even more money to win the war, even after inaugurating the Federal Income Tax. Realising this fact and knowing that the President could continue printing his own money, the banksters proposed a National Bank Act. They exerted their power over Congress once again to see the act passed and from this point onwards the entire US money supply was to be created out of debt by the banksters buying US Government bonds and issuing them from reserves for bank notes. The banksters by causing their trademark financial panics, had already destroyed many of their competitors in the form of 172 state banks, 177 private banks, 47 savings institutions, 13 loan and trust companies and 16 mortgage companies. With an election on the horizon however, Lincoln decided to wait until the following year and until he gained the necessary public support to reverse the National Bank Act, which he had been pressured into signing in the first place.

In the meantime, the banksters were constantly pressing for a gold standard, because gold was scarce and therefore easier to monopolise but Lincoln was as strongly opposed to this as he was to their demands for the re-establishment of a central bank.

Prior to the Lincoln administration, private commercial banks were able to issue paper money, 'State Banknotes,' but that all ended with the National Bank Act of 1863 which prohibited states from creating money and it began the movement to abolish redeemable currency. The Greenback was an emergency-issued currency that was not redeemable in silver until after the Civil War. In 1879 it became legal tender and the Greenbacks remained valid until they were discontinued in 1994.

But sadly, Lincoln was the last President to issue debt-free United States notes. In his own words, *"We gave the people of this republic the greatest blessing they ever had, their own paper money to pay their own debts."* The Rothschild/bankster controlled newspaper, '*The Times*' of London responded, rather predictably and defiantly…

"If that mischievous policy, which had its origin in the North American Republic, should become indurated down to a fixture, then that government will furnish its own money without cost. It will pay off debts and be without a debt. It will have all the money necessary to carry on its commerce. It will become prosperous beyond precedent in the history of civilised

governments of the world. The brains and the wealth of all countries will go to North America. That government must be destroyed or it will destroy every monarchy on the globe."

What the 'voice' of the British bankster Empire, was in effect saying, was that the head of state of another sovereign nation, the United States, President Abraham Lincoln had to be destroyed.

Despite the increased efforts of Rothschild agent August Belmont, who had already become Democratic Party Chairman and who backed General George McClellan as the Democratic nominee to run against him with the full support of the banksters, Lincoln was nevertheless re-elected to a second term in office. But two weeks later, Lincoln wrote to a friend …

"The money power preys upon the nations in times of peace and conspires against it in times of adversity. It is more despotic than monarchy, more insolent than autocracy, more selfish than bureaucracy."

And then, in a statement to Congress, Lincoln declared *"I have two great enemies, the Southern army in front of me and the financial institutions in the rear. Of the two, the one in my rear is my greatest foe."*

Salomon P Chase, Lincoln's Secretary to the Treasury, stated … *"My agency in promoting the passage of the National Banking Act was the greatest financial mistake in my life. It has built up a monopoly which affects every interest in the country."*

The statistics of this totally manufactured Rothschild/bankster war were staggering. It really was the first war of the modern industrialised age. It was a war that saw some 240 patented applications for military weapons, the first war to use telescopic gun-sights, the first to use land mines and the banksters profited greatly from all those arms sales too. This was also the first war to utilise the 200 rounds per minute unprecedented 'killing-power' of the Gatling gun. The world's first ever 'machine gun.'

The American Civil War cost the lives of over 600,000 men, with half of that total being from pneumonia and disease and a further 1 million were to die later from their injuries. There were 51,000 deaths alone, in the three days of the Battle of Gettysburg, 1st to 3rd July 1863, the bloodiest battle of the war. Staggeringly, more than 100,000 Union soldiers were under the age of 15 (drummer boys were often as young as 9.) Of the 60,000 documented surgeries of the war, most were amputations.

It is also staggering to report that twenty-five per cent of all military-aged men (18-45) in the South, died in the Civil War. The state of Mississippi in 1863 alone spent one-fifth of its annual budget on prosthetic limbs to accommodate its amputees from the war. The financial cost of the entire war, damages and pensions included, was estimated at close to $7 billion. A Union private was paid $13 per month, his Confederate counterpart, $11 per month. But in the North it was possible to legally buy yourself out of the draft for $300 (an extremely large sum in those days) and in the South you were exempt if you owned more than 20 slaves. Only one-in-five Southerners owned slaves and most of those usually just owned one or two.

In 1860, the US National Debt was $65 million. The Civil War saw this debt grow to $2.7 billion—a 40-fold increase. However, in 1789, the year George Washington took office, the US National Debt was $77 million. The only logical and reasonable conclusion to be drawn from those figures has to be that for this debt to actually decrease in those critical years for the young, growing United States from 1789—1860, that it must have been the direct result of the US Government rejecting the Rothschild created Second Bank of the United States in 1836 and its regaining control of its own money supply and hence its ability to repay the said debt.

Then, on the evening of 14th April 1865, forty-one days after his second inauguration and just five days after General Lee officially surrendered to General Grant at Appomattox court house, thus ending the four-year, bloody conflict, President Lincoln was shot in the back of the head at point-blank range by assassin and 33rd degree Freemason, John Wilkes Booth, at Ford's Theatre, Washington DC. He died of his injuries early the next morning and less than two weeks after the final end of the Civil War.

And thus did Abraham Lincoln become the first American President to be 'officially' assassinated in office. 'Officially,' because the widely-held belief among researchers, is that President William Henry Harrison was the first in 1841, when instead of dying of pneumonia as reported, he was believed to have been poisoned for defying the banksters. His successor John Tyler was also poisoned, but he recovered and quickly re-thought his opposition to the money powers.

So much has been written about the assassination of Lincoln, but as with much of history, the 'real truth' never emerges. As with all political assassinations, it is the cover-up, maintaining an 'official' story no matter how unbelievable or contrary to the evidence, that our so-called 'historians' record for posterity.

In this case, it was always known that there was a plot, a conspiracy to kill Lincoln and his assassin John Wilkes Booth was a major part of it. But in reality, no-one knew exactly how widespread a conspiracy it was or indeed how it could all be connected to a much higher power than appeared to be the case. That is of course until 1974, when researchers found among the papers of Edwin M. Stanton, Lincoln's Secretary of War, several letters describing the conspiracy cover-up that had been either communicated directly to Stanton or intercepted by him. It transpired that all three victims, Harrison, Tyler and Lincoln had been obstructing on-going bankster plans for the US Civil War (1861-1865.)

In fact, Booth was merely the 'front-man' for a much wider conspiracy, a fact that was widely acknowledged at the time but which has now been conveniently ignored and/or deleted from history. Four additional co-conspirators were hanged for the crime and two more received life sentences in jail. Lincoln's successor, Andrew Johnson, had just taken office as VP literally weeks before the assassination, replacing Hannibal Hamlin. Incidentally, Booth is commonly believed (according to official history) to have been silenced when he was killed whilst resisting arrest. But, according to an article by Mark Owen on the website *henrymakow.com,* Booth was actually killed by the 'outlaw' Jesse James a fellow high-ranking Freemason and member of the KGC, in 1903 for the heinous crime of breaking his masonic oath—a far more serious transgression of course for Freemasons, than assassinating the legally elected leader of a country.

It was also well known from the beginning, that in Booth's trunk in his Washington hotel room they found coded messages and the key to that code was found in the Richmond office of Rothschild agent, Judah P. Benjamin. Benjamin had already fled to England where he established for himself a comfortable living as a Queen's Counsel, a barrister at law. As a senior Rothschild agent, Benjamin through the *Knights of the Golden Circle* had laundered their gold and dollars through a Montreal bank. He had been running so many Confederate spies out of Montreal, that the city became known as the 'second Richmond.' Richmond itself of course being the capital of the Confederate States.

Furthermore, among Stanton's papers, they found 18 pages that had been removed from John Wilkes Booth's diary and which revealed the names of 70 people (some in code) who were directly or indirectly involved in the plot to kidnap or kill Lincoln. In addition to Stanton, other prominent names involved in the conspiracy were Charles A. Dana, Assistant Secretary of War, and Chief of the War Department's Telegraph office.

Journals and coded papers by Colonel Lafayette C. Baker, Chief of the National Detective Police, the forerunner of the US Secret Service, detailed Lincoln's kidnap and assassination conspiracy and subsequent cover-up. The plot included a group of Maryland farmers, a group of Confederates including Jefferson Davis (President of the Confederacy) and Judah P. Benjamin (the Confederate Secretary of War and Secretary of State), a group of Northern banking and industrial interests, including Rothschild agents Jay Cooke (Philadelphia financier) and Henry Cooke (Washington DC banker), Thurlow Weed (New York newspaper publisher) and a group of radical Republicans who did not want the South reunited with the North as states, but wanted to control them as military territories and these included among their number, Senator Benjamin Wade of Ohio, Senator Zechariah Chandler of Michigan and Senator John Conness of California.

All of the above groups, which were all connected to the *Knights of the Golden Circle*, pooled their efforts and it was then proposed to use the well-known actor and Confederate patriot John Wilkes Booth. The original plan called for the kidnapping of Lincoln, Vice-President Andrew Johnson, and Secretary of State William H. Seward but the National Detective Police discovered their plans and informed Stanton. The kidnap, which had been planned for January 18th, 1865, was thus foiled.

Captain James William Boyd, a secret agent for the Confederacy and a prisoner of war in the Old Capitol Prison, was used by the National Detective Police to report on the activities of the prisoners and to inform on crooked guards. He looked similar to Booth, aside from his red hair and moustache and coincidentally had the same initials.

Stanton had him released and Boyd took over the Northern end of the conspiracy which had been joined by the Police and the War Department. In other words, Boyd was being set-up as the 'patsy,' an essential part of any political assassination and he was what the intelligence community refers to as a 'useful idiot,' meaning in effect that he was unaware he was being used. The Northern group preferred to kill Lincoln outright while Booth was in favour of kidnapping him and using him as ransom to obtain the release of Confederate prisoners of war.

Booth failed in his kidnap quest on two occasions in March of 1865 and then eventually fatally shot Lincoln on 14th April at Ford's Theatre. Boyd, warned that he could be implicated, planned to flee to Maryland and was blamed for attacking Seward, which by the way, he did not. Indeed, Boyd was actually the one shot at Garrett's farm and deliberately misidentified as Booth. National Detective police agents Andrew and Luther Potter had been on his trail from the beginning and were called upon to identify the corpse. When the blanket over the face of the victim was removed they commented, *"He sure grew a moustache in a hurry—red too."*

Contrary to reports, not a single friend of Booth was called to the inquest to identify the body. A Washington doctor named John May had removed a tumour from Booth's neck several months prior to the Lincoln assassination and was summoned to view the corpse. On seeing it, he said *"There is no resemblance in that corpse to Booth nor can I believe it to be him."* May later changed his statement (probably under extreme duress) to conform to the official proclamation that Booth had been captured and killed.

The police and Stanton discovered the body was really Boyd's after it was announced to the nation that it was Booth, the only photograph taken of the body was found in Stanton's collection. It was removed by Colonel Lafayette Baker to the old Arsenal Penitentiary where it was buried in an unknown place under the concrete floor. Each of the 26 detectives that worked on the case received several thousand dollars each after signing disclaimers stating that they had no further interest in the case. This of course is a common modus operandus (operating method) in such cases and is still used to this day. After all, why change a successful strategy?

Baker and detectives Luther and Andrew Potter knew the case was not yet closed and had to find Booth to prevent him from 'talking.' They followed his trail to New York and later to Canada, England and India.

So what happened to John Wilkes Booth? The Knights of the Golden Circle spirited Booth away to Granbury, Texas, where he lived and worked for many years as 'John St. Helen.' His own granddaughter Izola Forrester affirmed this in her 1937 book, *'This One Mad Act'* and she further stated that it was common knowledge in the Booth family that he did not die as was claimed, in the barn. In 1872, St. Helen was operating a distillery in Glen Rose, Texas where he was pursued by revenue agents over whiskey taxes. He hired an attorney, Finis Bates to represent him and Bates, the grandfather of Hollywood actress Kathy Bates, later wrote his own book about St. Helen (Booth.)

One day, after contracting a dose of influenza, St. Helen was convinced that he was going to die and called Bates to his bedside where he confessed that his real identity was John Wilkes Booth and that he was the assassin of Abraham Lincoln. Bates was highly sceptical naturally, but St. Helen gave him a photograph of himself for future identification purposes and after making a full recovery from his ailment, St. Helen begged Bates to hold his confession in strict confidence.

Meanwhile, National Detective Police Chief Baker broke off relations with Stanton who was discharged from the Army and as head of the secret service in 1866. A year later, Baker in his book 'The History of the U.S. Secret Service,' admitted delivering Booth's diary to Stanton and on another occasion testified that the diary was intact when it was in his possession. This in effect means that Lincoln's Secretary of War, Edwin M. Stanton who was actually Baker's boss, as the National Detective Police came under the War Department of the Army, *removed* the pages to facilitate a cover-up of an assassination to which he was an accessory, because the pages were found in his collection. Col. Lafayette Baker, who directly reported to Stanton, but also to Lincoln, was totally devoted to the President and for that loyalty and therefore by definition being a threat to Stanton, he was slowly poisoned till he died in 1868.

In 1922, two Civil war veterans swore an affidavit stating that the body removed from the Garrett farm was not Booth. Joseph Zeigen and Wilson Kenzie said they had served with the cavalry troop that surrounded the barn and furthermore, that the man dragged from the barn wore a Confederate uniform and on his feet were yellow brogans, the service footwear of the Confederacy. Subsequently to this, the two were sworn to secrecy and again probably also subjected to threats.

But back to the main thrust of the story… In 1866 the banksters renewed their push for the re-institution of a central bank under their control and an American currency backed by gold. They chose gold as gold has always been relatively scarce and therefore a lot easier to monopolise, than, for example silver, which was plentiful in the United States and had been found in huge quantities with the opening of the American West.

So, on 12th April, Congress resumed work for the European central bankers. It passed the, "Contraction Act," which authorized the Secretary of the Treasury to contract the money supply by retiring some of the Greenbacks in circulation.

This money contraction and its disastrous results was explained by Theodore R. Thoren and Richard F. Walker, in their book, 'The Truth in Money Book,' in which they stated the following… *"The hard times which occurred after the Civil War could have been avoided if the Greenback legislation had continued as President Lincoln had intended. Instead there were a series of money panics, what we call recessions, which put pressure on Congress to enact legislation to place the banking system under centralised control. Eventually the Federal Reserve Act was passed on 23rd December 1913."*

The 'Contraction Act,' passed by Congress affected the economy by decreasing the money supply as currency is being withdrawn. In addition, it was announced that the support of the Russian fleet cost the country about $7.2 million. Johnson did not have the constitutional authority to pay money to a foreign government for services, so arrangements were made instead, to purchase Alaska from the Russians in April 1867. This became known as 'Seward's Folly,' but despite what the banksters' historians and the bankster-owned *Wikipedia* tell us, the US possession of Alaska was nevertheless engineered as part of a compensation payment for the Russian Navy.

As for the Russian Czar, Alexander II, in 1866 he survived an assassination attempt but in 1881 he did not, when he was killed by an exploding bomb. The wrath of the Rothschilds upon the Russian monarchy lingered on as they continued to make good on their threat to systematically destroy every member of the Romanov dynasty.

In August 1867, the 17th President of the United States Andrew Johnson, failed in his attempt to remove Stanton from office and impeachment proceedings were begun against him in February, 1868 by Stanton and the Radical Republicans. Johnson was charged with attempting to fire Stanton without Senate approval, for treason against Congress and public language 'indecent and unbecoming' as the nation's leader.

Senator Benjamin F. Wade, President *pro tempore* of the senate and next in line for Presidential succession, was so sure that Johnson would be impeached that he already had his cabinet picked and Stanton was named as his Secretary of the Treasury. However as it turned out, the 26th May vote was 35-19, one short of the necessary two-thirds majority needed to impeach Johnson.

Ernest Seyd was sent to America in 1872 on a mission from the Rothschild owned Bank of England. He was given $100,000 with which he was to bribe as many Congressmen as necessary, for the purposes of getting silver demonetised as it had been found in huge quantities in the American West, and would therefore cut into the Rothschild's profits. He obviously spent his money wisely, as Congress passed the *'Coinage Act,'* the very next year, which resulted in the immediate cessation of the minting of silver dollars. Furthermore, Representative Samuel Hooper, who introduced the bill in the House, even admitted that Ernest Seyd had actually drafted the legislation.

Even Seyd himself admitted that he was behind the demonetising of silver in America, when he made the following statement… *"I went to America in the winter of 1872-1873, authorised to secure, if I could, the passage of a bill demonetising silver. It was in the interests of those I represented, the governors of the Bank of England, to have it done. By 1873, gold coins were the only form of coin money."*

Due to the covert manipulation of the money supply in America, by 1876, one third of the workforce was unemployed and unrest was growing daily. There were even calls for a return to Greenback money or silver money and as a result, Congress created the, 'United States Silver Commission,' to investigate the problem.

The Commission clearly understood that the national and international bankers were the cause of the problem with their deliberately contrived contraction of the money supply. An excerpt of their report reads as follows, *"The disaster of the Dark Ages was caused by decreasing money and falling prices… Without money, civilisation could not have had a beginning, and with a diminishing supply, it must languish, and unless relieved, finally perish. At the start of the Christian era the metallic money of the Roman Empire amounted to $1,800,000,000. By the end of the 15th century it had shrunk to less than*

$200,000,000 ... History records no other such disastrous transition as that from the Roman Empire to the Dark Ages ... "

Despite this damning report from the Commission, Congress took no action. However, rioting broke-out from Pittsburgh to Chicago. The bankers eventually decided to watch and wait as they knew that despite the violence, they were now firmly back in control. At the meeting of the American Bankers Association they urged their membership to do everything in their power to shout-down any suggestion of a return to Greenbacks.

The American Bankers Association secretary, James Buell, even wrote a letter to the members in which he blatantly called-on the banks to subvert both Congress and the press. In this letter he stated, *"It is advisable to do all in your power to sustain such prominent daily and weekly newspapers, especially the Agricultural and Religious Press, as well as oppose the Greenback issue of paper money and that you will also withhold patronage from all applicants who are not willing to oppose the government issue of money ... To repeal the Act creating bank notes, or to restore to circulation issue of money will be to provide the people with money and will therefore seriously affect our individual profits as bankers and lenders. See your Congressman at once and engage him to support our interests that we may control legislation."*

Buell's letter clearly had some effect, as although pressure mounted in Congress for change, the press tried to turn the general public away from the truth. An example of this was from the *New York Tribune* in their 10th January edition in which is stated in a banksters' propaganda piece, *"The capital of the country is organised at last and we will see whether Congress will dare to fly in its face."*

This early control of the media did not work entirely nevertheless, as on 28th February 1878 Congress passed the 'Sherman Law,' which allowed the minting of a limited number of silver dollars, ending the five year hiatus. However, this did not mean that anyone who brought silver to the United States Mint could have it struck into silver dollars, free of charge, as in the period prior to Ernest Seyd's Coinage Act in 1873. Gold backing of the American currency also remained.

However, the Sherman Law did ensure that some money began to flow into the economy again, and coupled with the fact that the banksters now realised that they were still firmly in control, they started issuing loans again and thus the post-Civil War depression was finally ended.

Someone who did not much care for the banksters, but who knew all about silver, gold and American banking, was a certain Jesse Woodson James.

In addition to all you think you may know about him, further research that has surfaced in recent years, by writers such as Del Schrader with *'Jesse James Was One Of His Names,'* Mark Owen writing for *henrymakow.com* and Warren Getler and Bob Brewer with their book *'Rebel Gold,'* Ronald J. Pastore and John O'Melveny's *'Jesse James Secret Codes,'* the infamous outlaw and western legend Jesse James, did NOT die at the hand of his cousin Bob Ford in 1882 as is widely believed.

This may be even more difficult to accept, because the legend of Jesse James, the mythology and the books, the movies, the TV shows, have all instilled in us that he did die as 'history' tells us. But please consider the following...

It is now known for certain that Jesse James faked his death to escape the law and the Pinkerton detectives of the railroad barons. Remember that back in those days, fingerprint identification was still not perfected, photography was becoming popular but again was in its infancy, crime reporting tended towards 'pulp fiction' and law enforcement relied more on bounty hunters and private detectives to track-down their fugitives, especially if it was the banks, railroads and insurance companies putting-up the rewards. And as for trying to correctly identify someone, that was not so much a science as an art-form in itself. But, according to Bud Hardcastle (a Jesse James historian,) the man who was killed and identified as James, was in fact Charles Bigelow.

Bigelow had been claiming and bragging that he **was** Jesse James, in all the robberies in which he was involved and upon his death was then buried as Jesse James. It is further believed by Hardcastle and other historians, that Bigelow's wife, a prostitute, was bribed and pretended to be Mrs. Jesse James when she identified the corpse.

Firstly, so much of what we know about Jesse James is a lie or a fabrication. As with many legends, it was born out of hyperbole and exploitation. Jesse James was an extraordinary individual, who if researchers are to be believed, and there is enough reasonable evidence to confirm this, lived a very long and fascinating life.

As stated earlier, Jesse James belonged to the *Knights of the Golden Circle* (KGC), a secret society that had a very powerful influence over the Confederacy. Other members included General Bedford Forrest and Captain William Quantrill. James rode with Quantrill and his infamous 'raiders,' a Confederate guerrilla outfit, during the Civil War. They became known more for being renegades, and bush-whackers because of their brutal, sadistic tactics whilst Jesse James became very proficient in subversive fighting and was an excellent spy for the Confederacy and certainly, patriotically believed it would eventually rise again. James was also involved in smuggling arms and ammunition to the Plains Indians, as well as training in guerrilla tactics against their common enemy, General George Armstrong Custer and the Union Army.

After the surrender of General Robert E. Lee at Appomattox court house, the Confederacy immediately went 'underground' and the KGC became even more determined and vowed to continue the fight, covertly. A force of 2,000 Missouri cavalry and a full regiment of Confederate-led Red Bone Indians from East Texas, commanded by General J.O. Shelby, journeyed to Mexico to join their ally, the Emperor Ferdinand Maximilian. When threatened by Mexican patriots under the leadership of Benito Juarez, an elite force led by Colonel William Quantrill and Colonel Jesse James was despatched to their aid.

While in Mexico, James was enlisted in an operation to smuggle Maximilian's treasure out of Mexico but on their way back north, the James forces learned that Maximilian had apparently been executed by the Mexican patriots. He and several others had been shot by firing squad, then loaded into carts and carried away for burial.

But the gravesite ceremony was infiltrated by the Red Bone Indians, who noticed signs of life in Maximilian. The Indians talked the Mexicans into allowing them to give him a separate burial. Later he was nursed back to health and transported to East Texas.

According to writer Del Schrader, Maximilian changed his name to John Maxi and began living undercover in North America. For further services to Maxi (Maximilian,) the KGC was personally rewarded $12.5 million of which $5 million alone was given to Jesse James and who was able to gain even more favour by reuniting Maxi with his wife Carlota. With his new-found wealth, James was more than ready and able to transform his life by faking his own death and this completely fooled the authorities and indeed the whole world.

James then began living under the name of J. Frank Dalton. (The name Dalton was his mother's maiden name, the initial 'J' for Jesse and 'Frank' was his brother's name.) As Chief of the inner sanctum of the *Knights of the Golden Circle*, James was one of the most powerful men in America and exceptionally rich too.

It is now also believed that Jesse James was actually the comptroller of the Confederacy, in charge of all gold and silver bullion. Headquarters for the KGC was Nashville, Tennessee, the home of Jesse's brother Frank and many years later, it became the Dixie Tabernacle, original home of the 'Grand Ole Opry.'

The covert fight of the Confederacy through the efforts of the KGC continued on for 19 more years and the outlaw exploits of the James gang, his cousins the Dalton gang and also the Younger's, in robbing banks and trains were all for the benefit of and coordinated by the KGC. It was said by some that Jesse James later used his own personal fortune to 'buy into' oil in the early days of the Texas oil boom and even that he invested in the Hughes Tool Company, owned by Howard Hughes Sr. This could well be true, as there is no doubt at all that Jesse lived to the ripe old age of 107, finally dying in 1942 in Lawton, Oklahoma.

Whatever happened to the 'loot,' the buried treasure of the KGC became the stuff of legends too. Both Jesse James and John Wilkes Booth were not only KGC members, they were also Freemasons. Having firstly used the alias John St. Helen, Booth then became David George but through his heavy drinking and laudanum dependency, he began to boast of who really was and what he did to Lincoln and also for the KGC. For many years he had been living-off a generous annual pension of $3,600, in return for keeping a low profile. And so for his indiscretions and after numerous warnings, it was decided to silence him forever and it was Jesse James who traced him to the Grand Hotel in Enid, Oklahoma, one winter evening in 1903. He offered Booth a glass of lemonade laced with arsenic and made sure this time that Booth would be clearly identified as being the real John Wilkes Booth. It was a massive scoop for the press, as scores of reporters descended on Enid for such a sensational story and Finis Bates, Booth's attorney helped identify the corpse. The mortician W. B. Penniman later charged tourists 10 cents to view Booth's corpse and following that it was Bates who profited even more, by renting out the mummified body to carnivals and sideshows.

It was bad enough that Booth had been so indiscreet about the Lincoln plot, but breaking the secret oaths of both the KGC and the Freemasons was the 'last straw' it would seem. As for Jesse James, this story appeared in the San Antonio Express on 21st January 1950 along with a picture from 1942...

"Old Time Bandit Meets the Press—J. Frank Dalton, 107, in bed, who claims to be Jesse James, talks to reporters on his arrival in New York. With him are two of his witnesses, Bushy Bill Roberts, 90, who claims to be a member of the James gang, and Colonel James R. Davis, 109, who says he was a US Marshal for the Cherokee Indian Nation. Dalton says history incorrectly recorded his death in 1882, when the victim of Bob Ford's gun was actually another man."

Though his war against the South had been brutal and destructive, Lincoln's post war policy towards the defeated states was to have been one of reconciliation and rebuilding. With his sudden death however, a radical faction within the Republican Party, known literally as the 'Radical Republicans' were free to abuse and punish the Southern states for their audacious secession.

During Reconstruction, many supporters of the old Confederacy were banned from voting, while newly-freed slaves were given the vote before they could even be educated. Smooth talking 'carpetbaggers' from the North flooded the South, promising to give the ex-slaves '40 acres and a mule' in exchange for their votes but once installed in office, the carpetbaggers and their ex-slave allies raised heavy taxes on the conquered southerners. Criminal acts against southerners, as well as rapes of southern women, became commonplace.

So it was in this atmosphere of oppressive occupation that the Confederate Army veterans formed a secret society spin-off from the *Knights of the Golden Circle* known as the *Ku Klux Klan* (KKK.) Klan members, clad in intimidating white robes and hoods, holding burning crosses, served as vigilante groups. They restored order, protected white women from being raped, lynched known criminals, attacked radicals and prevented the ex-slaves from voting for the carpetbaggers.

More so than the Civil War itself, it was the vindictive oppression of the South during Reconstruction that incited racial tensions and left lasting scars that took more than a century to heal. Meanwhile, in Europe...the Franco-Prussian War, a conflict between the French Empire of Napoleon III (nephew of Napoleon Bonaparte) and the Germanic Kingdom of Prussia began. Prussia was aided by a confederation of many smaller German states and its swift victory thwarted French ambitions in central Europe and brought about the end of Napoleon III's rule.

True to form after the war, the Rothschilds of France stepped-in with a massive bail-out of the nearly bankrupted French government. The new government (The Third Republic) was again a 'democracy,' bought and paid for by the Rothschilds and is under their influence more so than it was under the at best only semi-controllable Napoleon III. This is yet another fine example indeed of the best democracy that money could buy.

The Prussian/German victory over France was the instigating factor in the unification of the all the disparate German states under Kaiser (King) Wilhelm I of Prussia. The establishment of the German Empire thus ended the 'balance of power' that had been created with the Congress of Vienna in 1815 and Germany suddenly became the main economic power in continental Europe with one of the most powerful and professional armies in the world.

But meanwhile, back in England, the Rothschilds plotted and schemed to check and control the new German nation. Although their friends, thee Jewish banksters were thriving in Germany, Germany (like Czar Alexander's Russia) now had the capacity to shape its own destiny and thwart the ambitions of the 'City of London,' the bankster capital and power-base. But the Rothschilds now had a problem. Not only was German politics totally outside of their control, but the fact that several German Royals were intermarried with British nobility complicated the City's ability to threaten Germany with British military might.

Otto Von Bismarck was installed as the Chancellor (political head) of the new German Reich under Kaiser Wilhelm I and through his skilled and energetic diplomacy, he kept Germany out of war and the rest of Europe at peace and soon after a united Germany was established, Bismarck's government became the first European nation to grant full citizenship rights to its Jewish population. Even Rothschild's England and France had yet to achieve this and the British, Jewish Prime Minister Benjamin Disraeli held office only because he had 'converted' to Anglican Christianity. However, Jews then began to thrive in the new 'liberal' Germany.

The German Chancellor Otto von Bismarck then negotiated an agreement between the monarchs of Austria-Hungary (Emperor Franz Joseph,) Russia (Czar Alexander II) and Germany (Kaiser Wilhelm I.) The alliance, known as 'The League of The Emperors,' had three key stated purposes . . .

1. The League served as a mutual defence against the growing Red (Communist) movements, which had menaced Europe with violence since 1848.
2. The League worked to avoid war amongst each other when diplomacy can suffice to resolve differences.
3. The League opposed the expansion of French power and French/British schemes to threaten the internal order of their countries.

The military and financial power of these three great Empires formed a Central-Southern-Eastern European power-base that unfortunately for them as it was soon to transpire, the Rothschild banksters and their British and French 'hit men' could not control!

The British Empire from the very beginning was a creation of the Rothschilds. It was at its zenith during the iconic reign of Queen Victoria, but all along it was never about anything other than promoting and enforcing the policies of the Rothschilds and their bankster friends and opening-up new profit opportunities. It was Lionel de Rothschild, through his trusted agent and prime asset, the British Prime Minister Benjamin Disraeli that controlled Queen Victoria. The Rothschilds used Disraeli to strengthen the British nation in order to fulfil their goals, to confront Russia, to promote democracy and reform as a 'winning hearts and minds' cover and to advance the newly established Zionist agenda for world power. In these ends, Benjamin Disraeli succeeded. Queen Victoria herself was greatly enriched from the Rothschild empire built on slavery, opium, exploitation and corruption and it was the British soldier, the 'mercenary' of the Rothschild's vaulting ambition that eventually changed the complexion of the whole world.

In 1875, Khedive Said of Egypt was in financial difficulties and he therefore desperately needed to sell his controlling interest in the Suez Canal whilst the Rothschilds needed to control the Suez Canal themselves in order to protect and enhance their huge investments in the Middle East. So, Lionel de Rothschild directed Prime Minister Disraeli to buy-up Said's shares for £4 million and even though Parliament was not even sitting at that time, he convinced Queen Victoria in a letter that this would be in the best interests of Britain, that he must hurry with the transaction and that the Rothschilds were the only available source of immediate funding.

Of course it was a huge lie and the Rothschilds thereby benefitted by £500,000 alone, whilst Disraeli and other political insiders such as Lord Derby, also collected their share.

The Rothschilds did not wish to own the canal themselves and as is the case with most of their business interests, they preferred to remain in the shadows. It was obviously preferable to them that a government that they control owned it, as the military would then protect it for them.

Then in 1877 the **Russo-Turkish War began. Fir**stly, Russia desired to reclaim vital Black Sea territory lost in the Rothschild-promulgated Crimean War twenty years earlier and her other objective was to liberate the Orthodox Christian Slavic populations of the Balkan states, currently under Muslim Turkish rule. Russia's Orthodox Christian and Slavic allies, Serbia, Montenegro, Romania and Bulgaria, all rebelled against Turkey and fought alongside Russia whilst Turkish mistreatment of Bulgarian Christians, further angered the Russians. It was Russia that dominated the conflict, probably unsurprisingly due to her size, and began advancing towards the Turkish capital, Constantinople. Dismayed that Russia may capture Palestine from the beaten Turkish Empire, Disraeli pressured Russia to accept a truce offered by Turkey and he sent British ships to the area to intimidate Russia and to force a peace conference in Berlin, Germany.

Then, just days before the important international conference was due to take place in Berlin, two assassination attempts were made against German Emperor, Kaiser Wilhelm I. On 11th May 1878 a Communist named Emil Max Hodel fired shots at the Emperor and his daughter as they travelled together in their carriage. Fortunately for them the 'marksman' was a poor shot and Hodel was captured and then executed in August that year.

Three weeks later, another 'Communist sympathiser' named Karl Nobiling fired a shot-gun at the Emperor. The 82 year old Kaiser was wounded, but he survived against the odds and Nobiling then shot himself and died of his wounds three months later. The banksters' secret war against the Three Emperors League and all of Europe's Christian Monarchs, was just beginning to be 'ramped-up.'

Prime Minister Benjamin Disraeli totally dominated the Berlin conference which was called into session in order to settle the Russo-Turkish war even though Germany, Austria-Hungary, Russia, France, Italy and Turkey were also all in attendance. The Ottoman Turks still controlled Palestine but Britain and its Rothschild masters were desperate to assume control themselves and this was their ultimate goal.

Just before the Congress opened, Disraeli had concluded a secret deal with Turkey against Russia, whereby Britain was allowed to occupy the strategic island of Cyprus. This gave Disraeli a distinct advantage during the Congress and led him to issue new threats of war with Russia if she refused to comply with the requests of the Turks (who lost the war!)

Another underhanded pre-conference deal had also been struck between the divisive Disraeli and Russia's ally, Austria-Hungary whereby orthodox Christians, including the Serbian population of Bosnia, were to be placed under Austria-Hungary's rule. Russia and its Slavic allies had won the war against Turkey but many of the Slavs were to be transferred from Turkish rule to Austro-Hungarian rule. This move caused deep resentment among the Slavic subjects of Austria-Hungry, especially the Serbians of Bosnia who were forbidden from uniting with the newly independent nation of Serbia. Court intriguers on all sides had now inserted a permanent wedge between Russia and Austria-Hungry.

The German Chancellor Bismarck tried to keep the Disraeli engineered controversies from breaking up the Three Emperors League, but the humiliation of Russia at the hands of Britain, Turkey and Austria-Hungary was too much for her to bear. Russia withdrew from the League in disgust and then instead of being allied with Germany (whom Disraeli also wanted to isolate), Russia was now isolated and placed in a position where it could be pitted against Germany's ally, Austria-Hungary—a classic 'divide and conquer' strategy.

The foundations of The Great War of 1914-1918 (World War I) were actually built at the Congress of Berlin, through the pure-evil plotting of the Rothschild-Zionist asset, Benjamin Disraeli. Upon his return to England, the deceitful Disraeli boasted of how he had killed the League of the Three Emperors and with the League now disbanded, Rothschild and Disraeli escalated their assault on Russia.

Queen Victoria reigned over the British / bankster Empire from June 1837, until her death in January, 1901. During that 64 year period, Britain was involved in no less than 37 wars and conflicts. From the Opium Wars, the Boxer Rebellion in China, to the Indian Mutiny, the Crimean and Boer Wars in Africa etc., none of which benefited the vast majority of British people who on the contrary, were themselves enslaved in poverty and misery. The wars were really about the capturing of trade markets and / or the securing of natural resources to benefit the banksters and capitalists (as are all wars) but of course they were sold to the masses as defending our rights and fighting for our 'freedom.' Echoes of today really, as the same modus operandi are still used even now. Why change a successful formula for deceiving the people, after all?

To demonstrate how much our present-day view of history is coloured by what we are told by complicit historians ... how many people today realise how unpopular a monarch Queen Victoria was? In fact she survived no less than seven assassination attempts between 1840 and 1882. So much then for the widely disseminated view of her being adored by her loyal peoples. Nothing could be further from the truth. And of course, there was always the constant threat of assassination of any monarch or political figure that stood against the edicts of the banksters.

The Victorian era was the age of both industrial and political revolution, of economic extremes and allegedly of unabashed patriotism. Millions of mere children toiled in the bowels of the earth, the factory sweatshops and the stately homes of the elite and even on the fields of battle in order to benefit their bankster masters.

After four previous attempts, on 13th March 1881, Rothschild's 'Red' terrorists finally succeeded in assassinating Czar Alexander II of Russia. In the presence of his son Alexander III and grandson Nicholas, the Communists hurled bombs at the Czar's carriage, blowing-off Alexander's legs and causing him to bleed to death. And so the Rothschild threat to utterly destroy the Russian monarchy continued apace.

Then America lost its second President in 16 years to an assassin's bullet. James Garfield was an Ohio Republican who had only been in office for three months. He was a brilliant scholar, talented orator and a vocal advocate of interest-free 'hard money' (gold) as a national currency. He was outspoken in his mistrust of the banksters and issued this warning only two weeks before he was assassinated:

"Whoever controls the volume of money in our country is absolute master of all industry and commerce ... and when you realise that the entire system is very easily controlled, one way or another by a few powerful men at the top, you will not have to be told how periods of inflation and depression originate."

So it was then that on the 2nd July 1881, the 20th President of the United States, James A. Garfield was shot at a railway station by 'another' 'crazed, lone gunman' Charles Guiteau. Garfield actually survived the attack and was slowly recovering, but his condition worsened after two months of doctors needlessly probing him to find the by-now harmless bullet. He finally died on the 19th of September, not from the bullet, but by infection caused by the probing of the very suspect, some may even say 'criminally incompetent' doctors.

Coincidentally maybe, 'incompetent' doctors also hastened the deaths of 9th President William Henry Harrison and 12th President, Zachary Taylor. Taylor only served as

President for just sixteen months, from 4th March 1849 to 9th July 1850, and was best known as a former general in the Mexican-American War. Rumours persisted at the time and since, that his death was no accident and that indeed it was an assassination, a poisoning in fact.

On 4th July 1850, President Taylor became feverish. To alleviate his symptoms, he drank 'a pitcher of milk' and ate 'a bowl of cherries and several pickles.' Five days later he died and despite the rumours of poisoning, historians blamed various ailments for his passing, including cholera, typhoid fever and even food poisoning. Then in the late 1980s, an author by the name of Professor Clara Rising, decided to challenge established history.

Professor Rising theorised that unknown persons assassinated President Zachary Taylor via poison, specifically arsenic. On 17th June 1991, his lead coffin was removed from the ground and soon afterwards, Dr. George Nichols and Dr. William Maples discovered that Taylor's remains were in remarkably good shape. They proceeded to gather tissue samples, where initial tests showed relatively high arsenic levels. However, they were proclaimed to be too low to indicate a deliberate poisoning. But the rumours did not end there. In 1999, Michael Parenti revisited the arsenic theory in his book '*History as Mystery*' and reported numerous flaws in the autopsy. He also provided a convincing mass of circumstantial evidence that pointed to a poisoning. For example, Zachary Taylor's hair showed a suspiciously large amount of antimony, which is poisonous. Also, the amount of arsenic revealed in a second analysis of his hair was found to be similar to that of other poison victims.

Then there was the case of the 15th President of the United States, James Buchanan. He was inaugurated on 4th March 1857, before the Civil War, but at a time when tensions over slavery and secession were still running high. Buchanan was known to be suffering from a serious illness at his inauguration and some very strange circumstances surrounding it, made it appear that the new President had also been poisoned.

An article in the *New York Times* on 2nd June 1857 made a case that the illness suffered by President Buchanan earlier that year was nothing ordinary. According to the newspaper article, president-elect Buchanan first arrived at the National Hotel in Washington, D.C. on 25th January 1857. The very next day, people at the hotel began complaining of symptoms of poisoning, which included inflammation of the intestines and a swollen tongue. Buchanan himself was affected and, feeling quite ill, returned to his farm in Pennsylvania. However, after Buchanan left the National Hotel, things quickly returned to normal and no new cases of the apparent poisoning were reported.

Presidential inaugurations in the 19th century always took place on the 4th March and on 2nd March 1857, Buchanan returned to Washington and again checked into the National Hotel. As Buchanan returned, so did reports of poisoning. In the days surrounding the inauguration more than 700 guests at the hotel, or guests at Buchanan's inauguration parties, complained of illnesses. And as many as 30 people, including some of Buchanan's relatives, died. James Buchanan was stricken and felt quite ill at his own inauguration, but he did survive. However, rumours of his death swept through Washington in the early days of his administration, and some newspapers even reported that the President had died.

The explanation offered for all the illness and apparent poisonings was that it was all a vermin extermination gone horribly wrong. Supposedly the National Hotel was infested with rats, and rat poison laid down for them somehow made its way into the hotel food. However, suspicions lingered throughout Buchanan's term that some dark conspiracy had targeted him. Or, using the principle of 'Occam's Razor,' could it simply be the fact, that none of these Presidents Buchanan included, were friendly to the banksters, or their aims?

Although the British-Rothschild agent Benjamin Disraeli had destroyed The Three Emperors League (Russia/Germany/Austria-Hungary,) the German Chancellor Bismarck continued to work for peace. To 'reinsure' the peace of Europe and to prevent British or French intrigue from starting more wars, Bismarck and Russia agree to a secret treaty known as *'The Reinsurance Treaty.'* Under the terms of this agreement, Germany and Russia agreed to remain neutral should either of the other become involved in war with a third nation. However, neutrality would not apply if Russia attacked Germany's ally, Austria-Hungary.

The two giants remained vulnerable to the Balkan controversy in Austria-Hungary *(Russia was the protector of the minority Slavic/Orthodox community under Austrian rule and also of small Slavic states like Serbia.)* Nonetheless, the 'Reinsurance Treaty' was regarded as a very good sign that Russia and Germany would be able to work out any future differences diplomatically. Then Kaiser Wilhelm I of Germany passed away in March of 1888 at the age of 91. He was succeeded by his son Frederick I, who died of throat cancer after a reign of just 3 months. Frederick's 29 year old son Wilhelm II then became Kaiser in June of 1888. Like so many young, 'educated' Europeans of the day, Wilhelm II (like his father Frederick) had been infected with the poison of 'liberalism.'

Whereas the 'Iron Chancellor' Bismarck believed in strong leadership and in smashing the Reds, young Wilhelm hesitated to crush the Communists and Socialist agitators as he had come to believe that if Germany became more 'democratic,' it should pacify the Red agitators. He also wanted better relations with Great Britain, the enemy of Russia and to that end, **Wilhelm, (possibly under the influence of NWO court intriguers) turned his back completely on Russia and refused repeated Russian requests to renew Bismarck's Reinsurance Treaty with Russia.**

These irreconcilable differences led Wilhelm to dismiss the legendary Bismarck in 1890. As the grandson of Britain's Queen Victoria, Wilhelm naively believed that he could trust and befriend Britain, *which unfortunately for him belonged to the Rothschilds, not Victoria.* He also believed that he could solve any potential future problems with Russia (over the Balkan controversy with Austria-Hungary) simply by direct negotiation. But Russia now felt isolated from Germany and mistrusted Germany's ally, Austria-Hungary. This left her very vulnerable to French and British intrigue.

By 1891 the banksters had spent the previous decade creating economic booms followed by depressions so that they could buy-up thousands of homes, businesses and farms for a fraction of their value. They were preparing to take the economy down again in the near future and in a shocking memo sent out by the American Bankers Association, which would appear in the Congressional Record more than twenty years later, the following was stated...

"On September 1st 1894 we will not renew our loans under any consideration. On September 1st we will demand our money. We will foreclose and become mortgages in possession. We can take two-thirds of the farms west of the Mississippi and thousands of them east of the Mississippi as well, at our own price... Then the farmers will become tenants as in England..." 1891 American Bankers Association, as printed in the Congressional Record 29th April 1913.

Feeling isolated from Germany and suspicious of Austria-Hungary, in 1894, Russia fell into a clever trap set by France. 'The Franco-Russian Alliance' created an entangling military alliance between the two nations and the Russian giant could now be used to create a deadly second front in any future war with Germany. This is exactly what Bismarck had worked so hard to avoid. The popular French President at the time, Marie Francois Sadi Carnot had a reputation for honesty and was untouched by the massive Panama Canal scandal of 1892. He also established a friendship with the Russian Czar Alexander III, receiving the Order of St. Andrew from the Czar himself.

But Carnot's popularity, immunity to blackmail and close friendship with the hated Czar made him difficult for the Rothschilds to control. At this point in history, it appears that the Zionists were removing some of their 'eggs' from the increasingly anti-Semitic French 'basket' and placing them in the increasingly Jewish-influenced German basket, *(as suggested by Jewish-French Captain Dreyfus passing secrets to Germany).* The one constant that remained was the Rothschild's hatred for Russia.

This may explain why Carnot was stabbed to death by Italian Anarchist, Sante Geronimo Caserio, a murder which engendered horror and outrage throughout France. No King or President was safe it would seem, from the Communist radicals and their bankster masters.

The central issue in the 1896 US Presidential campaign was the issuance of silver money. Senator William Jennings Bryan from Nebraska, a Democrat aged only 36, made an emotional speech at the Democratic National Convention in Chicago, entitled, 'Crown of Thorns and Cross of Gold.' Senator Bryan stated that, *"We will answer their demands for a gold standard by saying to them, you shall not press down upon the brow of labor this crown of thorns, and you shall not crucify mankind upon a cross of gold."*

The bankers naturally supported the Republican candidate, William McKinley who in return favoured the gold standard. Furthermore those in the McKinley camp, cajoled manufacturers and industrialists to inform their employees that if Bryan were elected, all factories and plants would close and there would be no work. This tactic succeeded well. McKinley beat Bryan, albeit by a small margin.

One of the banksters' great desires now was to destabilise Catholic Spain and turn it into a more controllable (by them) 'democracy.' **Antonio Canovas** was the conservative Prime Minister of Spain at the time and he was an advocate of a constitutional monarchy and a staunch supporter of the Catholic Church, making him a target of the Christian-hating Reds and their Rothschild masters.

Red terrorists had previously hurled a bomb at Canovas but the attempt on his life failed. While internal Red turmoil weakened Spain from within, external Globalist elements in the United States were agitating for war with Spain over control of its Cuban colony. Canovas however, did not live to see the disastrous Spanish-American War. He was shot dead by Italian 'anarchist' Michele Angiolillo, probably another Rothschild-sponsored 'lone-nut,' just months before the war with the US began.

The idea of a Jewish state being formed in Palestine had been mooted for decades and whenever Russia advanced its interests in the area, Rothschild's Britain would respond vehemently. It was the banksters' aim to seize Palestine as a base in the Middle East and they constantly plotted, and schemed and did anything they could, to get their hands on their prize. This had now become one of the fundamental tenets of the new creed of Zionism, the establishment of a Jewish base in Palestine and although that was the overt reason, the covert reason had more to do with establishing a country that they could use as a power-base to enable them to behave with the 'legal' protection and impunity of a nation-state.

The problem for the Zionists was that Palestine was 90-95% Arab and remained under the sovereignty of the Ottoman Turkish Empire and unless the Turks voluntarily agreed to cede Palestine to the Jews of Europe, the Zionist dream would never be realised.

In 1901, the bankster-Zionists had offered to arrange a reduction of Turkey's foreign debt (owed to Zionist bankers) in exchange for Palestine. The Sultan of Turkey, Abdul Hamid II bluntly refused the offer because he believed quite rightly, that giving away the Holy Land to the Jews of Europe would be a betrayal of Turkey's and Palestine's Muslim population. The Zionist leader, Theodor Herzl however, refused to concede defeat and the Zionist movement grew rapidly amongst both Jew and non-Jew alike.

The British then offered to the Jews, the African colony of Uganda but the Zionists refused, insisting upon Palestine. Prior to his death in 1904, Herzl predicted that a world body would one day give Palestine to the Jews and that he would go down in history as father of the Jewish State. For Herzl's dream to come true, a European military power would have to be manipulated into taking Palestine away from the Turks by force.

By this time, Bismarck was now 83 years old and in poor health. Kaiser Wilhelm II visited the ex-Chancellor for the last time in the December of 1897 and again, the wise old man warned the Kaiser to beware of the intrigues of courtiers around him and of a European disaster that may yet still come. Subsequently, Bismarck made these accurate predictions...

"The crash will come twenty years after my departure if things go on like this... One day, the great European War will come out of some damned foolish thing in the Balkans."

Bismarck had always worried about a Balkan crisis turning into a World War and an internal Red uprising. With his 'Three Emperor's League' and 'Reinsurance Treaty' with Russia now gone, he clearly saw that Germany was vulnerable to British and French intrigue as well as to Red revolutionaries. The 'Iron Chancellor' died the following July and his grim prophecy would be fulfilled as he predicted, almost to the month.

"On the one hand there is the party which holds the power because it holds the wealth, which has in its grasp all labour and all trade, which manipulates for its own benefit and its own purposes all the sources of supply, and which is powerfully represented in the councils of State itself. On the other side there is the needy and powerless multitude, sore and suffering. Rapacious usury, which, although more than once condemned by the Church, is nevertheless under a different form but with the same guilt, still practiced by avaricious and grasping men ... So that a small number of very rich men have been able to lay upon the masses of the poor a yoke little better than slavery itself." Pope Leo XIII.

This was the dawning of the era of so-called 'yellow journalism,' of false reporting, lies and whipped-up hysteria. This is a necessary state of affairs in order for a 'false-flag' event such as the one below to succeed. False flag operations are covert operations designed to deceive in such a way that the operations appear as though they are being carried out by other entities, usually the enemy of those who commit them. The name is derived from the common military deception of flying false colours, that is, deceptively flying the flag of a country other than one's own. False flag operations are not limited to war and counter-insurgency operations, as they are often used during peace-time too. (For a comprehensive list and report of false flag operations through the ages, please read *'The Falsification of History,'* also by this author.)

15th February 1898—America's first 'False-Flag Terrorist Event'—the sinking of USS Maine

So, in an atmosphere of feverish warmongering against the Spanish, by the Hearst and Pulitzer press, the *USS Maine* was 'strangely' ordered to sail into Cuba's Havana Harbour in January of 1898. Three weeks later, she 'conveniently' exploded and swiftly sank, killing 261 US sailors. The warmongers and yellow press quickly blamed the attack on a planted Spanish mine and demanded war against Spain. Spain denied any involvement of course, as it had absolutely nothing to do with the incident and many years later, even the US government acknowledged that Spain was wrongly accused, stating that the explosion was 'an accident'—which is about as far as any government will go towards admitting the truth when false flag operations are exposed.

The recently appointed Assistant Secretary of the Navy was an up-and-coming bankster-controlled, Globalist warmonger named Theodore Roosevelt. It was Roosevelt who, unknown to McKinley and at the request of his bankster masters, ordered the *USS Maine* to sail to Havana in order to set-up this 'false-flag' operation. But then, when the pressure from Congressional warmongers and the yellow press became too intense for McKinley to resist, the US declared war on Spain in April of 1898.

The rallying cry of this blatant warmonger was "Remember the Maine and to hell with Spain!" The war with Spain was both brief and one-sided and although the US nevertheless suffered 3000 casualties, it gained control over Guam and the Philippines. Her heavy defeat also dealt a severe psychological blow to Spain and undermined its monarchy. It also marked the beginning of America's gradual transition from a relatively peaceful, constitutional republic, to the violent, crazed 'global bully' we see today.

However even in those days, the Rothschilds and the banksters controlled the world media and the fact that it was the Spanish themselves who did their utmost to rescue the dead, dying and injured from the *USS Maine*, went largely unreported.

In order to guarantee the success of any false-flag operation, the controlled mainstream media has to 'sell' the lie to an ignorant, indifferent public. Pulitzer and Hearst's reports went well beyond exaggeration; they outright fabricated stories of horrific conditions and atrocities under Spanish rule. Following the age-old newspaper maxim, *'If it bleeds, it leads,'* their reporters were despatched to Cuba. However, upon their arrival they found a completely different situation to what they had been conditioned to believe was the case. The famous artist and correspondent, Frederick Remington wrote to Hearst... *"There is no war. Request to be recalled."* Hearst's famous reply was, *"Please remain. You furnish the pictures, I'll furnish the war."* And he certainly did.

"Mr. Roosevelt is the Tom Sawyer of the political world of the twentieth century; always showing off; always hunting for a chance to show off; in his frenzied imagination the Great Republic is a vast Barnum circus with him for a clown and the whole world for an audience; he would go to Halifax for half a chance to show off and he would go to hell for a whole one." Mark Twain.

Theodore Roosevelt's 'progressive ideas,' despite the patriotic hype and speeches, all emanated from the banksters and what most benefitted them. He proved his worth to them by greatly expanding the role of the US Government and exerting its muscle all around the globe. This indeed was the beginning of America's role as the world's first, greatest and now only, 'super-power.'

Aware of the strategic need for a short-cut between the Atlantic and Pacific to facilitate corporate trade and reduce both delivery costs and shipping times, it was Roosevelt who promulgated the construction of the Panama Canal. His corollary to the Monroe Doctrine prevented the establishment of foreign bases in the Caribbean and arrogated the sole right of intervention in Latin America to the United States.

The Spanish-American War also had the effect of launching Theodore Roosevelt into the national spotlight as a 'war hero.' As soon as war began, Roosevelt resigned his position as Assistant Navy Secretary and joined a cavalry unit dubbed the 'The Rough Riders.' The lackeys of the Pulitzer and Hearst press brigade wildly exaggerated Roosevelt's 'heroic charge on horseback' at the 'decisive' Battle of San Juan Hill which in reality was simply a minor skirmish in which the Americans, fighting on foot, outnumbered the Spaniards by fifteen to one. Roosevelt referred to the war of 1898 as 'a splendid little war,' which I believe tells us all we need to know about the odious little man. It was clear now that this insane warmonger, who had pushed hard for war with Spain and engineered the sinking of USS Maine, was being groomed for bigger and better things.

The Anglo-Boer War in Southern Africa, beginning in 1899, was destined to become the first, but not by a long stretch the last, major military clash of the 20th century. The Boers were the descendants of German, French and Dutch settlers who had arrived in South Africa in the 1600s. Hard working Boers ('Boer' is the Dutch word for farmer) had developed the virgin land and built prosperous and free republics for themselves. But the discovery of gold and diamonds in the 1800s attracts the banksters' interest and so of course that was all about to change.

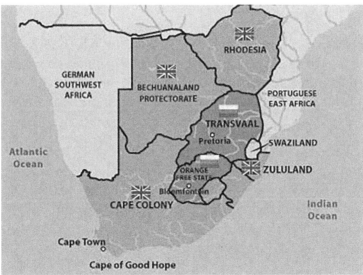

Rothschild agent Cecil Rhodes, for whom 'Rhodesia' and the 'Rhodes Scholarship' would later be named and former rival, rags-to-riches millionaire Barney Barnato, joined forces and made the DeBeers company, the world's largest diamond producer and consortium. Today it is owned by the Oppenheimer bankster family.

On 29th December 1895, a band of 500 British adventurers attempted to seize control of South Africa in an 'unofficial' armed takeover. The failed raid was led by Rhodes' personal friend, Leander Starr Jameson. Undaunted by the raid's failure, the UK-Jewish bankster alliance continued to foment war against the Boers, with Jewish newspapers in the UK being the most vocal of all. The Boers asked Britain to withdraw its troops, the Brits refused and so the Boer War began in earnest in October 1899.

The Rothschild-UK armies waged a brutal and cruel war, starving women and children in disease-ridden concentration camps and destroying farms. (Concentration camps were not invented by the Nazis.) These camps were originally designed for refugees whose farms had been destroyed by the brutal British 'scorched earth' policy (the burning-down of all Boer homesteads and farms.) Then, following Kitchener's new policy, many women and children were forcibly moved to prevent the Boers from re-supplying from their homes and more camps were built and converted to prisons.

Neither was this the first instance of concentration camps, however. The Spanish had used them in the Ten Years' War that later led to the Spanish-American War and the United States used them to devastate guerrilla forces during the Philippine-American War. But the concentration camp system of the British was on a much larger scale, there being a total of 45 tented camps built for Boer internees and 64 for black African ones. Of the 28,000 Boer men captured as prisoners of war, 25,630 were sent overseas. So, most Boers remaining in the local camps were women and children, but the native African ones held large numbers of men also.

The conditions in the camps were very unhealthy and the food rations were meagre and the wives and children of men who were still fighting were given smaller rations than others. The poor diet and inadequate hygiene led to endemic, contagious diseases such as measles, typhoid and dysentery. Coupled with a shortage of medical facilities, this led to large numbers of deaths.

A report after the war concluded that 27,927 Boers (of whom 22,074 were children under 16) and 14,154 black Africans had died of starvation, disease and exposure in the concentration camps. In all, about 25% of the Boer inmates and 12% of the black African ones died (although recent research suggests that the black African deaths were underestimated and may have actually been around 20,000).

When the British instigated and armed local black tribes to 'kill the Boers' (just as they had done with American Indian tribes against the rebellious American colonists of the 1770s,) the Boers finally submitted to British rule. This was yet another triumph for the banksters over a small self-sufficient, self-governing nation, now brought firmly under the banksters' heel along with their multitude of natural resources, now fully ripe and ready to be turned into bankster profits.

But meanwhile, back in America on the 21st November 1899, there was another suspicious, political 'sudden death.' After the onset of a strange illness, Vice President Garret Hobart died of heart failure at the age of 55. Like his good friend President McKinley, Hobart was a genuine constitutional conservative. His untimely death conveniently created an opening for the Progressive-Globalist faction that had now seriously infiltrated the Republican Party.

Whilst running the US Navy, Theodore Roosevelt's role in the false-flag destruction of the *USS Maine* conveniently positioned him for rapid 3-step career advancement:

1. Roosevelt's military record was *grossly* exaggerated by the yellow press (the mythical charge of San Juan Hill).
2. The 'war hero' was then catapulted into the Governorship of New York in 1899.
3. When Vice President Hobart died unexpectedly (almost certainly poisoned,) the Globalist-Zionist wing of the Republican Party forced the 'war hero' upon a reluctant McKinley as his new VP.

The Globalists were now just one step away from having their first puppet installed in the White House and subsequent events suggested that Hobart's oddly convenient death was part of a plan.

It is perhaps worthwhile now to summarise the modus operandi of the bankster plans for world domination...

The banksters overall plan, through their main entity the British Rothschild family, was to enslave the world with debt and to control all governments, finance, commerce and natural resources, until finally their hoped-for one-world totalitarian government was established.

To achieve this ultimate goal, they would instigate and prolong endless wars and conflicts, terrorist acts, assassinations and riots to further the indebtedness of nations, to divide and conquer peoples, to pit religions and political parties against each other. They would also create secret societies, capitalism, socialism, fascism and communism, all to do their bidding and to provide 'opposites' which may be set at each other's throats at will.

So, at the turn of the nineteenth century into the twentieth the banksters were busy reconfiguring the world and positioning it for their first global war. They were also preparing to re-establish and expand their control over America once again and in doing so, they would soon be ready to continue their long-term plans. They were only just getting started in fact...

Chapter 2
The Rise of the Banksters

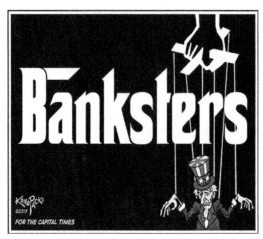

So, now that the scene has been set, the roots of the banksters' evil machinations have been covered in detail and the reason that the world is the way it is has been revealed, you are now hopefully somewhat better prepared to understand their further rise to ultimate power. Indeed, as we moved into the modern age, their crimes against humanity became even more horrific and much more brazen.

Given different circumstances, and with all the scientific advances of the past one hundred years or so, the 20th century should have been a 'perfect age' for mankind, a utopia if you will, that could so easily have been our reality. As different as we all are as human beings, we all have the same needs and desires, we share a common love for our families and for our countries. Most of us ask only to be left in peace to live our lives and to be prosperous enough to make a comfortable life for ourselves and our families without financial worry. How sad it is then that these are the very things that the majority are now denied by the banksters as they continue to 'bleed us dry' in every possible way they can.

But as we have already witnessed to a certain extent, the banksters never had any other plans for 'we, the people.' To them, we were and indeed still are, just another resource to be used and exploited. We are sheep to be fleeced and led to the slaughter. The banksters have corrupted our ideals and beliefs, set us against each other and all without most of us ever even suspecting it for a moment. They are the masters of deceit and deception and from the very beginning they have counted upon our collective ignorance, selfishness and our indifference to the plight of others. Our sense of right and wrong, our loyalties and trust, have all been turned upside-down and made us uncomprehending accomplices to their evil crimes. The banksters of course, could not have done any of this without our compliance, albeit unwittingly.

In stating categorically that the banksters are 'Zionists,' that they perpetrated all these wars, assassinations, frauds and depressions for some perverted political agenda called

Zionism, for clarification, it should be clearly understood that the everyday use of the word 'Zionism,' has little to do with Judaism or the Jewish religion itself, despite the implications to the contrary.

The banksters are however without doubt, mostly of Jewish origin and their crimes against humanity are to a large extent protected by the term 'anti-Semitism,' which they scatter around like confetti at a wedding, whenever their serious indiscretions are in danger of being exposed. Their greatest defence, their perfect alibi, has always been our ignorance of this fact and of the crimes that they have committed down the centuries. In addition to that, we must also consider the general wholly contrived, continued ignorance of the fact that Zionism and Judaism are virtually total opposites. They are almost diametrically opposed to each other and indeed orthodox Jews more than any other single group, vehemently oppose Zionism.

But do not simply take my word for this dear reader, I shall allow an organisation with far more credibility than myself to explain the difference. No, not the bankster/Zionist controlled *Wikipedia*™ or any other 'mainstream' media source, but *'Neturei Karta International—Jews United against Zionism,'* an organisation that has been in the forefront of the battle against Zionism for over a century...

"Judaism believes in One God who revealed the Torah. It affirms Divine Providence and, accordingly, views Jewish exile as a punishment for sin. Redemption may be achieved solely through prayer and penance. Judaism calls upon all Jews to obey the Torah in its entirety including the commandment to be patriotic citizens. Zionism rejects the Creator, His Revelation and reward and punishment. Among its fruits are the persecution of the Palestinian people and the spiritual and physical endangering of the Jewish people. It encourages treasonous, dual loyalty among unsuspecting Jews throughout the world. At its root Zionism sees reality as barren and de-sacralised. It is the antithesis of Torah Judaism."

In simple terms, the Zionist political movement was the creation of a Hungarian-Jewish journalist named Theodor Herzl, amongst whose ideas was the founding of a Jewish state. Upon hearing of this, the banksters, or more precisely *M.A. Rothschild & Fils* of Paris, and *N.M. Rothschild & Son* of London, decided that here was a 'useful idiot' that could be manipulated to their own purposes. It was Edmond de Rothschild who worked closely with Herzl, financing the Jewish settlements in Palestine and as Rothschild himself once remarked, *"Without me, Zionism would not have succeeded, but without Zionism my work would have been stuck to death."*

But to say that the banksters are Zionist in their beliefs is really untrue. Even though it has been the vehicle that has propagated their ideas AND protected them, banksters have merely used Zionism as a convenient front. Using it as a front, hiding behind the Jewish people, exaggerating and exploiting their 'suffering,' yet all the while promoting anti-Semitism to deflect and silence any and all debate and criticism of their actions, is how the banksters really utilise Zionism. Zionism is not confined simply to Jewish people, there are Christian-Zionists too and I shall cover this aspect later. Again, the banksters use everyone to their own advantage. They are for and against everything, depending on the circumstances of the moment and how it suits their purposes—or not, but their evil agenda is always slowly advanced, without the masses ever knowing it.

The 'label' of 'anti-Semitism' is actually utterly meaningless, yet it has been hijacked by a small group of people to inhibit us all from criticising their actions. To fully comprehend this point, it is firstly necessary for me to define three commonly misunderstood or even possibly unfamiliar terms.

Judaism—The Jewish *religion*. Jews can be split into two distinct sub-groups, Ashkenazi (Khazarian) Jews who comprise by far the majority (over 90%) and Sephardic Jews. These two sub-groups are racially as different as chalk and cheese and so, despite what you may believe or more accurately have been urged to believe; Judaism is a 'religion' and not a 'race.' In fact many people of Jewish background and parentage are not even religious and so their being described as 'Jews' is actually erroneous.

Zionism—a *political* movement that was originally established to lobby for a Jewish homeland and now exists to promote the superiority of Israel above all other countries, with the ultimate goal of a one-world government based in Tel Aviv. Zionism is comprised primarily of Jewish people, but many non-Jews are Zionists and indeed many Jews are anti-Zionist.

Semitism—Not the state of being Jewish as is generally believed and promoted by Zionism for its own ends but simply the racial group to which inhabitants of a small area of the Middle East belong. Semites may be Sephardic Jews or they may be Arabs, there is no *racial* difference between the two. However Ashkenazi Jews, despite their loud and raucous protestations to the contrary, are definitely not Semitic.

"It is important that you understand what Zionism really is. Zionist propaganda has led the American people to believe that Zionism and Judaism are one and the same and that they are religious in nature. This is a blatant lie." Jack Bernstein, assassinated by the Mossad.

"The meaning of the term 'anti-Semite' has significantly changed in recent years. There was a time when this term referred to those who despised Jews. Later, the term referred to those who promoted myths about a global Jewish conspiracy to rule the world. Today the term 'anti-Semite' is used by the ruling elite to lambast human rights activists who advocate equal rights between Jews, Christians and Muslims, the right of return of Palestinian refugees to their homeland and the vision of a common, democratic state for both Palestinians and Israelis. The word 'anti-Semite,' which initially conveyed a negative and even sinister meaning, refers now to positive and highly commendable attitudes that can be carried with honour. One may lament this change of meaning, but one should remember that a word does not carry any particular meaning. It is merely a conventional symbol that refers to external contents. By convention, society could agree to name animosity towards Jews 'xakaculca,' democracy 'zbzb' and elephants 'democracy.' Inasmuch as the term 'anti-Semite' now refers to human rights advocates and radical democrats, I declare myself a radical anti-Semite." Elias Davidsson, June 2011.

"Zionists from the beginning welcomed anti-Semitism as a means of undermining what Zionists believed was the sense of false security of Jews in western, liberal societies, and as the

means by which Jews would be kept in a permanent state of neurosis. Large and powerful organizations such as the US-based Anti-Defamation League of B'nai B'rith exist mainly for the purpose of exaggerating the extent of anti-Semitism in order to keep Jews under the Zionist heel and keep Israeli coffers filled." Rabbi Silverstein, 'The Lies of Zionism.'

"Anti-Semites will become our surest friends, anti-Semitic countries our allies." Theodor Herzl, founder of Zionism in the 19th century.

"Anti-Semitism is no longer the hatred of and discrimination against Jews as a religious or ethnic group; in the age of Zionism, we are told, anti-Semitism has metamorphosed into something that is more insidious. Today, Israel and its Western defenders insist genocidal anti-Semitism consists mainly of any attempt to take away and to refuse to uphold the absolute right of Israel to be a Jewish, racist state." Professor Joseph Maddad, palestineremembered.com, 5th May 2007

It is important here to make the point that Zionists are not the friends of the Jews in any way, despite what many Jews believe. Jews worldwide have been and continue to be used, often unknowingly in the Zionists plotting and scheming for world domination.

Ashkenazi Jews originated from the plains of South-Eastern Europe / Western Asia and were originally a large, war-like, nomadic tribe, the Khazars, who inhabited those regions in the Dark and early Middle Ages. They converted en-masse to Judaism, not through faith but simply in order to bring respectability to their previously god-less reputations when integration with other societies became necessary, more than a thousand years ago. This was the group of 'Jews' who were discriminated against for centuries and expelled from many European nations for their usury, anti-social practices and their own discriminatory practices against non-Jews. I repeat that these people had no racial or genetic ties to the 'Holy Land' whatsoever and so the oft-repeated cries for a Jewish state in their ancestral 'homeland' in the early to mid-twentieth century, was simply Zionist propaganda and deception. Sephardic Jews however, are native to the Holy Land or Palestine and were the original biblical Jews.

So, in effect the Zionists have deliberately blurred the boundaries, between race, religion and politics to prevent criticism of their actions. They have hi-jacked the term 'anti-Semitism,' strictly speaking an accusation of racism and managed over time to associate this with discrimination against Jews in general by deceitful social engineering, whilst also turning the distinction between 'Jewish' and 'Zionist' into a grey area, to the same effect. How have they achieved this? Their almost total control of banking, media and the entertainment industries makes this task fairly straightforward via their vast propaganda machine. Many Hollywood movies subtly promote the superiority of the Jews and the weakness and immorality of non-Jews. Anyone who criticises or stands up to them in any way is subtly and sometimes unfortunately, not so subtly, destroyed. At the very least their detractors are accused of being, (shock-horror,) anti-Semitic with all the attendant stigma this terminology carries. Anti-Semitism is closely related and linked to Nazism in the minds of most people today. The immense power of propaganda, social engineering and mind control should be underestimated only at one's peril.

"We must distinguish between political and racial anti-Semitism. It's obvious that organised Jewry has a political program synonymous with the Rothschild satanic world government agenda." Henry Makow, Jewish-born researcher and author of 'A Cruel Hoax.'

Think about this for a moment. Political criticism is valid today (at least for now anyway) whilst racial criticism (racism) is totally frowned upon and even legislated against. In making their cause a racial rather than a political one and by rendering the two distinctly separate terms 'Jewish' and 'Zionist' interchangeable, they have succeeded in duping the world and protecting their own insidious views and actions from any form of censure, on pain of being branded by them as an anti-Semite and therefore by implication, a Nazi.

So, an 'anti-Semite' strictly speaking, by definition is someone who discriminates against people of the area known as the 'Holy Land,' Palestinian Arabs and Sephardic Jew alike and not simply someone who is a 'Jew-hater' as it has been engineered to be construed.

Personally speaking, I am not anti-Semitic (or anti-Jewish, to be clear.) Jews have been duped and suffered at the hands of these wolves in sheep's clothing more than any other group and in many ways still are. I believe strongly in the freedom of all to do as they choose as long as it harms no-one, but I am definitely anti-Zionist politically, as their actions and beliefs are calculated to cause maximum harm to those who do not share their extreme racist views. However, the views expounded herein will no doubt see me labelled as 'anti-Semitic' by the Zionist attack-dogs. If anti-Semitism did not exist, the Zionists would have to invent it. Actually, they already have done so.

Of course there are anti-Jewish people in the world. To deny that fact would be ridiculous. But there are also anti-British, anti-American, anti-Muslim and anti-almost-anything-you-can-name elements abounding throughout the world today, too. However, in my view it is highly significant that to be anti-anything-else, does not carry the same stigma as being 'anti-Semitic.' This has been successfully inured into our culture to become a heinous act far more serious than any other form of prejudice.

The Dreyfus Affair

Theodor Herzl had no idea of the role he was about to play in history, or how he was totally used in a diabolical plan that began in 1894. Alfred Dreyfus was a Jewish-French artillery captain who was framed by Edmund de Rothschild, for passing secrets to the Germans. It was a Rothschild plan all along to stir-up hatred of the Jewish people and to show them as a threat to the French way of life.

The broad facts of '*l'Affaire*' are well known to history, but maybe not so much the real, hidden truth. In 1894, when France was still seeking revenge following her humiliating defeat in the Franco-Prussian war, Captain Alfred Dreyfus, a Jewish army officer from the 'lost provinces' of Alsace-Lorraine ceded to Germany after the defeat, was accused of passing military secrets to the German embassy in Paris. The only evidence against him was a slight resemblance between his handwriting and that on the *bordereau*, a torn up list of not very interesting items promised by a supposed traitor inside the French army that had been stolen from the Embassy's wastepaper basket by a 'cleaner,' employed by the French counter-intelligence agency.

Despite the clear lack of evidence, Dreyfus was the perfect scapegoat. He was aloof, pushily ambitious and unpopular with his peers, spoke good German and regularly visited the newly German-acquired 'lost provinces' to see his family. Above all perhaps, at a time when 'anti-Semitism' was rife, he was Jewish. The fact that he was also intensely patriotic and fanatically devoted to France and the army counted for nothing with his superior officers however, as it was they who condemned him.

Dreyfus was swiftly convicted of high treason by court martial, publicly degraded before a baying mob and dispatched to Devil's Island, the notorious penal colony off South America where he languished in misery for four years. Meanwhile his wealthy brother, Mathieu, campaigned tirelessly to re-open the case and to uncover the real traitor. After innumerable setbacks and several bribes paid to influential people, he succeeded in identifying another officer, the dissolute Major Charles Esterhazy, as the true author of the *bordereau*. As ever, though, it was not the original offence but the cover-up that was significant. A conspiracy of politicians, right-wing journalists, many of the Catholic clergy and the leading army generals had connived not only in convicting the innocent Dreyfus, but in using it as a vehicle to condemn France's entire Jewish community, along with its Freemasons, Protestants and left-wingers, as potential traitors. Only after repeated re-trials and setbacks was the full extent of the plot exposed, involving lies, forgeries, the inter-suicide of the forger, duels, passionate quarrels, riots, Emile Zola's immortal letter '*J'Accuse!*' and the death of its recipient, France's President Faure, in the Elysée Palace.

Carrying out complex, elaborate anti-Semitic schemes to confuse the authorities, the public and historians and ultimately to garner sympathy for the Jewish / Zionist cause which they of course were deceptively trying to render interchangeable, was to become a hallmark of the Rothschilds. The idea was to smear and humiliate the rival anti-Semitic, anti-Rothschild party. However in 1906, Dreyfus was fully vindicated and the real spy, the Rothschild agent, Esterhazy, fled to England. The army had known for some time that it was Esterhazy, but succeeded in covering it up. There was a deep loathing of Jews within the French army and this worked to the advantage of Baron Edmund Rothschild.

And so it was that the huge public outcry and rioting against Dreyfus, was the major factor that sparked Theodore Herzl and his Zionist beliefs. And just as with Dreyfus, Rothschild would make even greater use of Herzl, to the point where he helped to found the Zionist state that the banksters had wished-for all along. Ironically, Palestine was only sixth on the list for such a homeland at Theodor Herzl's First Zionist Congress in 1897, behind countries including Argentina, Uganda and Turkey. It was in fact the Christian Zionists who were orchestrating the takeover of Palestine from the beginning.

The First Zionist Congress was held in Basel, Switzerland and was chaired by Theodor

Herzl himself. Jewish delegates from across Europe soon agreed that Palestine should one day be given to them.

They adopted the former sign of the Rothschilds, the 'red hexagram,' the two interposed triangles, as the Zionist movement's emblem.

Herzl also stated in his diaries, *"It is essential that the sufferings of Jews ... become worse ... this will assist in realisation of our plans ... I have an excellent idea ... I shall induce anti-Semites to liquidate Jewish wealth ... The anti-Semites will assist us thereby, in that they will strengthen the persecution and oppression of Jews. The anti-Semites shall be our best friends."*

The death of President McKinley in the US in 1901 at the hands of an assassin launched the bankster puppet Theodore 'Teddy' Roosevelt into office, completing his amazing ascent from obscurity to the White House in just two years. McKinley's 'convenient' death marked the beginning of 'The Progressive Era,' in which the Federal government greatly expanded its power and foreign involvement, all of course at the behest of and to the benefit of the banksters.

President McKinley had begun his attack against the banksters, with his ally and Secretary of State John Sherman, younger brother of Civil War hero, General William Tecumseh Sherman. The legal tool used by President McKinley and Sherman against the banksters was the law known as the 'Sherman Anti-trust Act,' which was first brought to bear against the Rothschild-supported and funded JP Morgan financial empire known as the 'Northern Trust' which by the late 19th century owned nearly all of America's railway system.

But now let me introduce you to the one man who more than any other Zionist bankster, had the absolute greatest influence on not just American history, but also that of the entire World.

He was the foremost Jewish leader from 1880 to 1920 in what is now referred-to by Jewish-American historians as 'The Schiff Era.' He served as the Director of many important corporations, including the *National City Bank of New York, Equitable Life Assurance Society, Wells Fargo & Company*, and the *Union Pacific Railroad*. Schiff, who made his fortune from interest-bearing loans, was the main player behind the *'Hebrew Free Loan Society'* in 1892, an organisation which issued interest-free loans only to Jews and which is still in operation today.

There are so many dimensions to the banksters, so many layers of complexity and interconnection. It may help in comprehending the sheer scale of it all, to think of the huge banking dynasties as a large criminal family, inter-married and constantly growing and evolving with the passage of time. These are the ultimate 'movers and shakers,' and money, power and immense, obscene wealth is everything to them.

Jacob Schiff was born in 1847 in Frankfurt-am-Main, Germany, to Moses and Clara Schiff, members of a distinguished Ashkenazi Jewish rabbinical family that traced its lineage in Frankfurt back to 1370 and his father, Moses Schiff, was a broker for the Rothschilds. Schiff was educated in the schools of Frankfurt and was first employed in the banking and brokerage business as an apprentice in 1861.

After the US Civil War had ended in April 1865, Schiff came to the United States, arriving in New York City on 6th August. He was licensed as a broker on 21st November 1866, and joined the firm of *Budge, Schiff & Company* in 1867, eventually becoming a naturalised citizen of the United States in September 1870. He had been sent to America by the Rothschilds with instructions and the finance necessary to buy into a banking house, the purpose of which was to carry out four specific assignments...

1. The most important task, was to help acquire control of America's money system.
2. Find desirable men, who for a price would be willing to serve as stooges for the great conspiracy and promote them into high places in the Federal government, Congress, and the US Supreme Court and all Federal agencies.
3. Create strife throughout the nation, particularly between the whites and blacks.
4. Create a movement to destroy all religion in the United States, with Christianity the chief target.

Rothschild's greatest agent of them all, Jacob Schiff, went on to spectacularly succeed in all four of these tasks, as you will see...

He went on to finance John D. Rockefeller's *Standard Oil Company*, Edward H. Harriman's railroad empire that included *Union Pacific* and *Southern Pacific* and also the *Wells Fargo Express Company* and Schiff made Andrew Carnegie's steel empire possible too.

However, Schiff's most history-influencing accomplishment would have to be the role of 'Trojan Horse,' which he played in the late 1890s. At a time when Jewish influence in America was relatively minor and Jewish numbers were yet very small, it was Schiff's cajoling of the outgoing US President and former New York Governor, Grover Cleveland that prevented the massive wave of Jewish immigration to America from being shut-down completely.

The proposed Immigration Bill of 1897 would have required immigrants to undergo a literacy test; something that the vast majority of Russian Jews would not have been able to pass, due to their inherent low levels of literacy. But after passing both Houses of Congress, Cleveland's veto, induced by Schiff, saved the day for the incoming Communist-leaning and Zionist Jews of Russia.

The Jewish historian Lawrence J. Epstein wrote accurately... "*It is staggering to consider the alternative course American Jewish history would have* taken had this measure passed."

As a good Rothschild protégé, Schiff hated Christian Russia with a passion and worked tirelessly to overthrow the Romanov Dynasty and replace it with Jewish Reds

/ Communists. Towards that end he personally financed and sold bonds on behalf of, about 50% of the entire Japanese war effort during the Russo-Japanese War. As a result, the war ended with a Japanese victory.

Russia's loss was also facilitated by Schiff's puppet, Teddy Roosevelt, whose negotiating intervention clearly favoured Japan over Russia.

For his role in securing victory for Japan, Schiff was personally awarded a medal, the *Order of the Rising Sun*, by the Japanese Emperor. But unbeknown to the Emperor, Schiff, Roosevelt and their henchmen were at the time already plotting Japan's ultimate demise, a process which started with Roosevelt's escalating naval manoeuvres in the Pacific (Philippines, Midway, Guam, Pearl Harbor), and culminated with nephew Franklin's war and atomic bombs of 1945 *(actually dropped under Truman's orders, four months after FDR's death)*.

Schiff's Jewish agents in Russia successfully used the humiliating loss of the Russo-Japanese war as an opportunity to plan and launch the first Communist Russian revolution in 1905. This bloody Revolution ultimately failed, but the Czar's regime was left considerably weakened. Many of the returning Russian POWs from the war with Japan came home brainwashed after Schiff had arranged for them to be subjected to Communist propaganda, whilst in Japanese captivity. The final Bolshevik overthrow of Russia in 1917 in fact largely owed its success to the damage done to Russia by Jacob Schiff and Roosevelt in 1905.

Not content with flooding the North-eastern US with future Communists, Progressives and Zionists from Russia, Jacob Schiff founded and financed the 'Galveston Movement,' an attempt to settle Russian-Jewish immigrants in the south and west of the United States. Schiff himself described the effort in an article of 1914. He wrote . . .

"The committee placed itself promptly after its organization into communication with the Jewish Territorial Organization, of which Israel Zangwill is the head, and an arrangement was entered into between that organization and the Galveston Committee, under which the former undertook to make propaganda in Russia and Romania for acquainting intending emigrants with the advantages of going into the United States through Galveston (Texas), rather than to and through the overcrowded and congested North Atlantic ports."

Instead of confining the arrival of Jews to just the New York, New England, Pennsylvania and New Jersey areas, Schiff's clever scheme facilitated the spread of the liberal/progressive plague to even the most conservative parts of the country.

As was also the case during the Russo-Japanese War of 1905, the chaos of World War I enabled the Jewish-dominated Communists *(Bolsheviks)* to stage another uprising in 1917. Leading the diabolical efforts was Jacob Schiff's loyal agent, Leon Trotsky, newly re-established in Russia after having been in hiding in Brooklyn, New York throughout the previous decade. The Czar had been forced to abdicate earlier that same year and the provisional government was soon overthrown by the Jewish-led Bolsheviks.

The following year, Schiff's Bolshevik henchmen murdered Czar Nicholas II, his wife

Alexandra and his entire family and the subsequent reign of genocidal terror that the Soviets then engendered, was a stain on humanity for decades to come. Scores of millions, mainly Christians, were brutally exterminated, as many as 100 million at some estimates, and none of it could ever have happened without the tireless chicanery of the Rothschilds, Schiff and their subordinates. Soon after the Revolution, Schiff removed Russia (by this time the Soviet Union) from his 'do-not-lend-to' list.

From all the stock and banking fraud, to the crash of 1907 and the founding of the Federal Reserve Bank, Jacob Schiff was either indirectly or more often than not, directly responsible.

The NAACP *(National Association for the Advancement of Colored People)* is the most well-known Black-American organisation. What is not widely known is that its founders were ALL Zionist Marxists. Its Jewish co-founders included Julius Rosenwald, Lillian Wald, and Rabbi Emil Hirsch, however a black Communist named W.E. Dubois was deceptively installed as the NAACP's front man.

In 1914, Schiff became a Board member of the NAACP. With a 'giant' such as Schiff on board, the organisation was then ready to begin fulfilling its original shady objectives of undermining white superiority. Zionist money and influence has long dominated this 'civil rights' organisation, which did not elect its first non-Jewish President until 1975.

By design, Schiff's Jewish-controlled NAACP drew Blacks away from the positive influence of the Black-American conservative patriot Booker T. Washington, a dominant black political leader who believed in America's founding principles and genuinely sought to build bridges between whites and blacks. However, the liberal, Democrat NAACP represented the opposite of what B. T. Washington stood for, which was self-reliance. The NAACP was and is an anti-white Globalist-Marxist tool that serves to divide Americans whilst seducing radicalised black voters into the Leftist political camp. As a result of this policy, even today, 90-95% of black people blindly vote for Democrat candidates.

After carefully researching his options, Schiff bought a partnership in a firm that called itself *Kuhn and Loeb*. As was Schiff himself, Abraham Kuhn and Solomon Loeb were both immigrants from German-Jewish ghettos. They arrived in the US in the mid-1840s and both of them started their business careers as itinerant peddlers. In the early 1850s they pooled their resources and set-up a merchandise store in Lafayette, Indiana under the firm name of *Kuhn and Loeb* servicing the many covered-wagon settlers on their way west. In the years that followed they set up similar stores in Cincinnati and St. Louis and eventually added pawn-broking to their portfolio of interests. From that position to money-lending was a very short and simple step.

By the time Schiff arrived on the scene though, *Kuhn and Loeb* was a well-established private bank and this was the organisation into which he bought. Shortly after he became a partner in *Kuhn and Loeb*, Schiff married Loeb's daughter Teresa and then he bought out Kuhn's interests and moved the firm to New York and *Kuhn and Loeb* became *Kuhn, Loeb, and Company*, international bankers with Jacob Schiff, agent of the Rothschild's, ostensibly the sole owner. And throughout his career, this hybrid of Judas and Machiavelli, the first hierarch of the bankster's great conspiracy in America, posed as a generous philanthropist and a man of great virtue, which of course, was the cover-up policy promulgated by the banksters.

So, the first great step of the conspiracy was to be the hi-jacking of the entire American money system, but to achieve that objective, Schiff had to elicit the complete co-operation of the then big bankster elements in America and that was easier said than done. Even in those years, Wall Street was the heart of the American money markets and no less a figure than J.P. Morgan was its ultimate dictator.

John Pierpont Morgan was born in 1837, during the first money panic in the United States. Significantly, this had been caused by the *House of Rothschild*, with whom Morgan was later to become associated. *J.P. Morgan Company* began life as *George Peabody and Company*. George Peabody (1795-1869,) born in South Danvers, Massachusetts, began business in Georgetown, Washington D.C., in 1814 as *Peabody, Riggs and Company*, dealing in wholesale dry goods and in the operation of the Georgetown Slave Market.

But in 1815, to be closer to their source of supply, they moved to Baltimore, where they operated as *Peabody and Riggs*, from 1815 to 1835. Peabody found himself increasingly involved with business originating from London and so in 1835, he established the firm of *George Peabody and Company* in London. He had an excellent introduction into London business through another Baltimore firm established in Liverpool, *Brown Brothers*. Alexander Brown came to Baltimore in 1801, and established what is now known as the oldest banking house in the United States, still operating today as *Brown Brothers Harriman* of New York; *Brown, Shipley and Company* of England; and *Alex Brown and Son* of Baltimore.

Soon after he arrived in London, George Peabody was surprised to be summoned to an audience with the gruff, Baron Nathan Mayer Rothschild. Without mincing words, Rothschild revealed to Peabody, that much of the London aristocracy openly disliked him (Rothschild) and refused his invitations. He proposed that Peabody, a man of modest means, be established as a lavish host whose entertainments would soon be the talk of London. Rothschild would, of course, pay all the considerable expenses involved. Peabody naturally accepted the offer and soon became known as the most popular host in London.

His annual 'Fourth of July dinner,' celebrating American Independence, became extremely popular with the English aristocracy, many of whom, while drinking Peabody's wine, regaled each other with jokes about Rothschild's crudities and bad manners, without realising that everything they ate and drank had been paid for by Rothschild. It is hardly surprising therefore that the most popular host in London would also become a very successful businessman, particularly with the House of Rothschild supporting him behind the scenes.

His American agent was the Boston firm of *Beebe, Morgan and Company*, headed by Junius S. Morgan, father of John Pierpont Morgan. Peabody, who never married and had no-one to succeed him, was very favourably impressed by Junius Morgan and persuaded him to join him in London as a partner in George Peabody and Company in 1854. In 1860, the 23 year old John Pierpont Morgan had been taken on as an apprentice by the firm of *Duncan Sherman* in New York but he was not very well-regarded and in 1864, Morgan's father was outraged when *Duncan Sherman* refused to make his son a partner.

He promptly arranged for one of the chief employees of *Duncan Sherman*, Charles H. Dabney, to join John Pierpont Morgan in a new firm, *Dabney, Morgan and Company*. *Bankers* magazine of December 1864, noted that Peabody had withdrawn his account from *Duncan Sherman* and that other firms were expected to do so. The Peabody account, of course, went to *Dabney, Morgan Company.*

George Peabody found that he had chosen well in selecting Junius Morgan as his successor and Morgan agreed to continue the sub-rosa relationship with *N.M. Rothschild Company*, and soon expanded the firm's activities by shipping large quantities of railroad iron to the United States. It was Peabody iron which was the foundation for much of America's railroad tracks from 1860 to 1890.

In 1864, content to retire and leave his firm in the hands of Morgan, Peabody allowed the name to be changed to *Junius S. Morgan Company*. The Morgan firm then and since has always been directed from London whilst John Pierpont Morgan spent much of his time at his magnificent London mansion, 'Prince's Gate.'

The reason that the European Rothschilds preferred to operate anonymously in the United States behind the facade of *J.P. Morgan and Company* is that a considerable anti-Rothschild movement had developed in Europe and the United States which focussed on the highly-suspect banking activities of the Rothschild family. Even though they had a registered agent in the United States, August Schoenberg, who had changed his name to Belmont when he came to the United States as the representative of the Rothschilds in 1837, it was extremely advantageous for them to have an American representative who was not known as a Rothschild agent.

Although the London house of *Junius S. Morgan and Company* continued to be the dominant branch of the Morgan enterprises, with the death of the senior Morgan in 1890 in a carriage accident on the French Riviera, John Pierpont Morgan became the owner of the firm. After operating as the American representative of the London firm from 1864-1871 as *Dabney Morgan Company*, Morgan took on a new partner in 1871, Anthony Drexel of Philadelphia and operated as *Drexel Morgan and Company* until 1895, two years after Drexel's death. Only then, did Morgan change the name of the American branch to *J.P. Morgan and Company*.

Next in line were the Drexels and the Biddles of Philadelphia. All the various other financiers, large or small, were subservient to those three major dynasties; but particularly to that of Morgan. They were all three, proud, haughty and arrogant 'potentates.'

In the decades following the Civil War, America's industries really began to burgeon. There were great railroads being built nationwide and the fledgling oil, mining, steel and textile industries were all just beginning to prosper. All of those growth industries needed huge investment and much of that would come from abroad, from the *House of Rothschild* no less and this was where Schiff's machinations came into their own.

He played a very cute game indeed, financing John D. Rockefeller, Edward R. Harriman and Andrew Carnegie. He financed the *Standard Oil Company* for Rockefeller (the Rockefeller family are Rothschild descendants through a female bloodline,) the Railroad Empire for Harriman, and the Steel Empire for Carnegie. But instead of hogging all the other industries for *Kuhn, Loeb, and Company*, he opened the doors of the *House of Rothschild* to Morgan, Biddle, and Drexel. In turn, Rothschild arranged the instigation of London, Paris, European and other branches for those three, but always in partnership with Rothschild subordinates and Rothschild made it very clear to all those men that Jacob Schiff was the ultimate 'controller,' in New York.

Thus at the turn of the century, Schiff had secured control of the entire banking fraternity on Wall Street which by then, with Schiff's help, included *Lehman brothers*, *Goldman-Sachs*, and other internationalist banks that were headed by Rothschilds' place-men. This meant total control of the nation's money powers and the time was now almost right for the biggest coup de grace of all—the entrapment of the entire United States national money system.

Under the US Constitution at that time, the responsibility for control of the money system was vested solely with Congress, but Schiff needed to find a method by which he could seduce Congress to betray that Constitutional edict and thereby surrender that control to the hierarchy of the banksters' great conspiracy. In order to legalise that surrender and thus render 'the people' powerless to resist, it was necessary to entice Congress to enact special legislation.

In order to accomplish that, Schiff would have to install stooges into both houses of Congress, stooges powerful enough to influence Congress into passing the necessary legislation. Equally or even more importantly he would have to plant a stooge in the White House itself, a president that was totally without integrity or scruples and who would sign new legislation making the entire dastardly scheme possible.

So, he had to somehow gain control of either the Republican or the Democratic Party and the latter was the more vulnerable of the two options as it was desperate to gain power at this time. Except for one brief occasion, the Democrats had been out of office since before the Civil War. In the US at this period, there were considerably more Republican-minded voters than Democrats but Schiff was a smart and very shrewd man and his solution emphasised how very little the Jewish/Zionist internationalist banksters care about their own racial brethren.

In the late 1880s / early 1890s, a nationwide series of anti-Jewish 'pogroms' began to occur in Russia. The word 'pogrom' literally means 'riot' in Russian. Commonly, the term describes the semi-official persecution of Jews in the Russian Empire that began in the early 1880s and due to their situation in Russia becoming extremely uncomfortable, many Jewish families fled, the vast majority to America. Ultimately, almost two million people emigrated in the space of a few years.

These pogroms had originally begun after the Russian Empire (which previously had very few Jews) acquired territories with large Jewish populations during 1791-1835. These territories were designated *'the Pale of Settlement'* by the Russian government within which Jews were reluctantly permitted to live and it was there that these pogroms largely occurred. Most Jews were forbidden from moving to other parts of the Empire, unless they converted to Orthodox Christianity.

Many, many thousands of innocent Jews, men, women and children were slaughtered by the Cossacks and other armed peasant groups whilst the slaughter of innocent Jews also broke out in Poland, Rumania and Bulgaria. All those pogroms were fomented by Rothschild agents and ultimately had the desired effect . . . Millions of terrified Jewish refugees from all of those nations converged upon the United States and this trend continued throughout the next two decades as the pogroms continued mercilessly. All refugees were of course aided by self-styled 'humanitarian committees' set up by Schiff, the Rothschilds and their affiliates.

Most of the refugees entered the country via New York, but the Schiff-Rothschild humanitarian committees calculatingly dispersed many of them into many other large cities such as Chicago, Boston, Philadelphia, Detroit and Los Angeles, etc., and all of them without exception were rapidly made 'naturalised citizens' and brain-washed to support the Democratic party, 'in their best interests' of course. Thus most of the immigrants became Democratic voters in their respective communities, all controlled and manoeuvred by their 'benefactors.' And ultimately it was through the use of this methodology that Schiff installed men such as Nelson Aldrich into the Senate and Woodrow Wilson into the White House, as Rothschild puppets.

Another one of the important tasks assigned to Schiff when he was dispatched to America, was to instigate the destruction of the unity of the vast majority, white Christian American people by creating racial strife. By using the pogrom-driven Jewish refugees into America, Schiff created a ready-made minority group for that purpose but the Jewish people, as a whole a peaceful and non-aggressive group also made fearful by the pogroms, could not be depended upon to create the violence necessary to instigate racial violence and thereby destroy the unity of American people.

But this proved to be no real problem for Schiff and his controllers. Within America there was an already made-to-order, 'sleeping' yet large minority group, the Negroes, who could be sparked into demonstrations, rioting, looting, murder and every other type of lawlessness and all that was necessary to achieve this was to make them 'aware' of the injustices and oppression they suffered at the hands of 'whitey.' Schiff realised that together, those two minority groups, properly manipulated could be used to create exactly the mayhem in America that the banksters would need to accomplish their insidious objectives.

In 1904, the Russo-Japanese War began over disputes surrounding the control of Manchuria and Korea. In particular, Port Arthur on the Pacific coast was highly coveted by Russia and when negotiations stalled, war inevitably broke out. The Japanese stunned the world with their victory over Russia, but the result was maybe not that surprising considering that Japan's victory had been achieved with considerable assistance from the banksters via Jacob Schiff and the European Rothschilds who provided massive amounts of finance for the Japanese military effort.

In fact, the banksters had consciously used the Japanese in order to weaken their arch-enemy Russia as a stepping-stone to the overthrow of the Czar by internal communist subversives (also financed by Schiff and Rothschild.) Schiff had even arranged for Marxist reading materials to be given to 50,000 Russian prisoners-of-war being held in Japan and later, many of these 're-educated' soldiers turned against the Czar during the 1917 revolution. For all his efforts in helping them to defeat Russia, the Japanese government awarded Schiff with a medal.

Russia's Grand Duke, Sergei Alexandrovich was the brother of the late Czar Alexander III. Their father, Alexander II had been murdered by the 'Reds' in 1881 and the Grand Duke met exactly the same fate as his father, when a Red terrorist named Kalyayev, hurled a bomb into the Duke's carriage. The bomb landed in his lap and blew both the Duke and his carriage into very small pieces. Afterwards, Duchess Elizabeth, the Grand Duke's wife withdrew from public life, founded a convent and dedicated herself to helping the poor, only to become yet another victim of the communists along with her maid in 1918. And thus the Rothschilds continued their deadly vendetta against the Romanov family, begun almost a century earlier after the Czar's refusal to sanction the Rothschilds' plans for one world government.

It was the Rothschild's backing of German-Jewish philosopher, the 'useful idiot,' Karl Marx in 1848 that created organised Communism. Marx's 'Communist Manifesto' was in reality the first stage of the banksters' next plan for a one-world government. Marx's grandparents were actually related to the Rothschild family through marriage.

Marx's cult followers promoted violence, class envy and hostility towards free-markets, family, business, tradition and Christianity and in addition to the angry misfits and maladjusted criminals who followed Marx's 'teachings,' there were many well-meaning idealists who fell for his poisonous promises of a better world with prosperity and equality for all. The combined influence of both Communists and anarchists (known collectively as 'Reds') along with the cancerous spread of 'liberalism / progressivism' had really taken root by the late 19th century.

The attempted Russian Revolution of 1905 was a wave of political uprisings, massive labour strikes and terrorist acts against the government of Russia. The Reds, under orders from their Rothschild / Schiff masters, used the discontent surrounding the lost war with Japan to foment the revolution during and after which, Red revolutionaries murdered 7,300 people and wounded about 8,000. Though the Jewish-inspired and led 'Red Revolution' was eventually suppressed, Czar Nicholas II was forced to make 'democratic' concessions which weakened his power and set-up the monarchy for a future attempt at revolution. Nicholas made a critical mistake by showing mercy to the Red leaders, Lenin and Trotsky, but instead of executing them, the Marxist leaders were merely deported.

Lenin eventually made his way to Switzerland and Trotsky fled to New York after escaping from prison. These exiled Communists would one day return, financed by gold from the banksters, to terrorise Russia once again.

But meanwhile, the Royal bloodbath in Europe continued as Red assassins murdered King Carlos of Portugal along with his son and heir, Prince Luis Filipe. The assassins, linked to the secret Carbonaria Society, also attempted to kill the Queen in the hope of provoking a revolution in Portugal. Despite the widespread panic these acts provoked, a revolution did not materialise and Prince Manuel (the younger son of the King) succeeded his father.

All the crowned-heads of Europe were horrified by these events, partly due to King Carlos' popularity, as much as the manner in which the assassination was planned and orchestrated and not least because they now feared for their own safety too.

The Protocols of the Learned Elders of Zion

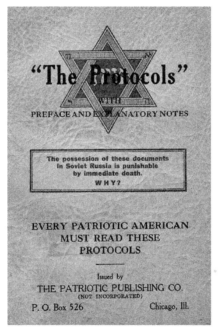

This document has been the centre of controversy from its very beginning, but then that was the intention. It was a Russian professor named Sergei Nilus that published it originally, the Protocols being the minutes of a secret meeting of Jewish elites towards the end of the 19th century. Within its pages are a detailed Zionist 100-year master plan for world domination, complete with precise details of the Zionist take-over of all banking, commerce, the media and many other aspects of our daily lives.

"I feel sorry for the innocent people who think Osama bin Laden was responsible for 9/11, that the media tells the truth and we live in a free country. We live in a world designed

and controlled by Satanist central bankers according to the blueprint of The Protocols of the Learned Elders of Zion. We are being harassed by terrorism, war, financial crises and viruses just as the Protocols promised. The purpose is to make us throw up our hands and accept world government, which is a euphemism for banker tyranny. Whether it is climate change, wars, bank bailouts or 'hate laws,' there is less distinction everyday between the perversity of the Illuminati bankers and the actions of our government." Sonia Sotomayor, a member of the all-female 'Belizean Club' which is the lesser-known, female equivalent of Bohemian Grove.

Today, the Protocols are widely claimed by the Zionist-controlled media as a huge 'anti-Semitic hoax,' but then this is unsurprising as we know that the banksters own the media too. And as you have already learned, they always strongly promote controversy as it distracts and divides and diverts attention from reality.

Below is a very brief synopsis of the contents of the Protocols:

- Destroy the Church and all Christianity
- Promote atheism
- Wage class warfare by setting labour against management
- Overthrow Czarist Russia
- Corrupt the morals of the people
- Promote meaningless, talentless 'modern art' and pornography
- Use anti-Semitism to keep 'lesser Jews' cohesive
- Manipulate women with ideas of 'liberation'
- Create economic depressions and inflations
- Create 'controlled opposition' to themselves
- Use national debt as a weapon to enslave countries
- Subvert and control all existing governments
- Install tainted politicians that can be easily blackmailed
- Manipulate college students with phony idealism
- Assassinate world leaders
- Spread deadly diseases
- Use balance of power politics to control nations
- Commit 'false flag' acts of terrorism
- Promote sports and games to divert people from seeking the truth
- Start a world war which will include the USA
- Set up world government after an economic crash

So, for a document written over a century ago, these so-called 'fake' Protocols were extremely accurate in their predictions.

But back to the main story; in the dawning, modern era of the 20th century, the flag-waving, 'all-American hero,' Theodore Roosevelt became the perfect prototype for political puppets controlled by the Zionist banksters. Theodore Roosevelt was groomed from a very young age. His father was an opium agent of the Rothschilds, using a plate-glass company as a 'front' for the operation. Indeed, all of the US opium and black slave agents of the Rothschilds used various business fronts such as tea importers and fur exporters.

Roosevelt was of Jewish ancestry, descended from Claes van Rosenvelt from Holland, who arrived in Boston in 1645 and eventually settled in New York. His even older ancestor, one Rossacampo was driven away from Spain during the Spanish Inquisition by the Alhambra decree in January 1492 and later settled in Holland. At this time, around 78,000 Jews were forced to leave Spain, a figure which somehow through the establishment media was inflated to 300,000 (*no surprise there then—JH.*) This had been instigated by the Catholic monarchs King Ferdinand and Queen Isabella acting upon a decree from the Pope -- also known as Papal bull—on 31st March 1492.

And so it was that 400 years later, the Rothschilds 'avenged' the Jews and punished Spain using their stooge in the USA, Theodore Roosevelt, by engineering the destruction of the Spanish Empire. The Spanish Empire was the first truly global empire, reaching its territorial zenith in the late 1700s. But by 1898, Spain was losing territories regularly. Cuba, 4000 miles away from Spain, was becoming increasingly more difficult to control and a minor revolution had broken out.

This was most unwelcome news to the Rothschilds as their US agents owned most of the Cuban sugar, tobacco and the clandestine drug cultivation (smuggled in huge Cuban cigars) and worth about $3bn today. In addition, the black slaves in Cuba were shipped-in by the Rothschilds using JP Morgan and many others as agents. Notably, on all Jewish holidays the slave trade was temporarily suspended.

So, on 15th February 1898 a US navy battleship the *USS Maine* was sabotaged and sunk in Havana Harbour, Cuba with terrible loss of American lives which was all stage-managed to perfection by the Rothschilds. There were 261 fatalities, 76 were seriously injured and only 19 uninjured.

Blaming Spain for committing this 'unprovoked act of war' was utterly ludicrous, nevertheless this did not stop the Americans from insisting that the only 'atonement' Spain could offer for the loss of the obsolete ship and hundreds of lives, was the granting of independence to Cuba and by transferring most of her colonies to the US for next to nothing. All the while encouraged by the 'yellow press,' who reported alleged Spanish atrocities in Cuba, the American public was driven almost to hysteria and Spain was certainly no match for the mighty military power of the United States.

Naturally the Cubans and the Spanish protested bitterly and loudly that they were not responsible for what had happened and there is no doubt that this was a false-flag operation, perpetrated by the Americans themselves in order to fulfil their agenda of destroying the Spanish Empire and taking-over Cuba.

National City Bank was America's most powerful bank at this time, with a board including representatives of the Rockefeller, Morgan and Rothschild interests. To finance the war, Assistant Treasury Secretary Frank Vanderlip negotiated a $200 million loan from *National City Bank* and afterwards, the bank made Vanderlip its president in yet another example of the 'rotating-door' policy operated constantly between the higher echelons of government and industry / commerce.

A new tax was soon announced to fund the war (or practically speaking, to reimburse *National City Bank*.) Since the Supreme Court had ruled income tax to be unconstitutional in 1895, a Federal excise tax was levied on telephone services. This tax remained in force for over a century, contributing towards the funding of both WWI and WWII, Korea and Vietnam until it was repealed in 2006. But although the Spanish-American War ended in 1898, the 'temporary tax,' over its 107 year lifetime, generated almost $94 billion, more than 230 times the cost of the Spanish-American War.

Even today, many people still believe the bankster-created image of America's youngest ever President, Theodore Roosevelt. In a famous letter written to the head of the *American Defense Society* on 3rd January 1919, three days before his death, Roosevelt expressed his views on immigration and immigrants. He felt that immigrants should assimilate, become loyal Americans and speak English . . .

"We should insist that if the immigrant who comes here does in good faith become an American and assimilates himself to us, he shall be treated on an exact equality with everyone else for it is an outrage to discriminate against any such man because of creed or birth-place or origin.

But this is predicated upon the man's becoming in very fact an American and nothing but an American. If he tries to keep segregated with men of his own origin and separated from the rest of America, then he isn't doing his part as an American. There can be no divided allegiance here. . . We have room for but one language here, and that is the English language, for we intend to see that the crucible turns our people out as Americans, of American nationality, and not as dwellers in a polyglot boarding-house; and we have room for but one soul loyalty, and that is loyalty to the American people."

Unfortunately Theodore Roosevelt chose not to live up to those fine words and like so many other of our 'revered' leaders, simply sold his soul to the banksters for fame and fortune.

Our distorted history tells us that the faceless banksters were the true 'Robber Barons,' the powerful men responsible for all our financial woes, as indeed they were, but the Rothschilds, the Rockefellers and men like Jacob Schiff are never spoken of in this respect. We never see their faces or even hear their names mentioned in connection with all the financial woes of the world brought to us courtesy of these banksters. Of course, this is exactly how it is meant to be. The banksters always have fronts and 'fall guys.' You are not supposed to know who the real puppet-masters, the real 'organ-grinders' are, only their monkeys. Most people believe that the Italian-Sicilian Mafia runs all the organised crime, the Columbian cartels the drug operations and so on. It is an illusion, a deliberate distraction from the ultimate criminals.

But in the first decade of the twentieth century, the Rothschilds and their bankster friends were finalising their plan to re-establish a central bank in the United States. First of all, certain events had to be engineered so that the masses would not only be easily duped into accepting it, but actually *welcome* it. It would be the same three-step process that the banksters frequently use; present the PROBLEM, wait for the REACTION then offer the SOLUTION. Otherwise known simply as the Hegelian Dialectic or 'problem, reaction, solution.'

In January 1907, Jacob Schiff addressed the *New York Chamber of Commerce* and warned, some may even say threatened that…

"Unless we have a Central Bank with control of credit resources, this country is going to undergo the most severe and far reaching money panic in its history."

And sure enough, in October of that year, the banksters duly delivered their promised panic. JP Morgan was responsible for creating 'The Panic of 1907,' whereby the stock market fell nearly 50% from its peak in 1906. The economy went into massive recession and there were numerous 'runs' on banks and trust companies. The primary cause of the panic was as usual, a retraction of loans that began in New York and rapidly spread across the nation, leading to the wholesale closing of banks and businesses. However, total ruin of the national economy was 'fortunately' averted when JP Morgan personally intervened by organising a team of bank and trust executives who re-directed money between banks, secured further international lines of credit and bought-up the now plummeting stocks of healthy corporations.

The bankster-owned press, such as the *New York Times*, owned by Zionist, Adolph Ochs, openly promoted an increase in the panic through the pages of his newspaper and strongly advocated the creation of another American central bank in order to 'prevent this panic from occurring again.'

JP Morgan also deliberately precipitated the panic by instigating and spreading wild rumours about the insolvency of the *Knickerbocker Trust Company*, one of the largest US banks. This mistrust soon spread throughout the industry and began to affect all the other banks and so by the use of these dubious tactics Morgan gained numerous large additions to his portfolio. Indeed it was he who was primarily responsible for generating a strong belief in the ordinary American people that a central bank would prevent another such panic in the banking system. Problem, reaction, solution, yet again.

The earlier financial crisis of 1893, had already been used by the banksters, especially the Rockefellers to literally monopolise the oil industry. As for JP Morgan, it enabled him to consolidate and expand his holdings in railways, electric power and the telephone industries but above all, it served to establish him as the most powerful bankster in the United States.

During 1908 the 'bankster-owned' President Theodore Roosevelt, appointed the 'bankster-owned' Senate Republican leader and 'financial expert,' Nelson Aldrich to head the National Monetary Commission set-up to investigate the causes of the panic which of course was all unnecessary as they already knew what had caused the panic. In fact Aldrich set up two commissions, one to study the American monetary system in depth and the other, headed by Aldrich himself, to study the already well-established European central-banking systems and submit a report on them.

Nelson Aldrich was a very powerful man indeed for he was the *de facto* leader of the small coterie of Senate Republicans who dominated the party caucus and who determined the action of the Senate on most issues between 1895 and 1910.

Initially, the concept of 'centralised banking' was met with much opposition from many politicians, who with knowledge of the previous failed attempts at this scheme were suspicious of a central bank-type scenario. There was also a small yet voluble group who asserted (correctly) that Aldrich was biased due to his close ties to wealthy bankers such as Morgan and Rockefeller. However, later that same year, Teddy Roosevelt surprisingly decided not to run for re-election. He instead pledged his support to his close friend, William Howard Taft who was duly elected President, but whose policies of limited constitutional government went against Roosevelt's 'big government' progressivism.

Taft irritated many with his policies but in all fairness, he always adhered to the law and the constitution. His administration continued Roosevelt's anti-trust policies bringing as many as 90 suits under the *Sherman Anti-trust Act*. However, whilst his predecessor had subjectively differentiated between 'good' and 'bad' monopolies, Taft concentrated solely on enforcing the laws. As a result, Taft's 'trust-busting' angered Theodore Roosevelt, big business, and the banksters themselves.

In 1911, the courts broke up John D. Rockefeller's *Standard Oil*. Taft also instigated a suit against JP Morgan's *US Steel*. The company produced nearly 70% of worldwide steel and enjoyed a 90% market share in the United States. Despite the *U.S. Steel* dominance, the government lost the case.

Former President Roosevelt approved of the *US Steel* combination. In his view, the monopoly did not violate the spirit of the *Sherman Anti-Trust Act*. He did not believe that the company represented a 'bad' monopoly. In fact, Roosevelt felt *US Steel* benefited Americans. When Taft attempted to crush the monopoly, it angered the former president because he could not understand Taft's motivations for attacking the institution. This action was one of many Taft policies which drove a wedge between the two presidents.

The antitrust suit angered the business community as well. As may be expected, big business opposed Taft's actions. He threatened their profits and independence and the 90 lawsuits represented the greatest governmental assault on the business community ever, up to that point in time.

Ironically, Taft somehow contrived to anger enemies of big business too. The President only wished to enforce the law and his motivations were more esoteric than the progressives who wanted to punish evil. Taft's conservative, legalistic rhetoric alienated him from the one group that should have rallied to his trust-busting. He firmly believed he was doing the 'right thing' by enforcing the law and busting monopolies but despite this, he managed to alienate almost everyone. Roosevelt was angered by

Taft's inability to distinguish between 'good' and 'bad' monopolies and the wider business community felt betrayed by the conservative President. Those in favour of reform were also opposed to Taft because he did not understand their motivations. So, despite all his actual achievements in the trust-busting realm, President Taft suffered politically, indeed he may well have been better regarded politically, through inaction.

Even then, there was only ever the 'illusion' of choice.

In 1909, a 'useful idiot' by the name of Cyrus Scofield had been chosen for leadership of the Christian-Zionist Movement. However, you will certainly not hear the truthful story of Cyrus Scofield from *Wikipedia*™ or any other 'establishment' source. As a young con-artist in Kansas after the Civil War, he had met-up with John Ingalls, an aging lawyer who had been instructed by the banksters some thirty years previously, to work on behalf of the abolitionist (of slavery) cause. Pulling strings both in Kansas and with his powerful masters, Ingalls assisted Scofield in gaining admission to the Bar, and procured his appointment as Federal Attorney for Kansas. Ingalls and Scofield then became partners in a railway scam which led to Scofield being forced to resign in 1873, and also serving time for criminal forgery.

Upon his release from prison, Scofield deserted his first wife and his two daughters, Abigail and Helen and took as his mistress a young girl from the St. Louis Flower Mission. He later abandoned her too, for Helen van Ward, whom he eventually married. Then, following his Zionist bankster connections to New York, he settled at the Lotus Club, which he listed as his address for the next twenty years. It was here that he presented his ideas for a new Christian Bible and was taken under the wing of a prominent New York attorney and Zionist bankster agent, Samuel Untermyer who became Scofield's 'handler.' Untermyer was also the man who played a similar role, keeping President Woodrow Wilson firmly in-line and under the tight control of the Zionist banksters.

Of course, Scofield's new version of the Bible was completely 'Zionised' and it is this aspect that induces many Christians today to believe that Jesus will one day return to save his followers from the 'end-times,' (the Rapture) after Israel has been established, and that 'God will bless those who bless Israel.' Published by the bankster-owned *Oxford University Press* in England, the Scofield bible became a powerful weapon for the Zionists in making millions of 'Evangelical' Christians even more fanatical Christian-Zionists through politics and religious beliefs, than their Jewish counterparts.

So, as you may now begin to see, the Rothschilds, the banksters, the ruling Zionist elite were well-prepared for carrying out their evil plans of world domination and enslavement as the twentieth century progressed. As difficult and unimaginable as all this may be to digest, it is one of the many reasons that these arch-criminal psychopaths have managed to conceal their evil crimes for centuries. It is so easy to simply dismiss everything presented here as simply an unbelievable 'conspiracy theory,' but what came next may appear to be more akin to something out of a cheap horror movie.

The Banksters' Secret Societies

On 1st May 1776, the very year that America 'won' its so-called 'independence' from British rule, a Crypto-Jew named Adam Weishaupt formed a secret society, the *'Order of Perfectibilists,'* a name that was later changed to the *'Illuminati'* meaning the 'enlightened ones.' As with numerous other societies and entities that were to follow, the sworn purpose of the *Illuminati* was and is to abolish Christianity, and overturn all civil government.

Weishaupt was the son of a Jewish rabbi but became a Jesuit priest prior to becoming an atheist and ultimately a Satanist. He studied in France where he met Maximilien de Robespierre, the future leader of the bloody, French Revolution. Weishaupt was also a student of the Eleusinian mysteries, Pythagoras, the Kabbalah, the Keys of Solomon and occult rituals. In 1773 he held a meeting with the bankster patriarch himself, the supreme master of usury and insider trading, Mayer Amschel Rothschild to discuss world revolution. The Rothschilds were already Freemasons and financially supported the *Illuminati*'s mission.

Weishaupt then infiltrated the *Continental Order of Freemasons* with his *'Illuminati'* doctrine and established lodges of the Grand Orient to be their secret headquarters, in the process recruiting some 2,000 paid followers including the most prominent men in the field of arts, education, science, finance and industry and who were all instructed to follow a detailed master-plan.

Similarly to *The Protocols of the Learned Elders of Zion* that would follow a hundred years later, the idea was to corrupt society using deception and subterfuge. Weishaupt laid-down the following goals for his loyal followers: 1) abolish all ordered government; 2) abolish private property; 3) abolish inheritance; 4) abolish patriotism; 5) abolish all religion; 6) abolish family and marriage; 7) encourage the creation of a 'one-world government.' In fact these goals were all an embryonic form of Communism. The reader should by now realise that all the preceding descriptions of banksters and their many crimes against humanity are in essence, unabashed and undiluted Communism.

Weishaupt instructed the Illuminati to act in secret and also took great satisfaction from deceiving Christians and other religions, into joining his order. Initiates were told that the Illuminati represented the highest ideals of the Church, that Christ himself was an Illuminist and that his secret mission was to restore people to the liberty that they lost in the Garden of Eden. Weishaupt also informed them that Christ despised riches and that they should prepare for the 'abolition of property ownership and the sharing of all possessions.' Where have we heard that one before?

Then in 1784, Weishaupt, issued a decree to the Illuminists in the form of a book, with instructions for the instigation of the French revolution by Maximilien de Robespierre. This book had been written by one of Weishaupt's associates, Xavier Zwack and was being sent by courier from Frankfurt to Paris. However, en route the courier was unfortunately (or not, depending on your viewpoint) struck by lightning and killed and the book was discovered by the authorities.

As a consequence, the authorities ordered the raiding of Weishaupt's Masonic Lodges of the Grand Orient and the homes of his most influential associates. Clearly, they were absolutely convinced that the book they discovered posed a very real threat to law and order and that it would promote complete anarchy and war. So as a result, the following year, the Bavarian government outlawed the Illuminati and closed-down all their Bavarian lodges of the Grand Orient and Mayer Amschel Rothschild moved his family to Frankfurt, to a house which he shared with the Schiff family.

In 1786 the Bavarian government published the details of the Illuminati plot in a document entitled, *'The Original Writings of the Order and Sect of the Illuminati.'* They then distributed this to all the heads of church and state throughout Europe, who sadly ignored this dire warning, resulting in the fomenting of the French Revolution in 1789.

"The Illuminati, operating in the guise of the Jacobins, forced the regime-change that historians now call the French Revolution." Andrew Smith, *henrymakow.com*

There is no doubt that the French Revolution, which utterly devastated France between 1787 and 1799, was inspired and instigated by Freemasonry and just as with the English Revolution, a century and a half earlier, things are not as portrayed by mainstream history. Although popularly believed to have begun due to a public uprising over widespread poverty and starvation and government representation, the real facts tell us that this starvation was instigated by cells of French Freemasonry and the German Illuminati.

In 1789, the Duke of Orleans purportedly bought-up much of the grain in France and either sold it abroad, secreted it away or destroyed it, thus engendering starvation amongst the French peasant classes. Galart de Montjoie, a contemporary, blamed the Revolution almost solely on the Duke of Orleans, writing that he *"was moved by that invisible hand which seems to have created all the events of our revolution in order to lead us towards a goal that we do not see at present..."*

"If, then, it is said that the [French] Revolution was prepared in the lodges of Freemasons—and many French Masons have boasted of the fact—let it always be added that it was Illuminised Freemasonry that made the Revolution and that the Masons who acclaim it are Illuminised Masons, inheritors of the same tradition introduced into the lodges of France in 1787 by the disciples of Weishaupt, patriarch of the Jacobins." Nesta Webster

In fact the revolution was a central banksters dream as it established a new constitution and passed laws that both forbade the Roman Church from levying taxes and also removed the Church's exemption from taxation. This was a period of radical upheaval in France. Unlike America's Revolution, which placed limits on governmental power, the atheistic radicals of France sought total power. Their rallying cries of *'Liberty, Fraternity, Equality,'* were empty words that attracted gullible mobs and their associated thugs.

From 1793-1794, the so-called *'Committee of Public Safety'* operated as the dictatorship in France. A 'reign of terror' was unleashed and King Louis XVI, Queen Marie

Antoinette and 40,000 others were publicly executed, by 'Madame Guillotine.' In addition, the Jacobin mobs also targeted priests and nuns as well as the wealthy.

Freemasonry

Freemasonry is a subject that guarantees controversy as it continues to play a critical role in so much of the evil that has prevailed throughout history, as evidenced by the fact that so many of the powerful, influential people involved in historical (and present day) intrigue are Freemasons. Indeed, it is a secret society like so many others that has been co-opted by the banksters without the majority of well-intentioned, decent, lower-level Freemasons ever knowing it.

The movement has a pyramid structure, as with most other institutions, the highest level being the 33rd degree. Most Freemasons never progress beyond the 3rd degree (many are even now, unaware that there are any degrees above the 3rd) and provide a 'cover' for all the nefarious activities occurring at high-level, through their community and charitable activities. The very top of the pyramid, degrees 31 to 33 are Illuminati through and through, whilst the bottom levels consist of the law abiding debt-slaves, the 'goyim' (Hebrew for cattle—which is how the 'common' people such as you and I are regarded).

Freemasonry probably had its original roots in the mediaeval crafts, whereby each trade had its own 'guild' or 'union' in modern parlance, to protect the interests of its members. In return for this protective presence the craftsman had to submit to the most rigorous regulation. He had to serve as an apprentice, usually without pay, for two to ten years (depending on the trade,) live with and obey the master craftsman who tutored him, and then finally once this long induction process was complete, the apprentice was free to start out alone, frequently taking one of his master's daughters as a wife.

With the expansion of economics, often came the need of the craftsman to borrow money to finance long-term undertakings and his willingness to pay interest for this benefit. The Christian Church condemned usury at this time and money-lending was permitted only by and to Jews, who were barred from guild membership by dint of their religious practices.

Stonemasons, by the very nature of their trade, were itinerant, constantly moving between villages and towns seeking employment. Their membership of the masonic craft guild was a reassurance to potential customers and employers that he was a bona fide craftsman who could be relied upon to provide a fair days work for a fair days pay. The insignia of their guild displayed representations of the tools of their trade and where language or literacy was a barrier to communication, served as a visual guarantee of ability. It was from these humble beginnings that secret symbols, restricted membership, oaths of secrecy and mutual aid evolved but eventually the guilds became entities that were no longer necessarily populated by those skilled in the crafts and trades their societies purported to represent, becoming almost entirely symbolic and totally unrepresentative of the craft or trade.

In 1645, the Royal Society, founded either in Oxford or in London depending on source, was created with the intention of promoting scientific enquiry rather than the simple, unthinking acceptance of received wisdom. Many facets of the society were based on the tenets of freemasonry and indeed many of the founders were freemasons—a state of affairs that still exists to this day. It was the brother-in-law of Oliver Cromwell, the future 'Lord Protector' of the Commonwealth of Great Britain who became its first chairman. Cromwell's uncle, Thomas Cromwell during the reign of Henry VIII a century earlier had already severed the ties between the Roman Catholic Church and the English monarchy and Oliver himself had managed to continue the process, by engineering the severing of King Charles I's head from his body.

In 1717, Freemasonry, now a new form of cult entirely distinct from the various existing creeds of Europe, spread rapidly to Paris, Florence, Rome and Berlin, where its deliberately syncretic rituals and décor, Solomon's temple's signs and symbols made it thoroughly cosmopolitan and religiously neutral. Nothing could better encapsulate the early spirit of the 'enlightenment.'

Andrew Ramsay, a Scottish Jacobite exiled in France, who was Chancellor of the French Grand Lodge in the 1730s, claimed that the first Freemasons had been stonemasons in the crusader states who had learned the secret rituals and gained the special wisdom of the ancient world. According to the German Freemasons, the Grand Masters of the Order had learned the secrets and acquired the treasure of the Jewish Essenes.

Either way, Freemasonry had now escaped its earlier guise of stonemasonry and in its new incarnation appealed to the intellectuals and the nobility. The early membership of 'free' masonic lodges included merchants and financiers, notaries and lawyers, doctors, diplomats and gentry, in other words men of substance and sound reputation. By the middle of the eighteenth century these included members of the French royal family, Frederick the Great, Maria Theresa's husband, Francis of Lorraine and her son, Joseph.

Freemasonry not only played an important role in the French Revolution, but also with regard to the American Revolution, in particular the lodges affiliated to the Grand Lodge of Scotland. Scottish Rite Freemasonry blossomed in North America and indeed Freemasonry could be found on both sides of the looming war between the colonists and the Crown and although there is no clear evidence of collusion amongst masons from opposing camps, the fact that the British made some extraordinary military errors arouses my suspicions in this regard.

Sir William Howe's failure to pursue Washington after expelling him from New York and Sir Henry Clinton's wilful failure to link up with Burgoyne's army marching south from Montreal in 1777 are the two most conspicuous examples. In both cases, it would seem that the American forces were handed a massive advantage that greatly helped their cause.

The Grand Master for North America was Joseph Warren and the Green Dragon coffee house in Union Street, Boston, purchased by the Provincial Grand Lodge is generally considered to be the site where one of its offshoots 'The Sons of Liberty' plotted the Boston Tea Party and carried it out in the guise of 'Red Indians,' now re-branded for the sake of political correctness as 'Native Americans.' So already there was an infiltration of the 'hidden hand,' as a secret society is an ideal vehicle for covert control. It was however, an infiltration of which many of its members were unaware.

One of the little known and least advertised facts about Freemasonry and the Masonic Lodge is its Jewish origin and nature. The religion of Judaism is based on the Babylonian Talmud and the Jewish Kabbalah formed the basis for the Scottish rites 33 ritual degree ceremonies.

"Masonry is based on Judaism. Eliminate the teaching of Judaism from the Masonic ritual and what is left?" The Jewish Tribune of New York, 28th October 1927

"Freemasonry is a Jewish establishment, whose history, grades, official appointments, passwords and explanations are Jewish from beginning to end." Rabbi Isaac Wis

Undoubtedly already under Jewish influence, Judeo-masonry in Europe became popular with the rise to power of the House of Rothschild. Adam Weishaupt who formed the Illuminati in 1776, founded the Lodge of Theodore in Munich and was befriended and funded by Meyer Rothschild, whose clerk in his Frankfurt office, Sigmund Geisenheimer, had extensive Masonic contacts and was a member of the French Grand Orient Lodge, 'l'Aurore Naissante.' With the help of Daniel Itzig (Court Jew to Frederick William II) and the merchant, Isaac Hildesheim (who changed his name to Justus Hiller) he founded the 'Judenloge' (Jewish Lodge.)

In 1802 the old established Jewish families including the Adler, Speyer, Reiss, Sichel, Ellison, Hanau and the Goldsmid families became members of the Judenloge and in 1803 Nathan Rothschild joined the Lodge of Emulation in England whilst his brother James Rothschild became a 33rd degree Mason in France.

The book on the Masons *'Morals and Dogma'*, authored by the late Sovereign Grand Commander of the Scottish rite, Albert Pike, states that...

"Masonry conceals secrets from all except the adepts and sages and uses false explanations and myth interpretation of its symbols to mislead."

The rise of Masons to political power in Israel dates back to the state's origins in 1948. David Ben Gurion, Israel's first Prime Minister, was a Freemason and indeed every Prime Minister since then has been a high level Mason, including Golda Meier who was a member of the women's organisation, the Co-Masons. Most Israeli judges and religious figures are Masons and the Rothschild-supported Hebrew University in Israel erected an Egyptian obelisk, an overt symbol of Freemasonry, in its courtyard.

Today, it is virtually impossible to obtain a state of high office in any sphere in virtually any nation without membership of this all-pervasive body. From politicians to law-makers, to police and security agencies, they are all heavily populated at the upper echelons by high-ranking Freemasons. All of which makes claims of democracy for our society, almost laughable, were it not so serious a subject. Freemasons must always and under all circumstances put their 'brethren' first in all matters, regardless of a nation's laws. How then can one conclude that any election, from political by-elections to the election of political party leaders to the appointment of public company directors and high-level civil servants, could possibly be fairly conducted?

The simple answer of course is that they cannot and thus we have as our default a system whereby exploitation and corruption is the norm and not the exception, whatever we may try to convince ourselves to the contrary.

In the 16th century, Sir Francis Bacon was the head of the secret societies in England and authored his famous book, *The New Atlantis*. Bacon's book was the blueprint for colonising the United States, advocating that America...

"...would become a paradise in which men would follow reason, become gods and work for a universal world republic that would then replicate the Utopian conditions of America throughout the known world."

Secret knowledge would be passed on through the generations by Freemasons and other secret societies. As Chief of the Rosicrucians and the first Grand Master of modern Freemasonry, Bacon sent his followers to the new world. A 1910 Newfoundland stamp with his image upon it reads; *"Lord Bacon: the Guiding Spirit in the Colonisation Scheme."*

Because of his influence, Francis Bacon is considered by some to be the real and true founder of America. For centuries, controversy has surrounded this figure who is believed by many to be the illegitimate son of Queen Elizabeth I, and secret author of the Shakespeare plays; the man whom Thomas Jefferson considered one of the three most influential men in history.

In 1733, Rosicrucian Freemasonry formally entered America when the St John's Lodge was established in Boston. It subsequently became the Masonic capital of Britain's colonies and by 1737 there were Lodges in Massachusetts, New York, Pennsylvania, and South Carolina, all of which were totally committed to implementing the plan for Bacon's Utopian *'New Atlantis.'* In February 1731, Benjamin Franklin became a Rosicrucian Mason and in 1734, Provincial Grand Master of Pennsylvania.

Franklin returned to England from 1764 to 1775 and discovered Baconian English Freemasonry's Secret Doctrine to create a New World or philosophical Atlantis in America and in 1775, Tom Paine, whom Franklin had sent to America to work on the *Pennsylvania Magazine*, argued that America should demand independence from England. Franklin returned to Philadelphia and printed Paine's *Common Sense* propaganda booklet, advocating American independence from Britain.

In fact, the federalism that finally united the 13 colonies into states was identical to the federalism of the Grand Lodge system of Masonic government which had been created in Anderson's Constitution of 1723.

One of the incidents in the prelude to the Revolution, the 'Boston Tea Party,' was an entirely Masonic-inspired event organised by the St Andrew's Lodge in Boston, of which John Hancock and Paul Revere were members, and supported by Virginia Masons, Patrick Henry and Richard Henry Lee. At nightfall on 17th December 1773, at least 120 Masons from the St Andrew's lodge, disguised as Mohawk Indians, boarded British ships and threw their cargo of tea (an expensive commodity at the time) into the harbour, allegedly to protest numerous unfair taxes levied by King George III. However, the reality was that this act was just one small step on the road to engineering the revolution.

Of the 56 signatories of the Declaration of Independence, according to some sources, 53 were Freemasons. The first President, George Washington was a Freemason and was elected Grand Master of the Templar Alexandria Lodge no. 22 in Virginia. There are several paintings of Washington wearing his ceremonial masonic apron and full masonic regalia, so we know that that at least is a fact. In addition, 31 out of 33 military generals under George Washington were also Freemasons and significantly, the entire British military hierarchy was also Freemasonic. Sir William Howe, Brigadier General Augustine Prevost, and 34 senior Colonels were all Masons.

When the French joined the fray on the side of the Americans, the Freemason Marquis de Lafayette joined battle with the Freemason General Cornwallis, commander of the British forces at Yorktown. Some sources in Britain openly blamed Templar Freemasonry for the humiliating British defeat, suggesting that Cornwallis, Clinton, and the Howe brothers were all Templar Freemasons and had conspired together to deliberately hand victory to their fellow Freemasons. In 1781 General Howe and Admiral Howe were accused by 'Cicero' of betraying their country to Benjamin Franklin, but it whilst remaining a distinct possibility, the real truth will probably never be known.

The first President (although that was never his official title) George Washington, was from a British aristocratic background and was of course, a 33rd degree Freemason. His initiation ceremony was in effect a Freemasonic ritual attended by all the Masonic hierarchy of the country in full masonic regalia, aprons et al.

Washington chose a marshy swamp as the site for the new nation's capital in 1790 and selected Freemason, Pierre Charles Enfant to design the new city, at that time named the 'Territory of Columbia.' In 1795 the Freemasonic Founding Fathers laid out the streets of Washington D.C. to form Masonic symbols: a compass, square, rule, pentagram and octagon.

On the 18th September 1793, Washington laid the foundation stone of the Capitol building in his full Masonic regalia and was surrounded by brother Masons. The foundation stones for the White House and other Federal buildings were also laid-down in a Masonic ceremony, designed to be the fulfilment of Bacon's dream of the '*New Atlantis.*'

The Illuminati emblem, their Great Seal, designed by Adam Weishaupt, was later placed on the US one dollar bill by Freemason, President Franklin Roosevelt in the 1930s.

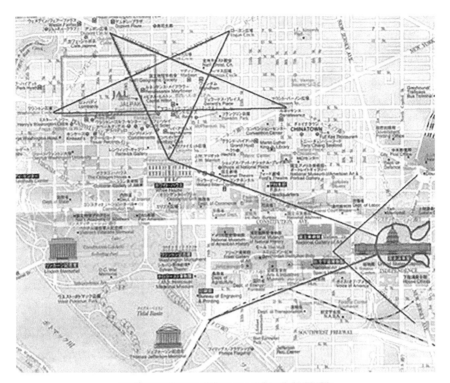

Thomas Jefferson, John Adams and Benjamin Franklin also adopted the Illuminati's ideals whilst in France in 1784, to negotiate a treaty with France. Significant evidence reveals that Benjamin Franklin was a Satanist, a member of the Hellfire Club, a secret society that conducted black masses and orgies. In 1998, workmen restoring Franklin's former London home, dug up the remains of six children and four adults hidden below the floor and the British *Sunday Times* reported that;

"Initial estimates are that the bones are about 200 years old and were buried at the time Franklin was living in the house, which was his home from 1757 to 1762 and from 1764 to 1775. Most of the bones show signs of having been dissected, sawn or cut. One skull has been drilled with several holes. Paul Knapman, the Westminster Coroner, said yesterday: 'I cannot totally discount the possibility of a crime. There is still a possibility that I may have to hold an inquest.'"

In fact, completely in-line with Freemasonry, the 'Founding Fathers' rejected all organised religion in favour of Deism. They believed... 1) in a supreme being; 2) the need to worship that being; 3) that the best form of worship was to lead a virtuous life; 4) that one must repent; 5) that one would be rewarded and/or punished after death. Any religious view contrary to nature and reason, such as a virgin birth and divine intervention in the affairs of men, is rejected by Deism as may be seen in the Deist works by Voltaire and Rousseau all of which were studied in detail by Washington et al. Benjamin Franklin, Thomas Paine, Thomas Jefferson, and John Adams were all openly Deists whilst George Washington and many other Founders posed as Christians but were clearly Deists as evidenced by their personal writings.

The reason that the Founding Fathers kept their Deism secret and retained the façade of Christianity was to unify the Catholic, Anglican, and Puritan settlers into one new nation-state as specified by Bacon in his writings. They also wanted to be sure of having a nation of trusting and passive followers and so religion served a utilitarian, rather than spiritual purpose.

It may be surprising to some to learn that in actuality, the United States of America has never been a country in its own right. It was established by British Freemasonry in conjunction with American Freemasonry in order to perpetuate the deception of 'freedom for the people,' to enable covert control of the masses and facilitate huge, ongoing profits at the expense of those masses.

In 1830 a certain Guiseppe Mazzini travelled to Tuscany, where he became a member of the *Carbonari*, a secret association with covert political aims and on the 31st October of that year he was arrested at Genoa and interned at Savona and during his imprisonment he devised the outlines of a new patriotic movement aiming to replace the unsuccessful *Carbonari*. Although freed in early 1831, he chose exile to Geneva in Switzerland rather than life confined to the small hamlet, which was what was ordered by the authorities.

Mazzini's ambition was to create a 'United States of Europe,' more than a century before the *European Union* came into existence. Globalism is Illuminism by another name after all and Mazzini was loyal to both. In 1860, he founded a group of revolutionaries by the name of *Young Italy* whose goal was to free Italy from the control of monarchy and the Pope. They succeeded and Mazzini was honoured as a patriot in Italy and in the process, the infamous Italian / Sicilian *Mafia* was born. The *Young Italy* revolutionaries needed money, and they supported themselves by robbing banks, looting or burning businesses if protection money was not paid and kidnapping for ransom. Throughout Italy the word spread that *'**M**azzini **A**utorizza **F**urti, **I**ncendi e **A**ttentati,'* meaning, 'Mazzini authorises theft, arson and kidnapping.' This phrase was later shortened to the acronym, MAFIA and thus organised crime was born.

Incidentally, Mazzini was also the founder of the Scottish Rite of Freemasonry in Italy.

Prior to his death in 1872, he made another revolutionary leader named Adrian Lemmy his successor. Lemmy was subsequently succeeded by Lenin and Trotsky, then by Stalin and the revolutionary activities of all these men were amply financed by the Rothschilds.

Mazzini was connected to numerous evil people, but none more deserving of that epithet than the always controversial and very shadowy Albert Pike. During his leadership, Mazzini enticed Pike into the by this time, formally disbanded but still covertly operating, Illuminati. Pike was fascinated by the idea of a one world government and when asked by Mazzini, readily agreed to write a ritual tome that outlined the transition from average-ranking Mason into a 33rd degree, Illuminati Mason. Since Mazzini also wanted Pike to head the Illuminati's American chapter, he clearly felt that Pike was worthy of such a task. Mazzini's intention was that once a Mason had made his way up the Freemasonic ladder and proven himself worthy, the highest ranking members would offer membership to the 'secret society within a secret society.'

It is for this reason that most Freemasons vehemently deny the evil intentions of their fraternity. Since the vast majority of members never come anywhere remotely close to reaching the 30th degree, let alone the 33rd degree, they are unaware of the real purpose behind Freemasonry.

In fact, Albert Pike was the most influential and controversial Freemason in the history of American Freemasonry and personally designed 30 initiation rituals for the advanced degrees he created inside Freemasonry, turning the original three degrees into 33, and investing great ceremonial magic into the culture, which he soon dominated as its American 'Grand Master.'

Pike was born on 20th December 1809, in Boston, Massachusetts, the son of an alcoholic father and a mother who tried to push him into the ministry. In 1825 he was sent to live with his uncle, who discovered that Pike had a photographic memory and was able to recall large volumes at will. He soon mastered several languages and passed his entrance exams for Harvard but unable to afford the tuition fees, he became a teacher in Gloucester, Massachusetts instead. In 1831 he moved to New Mexico and joined several expeditions there, finally settling in Fort Smith, Arkansas in 1833 and again taught in school for a year whilst he studied law. He opened his law practice in 1834.

Pike spent the next twenty or so years building his reputation before becoming politically active during the 1850s. He organised the *Know-Nothing Party* (Order of United Americans,) a reactionary political movement opposed to foreigners and believed strongly that the continuance of slavery was preferable to the practice of farmers importing cheap foreign labour. At the same time he was pro-Indian and as the representative of several tribes of Native Americans won some large settlements on their behalf, from the US government. At the beginning of the Civil War (1861) Pike, by this time living in New Orleans, was named Commissioner of Indian Affairs for the Confederacy.

Eventually he was proclaimed a brigadier general and he organised several regiments from the Arkansas tribes but unfortunately, some of his 'native' soldiers mutilated Union soldiers during a battle in 1862, which caused massive controversy. As a result of that controversy, he came into conflict with his superiors and accused the Confederacy of neglecting its treaty obligations to the Indian tribes. He was arrested for treason, but released when the war came to an end but by now hated by both sides, he fled to the Ozark Mountains and later to Montreal, Canada.

Pike was very influential in George Bickley's *Knights of the Golden Circle*, a Masonic front organisation for the Confederacy. The KGC immediately absorbed the Masonic operatives in Mazzini's *Young America* and became the pre-military organisation of the Confederacy. *The Knights of the Golden Circle* soon expanded westwards across Ohio, Indiana, and Illinois, then south along the Mississippi River to the Gulf of Mexico and east into Maryland and Virginia whilst along the way they recruited many new members. It was envisioned that the '*Golden Circle Empire*,' would spread-out from the Southern states and into Mexico, South America and the Caribbean. Albert Pike opened up a branch in New Orleans, through which Mazzini's Mafia later entered the United States following the Civil War.

One of the initiates into the *Knights of the Golden Circle* was General and Freemason P.T. Beauregard, a West Point graduate and the brother-in-law of one of Louisiana's political leaders, the Freemason, John Slidell. Beauregard was 'credited' with starting the Civil War with his surprise attack on Fort Sumter in 1861.

Long before Fort Sumter, however, Caleb Cushing realized that the anti-slavery north and the pro-slavery south were too far removed geographically to foment a civil war over slavery. A division between neighbours in close proximity had to be created before a war would break out nationally. Such a division was guaranteed by the first order of Congressional business during the Pierce Administration—the passage of the Kansas-Nebraska Act. This act called for the Nebraska Territory to be divided into the territories of Kansas and Nebraska, whose residents would then determine whether slavery would be permitted or not. When the bill passed, the terrible aftermath was utterly predictable. Outrageous acts of murder and arson were committed on both sides, by both the pro-slavery Missourians, and the white 'abolitionists' under the command of John Brown.

What is little known about John Brown is that he spent much of his adult life in secret societies, including the *Oddfellows, Sons of Temperance*, and the Freemasons. Brown was made a Master Mason in Hudson, Ohio on 11th May 1824 and he served as junior deacon from 1825 to 1826. However he renounced Freemasonry in 1830, when an anti-Masonic fervour swept the nation. Caleb Cushing however, viewed John Brown as the perfect candidate to bring about the insurrection of the Southern states. As an anti-Mason, Brown would never be suspected as being an agent of Freemasonry, he reasoned. Brown had joined Mazzini's *Young America* and was supported financially by the John Jacob Astor, Masonic interests in Boston and New York. After receiving his instructions from Caleb Cushing, John Brown deliberately set out to instigate civil war in America.

In January 1857, the Freemason James Buchanan was elected president to replace Franklin Pierce. John A. Quitman, the father of Mississippi Freemasonry and leader of the southern secessionists, was the representative from Mississippi in the House of Representatives. Quitman in fact was intended to be the next Sovereign Grand Commander of the Southern Jurisdiction of Scottish Rite Freemasonry, but on 17th July 1858, he suddenly died—by poisoning, according to Masonic authority and a common fate for those who oppose them. Quitman's close friend Albert Pike, the man groomed by Cushing to take over Southern Freemasonry, conducted a 'lodge of sorrows' in Quitman's memory and a year later was elected to fill the post that Quitman would have held. As a result, Albert Pike then found himself the leader of the Southern secessionists.

After Buchanan was elected president, he appointed to government posts only those who fanatically supported the Southern cause and who were therefore more likely to favour direct action against the North. Buchanan appointed Freemason Edwin M. Stanton of Pennsylvania to the post of Attorney General, and he would later be strongly implicated in the assassination of Abraham Lincoln. Buchanan also appointed Freemason Howell Cobb of Georgia as Secretary of the Treasury and in March 1860, Cobb was elevated to the 33rd degree and appointed by Albert Pike as leader of the secessionists in Georgia and chairman of the convention which organised the Confederacy in Montgomery, Alabama.

Buchanan's vice president was Freemason John C. Breckinridge of Kentucky. Breckinridge was in attendance at the 1860 national convention of the Democratic Party held at Charleston, South Carolina, the headquarters of the Southern Jurisdiction of Freemasonry. Presiding over the convention was Northern Jurisdiction Freemason Caleb Cushing and under his supervision, the Gulf States delegation staged a walkout, formed their own convention, and elected Cushing as its chairman. The secessionists then nominated Breckinridge as their candidate for president, while campaigning in Kentucky, and Breckinridge received his 33rd degree from Albert Pike.

Meanwhile, the newly-formed Republican Party, nominated Abraham Lincoln as its presidential candidate and Lincoln, although significantly **not** a Mason, duly won the election.

That same year Breckinridge was elected US Senator from Kentucky. At the beginning of the Civil War, he had defended the South in the Senate and entered the Confederate's service, for which act he was expelled from the Senate in December 1861. Freemason Jefferson Davis, President of the Confederate States, then duly appointed Breckinridge as his Secretary of War.

It seems highly likely that Albert Pike had instigated the process of secession immediately after Lincoln's election. Significantly, on 20th December 1860, the state of South Carolina, headquarters of the Southern Jurisdiction of Freemasonry, was the first state to secede from the Union.

On that same day, the state of Mississippi, whose secessionist organisation had been created by the late Scottish Rite leader, John A. Quitman, followed South Carolina's lead and again on that very same day, the Freemason John Floyd, Secretary of War under the still-presiding, yet outgoing President Buchanan, performed another act of treason by ordering the Allegheny arsenal at Pittsburgh to send 113 heavy cannons and eleven 32-pound cannons to the unfinished, undefended Union forts at Ship Island, Mississippi, and Galveston, Texas, where they could easily be seized by the insurrectionists.

On 22nd December 1860, the state of Florida seceded from the Union, led by US Senator David Levy Yulee, member of the Freemasonic Hayward Lodge, Gainesville, Florida. The state of Alabama also seceded on 24th December 1860. Then on 2nd January 1861, Georgia's secession was led by two Freemasons, Howell Cobb, President Buchanan's Secretary of the Treasury, and Robert Toombs, who became the first Secretary of State of the Confederacy. Both men received the honorary 33rd degree after the Civil War—how unsurprising. Louisiana then seceded next on 7th January 1861, led also by two Freemasons, John Slidell and Pierre Soule. Soule also received the honorary 33rd degree after the Civil War. Thousands of armed paramilitary *Knights of the Golden Circle* forced Governor of Texas and Freemason, Sam Houston to secede in February, 1861 and finally on the 12th April 1861, the Freemason, General P.T. Beauregard was ordered to attack Fort Sumter, South Carolina, thus instigating four years of horrific carnage and bloodshed. The bankster-created and backed American Civil War had finally begun.

After Lincoln unexpectedly ordered a national mobilisation to crush the rebellion, the *Knights of the Golden Circle* engaged in paramilitary and espionage operations in the North, along with parallel and successor groups under different names, none of which however, publicly carried their proper name, the *Ancient and Accepted Scottish Rite of Freemasonry.*

In total, only eleven Southern states seceded from the Union, yet the Confederate flag bore 13 stars, which is a sacred Masonic number, covertly signalling to those who knew the truth, that the secession of the Southern states was motivated by the Knights Templar's Southern Jurisdiction of the Scottish Rite of Freemasonry.

President Lincoln's inauguration was held on the 4th March 1861 but of all the appointments to his cabinet, he made one fatal error of judgement. He appointed the Freemason Edwin Stanton, Buchanan's former Attorney General, as his Secretary of War. When Lincoln arrived at Washington to assume the Presidency, Freemasonry's armed Knights of the Golden Circle were foiled by General Winfield Scott in their first of two attempts to assassinate Lincoln but Stanton would be implicated in the second and fatal attempt.

Albert Pike was also a part of the Ku Klux Klan, being the leader (or Grand Dragon) in Arkansas. After Lincoln's assassination, in one of his first acts as President, fellow Freemason Andrew Johnson awarded the Supreme Master Mason a complete pardon for all his 'war crimes.' Pike went from hiding-out in Canada in fear for his life, to being accorded full Masonic rites in the White House, recognising his prowess in the occult. Johnson was, after all, a committed and enthusiastic Freemason and as such, he considered Albert Pike as his mentor in all things Freemasonic.

Pike was also said to be a Satanist who indulged in the occult and he allegedly possessed a bracelet which he used to summon Lucifer, with whom it was said, he had constant communication. He was the Grand Master of a Luciferian group known as the Order of the Palladium (or Sovereign Council of Wisdom,) which had been founded in Paris in 1737. 'Palladism,' as it was known, had been brought to Greece from Egypt by Pythagoras in the fifth century BC, and it was this cult of Satan that was introduced to the inner circle of the Masonic lodges. It was aligned with the Palladium of the Templars. In 1801, Hyman Isaac Long brought a statue of Baphomet (Satan) to Charleston, South Carolina, where he helped to establish the Ancient and Accepted Scottish Rite. Long apparently chose Charleston because it was geographically located on the 33rd parallel of latitude (33 being a sacred masonic number) and this council is considered to be the Mother Supreme Council of all Masonic Lodges of the World.

Albert Pike made his mark before the war in Arkansas as a lawyer and writer, but as a Confederate Brigadier General, he was, according to the *Arkansas Democrat* of 31st July 1978, a complete 'wash-out,' not a hero. Yet, Pike is the only Confederate general with a statue on Federal property in Washington, DC. He was honoured, not as a military commander or even as a lawyer, but as the Southern regional leader of the Scottish Rite of Freemasonry. His statue stands on a pedestal near the foot of Capitol Hill between the 'Department of Labor' building and the Municipal Building, between 3rd and 4th Streets, on D Street. As for Pike's mentor, Guiseppe Mazzini, the founder of the 'Mafia' amongst all his other crimes against humanity, he has a bust statue in Central Park, New York City. Well, why not?

In 1871 Pike designed a plan for world conquest and wrote of it in a letter to Mazzini dated 15th August. In this letter he stated plainly that three future 'world wars' (a concept never considered before) would be instigated to prepare the people of the world for the New World Order. Albert Pike's plan for the bankster-Illuminati was simple and effective. He wrote that Communism, National Socialism, Political Zionism and other International political movements would be organised and used to foment the three global wars and three major revolutions. How prophetic.

World War I was to be fought so as to enable the Illuminati to overthrow the power of the Czars in Russia and turn that country into a stronghold of atheistic Communism whilst the Bolshevik / Jewish, 'Red' forces attempted to destroy Christianity by murdering upwards of 50 million of its adherents. The differences stirred-up by the agents of the Illuminati between the British and German Empires were to be used to instigate this bloody war.

World War II was to be engendered using the differences between Fascists and political Zionists to great effect. It was a war to destroy Fascism, the deadly enemy of the Communist banksters and the power of political Zionism increased to enable the sovereign state of Israel to be established in Palestine. During World War II International Communism was to be bolstered until it equalled the strength of united Christendom at which point it was to be contained and kept in check until required for the final societal cataclysm to come. Can any informed person deny that Roosevelt and Churchill put this policy into effect thus resulting in the 45 years-long 'Cold War'?

So according to Pike's letter of 1871, World War III is yet to come before the banksters' long-awaited and much-vaunted *New World Order* can come to pass. This is to be brought about by using the 'differences' between political Zionists and the leaders of the Muslim world. The war is to be directed in such a manner that Islam (the Arab World) and political Zionism (including the State of Israel) will destroy each other, whilst at the same time the remaining nations, once more divided against each other on this issue will be forced to fight themselves into a state of complete physical, mental, spiritual and economical exhaustion.

Some may sanitise Pike's 'accomplishments' and strongly deny and ridicule all this as absurd 'conspiracy theory,' in which case I would ask that they simply look at what is happening in the world right now. Those who aspire to undisputed world domination intend to provoke the greatest social cataclysm the world has ever known. I will let Pike's words speak for themselves...

"We shall unleash the Nihilists and Atheists and we shall provoke a formidable social cataclysm which in all its horror will show clearly to the nations the effect of absolute atheism, origin of savagery and of the most, bloody turmoil."

Only the banksters plan their crimes decades in advance. Only the banksters, have the means, motive and opportunity to carry out these crimes and only the banksters can cover their own tracks afterwards.

I sincerely hope that we can all wake-up soon too these nefarious crimes... Christians, Muslims, Buddhists and Atheists alike, but more than anyone, the Jewish people, the ones in whose name this atrocity is being perpetrated...

Indeed, we **ALL** have to wake-up to the crimes against humanity of the Zionist banksters.

Chapter 3
The Bank that Robbed the World

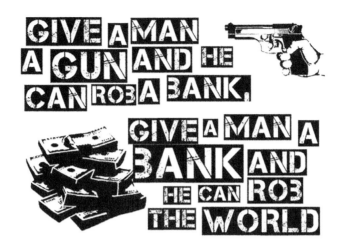

The Mechanics of Bank and Mortgage Fraud

The premise of all bank/building society loans should be that the bank has a sum of money in reserve and therefore available to loan and assuming you qualify as a borrower, then the bank will loan you money as long as you contract to repay it plus a fee (interest.) In order to ensure that the bank does not lose its money, the banksters will ask for beneficial interest (ie. ownership) in your property which is used as collateral for the loan, until the contract is fulfilled (the loan is fully repaid.)

This is how most of us are led to believe that any bank loan/mortgage transaction works, but unfortunately this is untrue. It is pure fantasy in fact.

Firstly, the bank does not much care if you qualify, when you can offer tangible property as collateral because they know that they can simply foreclose on the property without having actually risked anything to acquire it, and this adds significantly to their 'bottom line.' But they promote and maintain the illusion that the borrower 'qualifying' for credit is important, because this conceals their real activities.

Secondly, once a potential borrower has been approved, nothing then happens until he signs a 'promissory note,' usual in the form of a loan application form and returns it to the bank/building society.

But, how does the bank actually reflect this 'loan transaction' in its books? The borrower's note is deposited as an *asset* of the bank and is credited to the bank's asset base but according to the rules of double-entry bookkeeping, the bank must now also enter a *debit entry* to offset its *credit entry* thus 'zero-ising' the transaction. The account being *debited* is the bank's own 'chequing account,' or demand deposit account and in bookkeeping terms a debit is a liability. (Remember this important point, I will return to it shortly.)

Then, what the bank actually does is to deposit this 'promissory note' as 'money' on its books and they then transfer this 'money' into the bank's own account as if it were their own and they do so without the customer's permission. It is from this chequing (demand deposit) account that the bank then transfers the loan to the borrower. This is palpably fraud and common criminal conversion.

As stated before, a debit is a liability and the 'money' deposited into the bank's chequing account was a *debit* and therefore a liability and yet the bank then credits the borrower from that account. But if a debit is a liability and the borrowers account is credited from that debit account, then what the bank actually loaned them is a liability from the debit side of the double-entry ledger, and not an asset! This is all facilitated by the creation of money from nothing.

The next thing to recognise, is the fact that the bank deposits the borrowers' note as 'money' on its books. They transfer that same 'money' to another account and then return it to the borrower in the form of a bank transfer.

But, when we borrow money, do we not assume that we are borrowing the *bank's* money and not our *own*? We do indeed, but we are wrong, very wrong. We are being deceived. Not only are we being hoodwinked with deceptive and misleading advertising... 'Mortgages available here,' but they are also accruing interest from loaning a borrower his *own* money and forcing him to risk his own collateral for the privilege!

But, I hear you exclaim, '... this cannot be true. Our governments would never allow this fraud to continue.' Unfortunately you would be wrong. This scam has been perpetuated for centuries, with no legal or governmental interference whatsoever.

In fact, the *Federal Reserve*, representative of ALL banksters, tells us bluntly and unashamedly how this fraud works in their own publication entitled, *'Modern Money Mechanics,'* which is still (at the time of writing,) available online, here...

http://www.rayservers.com/images/ModernMoneyMechanics.pdf

They have no shame at all about their banking practices, knowing that not even the badly mis-informed or complicit, professional economists will question their methods, as is exhibited by the following excerpts from that publication...

"What Makes Money Valuable? In the United States, neither paper currency nor checking and savings deposits have value as commodities. Intrinsically, a dollar bill is just a piece of paper, deposits merely book entries. Coins do have some intrinsic value as metal but generally far less than their face value.

What then makes these instruments—checks, paper money, and coins acceptable at face value in payment of all debts and for other monetary use? Mainly it's the confidence people have that they will be able to exchange such money for other financial assets and for real goods and services wherever they choose to do so."

And it gets even worse...

"Who Creates Money? Bankers discovered that they could make loans merely by giving their promise to pay (liability in the form of a check [cheque] from a debit 'DDA' account) or bank notes (Federal Reserve Note) to borrowers. In this way, banks began to create money. More notes could be issued than the gold and coin on hand because only a portion of the notes outstanding would be presented for payment at any one time. Enough metallic money had to be kept on hand, of course, to redeem whatever volume of notes was presented for payment."

Transaction deposits are the modern counterpart of bank notes and it was a small step only from the printing of notes to making book entries crediting the deposits of borrowers to the bank's own accounts and which in turn could be 'lent' back to the borrowers, thereby in effect, printing their own money.

So, the Federal Reserve admits openly that the borrower creates his own money by depositing his note with the bank, so they are in effect lending money that does not belong to them and indeed does not exist. That 'money' or 'credit' is actually only 'created' by the signature of the borrower on his / her loan agreement.

The Federal Reserve (on behalf of all banksters, everywhere,) also informs us that the banksters make loans by giving their promise to the borrower (liability.) But this promise can never be paid.

The banksters make a transfer or write a cheque to the 'borrower' which can only be cashed in their own, worthless paper money, but paper money, one-dollar bills, five-pound notes etc. is nothing more than a promise to pay, in effect meaning that a bankster's promise to pay is only redeemable by the bankster's promises to pay. Paper money is no longer redeemable in anything of value by any bank so all we can expect from them is a promise to pay—which of course never does get paid—a liability that is passed-on but never settled.

The borrower assigns his property, a tangible asset of value as collateral to the banksters and signs a contract to pay the banksters back in assets, the hard earned fruits of his labour over many years, and all he receives in return is a liability. The banksters never had any money to loan the borrower in the first place, but instead loaned him money that he, himself had created…his own money! And then, in the case of a 30 year mortgage, the borrower is committed to paying the banksters three times the amount he loaned to himself. Where is the banksters' risk? What did the bankster do to earn 30 years of his labour? What did the bankster do to earn the right to steal the house from his family if he is made redundant, after making the 'loan' repayments faithfully for twenty years but is now temporarily unable to continue? Nothing at all.

Now let's examine this quote from *'Modern Money Mechanics'*… *"…only a portion of those notes outstanding would be presented for payment at any one time."*

This is absolutely false and misleading. The banksters now are dealing in banknotes which are non-redeemable, period. If you do not believe this, try taking one into any bank anywhere and ask them to redeem your £10 note / $10 bill. All you will be offered in exchange is more notes/bills or equally worthless coins representing the same value. Originally 'one pound' represented one pound of silver (sterling) but now one pound is only worth whatever the banksters themselves, deem it to be worth.

Ever thought you may be in the wrong business? The banksters have perfectly 'legal' liens on everyone's property, homes, cars, incomes etc., without ever having to risk a penny of their own and better still they know that their worthless bank notes can never be redeemed for anything of substance either! You or I would quickly be behind bars, sewing mailbags if we tried to promulgate this scam of all scams

And this one… "…*it was a small step from printing notes to making book entries.*" Money is nothing more than bookkeeping entries made by the banksters after they lock-in the borrower's collateral and promise to pay. They know that since they only created the principal amount of the loan in new 'money' and the money to pay the interest on all of their loans is never created. Then, by simple mathematics some people are guaranteed to renege on loan repayments and thereby will they acquire their collateral, the borrower's property, free and clear through foreclosure.

Since the borrower is, in effect printing (figuratively speaking) and borrowing his *own* money, the banksters are nothing more than paper-shufflers who will collect their collateral without risk on their part.

So, if a borrower actually creates money via his promissory note, that is, his signature on a mortgage agreement, could he not discharge his liability with another note, which is the current medium of exchange? In fact, this has been done in a few instances, but the banksters in collusion with their friends in the court and legal systems, have now put steps in place to counter this in every possible way, using their immense wealth to facilitate the blocking of these activities as per my comments in the 'Foreword' to this book.

To couch this in simplistic terms, as I know that when this information is encountered for the first time, it can be difficult to grasp, imagine firstly that the bank has a 'pot' of £10,000,000 available to 'lend' as mortgages.

Upon the customer signing a mortgage agreement for say, a loan of £100,000, one would assume that this sum is **deducted** from the pot total, leaving a balance of £9,900,000. Correct?

Wrong. That £100,000 is actually **added** to the total using their creative, fraudulent bookkeeping methods whilst also taking advantage of the fact that they are able to 'create' money at will in this manner. So, the bottom line is that not only is bank enriched by the capital sum of £100,000, they are also made considerably more rich by the accrual of all the interest pertaining to the 'loan' of that capital sum which usually amounts to at least three times the original sum.

Not only does the bank benefit to the tune of around £400,000, even if you fail to pay it cannot lose, because it also has a lien on your property and would not hesitate to use the bought-and-paid-for court system to 'steal' that property, should any individual renege on his payments at any time during the term.

Put another even more simple way, this process requires exactly the same set of bookkeeping entries that would occur in the event of a burglar stealing your property and then returning that stolen property back to you, and claiming it to be a 'loan' and you then being legally obligated to repay both the principal and interest accrued, to the thief.

All banksters should be charged, arrested and tried for these crimes; and banks' boards of directors should be the co-defendants in a civil, class-action suit brought by every homeowner that has ever been drawn into this fraudulent financial trap.

"The real truth of the matter is, as you and I know, that a financial element in the large centres has owned the government of the US since the days of Andrew Jackson." Franklin D. Roosevelt in a letter written 21st November 1933 to Colonel E. Mandel House

But it gets even worse, much worse. The above is only the platform upon which the real, heinous crimes can begin…

The Kingdom of the Banksters

The banksters continue to view humanity as just another natural resource to be exploited. What we are spoon-fed by our educational and legal institutions, what we are shown on TV and in the newspapers, that no one is above the law, that good always triumphs over evil—well, this simply does not apply to the banksters. Through their immense, unlimited wealth, they own the law. They appoint the judges, the prosecutors AND defenders, they even own the police AND they get to lie about it all in the history books.

The Rothschilds and their bankster friends waited, albeit impatiently, a long time to permanently re-establish a central bank in the United States. It took decades to install their 'friendly' politicians and key figures in place, in order to create the right circumstances for the banksters to really start making obscene profits from the people, the trusting, ignorant masses, whom they hold in such high contempt. Having totally engineered earlier stock market collapses, and bank panics such as the one in 1907, the banksters firstly created the PROBLEM, they watched the public and political REACTION and subtly instigated the call for banking reform and regulation, and then they were in position to present the SOLUTION, *their* desired solution. Another example of the Hegelian Dialectic used to perfection once again. Why change a successful formula?

On the evening of 22nd November 1910, a group of newspaper reporters stood disconsolately in the persistent rain at the railway station at Hoboken, New Jersey. They had just watched a delegation of the nation's leading financiers leave the station on a secret mission but it would be several years before they discovered what that mission was, and even then they would not understand that the history of the United States had undergone such a dramatic change after that miserable night in Hoboken. Many, the majority in fact, still do not.

The delegation had left in a sealed, private railway carriage, with blinds drawn, for an undisclosed destination, led by the Republican Senator for Rhode Island, Nelson Aldrich, head of the National Monetary Commission.

The banksters' 'puppet,' President Theodore Roosevelt as directed, had signed into law the bill creating the National Monetary Commission in 1908, after the tragic *Panic of 1907* had resulted in a bankster-induced public outcry that the nation's monetary system be 'stabilised.' Aldrich had led the members of the Commission on a two-year tour of Europe, spending some three hundred thousand dollars of public money but he had not yet made a report on the results of this trip, nor had he proffered any plan for banking reform.

Accompanying Senator Aldrich at the Hoboken train station were his private secretary, Shelton, A. Piatt Andrew, Assistant Secretary of the Treasury, and Special Assistant of the National Monetary Commission, Frank Vanderlip, Rockefeller's personal representative and president of the Rockefeller's *National City Bank of New York*, Henry P. Davison, senior partner of J.P. Morgan Company and generally regarded as Morgan's personal emissary, and Charles D. Norton, president of the Morgan-dominated *First National Bank of New York*. Joining the group just before the train left the station were Benjamin Strong, also known to be a 'lieutenant' of J.P. Morgan and Paul Warburg, a recent immigrant from Germany who had joined the banking house of *Kuhn, Loeb & Co*, representing the Rothschilds of Europe.

The Rothschilds, the Rockefellers and the J.P. Morgan bankster-interests, although they competed with each other, often acted in unison when it was in their best and certainly most profitable interest to do so.

Six years later, a financial writer named Bertie Charles Forbes (who later founded *Forbes* Magazine), wrote:

"Picture a party of the nation's greatest bankers stealing out of New York on a private railroad car under cover of darkness, stealthily hurrying hundreds of miles South, embarking on a mysterious launch, sneaking onto an island deserted by all but a few servants, living there a full week under such rigid secrecy that the names of not one of them was once mentioned lest the servants learn the identity and disclose to the world this strangest, most secret expedition in the history of American finance. I am not romancing; I am giving to the world, for the first time, the real story of how the famous Aldrich currency report, the foundation of our new currency system, was written . . .

The utmost secrecy was enjoined upon all. The public must not glean a hint of what was to be done. Senator Aldrich notified each one to go quietly into a private car of which the railroad had received orders to draw up on an unfrequented platform. Off the party set, New York's ubiquitous reporters had been foiled . . . Nelson (Aldrich) had confided to Henry, Frank, Paul and Piatt that he was to keep them locked up at Jekyll Island, out of the rest of the world, until they had evolved and compiled a scientific currency system for the United States, the real birth of the present Federal Reserve System, the plan done on Jekyll Island in the conference with Paul, Frank and Henry . . . Warburg is the link that binds the Aldrich *system and the present system together. He more than any one man, has made the system possible as a working reality."*

Aldrich's private carriage, which had left Hoboken station with its shades drawn, had actually taken the financiers to Jekyll Island, Georgia which some years earlier, a very exclusive group of millionaires, led by JP Morgan, had purchased as a winter retreat.

They called themselves the *Jekyll Island Hunt Club* and at first the island was used only for hunting expeditions, until the millionaires realised that its pleasant climate offered a warm retreat from the rigours of New York winters and began to build huge mansions which they euphemistically referred to as 'cottages,' for their families' winter vacations. The club building itself, being quite isolated, was sometimes in demand for parties and certain other secret pursuits unrelated to hunting. On such occasions, the club members who were not invited to these specific events were asked not to attend for a certain number of days. Before Nelson Aldrich's party had left New York, the club's members had been notified that the club would be 'occupied' and therefore 'out of bounds' for the next two weeks. The Jekyll Island Club was chosen as the place to draft the plan for the banksters' usurpation of the control of the money and credit of the United States not simply because of its idyllic isolation and climate, but also because it was the private preserve of the people who were drafting the plan.

The *New York Times* later noted, on 3rd May 1931, in commenting on the death of George F. Baker, one of JP Morgan's closest associates that *"The Jekyll Island Club has lost one of its most distinguished members. One-sixth of the total wealth of the world is represented by the members of the Jekyll Island Club."* Membership was strictly by inheritance only.

However, the Aldrich group had no interest whatsoever in hunting, on this particular occasion. Jekyll Island was chosen for the site of the preparation of the proposed new Central bank because it offered complete privacy and also because there were no snooping journalists within fifty miles. Such was the need for secrecy that the members of the party agreed before arriving at Jekyll Island, that no last names would be used at any time during their two week stay. The group later referred to themselves as the *First Name Club,* as the names Warburg, Strong, Vanderlip and the others were prohibited during their stay as being instantly recognisable. The regular club attendees had been given two-week vacations from the club and servants who did not know the names of any of those present were shipped-in from the mainland for the duration. Even had they been interrogated after the Aldrich party departed back to New York, they could not have given their names to any nosy reporters.

So why all the secrecy? Why the two thousand mile round trip in a secluded carriage to a remote hunting club? Ostensibly, it was to initiate a programme of public service, to prepare banking reform which would be a blessing to the people of the United States, as ordered by the National Monetary Commission. The participants were no strangers to public benefaction and usually, their names were inscribed on brass plaques, or on the exteriors of buildings which they had sponsored. This was all contrary to the procedure they followed at Jekyll Island. No brass plaque was ever erected to mark the 'selfless' actions of those who met at their private hunting club in 1910 to ostensibly, 'improve the lot of every citizen of the United States.'

In fact, nothing beneficial to the nation or its people took place at Jekyll Island, whatsoever. The Aldrich group journeyed there in private to compose the banking and currency legislation which the National Monetary Commission had been ordered to prepare in public. At stake was the future control of the money and credit of the United States and if any genuine monetary reform had been prepared and presented to Congress, it would have immediately ended the power of the elitist one-world money-creators—the banksters. But in fact, the Jekyll Island meeting ensured that a central bank *would* be established in the United States and thus provide the banksters with everything they had always wanted.

As the most technically proficient of those present, Paul Warburg was charged with the actual drafting of the plan. His work would then be discussed and reviewed by the rest of the group. Senator Nelson Aldrich was present to ensure that the completed plan would appear in a form that would be guaranteed to be approved by Congress and the other bankers were there to include whatever details would be needed to make certain that they got their share of everything they wanted too, in a finished draft composed during a one-off stay. They well knew that after they returned to New York, there would be no further opportunity to rework their plan and they could not hope to obtain such secrecy of action on a second trip to Jekyll Island.

The infamous 'Federal Reserve room' Jekyll Island Hotel

The Jekyll Island group remained at the club for nine full days, working furiously to complete their dirty task. Despite the common interests of those present, the work did not proceed without friction. Senator Aldrich, a domineering character, became the self-appointed leader of the group and could not restrain himself from ordering the others around. Aldrich also felt somewhat out of place as the only member of the group who was not a professional banker. He had enjoyed substantial banking interests throughout his career, but only as an individual who had profited from the ownership of bank stocks. He knew very little about the technical aspects of financial operations.

His opposite number, Paul Warburg, believed that every question raised by the group demanded, not merely an answer, but a lecture. He rarely lost an opportunity to give the members a long discourse designed to impress them with the extent of his knowledge of banking. This was much resented by the others and often drew barbed remarks from Aldrich. It was only the natural diplomacy of Henry P. Davison that proved to be the catalyst which kept them cohesive. Warburg's strong German accent irritated them intensely but they knew they had to accept his presence if a central bank plan was to be devised which would guarantee them their riches beyond all wildest dreams. Warburg himself made little effort to assuage their prejudices and confronted them on every possible occasion on technical banking questions, which he considered his private preserve.

The '*Monetary Reform Plan*,' later to become the '*Aldrich Plan*,' prepared at Jekyll Island was to be presented to Congress as the completed work of the National Monetary Commission. It was imperative that the *real* authors of the bill remain hidden.

So great was popular resentment against bankers since the *Panic of 1907* that no Congressman would dare to vote for a bill with any connection whatsoever to the banking industry, so the Jekyll Island plan was a central bank plan disguised as a government initiative due also to the fact that in America there was a long tradition of opposition to the imposing of a central bank on the American people. This had all begun with Thomas Jefferson's fight against Alexander Hamilton's scheme for the First Bank of the United States, backed by James Rothschild and had continued with Andrew Jackson's successful war against Alexander Hamilton's scheme for the Second Bank of the United States, in which Nicholas Biddle was acting as the agent for James Rothschild of Paris. The result of that struggle was the creation of the Independent Sub-Treasury System, which supposedly had served to keep the funds of the United States (and its people,) well away from the clutches of the banksters.

A serious study of the panics of 1873, 1893 and 1907 indicated that these panics were the result of the international banksters' machinations in London. The public was demanding in 1908 that Congress enact legislation to prevent the recurrence of artificially induced money panics and such monetary reform now seemed inevitable. It was in order to control such reform that the National Monetary Commission had been set-up with Nelson Aldrich at its head, since he was majority leader of the Senate.

However, the main problem, as Paul Warburg informed his colleagues, was to avoid the label of 'central bank,' which would no doubt raise the suspicions and antagonisms of the public and politicians alike. For that very reason, he had decided upon the designation of '*Federal Reserve System*' which ought to be sufficient to deceive the people into thinking it was not a central bank, but one under the absolute control of the Federal authorities. But regardless of this, the Jekyll Island plan certainly would be a central bank in all but name, fulfilling all the usual functions of a central bank and would also be owned by private individuals who would profit from ownership of shares. Finally, as an 'issuing' bank, it would also control **all** the nation's money and credit.

Although a major player in German finance, after frequent business trips to New York, Warburg settled there in 1902 as a partner in *Kuhn, Loeb & Co.*, where the influential Jacob Schiff, his wife's brother-in-law, was senior partner. Warburg remained a partner in the family firm in Hamburg, but he became a naturalised American citizen in 1911. His salary was purportedly $500,000 per annum from the Rothschild-owned *Kuhn, Loeb & Co*, where his primary function was to lobby for the creation of the central bank.

Paul's brother, Max was the financial advisor to Kaiser Wilhelm prior to World War I and was also director of the *Reichsbank*, the central bank of Germany.

So, in order to impose the so-called *Aldrich Plan* upon a highly sceptical public, the banksters centred on the Rockefeller-Morgan-Rothschild nexus and mobilised their considerable combined resources in order to inculcate it into the American consciousness. Leading this propaganda onslaught were the national banks, which collectively contributed five million dollars to a 'fighting fund' to be used to persuade the American public that the plan for a central bank was in their best interests and should definitely be enacted into law by Congress.

Moreover, three of the leading American universities, Princeton, Harvard plus the University of Chicago and certain academics of standing, teaching therein, were used as the rallying points and apologists for this propaganda. Most notable of them all perhaps, was Woodrow Wilson, former president of Princeton University, governor of New Jersey and future President of the United States. The plotters used a large portion of the five million dollar 'slush fund' in their lobby group known as the *National Citizens' League* and composed of college professors of whom Professor O.M. Sprague of Harvard and J. Laurence Laughlin of the University of Chicago proved the most tireless propagandists for the insidious Aldrich Plan.

Further emphasis was placed upon the spurious assertion in the Plan that it contained a reform of the nation's monetary system as well as providing stability for the US currency by taking control of it away from the banksters. Of course, the reality was quite the reverse. The Aldrich Plan was written by the banksters, for the banksters, whose primary aim was the consolidation of their control over US currency and credit and the gargantuan, obscene profits that that would realise. But this reality was carefully concealed from the public and unwary politicians, and those who were perceived as a threat in any way to the Plan's enactment into law were berated, threatened, blackmailed or maybe worst of all, simply ignored.

There were many dissenting voices raised against the plan and its grave implications for America and her people. For instance, Charles A. Lindbergh Sr., the father of the famous flyer and Congressman for 6th District of Minnesota (1907-1917), who also opposed the US entry into World War I, was an arch opponent of the Federal Reserve System.

In his testimony before the Committee on Rules on 15th December 1911, after the Aldrich Plan had been introduced in Congress, Lindbergh stated . . .

"Our financial system is a false one and a huge burden on the people . . . I have alleged that there is a Money Trust. The Aldrich plan is a scheme plainly in the interest of the Trust . . . Why does the Money Trust press so hard for the Aldrich Plan now, before the people know what the money trust has been doing? . . . The Aldrich Plan is the Wall Street Plan. It is a broad challenge to the Government by the champion of the Money Trust. It means another panic, if necessary, to intimidate the people. Aldrich, paid by the Government to represent the people, proposes a plan for the trusts instead. It was by a very clever move that the National Monetary Commission was created. In 1907 nature responded most beautifully and gave this country the most bountiful crop it had ever had.

Other industries were busy too, and from a natural standpoint all the conditions were right for a most prosperous year. Instead, a panic entailed enormous losses upon us. Wall Street knew the American people were demanding a remedy against the recurrence of such a ridiculously unnatural condition. Most Senators and Representatives fell into the Wall Street trap and passed the Aldrich Vreeland Emergency Currency Bill. But the real purpose was to get a monetary commission which would frame a proposition for amendments to our currency and banking laws which would suit the Money Trust. The interests are now busy everywhere educating the people in favour of the Aldrich Plan. It is reported that a large sum of money has been raised for this purpose. Wall Street speculation brought on the Panic of 1907. The depositors' funds were loaned to gamblers and anybody the Money Trust wanted to favour. Then when the depositors wanted their money, the banks did not have it. That made the panic."

Strong criticism of the Aldrich Bill was also evident in testimony given during the *House Banking and Currency Committee* of the *American Bankers Association* under the chairmanship of Carter Glass. Glass was a lifelong Democrat and served in the US House of Representatives (1902—18,) where his most notable contribution was helping to compose and sponsor the Federal Reserve Act via his chairmanship of said *House Banking and Currency Committee*. For example, Andrew Frame who represented a group of Western bankers who opposed the Aldrich Plan, testified before the *House Banking and Currency Committee* of the *American Bankers Association*, having exposed the connivance of the schemers and plotters behind the Aldrich Plan, to have it scurrilously endorsed in 1911 by the *American Bankers Association* but which in 1912 did not even dare to have the Association *"reiterate its endorsement of the plan of the National Monetary Commission"* for fear of an honest and open discussion exposing its patently treasonous nature.

Another dissenting voice giving testimony to this committee was Leslie Shaw, a banker from Philadelphia. Shaw was especially aggrieved by the question of the supposed 'decentralisation' of the proposed System . . .

"Under the Aldrich Plan the bankers are to have local associations and district associations, and when you have a local organisation, the centred control is assured. Suppose we have a local association in Indianapolis; can you not name the three men who will dominate

that association? And then can you not name the one man everywhere else. When you have hooked the banks together, they can have the biggest influence of anything in this country, with the exception of the newspapers."

Chairman Carter Glass's House Report in 1913 was not only critical of Aldrich and the Bill bearing his name but of the process involved in its supposed drafting and the role (or lack of one) played by the *National Monetary Commission*.

Glass's dismay is obvious in this statement...

"Senator MacVeagh fixes the cost of the National Monetary Commission to May 12, 1911 at $207,130. They have since spent another hundred thousand dollars of the taxpayer's money. The work done at such cost cannot be ignored, but, having examined the extensive literature published by the Commission, the Banking and Currency Committee finds little that bears upon the present state of the credit market of the United States. We object to the Aldrich Bill on the following points: Its entire lack of adequate government or public control of the banking mechanism it sets up; It's tendency to throw voting control into the hands of the large banks of the system; The extreme danger of inflation of currency inherent in the system; The insincerity of the bond-funding plan provided for by the measure, there being a bare-faced pretence that this system was to cost the government nothing; The dangerous monopolistic aspects of the bill; Our Committee at the outset of its work was met by a well-defined sentiment in favour of a central bank which was the manifest outgrowth of the work that had been done by the National Monetary Commission."

The *Aldrich Plan* was never voted upon in Congress because its sponsors, Aldrich and his Republicans lost control of the House in 1910, then the Senate and ultimately the Presidency in 1912. However, although the animosity of Glass and his committee towards the Aldrich Plan was predicated upon their professed dislike of central banking and all it involves, Glass was all the while promulgating his own Bill, the *Federal Reserve Act*. This was an Act that would not only satisfy all Aldrich and his secret backers' requirements but also give such powers to a centralised authority that would fulfil all the functions of a central bank. Thus, although Congress had rejected Aldrich it would consent to Glass's *Federal Reserve Act* and thereby condemn America and its people to the consequences of the whims and scheming of international financiers, via their control of the central bank of United States.

However, there were a number of other powerful men who were also not in favour of the proposed Aldrich / Glass bankster *Federal Reserve Banking System*. Benjamin Guggenheim, Isidor Straus and John Jacob Astor were the most prominent among those who opposed the formation of this abomination. They were amongst the richest men in the world, but their money was accrued through industrial, retail and leisure interests, rather than through the financial sector and they stood firmly in the way of Glass and Aldrich.

Benjamin Guggenheim (1865-1912) was born in Philadelphia as the fifth of the seven sons of the wealthy Meyer Guggenheim. When Benjamin was twenty, he began managing the family's silver-mining operation in Leadville, Colorado, where he acquired his nickname the 'Silver Prince.' Whilst in Leadville, Guggenheim first saw the great potential of the smelting industry and with his family's backing, built the first smelting plant in Pueblo, Colorado and established the Philadelphia Smelting and Refining Company.

Benjamin Guggenheim John Jacob Astor IV Isidor Straus and wife, Ida

Following the first plant's enormous success, several more plants were built in locations around the United States. The company's mining and smelting silver, lead, and copper proved profitable and became the focus of the Guggenheim family's business. He and the rest of his family were made incredibly wealthy by the success of the company and at the time of his death, Guggenheim was estimated to be worth around $95,000,000.

Isidor Straus (1845-1912) was a German born, prominent New York businessman. During the American Civil War he worked in his father Lazarus' store for about 18 months whilst his father's business partner served in the Confederate, 4th Georgia Regiment. When his father's partner returned from the war, discharged owing to physical disability, Straus became the secretary to a foreign group whose intention was to import cotton to Europe. It was proposed that the proceeds would be used to build blockade-running ships but although Straus travelled to Europe, the enterprise never really got off the ground. In fact he remained in Europe for the remainder of the war and returned to the United States with $12,000 in gold he'd earned, trading in Confederate bonds.

Following the war, the Straus family moved to New York City where Lazarus and Isidor formed *L. Straus & Son*, importers of crockery, china and porcelain. In 1874 his brother Nathan, who by then had completed his education and joined the family firm, convinced Rowland Hussey Macy to allow *L. Straus & Sons* to open a crockery department in the basement of his store under licence. In 1895, the Strauss brothers purchased *R.H. Macy & Co*, and renamed it simply, '*Macy's*.'

John Jacob Astor IV (1866-1912) was the great-grandson of the John Jacob Astor who came to New York in the 18th century and made a fortune in beaver pelts and opium. Astor IV (commonly known as 'Jack') was a talented writer, writing amongst other things, *A Journey in Other Worlds*, an 1894 science fiction novel about life in the year 2000 on the planets Saturn and Jupiter.

Astor was also a lieutenant-colonel during the Spanish-American War and a prolific inventor. He patented several inventions, including a bicycle brake in 1898, a 'vibratory disintegrator' used to produce gas from peat moss, a pneumatic 'road—improver' and helped develop a turbine engine. In addition, Astor made millions in real estate and in 1897, built the Astoria Hotel which adjoined Astor's cousin, William Waldorf Astor's, Waldorf Hotel in New York City. The complex subsequently became known as the Waldorf-Astoria Hotel. He was also the creator of the Astor Theater.

With a net worth of well over $85 million, three times that of JP Morgan, Astor was commonly regarded as 'the wealthiest man in the world,' thanks to the Rothschilds and their bankster cohorts always ensuring that their wealth is NEVER, ever disclosed on any rich list, or even having their names mentioned.

Whilst at the 1893 World's Fair in Chicago, John Jacob Astor met a fellow exhibitor and inventor by the name of Nikola Tesla. For those not familiar with the name, Tesla was **the** absolute genius where electricity was concerned. He was the inventor of the alternating current, power system in use all over the world today and his discovery of the rotating magnetic field was almost as *revolutionary* as the Morse telegraph. He truly electrified the world.

Nikola Tesla (1856-1943)

In 1884, as a poor Serbian immigrant, he arrived in the United States and although he was poor in terms of money and possessions he was certainly rich in ideas. Ideas that would eventually light up the United States . . . and indeed the entire world.

At this time, the most famous inventor in the world was Thomas Alva Edison—the so-called '*Wizard* of Menlo Park.' Edison was credited with the invention of the DC dynamo and the electric light bulb, but the only thing he ever really invented was the electric chair. Edison was fixed firmly in the direct current (DC) camp and would not consider any other system at all. DC had very severe limitations and was totally impractical for long distance electrical transmission.

Almost immediately after entering the US, Tesla went to work for Edison. Edison was totally unaware of the great benefits of AC until Tesla showed him plans for his induction motor. Edison's DC system was extremely unwieldy and only worked over very short distances but Edison and his boss JP Morgan (yes, the banksters control technology too,) completely rejected this *revolutionary* invention.

Edison set him to work fixing the many problems with DC dynamos. Tesla had remarkable mechanical and electrical ability, and Edison promised him $50,000 if he could fix a particularly perplexing problem with his dynamo. Tesla worked for many months and finally the problem was solved but Edison reneged on his promise to pay him for all his hard work, resulting in Tesla leaving the *Edison Company* in anger and disgust.

"For a paltry few thousand dollars they lost not only a man who would have saved them many times that amount each year, but they also lost an opportunity to obtain world control of the greatest and most profitable electrical invention ever made." O' Neill, *Prodigal Genius*, p. 58

After leaving the *Edison Company*, Tesla had to work as a manual labourer for a year, ironically digging the streets of New York to lay Edison's cables. This was the worst time of his life as a poor man in a strange land but he was befriended by the foreman of his work-gang who persuaded him to form his own company. In spite of all the advantages of the AC system, Edison still refused to acknowledge its superiority and eventually inventor George Westinghouse of Pittsburgh came to Tesla's rescue. At this time, Edison and his boss Morgan sulked like spoilt children and began what became known in history as the *War of the Currents* or the battles between AC and DC.

George Westinghouse (1846-1914)

By 1886, the Westinghouse Company was one of the biggest and most successful in the entire world. Westinghouse was a Protestant, Christian gentleman and totally dissimilar to the robber barons of that era. His employees shared in the success of his company and he believed in doing his good works in secret and many charities throughout the country were helped by his generosity.

He offered to buy all the AC patents from Tesla for the staggering sum of $1m and royalties of $1.00 per horsepower of electricity produced. Unlike Edison, George Westinghouse was a man of his word and paid Tesla this staggering sum for all his AC patents. So favourably impressed was Westinghouse that he decided to act quickly. The story was related to author and close friend John O'Neill by Tesla ...

"'I will give you one million dollars cash for your alternating current patents, plus royalty,' Westinghouse blurted at the startled Tesla. This tall, suave gentleman, however, gave no outward sign that he had almost been bowled over by surprise.

'If you will make the royalty one dollar per horsepower, I will accept the offer,' Tesla replied. 'A million cash, a dollar a horsepower royalty,' Westinghouse repeated.

'That is acceptable,' said Tesla.

'Sold,' said Westinghouse.

'You will receive a check and a contract in a few days.' Here was a case of two great men, each possessed with the power of seeing visions of the future on a gigantic panorama, and each with complete faith in the other, arranging a tremendous transaction with utter disregard of details." O'Neill, *Prodigal Genius*, pp. 74-75

Edison's decision to inflict alternating current upon the world put George Westinghouse and Tesla on a collision course with both Morgan and Edison and no dirty trick was beneath that pair in their attempts to ruin Westinghouse and Tesla.

Thomas Alva Edison (1847-1931)

In 1895, the Westinghouse Company and Nicola Tesla built the first hydro-electric alternating current system at Niagara Falls. Tesla was determined that the awesome power of the falls should be harnessed to the awesome power of poly-phase alternating current and without using a single drawing, Tesla was able to work out the whole plan of electrification in his head. Everything worked perfectly the first time, but Tesla was determined to take it one dramatic step further and transmit electricity without cumbersome and unsightly wires.

It was also that year Tesla's laboratory in New York City was very suspiciously, totally destroyed by fire and a lifetime of priceless inventions were destroyed. Tesla usually worked through the night, but that particular night he was not in his office and so miraculously escaped death.

By 1897, the *War of the Currents* between Westinghouse and Edison had continued to escalate. Mergers had taken place between JP Morgan and Rockefeller-controlled companies such as *Thomson-Houston* and *Edison General Electric* to form the present day *General Electric Company*. This new *General Electric Company* tried to take-over *Westinghouse* and force them to abandon AC. They also insisted that Westinghouse stop paying royalties to Tesla.

"One of the requirements was that Westinghouse, get rid of the contract with Tesla calling for

royalty payments of $1.00 per horsepower on all alternating current articles sold under his patents. Financial advisers pointed out that if the business which Westinghouse expected the company would do under the Tesla patents in the ensuing year was anywhere near as great as estimated, the amount to be paid out under this contract would be tremendous, totalling millions of dollars; and this, at the time of reorganisation, appeared a dangerous burden, imperilling the ability which they were trying to attain for the new organization. Westinghouse strenuously objected to the procedure. This patent-royalty payment, he insisted, was in accordance with usual procedures and would not be a burden on the company, as it was included in costs of production, was paid for by the customers, and did not come out of the company's earnings. Westinghouse, himself an inventor of first magnitude, had a strong sense of justice in his dealings with inventors." O'Neill, *Prodigal Genius*, p. 79

By cheating him out of millions in royalty payments, Morgan and Rockefeller placed a financial 'squeeze' on the great inventor. Tesla had already lost a fortune because of the arson to his laboratory and now he was too short of cash to perfect his latest inventions. The arsonists could certainly hamper him financially, but they could never stop the torrent of new inventions that kept-on flowing from his fertile brain.

At the beginning of 1900, Tesla was extremely optimistic that he would be able to give the world wireless transmission of electricity and *data*. Unfortunately, that was not to be the case, Tesla was virtually penniless from losing his royalties on his AC patents and he had to approach his arch enemy JP Morgan for funding.

"Morgan made inquiries of Tesla concerning his financial structure. There were, in those days, a limited number of strong financial groups who were playing a terrestrial game of chess with the world's economic resources; the discoveries of a genius like Tesla might well have a profound effect on the destinies of one or more of these groups, and it would be well for an operator in this field to know more of the inventor's commitments. Undoubtedly, it was a source of surprise and satisfaction to Morgan when he learned that Tesla was a lone operator and now entirely without funds needed to carry on his researches." O'Neill, *Prodigal Genius*, p. 197

Morgan and his Rothschild backers at the *Bank of England* realised the deadly military possibilities of using electricity as a weapon and Tesla had already discussed the possibility of using electricity to bring rainfall to the desert areas of the planet. A 'weather weapon' is the most diabolically clever of all methods of warfare because no-one can ever prove that the weather is not a natural phenomenon. Meanwhile, Tesla lived at the *Waldorf Astoria* hotel and commuted daily to his laboratory in Manhattan. The hotel was owned by millionaire John Jacob Astor IV who was also a close friend and financier of Tesla.

The Waldorf-Astoria was the tallest hotel in the world and it was the permanent or temporary residence of some of the wealthiest and most eminent citizens of the day. Making his home there became a goal to which Tesla aspired and this he achieved in 1898 and he lived there for the next two decades.

"Col. John Jacob Astor, owner of the Waldorf Astoria, held his famous dining-room guest

in the highest esteem as a personal friend, and kept in close touch with the progress of his investigations. When he heard that his researches were being halted through lack of funds, he made available to Tesla the $30,000 he needed in order to take advantage of Curtis' offer and build a temporary plant at Colorado Springs. Tesla arrived in Colorado in May 1899, bringing with him some of his laboratory workers, and accompanied by an engineering associate, Fritz Lowenstein." O'Neill, *Prodigal Genius, p. 176*

In 1899 in Pike's Peak, Colorado, Tesla demonstrated the feasibility of safely transmitting electricity through the Earth *without* the use of wires (wireless electricity.) He chose Pike's Peak because of its remote location and the availability of electricity from a local power station, however he was also to discover that tremendously destructive forces could be unleashed upon the Earth by means of uncontrolled electrical resonance.

According to the establishment/bankster-controlled history books, it was Guglielmo Marconi (1874-1937) who discovered radio transmission. However in reality, it was Nikola Tesla's patents and research that Marconi was using. Marconi was one of JP Morgan's 'stable' of inventors, his company was the British *Marconi Company* and was financed and controlled totally by Morgan.

Marconi was deeply connected with the powerful dark forces of the British establishment, whereas Tesla was a dedicated, down-to-earth, honest and decent man who only wished to benefit mankind with his inventions. It was the *Marconi Company* that gained an exclusive contract, through bribery and insider-trading to set-up the British/bankster Empire's wireless communication system. Marconi was 'partnered' with the British military-industrial complex, and it was during the Boer War of 1899-1901, that radio technology was successfully used for the first time.

As well as Marconi, Edison was also the consummate businessman, measuring the success of his patents based on the amount of money each made. Whilst Tesla was passionate about discovering and inventing new and revolutionary processes, he was first and foremost a scientist, not a businessman. Once he had discovered something worthwhile, he often lost interest and often did not even patent his breakthroughs, however he still managed to register more than 700 patents. When told that Marconi had done something amazing with radio transmission by sending the first trans-Atlantic message, Tesla replied, *"Marconi is a good fellow. Let him continue. He is using 17 of my patents."*

Many years later of course, radar was developed. It was 'officially' invented in 1935, but 18 years previously, Tesla had outlined how it would work. It was he who had originally pitched the idea to the US Navy, who turned it down out of hand. And who was head of Research and Development for the Navy at the time? Unsurprisingly, none other than Thomas Edison.

The official inventor of X-Rays was the German physicist Wilhelm Röntgen, but it was Tesla who also warned that they were extremely dangerous and who outlined the science years before Röntgen did.

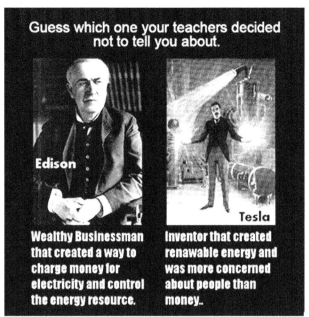

And who built the first hydro-electric plant? Nikola Tesla. Who was the first person to record radio waves from outer space? Who invented remote control? Who invented neon lighting? All of those were Tesla's inventions. He also formulated a scheme to provide free electricity for everyone, drawing it from the ionosphere but of course, JP Morgan was not too happy with that idea. Morgan had already developed a great business opportunity in generating electricity, metering and charging for it and as the use of electricity expanded exponentially during the early part of the twentieth century, so did Morgan's profits.

But it was in John Jacob Astor, that Nikola Tesla had found the ideal financial backer and friend. Of course Astor was no saint, he was a hard-headed businessman and had divorced his wife for a girl young enough to be his daughter. But he was not a greedy, treacherous, psychopathic bloodsucker like Morgan, and was working diligently alongside Tesla to bring their 'free electricity for all' scheme to early fruition.

And so, with the struggle to establish the Federal Reserve Bank AND the free electricity project firmly in Morgan's thoughts, John Jacob Astor, Benjamin Guggenheim and Isidor Straus, who had a combined wealth of well over $500 million and who were all strongly and vocally opposed to the creation of a central bank, were personally invited by Morgan to join him on the maiden voyage of his new state-of-the-art, luxurious, hailed as the world's first 'unsinkable' ship ... *RMS Titanic*

RMS Titanic

Maybe most of you can now guess the next part of the story, but there is more than enough compelling evidence to show that *RMS Titanic* was deliberately sunk by its owner JP Morgan and his Rothschild/bankster friends as part of an elaborate long-term plan that firstly required the eliminating of the main opposition to their central bank takeover of America's money supply. In addition to that, there was another motive for Morgan, massive insurance fraud. The deaths, or rather murders of more than 1,500 of the ship's passengers and crew, were all inconsequential to him, except of course for those of Guggenheim, Straus and Astor.

Only, where Astor was concerned, there was an additional motive, the elimination of Nikola Tesla's independent financing and close friendship. Tesla's revolutionary technological ideas and the possibility of future inventions that would greatly benefit mankind, rather than the banksters wallets, were conveniently, almost literally 'sunk without trace' along with the rest of the 46,000 ton ship.

Again, this is a question of suspension of cognitive dissonance, asking you to consider a possible, radical alternative to what our history books and Hollywood have always told us about *Titanic* sinking after a collision with that infamous iceberg. John Pierpont Morgan was in control of the British-based *White Star* shipping line as well as a significant portion of all American finance and commerce and in 1908, he took the decision to build a new, exclusive class of liners to enable the wealthy to cross the Atlantic in absolute luxury.

This class of ships was to be named the '*Olympic*' class and so construction of the giant vessels, the '*Olympic*,' the '*Titanic*' and the '*Britannic*,' began in 1909 at the *Harland and Wolff* shipyard in Belfast, Ireland.

However, rather unfortunately for Morgan and his personal bank balance, this money-making venture stalled somewhat. The *Olympic*, the first one of the proposed three sister-ships to be completed was involved in a heavy collision with the British Royal Navy cruiser, *HMS Hawke* in September 1911 off the south coast of England, a few weeks after its maiden voyage and had to be extensively 'patched-up' before embarking on the return journey to *Harland and Wolff*'s shipyard in Belfast, Ireland in order to undergo full damage assessment and proper repair work. At this time, the only dry dock in the world large enough to take her was in Belfast.

It is worth noting at this point that although the *Olympic* was the first of the virtually identical triplet 'sisters' to be completed and enter service, she was never given the publicity, nor enjoyed the huge public acclaim that her younger sister enjoyed, the following year? Why would that be? Surely the big fanfare and carnival-like atmosphere surrounding the maiden voyage of these 'floating wonders of the age' should have been reserved for the first one to enter service, *Olympic* not the second one, *Titanic*? Indeed, in comparison, the occasion of *Olympic*'s maiden voyage in 1911 passed relatively quietly. Could the huge accolades and publicity accorded to *Titanic*'s maiden voyage, possibly have been part of this bankster conspiracy to entice the rich and famous, such as Guggenheim, Straus and Astor to her maiden voyage?

In the meantime a Royal Navy enquiry into the *RMS Olympic* accident, not unexpectedly, found the crew of the *Olympic* and thus the *White Star Line* culpable for the collision and this in effect meant that the *White Star Line*'s insurance was null and void and the company would therefore be liable to pay for all the costs of the repairs to BOTH ships themselves, despite the fact that it was patently obvious from the enquiry transcripts that it was the helmsman of *HMS Hawke* who bore all the guilt for the incident. But to make a long story short, this meant that *White Star* was out of pocket to the tune of at least $3.2 million for repairs and lost revenues whilst the ship was unable to 'earn its keep.'

Obviously, the massive financial investment of the *White Star Line* (and Morgan) needed to be recouped as soon as possible and this therefore placed severe pressure on the organisation and impacted upon the final completion of the *Titanic*, further contributing to the financial black hole in which *White Star* now found itself increasingly being consumed.

However, for Morgan and *White Star*, even worse news was to come. The damage to the *Olympic* was far more severe than anyone had expected and the situation was even further exacerbated by the *Olympic* being involved in yet another incident involving a partially submerged wreck. Although the damage inflicted in the *Hawke* incident had been shored-up as well as it could have been, there were strong and persistent rumours circulating amongst the *Harland and Wolff* workforce and the *White Star* crews that all was not well with *Olympic* and this was confirmed beyond doubt when it lost a propeller blade in the above episode, causing further severe vibrational damage to the already damaged ship. I believe that the keel of the ship was actually twisted and therefore damaged beyond economic repair, which would have effectively meant a one-way trip to the breakers yard for her. As this was almost certainly the case, it is virtually certain that the *White Star Line* would have been bankrupted, given it's by now, precarious financial situation.

"*…it took a fortnight [two weeks] of emergency patching to Olympic's hull before she was in any fit state to attempt the journey from Southampton to Belfast for more complete repairs. Able to use only one main engine, the crippled liner made the voyage at an average speed of 10 knots, wasting the exhaust steam from the one usable engine. This steam would normally have driven the central turbine engine, which shows that this engine, its mountings or shafting had been damaged in the collision. As this engine sat on the centreline of the vessel, immediately above the keel, which the propeller shaft ran through, we can reasonably assume that the keel was damaged.*" Robin Gardiner, '*Titanic, the Ship that Never Sank?*'

If Gardiner's hypothesis is correct, then the seeds had been sown for a truly remarkable, yet little known event; the surreptitious switching of the identities of the two ships, *Olympic* and *Titanic* in order to facilitate massive insurance fraud and dispose of the Federal Reserve bill's detractors and also the now worthless, virtual wreck *RMS Olympic* in the guise of its younger sister, *Titanic*.

Olympic left, Titanic right

Gardiner presents a long, well-researched series of credible testimonies, indisputable facts and evidence, both written and photographic, that would seem to point to the fact that the two ships were indeed switched with a view to staging an iceberg collision or other fatal event, with the *Titanic* (originally the *Olympic*) and many of its passengers and crew being sacrificed in an audacious insurance scam which would save White Star from financial ruin.

The alleged switch could have easily been accomplished over a weekend, with very little alteration. Even if some workers had realised what was going-on, none would dare risk losing their precious jobs in such depressed times and run the risk of never finding work in Belfast again. So secrecy would have been no problem, besides who would believe them, and what newspaper editor would dare 'cross' his bankster masters?

According to Gardner, *"Almost two months after the Hawke/Olympic collision, the reconverted Titanic, now superficially identical to her sister except for the C deck portholes, quietly left Belfast for Southampton to begin a very successful 25 year career as the Olympic. Back in the builders' yard, work progressed steadily on the battered hulk of Olympic. The decision to dispose of the damaged vessel would already have been taken. It must have been obvious from quite early on that the vessel was beyond economic repair, so these repairs need not have been quite as thorough as they otherwise might have been. Instead of replacing the damaged section of keel, longitudinal bulkheads were installed to brace it."*

How significant then in the light of this statement, that when the wreck of the *Titanic* was first investigated by Robert Ballard and his crew after its discovery in 1985, that the first explorations of the wreckage revealed (completely undocumented in the ships original blueprints) iron support structures in place, which appeared to be supporting and bracing the keel. This was never satisfactorily explained either at the time or subsequently but would certainly be significant if correct and there is absolutely no reason to believe that it is not correct, as it was reported by the puzzled Ballard himself who of course at that time knew nothing about the alleged switching of the two ships' identities.

Simply arranging for all three men to undergo separate 'accidents' would have appeared far too suspicious, so they decided to lure them to the same place at the same time and

Titanic's pre-determined, ill-fated maiden voyage was the ideal solution. The separate 'accidental' deaths of three such prominent men would have raised far too many questions and would have been far too risky to even contemplate as a possible solution to Morgan's problems. There is little doubt in my mind that this was the real reason for all the 'hype' surrounding *Titanic*'s maiden voyage despite the fact that the *Olympic* was accorded a much less publicised or flamboyant 'send-off' on the 14th June 1911, even though she was after-all, the first of the 'sisters' off the production line.

Morgan himself also had a reservation to travel on the ship, but as was always intended, he had a 'last minute change of plan' due to a so-called 'bout of ill health' and significantly failed to show at Southampton at the appointed time and so his personal stateroom remained empty as the giant vessel pulled away from Southampton docks on the afternoon of the 10th April 1912, to the delight of the cheering crowds on the quayside.

Is it possibly also significant that Morgan ordered that an expensive collection of bronzes that he had purchased in Paris, should be unloaded from the ship at the last minute, too? And incidentally, Morgan was seen a few days later in his favourite French holiday resort, Aix les Bains, with his mistress, appearing to be in the best of health.

Another strange anomaly is that *Titanic* actually set sail on her maiden voyage only around half-full with 2,224 passengers, in the midst of a month-long coal strike in Britain that had in effect prevented 95% of scheduled Atlantic crossings taking place. Many applicants for first-class tickets were inexplicably only offered second-class cabins despite the fact that many first-class cabins remained empty, thus discouraging many would-be passengers from sailing.

And as is now well known and documented, there were not enough lifeboats for the full complement of passengers and crew and some of them left the ship as little as only one quarter full in any case and this fact could well have been used to its full advantage in the execution of Morgan's master plan.

The Captain strangely ordered white flares to be launched, knowing full well that the international standard colour of distress flares was red. Titanic possessed a full complement of white, blue AND red flares. Other ships without wireless transmitters, passing within sight of these flares were intentionally confused and thought that maybe those aboard *Titanic* were having a fireworks party. This of course was also all part of the scheme.

The book and feature film of the same name most responsible for the ubiquitous *Titanic* myths prevalent today, published in the 1950s and the feature film of the same name, '*A Night to Remember*' was published by *Longmans, Green & Co*, in 1955 and written by Walter Lord.

Lord was well-known to be a 'former' member of the US intelligence services (OSS and CIA) but given the fact that that anyone who has ever *been* a member of these organisations always in effect remains a member, can we really rely on his accounts or are they just more subterfuge amongst a morass of contradictory stories surrounding the event? What would motivate a 'former' member of one of the world's elite security services to write a book about an accident involving an ocean liner, forty years previously? As always seems to be the modus operandus in any suspected 'conspiracy,' we are bombarded with these so-called 'facts' by the bankster controlled media, to such an extent that we believe that they cannot possibly be untrue or deliberately misleading.

However, many of the major *Titanic* 'facts' have subsequently been proven to be false but somehow the same version of the story still persists as the absolute de facto truth. Such is the power of propaganda on the human mind and significantly, symptomatic of the methodology by which most of our history is perverted.

"As I delved deeper into the story, more and more inconsistencies became apparent. Inconsistencies that individually meant little but collectively pointed to a grimmer reality than that usually depicted in the heroic legend. Officers who were later acclaimed as heroes were exposed as anything but. One in particular removed a little boy from a lifeboat at gunpoint, before escaping in that same boat himself. Descriptions of the collision and damage supposedly sustained by Titanic do not agree. The 'slight scrape' with the ice that was hardly noticed by most aboard contradicts solid evidence of structural damage at least 5½ feet within the outer hull of the vessel. Then came evidence to show that the ice the ship encountered was seen first not 500 yards ahead but more like 11 miles. I began to wonder if perhaps the sinking of the Titanic might not have been an accident after all." Robin Gardner, *'Titanic, the ship that never sank?'*

Indeed, did *Titanic* actually strike an iceberg at all? We only have the eye-witness testimony of four people believe it or not, with which to confirm or deny this fact. First Officer Murdoch would have been the fifth witness but 'fortunately' for the perpetrators he did not live to tell his story. Is it not more than possible that the copious amounts of ice on the deck of *Titanic* reported by many survivors could easily have been the result of *any* collision dislodging the icy build-up on masts, funnels etc. or it could even have been easily shaken loose from the hundreds of yards of overhead rigging and wiring by the thrusting of the ships engines abruptly into reverse? It was after all, an extremely cold, still night with temperatures below freezing.

The point here is that there exist so many different reasons to believe that the official story is probably just an elaborate fabrication. Both the American and British official inquiries were even thought at the time to be pretty much 'whitewashes,' with much evidence either ignored and eye-witness testimonies being twisted or indeed fabricated to fit the 'official' story.

It is staggering also to report that of the 102 witnesses called to the British enquiry, only two were passengers (the influential Gordons of the famous London gin company) and it is even more surprising to learn that none of the witnesses (crew or passengers) were allowed to offer their own first-hand evidence of any kind and were strictly restricted to the simple answering of fixed, standard questions without elaboration. By any standards at all, this sounds very much like a 'whitewash.'

The passage of time has also served to cloud the mystery still further and we should also note that amongst all the myriad of (probably) deliberately conflicting information unearthed by the two inquiries, the most puzzling of all is the situation regarding the 'yellow-funnelled steamer' observed in the proximity of *Titanic* by several officers and passengers at around the time of the incident and which has never been either identified or explained away at all. Significantly, this odd occurrence does not even warrant a mention in any surviving *Titanic* legends—very strange to say the least, despite its appearance in several contemporary newspapers. The crew of this ship (who or whatever she was) must have been aware that they were in the approximate area of the *Titanic's* demise at the same time, so why did no-one from the ship come forward after the event to volunteer any evidence or information or simply to state that they had seen nothing significant, instead of disappearing into the mists of history forever? It also begs the question as to why no attempts were made to discover the identity of this ship either by the inquiries or subsequently by independent investigators. Even if attempts were made at the time, as far as I am able to tell, they have been very successfully covered-up and no evidence remains today.

Indeed, could this mysterious 'yellow-funnelled' vessel have been responsible for the devastating damage to *Titanic* in any way? I personally believe it is a very strong possibility and that the 'iceberg collision' is just a cover story concocted to protect the guilty. This vessel was also seen by the crew of the *Californian*, who were to become the 'scapegoats' of the official story.

"…I saw another steamer approaching, and asked [the wireless operator] what vessels he had within reach; he replied: 'The Titanic', whereupon I replied, 'that is not the Titanic, she is too small and hasn't enough lights.' Shortly afterwards this steamer stopped and was bearing S.S.E. about five or six miles from our position. … the chief officer was sweeping the southern horizon with his glasses, and finally reported he saw a four-mast steamer with a yellow funnel to the southward of us, and asked if we should try to get down to have a look at her." Captain Lord of *SS Californian* interviewed by an American newspaper, 1914.

SS Californian Captain Stanley Lord

Lord became the official scapegoat for the disaster for his so-called 'negligence' in not rushing sooner to *Titanic's* aid as the *Californian* was probably only 'about 11 miles' from her when she went down.

The following extract from a report that appeared in the *Boston Globe* newspaper, four days subsequent to the disaster would seem to cast even more doubt on the veracity of the official version of events …

*"Captain Lord was asked in what latitude and longitude he was when he first received the SOS message from the Virginian, and his reply was that he could not give out **'state secrets'** and that the question would have to be answered by those in the office."*

"...the reporters were requesting what he termed 'state secrets' and that the information would have to come from the company's office. Ordinarily when a steamer reaches port and has anything to report, figures giving exact positions reckoned in latitude and longitude have always been obtainable from the ship's officers...." The Boston Globe, 19th April 1912

I think any comments from me on the above would be superfluous to requirements and I will credit the readers own common-sense with providing the answer as to whether there was a conspiracy involving the highest echelons of governments, being perpetrated.

Furthermore, upon arriving back in England at Plymouth docks, from New York aboard the steamer *Lapland*, two weeks after the disaster, 173 of the surviving crew members both male and female were firstly, illegally denied their rights to speak with their legal and trade union representatives. Then in addition they were also illegally detained overnight against their wishes (the common terminology for this act is unlawful imprisonment or even kidnapping) in a containing area within the dockyard itself where they were forced to sign a document that they believed was the 'Official Secrets Act', promising to keep secret forever, the actual events of the night of 14th / 15th April. Otherwise, they were told, they would be prosecuted and 'never work again,' not just for *White Star* but for any other employer at all.

In those now long-gone days, the inability to procure gainful employment could be almost a death sentence to the crews *and* their families. So, make of that what you will, but there is no apparent reason why this should happen if the official story was the truth. It is also worth noting that also in those distant days it was far easier without mass and instantaneous communication devices, to invent or twist facts and bury individuals' own stories. Today of course, any of the survivors' personal experiences would be viral on the Internet within hours of the event.

So did Captain Smith deliberately steer *Titanic* into a huge ice-field without reducing speed in order to create the cover-story of the iceberg collision knowing that he was setting-up *Titanic* to be rammed by the yellow-funnelled mystery ship, in fulfilment of the banksters' dastardly plot? There were hardly any eye-witnesses to what actually happened after all, so this proposition seems very plausible given all the circumstantial evidence. Along with the officer on duty on the Bridge at that time, First Officer William Murdoch and Quartermaster Hichens plus Quartermaster George Rowe on the after-bridge, lookouts Frederick Fleet and Reginald Lee were the only other ones known to have personally witnessed the appalling events.

And of these five witnesses, only four survived, significantly all of them 'lower-class' people and placing undue pressure on four working-class people to keep quiet over a century ago, would have been a relatively simple task. First Officer Murdoch is perhaps also significantly but certainly conveniently, said to have 'committed suicide' in the aftermath of the collision whilst the ship was being abandoned, however there is no solid evidence available with which to corroborate this fact.

Why would he do this? He has also been accused of shooting passengers before turning a gun on himself, something that his family and descendants have disputed vehemently ever since and so could there be a more sinister explanation for his demise along with that of Captain Smith? Down the years, suicide has always been a very convenient cover-story for many a silencing-murder and in addition it is perhaps significant that none of Guggenheim, Straus and Astor survived to tell their stories either. Indeed Straus and Guggenheim's bodies were never found and Astor's was picked-up a few weeks later with his face battered beyond recognition and only identifiable by the contents of his pockets.

So why would Morgan not have simply had Astor, Guggenheim and Straus shot or poisoned, that certainly would have been easier than sinking an entire ship? But to reiterate and re-emphasise the previous point, had this been the case, there would no doubt have been very awkward, intense high-level investigations into their simultaneous murders, due to their prominent positions in society.

But how could Morgan guarantee that Astor, Guggenheim and Straus would be on the ship? Maybe there were behind-the-scenes events, put in place by Morgan, to ensure those men would be on the ship. In addition, how could Morgan be sure Astor, Guggenheim and Straus would go down with the ship and not get off onto lifeboats? Maybe Morgan knew that Astor was a decent, chivalrous character who would not even dream of putting his own safety before women and children... "*Colonel Astor was another of the heroes of the awful night. Effort was made to persuade him to take a place in one of the life-boats, but he emphatically refused to do so until every woman and child on board had been provided for, not excepting the women members of the ship's company.*" Apparently, Guggenheim and Straus's actions were similar.

Or alternatively, how easy would it have been under the circumstances and in the post-collision mayhem and confusion, for a paid assassin to dispose of Messrs Smith, Murdoch, Guggenheim, Straus and Astor, in order to make absolutely certain that none of them escaped their planned fates against all the odds?

It also has to be stated that Morgan's switching of the ships, the massive insurance fraud, was more than merely just suspected by both the bankster-controlled governments of Britain and the United States. If the Morgan-owned *White Star Line* had gone bankrupt, then so would the *Harland & Wolff* shipyard that built their ships, and that would have laid-off thousands of workers, and affected the political situation as a result. The British Prime Minister at the time was H. H. Asquith and his Liberal government had an extremely slender majority in Parliament. Had the two companies folded, creating further massive unemployment and public unrest, the impact upon the government would have been disastrous and would probably have meant the end of Asquith's reign as PM.

To return to the question of the alleged insurance fraud, *Titanic*'s insurers promptly paid-out over $12 million on a ship that cost $10 million, thanks to Morgan's psychic prudence in over-insuring it. This was strange enough in itself as Morgan's usual practice was to insure ships for 75% of their value—not 120%! At the time, this was the biggest maritime insurance claim ever.

And as for the '*real*' *Titanic*, the one that had been switched and bore the name *RMS Olympic*, she went on to serve as a troop transport in World War I, and earned the nickname 'Old Reliable.' Following the end of the war in 1918, she again became a passenger liner, plying the Atlantic route for many years. She was retired from service in 1935 and sold to Sir John Jarvis for $100,000 and was stripped of all fixtures and fittings, many of which were recycled and the remainder scrapped.

Executing a diabolical plan such as this and in addition killing fifteen hundred innocent people to advance an agenda for huge financial gain, as will become evident, is absolutely commonplace. In fact, the banksters have made something of a science of it down the long years.

To this day, in our history books, the movies and in all those so-called documentaries on the *History Channel* and *National Geographic* channels etc., the official story will always be the one being promoted, in order to continue to protect the guilty. Occasionally these 'outrageous conspiracy theories' may get an airing, not in a balanced way but only in such a way as to 'debunk' them and divert the people from the real truth. The iconic BIG LIE has to be perpetuated after all. If the 'masses' ever discovered the real truth, that they had been fooled all along, then they may just start questioning everything else…such as JFK, 9/11, Princess Diana, the war on terror and far too many more incidents to list here.

So, with the elimination of the those three vocal, mega-rich businessmen, the so-called *Aldrich Plan* for a central bank slowly made its way through the 62nd Congress in 1912, but it nevertheless met with critical opposition from the Progressive Democrats over the banksters having a controlling interest with virtually no public scrutiny—and thus stalled temporarily. So in 1913, the central bank bill was re-introduced once again by the persistent banksters and given the revised, deceptive title '*The Federal Reserve Act,*' in order to mask its real purpose, the creation of a national financial system owned in its entirety by private individuals. Furthermore, the Federal Reserve Board would be composed of twelve districts and one director, the Federal Reserve Chairman, who would in effect be able to manipulate the nation's entire financial resources by controlling the money supply and available credit at will and by holding the government to ransom, through borrowing.

The banksters still had a small problem, however. President William Howard Taft had already made it clear that he would veto such a bill if it was introduced and so they simply had to make sure he would not win re-election, at any cost.

History records the 1912 Presidential campaign as one of the more dramatic political upsets of all time. The incumbent, President Taft, was a popular president and the Republicans, in a period of general prosperity were firmly in control of the government through their majority in both houses. The Democratic challenger, Woodrow Wilson, Governor of New Jersey, had no national recognition whatsoever and was a staid, austere man with no charisma and who engendered little public support.

Both parties had included a monetary reform bill in their manifestos. The Republicans were committed to the *Aldrich Plan*, which had already been denounced as a bankster plan and the Democrats had the *Federal Reserve Act* in their portfolio however, perhaps unsurprisingly, neither party took the trouble to inform the public that the bills were almost identical except for the names.

In retrospect, it now seems obvious that the banksters decided to dump Taft and go with Wilson. How do we know this? Taft seemed certain of re-election and Wilson would no doubt have returned to the obscurity from which he came, but suddenly, Theodore Roosevelt re-appeared on the scene. He announced that he was running as a third party candidate, the 'Bull Moose.' His candidacy would have been utterly ludicrous had it not been for the fact that he was exceptionally well-financed.

Moreover, he was given totally unlimited coverage by the bankster-sponsored and owned, press, indeed more than Taft and Wilson combined. As a Republican ex-president, it was obvious that Roosevelt would decimate Taft's potential vote and divide the Republicans. This eventually proved to be the case and Wilson won the election by a landslide and yet to this day, no-one can say what Roosevelt's agenda actually was, or why he would sabotage his own party's prospects in that way. My personal guess is that it was a five-letter word beginning with 'M' and ending in 'Y' ... and plenty of it!

Since the banksters were financing all three candidates, they were certain of victory regardless of the outcome but there is no doubt that Wilson, in this instance, was their preferred option. Later Congressional testimony showed that in the firm of *Kuhn Loeb & Co*, Felix Warburg was supporting Taft, Paul Warburg and Jacob Schiff were supporting Wilson and Otto Kahn was supporting Roosevelt. It really made no difference which party won the election in the end (as far as the central bank plans were concerned, apart from the fact that Wilson may have been more amenable to the banksters' aims on other issues). Anyway, the overall result was that a Democratic Congress and a 'bankster-friendly' Democratic President were elected in 1912 in order to get the central bank legislation passed. It seems probable that the identification of the *Aldrich Plan* as a bankster-sponsored operation ensured that it would have a difficult passage through Congress, as the Democrats would solidly oppose it, whereas a successful Democratic candidate, supported by a Democratic Congress, would facilitate the acceptance of the *Federal Reserve* plan.

Taft was brutally discarded because the banksters doubted that he could deliver on the *Aldrich Plan* and Roosevelt's entirely engineered candidacy was the instrument of his demise.

In order to further confuse the American people and deceive them as to the real purpose of the proposed *Federal Reserve Act*, the architects of the *Aldrich Plan*, the powerful Nelson Aldrich, although no longer a senator and Frank Vanderlip, president of the National City Bank, set up a campaign against the Bill. They gave interviews whenever they could find an audience denouncing the proposed *Federal Reserve Act* as inimical to banking and to good governance.

'The Nation,' on 23rd October 1913, pointed out that, *"Mr. Aldrich himself raised a hue and cry over the issue of government 'fiat money,' that is, money issued without gold or bullion back of it, although a bill to do precisely that had been passed in 1908 with his own name as author, and he knew besides, that the 'government' had nothing to do with it, that the Federal Reserve Board would have full charge of the issuing of such moneys."*

Frank Vanderlip's claims were so bizarre that Senator Robert L. Owen, chairman of the newly formed *Senate Banking and Currency Committee*, which had been formed on 18th March 1913, accused him of openly conducting a campaign of misrepresentation about the Bill. The interests of the public, or so Carter Glass claimed in a speech in September 1913 to Congress, would be protected by an advisory council of bankers. *"There can be nothing sinister about its transactions. Meeting with it at least four times a year will be a bankers' advisory council representing every regional reserve district in the system. How could we have exercised greater caution in safeguarding the public interests?"*

In the next phase of the scheme, shortly after President Wilson's first inauguration, he received a visitor to the White House by the name of Samuel Untermyer, who was a prominent New York City attorney who contributed generously to the National Democratic Committee that installed Wilson in the White House in Washington in the 1912 election. As you may recall from earlier, Untermyer was the bankster 'handler' for Cyrus Scofield and the Zionised bible.

At first, President Wilson was extremely pleased to welcome Untermyer to the White House, having met him previously, during the campaign. However, Untermyer surprised Wilson when he eventually informed him of the real purpose of his visit. Untermyer explained to Wilson that he had been retained to bring a breach of promise action against him but that his client was willing to accept $40,000 in lieu of commencing the breach of promise action.

Untermyer then produced a pack of letters from his pocket, written by President Wilson to a former colleague's wife when they were professors together at Princeton University. These letters firmly established the illicit relationship which had existed between Wilson and the woman in question and unfortunately for him, he had apparently written dozens of endearing letters to her, many of which she never destroyed. Wilson reluctantly acknowledged his authorship of the letters after examining them.

Wilson had left Princeton University to become the Governor of New Jersey and in 1912, he had been elected to his first term as President of the United States. However in the interim period, his former, illicit lover had divorced her husband and married again. Untermyer explained that her second husband had a grown-up son who was in the employ of one of the leading banks in Washington and furthermore his former sweetheart was very fond of her step-son. Apparently this man was now in financial trouble and suddenly needed $40,000 (around half a million dollars today) in order to satisfy a pressing liability to the bank for which he worked.

The full details are not particularly relevant other than to say that the step-son of Wilson's ex-lover needed the money badly and quickly and Wilson was the logical prospect for that $40,000. Wilson expressed his gratitude for the good fortune that his former lover had approached Untermyer to seek his assistance, otherwise the publicity could have proven very embarrassing had the woman chosen to instead consult a Republican attorney.

However Wilson simply did not have that amount of money and informed Untermyer of this fact. Untermyer therefore suggested that Wilson should consider the matter and that he would return in a few days' time to discuss the matter further. In fact, Untermyer used the next few days in Washington investigating the credibility of the stepson's story of his pressing need for $40,000 and learned that the story had not been misrepresented in any way to him.

Untermyer visited Wilson again, a few days later as promised and Wilson appeared irritated yet confessed once again that he simply did not have $40,000 to pay his would-be blackmailer. Untermyer appeared to consider the matter a few moments before offering his already pre-conceived solution, but Wilson was completely taken aback by Untermyer's proposal.

Untermyer offered to pay the $40,000 himself on one condition, that Wilson would promise to appoint a nominee recommended to Wilson by Untermyer to the first vacancy on the United States Supreme Court. Wilson was ecstatic and thought it a small price to have to pay to be relieved of his 'difficulty,' finally resolving once and for all the issue of the breach of promise suit which was never mentioned again from that point on. As an insurance policy against any further dissension from Wilson against bankster's wishes, Untermyer permanently retained the incriminatory letters in his possession.

Untermyer was indeed a man of great wealth. The law firm in New York of which he was the leading partner, *Guggenheim, Untermyer and Marshall*, is still today one of the nation's most prominent and most prosperous law firms. He was also a committed Zionist who worked assiduously for the dark powers to help bring about the creation of the State of Israel in line with Zionist goals.

During the so-called *Pujo Committee* it was the voice of Special Counsel Untermyer that was heard over all others, even that of Chairman Pujo. Thus from the commencement of the hearings to their conclusion it was Untermyer who called the tune. Moreover, Untermyer steadfastly refused to ask either Senator LaFollette or Congressman Lindbergh, the two principal political opponents of the banking trust, to testify in the investigation which they above all others had pressured Congress to hold. Instead the committee under the stewardship of Untermyer called a steady stream of men sympathetic to banking, the banksters and the concept of central and fractional reserve banking. Thus, during the course of the charade that was the Pujo investigation, banksters upon the invitation of Untermyer made the trip from New York to Washington to testify before the Committee.

They all solemnly declared that although they were indeed bankers they always operated in the public interest; indeed, they claimed that they were motivated only by the highest ideals of public service just as were the Congressmen before whom they were testifying.

Another telling fact that confirmed the Pujo investigation as the farce it undoubtedly was, is what Untermyer, the slickest corporate lawyer in town, did **not** ask any of the bankers *vis-a-vis* the web of interlocking directorates by which they controlled industry. Nor did he allude to the international gold movements, a known factor in money panics, or, more importantly, the intimate relationships between American bankers and European bankers and especially the Jewish banking families whose influence he knew all too well. Thus, the influence of Jewish banking houses such as *Kuhn Loeb, J. & W. Seligman, Ladenburg Thalmann, Speyer Brothers, M. M. Warburg, Eugene Meyer, Lazard Freres* and the *Rothschild Brothers*, which transcended national interests and the interests of nations and their peoples was never alluded to whatsoever by Samuel Untermyer.

This was hardly surprising given Untermyer's penchant for Zionism and all that this insidious philosophy entails. An example of Untermyer's duplicity was the sympathetic treatment given to another Zionist intriguer, Jacob Schiff, senior partner in the banking house of *Kuhn Loeb & Company*. Schiff with the connivance of Untermyer talked for many minutes on generalities of banking without revealing anything substantive or particular about the operations of the very powerful banking house of which he was the prime mover. A bank moreover that Senator Robert Owen had identified as the representative in the United States of the most powerful Jewish interests in the world, the Rothschilds.

The Founding Fathers had attempted to safeguard the sovereign Republic they had fought hard to create by safeguarding the liberties and prosperity of the people by special provisions concerning the control of money issue and credit. Thus, Article 1, Section 8 of the Constitution whereby the people of the United States granted to Congress the power *"to coin Money, regulate the Value thereof, and of foreign Coin, and fix the standard of Weights and Measures."*

That is why it was made manifest that Congress was refused the constitutional power to delegate money-creation and its regulating responsibility to any private group. This imperative endured until the fateful night of 23rd December 1913, during a hurried, harassed debate, when congressmen eager to head home early for Christmas, incautiously and inadvisably passed the *Federal Reserve Act* into law. Seemingly, a piece of *ad libitum* governance that became known as 'the Christmas Massacre,' this legislation created the cartel of private banks (i.e. the Federal Reserve System consisting of 12 Federal Reserve banks, the Federal Open Market Committee, the Federal Advisory Council, and, since 1976, a Consumer Advisory Council), managed by a Board of Governors appointed to their long terms of office by the President. This group of privately-owned and controlled banks thereby became the sole issuer of US money and credit, with full control over its quantity and thus its value.

Moreover, the unprecedented speed with which the *Federal Reserve Act* had been passed by Congress had also taken President Wilson unawares, since he, like many others had been assured by Congress, as well as those powerbrokers outside Congress, that the bill would not come up for voting until after the Christmas break. Wilson initially refused to sign the Act, however, he relented when pressured by another Zionist intriguer and international financier Bernard Baruch, a principal contributor to Wilson's campaign fund, who reassured Wilson that his concern was a trifling matter, which could be easily remedied later via 'administrative processes.' The imperative of the central bank schemers was to get the *Federal Reserve Act* signed into law in haste, before a less distracted Congress could give their considered, critical judgment of this piece of pernicious legislation.

Wilson as promised, in return for the banksters campaign financing and 'hush money,' and suitably assured by Baruch's promises, duly signed the Federal Reserve Act into law and by doing so effectively handed over the destiny of the United States of America and its people to the dark powers of International usury—**the banksters!**

It was the *Federal Reserve Act* that had destroyed the very thing that the Founding Fathers had feared and presciently attempted to obviate against, by authoring Article 1, Section 8 of the Constitution. That is that the *Constitution* itself, the lawful safeguard of the United States of America and the liberties of its people, would be circumvented by the banksters and would cease to be the governing covenant of the American people. Moreover, that consequently, the liberties of the American people would be handed over to a small, shadowy cabal of international private bankers.

It is a supreme irony that although those present at the signing of the bill included Vice President Marshall, Secretary Bryan, Carter Glass, Secretary McAdoo, Senator Owen, Speaker Clark and other Treasury officials, none of the real authors of the bill, the participants at the secret meeting on Jekyll Island, were present. Like all the real powerbrokers who control the destiny of the world, the true writers of the *Federal Reserve Act* chose to remain hidden from public scrutiny and so prudently absented themselves from the scene of their victory, the White House, when Wilson signed the Act into law.

Congressman Charles Lindbergh said on the day that the *Federal Reserve Act* was passed, to the House…

"This Act establishes the most gigantic trust on earth. When the President signs this bill, the invisible government by the Monetary Power will be legalised. The people may not know it immediately, but the day of reckoning is only a few years removed. The trusts will soon realise that they have gone too far even for their own good. The people must make a declaration of independence to relieve themselves from the Monetary Power. This they will be able to do by taking control of Congress. Wall Streeters could not cheat us if you Senators and Representatives did not make a humbug of Congress. . . . If we had a people's Congress, there would be stability. The greatest crime of Congress is its currency system. The worst legislative crime of the ages is perpetrated by this banking bill. The caucus and the party bosses have again operated and prevented the people from getting the benefit of their own government."

The 24th December 1913 *New York Times'* editorial response, in contrast to Congressman Lindbergh's criticism of the bill was, *"The Banking and Currency Bill became better and sounder every time it was sent from one end of the Capitol to the other. Congress worked under public supervision in making the bill."*

By 'public supervision,' the *Times* apparently meant 'Paul Warburg,' who for several days had maintained a small office in the Capitol building, where he directed the successful pre-Christmas campaign to pass the bill and where Senators and Congressmen came hourly at his bidding to carry out his strategy.

Two of these secretive 'masters of the universe' after the event, corresponded on their success in subverting the Constitution and the stealing of the credit of both the United States and its people. On 24th December 1913, Zionist conspirator Jacob Schiff head of the investment banking firm of *Kuhn, Loeb & Co*, wrote to Edward Mandel House (1858-1938), President Wilson's supposedly most trusted adviser but who actually was an intriguer for the forces behind international usury and who repeatedly betrayed Wilson to these forces ... *"My dear Colonel House, I want to say a word to you for the silent, but no doubt effective work you have done in the interest of currency legislation and to congratulate you that the measure has finally been enacted into law. I am with good wishes, faithfully yours, Jacob Schiff."*

There is no doubt that Edward Mandel House was an arch-intriguer who could not resist telling the world of what he knew of the grand conspiracy and his part in it. He achieved this by publishing a book, *'Philip Dru, Administrator'* which was published in the guise of a novel and although House initially disclaimed authorship he later admitted it was his own work. In earlier times, those such as House were, privy to the ancient and grand design of the conspiracy emanating from the occult underworld who, taking the blood oaths to conceal its dark secrets away from the masses, would usually have paid the ultimate price and forfeited their lives via assassination. However, by the time House had written his book, the leaders of the conspirators had deemed their efforts such a success and their position so unassailable that it was appropriate to begin to reveal the enormity of their deception and indeed revel in it. House, therefore was given free rein to benefit and allowed to live out his natural life span.

The book described in fictional form what the author, House referred to as a conspiracy which had succeeded in electing a puppet-president by means of 'deception regarding his real opinions and intentions.' The book also described this utopia of the future as akin to the *". . . socialism as dreamed of by Karl Marx (with a) spiritual element (which will be the salvation of all those) unhappy many who have lived and died lacking opportunity, because, in the starting, the world-wide social structure was wrongly begun."*

Philip Dru, Administrator, ostensibly a novel, was actually a detailed plan for the future government of the United States of America in which 'Socialism as dreamed of by Karl Marx' is established as the ruling ideology. House's novel anticipated the creeping 'socialisation' (communism) of America and the necessary legislation required, as its title character and protagonist Dru enacted.

Socialist legislation that 'Dru the dictator' enacted, included graduated income tax, old age pension provision, unemployment insurance, co-operative markets, a federal reserve banking system, flexible currency system, national employment bureaus and an excess profits tax. This was in effect a blueprint for the Woodrow Wilson and Franklin D Roosevelt 'liberal' administrations. Thus, it was no coincidence that House, who imagined himself as Dru, managed to position himself as the confidential advisor to two Presidents of the United States, Wilson and Roosevelt, whose administrations laid the foundations of the future Socialist tyranny which is now about to entrap the people of America. But then, House was so privileged because he was sponsored by and the representative of very a powerful faction that has become almost unassailable, the dark forces behind the conspiracy for the creation of the *New World Order*. And, crucial to this dark agenda was the co-opting of America, her people and her wealth-creating capacity.

The Socialist (Communist) tyrant Lenin said that the establishment of a central bank is 90% of 'communising' a country and another of his ilk, Karl Marx in the *Communist Manifesto* called for *"the centralisation of wealth in the hands of the state by means of a national bank with an exclusive monopoly."*

During this time, President Wilson's closest 'advisor,' Edward Mandel House's power was enormous. He was involved not only in selecting the President's Cabinet but also virtually ran the State Department single-handedly. Wilson's great dependence on House was described by Wilson himself. *"Mr. House is my second personality. He is my independent self. His thoughts and mine are one."* Indeed so.

Thus, the unfortunate Wilson, the twenty-eighth president of the United States and no doubt a man of 'some' honour and integrity although sadly lacking in independence of thought, had in House, his 'second personality,' a man whose loyalties lay elsewhere and whose betrayal of personal friendship to the secret agenda of his masters was complete and unconditional. Wilson could therefore claim the dubious distinction of being the first of the puppet-Presidents placed into power by the banksters, who were obliged to do what they were told and by doing so, completely lost their moral focus.

Most of the policies to which Wilson attached his name and what in retrospect brought him into disrepute were products of the unholy alliance betwixt banksters and state. These were the shared 'liberal and progressive ideas' that he and House ensured were translated into legislation, for example Wilson's welcome, endorsement and financial support for the murderous Bolshevik Revolution in Russia as well as his introduction of the immoral graduated income tax as recommended by another internationalist bankster-puppet, Karl Marx, in his *Communist Manifesto*.

But perhaps more pertinent to modern times was his complicity in the creation of America's privately owned central bank, the Federal Reserve, through his sponsoring of the *Federal Reserve Act*. We may only now begin to understand why such a lengthy campaign of planned deception was necessary, from the secret conference at Jekyll Island to the identical 'reform' plans proposed by the Democratic and Republican parties under different names. The banksters could not wrest control of the issuance of money from the citizens of the United States, to whom it had been designated through its Congress by the Constitution, until Congress itself usurped the Constitution and handed them their monopoly on a plate.

Like most of the 'behind-the-scenes operators' named in this book, House had an almost obligatory 'London connection.' Originally from a Dutch family named Huis, his ancestors had lived in England for three hundred years and at some point in the past had 'anglicised' their surname. House's father had emigrated to and settled his family in Texas, where he made a fortune in blockade-running during the Civil War, shipping cotton and other contraband to his British connections, including the Rothschilds and bringing back much-needed supplies for the beleaguered Texans.

House senior, not trusting the volatile Texas situation, prudently deposited all his profits from his blockade-running in gold with the *Barings* banking house in London and by the end of the Civil War in 1865, he was one of the wealthiest men in Texas. Upon his death in 1880, his estate was distributed among his sons as follows: Thomas got the banking business, John, the sugar plantation and Edward, the cotton plantations, which brought him a more than comfortable income of $20,000 a year.

By the age of twelve, the young Edward Mandel House had contracted 'brain fever,' and was later further crippled by sunstroke. As a result, he was a semi-invalid for the rest of his life and his ailments gave him an odd, Oriental-appearance. He never entered any profession, but used his father's money to become the 'kingmaker' of Texas politics, successively electing five governors from 1893 to 1911. Then, in 1911 he began to support Wilson for President and levered the crucial Texas delegation to him which in effect secured his nomination.

And so, the *Federal Reserve System* began its operations in 1914 with the activity of the Organisation Committee appointed personally by Woodrow Wilson and composed of Secretary of the Treasury William McAdoo, who was his son-in-law, Secretary of Agriculture Houston, and Comptroller of the Currency, John Skelton Williams. Then on 6th January 1914, JP Morgan met with the Organising Committee in New York and informed them that there should not be more than seven regional districts in the new system. This committee was to select the locations of the 'decentralised' reserve banks and was empowered to select from between eight to twelve reserve banks, although JP Morgan had testified he thought that not more than four should be selected.

Much politicking went into the selection of these sites, as the twelve cities thus favoured would become enormously important as financial hubs. New York, of course, was a foregone conclusion. Richmond was the next selection, as a pay-off to Carter Glass and Woodrow Wilson, the two Virginians who had been given political credit for the *Federal Reserve Act*. The other selections of the Committee were Boston, Philadelphia, Cleveland, Chicago, St. Louis, Atlanta, Dallas, Minneapolis, Kansas City and San Francisco. All of these cities later developed important financial districts as the result of their selection.

These local battles, however, paled in view of the complete dominance of the *Federal Reserve Bank of New York* in the system.

"In practice, the Federal Reserve Bank of New York became the fountainhead of the system of twelve regional banks, for New York was the money market of the nation. The other eleven banks were so many expensive mausoleums erected to salve the local pride and quell the Jacksonian fears of the hinterland.

Benjamin Strong, president of the Bankers Trust (JP Morgan) was selected as the first Governor of the New York Federal Reserve Bank. Adept in high finance, Strong, for many years manipulated the country's monetary system at the discretion of directors representing the leading New York banks. Under Strong, the Reserve System was brought into interlocking relations with the Bank of England and the Bank of France. Benjamin Strong held his position as Governor of the Federal Reserve Bank of New York until his sudden death in 1928, during a Congressional investigation of the secret meetings between Reserve Governors and heads of European central banks which brought on the Great Depression of 1929-31." Ferdinand Lundberg, 'America's Sixty Families'

Strong had married the daughter of the President of Bankers Trust, which brought him into the line of succession in the dynastic intrigues which play such an important role in the world of high finance. He also had been a member of the original Jekyll Island group, the 'First Name Club,' and was thus qualified for the highest position in the Federal Reserve System, as the Governor of the *Federal Reserve Bank of New York* which dominated the entire system.

Because the *Federal Reserve Bank of New York* was to set the interest rates and direct open market operations, thus controlling the daily supply and price of money throughout the United States, it is the stockholders of that particular bank who are the 'real' directors of the whole network.

The Federal Reserve Bank of New York issued 203,053 shares, and as filed with the Comptroller of the Currency 19th May 1914, the large New York City banks took more than half of the outstanding shares. The Rockefeller and *Kuhn, Loeb* controlled *National City Bank* took the largest number of shares of any bank, 30,000 shares whilst JP Morgan's *First National Bank* took 15,000 shares. When these two banks merged in 1955, they owned in one block almost one quarter of the shares in the *Federal Reserve Bank of New York*, which controlled the entire system and thus they could name whoever they chose, to be Chairman of the Federal Reserve Board of Governors.

Chase National Bank took 6,000 shares and the *Marine National Bank of Buffalo*, later known as *Marine Midland*, took 6,000 shares. This bank was owned by the Schoellkopf family, which controlled the *Niagara Power Company* and other large interests. *National Bank of Commerce* of New York City took 21,000 shares.

The shareholders of these banks which own the stock of the *Federal Reserve Bank of New York* are the people who have controlled the political and economic destiny of the USA since 1914. They are specifically, the Rothschilds of Europe, *Lazard Freres, Kuhn Loeb Company, (M.M. Warburg Company,) Lehman Brothers, Goldman Sachs*, the Rockefeller family, and the *J.P. Morgan* interests. These interests have merged and consolidated in recent years, so that the control is now much more concentrated and in far fewer hands. *National Bank of Commerce* is now *Morgan Guaranty Trust Company*. *Lehman Brothers* has merged with *Kuhn, Loeb Company, First National Bank* has merged with the *National City Bank*, and in the other eleven Federal Reserve Districts, these same shareholders indirectly own or control shares in those banks, with the other shares owned by the leading families in those areas who own or control the principal industries in these regions.

The 'local' families set up regional councils on orders from New York, of such groups as the *Council on Foreign Relations, Trilateral Commission*, and other instruments of control devised by their masters. They finance and control political developments in their area, name candidates and are seldom successfully opposed in their plans.

These developments following the passage of the Federal Reserve Act proved every one of the allegations Thomas Jefferson had made against central banks as far back as 1791; that the subscribers to the *Federal Reserve Bank* stock had formed a corporation, whose stock could be and was held by aliens; that this stock would be transmitted to a certain line of successors; that it would be placed beyond forfeiture and escheat; that they would receive a monopoly of banking, which was against the laws of monopoly; and that they now had the power to make laws, superior to the laws of the individual States.

No state legislature can countermand any of the laws or regulations laid down by the Federal Reserve Board of Governors for the benefit of their private stockholders. This board issues laws as to what the interest rate shall be, what the quantity of money shall be and what the price of money shall be. All of these powers abrogate the powers of the state legislatures and their responsibility to the citizens of those states and thus riding roughshod over the Constitution.

The bankster-owned *New York Times* stated that the Federal Reserve Banks would be ready for business on 1st August 1914, but they did not actually begin operations until 16th November. At that time, their total assets were listed at $143m from the sale of their shares to stockholders of the national banks which subscribed to it. However, the actual amount of this $143m which was paid-in for these shares remains shrouded in mystery. Some historians state that the shareholders only paid about half of the amount in cash whilst others believe that they paid in no cash at all, but merely paid by cheque, which they drew on the national banks which they themselves owned. This latter option seems most likely and that from the very outset, the *Federal Reserve* operations were 'paper issued against paper,' that book-keeping entries comprised the only values which changed hands. Indeed this would dovetail nicely with the way in which these entities operate anyway.

As previously stated, the *Federal Reserve System* was a name carefully selected and designed to deceive. The word 'Federal' conjures an image of a governmental organisation whilst 'Reserve' implies that the currency is being backed by gold and silver. 'System' was used in lieu of the word 'bank' so that no-one would conclude that a new central bank had been created. In reality, the act created a 'for-profit,' central-banking corporation owned by a cartel of private-owned banks.

The Ten Member Banks of the Federal Reserve System...

- *Rothschild Bank of London*
- *Warburg Bank of Hamburg*
- *Rothschild Bank of Berlin*
- *Lehman Brothers of New York*
- *Lazard Brothers of Paris*
- *Kuhn Loeb Bank of New York*
- *Israel Moses Seif Banks of Italy*
- *Goldman, Sachs of New York*
- *Warburg Bank of Amsterdam*
- *Chase Manhattan Bank of New York*

In 1977 *Kuhn Loeb* and *Lehman Brothers* merged to create *Kuhn Loeb, Lehman Brothers, Inc.*

Are you aware that the FRB is the only for-profit corporation in America that is exempt from both federal and state taxes? The FRB takes in about one trillion dollars per year tax free, under law 12 USC 531, and the bankster dynasties as listed above receive a share of **all** that money.

In addition 100% of the taxes that US citizens pay, goes directly to the Federal Reserve. On the back of any cheque (check) made payable to the Internal Revenue Service it is endorsed as *'Pay Any F.R.B. Branch or Gen. Depository for Credit U.S. Treas. This is in Payment of U.S. Oblig.'*

To reiterate, every penny paid in income taxes is given to these private bankster families, commonly known as the 'Fed'...tax free! And this corrupt, criminal robbery and extortion is repeated in every country of the world, except, as at time of writing, North Korea, Cuba and Iran. Until recently you could also have added Iraq, Libya and Syria to that list. Can you spot the connection at all? Is it a coincidence that these are the very same countries currently being constantly vilified and/or under threat of attack from our bankster-owned governments via the military-industrial complex? Personally speaking I am not a great believer in coincidence, how about you?

For most of us the subject of the inner workings of our financial system and the question of how money comes into being and the part it plays in everyday banking, always sounds so boring, uninteresting and complicated. And that is exactly how the banksters like it... You are not meant to figure it all out or supposed to discover exactly how spectacularly simple the subject really is.

Indeed the banksters literally create money from nothing, out of 'thin air' if you will. Forget all the media 'talking heads,' the so-called economists, financial experts and government officials, because they are all working at the bankers behest, some knowingly and others are simply deceived by their so-called 'education' and/or are propagandised by their superiors all the way down the 'food chain.' With an authoritative air, they stand before us, spouting endless, incomprehensible gibberish that they have heard second-hand or learned off-pat from a bankster-written textbook, specifically designed to hide and confuse how we are all 'robbed,' each and every day. Indeed most of them are just programmed 'repeaters,' endlessly repeating so-called 'facts' they have been told or read.

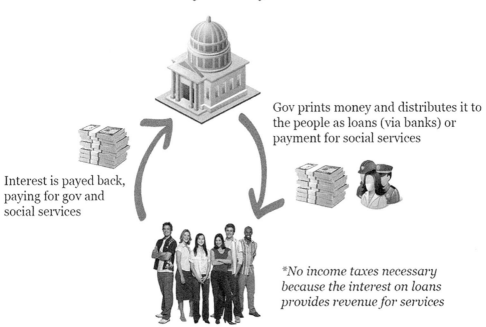

An honest, healthy, uncorrupted financial system is simplicity itself. It requires no taxation and is self-sustaining, generating no debt!

Again I would ask, how is money created? If the average Joe on the street is asked this question, most of them have absolutely no idea. This is rather odd, because we all use money—constantly. One would assume that it would only be natural for us to know whence it comes. So what is the answer? Many people assume that in the USA, the federal government creates the money, but that is absolutely not the case. If the US government and indeed any country's government could just print and spend whatever money it needed-to, the national debt would be zero. But instead, to take the US national debt as an example, as of 1st January 2015, this stood at $18,096,707,199,355.91. That is over $18 trillion or put another way, $56,000 per citizen and this is growing at the rate of $2.43 billion daily.

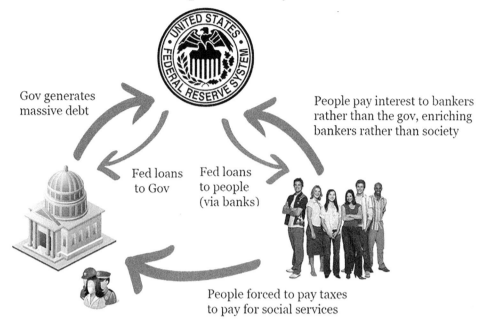

We often hear these huge figures being bandied around, by financial 'talking heads,' but do any of us have any real concept of them? For example, what does a million dollars (pounds) look like? Or a billion, and what about a trillion? It is fair to say that most people have never even seen $10,000 or £10,000 let alone these telephone number-like sums we hear so much about on a daily basis.

The following illustrations provide some idea of the reality of the sums involved ... so strap-in and prepare to be shocked.

One Million Dollars
$1,000,000 - Not as big of a pile as you thought, huh?
Still, this is 92 years of work for the average human on earth.

One Hundred Million Dollars
$100,000,000 - Plenty to go around for everyone.
Fits nicely on an ISO / Military standard sized pallet.

The couch is worth $46.7 million. Made out of crispy $100 bills.

However, now we are getting a little more serious. Below is $1bn…

However, here is $1 trillion… These are the kind of numbers to which I refer…

The 2011 US federal deficit was $1.412 trillion, 41% more than is depicted above. If you had spent $1m a day since the day Jesus was born, you would still not have spent $1 trillion by now, but only a 'mere' $700 billion which by coincidence, just happens to be the same amount that the banks received in their recent bailout.

The Statue of Liberty seems rather worried as the United States national debt is soon to pass 20% of the entire world's combined economy (GDP / Gross Domestic Product).

If the national debt could be laid in a single line of $1 bills, it would stretch out from Earth, all the way past Uranus, a distance of some 2 billion miles.

And to whom is this vast sum of money owed ... Yes, that is correct, to the banksters, those nice, benevolent people who lend us 'their' money to buy cars and houses and to whom the governments of the world owe every penny of money currently in circulation

But why does any government need to borrow money from anyone?

The truth is that in a healthy, uncorrupted society a government does not have to borrow anything from anyone. But under the central banking paradigm, governments have allowed themselves to be subjugated to a financial system which requires the constant, ongoing borrowing of ever larger and larger amounts of money. Obviously, this arrangement is not permanently sustainable and the inherent structural problems caused by such a system are at the very heart of all our national debts and monetary crises of today.

To use the US government as a convenient example once again; if it wants to issue $1 billion, it has to go 'cap in hand' to the FRB to borrow the money. The FRB then contacts the Treasury and instructs them print 10,000,000 Federal Reserve Notes in units of one hundred dollars. The Treasury charges the FRB 2.3 cents for each note, resulting in a total of $230,000 for the 10,000,000 FRNs. The FRB then **lends** the $1 billion to the government at face value plus interest. To add insult to injury, the government then has to create a bond for $1 billion as security for the loan. And thus do the banksters enrich themselves. However, in reality the FRB does not even print the money, it is simply a computer entry in their accounting system.

"It is absurd to say that our country can issue $30,000,000 in bonds and not $30,000,000 in currency. Both are promises to pay; but one promise fattens the usurer, and the other helps the people." Benjamin Franklin

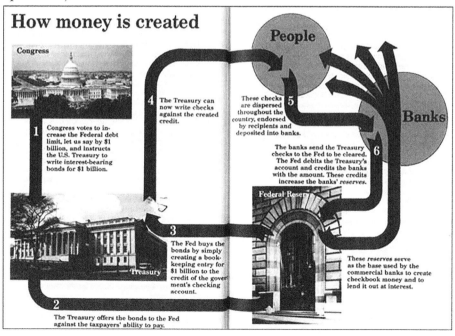

All banks in the US are members of the Federal Reserve Banking System and worldwide are affiliated to their own country's respective central bank. This membership makes it LEGAL for them to create money from nothing and lend it to us. Like the goldsmiths of old, they know that only a small fraction of the money deposited in their banks is ever actually withdrawn in the form of cash. Only about 4% of all the money that exists is in the form of currency. The rest of it is simply a computer entry, it exists DIGITALLY only.

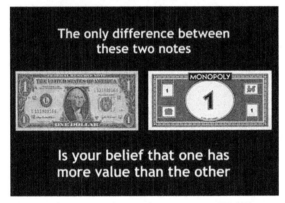

Our worldwide monetary system is what is known as a FIAT currency.

Imagine sitting down to play Monopoly and having a friend claim that they are going to act as both the bank and a player. Then when the game starts and your friend, using *bank money*, buys every single property and fills them with every hotel. You and the other players would be quickly bankrupted because your friend has taken all your money and now owns everything. Who would ever play the game that way? Unfortunately, *we all do*. In 1913 and as previously related at length, the US financial system, like so many others before and since, was hijacked in much the same way as that Monopoly game when private banksters bribed, coerced and cajoled politicians into granting them the legal right to create money. It is illegal for you and I to print our own money, but our government willingly lets the banksters create money out of thin air and then unbelievably, *borrows it back from them* in the form of interest-bearing loans. This is the ONE AND ONLY reason for the massive national debt and its spiralling increase and NOT government overspending or trade deficits or anything similar, as we are constantly being told. We are being lied to by the banksters and their professional apologists 24/7, I'm afraid.

In a FIAT money system, money is not backed by a physical commodity (ie. gold or silver.) Instead, the only thing that gives the money value is its relative scarcity and the faith placed in it by the people that use it. In addition, there is no restriction on the amount of money that can be created. This allows for unlimited credit creation, initially leading to the mistaken belief that this represents solid economic growth, as spending and business profits grow and frequently there is a rapid growth in equity prices. In the long term however, the economy suffers even more by the following, inevitable contraction than it ever gained from the expansion in credit.

In most cases, a fiat monetary system comes into existence as a result of excessive public debt. When a government is unable to repay all its debt in gold or silver, the temptation to remove physical backing rather than to simply default becomes irresistible. This was the case in 18th century France as well as in the 1930s and more recently in the 1970s in the US, when President Nixon removed the last link between the dollar and gold and which is still in effect today.

Hyper-inflation is the terminal stage of any fiat currency. With hyper-inflation, money loses most of its value very quickly indeed. It often occurs as the result of increasing regular inflation to the point where all confidence in money is lost. In a fiat monetary system, the value of money is based on confidence and once that confidence is gone, money rapidly becomes worthless, usually irreversibly, regardless of its scarcity. The United States has so far avoided hyper-inflation by shifting between a fiat and gold standard over the past 200 years.

THE BASIC FRACTIONAL RESERVE BANKING CYCLE

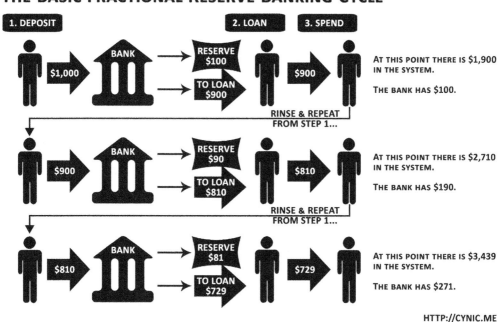

While fractional reserve banking mechanics are surprisingly simple, the implications of the system are not. Mechanically, fractional reserve banking depends on 3 factors:

Initial deposit: The amount of the initial deposit

Reserve requirement: The fractional reserve requirement is a number between 0 and 1

Iterations: The number of times that money is deposited or cycled through the system.

The initial deposit into the fractional reserve banking system comes from the government when they issue bonds and deliver them to the bank. These bonds are in effect 'IOUs' from the government as a promise to pay the amount of the bond back—with interest.

The reserve requirement is a number between 0 and 1 and sets the ratio of the amount of money that they bank can 'print' to loan out. For example, if the reserve requirement is 0.1 (10%) and the bank receives $100 in government bonds, then the bank can loan out $100 × (1 − 0.1) = $100 × 0.9 = $90.

So the basic mathematics of the system are extremely simple. Generally:

Loan = Deposit × (1 − Reserve Requirement)

eg. $90 = $100 × (1 − 0.1)

Or, in terms of what the bank must keep in reserve, i.e. the amount of money that it cannot loan:

Reserve = Deposit × Reserve Requirement

e.g. $10 = $100 × 0.1

But it does not stop there. Once a loan is made, the person that receives the loaned money spends it to obtain some form of wealth in the real world. That could be absolutely anything, a house, a car, groceries, a meal at a restaurant, etc. etc. The seller of the product or service then takes that money, goes back to the bank, and deposits it. That deposit is then subject to the same reserve requirement with the remainder being made available for the bank to loan out again.

"The study of money, above all other fields in economics, is one in which complexity is used to disguise truth or to evade truth, not to reveal it. The process by which banks create money is so simple the mind is repelled. With something so important, a deeper mystery seems only decent." John Kenneth Galbraith, Professor of Economics at Harvard

"It is well enough that people of the nation do not understand our banking and money system, for if they did, I believe there would be a revolution before tomorrow morning." Henry Ford, founder of the Ford Motor Company.

The Federal Reserve Bank only *creates* the Principal, not the usury or interest that it lends to the US government. Therefore the interest can NEVER be repaid and the debt continues to spiral out of control and the end result is inevitably foreclosure and bankruptcy.

This provides the banksters with an incredible engine for wealth generation, which would not be at all possible in an ordinary economy. Imagine consistently loaning-out 9 times as much money as you actually possessed, how long would that be sustainable?

But in our corrupted system, it all works out because the FRB is always able to create more money from nothing to keep it all going.

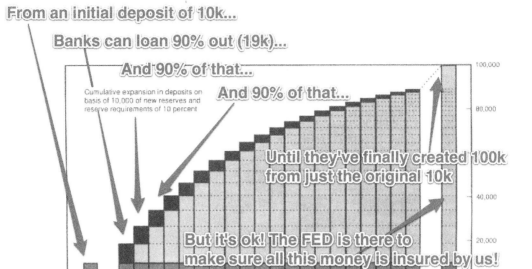

In her book '*Web of Debt*,' author Ellen Brown provides a good example of just how profitable this is for the banks...

"You live in a small town with only one bank. You sell your house for $100,000 and deposit the money into your checking account at the bank. The bank then advances 90 percent of this sum, or $90,000, to Miss White to buy a house from Mr. Black. The bank proceeds to collect from Miss White both the interest and the principal on this loan. Assume the prevailing interest is 6.25 percent. Interest at 6.25 percent on $90,000 over the life of a 30-year mortgage comes to $109,490. Miss White thus winds up owing $199,490 in principle and interest on the loan—not to you, whose money it allegedly was in the first place, but to the bank. Legally, Miss White has title to the house; but the bank becomes the effective owner until she pays off her mortgage.

Mr. Black now takes the $90,000 Miss White paid him for his house and deposits it into his checking account at the town bank. The bank adds the $90,000 to its reserve balance at its Federal Reserve Bank and advances 90 percent of this sum, or $81,000 to Mrs. Green, who wants to buy a house from Mr. Grey. Over 30 years, Mrs. Green owes the bank $81,000 in principle plus $98,541 in interest, or $179,541; and the bank has become the effective owner of another house until the loan is paid off. Mr. Grey then deposits Mrs. Green's money into his checking account. The process continues until the bank has 'lent' $900,000, on which it collects $900,000 in principal and $985,410 in interest, for a total of $1,885,410. The bank has thus created $900,000 out of thin air and has acquired effective ownership of a string of houses, at least temporarily, all from an initial $100,000 deposit; and it is owed $985,410 in interest on this loan. The $900,000 principle is extinguished by an entry on the credit side of the ledger when the loans are paid off; but the other half of this conjured $2 million—the interest—remains solidly in the coffers of the bank, *and if any of the borrowers should default on their loans, the bank becomes the owner of the mortgaged property."*

So imagine if we borrow £10,000 to make some home improvements. The bank did not actually take £10,000 from its pile of cash and put it into your pile, they simply went to their computer and input an entry of £10,000 into your account in effect creating from nothing a debt which you have to secure with an asset and repay with interest. The bank is allowed to create and lend as much debt as they want, as long as they do not exceed the 10:1 ratio imposed by the FRB.

You buy a 100k house.

Price goes up 10k over 1 year.

No leverage 1:1

Pay 100k for house → You made 10% on your money

Partial Leverage 10:1

Pay $10k and finance $90k at 6% → You made 65% on your money

Max leverage 100:1

Pay $1k and finance $99,000 at 6% → You made 144% on your money

As we can see, betting with 100 times the amount of money you actually possess, can turn an outrageous profit when you're winning, but even the slightest downturn can destroy you, which is exactly what happened to the banks during the last financial crisis. Of course this is not news, the biggest players know exactly how this game is played. In fact, the more volatile the market is, the more profit that can be made.

So whilst ordinary citizens are being ruined by boom and bust cycles, the reality is that the markets are behaving exactly as intended and money is constantly being siphoned-off by those privy to the scam.

"The few who understand the system, will either be so interested from its profits or so dependent on its favours, that there will be no opposition from that class." Rothschild Brothers of London, 1863

There are many other examples of rigging the system such as the LIBOR scandal, or the more recent ISDA fix scandal, where banks were essentially caught colluding to manipulate global markets. But all that is not even the worst aspect of the scam. Whatever system of finance we use there will always be a minority who sell their souls, one way or another or lie and cheat to become obscenely rich, but the worst and most pernicious aspect of *this* scam by far, is inflation, because it attacks the wealth and well-being of every ordinary, honest, hard-working person.

Consider this... If all money is created as debt, which is being loaned out at interest, how is there ever enough money in the system to cover the interest accruing? The simple answer is that there is not. By definition, there is always more money owed-back than was created in the first place and that ever-escalating debt creates a mathematical inevitability where the harder we struggle to break even, the more indebted we become.

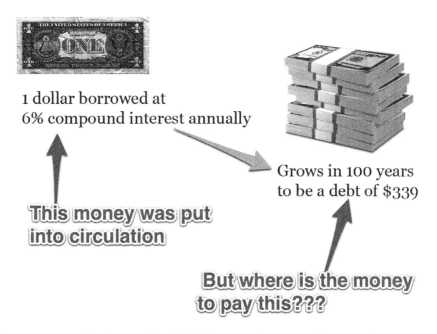

Since the money required to pay back the interest does not exist, more loans are required and then more loans and more loans, a process which ultimately inflates the value of currency, drives prices higher and higher, and cripples a nation with debt.

This in fact is the sole reason that people such as Charles Lindbergh Sr., John Jacob Astor IV, Benjamin Guggenheim, Isidor Straus and indeed many other wealthy individuals were so opposed to the Federal Reserve Act. They knew, as we now know to our great cost, that this system absolutely destroys the wealth of every individual by removing it into the already overflowing coffers of the banking industry. As people such as those mentioned above had so much more to lose than most, the reason for their vehement opposition to the banksters' plans now becomes very apparent.

"If the American people ever allow private banks to control issue of their currency, first by inflation, then by deflation, the banks and the corporations that will grow-up around them, will deprive the people of all property until their children wake up homeless on the continent their fathers conquered. The issuing power should be taken from the banks and restored to 'the people,' to whom it properly belongs." Thomas Jefferson

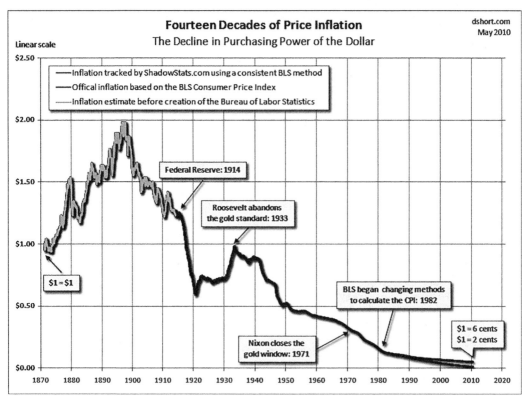

Sadly, the warning issued by Jefferson went unheeded by those who could have prevented the abomination of the FRB from becoming a reality. It is a fact that back in the 1970s with just an 'ordinary,' what is now termed a 'minimum wage' job, it was easily possible to buy a house AND support a family. But today, despite working at *two* jobs in some cases, many families do not have enough to put food on the table every day. Homelessness is becoming endemic and there are now (2015) almost 50 million people in the US living below the 'poverty line.' In addition it was recently stated that there are approximately (the exact figures are unknown) 150,000 homeless people living on the streets of Los Angeles, alone. These trends run totally contrary to any reasonable standard of 'progress' to be expected from a society with a benevolent economy, especially considering all the many technological advancements of the last century. So much for 'your friendly bank,' eh?

To reiterate: Money is created from nothing at all and every time a loan is made, money is created out of debt.

People fear what they do not understand and it is far easier to delude and control them when they are 'ignorant' and afraid.

Interestingly, in October 1913, in the last days of the Taft administration, the US Congress finally passed a bill legalising direct income tax of the people. This was in the form of a Bill pushed through by Senator Aldrich, which is now commonly known as the 16th amendment to the Constitution. The income tax law was fundamental to the workings of the Federal Reserve Bank because the FRB was a system which would generate an unlimited Federal debt. The only way to guarantee the payment of interest on this debt was to directly tax the people's incomes, as had been the case in England, with the Bank of England and indeed every other country in the world (bar the three aforementioned.)

The US *Internal Revenue Service* (IRS) and in England the *Inland Revenue*, are merely collection agencies for the central bank. The US government obtains its authority to collect income tax through the 16th Amendment, the Federal income tax amendment, which was allegedly ratified in 1913.

"The Congress shall have power to lay and collect taxes on incomes, from whatever source derived, without apportionment among the several States, and without regard to any census or enumeration." The 16th Amendment to the Constitution of the United States of America

Over the years, numerous researchers such as for example, William J. Benson, discovered that the 16th Amendment was never ratified by the requisite 75% of the states and that regardless of this fact, Secretary of State Philander Knox had fraudulently declared ratification. Article V of the US Constitution defines the ratification process and requires three-quarters of the states to ratify any amendment proposed by Congress.

In 1913, there were forty eight states in the American Union, meaning that affirmative action of thirty six of those forty eight was necessary for ratification and in February 1913, Secretary of State Philander Knox proclaimed that thirty-eight had ratified the Amendment.

In 1984 Bill Benson began a research project, never before undertaken, to investigate the process of ratification of the 16th Amendment. After travelling to the capitols of the New England States and reviewing the journals of the State legislative bodies, he discovered that many states had not ratified the proposed amendment and continued his research at the National Archives in Washington, DC. This damning piece of evidence is a 16 page memorandum from the Solicitor of the Department of State, among whose duties is the provision of legal opinions for the Secretary of State. In this memorandum, the Solicitor listed the many errors he found in the ratification process.

The following states are among the thirty eight from which Philander Knox claimed ratification:

California: The legislature never recorded any vote on any proposal to adopt the amendment proposed by Congress.

Kentucky: The Senate voted on the resolution, but rejected it by a vote of nine in favour and twenty two against.

Minnesota: The State sent nothing at all to the Secretary of State in Washington.

Oklahoma: The Senate amended the language of the 16th Amendment to convey the precisely opposite meaning to that intended.

At the end of his project in 1984, Benson had visited the capitol of every state from 1913 and knew that not a single one had actually or legally, ratified the proposal to amend the Constitution. Thirty three states engaged in the unauthorised activity of altering the language of an amendment proposed by Congress, a power that the individual States do not possess.

Since the approval of thirty six states was needed for ratification, the failure of thirteen to ratify should have been fatal to the Amendment. In fact there were only two states that provably, successfully ratified.

It is a little-known fact that the greatest period of economic growth in American history was during a time when there was absolutely no federal income tax. Between the end of the Civil War and 1913, there was an economic boom in the United States unlike anything ever seen before or since.

Most people, in all countries, simply assume that there is no other option to an income tax and assume that it has always been with us and that it will always be with us. Every year, the American people 'lose' in excess of $4 trillion in State and Federal income taxes and this figure is equivalent to approximately 30% of **all** income earned.

But would governments suddenly go bankrupt if there was no income tax? No, actually the truth is that governments had no financial problems at all prior to the advent of an income tax. In fact, the US national debt for example, has grown **5000 times larger** since the Federal income tax and the FRB were created by the corrupted Congress and since then, the dollar has lost 97% of its value.

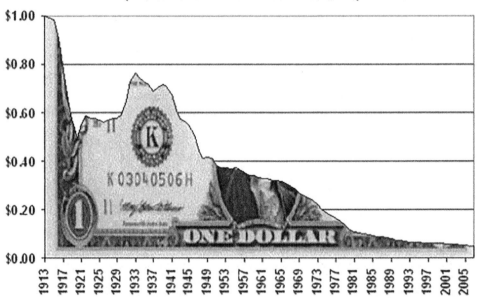

The Federal Reserve system was actually designed to trap the United States in a debt spiral from which it could never possibly escape, and the federal income tax was needed to greatly expand the size of the federal government and to deprive the American people of the funds necessary to service that debt. But it does not have to be this way. America was once much better-off before the income tax and the Federal Reserve were created, and could easily revert to such a system once again.

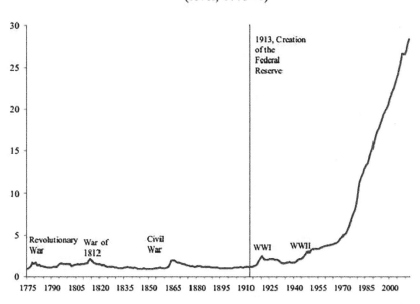

Figure 1. Consumer Price Index, United States, 1775-2012 (level, 1775=1)

Sources: Bureau of Labor Statistics, Historical Statistics of the United States, and Reinhart and Rogoff (2009).

The Federal Reserve has brought nothing but massive inflation, and much more massive debt not just to the people of the United States, but to the world itself. In pre-Federal Reserve 1910, the US national debt was $2.6bn yet today it is more than 5,000 times that amount at almost $17 trillion. That is $17,000,000,000,000! Combined with the other bankster-owned central banks of the world, we can only wonder what all that stolen money and all those illegal taxes could have done to benefit mankind in general instead of the tiny minority who keep it ALL for themselves.

What you are about to read should absolutely astound you. During the last financial crisis, the Federal Reserve secretly conducted the biggest bailout in the history of the world and the FRB fought in court for several years to keep it a secret. We can all remember the TARP bailout, and the American people were absolutely outraged that the Federal government spent $700bn bailing out the 'too big to fail' banks. But that bailout was pocket change compared to what the Federal Reserve did.

The Federal Reserve actually handed more than $16 trillion in almost interest-free money to the 'too big to fail' banks between 2007 and 2010. But of course this is never reported in the bankster-controlled mainstream media.

According to the limited GAO audit of the Federal Reserve that was mandated by the Dodd-Frank Wall Street Reform and Consumer Protection Act, the grand total of all the secret bailouts conducted by the Federal Reserve during the last financial crisis comes to a whopping $16.1 trillion.

This is an astonishing amount of money. (Please refer back to the diagrams on the previous pages to put this into full perspective). It is also put into sharp perspective by noting that the entire GDP (gross domestic product), in other words all the money generated in the United States for the entire year of 2010 was only $14.58 trillion. But, according to the GAO audit, $16.1 trillion in secret loans were made by the Federal Reserve between December 2007 and July 2010.

The following list of banks and the amount of money that they received was taken directly from page 131 of the GAO audit report…

- Citigroup—$2.513 trillion
- Morgan Stanley—$2.041 trillion
- Merrill Lynch—$1.949 trillion
- Bank of America—$1.344 trillion
- Barclays plc—$868 billion
- Bear Sterns—$853 billion
- Goldman Sachs—$814 billion
- Royal Bank of Scotland—$541 billion
- JP Morgan Chase—$391 billion
- Deutsche Bank—$354 billion
- UBS—$287 billion
- Credit Suisse—$262 billion
- Lehman Brothers—$183 billion
- Bank of Scotland—$181 billion
- BNP Paribas—$175 billion
- Wells Fargo—$159 billion
- Dexia—$159 billion
- Wachovia—$142 billion
- Dresdner Bank—$135 billion
- Societé Generale—$124 billion
- All Other Borrowers—$2.639 trillion

Not only did the Federal Reserve give $16.1 trillion in virtually interest-free loans to the 'too big to fail' banks, the Fed also paid them over $600 million to help run the emergency lending program. According to the GAO, the Federal Reserve shelled-out an astounding $659.4 million in 'fees' to the very financial institutions which caused the financial crisis in the first place.

If the FRB can afford to 'lend' more than $16tn to all the other parasites in the financial system, how much 'money' do you think they actually have in their possession in total? This is obviously not public domain information but my guess would be 'considerably more than actually physically exists in the entire world.' But of course we already know now that most 'money' exists only theoretically anyway.

So as is now evident, the 'licensed to steal' bankster-run central banks routinely bail out their member banks and their 'friends' but the taxpayers always get presented with the bill. A bill commonly known as the 'national debt.' Except in reality, there is no national debt. It is all an **illusion**, a massive **fraud** but the banksters down the centuries have brainwashed us all into thinking it is **REALLY** owed to them. It's a lie.

Here is an amusing, fictional anecdote that illustrates just how much of an illusion it all is . . .

"It is the month of August; a resort town sits next to the shores of a lake. It is raining, and the little town looks totally deserted. It is in the toughest times since 1934, everybody is in debt, and everybody lives on credit; mostly from each other.

Suddenly, a rich tourist comes to town. 'Oh boy!' Everyone says to themselves when they spot his limousine. 'How long can we keep this rich guy in town?'

The limo stops, the back door opens and the bigshot enters the only hotel. He drops a 100-dollar bill on the reception counter, and asks to inspect the rooms upstairs in order to pick one he might like.

The moment the elevator closes taking the new customer upstairs, the hotel proprietor takes the 100-dollar bill and sprints four doors down the sidewalk to pay his debt to the butcher. The butcher takes the 100-dollar bill, and runs out back to pay his debt to the pig farmer. The pig farmer takes the 100-dollar bill, and hurries to pay his debt to the supplier of his feed and fuel. The supplier of feed and fuel takes the 100-dollar bill and hurries to pay his debt to the town's prostitute that in these hard times, gave her services on credit. The hooker runs to the hotel, and pays off her debt with the 100-dollar bill to the hotel proprietor to pay for the rooms that she rented when she brought her clients there.

It all happened in less than 10 minutes, and the hotel proprietor promptly placed the 100-dollar bill back on the counter so that the rich tourist would not suspect anything.

And it was just in time, too, because only a moment later, the rich tourist came down after inspecting the rooms, picked up his 100-dollar bill, remarked that he did not like any of the rooms, and left town.

No one earned anything. However, the whole town was suddenly without debt, and was looking to the future with a lot of optimism.

And now you have seen a quick snapshot of how the federal government . . . via the handy Federal Reserve credit machine, operates in our society." Pat Shannan, *'Everything They Ever Told Me was a Lie.'* 2010.

The banksters certainly do not have to point a gun at us to get our money. As they own the law and everything else besides, we pay them out of fear of the consequences of non-compliance!

Chapter 4
The Elite Money Power

As with any investigation into culpability, we should always 'follow the money' and in this case it leads to the ultra-powerful, elite bankster families. We will later see further evidence of how they operate, how they enslave humanity and kill millions; crimes that in truth, only the satanically-influenced or psychopathically-minded would be capable of perpetrating.

In 1776, as already related, the *Order of the Illuminati* was founded by Adam Weishaupt in Bavaria. It was and indeed still is, powerfully connected to the ruling financial elite (banksters) who possess the lion's share of the world's wealth. The Rothschilds for instance, played a major role in the financing and support of the Bavarian Illuminati in its formative years, but there are also several other families involved.

Over the years, this organisation of pure evil has spread its despicable tentacles into every country of note but remains largely hidden from view because the Illuminati is after all, a 'secret society,' along with its equally repugnant 'bedfellow,' Freemasonry. Indeed at the senior levels of Freemasonry, the boundaries between the two, if they exist at all, become exceedingly blurred. The 13 major Illuminati bloodlines exist as a mirror of the 13 levels of the pyramid as denoted on the seal on the reverse side of the US $1 bill and these wealthy families, who are without doubt the **real** rulers of the world, were thrust into prominence and empowered in the Satanic master plan carried out by the Illuminati.

There are in total, 13 families who are Illuminati but the membership however, is not completely static. 13 of course, is regarded by them as a Satanic number with magical, occult power and is very much to the forefront of all Illuminati planning yet often used in 'plain sight' in their various subterfuges.

There is little doubt of the existence of a long-term plan by the international financial elite to enslave humanity in order to bring about their oft-quoted 'New World Order.' This conspiracy is often attributed to various factions including, but not exclusively, the Illuminati themselves, Jews, Zionists, the Vatican, Jesuits, Freemasons the Black

Nobility and the Bilderbergers etc. However the truth is that it is a complex hybrid of all these elements that make up the whole sorry group.

But the real villains are those at the heart of our economic and cultural life. They are the dynastic families, the 'Royals,' the owners of the Bank of England, the US Federal Reserve and associated cartels. They also control the World Bank and IMF and most of the world's Intelligence agencies. Their identity is meant to be secret but the Rothschilds are certainly among their number. We should never forget that money is power and this power rests largely in the 'City of London.'

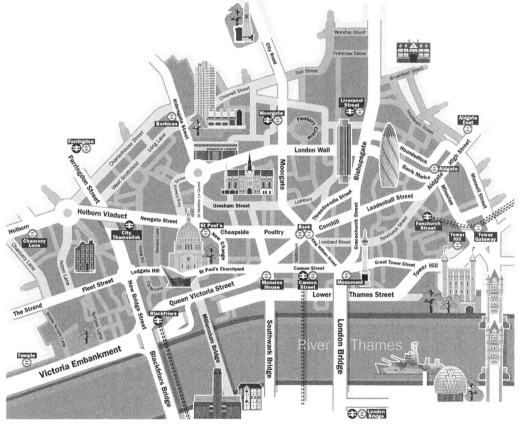

The 'City of London'

The great majority of people assume that the phrases 'the Crown' and 'the City' in reference to London, refer to the Queen or the capital of England.

However, this is not so. 'The City' is in fact a privately owned Corporation and Sovereign State occupying an irregular rectangle of 677 acres, approximately one square mile, and located right in the heart of the 610 square mile Greater London area. The population of 'the City' is listed at just over four thousand, whereas the population of the 32 Boroughs of Greater London is approximately seven and a half million. This square mile that constitutes the 'City' has its own mayor, laws, courts, flag, police force and newspapers, characteristic of all three independent 'City States,' the City of London, Washington DC and Vatican City. They are in effect countries within countries, but only Vatican City is officially accorded the title of 'country.'

The true identity of 'the Crown' however is kept most secret, but nevertheless it was the Crown-controlled Bank of England that took and assumed control of the United States during the Theodore Roosevelt Administration (1901-1909) when its agent, who was in reality a Crown agent (*J. P. Morgan and Co.*), assumed control of 25% of American business interests.

'The Crown' has never referred to the King or Queen of England, not since the establishment of the corporate body, but the British Monarchy is a figurehead for 'the Crown,' rules parliament in Great Britain and has absolute authority over the Prime Minister and his government through a Vatican knighthood by the name of the *Order of the Garter*. Despite its many sycophantic apologists, encouraged all the while by the compliant media and the political hierarchy, who claim that the Royal family are just 'figureheads,' unfortunately this is absolutely, categorically NOT the case at all.

The Crown is the directorate of the corporation, and Great Britain is ruled by the Crown, the City of London which controls the Bank of England—a private corporation. In other words 'the City' is a 'private' state existing in Britain within the very heart of London. It became a sovereign-state in its own right in 1694 when King William III sanctioned the privatisation of the *Bank of England*, and handed it over to the banksters who today rule the financial world ... in exactly the same way that the FRB banksters were freely given the ultimate control of money in the US in 1913.

Today, the City State of London is the world's ultimate centre of financial power and the wealthiest square mile on the planet. The City is also unsurprisingly, home to the privatised Bank of England, Lloyd's of London, the London Stock Exchange and the headquarters of all British-based and many foreign banks. It is home to the branch offices of 385 foreign banks plus 70 US banks, as well as many newspapers and publishing monopolies. It controls the world media and the world's intelligence services and it is from within the Crown City of London that British Freemasonry, overseen by the British Monarchy specifically the Duke of Kent (Freemasonic Grand Master), and indeed World Freemasonry is governed. This includes the Grand Orient Masonic Order and the Washington DC version, 'Scottish Rite Freemasonry.' All a coincidence? I think not.

'The Crown' is a committee of twelve men who rule the independent sovereign state known as 'the City.' 'The City' is not part of England and not subject to the Sovereign ruler of Great Britain and its Commonwealth. Neither is it under the rule of the British parliament, it is a separate, independent state, presided over by a Lord Mayor.

The Lord Mayor and his council serve as proxies or representatives who in effect deputise for the world's wealthiest, most powerful banking families, including the Rothschild family, the Warburg family, the Oppenheimer family and the Schiff family. These families and their descendants own and run the Crown Corporation of London. The Lord Mayor, who is elected for a one year term, is the absolute 'monarch' in the City.

"The relation of this monarch of the City to the monarch of the realm [Queen] is curious and tells much. When the Queen of England goes to visit the City she is met by the Lord Mayor at Temple Bar, the symbolic gate of the City. She bows and asks for permission to enter his private, sovereign State. During such State visits the Lord Mayor in his robes and chain, and his entourage in medieval costume, outshines the royal party, which can dress up no further than service uniforms." Aubrey Menen, *Time-Life*, 1976, p. 16

So, the Lord Mayor leads the Queen into **his** city. We may think this is simply 'quaint' and part of the long British Heritage, no longer to be taken seriously, but simply an age-old ceremony kept as tradition. This is exactly what we are meant to believe but the symbolism is clear; the Lord Mayor is the monarch and the Queen is his subject. The Queen is subordinate to the Mayor only in the City but outside of the City of London he bows to her and furthermore, this exclusive clique who rule the City dictate to the British Parliament, despite the fact that in theory, Britain is ruled by a Prime Minister and a Cabinet of Ministers. These 'fronts' go to great lengths to create the impression that they are running the country but, in reality, they are mere puppets whose strings are pulled by the shadowy characters who dominate behind the scenes.

As the former British Prime Minister of England during the late 1800s, Benjamin Disraeli wrote … *"So you see … the world is governed by very different personages from what is imagined by those who are not behind the scenes"* 'Coningsby,' The Century Co., 1907, p233

The City of London is the only part of the United Kingdom, over which parliament has no authority whatsoever and in one respect at least, the Corporation acts as the superior body of the two. It imposes on the House of Commons a figure referred-to as the 'Remembrancer,' an official lobbyist who sits behind the Speaker's chair and ensures that, whatever we or our elected representatives might think, the City's rights and privileges are fully protected.

The now greatly depleted British Empire was an extension of banksters' financial interests. Indeed, all the colonies were 'Crown Colonies.' They belonged to the City and were not subject to British law although British citizens were expected to shed blood (often their own) and conquer and pay for them. One key aspect of the colonial period is generally omitted or air-brushed from official history and that is the fact that all the Crown colonies were established on a corporate model with financial ties to the City of London, not to the nation of the United Kingdom (the official name of the political entity consisting of England, Scotland, Wales and Northern Ireland.) The UK is a Crown colony but the City of London is not.

The directorate of the Crown, had and has no loyalty to any nation, they were and are, devoted entirely to their own philosophy, which seeks absolute power and wealth. For more than 250 years, the 'servants' of the Crown brought untold wealth back from the colonies to the British Isles—to enrich their bankster masters only. The general population of the United Kingdom received very little wealth as a result of these exploits, if any at all, despite the fact that it was they who provided the finance through taxation and the 'cannon fodder' in the form of the armed forces, to enable the subjugation of foreign powers in order that the banksters could profit from the altruistic exploits of the armed forces.

These servicemen were invaluable assets of the Crown, but they did not know whom or what they served—and indeed still do not. (None are more hopelessly enslaved than those who falsely believe they are free.) Historian Jeffrey Steinberg could also have been referring to the US, Canada or Australia (or any other country you care to name) when he wrote that … *"England, Scotland, Wales, and Northern Ireland, are today little more than slave plantations and social engineering laboratories, serving the needs of the Crown/City of London."*

According to the *American Almanac*, the Crown and their associated banksters are part of a network with an estimated $10 trillion in physical assets (as opposed to non-existent paper and money in its various electronic forms.) The Crown is in total control of such corporate giants as *Royal Dutch Shell*, the former companies comprising the giant *Imperial Chemical Industries*, (now 'rationalised' into many different organisations), *Lloyds of London, Unilever, Lonrho, Rio Tinto Zinc,* and *Anglo-American DeBeers*. It completely dominates the world supply of oil, gold, diamonds, and many other vital raw materials.

The Crown/City of London also dominates the world's speculative markets. A tightly interlocking group of corporations involved in raw materials extraction, finance, insurance, transportation and food production, controls the lion's share of the world's markets and exerts supreme control over world industry. In order to understand the genuine motives for particular actions and events in history we already know to 'follow the money,' but that is only part of the story, we must also follow the philosophy and the religious beliefs of those in control. For purposes of clarity, 'the Crown' always refers here to a stealthy circle of power-brokers (the banksters) who all believe in the Freemasonic philosophy of the 'brotherhood of man' ruled by philosopher kings (or adepts) in league with the God of Masonry. This point is not up for debate, it is only necessary to read some of the cumbersome histories of Masonry and also read Albert Pike's *Morals and Dogma* to understand explicitly that this power-philosophy encompasses virtually all the religious ideas ever imagined by man.

Ordinary members of Masonic lodges, those of the so-called 'blue degrees,' numbered 1-3 or the three overt levels, the only ones to which most Masons can aspire, are to these adepts and their goals what the people of the Western civilisations are to the directors of the Crown, that is 'useful idiots.' This ultra-secretive, all-pervasive cabal is represented by the dominant political, economic and cultural institutions across the world. Indeed, western society has been thoroughly subverted and western culture is morally bankrupt, whilst our so-called democracies are a subtle form of social control and the mass media and our so-called education systems are nothing more than a sham, or at best, covert forms of indoctrination.

The British government is the bonded slave of the 'invisible and inaudible' force centred in the City and the City is the master of all. The 'visible and audible leaders' i.e. 'elected' politicians, are mere puppets who dance to the tunes of the real powers-that-be. They have no real power and no authority and in spite of the outward show to the contrary, they are mere pawns in the on-going game being played-out by the financial elite, the banksters.

It is important to recognise the fact that two separate empires were operating under the guise of the British Empire, one was the Crown Empire and the other the British Empire. The colonial possessions that consisted primarily of white people were under the jurisdiction of the Sovereign i.e. under the authority of the British government, that is, such nations as the Union of South Africa, Australia, New Zealand and Canada were governed under British law. However, these only represented around 13% of the people who made up the inhabitants of the British Empire.

All the other elements of the Empire, nations such as India, Egypt, Bermuda, Malta, Cyprus and colonies in Central Africa, Singapore and Hong Kong were all Crown Colonies. These were not under British rule and parliament had no authority over them. As the Crown owned the committee known as the British government there was no problem whatsoever in convincing the British taxpayer of the need to pay for naval and military forces to maintain the Crown's supremacy in these countries.

The City reaped enormous profits from its operations conducted under the protection of the British armed forces however, but this was not British commerce and British wealth it was the international banksters, prosperous merchants and those members of the aristocracy who were part of the 'City' machine that accumulated vast fortunes, especially as the 'City' is also a tax haven for them. In fact it is linked to other satellite tax havens across most time zones, ranging from Hong Kong and Singapore in the East, to the British Virgin Islands, the Turks and Caicos Islands, Bermuda and the Cayman Islands and the Bahamas in the West. All of these havens are Frankenstein creations of the City, as are the Crown Dependency islands of Guernsey, Isle of Man and Jersey. Is it any surprise that the rich just keep getting richer!?

The Knights Templar

The Crown, the Crown Temple or Crown Templar are all synonymous and date back to the Knights Templar Church. But please understand that this whole pompous, title-ridden nonsense, is just a front for a historically long established, institutionalised criminal and financial oligarchy that has been deceiving and robbing the masses for centuries. The Temple Church was built by the Knights Templar in two parts; the

Round and the Chancel. The Round Church was consecrated in 1185 and modelled on the circular Church of the Holy Sepulchre in Jerusalem and the Chancel was completed in 1240. The Temple Church serves the both Inner and Middle Temple and its grounds are also home to the Crown offices at Crown Office Row. This Temple 'Church' is significantly outside of any Canonical jurisdiction.

Between 1095 and 1291 AD, the Roman Catholic Church instigated seven enormous bloodbaths now referred to as 'the Crusades,' which were nothing more than a convenient excuse for torturing, maiming, beheading and committing genocide against millions of Muslims in 'the name of God.' The Church's brutal soldiers were named the 'Knights Templar' or 'Knights of the Temple of Solomon' and eventually evolved into today's secretive brotherhood, the Freemasons after the order was 'dissolved' in the early 14th century.

The Knights Templar were a pseudo-Christian group of Crusaders, who took up residence in Solomon's Temple in Jerusalem and spent many years digging a tunnel in an attempt to find the Ark of the Covenant, because it was believed that whoever held this ancient treasure, would have the power to rule the whole world, and hence the various legends prevailing throughout recorded history regarding the search for the Ark. Incidentally, the red cross and sword on the flag of the city of London and the red cross on the flag of England (the cross of St. George, below) is actually the Knights Templar's symbol and is overtly and prominently displayed by many corporate and other entities, for example by the Italian car manufacturer, *Alfa Romeo* and more significantly by the *Red Cross* organisation itself, from whence it gets its name. The Cross of St. George also appears on the flags of several nations.

Between 1450 and 1700, the Catholic Church followed-up their 'holy' terror campaign with the Spanish Inquisition. Based on rumours and accusations of practicing witchcraft, the Catholic Church hunted down, tortured and burned-alive tens of thousands of innocent men and women who were allegedly practising the black art of witchcraft.

And more recently, over the course of the last five decades, more than fifteen hundred

Catholic priests and bishops have been identified in the sexual assault of tens of thousands of boys and girls in their trusting congregations and orphanages. Whilst preaching spiritual values of poverty and chastity, the Catholic Church accumulated all its immense wealth by placing a price-tag on sin. Many bishops and popes actively marketed guilt, sin and fear for profit, by selling 'indulgences,' in effect licences to sin and be subsequently forgiven. Worshippers were encouraged to pre-pay for sins that had not yet been committed and obtained a pardon for them in advance and those who did not pay were threatened with eternal damnation and excommunication. Another method of money extraction was to entice wealthy land owners to bequeath their land and fortunes to the church on their death-bed, in exchange for a blessing which would supposedly enable them to go to heaven. Pope Leo V actually rebuilt St. Peter's Basilica, by selling tickets to heaven.

The Knights Templar, were originally named 'the Poor Fellow-Soldiers of Christ and the Temple of Solomon.' This is a blatantly misleading title, considering the immense wealth and power of the Templars, who operated 9,000 manors across Europe and owned the majority of the mills and markets. It was the Templars that issued the first paper money for public use in Europe, thus establishing the fiat banking system we know today and being the predecessors of today's banksters. In England, they established their headquarters at a London temple, which still exists today, Temple Bar (Crown Temple.) This is located in the City of London, between Fleet Street and Victoria Embankment and the aforementioned 'Crown,' to be precise, is the Knights Templar church, also known as the Crown Temple.

The Temple Bar consists of what are known as 'Inns of Court' of which there are four; *Inner Temple, Middle Temple, Lincoln's Inn* and *Gray's Inn*. It is believed that the Inner Temple is the core group that governs the City of London Corporation, and controls the legal system of Canada and Britain while the Middle Temple controls the legal system of the United States, although all Inns are themselves controlled by the same elite group at the very top of the pyramid, of course.

The logo of the Inner Temple is a white horse on the sunburst seal of the Jesuit Order. The white horse is a symbol of the British Empire / Order of the Garter / Crown Corporation and is the same white horse which is also the symbol of the American-based CFR (Council on Foreign Relations). The white horse is in fact a Jesuit symbol—Pegasus. It is the Jesuit Order that governs the Honourable Society of the Inner Temple.

The Master of The Temple is appointed and takes his place by sealed (non-public) patent, without induction or institution. All licensed Bar Attorneys or Attorners, in Britain, the United States and indeed everywhere else, owe their allegiance and give their solemn oath, in pledge to the Crown Temple, whether they realise this or not. In fact most do not. This is because all Bar Associations throughout the world are signatories and franchises to the International Bar Association located at the Inns of Court at Crown Temple, which are physically located at Chancery Lane behind Fleet Street in London. The American Bar Associations are all franchises to the Crown.

The Bar Association is a British-Masonic system that has nothing to do with the country's sovereignty or the constitutional rights of its people. This is why, all flags displayed in UK or US courts, have a gold fringe around the edges denoting international and/or maritime law as these courts have no jurisdiction whatsoever on dry land in these Sovereign territories despite their pretence to the contrary.

The governments of the United States, Canada and Britain are all subsidiaries of the Crown, as is the Federal Reserve in the US and Canada (aka the 13th Federal Reserve.) The ruling Monarch in England is also subordinate to the Crown and the global financial and legal system is controlled from the City of London by the Crown.

Declaration of Independence and the US Constitution

Most people believe that the US declared independence from Britain in in 1776, thanks to our 'education' system and the lies and half-truths peddled to us down the centuries by ignorant, propagandised academics—and also the mainstream media. Even a cursory examination of the US currency reveals all the Masonic symbolism and of the signatories to the Declaration of Independence, at least five of which were Temple Bar attorneys and all of whom had sworn allegiance to the Crown.

Alexander Hamilton was one of the Middle Inn Crown agents during the formation of the US, and was assigned to set up the American banking system, on explicit orders from the Crown, to control the United States. In fact, a 'State' is a legal entity of the Crown. This is also true of the 'State' of Israel. In total, seven members of the Constitution Convention that signed the United States (actually estates, as in property) Constitution were Middle Inn Templars and today, copies of both the Declaration of Independence and US Constitution still hang on the wall, in the library of the Middle Temple, in London. Thus, any American that believes that they live in an independent republic is badly misinformed to say the least.

The Queen of England, Elizabeth Windsor, through her covert partnership with the Crown Temple, is the largest landowner on Earth. She is the Head of State of the United Kingdom and thirty-one other 'sovereign' states and territories and the legal owner of just under 7 billion acres of land, one sixth of the Earth's land surface—or to put it another way—she owns an acre of land for every person currently living. Most of this land is in Canada, the second-largest country on Earth, where she holds title to 2,467 million acres. In addition she 'owns' 1,900 million acres in Australia, 114 million acres in Papua New Guinea, 66 million acres in New Zealand and 60 million acres in the UK.

The City States of 'The Vatican,' 'The District of Columbia' and 'The City of London' form one interlocking Empire and these three 'City State' corporations control the world economically, through the City of London Corporation, militarily through Washington DC, and spiritually through the Vatican. They pay no taxes, are under no National Authority, have their own Independent Flag, their own Separate Laws and their own Police Force and have totally independent identities to the rest of the outside world.

Adorning the walls of St. Peter's Basilica, is the Vatican-approved image of God, an angry, bearded man in the sky painted by Michelangelo. Cruel and violent images of Gods tortured Son, suffering, bleeding and dying with a crown of vicious-looking thorns on his head and nails pounded through his feet and hands are on display throughout the Vatican. These images serve as reminders that 'God allowed His Son to be tortured and killed to save the souls of human beings who are all born sinners.'

The Vatican and the Catholic Church it controls, rules over approximately 2 billion of the world's 7 billion people and has been in existence virtually since the birth of Christianity, but the 110 acre Vatican City itself, only came into being when it became an independent state in 1929, through the Lateran Treaty signed by Cardinal Secretary of State Pietro Casparri on behalf of the Holy See and by Prime Minister Benito Mussolini on behalf of the Kingdom of Italy. Whilst two-thirds of the world earns less than £1 a day and one-fifth of the world is underfed or starving, the Vatican hoards billions in solid gold bullion, within the vaults of the Bank of England and the US Federal Reserve Bank. In addition, the Catholic Church has huge investments with many multi-national corporations.

During the Dark Ages, the Catholic Church not only hoarded the wealth they collected from the poor, but they hoarded knowledge too. They kept the 'masses' ignorant by denying them a basic education and also prohibited anyone from reading or even possessing a Bible, under pain of death.

As with the city states of London and the Vatican, the city state of the District of Columbia was officially created in 1871 and is located on ten square miles of land in the heart of Washington. The District of Columbia has its own flag and its own independent constitution. This constitution operates under a tyrannical Roman law known as *Lex Fori*, which bears no resemblance at all to the US Constitution and the name Capitol Hill derives from Capitoline Hill, which was the seat of government for the Roman Empire. When Congress passed the Act of 1871 it created a separate corporation known as The United States and corporate government for the District of Columbia. This treasonous act allowed the District of Columbia to operate as a corporation outside the original constitution of the United States and contrary to the best interests of the American people.

The United States (United British Estates), was established as a corporation under the rule of Washington DC (which is itself subservient to The City of London) with the passage of the Act of 1871. Corporations are run by Presidents hence we have the 'President' of the United States and the fact remains that the US President is nothing more than a figurehead for the central banksters and the transnational corporations, both of which are controlled by High Freemasonry that *really* controls America, Canada and many other countries.

At the centre of each of the three city states is a towering phallic-shaped stone monument, an obelisk. The 187 ton, 69 foot tall London obelisk (aka Cleopatra's Needle) was transported to London from Egypt and erected on the banks of the River Thames at Victoria Embankment in 1878, during the reign of Queen Victoria. The obelisk originally stood in the Egyptian city of On, or Heliopolis (the City of the Sun.) The Knights Templar's land extended to this area of the Thames embankment, where the Templars had their own, private docks.

In Vatican City, another Egyptian obelisk towers high above St. Peter's Square. It was relocated there in 1586, by Pope Sixtus V and is the only obelisk in Rome that has stood since Roman times. Rome originally had the most obelisks of any city, with eight Egyptian and five ancient Roman examples. Obelisks are phallic symbols honouring the pagan sun god of ancient Egypt, *Amen Ra*. The circle on the ground upon which it stands represents the female vagina, whilst the obelisk itself is the male penis. This is common occult symbolism and the spirit of Amen Ra is said to reside within the obelisk.

In Washington DC, the obelisk known as the Washington Monument was dedicated to the Freemason George Washington by the Freemasonic grand lodge of the District of Columbia. 250 Masonic lodges financed the Washington obelisk monument, including the Knights Templar Masonic order.

Standing at 555 feet, the Washington Monument is the tallest obelisk in the world and also the tallest free-standing structure in Washington DC. The monument's cornerstone, a 12-ton slab of marble, was donated by the Grand Lodge of Freemasons. As is the Vatican obelisk, the Washington monument too is surrounded by a circle denoting the female and the reflecting pool in front of the monument signifies the ancient Masonic/Kabbalistic dictum, 'as above, so below.'

Any study of the signed treaties and charters between Britain and the United States will reveal the inescapable truth that the United States has always been and still is a British Crown colony. This is the primary reason that British and US Presidents and politicians alike always refer to the 'special relationship' that exists between the two countries.

King James I was famous not only for the rewriting of the Bible into the 'King James Version,' but also for his signing of the first charter of Virginia in 1606. That charter granted America's British forefathers a licence to settle and colonise America and also guaranteed the future kings and queens of England, sovereign authority over all the citizens and colonised land in America stolen from the Indians. After America declared its independence from Great Britain, the Treaty of 1783 was signed. This treaty specifically identifies the king of England as the 'Prince of the United States' and contradicts the belief that America 'won' the war of independence. Although King George III of England relinquished most of his claims over American colonies, he kept his right to continue receiving payment for his business venture in colonising America.

Had America really won the War of Independence, they would never have agreed to pay debts and reparations to the king of England. In fact, the war actually bankrupted America and turned its citizens into permanent debt slaves of the king. Then more than twenty years later, in the war of 1812, the British burned the White House to the ground and also many US government buildings, in the process conveniently destroying all ratification records of the US Constitution.

Most people believe that the United States is an independent country and that the President is the most powerful man on earth, but in reality, the United States is not a country, it is a corporation and the President is President of the corporation of the United States and his 'elected' officials work for the corporation, not for the American people. But if indeed the United States is a corporation, it begs the question as to who owns it.

Similarly to Canada and Australia whose leaders are prime ministers of the Queen and whose land is Crown-owned land, the United States is just another Crown colony. Crown colonies are controlled by the Empire of the three City States, an Empire 'hidden' in plain sight, unbeknown to the masses.

The Round Table

The organisation was founded by Cecil Rhodes and although based in the UK, this financial empire extends its influence via a worldwide network, whose supreme council is headed by the Rothschilds of Britain and France. A generational seat is also accorded to a descendant of the Hapsburgs, and to the ruling families of England and France. In America, the Illuminati are represented by old-money families, such as the Rockefellers, Mellons and Carnegies.

The siphoning of the British people's wealth into the coffers of the Illuminati in the City of London, created severe economic inequalities and stifled the nation's ability to adapt technologically at a pace similar to that of the rapidly expanding nation of Germany. And so, by the 1870s, the British Empire reached its absolute zenith and England began the longest economic depression in its history, one from which it was not to recover until the 1890s. Therefore, the country of Britain no longer provided the economic capacity to support the global ambitions of the Illuminati and so it was at that point that the Illuminati sought to confer increasing power upon its branches in the United States, which it could rule by proxy in the coming century, while still based financially in Britain.

"I know quite well that whether Mr. Rhodes is the lofty and worshipful patriot and statesman that multitudes believe him to be, or Satan come again, as the rest of the world account him, he is still the most imposing figure in the British Empire outside of England. When he stands on the Cape of Good Hope, his shadow falls to the Zambesi. He is the only colonial in the British dominions whose goings and comings are chronicled and discussed under all the globe's meridians, and whose speeches, unclipped, are cabled from the ends of the earth; and he is the only unroyal outsider whose arrival in London can compete for attention with an eclipse." Mark Twain on Cecil Rhodes

The son of Baron Lionel Rothschild, Nathaniel Mayer, also known as 'Natty' de Rothschild, became head of NM Rothschild and Sons after his father's death in 1879. Natty also funded Cecil Rhodes in the development of the British South Africa Company and the De Beers diamond conglomerate. He administered Rhodes' estate after his death in 1902, and helped to set up the *Rhodes Scholarship* at Oxford University.

In the first of his seven wills, Cecil Rhodes called for the formation of a 'secret society,' devoted to *'the extension of British rule throughout the world.'* Rhodes also posited that only the 'British elite' should be entitled to rule the world for the benefit of mankind. In other words, the Illuminati of the City of London would exploit the expansion of British imperialism, to increase their control over gold, the seas, the world's raw materials, but most importantly, after the turn of the century, a precious, new commodity, oil.

The goals Rhodes articulated included the *"the ultimate recovery of the United States as an integral part of the British Empire [which] would culminate in consolidation of the whole Empire, the inauguration of a system of Colonial Representation in the Imperial Parliament which may tend to weld together the disjointed members of the Empire, and finally the foundation of so great a power as to hereafter render wars impossible and promote the best interests of humanity."*

In his third will, Rhodes left his entire estate to the prominent Freemason Lord Nathaniel Rothschild as trustee. Rhodes had also been initiated into Freemasonry in 1877, shortly after arriving at Oxford and joined a Scottish Rite Lodge. To chair Rhodes' secret society, Lord Nathaniel Rothschild appointed Alfred Milner, who then recruited a group of young men from Oxford and Toynbee Hall. All were well-known English Freemasons, among them Rudyard Kipling, Arthur Balfour, also Lord Rothschild and other Oxford graduates, known collectively as 'Milner's Kindergarten.' And they, together with a number of other English Freemasons, founded the *Round Table*.

The man charged by the *Round Table* with bringing the United States within the financial control of the Rothschilds was Jacob Schiff who also financed the *Standard Oil Company* for John D. Rockefeller. One thing that we must always bear in mind is that the Illuminati and the powerful families of world banking are one and the same.

As close as may be ascertained, the current list of thirteen families of which the Illuminati/banksters is composed is as follows:

Rockefeller.
Money, Oil, Medical, Education, Think Tanks and Foundations.

John D. Rockefeller Sr. was tasked by the Rothschilds, through their agents John Jacob Astor and Jacob Schiff, to gain control of the American oil industry. The Rockefellers are themselves an important Illuminati family, being Marranos (crypto-Jews), who initially moved to Ottoman Turkey, and then France, before arriving in the US.

John D. Rockefeller Sr. founded Standard Oil, which, through the second half of the nineteenth century, achieved infamy for its ruthless practices. Growing public hostility toward monopolies, of which the *Standard Oil Trust* was the most egregious example, caused a number of states to enact anti-monopoly laws, leading to the passage of the *Sherman Antitrust Act* by Congress in 1890.

In 1892, the Ohio Supreme Court decided that *Standard Oil* was in violation of its monopoly laws but Rockefeller evaded the decision by dissolving the trust and transferring its properties to companies in other states, with interlocking directorates, so that the same men continued to control its operations. In 1899, these companies were re-united in a holding company, *Standard Oil Company of New Jersey*, which existed until 1911, when the *US Supreme Court* again declared it in violation of the *Sherman Antitrust Act*, and therefore illegal. The splintered company, although using various names, continued to be run by Rockefeller.

The history of the Rockefeller family began, with John D. Rockefeller Sr.'s father, William Avery Rockefeller. 'Big Bill,' was a travelling salesman who advertised himself as a 'William Rockefeller, the Celebrated Cancer Specialist' and who hawked 'herbal remedies and other bottled medicines.'

He guaranteed *'all cases of cancer cured unless they are too far gone,'* and these outrageous claims allowed him to charge $25 for his magic cancer cure, a sum then equivalent to two month's wages. The 'cure' survived until quite recently as '*Nujol*,' consisting principally of petroleum and peddled as a laxative. *Nujol* was manufactured by a subsidiary of Standard Oil of New Jersey, *Stanco*, whose only other product, manufactured on the same premises, was the insecticide, *'Flit.'*

Big Bill fled from a number of indictments for horse stealing, eventually disappearing altogether as William Rockefeller and re-emerging as 'Dr. William Levingston of Philadelphia,' a name which he retained for the rest of his life. An investigative reporter at Joseph Pulitzer's *New York World* newspaper, later disclosed that William Avery Rockefeller had died 11th May 1906 in Freeport, Illinois, where he was interred in an unmarked grave as the aforesaid 'Dr. William Levingston.'

He married Eliza Davison in 1837 and shortly thereafter engaged Nancy Brown as his 'housekeeper,' who became his lover and who also bore his children. On June 28, 1849, he was indicted for raping a hired girl in Cayuga, New York and later was found to be residing in Oswego, New York and was forced once again to flee. He had no difficulty in financing his 'womanising' from the sale of his miraculous cancer cure and from another product, his '*Wonder Working Liniment*,' which he offered at only $2 a bottle. It consisted of crude petroleum from which the lighter oils had been boiled away, leaving a heavy solution of paraffin, lube oil and tar, which comprised the 'liniment.'

From small beginnings in Cleveland, Ohio, John D. Rockefeller started his career as a bookkeeper and from there he then went into partnership in a refinery with the Clark brothers and eventually bought the company from them, taking great delight in the title of the 'Most Ruthless American.'

He was a profiteer during the Civil War, selling liquor to Federal troops at a high profit, gaining the initial capital to embark on his drive for a monopoly in the oil business and then in 1870, Rockefeller, along with his associates and older brother William, incorporated his petroleum holdings into the *Standard Oil Company (Ohio.)* He would buy-out his competitors or put them out of business through tactics that included price-cutting and the acquisition of such supporting enterprises as pipelines, oil terminals, and cooperage plants.

"He expanded with great daring. Borrowing wherever he could, and bringing in new partners. He realized that the only way to dominate the industry was not by producing oil, but by refining and distributing it, and undercutting his rivals by cheaper transport. With the help of a new partner, Henry Flagler, he persuaded the railroads to give secret rebates to his oil, extending the existing practice of allowing discounts for large quantities of freight." Anthony Sampson, 'The Seven Sisters.'

When Rockefeller secretly bought out rival oil companies, the executives pretended to be Rockefeller competitors and reported what other rival company executives told them. By 1870 he established a joint-stock company, called the Standard Oil Company, with a capital of a million dollars, of which he owned 27 percent. Standard Oil was already, by this time producing one tenth of the oil in America.

By 1875, Rockefeller, as president of the refiners' *Central Association*, had become the leader of the refiners. The refiners effectively took control from the producers and drillers and he formed the *Standard Oil Trust* in 1883, trading across the entire continent.

"Through the device of a trust, which held shares in each component company, Rockefeller was able to circumvent the laws which then prohibited a company in one state from owning shares in another; at the same time, he could and did pretend that all the companies were independent. He had no personal doubts about the rightness and need for this kind of concentration: 'this movement,' he said later, in a famous passage, 'was the origin of the whole system of modern economic administration. It has revolutionized the way of doing business all over the world. The time was ripe for it. It had to come. Although all we saw at the moment was to save ourselves from wasteful conditions . . . The day of combination is here to stay. Individualism has gone, never to return.'" Anthony Sampson, 'The Seven Sisters.'

From his operational hub at 26, Broadway in New York City, Rockefeller bought oilfields as well as refineries as the industry moved from Pennsylvania to Ohio, to Kansas, and on to California. *Standard Oil*'s income was larger than most states and it often 'bought' federal and state politicians in order to consolidate its position. With its huge profits, *Standard Oil* could finance its own expansion, remaining free from the grip of the banksters, whom Rockefeller resented. *Standard Oil* began exporting oil to the Middle East, the Far East and Europe and by 1885, 70% of its business was overseas.

Standard had its own network of agents throughout the world, its own intelligence service which provided information about its competitors and about political leaders in all the target market countries. The ruthlessness of Rockefeller's tactics against his competitors and his own workers (when they dared to demand a living wage,) became the focus for serious condemnation of Rockefeller and his sordid tactics. And indeed, Ida Tarbell's *'History of Standard Oil'* turned the public against the monopolistic excesses of Rockefeller.

Then in 1890, the *Sherman Anti-Trust Act* was passed but was only brought to bear much later, during Theodore Roosevelt's presidency. In 1907 a report was published by the Commissioner of Corporations and a special prosecutor, Frank Kellogg, began to detail the evidence of Standard's illegal monopoly and exorbitant profiteering—nearly a billion dollars in a quarter-century. The case was appealed in the Supreme Court which in 1911 decreed that *Standard Oil* must divest itself of all its subsidiaries.

John Davison Rockefeller, Jr., (1874-1960) was the only son and heir of John D. Rockefeller, Sr. After graduating from Brown University in 1897, he worked in family enterprises eventually personally financing the Rockefeller Centre in New York City. Also, by donating land in New York City, Rockefeller was influential in the decision to locate the United Nations headquarters in the United States. He had one daughter, Abby (born 1903), and five sons; John D. III, Nelson, Laurence, Winthrop, and David, who is still alive at the time of writing, aged 100 (b. June 1915) and to whom I will return my attention shortly.

Standard Oil today consists of…

- *Standard Oil Company of New Jersey (EXXON)*
- *Standard Oil Company of New York (MOBIL)*
- *Standard Oil Company of California (SOCAL)*
- *GULF Oil Company*
- *Texas Company (TEXACO)*

The total value of the assets of all living descendants of John D. Rockefeller is now estimated to be around 2 trillion dollars.

Astor. *Money, Drugs, Real Estate, Politics.*

The original founder of the Astor fortune was John Jacob Astor I, who was born in Waldorf, in the Duchy of Baden (Germany) of a Jewish bloodline. Their Jewish origins have been deliberately well hidden and various false stories of the Astor heritage have been circulated by them. John Jacob Astor I was a butcher in Waldorf and in 1784 he immigrated to America after a brief stopover in London, England.

The story goes, that he arrived in America penniless, and that may well be true, however he soon joined the Freemasons and within three years had become the Master of the Holland Lodge No. 8 in New York City. (This Holland Lodge is notable in that many of its members have good connections to the Illuminati elite.)

An example of a Lodge no. 8 member was Archibald Russell, 1811—1871, whose father was President of a real hotbed of Illuminati activity for many years, *The Royal Society*, of Edinburgh. By 1788, Astor was master of the lodge and this in itself is rather interesting considering that Astor allegedly could not speak English when he arrived in America, and was supposedly 'very poor.'

The first John Jacob Astor was notorious for being cold-hearted and anti-social, 'a man who had no charm, wit or grace,' according to a member of the DuPont family, who wrote a sympathetic biography entitled *The Astor Family.*

The original financial breakthrough for Astor came when he undertook a series of shady and some say, crooked real estate deals in the New York City area and following that, two men awarded John Jacob Astor a special government privilege. Those two men were President Jefferson and Secretary Gallatin, who were both Illuminati members. The United States government had placed an embargo on all US ships from sailing with goods in 1807, but Astor was granted special permission from these two men for his ship to sail with its cargo. From this enterprise he made almost $200,000 profit in 1807 money values—an absolute fortune. Astor was also able to make huge profits from the War of 1812, which crippled almost all the other American shippers. He also worked together with George Clinton, another member of the Illuminati, on land deals.

Sometime prior to 1817, John Jacob Astor I entered into the fur trade and became the biggest player of all until he sold his interests in 1834. Over the years, he had somehow managed to build up a monopoly but quite how he had managed to exclude everyone else is a very pertinent question. Bearing in mind that white people had been trapping furs in North America for several centuries and the native Indians for many centuries before that, Astor arrived and in a few short years completely owned the entire industry. This could only have been possible because of the undue influence of his friends in high places. If his position in the hierarchy had not been a privileged one then there is no doubt that the families that originally controlled the fur trade would not have allowed him to 'muscle-in' on their territory.

As a direct result of the expansion of his fur company the town of Astoria, Oregon was born and even today, perhaps in honour of the family that originally founded it, Astoria is a veritable 'hot-bed' of satanic covens. Astor however, unsurprisingly, was also on very good terms with the influential politicians of the day, perhaps because most of them were Freemasons and adepts of Satanism too. He had also been very active in the opium trade, but in 1818 he made a great public show of ending his interest in running opium to China.

"John Jacob Astor made a huge fortune out of the China opium trade, it was the Committee of 300 who chose who would be allowed to participate in the fabulously lucrative China opium trade, through its monopolistic BEIC, and the beneficiaries of their largess remained forever wedded to the Committee of 300." John Coleman, 'The Conspirator's Hierarchy: The Story of the Committee of 300,' p. 131

Interestingly another of the thirteen bloodlines, the Russells, was also one of the 'lucky' few to obtain a slice of the Chinese opium trade. It is clear from written history that Astor was repeatedly privy to inside information, and maintained his own opium courier system.

Another speculative venture that succeeded for him, was his purchase of large amounts of land in New York which rapidly increased in value. In addition the great financial panic of 1837 (yes, another one!) allowed him to foreclose on a large number of mortgages thus massively increasing his assets.

And so Astor's wealth continued to skyrocket and as one biographer wrote, *"When it came to a question of principle versus profit, Astor was a practical man."* Put simply, he had no morals or scruples whatsoever and yet despite his enormous wealth he also acquired a deserved reputation for reneging upon his legitimate debts.

Astor eventually became a bankster himself and sat on the board of five directors of the new, yet short-lived central bank, the *Bank of the United States*. How ironic that his great grandson, John Jacob Astor IV was to be such a vocal opponent of the 3rd (and successful) attempt to set up a permanent central bank, 80 years later. There is no doubt that he had become the richest man in the United States, his wealth represented approximately one-fifteenth of the whole amount invested throughout the territory of the United States.

John Jacob Astor I's descendants had a penchant for secrecy and shunned the limelight, preferring to keep a very low profile whilst others became the public faces of their enterprises. In contrast to some of the other bloodline families, the Astors often chose not to sit on boards of corporations they controlled yet nevertheless in 1890, a real estate expert calculated that they owned 5% of ALL New York City real estate. But now, after making their fortune whilst residing in the New York area, the Astors have largely all immigrated to England. However they still wield great financial power in the United States through proxies, and their collective fortune is estimated to be about £25 billion today.

William Backhouse Astor was the son of John Jacob Astor I. In the 19th Century he was infamous as a 'slum landlord' and for his deplorable treatment of thousands of people who rented from him in New York. There were repeated riots and protests by tenants who were forced to exist in terrible conditions in the slums owned by Astor, but their complaints were consistently ignored and of course the protests were brutally suppressed by the authorities who as always, act on behalf of the rich, against the poor. Only around 50% of the children of his tenants attained adulthood, a very poor ratio, even for those days.

John Jacob Astor III was the son of William Backhouse Astor, and was just as haughty, cruel and corrupt as his father and grandfather before him had been. He created and ran 'sweat shops' for the poor masses living in his New York tenements and openly supported corrupt politicians such as the criminal, 'Boss' Mayor Tweed who effectively ran New York City for his own unseemly ends. 'The Tweed Ring' stole millions of dollars from the city of New York before they were finally caught and sent to prison for the embezzlement of more than $200 million of the city's money, a vast sum in those days. The power of the Astor family and its fortune allowed JJ Astor III's involvement to remain overlooked and un-reported by the compliant press, whilst Tweed went to prison for life.

On the corner of 33rd Street and 5th Avenue, New York, the original Waldorf Hotel was built by William Waldorf, and opened in 1893. It was contemporarily described as 'the ultimate in snob appeal.' Later two Astor cousins built the Astoria in New York which opened in 1897 and the two hotels eventually merged to create the luxurious Waldorf-Astoria hotel complex.

The Astors are also very prominent in the 'Group' which is Britain's equivalent to the *Skull and Bones* secret society of which the Bush family are famously members. In Britain, the Astors, along with about 20 other families dominate the Group, just as certain families such as the Whitneys in the US, dominate the *Order of Skull and Bones*.

In 1919, the *Royal Institute of International Affairs* (RIIA) was created as a prominent arm of the Illuminati and the Astors were its major financial backers. The RIIA is in effect the British equivalent to the Council on Foreign Relations (CFR) which plays a major role in the political policy-making process in the US, albeit behind the scenes and by unelected members. Just above the CFR/RIIA in the overall hierarchy are Round Table groups which were initially named by Cecil Rhodes as the '*Association of Helpers.*' Rhodes set up the Rhodes Scholarships to recruit and bring young men from the bloodline families to Oxford University, to be initiated into the Illuminati and to be instructed in the tenets of and the furtherance of the *New World Order* agenda.

The Astor family in London eventually split into two powerful segments with one branch of the family based on the Cliveden Estate and the other becoming 'Barons,' the Astors of Hever. William Waldorf Astor owned the *Pall Mall Gazette*, the *Observer*, and the *Pall Mall* Magazine and in addition, the *Times* of London has been controlled by the Astors since 1922. However, most of the assets and wealth of the 13 bloodline families is hidden in order to avoid identification of the source.

The Astor dominated *Institute for Pacific Relations* (IPR) was the group that was behind the Illuminati's decision to allow Red China to share in the opium trade and also helped lay the groundwork for the Pearl Harbor attack. The Astors also were instrumental in the appeasement policy in Europe which allowed Hitler to re-arm Germany and threaten British interests, the ultimate pre-cursor to World War II.

They were also involved in the temperance movement against alcoholic drink which was ostensibly begun by the *Women's Christian Temperance Union*. The Temperance movement was an elite-creation which allowed families such as the Kennedys and Onassis, also two of the thirteen Illuminati families to become immensely rich by virtue of control of the 'bootlegging industry' in the 1920s and 30s. Today's equivalent of the Temperance movement is the drug trade, another illuminati-controlled enterprise worth hundreds of millions, if not billions, annually.

As do their partners in crime, the Rothschilds, DuPonts and Rockefellers, the Astors always select a patriarch, the eldest male and this privilege is passed down from generation to generation as a birth-right within the different branches of the family, just as a king passes on the throne to the eldest male heir.

Russell. *Money, Drugs, Skull and Bones.*

The story of the Russell family begins at Yale University, where three elements of American social history, espionage, drug smuggling and secret societies, become one.

Elihu Yale for whom the University is named, was born near Boston, educated in London and served with the British East India Company, eventually becoming governor of Fort Saint George, Madras, in 1687. He amassed a great fortune from trade and returned to England in 1699. Yale became known as quite a philanthropist and upon receiving a request from the Collegiate School in Connecticut, he sent a donation and a gift of books. After further, subsequent bequests, it was proposed in 1718 that the school be named Yale College.

A statue of Nathan Hale stands on Old Campus at Yale University with an identical copy in front of the CIA headquarters in Langley, Virginia. Yet another stands in front of Phillips Academy in Andover, Massachusetts (where George Bush the elder went to prep school and joined a secret society at age twelve.) Nathan Hale, along with three other Yale graduates, was a member of the 'Culper Ring,' one of America's first intelligence operations, established by George Washington and effective throughout the Revolutionary War. Nathan Hale was its only operative to be captured by the British, and after making public his famous 'regrets,' he was hanged in 1776. Since the founding of the American nation, the relationship between Yale and the 'intelligence community,' has been particularly strong.

Then in 1823, Samuel Russell established *Russell and Company* for the primary purpose of acquiring opium in Turkey and smuggling it into China, later merging with the Perkins (Boston) syndicate in 1830 and becoming the primary American opium dealer. Indeed many great American and European fortunes were built on the China opium trade.

One of *Russell and Company's* Chief of Operations in Canton was Warren Delano, Jr., grandfather of Franklin Delano Roosevelt. Other Russell partners included John Cleve Green (who financed Princeton University,) Abel Low (who financed construction of Columbia University,) Joseph Coolidge and the Perkins, Sturgis and Forbes families. (Coolidge's son founded the *United Fruit Company*, and his grandson, Archibald C. Coolidge, was a co-founder of the *Council on Foreign Relations*.)

William Huntington Russell, Samuel's cousin, studied in Prussia (now part of modern-day Germany) in 1831-32, a period when the region was a hotbed of new ideas. It was at this time that the 'scientific method' was being freely applied to all forms of human endeavour and as a result, Prussia, which blamed the defeat of its forces by Napoleon in 1806 on soldiers only thinking about themselves in the stress of battle, took the principles set forth by John Locke and Jean Rousseau and created a new educational system. Johan Fitche, in his address to the German People, declared that the children would be taken over by the State and told what to think and how to think it, an early form of Marxism / Communism.

Georg Wilhelm Friedrich Hegel took over Fitche's chair at the University Of Berlin in 1817 and was a professor there until his death in 1831. Hegel was the embodiment of the Prussian idealistic philosophy school of Immanuel Kant and to him, the world was a world 'of reason.' The state was 'Absolute Reason' and the citizen could achieve true freedom only by worship and obedience to the state. Hegel called the state the 'march of God in the world' and 'the final end.' This final end, Hegel declared, 'has supreme right against the individual, whose supreme duty is to be a member of the state.' Communism has its philosophical roots in Hegelianism and this philosophy was very much in vogue during William Russell's time in Prussia. The 'Hegelian Dialectic,' otherwise known as 'Problem, Reaction and Solution' is also a product of Hegel's philosophy.

Upon Russell's return to Yale in 1832, he formed a secret society with Alphonso Taft, the *Order of Skull and Bones* and according to information acquired from a break-in to the 'tomb' (the Skull and Bones meeting hall) in 1876, '... Bones is a chapter of a corps in a German University... General Russell, its founder, was in Germany before his Senior Year and formed a warm friendship with a leading member of a German society. He brought back with him to college, authority to found a chapter here.' So class valedictorian William H. Russell, along with fourteen others, became the founding members of '*The Order of Skull and Bones.*'

In 1833, the young members adopted the skull and bones symbol as their 'logo' and at the same time, the number 322 became part of the emblem of the organisation. 322 BCE was actually the year in which the Greek orator Demosthenes died.

In 1856, Skull and Bones was officially registered under the name *Russell Trust*, owned by William H. Russell and on 13th March of the same year, the organisation moved its headquarters into a sinister mausoleum-like building within the confines of Yale University and appropriately named 'the Tomb.' Allegedly, there are innumerable human skulls and bones in the 'tomb,' the keeping of which, is illegal under Connecticut law.

Each year one of the responsibilities of the cohort of fifteen seniors is to select fifteen new junior members to replace them. This is known as being 'tapped' (selected) for the society. To be tapped for Skull and Bones is seen by many Yale students as the highest honour that can be attained, though occasionally some do refuse. 'Bones' members meet at least weekly and conduct an ongoing analysis of each other, including revealing their innermost secrets and their sexual activities, aimed at creating a long term bond between them, which continues after leaving university and taking their place in society. However this is also used as a lever for blackmail to keep the member 'in order.' Within the Bones 'tomb' are rooms which some believe to be used for satanic worship and other occult practices. Kris Milligan claimed that the room is arranged to represent an entrance into a higher level of the Bavarian Illuminati.

In the tomb, members dine from a china dinner service and using silverware formerly belonging to Adolf Hitler and consume expensive gourmet meals cooked for them by their own personal chefs. Each member is given a secret code-name and refer to themselves as 'knights' and to outsiders as 'barbarians.'

The Order encourages members to view the world outside of Skull and Bones in a desensitised and dispassionate way, thus allowing them to treat the rest of humanity in a scornful and derisive manner, totally devoid of empathy or compassion. The clocks in the 'tomb' are intentionally set five minutes ahead of the rest of their time zone in order that the 'Bonesmen' may feel an ongoing sense of existing in a totally separate world from the 'barbarians.'

'Tapping' is partially a response to visible or anticipated future excellence, thus it could be considered meritocratic. However, a the great majority of members are repeatedly drawn from the same core families thus rendering it a typical nested, generational-driven secret society with little chance of gaining access unless born into certain privileged families.

The family names of Skull and Bones-men roll off the tongue like a 'Who's Who' of American high society. Whitney, Taft, Jay, Bundy, Harriman, Weyerhaeuser, Pinchot, Rockefeller, Goodyear, Sloane, Stimson, Phelps, Perkins, Pilsbury, Kellogg, Vanderbilt, Bush and Kerry. Both John Kerry and George W. Bush are members of Skull and Bones and Bush famously refused to talk about their common membership in the Order of Death during his 9th February 2004 appearance on NBC's 'Meet the Press.' In another interview, when Bush was asked what he could reveal about Skull and Bones, he said, *'Well not much, because it's a secret...Sorry, I wish there was something I could manifest...'* before quickly changing the subject. Bush appointed eleven Skull and Bones members to his Administration in his first term alone.

William Russell went on to become a general and a state legislator in Connecticut. Alphonso Taft was appointed US Attorney General, Secretary of War (a post many 'Bonesmen' have held throughout the decades), Ambassador to Austria, and Ambassador to Russia (another post held by many 'Bonesmen.') His son, William Howard Taft was the only man to become both President of the United States and Chief Justice of the Supreme Court.

Li. *Money, Drugs, Politics and Vice*

The Rothschild and the Rockefeller families hold a very great respect for the Chinese and Japanese people and so China and Japan have been offered the chance to become important players in the '*New World Order.*'

The Li family has a long history in China, for example, during the Tang Dynasty around 15 different families were given the honour of using the name. Li Yuan was the founder of the Tang Dynasty which lasted from 618 to 906 AD and his son who succeeded him was Li Shimin. It was ironically during this dynasty that printing and paper money were introduced to China.

Today, the Lis control Red China, Hong Kong and Singapore and hold important positions in Taiwan. If the Lis which control these various nations are related, which is suspected by many researchers to be the case, then this is certainly one of the most powerful families in the world. In fact in terms of power, they are equally as influential as the Rockefellers in America.

They are also connected to several secretive, Chinese occult societies and as far as can be ascertained, the Li family In Hong Kong is part of the satanic hierarchy and works hand in glove with the British and American elite bankster families as well as being inextricably linked to the *Triads*, the Chinese 'Mafia.'

The Triads have an extremely long, colourful and even sordid history. They are a secret fraternity much like the Freemasons, yet they also have the appearance of a revolutionary army combined with the Mafia. They are all these things in one package and so are a much more complex group to attempt to understand. Their heritage and history make them almost a sub-culture and a sub-culture that is extremely difficult for law enforcement agencies to infiltrate, and their blood oaths and traditions bind them together and create a virtually impenetrable barrier to 'outsiders.'

Before Mao Tse Tung and his Communists took over in 1949, the Triads virtually ran China unopposed. For instance, it was discovered that in 1917, the Triads, along with the then Vice-President of the Republic of China were embezzling public funds on a large scale, to purchase opium in order to compete in the drug trade with the British and other western interests. Indeed many leaders of China prior to the Communist takeover were Triad leaders as well as also being Freemasons.

But, after the Communists took power, the Triads were forced 'underground.' The Communists made no attempt to eliminate the Triads altogether, but they did suppress their activities, forcing them to operate in secrecy rather than overtly. After the Tiananmen Square Massacre in 1989, the Triads smuggled the leaders of the democratic movement out of Red China but as already stated, the Communists have never quite managed to destroy their immense power.

In fact, the Triads are the most powerful criminal fraternity in the world, except for the Illuminati families that make up the Illuminati's 'Committee of 300.' The Mafia are mere 'newbies' and amateurs in comparison with the Triads who are almost 'untouchable' by any law enforcement group and they have operated with impunity in the United States for over 100 years, are major drug suppliers working in co-operation with the Illuminati, yet most Americans do not even know of their existence. And although America has many citizens of Chinese descent, they generally are unfamiliar with the Chinese dialects that any would-be undercover agents would have to know to infiltrate the Triad operations.

By 1931, there were eight main Triad groups and they had divided-up Hong Kong into geographic areas and ethnic groups for which each was responsible. These groups were the *Wo*, the *Rung*, the *Tung*, the *Chuen*, the *Shing*, the *Fuk Yee Hing*, the *Yee On*, and the *Luen*. Each had its own headquarters, its own sub-societies, and its own seemingly innocuous public 'covers.' The Fuk Yee Hing's cover for example, was that it was registered as a workers benevolent society. It consisted of 12 branch offices and a membership of 10,000.

Yee On's cover was as the '*Yee On Commercial and Industrial Guild.*' The Wo operated as a death gratuity association and in a similar way they were all disguised by their totally innocent-sounding names. Many martial arts clubs and organisations were also fronts for, or had affiliations with the Triads, and indeed continue to be associated with them, not only in Hong Kong but to some degree in all other countries too. The Triad group that works most closely with the Illuminati is the *Yee On Commercial and Industrial Guild*, which is the prime controller of the Kowloon Walled City which produced sex toys for the international market.

Today in Hong Kong there may be as many as 60 different Triad Societies operating. The largest numerically is the Yee On, with 33,000 members but the overall Triad influence is widespread, Vancouver, San Francisco, New York, London, Manchester and Amsterdam (not to mention Macao and Hong Kong) are just some of the bases of Triad Operation. Their money is made by extortion, gambling, prostitution and drugs and the Triads have collaborated closely with the CIA in creating the drug network. The creation of the Golden Triangle as a source for drugs was a joint CIA-Triad operation. Indeed, with the advent of the 1960s CIA-instigated drug culture the Triads introduced 'Pure No. 4' heroin into England to replace the 'Brown Sugar' that the Rolling Stones had famously sung about.

Every city In Britain where a sizeable group of ethnic Chinese are located, the Triads have a foothold, which in effect means **all** British cities. Most of the couriers for the Triads today are in fact Europeans and they are now using British banks rather than the Hong Kong banks in order to 'launder' their dirty money.

In addition, the Triads control the drug trade in New York City almost totally now and the only possible way that this could have been achieved was through the co-operation and goodwill of the major Illuminati families. Without this co-operation from 'above,' the Triads would quickly find themselves out of business.

So, in conclusion, the Li family controls Hong Kong through the Triads and the Triads are an occult fraternity, far bigger than Freemasonry, but less well-known despite their close ties to the Illuminati. Li Ka-Shing is the billionaire, de-facto ruler of Hong Kong and a major figure in the occult world. It was the Illuminati that assisted the Li's in establishing the *Li Commercial Bank* in New York, most likely as a reward for General Li Mi and his successor, Li Wen-Huan for having originally planted the poppy-growing fields in the Golden Triangle in order to produce the drugs marketed by the other Elite, bankster families.

We only need to observe known members of the Illuminati, such as *Skull and Bones* George Bush treat the Chinese Lis with such respect and friendship, even when it was Li Peng that crushed innocent people at Tiananmen Square, to realise that the Li family in China is also part of the Illuminati. Why else would the Rockefellers and Rothschilds also have such a cosy relationship with them and why does the Premier of the People's Republic of China, Li Peng always socialise with the Rockefellers and several other capitalists when he visits New York City, if he is such a hard-line communist?

Are the 'filthy capitalists' not the communists' sworn enemies? It is all one big illusion, one big 'game' I'm afraid, and we are the innocent dupes who lose every time.

Bundy. *Money, Politics*

The Bundy family, has a long history of connection with the world of occult and NWO organisations and are active members of the class of aristocracy sometimes referred to as the 'Boston Brahmin.' Throughout the last two centuries, they have been in highly influential positions within the governmental hierarchy of the United States, at various levels.

Jonas Mills Bundy (1835-1891) was a key advisor to President Grant, President Garfield and President Chester Arthur.

Harvey Hollister Bundy (1888-1963) was inducted into Skull and Bones in 1909. He was the 'Special Assistant' to Secretary of War, Henry Stimson (also Skull and Bones), a law clerk for Justice Oliver Wendell Holmes, the key Pentagon man on the *Manhattan Project*, secretary of the *US Sugar Equalization Board*, Chairman of the *Panama Railway Co.*, Chairman of *Boston Personal Property Trust*, director of *Boston Five Cents Savings Bank*, director of *State Street and Union Trust Companies*, director of *New England Merchants* and director of *R.M. Bradley Co.* In 1952, he became the chairman of the *Carnegie Endowment for International Peace*, chairman of *Foreign Bondholders Protective Council*, trustee and president of the *World Peace Foundation*, chairman of *Wellesley College* and chairman of the *New England Rhodes Scholarships Selection Committee*.

Harvey H. Bundy was one of the most prominent figures in the supervision of the *Manhattan Project*, responsible for developing the Atomic bomb. He was also the liaison between the *War Department* and the *Office of Scientific Research and Development.*

Then in *1952*, Harvey assumed control of the *Carnegie Endowment for Peace* from John Foster Dulles. *The Carnegie Endowment for Peace* has been a major vehicle for the Illuminati in the covert financing of various 'tax-free' projects. For example, in 1971, the organisation spent over $2 million, and had assets of $41 million. The stated object of the foundation is 'to promote international peace,' or at least reading between the lines, the kind of 'peace' that President George Bush told the United Nations that the world needed and that of course is the 'One World Government' (NWO) type of 'peace.'

Frederick McGeorge Bundy was initiated into Skull and Bones in 1921 and McGeorge Bundy, son of Frederick, was initiated in 1940 later becoming a member of the Council on Foreign Relations (CFR) and the Bilderberger Group. His brother, William Putnam Bundy, a 1939 Skull and Bones inductee, edited the Council on Foreign Relations magazine, *Foreign Affairs* and was a permanent member of the Bilderberger steering committee. He was also a partner in the law firm, *Covington and Burling,* a firm that represents many of the bankster and Illuminati Elite in Washington, D.C. *Covington and Burling* also appears to have been a front for the Illuminati in creating an extreme left-wing political movement in the US. In 1951 he quit *Covington and*

Burling to join the CIA as an analyst eventually attaining the position of Assistant to the Deputy Director of the CIA.

Most people would not necessarily recognise the Bundy name as that of a powerful Elite family, however, in the 1960s the two Bundy brothers (above) held the key positions that controlled most of the information that was fed to US Presidents, Kennedy and Johnson during their terms of office. When Johnson attained the highest office in the wake of JFK's assassination, McGeorge Bundy occupied the key position of National Security Advisor, a post which determined precisely what information reached the President's eyes and ears. His brother was also in a key State Department position and significantly, both Bundy brothers were also fraternal brothers of the Illuminati Order of the Skull and Bones. In addition to the above, McGeorge Bundy sat on MJ-12, which is the council of 'wise men' that covertly rules the United States.

Harry W. Bundy was also known to be a practising satanist and 'Chief Adept' of the Rosicrucians, another secretive sect with strong links to the Illuminati.

In 1953, Senator Joseph McCarthy became notorious almost overnight for his alleged 'commie hunting' activities throughout American politics, even dragging Hollywood into his net along the way. He has ever-since been vilified by the compliant mainstream media as some sort of 'crazy' or 'fanatic' for his actions. However the real, unreported truth is that McCarthy had discovered and tapped into the New World Order conspiracy and recognised its communistic leanings and the danger to the US constitution that it posed. He was, as it turns out, a patriot merely trying to get to the truth about what was really going on in the upper echelons of American politics and society and it is absolutely clear from his own writings that it was the NWO that he was opposing, not simply 'individuals with communist tendencies,' as has been falsely portrayed in order to discredit him and his actions. One of McCarthy's 'victims' at his *House Un-American Activities Committee* hearings just happened to be William P. Bundy, whom he had subpoenaed to testify.

The subpoena was instigated because McCarthy discovered that Bundy had donated at least $500 to help the infamous communist spy, Alger Hiss defend himself. Hiss's brother Donald incidentally, had also worked for *Covington and Burling* alongside Bundy and Senator McCarthy knew that if Bundy was questioned, it would help him expose the truth although he also realised that he would almost certainly lie under oath to protect himself and his fellow conspirators. However, Allen Dulles, the notorious CIA chief who was also Illuminati, arranged to smuggle Bundy out of the country so that he would not have to face McCarthy's intrusive questioning. The State Department had issued an arrest warrant for Bundy but as he was about to be detained at New York docks, Dulles somehow contrived to get the State Department to cancel the arrest by the 'calling-in' of a favour allowing Bundy to sail away, unmolested into the sunset on the liner *Queen Mary*.

"I note your refusal to give us any answers to our questions. Your insistence is very revealing. It would seem that the last man in the world who would try to protect and hide the facts about one of his top officers' association with, and contributions to, a convicted traitor

would be the head of the CIA. I think it necessary for me to call your attention to the tremendous damage you thereby do to this organization. That the matter cannot and will not rest here is, of course, obvious." Senator Joseph McCarthy's subsequent letter to CIA Director, Alan Dulles.

Lou Russell who was an important figure in McCarthy's *House Un-American Activities Committee* (HUAC) was also, significantly, part of the Illuminati power structure. This is not an unusual occurrence and is one of the Elite's usual tactics i.e. infiltrate the 'enemy' and thereby control them from the inside—or at least be aware of their every move. But by attempting to subject a member of one of the top 13 Illuminati families to Congressional questioning, McCarthy had in effect signed his own death warrant and the execution was soon expedited. McCarthy has been thoroughly demonised down the generations even though his only crime was that of attempting to protect America from the insidious NWO / bankster agenda. Skull and Bones' most famous son, George H. W. Bush was still denigrating McCarthy even during his 1992 Presidential campaign, forty years after the event.

Whilst the Hiss/Bundy affair led to McCarthy, who was a genuine American patriot, being thoroughly discredited and murdered, conversely a closet communist and lackey of the CFR was given wide publicity as an anti-communist hero. Richard Nixon (member of CFR) was falsely credited for helping to convict Hiss (also CFR) in order to build a false public image for him as an anti-communist crusader. However as President and protected by his 'anti-communist' reputation, Nixon officially recognised Red China, amongst many other pro-communist, NWO-friendly acts.

As for William P. Bundy himself, he later commented on the help Allen Dulles gave him throughout the Hiss affair... *"I guess there was an element of tribal loyalty in the way Allen handled this, that he knew me, he knew my brother, a sort of fellow feeling, a feeling for the comradeship of the CIA but also a tribal feeling toward a set of people who were in law firms, entered government when the need was felt, could be invited back to the house."*

Yes indeed, that 'set of people' is better known as the Illuminati banksters.

In 1960, Bundy whilst still with the CIA was named as the Staff Director of the new *Presidential Commission on National Goals.* If national goals are seriously being set, then that implies that something is happening above and beyond the democratic process, Congressmen voting in Congress and the market-place simply functioning unaided. However it is blatantly obvious that there is a 'guiding hand' behind all events. Nothing in politics or high-finance ever happens by accident and this is all leading us down a pre-planned route to achieve Illuminati and bankster goals, primarily the inception of their long-awaited *'New World Order.'*

Bundy's *Presidential Commission on National Goals* set-out objectives that are pure Hegelian philosophy. These goals stated that the individual has a duty to advance the will of the state and that the state...

"... is to stimulate changes of attitude... and the American citizen in the years ahead

ought to devote a larger portion of his time and energy directly to solution of the nation's problems ... many ways are open for citizens to participate in the attainment of national goals." Dr. Anthony Sutton, *'America's Secret Establishment'* p.50

In the late Dr. Sutton's excellent book which thoroughly dissects the *Order of Skull and Bones*, he describes how McGeorge Bundy received preferential treatment all through his life. Consistently, McGeorge Bundy was offered jobs for which there were many better qualified candidates. Bundy was initiated into the Skull and Bones in 1940 and subsequently joined the US Army as a Private. However, very few Privates ever achieve the rate of promotion that Bundy achieved. Within a year of enlisting as a Private he was already a Captain but not only was he promoted to Captain, he was also placed on the committee involved in planning the logistics of the invasions of both Sicily and Normandy. Truly incredible, as I am sure you would agree.

As Sutton pointed out on page 51 of his book ... *"Can a 23 year-old, with no military experience, undertake planning for amphibious operations? The answer is obviously no, even if his father (also Skull and Bones) ... is an aide to the Secretary of War (unsurprisingly, also Skull and Bones)."*

In 1945, he became assistant to the Secretary of War and co-authored a book with Stimson and after the war, Bundy continued his phenomenal climb up the ladder, from job to job to even more important role, often with no credentials qualifying him for such positions. Then in 1949, Bundy was invited to Harvard University to teach as an assistant professor and within four years was made the Dean of the Faculty of Arts and Sciences at Harvard! How does anyone become Dean of a prestigious University department after a mere four years of teaching? Not only was he regarded as an instant military genius and an economic whizz-kid, now he was suddenly head of Arts and Sciences at what is probably the most prestigious seat of learning in the entire country, if not the world.

Unsurprisingly given his ongoing track record, by 1961 he had become the Special Assistant for National Security Affairs to the President, holding the power of veto as to what the President is or is not made privy. For example, on pages 177-178 of *America's Secret Establishment*, Sutton quotes a conversation between McGeorge Bundy, Dean Achison (Scroll and Key—another Illuminati, college secret society akin to Skull and Bones) and President Kennedy, recorded in a memorandum. Kennedy was deceptively led to believe that the United States had deserted its ally of Portugal to aid nationalists in Angola, when in fact the US was supporting Marxist guerrillas in the same conflict.

In 1966, Bundy was appointed President of the *Ford Foundation*, another Illuminati foundation that now promotes the NWO agenda thanks to Bundy's infiltration. He then appointed Harold Howe to be his Vice President, a position for which Howe was singularly unqualified, except of course that Howe was another Skull and Bones inductee and was an NWO 'team player' that would help further the New World Order with all its inherent Hegelian philosophy and so-called 'socialism.' Incidentally, both of the Fords on the Foundation board resigned in disgust at the way the infiltrating 'Bonesmen' were using the Ford Foundation to further their own (i.e. the NWO) agenda.

Onassis. *Money, Oil, Drugs, Politics*

Aristotle Socrates Onassis—named after two Greek philosophers, went from being totally penniless at age 21 to being a millionaire at age 23. He was an Illuminati 'king,' a shipping tycoon, an intelligent, ruthless, driven man who spoke several languages; Greek, French, Spanish, English, Italian and Turkish.

Aristotle's father had planned to send him to Oxford University, but the Turkish genocide of the ethnic Greek Turks changed his plans and instead he set sail to Argentina, supposedly stateless and broke. It was said that he finally found a job as a dishwasher in a bar in Buenos Aires and then shortly afterwards in 1924, he was offered a position with the *British United River Plate Telephone Co.* (Argentina was often at this time referred to as the 'fifth British Dominion' because the British Rothschilds and other British investors owned so much of Argentina). Over the course of the next few years, Onassis proved himself very capable and in the background had been developing a successful tobacco importing organisation using his father's contacts and influence, supplied via Greece. Although profitable in its own right, the importing of tobacco was merely the cover for a vastly more profitable, opium running enterprise.

After two years of successful trading, Onassis began manufacturing cigarettes, thus removing the need for importing the tobacco. Again this was a cover but Onassis illegally 'borrowed' the name of a famous Argentine brand of cigarettes, BIS, and labelled his own cigarettes as such. However, the owner of BIS sued Onassis for using his company's name and won an injunction against him ultimately causing the business to fail. Regardless of this fact, history and Onassis's biographers still credit cigarette manufacturing as being the source of his vast wealth, whilst at the same time acknowledging that he lost money from it and had to withdraw because of its unprofitability—a contradiction no doubt designed to obscure his large scale involvement in the drugs trade.

Onassis associated with many powerful people and the fact that he mixed with establishment figures with Elite connections is unsurprising of a man of his wealth. However, it is the nature of his involvement with other Illuminati figures that reveals his true standing.

"Onassis dropping-in on Prince Alfonso Hoheiohe's Marbella Club in southern Spain and lunching with Baron and Baroness Guy de Rothschild (amidst rumours that it was Rothschild money that had supplanted his own in Monte Carlo) was obviously a noteworthy social incident." 'Onassis,' p. 255

During WWII, Onassis was a regular guest of the movie mogul Spyros Skouras at Mamaroneck on Long Island and amongst many other famous, close friends of Onassis was Eva Peron, the wife of the Argentinian dictator and with whom Onassis allegedly had an affair. He also had extensive Nazi connections that continued throughout his entire life, as indeed did the Perons. For instance, one of Onassis' Nazi associates was

Hjalmar Schacht, president of Hitler's *Reichbank*, who Onassis hired after the war. Schacht was employed by Onassis' shipyards in Germany, engaged in the building of oil-tankers after WWII.

Another extremely close friend of his was Winston Churchill. The mass-murderer and Freemason Churchill, was from a family (Churchill / Marlborough) that has long-been part of the ruling Elite that secretly runs the world. On several occasions, during Churchill's many holidays on Onassis' yacht *Christina* he informed Onassis that the only person that he could trust during WWII was Josef Stalin and this of course is very far from being the story portrayed in our history books. Onassis was also friendly with Winston Churchill's friend, Bernard Baruch.

It is widely believed that Baruch was the man who convinced Winston Churchill to join the Illuminati (NWO) conspiracy and he achieved this by demonstrating in New York in 1929, how the banksters could destroy the Stock Market at will. It was this dramatic demonstration of their ultimate power that brought Churchill on board.

Two more of Onassis' Illuminati friends were Joseph Kennedy (the father of JFK) and Peter Grace. Both men also were an intrinsic part of the thirteen Illuminati bloodline families. Gianni Agnelli, the owner of the Italian, *Fiat* car manufacturer and a powerful man in the Illuminati, also spent time on a number of occasions on Onassis' yacht *Christina* while it was in the Mediterranean Sea.

In 1928, the Illuminati owners of all the world's major oil companies had come together at Achnacarry Castle and formally created the '*Achnacarry Agreement,*' which in effect created a worldwide international oil cartel. This covert monopoly may be recognised by the fact that the same oil-tanker truck will often deliver to several different fuel stations in an area, regardless of whether it may be for example, a BP station (Rothschild) or an Exxon (Esso) station (Rockefeller.) Understanding this one fact, that the world's oil has been totally controlled by an Illuminati monopoly since 1928, will also help in the understanding that Onassis, the man who built the largest fleet of oil-tanker ships was also Illuminati, through and through.

In 1932, during the depths of the Great Depression, Onassis somehow bought his first six tankers for a fraction of their actual value (many, many more were soon to follow,) and then during the war he leased his tankers and other vessels to the Allies, making an absolute fortune in the process. Then, following the war, Onassis bought 23 surplus Liberty ships from the United States and embarked on a programme to build progressively larger oil tankers, soon becoming the world's foremost transporter of oil and petroleum. It was in fact he, who initiated the construction of a new breed of 'supertankers,' in 1954 alone, commissioning the building of seventeen such vessels. During the Arab-Israeli wars in 1956 and 1967, his tankers reaped immense profits transporting oil from the Middle East via the Cape of Good Hope route after the Suez Canal had been closed.

In 1953 Onassis purchased a controlling interest in the *Société des Bains de Mer*, which owned the casino, hotels and much other real estate in the upper-crust resort of Monte

Carlo. From 1957 to 1974 he also owned and operated *Olympic Airways*, the Greek national airlines, under concession from the Greek government.

Du Pont. *Money, Chemicals, Politics*

The family tend to spell their name as 'du Pont,' yet the official business name is written 'DuPont.'

E. I. du Pont was born Éleuthère Irénée du Pont de Nemours on 24th June 1771, in Paris. His father, Pierre du Pont de Nemours, was a watchmaker by trade and later a publisher. In the years before the French Revolution, Pierre was also an advisor to the monarchy on economic matters.

In his youth, du Pont was not interested in academic subjects, but had a fascination with explosives, engaging in his own independent research. At the age of 14, he entered the Royal College in Paris, where he became an apprentice to the renowned French chemist Antoine-Laurent Lavoisier. Lavoisier rapidly advanced the young du Pont's knowledge of chemistry as well as botany and agriculture and a few years later, after completing his apprenticeship, du Pont began to manage his father's publishing house. It was around this time that du Pont met Sophie Madeleine Dalmas and they married in 1791 and went on to have eight children.

Like his father, du Pont initially supported the French Revolution, believing that the government could undergo a peaceful transition to 'democracy,' but as events spiralled out of control in 1792, du Pont and members of his family found themselves defending the king from a mob besieging the Tuileries Palace in Paris. Although they succeeded in saving the king, this action made them some deadly enemies within the revolutionary movement and as the Reign of Terror raged, Pierre du Pont narrowly escaped the guillotine in 1794.

Éleuthère and Pierre du Pont decided to flee to the United States in order to seek safety for the family, landing in Rhode Island on 1st January 1800. Eventually the rest of the family followed and they all re-settled in Delaware. It was whilst hunting with a friend, Colonel Louis de Toussard that Éleuthère noticed that American-made gunpowder was comparatively poor in quality and very expensive and so, sensing an opportunity, du Pont travelled back to France with his brother, Victor, to obtain plans, machinery and financial support to start a gunpowder business in the United States. In 1803, he established *E.I. du Pont, de Nemours and Co.* on the Brandywine River near Wilmington, Delaware.

In order to challenge England's domination of the global gunpowder trade, it was Napoleon Bonaparte himself who helped finance du Pont in the establishment of his American gunpowder business in 1802. The first sale of gunpowder of the newly established company was to a close family friend, President Thomas Jefferson.

Du Pont was fanatical about the quality of his product and by 1811, all his diligence in that regard had resulted in his company becoming the largest manufacturer of gunpowder in the United States. The du Ponts continued to diversify their business, opening a woollen mill on the Brandywine River, as well as a cotton mill and a tannery, all of which were very successful. Helped by a massive boost in sales during the War of 1812, du Pont invested most of his profits back into the now rapidly expanding business conglomerate.

However, the company did have an occasional setback. Two explosions during the years 1815 and 1818 resulted in nearly 50 deaths and considerable financial losses, but the company rebounded and continued to prosper.

The company continued to expand quickly and by the mid-19th century had become the largest supplier of gunpowder to the United States military, supplying over half the gunpowder used by the Union Army during the Civil War.

Du Pont was the major supplier of gunpowder during many wars, including:

- War of 1812 (supplying the US against Britain/Canada)
- Mexican-American War, 1846 (supplying the US)
- Indian Wars, 1827-1896 (supplying the genocidal westward expansion)
- Crimean War, 1854 (supplying both England and Russia)
- Spanish-American War, 1898 (supplying the US)
- WWI, 1914-1918 (supplied all US orders and 40% of the Allies' total requirements)

The DuPont gunpowder factories totally dominated the industry. Henry du Pont (1812-1889) took control of gunpowder manufacturing when he was thirty-eight. However, he was an authoritarian and was known as 'Boss Henry' to his maligned and downtrodden workforce. His narrow-minded, backward and Machiavellian ideas almost ran the DuPont Company into the ground in spite of their virtual monopoly of the gunpowder market.

When he died, family members Alfred I. du Pont, Pierre Samuel du Pont II (1870-1954), and Thomas Coleman du Pont (1863-1930) assumed control of various DuPont interests and together revived the flagging fortunes of the now-aging Du Pont factories. They also contrived to buy-out their few remaining competitors, thus giving them an absolute monopoly in the munitions industry.

DuPont does not subscribe to capitalism. As is the case with all Elite-run corporations, its goal is absolute monopoly—which is tantamount to communism. Of course this is dressed-up in palatable yet deceptive terms such as 'bringing order and stability to a fragmented and chaotic industry.' They will attempt to achieve this legally (or often illegally) by creatively circumventing 'anti-trust' laws and employing armies of highly paid lawyers to further their ends in this respect.

In 1897, when it was illegally agreed with European competitors to divide-up the world and become a cartel, DuPont was awarded exclusive control of gunpowder sales in the Americas and by 1905, the company had assets of $60 million and was the automatic recipient of all US government gunpowder orders. DuPont then eventually diversified into newspaper publishing, chemicals, paints, varnishes, cellophane and rayon. During WWI the world's largest producer of dynamite and smokeless gunpowder, made hitherto unheard-of net profits of $250 million.

Between the wars, DuPont became the world's leading manufacturer of explosives, the world's foremost chemical company and the greatest producer of cars (General Motors) and synthetic rubber, another strategic war material. By the 1930s, it owned Mexican and Chilean explosive companies and a Canadian chemical company. Although still by this time the top US gunpowder supplier, this product represented only 2% of its total turnover.

DuPont's *General Motors* notoriously funded a vigilante / terrorist organisation to oppose unionisation of its Midwestern factories. Known as the *Black Legion*, its members wore black robes decorated with a white skull and crossbones. Anonymous behind their slitted hoods, this KKK-like network of thugs planted bombs in union meeting-halls, set fire to labour activists' homes, tortured union representatives, in the process killing at least 50 in Detroit alone. Many of their victims were black people lured North by the false promises of well-paid jobs in the blossoming car manufacturing industry. One of their victims, the Reverend Earl Little, was murdered in 1931 and his son, later known as Malcolm X, was then six years old. He would later say that his earliest memory was the night-time raid in 1929 when the *Black Legion* burnt down their house.

The *Black Legion*, claiming 200,000 members in Michigan alone, was divided into distinct squads, each focused on a different aspect of their work for DuPont; arson, bombing and execution.

Thanks to a Senate Munitions Investigating Committee (1934-1936) that examined criminal, war profiteering practices of armaments manufacturing companies during WWI, the public learned that DuPont had led munitions companies in sabotaging a League of Nations' disarmament conference in Geneva.

The committee's chairman, Gerald Nye, said that, "*... once the munitions people of the world had made the treaty a satisfactory one to themselves, Colonel Simons [of DuPont] is reporting that even the State Department realised, in effect, who controlled the Nation.*"

The du Ponts fought back against widespread public condemnation that rightly labelled them as the 'merchants of death,' they surely were. They claimed that 'communists' were behind the Senate hearings and blamed the Committee for undermining US military power. In response, Chairman Nye, a Republican from North Dakota, pointed-out that DuPont had made six times more profit during WWI than during the preceding four years ... "*...so naturally Mr. du Pont sees red when he sees these profits attacked by international peace.*"

In 1929, GM acquired Adam Opel, Germany's largest car manufacturer and in 1974, a Senate Subcommittee on Anti-trust and Monopoly heard evidence from researcher Bradford Snell proving that that in 1935, GM had opened an Opel factory to supply the Nazis with 'Blitz' military trucks. In appreciation, for this help, Adolf Hitler awarded GM's chief executive for overseas operations, James Mooney, with the Order of the German Eagle (first class.) Besides military trucks, Germany's GM workers also produced armoured cars, tanks and bomber engines.

DuPont's GM and Rockefeller's *Standard Oil of New Jersey* both collaborated with *I.G. Farben*, the Nazi chemical cartel, to form *Ethyl GmbH*. This subsidiary, now called Ethyl Inc., built German factories to provide the Nazis with leaded fuel for their military vehicles. Snell quotes from German records captured during the war ... *"The fact that since the beginning of the war we could produce lead-tetraethyl is entirely due to the circumstances that, shortly before, the Americans [Du Pont, GM and Standard Oil] had presented us with the production plants complete with experimental knowledge. Without lead-tetraethyl the present method of warfare would be unthinkable."*

In outright defiance of Roosevelt's desire to improve working conditions for the average man, GM and DuPont instituted the 'speedup systems.' These forced men to work at terrifying speeds on the assembly lines. Many died of the heat and pressure, greatly exacerbated by fear of losing their jobs. Irénée du Pont notoriously paid almost $1 million from his own pocket for armed and gas-equipped 'storm troopers' to supervise the plants and 'deal with' anyone who proved rebellious. He also hired the Pinkerton Agency to dispatch its detectives through his whole empire, in order to spy on suspected disruptive elements.

Since WWII, DuPont has continued to be an instrument of US government weapons production. Besides supplying plastics, rubber and textiles to military contractors, it invented various new forms of explosives and rocket propellants, manufactured numerous chemical weapons and was instrumental in building the world's first plutonium production plant for the atomic bomb. It was also responsible for the production of the infamous *Agent Orange* and Napalm, thus destroying millions of lives, livelihoods and whole ecosystems in Southeast Asia.

DuPonts 1939 slogan, *"Better Things for Better Living ... Through Chemistry,"* belies a destructive legacy that will last thousands of generations. One of the globe's worst polluters of all time, it pioneered the creation, marketing and cover-up of almost every dangerous chemical toxin ever known and is currently fighting countless lawsuits for the adversity to health and environmental effects of its products, the unsafe working conditions in its factories and the foolhardy, disposal practices it flaunts as solutions for its waste products.

Here is a small sample of DuPont's legacy to the planet:

- Sulphur dioxide and leaded paint.
- CFCs: 25% of the world's supply and almost 50% of the US market.
- Herbicides and pesticides: brain damage, hormone system disruption.
- Formaldehyde: cancer and respiratory illnesses.

- Dioxins: Leading the way to create these carcinogens, DuPont then suppressed data on their deadly effects.
- Highly-processed, non-nutritious products marketed as 'healthy food.'
- Genetically modified foods (GMOs) and 'terminator seeds' which threaten livelihoods and food security for 1.4 billion people who depend on replenishment of seeds.
- Patenting plant genes and stealing the third world's genetic resources.
- Using US prison labour, third world virtual slave labour and running factories in many oppressive regimes.
- Its oil subsidiary, Conoco, provided petrochemical raw materials and caused environmental devastation.
- DuPont is one of the world's biggest producers of greenhouse gases.
- Sold for 33 years, the fungicide *Benlate* destroyed crops, shrimp farms and caused birth defects.

Since the 1920s, DuPont produced leaded gas which is responsible for 80-90% of the world's environmental lead contamination.

Kennedy. *Money, Bootlegging, Movies, Politics*

In terms of both Elite connections and corruption, Joseph P. Kennedy, the father of JFK certainly had few peers.

Kennedy was a corporate tycoon, a politician, an entertainment executive who had *de facto* religious influence and was also intrinsically involved in military affairs. Two of his sons were military 'heroes,' his eldest son Joe junior being killed in action in WWII and he was also responsible for the orchestration of a concerted public relations campaign that inflated second son, John's naval 'heroics' so far out of proportion that it greatly contributed to his rapid rise to power.

In addition, Joe Kennedy was for all practical purposes a 'mob' figurehead for several decades, although his participation in illegal activities was more carefully hidden than the Sicilian families, who chose to run their businesses rather more publicly than Kennedy. When American youths were dying by the thousands in WWI, Joe was already enriching himself through his covert, dubious business practices, somehow managing to avoid the draft. During the subsequent Great Depression, many Americans lost everything while Kennedy continued to enrich himself further through business practices that directly benefited from the losses of others.

Down the decades, the Kennedys have experienced several tragedies, some intensely personal, some as a result of their high profile, and this became known as the 'Kennedy curse.' If there is such a thing as 'karma,' its effects could well be attributable to the despicable actions of the younger Joe Kennedy, who in the latter days of his life was firstly rendered all but helpless by a stroke and subsequently endured two of his sons being taken from him by assassin's bullets. Joe Kennedy however, was indeed the very personification of evil.

What is speculative is the considered possibility that the 20th Century 'success' of the Kennedys resulted from Joe Kennedy calling forth Satan and making a deal with the devil.

The following are excerpts from *'The Sins of the Father,'* by Ronald Kessler and *'The Kennedy Men: Three Generations of Sex, Scandal, and Secrets,'* by Nellie Bly . . .

"Joe's father, P.J. Kennedy, was a saloon owner who used his bar as a launching pad for his political career. In 1885, P.J. was elected to the Massachusetts House of Representatives, due in large part to the strong backing he received from the liquor lobby which was worried about the temperance movement. P.J. would serve five terms as a state representative before being elected to the Massachusetts Senate. P.J. skillfully used his political power to enrich himself and advance the career of his son Joseph P. Kennedy.

When Joe Kennedy was fresh out of college in 1912, his father got him a job as a state bank examiner. Here, Joe had access to useful information about the confidential affairs of companies and individuals who had credit lines with major Boston banks. He found out which companies were in trouble and which had extra cash, who was planning new products or acquisitions and who was about to be liquidated. A former Harvard classmate, Ralph Lowell, said, 'That bank examiner's job took him all over the state and laid bare the condition of every bank he visited. He acquired information of value to himself and others.'

Joe's strategy was to obtain inside information about troubled companies from banks, then drive their stock down so he could buy them more cheaply. While still on the state payroll as a bank examiner, Joe made an acquisition that was aided by inside information. He bought a Boston investment company called Old Colony Realty Associates, Inc. Joe turned the company from an old-line investment firm into one that made money on the misery of others.

Under Joe's direction, the company specialized in taking over defaulted home mortgages. He would then paint the houses, and resell them at far higher prices. By the time the company was dissolved, Joe's $1,000 investment had grown to $75,000.

Joe began cultivating strong alliances with members of the press, including William Randolph Hearst, who would print glowing stories about Kennedy's successes. In January 1914, when Joe was elected president of Columbia Trust, Hearst ran a series praising Joe as the youngest bank president in the country. The stories neglected to mention that Columbia Trust was owned by Joe's father and his friends.

Joe eventually assumed control of Columbia Trust by borrowing money from other family members who were never repaid. Kerry McCarthy, Joe's grandniece who interviewed some of those people for a research paper, said, 'I found money was loaned to him by family members and not repaid. Since it was family, he didn't feel there was a need to.'

In June of 1914, Joe married Rose Fitzgerald, daughter of Boston mayor John Fitzgerald. Joe would use this new connection for all it was worth. In 1917, with World War I already in progress, the United States government announced that young men would be drafted into military service, and that draft resisters would be executed. Although most of Joe's friends from Harvard had already volunteered to serve, Joe had no intention of fighting. Joe had already been placed in Class 1 and was subject to immediate call-up, when his father-in-law Mayor Fitzgerald, acquired a job for him at the Bethlehem Shipbuilding Corporation in Quincy, Massachusetts. Although Joe knew nothing about shipbuilding, he was made general manager, a job which effectively kept him out of the war.

Daniel Strohmeier, vice president of Bethlehem Steel, said, 'Joe was accommodated to skip the draft during World War I because of a lot of pressure from his father-in-law.' Seven months after the armistice was signed to end World War I, Joe left the shipyard. Having avoided the draft, he had no more need to work there. Joe was given a job with the venerable Boston stock brokerage firm Hayden, Stone and Company, after Mayor Fitzgerald promised to swing business to the firm if they hired his son-in-law.

Galen Stone, a friend of Joe's father-in-law, taught his protégé how to make huge sums of money off unsuspecting investors by trading on inside information. While the practice of using inside information was not then illegal, it was unethical. Stone breached his fiduciary duty to his stockholders, while Joe made money because of his privileged position at Hayden, Stone. Joe told one Harvard friend, 'It's so easy to make money in the market we'd better get in before they pass a law against it.' It was easy, as long as one was willing to breach trust.

Besides using inside information improperly, Joe made fabulous sums through what were known as stock pools. This was a way of manipulating the market by forming a syndicate and arranging for the members to trade stock back and forth. By bidding the price of the stock higher, the pool members created the appearance that the public was bidding up the price. In fact, the syndicate members retained the profits, and when the trading public bit by joining the action, the syndicate members sold out, leaving the public with losses. Joe called the practice 'advertising' the stock.

On January 29, 1919, the 18th Amendment was ratified. It prohibited the manufacture, sale, transportation, or importation of 'intoxicating liquors' for 'beverage purposes.' For Joe, the law represented an opportunity to make huge profits. He formed alliances with crime bosses in major markets, among them Boston, New York, Chicago, and New Orleans. These would come in handy years later when his son was running for national office. Among his mob associates was Frank Costello, former boss of the Luciano crime family, who bragged, 'I helped Joe Kennedy get rich.' Sam Giancana, who would later figure prominently in JFK's presidency, called Joe 'one of the biggest crooks who ever lived.'

Joe bought liquor from overseas distillers and supplied it to organized crime syndicates that picked up the liquor on the shore. Frank Costello would later confirm that Joe had approached him for help in smuggling liquor. Joe would have the liquor dumped at a so-called Rum Row—a trans-shipment point where police were paid to look the other way—and Costello and other mobsters would then take over. They distributed the liquor, fixed the prices, established quotas, and paid off law enforcement and politicians. They enforced their own law with machine guns, usually calling on experts who did bloody hits on contract.

By the mid-1920s, 'Fortune' estimated Joe's wealth at $2 million. Yet since Joe had left Hayden, Stone in 1922, he had had no visible job. While he made hundreds of thousands of dollars manipulating the market, only bootlegging on a sizable scale would account for such sudden and fabulous wealth."

One of the 'overseas distillers' with strong links to Kennedy and that authors and historians tend to gloss over, was the Jewish Bronfman family of bootleggers and whorehouse owners, who had made a fortune in Canada in the Prohibition era. The Bronfmans were major players in establishing the central, Bank of Canada (via the 1934 Bank of Canada Act,) as the sole issuer of banknotes in the country and the central bank for the Canadian dollar, and was a ploy consolidated by the banksters who arranged for the Bank of Canada to be designated a 'Crown' corporation, during the tenure of Canada's Prime Minister, Mackenzie King.

While that was ostensibly leaving the bank's share capital with Canada's Minister of Finance and the Canadian people, it was in reality transferring it to so-called 'Crown accounts,' which are in the domain of the private corporation of the City of London and presided over by a committee of about a dozen 'Judaised' financiers representing several banks in the City, headed of course, by the Bank of England.

Jews in Canada vociferously backed Mackenzie King's election as Canada's Prime Minister in 1921, because they knew that he had worked in the USA for the Rockefellers and was John D. Rockefeller Jr.'s close friend and confidant.

In Yiddish, Bronfman aptly means 'liquorman' and the hotel business put the Bronfmans in prime position to take advantage of the 1915 advent of Canadian prohibition. Bronfman hotels soon became 'boozeriums.' Prohibition, enacted on orders from the Privy Council as the prelude to the 1920s US Prohibition era and the birth of organised crime, catapulted the Bronfmans into the multi-millionaire bracket and to the status of 'untouchable' kingpins of crime in North America.

During Canada's four dry years from 1915 to 1919, the Bronfmans established their contacts with US organised criminals in preparation for illegally importing liquor into Canada. Then in 1916, they established their first link with the opium trade. Samuel and Abe Bronfman collaborated with the *Hudson Bay Company*, in which the Keswick family of *Jardine Matheson* had controlling interest, to buy the Canadian *Pure Drug Company*.

When prohibition in Canada ended in 1919 and Prohibition in the United States began, they simply turned from whiskey importing to whiskey exporting and after it was all over, in May 1936 they agreed to pay $1.5 million to settle their account with the US Treasury. This payment amounted to a subtle admission that half the liquor that flowed into the United States during Prohibition was from the Bronfmans.

A little reported fact is that the 'booze' that the family poured across the border was actually a dangerous poison, being a mixture of pure alcohol, sulphuric acid, caramel, water and aged rye whiskey, that in many cases left its victims paralysed. Between 1920 and 1930, 34,000 Americans died from alcohol poisoning, despite there being a ban on all alcoholic drinks.

A refusal to deal with the Bronfman gang on their terms usually meant death, and several independently-minded gang bosses were often executed by their lieutenants on the Bronfman's orders.

Since 1920 the Bronfmans had been importing British whiskey from the Distillery Company of London, which controlled more than half the world market in Scotch whisky. Owned by the higher echelons of the British society including Field Marshal Haig, Lord Dewar, Lord Woolavington, and others, the dispensation of distribution rights was a decision made by King George V.

But back now to Joseph Kennedy. He used the profits from his bootlegging operations to fuel his continued stock market speculations and to finance his fledgling efforts in the film industry.

By 1930 Kennedy was an extremely wealthy man. He had known that the Great Depression was coming and as Black Tuesday (the Wall Street Crash) approached, Joe being on the 'inside,' had liquidated his longer-term investments while continuing to make money on the declining market by selling short. In this way Kennedy made an estimated $1 million and contributed to the eventual market crash by forcing prices down. The fact that the market was totally unregulated had presented an opportunity to the unscrupulous bankers to manipulate it to their own ends and this is precisely what they did and in doing so made themselves obscenely wealthy whilst simultaneously causing widespread hunger, death and misery for years to come.

Stock pools such as those perfected by Joe Kennedy had defrauded legitimate investors and reporters and columnists had acted as shills for companies peddling stocks in return for payoffs. The crash instigated a worldwide financial panic and Depression that would last for many years and by 1932, 12 million Americans were jobless. Governments responded with strict tariff restrictions that stifled world trade, further contributing to the ongoing downward spiral.

Considerably richer because of his short selling, Joe Kennedy told friends that he had sold off his Wall Street holdings before the bottom dropped out of the stock market. He said he was now waiting to pick up the pieces left by 'dumb people.' His wealth was by this time estimated at over $100 million and yet by 1933, he was again manipulating the stock market to his advantage, even as Federal investigators were trying to expose the conditions that had led to the crash.

By 1933 the US had taken the first tentative steps towards repealing Prohibition, and with his usual foresight, Joe could see it was only a matter of time before the 18th Amendment was repealed and alcohol flowed freely again. So, he used his connections in Washington to obtain permits to import ridiculously large quantities of whisky for 'medicinal purposes' and stockpiled it in warehouses so that when Prohibition ended, he would have millions of dollars' worth of high-quality liquor in stock, all ready to make yet another fortune for himself.

After making his illicit fortune, Kennedy was one of the first 'Eastern' businessmen to grasp the potential of the movie business which was now firmly established on the west coast and by the mid-1920s, the American film industry was turning out 800 films a year and employed as many people as the car industry. This was indeed a 'gold mine,' as Joe had told several friends.

After buying a chain of small movie theatres, Joe eventually realised that the way to make real money was actually on the production side rather than the retail side. Moreover, he was also attracted to the glamour of Hollywood as not only could he influence the way films were made, he could also meet desperate young women, would-be movie stars who would do almost anything in return for a part in a film.

Whilst his wife Rose was back home in Boston, pregnant with their eighth child, Kennedy was in Hollywood, engaged in his notorious liaison with the 'superstar' Gloria Swanson. Swanson was by no means Kennedy's first extra-marital adventure, but she was the perfect 'trophy' to symbolise the great success he had achieved for himself.

Joe Kennedy used the profits from his first company, FBO to purchase the Radio Corporation of America (RCA) who had a new system for making motion pictures with sound. Now that Joe headed a studio, he wanted to buy a cinema chain to facilitate the distribution of his pictures and this would eventually lead directly to the infamous 'Pantages Scandal.'

Kennedy's eldest daughter Rosemary, was considered shy and mentally limited, exhibiting symptoms of what many now suspect was nothing more than simple dyslexia. For many years the family had dealt with the problem by sending her away to various special schools and convents but by the age of 21 she had deteriorated greatly, giving way to tantrums, rages and violent behaviour, probably at least partly due to extreme frustration at her treatment. She was beginning to understand that she would never 'measure up' to her siblings and the resulting frustration led to physical fights and worse, long absences at night when she would be out wandering the streets alone.

Rosemary increasingly became to be seen as a liability to Kennedy's increasing political ambitions and so it was that in 1942, he attempted to deal with the problem by arranging Rosemary to undergo a prefrontal lobotomy at St. Elizabeth's Hospital in Washington, DC. The experimental operation was believed to be extremely beneficial to people who had emotional problems but In Rosemary's case it was a complete disaster and left her permanently disabled, paralysed on one side, incontinent and unable to speak coherently. She was never allowed to return home, but instead was spirited away to St. Coletta's School in Wisconsin.

As late as 1958 the family was still maintaining the fiction that Rosemary had become a nun in Wisconsin, content to renounce the glamorous world of her siblings to teach less fortunate children. Today the official family version is that she was born retarded and that only her mother's Herculean efforts had made it possible for her to appear normal. All total fabrications of course.

Joe Kennedy's entry into politics began when a mutual friend arranged a meeting between Kennedy and then-Governor of New York, Franklin Roosevelt. Having just won re-election as Governor, Roosevelt was already being described as a contender for President. As a 'pragmatist,' willing to obtain support from almost any quarter, he saw Joe Kennedy as both a potential source of major campaign contributions and someone who could influence Wall Street and conservative Democrats. At their first meeting, Kennedy and Roosevelt forged a political alliance. Joe would contribute to his campaign and open doors to him on Wall Street whilst Roosevelt would bring Joe into his inner circle of advisers and include him in his Cabinet.

Once the campaign got under way, Kennedy not only contributed large sums of money directly to Roosevelt, but he also became Roosevelt's 'money collector' or 'bag-man,' collecting cash from those who wanted to hide their identities. Kennedy was also of further value to Roosevelt because of his close relationships with many newspaper publishers, who of course could be critically important to any 'democratic' election process. Not only could they promote the attributes of any candidates in their papers, they often used their political clout to choose candidates in the first place. Chief among these media power-brokers was Kennedy's old friend, William Randolph Hearst, the owner of no less than 33 newspapers with a daily circulation of 11 million. He also controlled 86 delegates to the Democratic nominating convention, nearly all whom hailed from the critical states of California and Texas. In a crucial, last-gasp move, Kennedy persuaded Hearst to back Roosevelt.

Hearst not only provided a huge campaign contribution, but he also swung his delegates toward Roosevelt. Kennedy justifiably claimed later that he had personally won the nomination for Roosevelt himself. However, more than a year after Roosevelt was elected President, Kennedy was still without his promised Cabinet post.

The stock market crash and resulting panic eventually led to the creation of the *Securities and Exchange Commission* in 1934, to which Kennedy was appointed head by President Franklin Roosevelt. This is akin to placing a fox in charge of the henhouse or like appointing Al Capone as head of a task force to combat organised crime and the appointment drew strong criticism from those who felt that Joe Kennedy symbolised everything the SEC had been set up to eradicate. Roosevelt, however stood firm, telling one advisor that it needed 'a thief to catch a thief.' Roosevelt also knew that Kennedy's financial backing had been critical to his election and he hoped that by giving Kennedy the SEC chairmanship it would secure his financial support for the next election as well.

The SEC, under Kennedy's stewardship outlawed most of the practices that had made Kennedy his fortune, including a ban on short-selling, one of his preferred ways of making money. For almost two years, an almost constant stream of Wall Street stalwarts took to the witness stand and described their roles in their seamy dealings and even though Kennedy's extensive, unethical (now illegal) transactions were revealed during the hearings, he was unsurprisingly never requested to appear.

However, Kennedy had ambitions for himself and his sons that went way beyond the trifling SEC and he duly resigned his post in September 1935.

Then by 1937, Kennedy had begun hinting to Roosevelt that he still 'deserved' some tangible form of recognition for his role in the election and so Roosevelt, who had by then become mistrustful of Kennedy, appointed him ambassador to England. His Ambassadorship coincided almost exactly with the beginning of World War II in Europe and throughout his three-years in office argued against American and British involvement in the war. Joe steadfastly maintained his position of appeasement toward Germany but in May 1940, Winston Churchill was elected British Prime Minister and this brought an end to appeasement (at the bankers behest no doubt) and hastened Kennedy's fall from favour. The 'final nail in his coffin' was Kennedy's public statement to the effect that 'Democracy is finished in England,' thereby giving Roosevelt no choice but to ask for his resignation.

JFK was named in honour of Rose's father, John Francis Fitzgerald, who in his day had been a popular Boston Mayor. Jack was an unhealthy baby who had suffered from whooping cough, measles, chicken pox and even scarlet fever. His father attended the hospital every day to be by his son's side and eventually Jack recovered but his health remained an issue for the rest of his life. The family joke was that if a mosquito bit him, the mosquito would die.

The family settled in Brookline, just outside Boston but as well as this, the family also owned property in the exclusive enclave of West Palm Beach, Florida. Summers were spent in Hyannis Port, Cape Cod where they swam, sailed, and played sports. The children played hard and were extremely competitive, encouraged all the while by their father who pitted them against each other in an attempt to 'toughen them up.' However whilst the children had everything they needed and wanted materially, they were not 'spoiled.' The boys especially, faced very high expectations in sports, education and all other activities.

Jack (JFK) attended Choate, an exclusive boarding school in Connecticut. He played tennis, basketball, football, and golf and read voraciously in those pre-TV days. He even subscribed to the *New York Times*, which was (and still is) unusual for a teenager. The principal of the school recalled later that he had a 'clever, individualist mind.' He was not the best student, but he took his education very seriously, especially history and English, which were his favourite subjects.

After his graduation from Choate, Jack entered Harvard where he regularly played football. He was not a very talented athlete but he persisted until rupturing a disk in his spine. This injury caused him severe pain for the rest of his life and he was permanently on medication, in order to alleviate his suffering.

On 3rd September 1939 World War II began and whilst still a student at Harvard wrote his thesis, '*Why England Slept,*' on Britain's lack of preparedness for war. It was a well-written book which was worthy of publication in its own right and Joe made sure of this through one of his contacts in the world of publishing.

Then, in June, 1940 Jack graduated from Harvard and headed to California, where he entered Stanford Business School. He had been given $1 million by his father and according to legend, bedded almost half the eligible females on the West Coast from San Francisco to Hollywood. However his playboy lifestyle was soon cut short by the attack on Pearl Harbor by the Japanese in December 1941.

Much more of the Kennedys later...

Reynolds. *Money, Tobacco, Metals, Politics*

Richard Joshua, 'R.J.' Reynolds, son of prosperous tobacco manufacturer Hardin W. Reynolds of Patrick County, Virginia, sold his part interest in a tobacco business he had with his father and in 1874 moved 60 miles south to Winston, North Carolina. Reynolds invested $7,500 in land and built and equipped a small factory there to manufacture 'flat plug' chewing tobacco. During his first year of operation, Reynolds produced 150,000 pounds of tobacco that was sold primarily, locally in the Carolinas and Virginia.

In 1879 the *R.J. Reynolds Tobacco Company* was incorporated in North Carolina but initially Reynolds faced stiff competition from rival manufacturers in Winston and its neighboring city of Salem. Reynolds, along with his brother William Neal Reynolds, who joined the firm in 1884, controlled the company.

R.J. Reynolds' eldest brother and rival, Abram Reynolds, founded his own, separate company manufacturing tobacco products and later became an early advocate of prohibition. Abram however, eventually sold his tobacco company and founded the *Lustre Bubbles Soap Company* as his land was rich in bauxite, an ingredient in both soap and aluminium. His son R.S. Reynolds, went on to later found *Reynolds Metals* and helped popularise aluminium foil.

Following their father's example, all five Reynolds brothers entered the tobacco business, some of them with R.J. and others with Abram. Then in 1890 the company went public and issued its first stock, with R.J. Reynolds himself owning almost 90% of the company. He was elected president, with one of his brothers serving as vice-president.

Reynolds was one of the first companies to introduce saccharin as a sweetening agent in chewing tobacco and by 1894 Reynolds had begun to experiment with smoking tobacco to compete with James Buchanan Duke's profitable brands and also in an attempt to turn 'scrap' tobacco into a profitable line. In 1895 the company introduced its first smoking tobacco brand, 'Naturally Sweet Cut Plug.' By 1898 the company's assets were valued at more than $1 million.

Due to considerable expansion in the late 1890s, Reynolds was in great need of working capital and so reluctantly, he turned to his rival, Duke for help. In 1898 Duke's *American Tobacco Company* established a subsidiary, *Continental Tobacco Company*, in an attempt to monopolise the nation's chewing tobacco business and then in April 1899 Reynolds sold two-thirds of his stock to Continental, but retained his position as president of the *R.J. Reynolds Tobacco Company*. Reynolds insisted upon maintaining his independence in Duke's tobacco trust and reportedly told friends that, '... *if Buck Duke tries to swallow me, he will get the bellyache of his life.*'

Duke allowed Reynolds his independence as long as he acquired chewing tobacco companies in the Virginia and Carolina area for the trust and Reynolds, as instructed, acquired ten companies but by 1905 he had also demonstrated his independence from the trust by producing five different brands of smoking tobacco.

The tobacco trust, like most trusts during the first decade of the 20th Century, proved to be highly unpopular and so in 1911 a US Circuit Court judge ordered the dissolution of the *American Tobacco Company* and it was forced to divest itself of all Reynolds stock. R.J. Reynolds and members of his family re-acquired some of the company's stock, hired aggressive new managers, and increased production and sales almost five-fold during the trust period. By this time, the *R.J. Reynolds Tobacco Company* was the smallest of the 'big four' tobacco manufacturers, but this was about to change.

Soon after achieving independence from the trust, Reynolds instituted a plan to place the company's stock into the hands of friendly investors. A company edict encouraged Reynolds' employees to buy company stock and the board of directors approved lending of surplus funds and profits to employees for the purchase of 'voting' stock. By 1924 the majority of the company's voting stock was in the hands of people who worked for the company and very soon all tobacco businesses began to emulate the Reynolds stock purchase model.

By July 1913, Reynolds had manufactured the company's first cigarette, producing three different cigarette brands simultaneously in order to test which one had the greatest public demand. The brand that proved most popular, *Camel* became an instant success because of its blend, pricing, and advertising. In fact Reynolds recognised the power of advertising and spent more than $2 million in 1915 in an aggressive national advertising campaign and it was Reynolds who adopted the then radical idea of selling cigarettes by the carton. Subsequently, profits soared from $2.75 million in 1912 to nearly $24 million in 1924, largely because of the phenomenal success of the *Camel* brand. By 1924 the *R.J. Reynolds Tobacco Company* net profits had surpassed the nation's largest manufacturer, the *American Tobacco Company*.

The company prospered under R.J. Reynolds's paternalistic leadership and continued to do so for decades after his death in 1918. William Neal Reynolds assumed the presidency after his brother's demise and remained in that position until 1924 when he was elected chairman of the board of directors, with Bowman Gray, Sr., appointed president. This ensured the perpetuation of R.J. Reynolds' management philosophy and ensured a continuity of leadership from people within the company. Before R.J. Reynolds's death he had begun the process that led to the company's listing on the New York Stock Exchange, issuing preferred stock in 1922 and common stock in 1927.

William Neal Reynolds retired as chairman in 1931 to be replaced by Bowman Gray, Sr. Under Gray's stewardship, in 1931, the company introduced moisture proof cellophane as a wrapper to preserve freshness in cigarettes—an innovation that other companies soon adopted. The company also began to manufacture its own tinfoil and paper from factories in North Carolina to reduce dependence on foreign supplies and developed a new sales policy that concentrated on mass sales based on brand-name recognition and customer loyalty. During the 1930s, Reynolds invested heavily in a series of advertising campaigns that emphasised the pleasures of smoking. By 1938 the company produced 84 brands of chewing tobacco, 12 brands of smoking tobacco and one primary brand of cigarette, *Camel*.

In 1948 a major anti-trust suit against the tobacco industry went to trial and several senior R.J. Reynolds employees were convicted and fined on charges of monopolistic practices, although they strongly asserted their innocence. The company itself also was convicted of the same charges. The following year, 1949, Reynolds introduced a major new cigarette brand, Cavalier which turned out to be a disaster and cost the company $30 million in five years.

However, the innovative John Clarke Whitaker assumed the presidency in 1949 and during his tenure Reynolds rebounded and prospered. Technical advances increased the amount of tobacco suitable for cigarette manufacturing, which helped the company's output double from 1944 to 1958. Reynolds also instituted an active merchandising campaign by using display racks of cigarettes in supermarkets. And in addition, company by-laws that had resulted in the concentration of stock in the hands of employees were gradually eased, making the shares available more widely.

It was during the 1950s though, that the tobacco industry experienced critical attacks centred on the issue of smoking and health, for the first time. In 1952 an article entitled '*Cancer by the Carton*' appeared in *Reader's Digest* and the following year the *Sloan-Kettering Cancer Institute* announced that its research showed a clear correlation between cancer and tobacco. The development of filter-tipped cigarettes was partly a response to health concerns and the board of directors also responded by appointing a diversification committee in 1957, to study possible investment in non-tobacco areas and to consider expansion of tobacco operations overseas.

Alexander H. Galloway became president in 1960 and, along with Chairman Bowman Gray, Jr., led the company into a period of unparalleled growth and diversification. The corporate diversification strategy initially focused on acquisitions in food-related industries.

Tobacco, however, continued to be the mainstay of Reynolds, despite the fact that in the 1960s the smoking and health controversy had intensified. In 1964 the US Surgeon General issued a report linking smoking with lung cancer and heart disease and in 1965, Congress passed the 'Cigarette Advertising and Labeling Act,' which required tobacco companies to place health warnings on cigarette packs. Cigarette advertising was also banned from radio and television from 1971 and the Federal cigarette tax was doubled in 1983.

When incriminating industry documents became public in the mid-1990s, *R.J. Reynolds* and competitors *Philip Morris* and *BAT Industries* were sued by dozens of state attorneys-general for costs associated with treating tobacco-related illnesses. Although the trio agreed to a settlement in 1997, the deal disintegrated during the Congressional approval process. In the meantime, the tobacco companies raised cigarette prices significantly, in anticipation of a large settlement payout. Finally, late in 1998 the cigarette makers agreed to pay states $206 billion. Although the final amount was less than that agreed, R.J. Reynolds and rivals did not win protection from private class-action suits, a condition for which they had lobbied strongly.

R.J. Reynolds' international operations suffered in the mid- to late 1990s. The company reduced its staff by ten percent in 1997 in an effort to apply the saving to the international business. However, *R.J. Reynolds Tobacco International* remained weak, and the holding company sold it to *Japan Tobacco, Inc.*, for $8 billion in May 1999. Terms of the sale included trademarks of *R.J. Reynolds Tobacco International* and international rights to Camel, Winston, and Salem brands. At the same time, *RJR Nabisco* spun-off the domestic tobacco business through a stock distribution to *RJR Nabisco* shareholders.

All the above information is obviously public knowledge, but what is really kept secret, is the Reynolds family involvement with the bankster-controlled Illuminati. Much of the family's money has been well-hidden behind fronts, holding companies, etc., and the Reynolds family have been involved in high-level drug dealing for many years. They have also had a major interest in banking.

Richard S. Reynolds, Jr. has been a board chairman of *Robertshaw Controls Company*, which has a strict monopoly on manufacturing car thermostats and other car parts. The big three American auto manufacturers all buy from *Robertshaw Controls Company* but then since all 3 of the American auto manufacturers are also Illuminati-controlled, this is no coincidence. *Cadence* which owns theatres and has published occult comic books such as the series, '*Journey into Mystery with the Mighty Thor*,' is also closely tied to the Reynolds family.

The Reynolds family also controls several Aluminium companies which form a large part of the bankster-controlled Aluminium cartel. The Mellon family works closely with the Reynolds in this Aluminium cartel and the Mellons have strong links to the British Royal family.

As previously related, the British Elite were heavily involved in the shipping and supply of opium. The British bankster Empire's military might and political clout was used to force China to allow the opium trade and what is perhaps less well-known is that before the communists took over China, the British Illuminati families hid their opium trade behind the cover of the *British American Tobacco Co*. Later the Red Chinese would hide their opium trading behind the same front, tobacco, with their state-run People's Republic of China Tobacco Bureau. In fact, the Red Chinese opium trade was conrolled by another Illuminati member, the Chinese President Li Xiannian from the occult Li family who are the leading oriental satanic family.

President Li, a drug lord was also finance minister of Red China from 1957-75. He sold so much opium to the west that he was able to help Red China pay off its debts and he was nicknamed 'the money god.' *R.J. Reynolds* was a partner with *British American Tobacco Co.* and was also involved in trading in opium for many years. It is strongly suspected that the family later also became involved in running cocaine and as described previously, Onassis also concealed his early drug smuggling behind tobacco importing.

The Reynolds, along with their fellow-illuminati families, use tax-free foundations as a vehicle to evade taxes and hide their true wealth whilst maintaining their financial power. The illuminati-controlled mainstream press heavily promotes them as 'charitable,' when most of the grants by these foundations are self-serving and only used for the benefit of the Elite. Examples of these foundations are the *Z. Smith Reynolds Foundation,* the *Kate B. Reynolds Foundation,* the *Richard S. Reynolds* Foundation and the *Mary Reynolds Babcock Foundation.* All of these foundations function only to benefit the banksters themselves.

Significantly however, a number of government agencies receive money from the Reynolds Foundations, especially those dealing with children such as the Social Services, and even Police Departments. One wonders why—or maybe not.

J.P. Sticht, a director of *R.J. Reynolds,* who has acted as a liaison between the Reynolds, Duke and Rockefeller dynasties is also a member of Rockefeller University Council and a member of the board of visitors to Duke University. Leighton Hammond Coleman, who is also Illuminati and part of the satanic Coleman family, also acts as emeritus director of *R.J. Reynolds Industries*. Both he and his father, were part of the *Pilgrim Society*, which is a level above the CFR in the Illuminati hierarchy.

Another director of *R.J. Reynolds Industries* was John D. Macomber, a Yale graduate. Macomber married into the Illuminati Morgan family and was also a member of the *Pilgrim Society*. Besides being a director of Reynolds, he also served the Rockefellers as a director of Chase Manhattan Bank. Gordon Gray, of the satanic Gray family, was also on the Reynolds board, and both Gray and Macomber were linked with the CFR.

The multitude of connections of Reynolds to the Elite, is quite overwhelming. Many of the institutions in the Middle South connect back to the Illuminati and their front organisations such as the Freemasons and the Chambers of Commerce, the CFR etc. etc. Companies with which *R.J. Reynolds Industries* interlock are *Arista Co., Avon Products, Federal Reserve Bank of Richmond, Dun and Bradstreet Companies, Foremost-McKesson Inc., Hatteras Income Securities, Hayes-Albion Corp., Jefferson Pilot Corp., McClean Industries, Northwestern Mutual Life Insurance, Perkin Elmer Corp., Richardson-Merrell Inc., S.C. Johnson and Sons Inc., Southern Broadcasting Inc., Standard Oil Co. of Indiana, Standard Savings and Loan, Stauffer Chemical Co., United States Filter Corp., United States Steel Corp., Wachovia Corp.*—to name just a sample.

Krupp. *Money, Military, Steel, Chemicals, Politics*

During the age of discovery when the New World was first being explored, the powerful occult oligarchies of Europe set up trading companies to divide-up control of the world. The *East India Company* was one of the most notable of these Elite-controlled trading companies. They were intrinsically connected to the occult world's leadership and the formation of drug cartels during the age of discovery. The 13 Illuminati families were all participants in the narcotics cartel that was instigated several centuries ago, its roots being traceable back as far as the Knights Templar and the Knights of Malta.

This drug cartel has persisted down through the centuries. For example, *I.G. Farben* was a 20th Century part of the German element of the cartel and a complete history of the Krupp family would include its links with I.G. Farben and the worldwide chemical monopoly that the Illuminati families have created.

The Krupp family first appeared in the form of Arndt Krupp, whom it is thought arrived in Essen, (now Germany) in 1587, from Holland and soon became a wealthy merchant in the area. His son Anton however, became a military arms dealer, probably at least partly due to the fact that his father-in-law ran a gunsmith company. By around 1650, the Krupps were Essen's most prominent family and it was said that they covertly controlled the city government. At this point in history, Germany was simply a collection of autonomous, individual 'states' and not a country per se. By 1800, the Krupps had diversified into steel and coal as well as military armaments.

Two of the most important advisors to Adolf Hitler during WWII were Gustav and Alfred Krupp and but for Gustav Krupp, Hitler would never have come to power. During 1932, the Nazi Party had little popular support and had lost heavily in the elections. Many of their largest financial contributors had withdrawn their support and seemed as though the party was about to die a slow, lingering death.

Josef Goebbels wrote at this time, "*…we are all very discouraged, particularly in the face of the present danger that the entire party may collapse and all our work be in vain. We are now facing the decisive test.*" Soon afterwards he also wrote, "*The financial situation in Berlin is hopeless. Nothing but debts and obligations,*" However, Gustav Krupp suddenly brought to bear his huge influence and wealth (100,000,000 German Marks) into saving the Nazi party from their 'hopeless' position. Gustav Krupp was perhaps the most powerful industrialist in Germany at the time and the weight of his great influence helped restore the Nazi party's fortunes and led to electoral victory later that year. When Krupp's financial contribution had been received, Hitler assigned Martin Bormann to control the money and from then on, Hitler's personal finances as well as the party's finances were totally within the power of Bormann, significantly also a member of the Illuminati.

Gustav Krupp was the sole owner of all his companies, there were no shareholders. He owned a vast array of corporations and companies and properties all over the world. The full extent of his holdings are unknown but this immense wealth ensured that his son, who was the sole inheritor of all the Krupp fortune was able to quickly rebuild his factories, totally destroyed by the allies in WWII, by using the money derived from foreign (non-German) holdings all over the world.

Was Hitler really the driving force of Germany's re-armament in the aftermath of

WWI or does it seem more likely that it was in fact Gustav Krupp who began secretly re-arming Germany in a scheme that perpetuated the immense profitability of his companies. In fact, the documentation that proves that Krupp began planning and secretly rebuilding German armaments on his own initiative, in preparation for WWII immediately after WWI, is absolutely incontrovertible.

When Hitler eventually gained power, Gustav Krupp immediately billed the new Nazi government 300 million marks for the cost of having secretly re-built the German war machine during the 1920s and the Nazis promptly paid him without question.

At the Nuremberg, so-called 'war-crime' trials in 1946, Gustav and Alfred Krupp were two of the Nazi defendants. However, Gustav was declared unfit for trial due to 'ill health' and Alfred was given very lenient treatment indeed. Many of the other Nazi defendants were in fact sentenced to death with far less evidence against them, than Alfred. As members of the Illuminati, were they being allowed 'special treatment?' This particular topic is discussed more fully in a later chapter.

When the war ended, Gustav was at Blumenbach Castle which is located in a remote site in the Austrian Alps and coincidentally, the American officer who captured the castle was Chip Bohlen's brother-in-law, Colonel Charles W. Thayer (in other words a relative of Gustav Krupp,) who made sure that the American troops did not loot the castle. This is a very strange coincidence indeed, that of all the millions of allied troops, it was actually a relative of the Krupps who was on hand to capture Gustav Krupp's castle.

The Illuminati's controlled mass media was eager to portray Gustav's son Alfred as a 'victim' of the Nuremberg trials, even though mountains of documents proved beyond doubt that he was more of a 'war criminal' than Adolf Hitler and his closest confidantes. Indeed, the copious documents relating specifically to the Nuremberg trial of Alfred Krupp were never printed in Germany and even today the truth about Krupp is concealed. History is constantly re-written by the controlled media and not least to portray Alfred Krupp as a victim of Nazism, rather than to tell the truth about how he ran the Krupp Empire with brutality and was actively involved in the torture of countless slave labourers in his factories.

Hitler had decreed that slave-workers were to be properly fed in accordance with their workloads but Krupp's slaves were systematically starved to death while being forced to undertake hard labour. There was an acute shortage of slave labour and pressing needs for tanks, ships, artillery, submarines and other Krupp-produced weapons, so it was ironic that Krupp's personal factory guards starved and beat slaves to death on a regular basis. The horrendous abuse that the slaves received indeed often inhibited the Krupp factories and prevented them from attaining their production goals.

These slave labourers were tortured in the basement of Krupp's 'Hauptverwaltungsgebaude,' the executive corporation office building in Essen. Several unimpeachable witnesses declared that some of the most despicable torture of slaves occurred within the hearing of Alfred Krupp's own office. Krupp's secretaries could certainly hear the screams of people being tortured and there is no doubt that if they could hear them, then so could he.

Later John J. McCloy, head of the *Council of Foreign Relations*, and member of the Illuminati, (more of him later, too) was given the job of High Commissioner, overseeing occupied Germany. He overturned the Nuremberg Trial decisions, ignoring the legalities (the law is only for lesser mortals to obey, of course) and freed Alfred Krupp from prison and fully exonerated him of 'war crimes.'

In total, the trial of Alfred Krupp's WWII crimes had taken five years, and was represented by 330,000 pages of court transcripts and all that time and effort was simply brushed-aside by McCloy. Krupp in fact had employed a team of thirty seven of the very best lawyers who had done everything in their powers both legally and illegally to free him. They even had witnesses murdered and contrived to suppress important, incriminating evidence. In fact, the mainstream newspapers in Europe and the US portrayed Krupp as having been denied adequate legal advice but this was far from the truth—he was the best-defended Nuremberg 'criminal' of all.

The Illuminati were always above the law and indeed still are. Friedrich Alfred Krupp was the head of the Fried-Krupp Industrial Empire but was also a homosexual paedophile who used little boys for sex. When he travelled on business he would always obtain boys to satisfy his distasteful urges. The proprietor of the *Hotel Bristol* in Berlin discovered Friedrich Krupp's sexual preferences when he was asked by Krupp to supply him with young boys at the Hotel. Utterly disgusted by this, he immediately contacted the Berlin police, who advised him to keep quiet in his own interests. Not only was Krupp above the law, but he also had friends in high places in the form of Kaiser Wilhelm, who was the grandson of Queen Victoria of England and a great friend and protector of the Krupps.

On the island of Capri, Italy a grotto was transformed into Krupp's own private sex den where countless numbers of young Italian boys regularly performed sexual services for Krupp. The owner of the grotto was also a prominent politician who could therefore protect Krupp's activities from unwanted intrusion. Solid gold pins shaped like artillery shells or two crossed forks (both designed by Krupp) were allegedly given to the young boys if they performed well.

Krupp also arranged for explicit pornographic photos to be taken of his abhorrent activities but these somehow leaked into the public domain and this, and all the many witnesses to Krupp's criminal, sexual activities, caused the Italian government to order Krupp to leave Italy. Any 'ordinary' person would have been arrested and thrown into jail, but Krupp was simply asked to leave. However, the press in Italy had got wind of this 'juicy' story and it was not too long before all of Europe knew of Krupp's paedophilia. That is except for Germany where the government and the controlled media kept it a secret. A few German journalists did attempt to get the story published in Germany but were arrested for their troubles.

When Krupp's wife learned of the scandal she was incredibly distressed and informed the authorities who immediately contrived to have her declared insane in order to silence her too. However, committing her to a mental asylum was never going to cover-up the scandal, it had grown completely out of control and after a short period spent fighting a desperate, losing battle, in November 1902 Friedrich Krupp committed suicide. The suicide was also covered up, and his body was placed in a concealed casket and in direct contravention of the law, no autopsy was ever performed.

No-one, not even Friedrich Krupp's close relatives were allowed to see the body and after a 'respectful' period of three days, there was a great remembrance ceremony for Krupp which included the participation of the Kaiser, followed by his remains being laid to rest in a guarded cemetery. The case of Friedrich Krupp's improprieties and the resulting scandal, suicide and cover-up, clearly demonstrate that these powerful men are absolutely above and beyond the law.

As with all the Illuminati families, the Krupps maintain extensive networks with all the Elite. For example, the Krupps are able at will, to hire or fire corporate leaders in many of Germany's major corporations, because their controlled banks hold the entire purse strings of Germany.

In July, 1944, the Illuminati's economic 'thinkers' quietly established the *World Bank* at Bretton Woods, New Hampshire, USA and Illuminatus John J. McCloy, the man who illegally set Krupp free, became its first president.

In more recent times, two Illuminati from the Krupp family were Alfred Krupp von Bohlen und Halsbach (1907-1967) and Charles 'Chip' Bohlen (1904-1974.) Chip Bohlen's grandfather and Alfred Krupp's great-grandfather were brothers. Alfred Krupp was one of the most powerful and richest men in Europe during the 1960s and 'Chip' Bohlen was one of the most powerful political figures of the United States serving as the US ambassador to the USSR for many years.

In 1967, upon Alfred Krupp's death, the Illuminati ceded control of Krupp's vast industrial empire to its International banksters.

Rothschild. *Money, Politics, Power-broking*

Much of the Rothschild family history has already been covered and their activities will continue to be a central theme throughout the remainder of this book.

Secret Societies

Most modern secret societies and especially those that practice degrees of initiation, and this is the key factor, are really one society with one purpose. We may refer to them however we wish, the Order of the Quest, the JASON Society, the Roshaniya, the Qabbalah, the Knights Templar, the Knights of Malta, the Knights of Columbus, the Jesuits, the Freemasons, the Ancient and Mystical Order of Rosae Crucis (Rosicrucians,) the Illuminati, the Communist Party, the Council on Foreign Relations, The Group, the Brotherhood of the Dragon, the Royal Institute of International Affairs, the Trilateral Commission, the Bilderberg Group, the Vatican, the Russell Trust, the Skull and Bones, the Scroll and Key, the Order, the Round Table; they are all essentially linked and all work toward the same ultimate goal, the New World Order.

You may believe that some of those organisations listed above do not, or so it appears, practice degrees of initiation. However, that is just the public view, for public consumption only. For example, many members of the Council on Foreign Relations, in fact the majority, never serve on the executive committees and never go through any initiation ceremony of any kind. They are simply the power base and are used to gain a consensus of opinion. These are not 'true' members as such but are deliberately given the impression that they are.

The Executive Committee is an inner core of intimate associates, members of a secret society called the Order of the Quest, also known as the JASON Society, devoted to a common goal. The ordinary members are an outer circle on whom the inner core acts by personal persuasion, patronage and social pressure. Anyone in the outer circle who does not conform is summarily expelled and this lesson is not lost on those who remain. Only members of the Order are initiated into the Order of the Quest, the JASON Society that makes up the executive members of the Council on Foreign Relations and, in fact, the Trilateral Commission as well. The executive members of these insidious organisations are the true world powers—and not governments.

These 'executives' are recruited, almost without exception from the fraternal secret societies of Yale and Harvard, known as the *Skull and Bones* and the *Scroll and Key*, respectively.

Both societies are secret branches (also called the Brotherhood of Death) of what is otherwise historically known as the Illuminati. They are connected to parent organisations in England (The Group of Oxford University and especially All Souls College,) and Germany (the Thule Society, also called the Brotherhood of Death.)

It is important to understand that the members of these Orders take an oath that absolves them from any allegiance to any nation or king or government or constitution, and that includes the negating of any subsequent oath of allegiance which they may be required to take. They swear allegiance only to the Order, its leaders and its goal of a New World Order.

Clinton, Bush, Obama et al are not loyal citizens of the United States, but instead are loyal only to the destruction of the United States and to the inception of the New World Order. According to the oath Bush took when he was initiated into Skull and Bones, his oath of office as President of the United States of America means nothing.

The Trilateral Commission

The Trilateral Commission is an elite group of some 300 very prominent business, political and intellectual decision-makers of Western Europe, North America, and Japan. This enterprise is a private agency that works to engender political and economic co-operation among the three regions. Its great objective, which it no longer hides, is the foundation of a New World Order.

The Trilateral Commission was the idea of its founder, the American bankster, David Rockefeller. The real reason for its formation was the decline of the Council on Foreign Relation's power as a result of the people's dissatisfaction with the Vietnam War. The reasoning behind the move toward the Trilateral Commission was the same principal as entering two horses in the same race, that is, it doubles the chances of winning. The real power has always remained solidly in the hands of the Council on Foreign Relations, however, the Rockefeller family was, is and always will be both the benefactor and power behind both organisations.

A key clue to the real danger presented by the Trilateral Commission is its 'Seminal Peace' document, written for them by Harvard Professor Samuel P. Huntington in the mid-1970s. In his paper Huntington recommended that democracy and economic development be discarded as outdated ideas. He wrote as co-author of the book '*The Crisis of Democracy,*' "*We have come to recognize that there are potential desirable limits to economic growth. There are also potentially desirable limits to the indefinite extension of political democracy. A government which lacks authority will have little ability short of cataclysmic crisis to impose on its people the sacrifices which may be necessary.*"

The philosophical underpinnings of the Trilateral Commission *are pro-Marxist. They are solidly set against the nation-state* and in particular, the Constitution of the United States. Thus, *national sovereignty must be abolished altogether in order to make way for the New World Order that will be governed by an unelected global Elite* with their self-created legal framework.

The Trilateral Commission established a firm grip on the Executive Branch of the US government with the election of Jimmy Carter in 1976 who was personally tutored in globalist philosophy and foreign policy by Zbigniew Brzezinski himself. Subsequently, when Carter was sworn in as President, he appointed no less than one-third of the US members of the TC to his Cabinet and other high-level posts in his Administration.

Thus, every Administration since Carter has had top-level Trilateral Commission representation either through the President or Vice-president.

The JASON Society

The JASON Society takes its name from the story of *Jason and the Golden Fleece* and it is a branch of the Order of the Quest, one of the most influential elements in the Illuminati. The Golden Fleece takes on the role of truth to JASON members and Jason represents the search for the truth. Therefore the name JASON Society denotes a group of men who are engaged in a search for the truth. The name Jason is always spelled with capital letters when used as the name of the JASON Society.

Founders of the JASON Group include members of the famous Manhattan Project, which brought together almost every leading physicist to build the atomic bomb during World War II. The group consists mostly of theoretical physicists and is the most elite gathering of scientific minds in the United States. As of 1987, the membership included four Nobel Prize winners and today JASON continues to offer scientific help the government cannot source elsewhere. They are probably the only group of scientists in the United States that know the true state of available technology.

JASON is shrouded in what appears to be unnecessary secrecy. For example, the group refuses to release its membership list and none of the members list JASON membership on their official resumés. Working completely 'behind the scenes,' JASON has guided the nation's most important security decisions and these include, but are not limited to, Star Wars, submarine warfare, and predictions about the greenhouse effect. According to the Pentagon, the JASONS hold the highest and most restrictive security clearances in the nation and are allocated the protocol rank of Rear Admiral when they visit or travel aboard ships or visit military bases.

The veil of secrecy drawn around the JASON Group has been so tight and so leak-proof since its inception that those who believe that the government cannot keep a secret may need to re-examine that position.

The Council on Foreign Relations (CFR)

The Council on Foreign Relations has been the leading edge of America's foreign-policy establishment for more than half a century. It is a private organisation of business executives, scholars and political leaders that studies global problems and plays a key role in developing US foreign policy. The CFR is one of the most powerful semi-official groups concerned with America's role in international affairs and is controlled by an unelected group of men recruited from the Skull and Bones and the Scroll and Key societies of Harvard and Yale, which are both chapters of a secret branch of the Illuminati.

The Council on Foreign Relations is a sister organisation, an off-shoot of the British, Royal Institute of International Affairs whose ultimate goal is also the New World Order. Although it existed originally as a 'diner's club' in New York, it did not take on its present form until 1921, when it merged with the Royal Institute of International Affairs and received its financial backing from JP Morgan, the Carnegie Endowment, the Rockefeller family, and other Wall Street bankster interests.

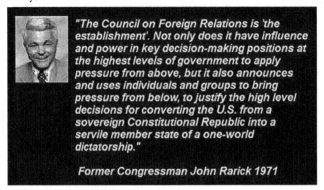

"The Council on Foreign Relations is 'the establishment'. Not only does it have influence and power in key decision-making positions at the highest levels of government to apply pressure from above, but it also announces and uses individuals and groups to bring pressure from below, to justify the high level decisions for converting the U.S. from a sovereign Constitutional Republic into a servile member state of a one-world dictatorship."

Former Congressman John Rarick 1971

The Council on Foreign Relations (along with the TC and the RIIA) controls our governments. Through the years its members have infiltrated the entire executive branch, State Department, Justice Department, CIA and the top ranks of the military. Every director of the Central Intelligence Agency has been a member of the CFR and indeed all presidents since Roosevelt have been members. The members of the CFR dominate ownership of the press and most, if not all, of America's leading journalists are members. The CFR does not conform to government policy, the government conforms to CFR policy.

The Bilderberg Group

The most powerful 'secret' organisation in the world is the Bilderberg Group, created in 1952 and named after the hotel where its first meeting took place in 1954. The man who instigated the Bilderberg Group, Prince Bernhard of the Netherlands, has the power to veto the Vatican's choice of any Pope it selects because his family, the Hapsburgs, are descended from the Holy Roman Emperors.

Prince Bernhard, with the assistance of the CIA, brought the hidden ruling body of the Illuminati into the public domain as the Bilderberg Group. This is the official alliance that makes up the true world governing body. It is an annual conference of Elites so secretive that it was nameless until being coined 'The Bilderberg Group,' after its original meeting place. They first convened in 1954 at the Bilderberg hotel in Holland under direction of the former Nazi, Prince Bernhard and David Rockefeller.

At the core of the organisation is three committees made up of thirteen members each. Thus the heart of the Bilderberg Group consists of 39 members with around 130 politicians, bankers, businessmen and senior media executives invited each year. The three committees are made up exclusively of members of all the different secret groups that make up the Illuminati, the Freemasons, the Vatican, and the Black Nobility. This committee works year-round in offices in Switzerland and absolutely determines who is to be invited to the annual meeting and what policies and plans will be discussed.

Every proposal or plan that has ever been discussed at an annual meeting of the Bilderberg Group has come to pass usually within one or two years following the meeting. It directs the 'silent war' that is being waged against us all. These are the men who really rule the world.

"Surely senior officials of the World Trade Organization, Federal Reserve, Financial Institutions like Rockefeller (the man himself,) the EU and UN World Government models, and corporate oil conglomerates couldn't belong to the same group as the leading politicians and the media? Well, they do. They all belong to the Bilderberg Group." Paul Joseph Watson, 'Order Out of Chaos'

"In 1954 the elite of the planet met in secret at the Bilderberg Hotel in Holland. The Bilderberg Group would later admit that their mission was the formation of the EU. Once the EU was established, under the guise of trade deals, a North American Union and Asian Union would be formed. The three interlocking super-states form the core of the global government, while the United Nations would serve as a world regulatory and enforcement body over the third-world sub-regions. The Bilderberg Group consists of the heads of all the managing Round Table groups that steer individual countries. Picture the elite power structure of the world as a giant pyramid with only the elite of the elite at the tip-top of the capstone. The group has been so secretive that until the mid-1980s the controlled corporate media denied its existence. Into the late 1990s coverage only consisted of rare one-line mentions, but with the rise of the alternative media, their strangle-hold on information has begun to slip." Alex Jones, 'Endgame'

In the Illuminati hierarchy, the Bilderberg Group sits above and controls the CFR, RIIA, and Trilateral Commission. It is composed of Kings, Queens, Princes and Princesses, Presidents and Prime Ministers from all over the world, IMF / World Bank / Federal Reserve heads, US Senators, CFR members, EU Commissioners, Rockefellers, Rothschilds, Journalists, TV News Anchors, CEOs and more. The last six heads of NATO have all been Bilderberg Group members.

In 1991 Bill Clinton was invited and the next year became President. Coincidence? You decide. Other notable attendees include, Margaret Thatcher, Tony Blair, Gordon Brown, Dan Quayle, Alan Greenspan, Gerald Ford, Henry Kissinger, Richard Pearle, Donald Rumsfeld, Colin Powell, William Perry, Prince Charles, Prince Philip, King Juan Carlos and Queen Sophia of Spain, Queen Beatrix and Prince Bernhard of the Netherlands, Peter Jennings, Rupert Murdoch, William F. Buckley Jr., Nelson, Jay and David Rockefeller, Jacob, Guy, Evelyn, Emma, and Lynn Forester Rothschild, Sigmund and Eric Warburg.

"The Bilderbergers meet once or sometimes twice a year. Those in attendance include leading political and financial figures from the United States and Western Europe. Prince Bernhard makes no effort to hide the fact that the ultimate goal of the Bilderbergers is a world government. In the meantime, while the 'New World Order' is being built, the Bilderbergers coordinate the efforts of the European and American power Elites. Prince Bernhard's

counterpart among the American Bilderbergers is David Rockefeller, chairman of the board of the CFR, whose economic base is the giant Chase Manhattan Bank and Standard Oil. Among the other Bilderbergers from the world of ultra-high finance are Baron Edmund de Rothschild of the House of Rothschild, C. Douglas Dillon of Dillon Read and Co., Robert McNamara of the World Bank, Sir Eric Roll of S. G. Warburg and Co., Ltd., Pierce Paul Schweitzer of the International Monetary Fund, and George Ball of Lehman Brothers. Every single one of those named as past and present members of the Bilderberger Steering Committee is or was a member of the Council on Foreign Relations." Gary Allen, 'None Dare Call it Conspiracy'

If you have never heard of Bilderberg it is probably because the heads of *CNN*, *Fox News*, *Newsweek*, *Time*, *The Washington Post*, The *Wall Street Journal* and many other media outlets are regular attendees. Protestors and 'lesser' journalists are kept at bay by private police, no one is allowed anywhere near the venue and no minutes of the meetings are ever made public.

"Now the Bilderberg Group in Reuters (which they own) has gone public that it actually grooms our presidents and our prime ministers; that, yes, its members really are international banksters; yes, royal families are involved; yes, the Bilderberg Group runs the central banks; and, yes, the elitists see us as the property of a global super-state (Reuters, May 23, 2001, Secretive Bilderberg Group to Meet in Sweden). Bilderberg member Prince Philip, in his own publication 'If I Were an Animal,' brags about how he would kill eighty percent of the population; how his great dream is to come back as a virus." Alex Jones, *'9-11, Descent into Tyranny.'* Alex Jones, despite his role as 'gatekeeper to Zionism,' does occasionally produce some valuable insight, too.

The late Jim Tucker made it his life's mission, to expose the criminal globalist organisation, known as *The Bilderberg Group*. Jim tracked their every move for over 25 years, reporting their clandestine meetings, *via several 'inside sources'* and he is largely the reason that we know so much about this criminal cartel now.

Despite all his years in the media, Tucker had never once heard of Bilderberg and once he discovered them, he realised immediately, as any real journalist should, that there was something wrong. As Tucker summarised it, quite correctly, time and again over the years, *"If a hundred of the world's best known sports figures or film stars were gathered at some exclusive resort behind closed doors for a private meeting, the entirety of the mass media would be on hand, clamouring for admittance and demanding to know what was going on. But when the world's richest banksters, media barons, industrialists, members of royalty, and political leaders were meeting secretly and discussing public policy matters that impacted on the course of the world's affairs, the establishment press never said a word."*

Best known for having tracked the aforementioned Rockefeller and the members of such high-level power groups such as the Council on Foreign Relations, the Trilateral Commission and, most notably, the Bilderberg Group, literally all over the planet for decades, the legacy of Tucker, self-described 'country boy' as a brave, no-nonsense investigative reporter is one that is difficult to deny.

The world is indeed a poorer place without him. R.I.P. Jim.

Chapter 5
The British Royal Bankster Family

An apt question at this point may well be; why include a section on the royal family in a book about the 'banksters?' The simple answer is that even though the myriad of Central Banks existing throughout the world never fully disclose their shareholders, much circumstantial evidence points to the fact that the royals pull many of the strings and are heavily financially involved 'behind the scenes' in central banking. In short, they themselves are banksters too.

The Royal families of Britain and Europe hold a special place in the hearts of many people who seem to absolutely believe the propaganda directed at us daily from the fawning media in all its forms. This insidious propaganda holds that these people are not far removed from being Gods or angels as well as being incapable of committing any wrongdoing whatsoever.

It also tells us that the existence of the Royal family is absolutely essential to the British economy and that without the 'tourism' engendered solely by these living Gods, that somehow we would all be living in abject poverty by now. Maybe a slight exaggeration by me, but I think you get the picture?

Actually it is all LIES . . . Unfortunately, I have to inform anyone who still lives in this fool's paradise regarding these genocidal parasites, that they have almost single-handedly been responsible for more deaths, murders and yes, even genocide down the centuries than any other family you could care to name. And this is not just simply 'all in the past' either, it continues to this day.

". . . this is the result of aeons of propaganda which has been perpetrated by the royal-political elite, who use pomp and circumstance, parades, fly-bys, flag-waving, national anthems, patriotism, royal weddings and the kissing of babies, as a tool to fool people into thinking that they have some kind of group membership to a nation which has at its head either a king, queen or president that represents their wishes and protects their families. It's a lie."
Chris Everard, British researcher and film director

It is actually provable that these burdens on our economy do not even pay for themselves via so-called tourism, let alone bring a huge bounty into the country from foreigners eager to spend millions and attracted only by thoughts of catching a glimpse of a 'minor royal' shopping in Harrods or catching a number 54 bus down to Portobello Road market to do bit of Saturday afternoon bargain-hunting.

Firstly, think about this . . . So what, if Buckingham Palace and other royal residences attract huge numbers of visitors every year? Where does all that money generated actually go? Back into the royal coffers and not into some communal 'pot' to be shared-out equally between all the citizens of the United Kingdom, I would suggest. The only group that actually benefits from 'royal' tourism are the royals themselves and there is no proof in the statement often made, that large numbers of people only visit London each year because of the royal connection, thereby contributing to the economy in many other ways.

In fact, secondly, think about this too...even if it was that the royals were almost solely responsible for the attraction of all that supposed foreign money flowing into the country, who actually benefits from all that 'extra' tourism income? Certainly not you or I, not at all. Maybe the large corporate hotel chains and the huge chain stores that abound in London or maybe even the theatre and entertainment industry, but we 'ordinary' folk? No, not a chance. We never see any of this supposed foreign bounty, ever, it only goes to businesses and gets re-cycled in that way. In other words it only goes directly to the already filthy rich (the banksters, who else?) to increase their already considerable fortunes—and NOT to the likes of you or I.

Royal Intrigue

The noted New Zealand researcher and author, Greg Hallet has spent almost a lifetime enquiring and probing into the murky, hidden realms of European royalty and his findings are an absolute revelation. Albeit, maybe an unbelievable revelation to those who will not hear a bad word spoken about our wonderful Royal families. So, what follows is not all my own research but mainly consists of Hallet's own findings, sometimes verbatim and sometimes paraphrased and edited by myself.

In an earlier chapter, I stated that the legendary, 'glorious' British Empire presided over by Queen Victoria, was in reality the British bankster Empire that was ruled primarily by the Rothschilds.

Nathan Mayer Rothschild wanted more than to just simply control the flow and production of money. He had accomplished that already by assuming firm control of the Bank of England in 1815, but he also wanted to control the royal bloodlines too. As the monarchs and nobility of Europe always seemed to be short of funds to service their utterly extravagant lifestyles and to maintain their strings of homes and palaces, it was no surprise that Prince Edward, Duke of Kent and Strathearn, was unable to pay his gambling debts, let alone maintain his string of mistresses with expensive tastes and expectations. As the fourth son of British King George III, Prince Edward was created Duke of Kent and Strathearn and Earl of Dublin on 23rd April 1799 and a few weeks later, was appointed a General and commander-in-chief of British forces in North America.

On 23rd March 1802 he was appointed Governor of Gibraltar and nominally retained that post until his death. Prince Edward was appointed Field-Marshal of the British forces on 3rd September 1805 and became the first member of the royal family to live in North America for more than just simply a short visit (1791-1800) and the first prince to enter the United States, travelling to Boston by foot from Lower Canada after American independence in 1794.

Virtually bankrupt, he was approached by Nathan Mayer Rothschild who offered to pay-off all his debts in return for certain breeding rights. 'Breeding' has always been an issue with royalty, but now, it seemed that the Rothschilds also wanted to follow suit and create an exclusive bloodline similar to the royal line.

Mary Louise Victoire, born 17th August 1786, was the fourth daughter and seventh child of Franz Frederick Anton, Duke of Saxe-Coburg-Saalfeld, and Countess Augusta of Reuss-Ebersdorf. On 21 December 1803 at Coburg, she married (as his second wife) Charles, Prince of Leiningen (1763—1814), whose first wife, Henrietta of Reuss-Ebersdorf, was her aunt. Charles and Victoria had two children, Carl Friedrich Wilhelm Emich and Princess Anna Fedora Auguste Charlotte Wilhelmine.

Through her first marriage, she was a direct matrilineal ancestor to various members of royalty in Europe, including Carl XVI Gustaf of Sweden, Felipe, Prince of Asturias and Constantine II of Greece. On 29th May 1818 at Amorbach she married Prince Edward, Duke of Kent and Strathearn, and became Princess Mary Louise Victoria of Saxe-Coburg-Saalfeld, Princess of Leiningen, Duchess of Kent and Strathearn.

Mainstream history relates that Edward and Victoria had one child together and that child would eventually become the legendary Queen Victoria, ruler of the British Empire. However there is evidence to suggest the true father was none other than Nathan Mayer Rothschild.

Alexandrina Victoria was born on 24th May 1819, and she was born illegitimate, fifth in the line of succession after her father and his three older brothers; the Prince Regent, the Duke of York and the Duke of Clarence (later King William IV.) The Prince Regent and the Duke of York were estranged from their wives, who were both past child-bearing age anyway and so the two eldest brothers were unlikely to have any further children. The Dukes of Kent and Clarence married on the same day, one year before Victoria's birth, but both of Clarence's daughters (born in 1819 and 1820 respectively) died as infants. Victoria's grandfather and father died in 1820 within a week of each other, and the Duke of York died in 1827.

On the death of her uncle, King George IV in 1830, Victoria became heiress presumptive to her next surviving uncle, King William IV. The Regency Act of 1830 made special provision for the Duchess of Kent to act as regent in the event of William's death whilst Victoria was still a minor. However, William was not at all confident in the Duchess's ability to act as Regent and in 1836 declared in her presence that he wished to live until Victoria's 18th birthday, so that a Regency could be avoided.

Just eight months after Alexandrina Victoria's birth, her 'official' father, Prince Edward, the Duke of Kent died suddenly—and strangely—of 'pneumonia,' a few days before his father, King George III. The widowed Duchess had little cause to remain in the United Kingdom, being unable to speak English and having a palace back home in Coburg, where she could live on the incomes of her first husband, the late Prince of Leiningen.

However, the Duchess decided that she would be better served by 'gambling' on her daughter's accession than by living quietly in Coburg and sought support from the British government, having inherited her second husband's considerable debts. After the death of Edward and his father, the young Princess Alexandrina Victoria was still only third in line to the throne and Parliament was not inclined to support yet another impoverished royal. The Duchess of Kent was allowed a suite of rooms in the by this time, dilapidated Kensington Palace, along with several other impoverished nobles. There she raised her daughter, Victoria, who on 20th June 1837, was to become Queen of the United Kingdoms of Great Britain and Ireland, and eventually Empress of India.

Queen Victoria eventually began to suspect that her mother's lover and her 'father's' comptroller, Sir John Ponsonby Conroy, whom she absolutely detested, was somehow involved in the very strange circumstances of her father's death. Although her father at the time of his untimely death was fifty three years of age, he was nevertheless fit and strong. The fact that he was suddenly laid-low by what was little more than a bad cold is acceptable, but that he actually died from this condition is very odd indeed. It certainly was extremely convenient for him to die suddenly at that time. As both an agent for Nathan Mayer Rothschild and a 'handler' for the Duchess, Sir John Conroy had been conducting a long-term affair with the Duchess.

The Duchess may well have given birth to his child, the next in line to the throne, but knowing the highly efficient spy network of the Rothschilds and their utter ruthlessness, it is unlikely that Sir John would have been stupid enough to 'cross' them in any way.

Sir John or rather Nathan Rothschild, had gained almost complete control of the Duchess, except for the fact that her husband, the Duke, was still alive. The Duke was quite an obstacle. He was financially insolvent, unstable, hugely disliked and feared by the royal household and most crucially, he was about to expose his wife's illicit liaison, send the Duchess back to Europe and take complete charge of the young princess.

It is strange to note that the Duke's entire household packed-up and moved to a remote, basic country cottage in the middle of one the coldest winters ever known. Sir John had arranged this bizarre move to save money, or so he said. Sir John being the Duke's equerry was in control of all the Duke's business.

He had been highly instrumental in the Duke's convenient and speedily arranged marriage to an unknown princess of an obscure German state. The Duke was unusually childless whilst his brothers had numerous illegitimate offspring from their various mistresses. The situation in Britain was, at that time extraordinary also in that King George III had thirteen children and yet not one of them had produced a legitimate child between them. There was no heir to the throne at all and so it was rather surprising that only a few months after the royal marriage the Duke and Duchess announced that an heir to the throne was expected. It was even more suspect, that so soon after Princess Victoria's birth, that the Duke of Kent succumbed to a 'cold,' dying very suddenly indeed. This left the baby princess not only the heir to the throne of Great Britain but her hopeless mother, the possible Regent of Britain and Sir John totally in control of both of them.

In 1833 at age fourteen, Princess Victoria, soon to be Queen Victoria and the sixty-four year old Duke of Wellington, victor over Napoleon's forces at Waterloo, the 'Iron Duke,' fell in love and secretly married and the fruit of their forbidden, secret love was a son who eventually became Prince Marcos Manoel. The Duke of Wellington's wife, Catherine Sarah Dorothea Wellesley, Duchess of Wellington, had died two years previously, so the secret marriage and the child heir were both absolutely 'legitimate.'

However, the boy was sent into exile in Portugal and given a Portuguese name as part of the elaborate cover-up but nevertheless, being the first-born son of Victoria, Marcos Manoel should have ascended to the English throne when the Queen died in 1901. But significantly, from this date onwards, a wave of destruction of the letters and diaries of Victoria began. Sir Philip Magnus, King Edward VII's biographer, expressed his regrets for this 'irreparable loss' to history.

In the 1920s the descendants of Marcos Manoel were seriously threatened and this is the reason that Francisco Manoel, first representative of the primogeniture of Queen Victoria, took the initiative of disclosing the British Crown's great secret.

Victoria never divorced Wellington and so in 1840, when she married Prince Albert of Saxe Coburg, it was therefore a bigamous marriage. Prince Albert was a closet homosexual and he too was illegitimate. His mother was Princess Louise of Saxe Coburg and his father was a stable boy called Alex Hanstein who later became Baron von Hanstein and the Count of Polzig. Alex Hanstein was himself the illegitimate son of Baron Karl von Hanstein.

Prince Albert always wore what was eventually named after him, a 'Prince Albert,' which was a chain linked to a piercing through his penis, drawn-up and around his waist, so in effect his penis was always vertical, but he was totally incapable of fathering a child. Queen Victoria's children were in fact fathered by Lionel Nathan de Rothschild who was Nathan Mayer Rothschild's son. Lionel Nathan de Rothschild through his immense power and influence eventually became the first Jewish Member of Parliament.

Benjamin Disraeli was the principal agent through whom Lionel Rothschild, by granting financial and other favours to numerous traitors, at last and after many failures, secured 'emancipation' for the Jews, complete with the right to sit in the House of Commons after taking a Jewish, not a Christian, oath. Lionel was first elected in 1847 as Member for the City of London, but as the House of Lords refused for years to pass Bills for Jewish Emancipation which had already been passed in the lower House, he was unable to take his seat. His constituents however, returned him to the Commons five times in succession, regardless of this fact. It was not until 1858 that he was enabled by law to take his oath in the Jewish form with his head covered. In 1850, he actually had the effrontery to try and 'con' the House by substituting the words, *"So help me, God,"* for *"…on the true faith of a Christian,"* but was ordered to withdraw by the Speaker.

As did Queen Victoria's father, Prince Edward, her 'official' husband Prince Albert, also died of 'pneumonia' in 1861.

Upon his death, and for the rest of her long life, she was a black-clad, virtual recluse. The elderly monarch lived in an atmosphere of grim silence in her castle at Balmoral, Scotland. She had as little contact with her staff as possible; if they needed to tell her something, they wrote a short note and placed it inside a sealed envelope and if their paths crossed in the house or gardens, they were expected to hide behind a convenient piece of furniture or if outside, the nearest bush.

It was at this time that John Brown, a dour Scotsman, entered her life. At first he was only employed as Victoria's fishing and hunting guide (a ghillie,) but as time passed and they grew closer, he accompanied her almost everywhere and was her constant companion. Brown was also given duties as Victoria's bodyguard, responsible for her safety on her rare public appearances. There had been several assassination attempts whilst Victoria rode in her carriage and contrary to the common myth that she was a well-loved and respected queen, the real truth was that she was hated by many, and during her reign Britain had never been closer to revolution in the previous two hundred years, such was the strong revulsion for her at the time.

Brown was born in 1826 and he died in 1883, aged 56. He treated Victoria somewhat differently than did all the other servants. He was altogether more informal, indeed more like a friend than a servant and in fact many believe that he was actually her lover.

After John Brown, Victoria eventually acquired another servant / confidante in the form of her Indian manservant, Abdul Karim.

In the Queen's Diamond Jubilee year of 1897, the Prince of Wales, the future Edward VII actually threatened to have his mother declared insane. Unthinkable? Well, that is exactly what happened after her Royal Household refused to condone the Queen's shockingly intimate friendship with Karim.

Victoria had become very fond of India and everything Indian and maybe this was the initial attraction for her, in this 'romantic' man of mystery. In fact she became so infatuated with the tall, handsome Muslim, Abdul Karim that senior royal advisers plotted to have her declared insane just days before her Jubilee unless she halted a controversial plan to knight him.

The young waiter—he was just 24—had begun serving at the Queen's table in June 1887 after being sent to London as a 'gift' from her Indian subjects. He soon began bewitching her with romantic tales of mysterious India and cooking up delicious curries for her in the royal kitchens.

Queen Victoria's Diamond Jubilee London, 1897

Victoria promoted Abdul from waiter to her personal teacher or 'Munshi' and after he began to teach her a few words in Hindi, the pair grew even closer. She had been starved of affection since the death of John Brown, and Abdul Karim's great-grandson, Javed Mahmood, recently said it is not difficult to see why she fell for his great-grandfather. He said, *"Abdul was a very warm man. He was very jolly, entertaining — a very human person. Maybe those were the traits that attracted the Queen eventually, because he came across as a man of flesh and blood, and she wasn't used to real people around her."*

Obviously, their growing intimacy was not well received in the strict, hierarchical world of the royal household. Nevertheless, in 1894, Abdul was elevated to the position of the queen's Indian Secretary making him an official member of the 'inner circle.' The idea that a servant, an outsider who has no pedigree or background, could suddenly attain a position of great closeness with the Queen was not very well received by the rest of her courtiers. And i*t wasn't just Abdul's 'class' that troubled the Queen's advisers, they were also scandalised by his 'race' too.*

But the more the royal household attacked Abdul, the more the Queen defended him. She sent an angry memo to her Private Secretary, Sir Henry Ponsonby, saying, *"As for Abdul Karim, the Queen cannot praise him highly enough. He's zealous and attentive, a thorough gentleman."*

The Royal household retaliated by sending investigators to India who returned with 'alarming' information about Abdul's origins. He was not, as he had claimed, the son of an important military doctor, in fact, his father was a lowly pharmacist who worked in Agra jail where Abdul himself had worked as a clerk. *But these revelations only served to push the Queen closer to Abdul.* She took a stance that was astonishing at the time—accusing her household of racial prejudice. In another memo to Ponsonby she wrote, *"To make out that the Munshi is low is outrageous. Abdul feels cut to the heart to be thus spoken of. The Queen is so sorry for the poor Munshi's sensitive feelings."*

Rumours soon began to circulate to the effect that Abdul was passing Victoria inflammatory advice about India and that he was a spy, leaking secret foreign policy information. Then in 1897, just a few weeks before Victoria's Diamond Jubilee celebrations, the Queen announced she planned to knight Abdul.

*This 'bombshell' was one step too far for her ministers and courtiers and even t*he Viceroy of India joined forces with the Prime Minister to oppose the move. In response, Victoria threatened to pull out of the Jubilee celebrations. With possibly the most prestigious public event that the British monarchy had ever seen, now under serious threat, the Queen's eldest son, Bertie, later Edward VII, assumed control of the situation. He hatched a plan with the Queen's doctor, Sir James Reid, who wrote to her, saying...

"There are people in high places who know your majesty well and say to me the only charitable explanation that can be given is that your majesty is not sane, and that at some time it will be necessary for me to come forward and say so. I have seen the Prince of Wales yesterday and he has said he is quite ready to come forward, because it affects the throne."

Victoria was angry but knew that she had to admit defeat and Abdul did not get his knighthood after all, but he was her constant companion during the Jubilee celebration and for the remaining four years of Victoria's life, she was inseparable from her beloved servant.

But when she finally died in early 1901, the protection Abdul had enjoyed came to a sudden end. Early one cold, February morning, around one month after Victoria's death, the inhabitants of a small cottage on the Windsor Castle estate were startled by a loud banging at the door. Tired and dazed, the head of the household, Abdul Karim, opened the front door to find a group of soldiers standing outside. They were accompanied by Queen Alexandra, wife of the new king, Edward VII and by Princess Beatrice, youngest daughter of the late Queen Victoria.

Much to Karim's astonishment, the party ordered him to hand over every letter, note and memo that the late Queen had sent him over the 13 years he had served her. She had written him many letters, sometimes several in a day, and often signing them 'your affectionate mother' and Karim had treasured them. Now the new King wanted them destroyed and so a bonfire was started outside the cottage and Karim watched in horror and sadness as every piece of paper bearing the Queen's handwriting was consumed by the flames.

Karim and his family were then ordered to pack their bags and leave for India immediately. The fairy-tale had ended and 8 years later, Karim died heart-broken in Agra, aged only 46.

His descendants left for Pakistan when the country was partitioned in 1947, leaving behind all the land and exquisite gifts given to Abdul Karim by Queen Victoria and other European royalty. Only a diary and a few items of memorabilia survived. A lonely grave in Agra, some portraits in Osborne House, the Hindustani journals they wrote for 13 years and a house that bears his name in Balmoral, are all that remain today of the Queen's closest confidant. Yet the story still remains and as yet has still not quite been erased from the history books.

Victoria and 'Albert's' eldest son, Albert Edward, was king of the United Kingdom and the British Dominions and Emperor of India from 22nd January 1901 until his death in 1910. He was the first British monarch of the House of Saxe-Coburg and Gotha.

Before his accession to the throne, he served as heir apparent and held the title of Prince of Wales for longer than any of his predecessors. During the long reign of his mother, Queen Victoria, he was largely excluded from political power and came to personify the fashionable, 'idle rich.'

The Edwardian era coincided with the start of a new century and heralded significant changes in technology and society, including powered flight and the rise of socialism/communism. Edward played a role in the modernisation of the British Home Fleet, the reform of the Army Medical Services and the reorganisation of the British Army after the Second Boer War. He also fostered good relations between Great Britain and other European countries, especially France, for which he was popularly called 'Peacemaker.'

Shortly after his accession, King Edward VII, discovered that his elder, legitimate half-brother, Marcos Manoel was still alive, causing his coronation to be delayed for 18 months from the 22nd January 1901 to the 9th August 1902. It was for this reason—that is to remove the threat posed by the legitimate heir to the throne—that King Edward VII personally ordered the murder of Marcos Manoel and then passed-on instructions to his son, King George V, who reigned from 1910 to 1936, to assassinate the exiled King of Portugal, King Manuel II, in Twickenham, south London. This destroyed the remainder of the Portuguese Royal Family and thereby eliminating the threat to Edward's bloodline.

Edward VII was a serial womaniser, and also bisexual, but he, despite the sobriquet of 'peacemaker,' far more than any other single human being, was the instigator of the First World War and thus brought about what was probably the most destructive single event in the history of western civilisation, to that point in history. When Edward VII married, he chose Princess Alexandra of the Danish Royal family, who had her own anti-German sentiments, because of Bismarck's war against Denmark in 1864.

Edward set up a discreet household in Marlborough House in London and began his long career as a royal rake. He became the undisputed leader of British high society and a legendary hedonist and sex maniac whose mistresses included Lillie Langtry, Daisy Countess of Warwick, Lady Brooke, Mrs. George Keppel and many others, too numerous to mention. Some of the can-can dancers painted by Toulouse-Lautrec had also been amongst Edward's hundreds of conquests.

There was also a fling with Sarah Bernhardt, the French actress. When Bernhardt was appearing in '*Fedora*' in Paris, Edward confided to her that he had always wanted to be an actor and so, the next night, in the scene in which Fedora comes upon the dead body of her lover, no-one recognised the heir to the British throne who was making his stage debut . . . as a corpse.

Edward's home at Marlborough House in London was also a centre of the 'Homintern,' the hub of the homosexual activities of London's high society, of which Edward was also an active and enthusiastic member. In fact, one of Edward's friends, Lord Arthur Somerset, known to his friends as 'Podge,' was arrested during a police raid on one of London's numerous homosexual brothels.

Prince Felix Yussupov was a prominent member of the Russian royal family and was also considered the most beautiful transvestite in Europe. One evening, Yussupov, dressed as usual as a woman, attended the theatre in Paris and soon noticed a portly, whiskered gentleman ogling him through an opera glass from one of the box seats. Within minutes, Yussupov received a propositioning note, signed King Edward VII. Yussupov was later to become one of the assassins of Rasputin, the 'mad monk' and reputed German agent, in December 1916.

The 'Royal' Jack the Ripper Murders

Edward VII's first-born son was Prince Albert Victor Edward, known to the family as 'Prince Eddy' and more formally as the Duke of Clarence and Avondale. Eddy was therefore the grandson of the reigning monarch, Queen Victoria and older brother of the future king of England, King George V and as such would have been first in line to the throne before George, had fate not overtaken him.

Unfortunately, due to centuries of Royal in-breeding, Eddy was partially deaf and of well below average intelligence and was thus shunned by the majority of his cold-hearted family.

Prince Eddy was arrested at least once in a homosexual brothel but his main claim to infamy today is that he had an indirect involvement in the 'Jack the Ripper' murders. This grisly series of crimes involved the murder of five prostitutes in the slums of the Whitechapel area of London in 1888. At the time of the murders, rumours were rife of the involvement of a member of the royal family and of freemasonic intrigue.

Prince Albert Victor Edward (Eddy) (1864-1933)

The story began in the late summer of 1888, the heyday of Queen Victoria's reign, in the gas-lit streets of London, when a young woman's horrifically mutilated body was discovered in a tawdry slum street, in the run-down Whitechapel area of London . . . .

On the evening of the 31st August 1888 the body of Mary Ann Nicholls, a common prostitute, was found prostrate on a pavement in the Whitechapel district in the East End of London. She had been brutally hacked to death, her throat having been slit and devastating cuts to her torso revealed her exposed internal organs. She was to be the first of a series of five victims of the now legendary killer who came to be known in popular folklore as 'Jack the Ripper.'

The so-called 'Ripper' murders came under the jurisdiction of the London Metropolitan Police Force and in particular an Inspector by the name of Frederick George Abberline, who was tasked with the overseeing of the investigation. It is important to note that the diaries of Frederick Abberline did not see light of day until around 70 years after the unsolved murders, being in the possession during this time, firstly of Walter Sickert (1860-1942), the famous artist of the time and latterly of Joseph Sickert, his son. The full significance of this will become apparent later.

Walter Sickert had been employed by the royal family in the 1880s to provide private art lessons to their son and heir, Prince Albert Victor, the Duke of Clarence, otherwise known by his colloquial name of 'Prince Eddy.' Eddy was in fact the eldest son of Albert Edward the Prince of Wales (later King Edward VII) and Princess Alexandra (later Queen Alexandra), the eldest grandson of the reigning monarch, Queen Victoria and older brother of the future king of England, King George V and as such would eventually have been first in line to the throne. Unfortunately however, Eddy was not in the best of health. He had been born, mainly due to centuries of royal in-breeding, partially deaf and of well below average intelligence and was thus shunned by the majority of his cold-hearted family.

Queen Victoria, the reigning monarch at the time was a great supporter and patron of freemasonry, as were all the Royal males of the age (and as they still are today.) Indeed it was the Saxe-Coburg-Gotha family (the current British royals) that had sponsored the rise of Adam Weishaupt, the founder of the Illuminati, originally a freemasonry offshoot, in Bavaria in the 18th century. Weishaupt himself was born and raised in the Bavarian town of Gotha.

It is a little known or reported fact that there are several masonic lodges in the royal palaces of Britain, the most significant one perhaps being the Royal Alpha Lodge in Kensington Palace. In 1885 Prince Eddy was initiated into the Royal Alpha Lodge at the behest of his father.

As well as his membership of the lodge, Eddy was also a regular attendee at a homosexual-paedophile brothel in Cleveland Street, London and indiscreetly instigated a series of explicit love-letters with a young boy employed at these most vile of premises. The well-known Satanist, Aleister Crowley had these letters in his possession for many years but eventually they were lost or more likely destroyed and have never since seen the light of day. This incident alone had the potential to become a huge national scandal if made public, but events took a turn for the worse when it was discovered that Eddy had also made a young Catholic 'commoner' of Irish descent by the name of Annie Elizabeth Crook, pregnant with his child. Eddy also, as it turned out, had foolishly married her in a clandestine church service and this in effect barred him from ever becoming king, as royal protocol does not permit British royals to marry Catholics, let alone one who is deemed to be a commoner and bearing a child conceived out of wedlock.

In 1883, Eddy's mother, Princess Alexandra, had asked the young painter Walter Sickert to introduce Eddy to the artistic and literary life of London. Sickert's studio, where he spent most of his time, was at 15 Cleveland Street near to Tottenham Court Road in north London. He duly introduced the teenage Prince to many of the area's 'bohemian types,' including the theatrical friends he had made when, for four years, he had been a minor member of the Lyceum Theatre Company. Sickert also introduced Eddy to one of his models, a pretty Irish Catholic girl, the afore-mentioned Annie Crook who lived nearby at 6 Cleveland Street, and who worked by day in a local confectioners shop. They fell for each other and, according to Sickert, went through two clandestine marriage ceremonies, one Anglican and one Catholic. Soon afterwards, due to Annie's pregnancy, her employer needed someone to deputise for her during her confinement.

Walter Sickert was asked if he knew anyone suitable and, after consulting friends, found a young girl by the name of Mary Jean (Marie Jeanette) Kelly, from the Providence Row Night Refuge for Women in Whitechapel. For some months, Mary worked alongside Annie Crook in the shop and the two became friends. In due course, on the 18th April 1885, Annie gave birth to Eddy's daughter, Alice Margaret and when she returned home, her new friend Mary Kelly moved-in as the child's nursemaid. Mary also worked as a prostitute in the evenings to supplement her meagre income.

Annie Crook—Walter Sickert's portrait

Naturally, Eddy absolutely enraged the establishment with his 'illicit' marriage and this combined with the incident of the love-letters, threatened to tear apart the monarchy and spark a constitutional crisis of major proportions. So, as is always the case, the monarchy set in motion a huge cover-up operation as part of the damage limitation process. Annie was kidnapped from the small apartment in Cleveland Street where she lived and in which Eddy spent time with her, and at the same time Eddy was abducted into a carriage headed for Buckingham Palace where he was instructed, in no uncertain terms, to remain 'under house arrest,' until further notice.

Fortunately, fearing the worst, Annie had already given the child, Alice to Walter Sickert for safekeeping shortly before she was forcefully taken to Guy's Hospital in London. She remained there for five months and whilst she was there, Sir William Gull, the Queen's personal physician performed a partial frontal lobotomy on her, in effect rendering her docile and compliant and thus easily controlled by these inhuman monsters. Subsequently certified insane by Gull, Annie lived for the rest of her life in institutions, spending her last days in the Lunacy Observation ward of St George's Union Workhouse, Chelsea and dying there in obscurity in early 1920 at the age of 57.

This was not the first time that Sir William Gull had been implicated in a scandalous royal cover-up operation. Around twenty years prior to this, the future King Edward VII, the father of Prince Eddy, had been involved in a series of extra-marital affairs, one of which was with the young Lady Harriet Mordaunt. One day she foolishly confessed to her husband, Sir Charles Mordaunt, that she had been unfaithful with several men, one of whom was the Prince of Wales.

Sir Charles was absolutely incensed and he let it be known that he intended to sue for divorce, citing the Prince as a co-respondent. The Prince of Wales was rightly nervous about giving evidence in court as it would bring shame upon the entire royal family and cause an unacceptable public scandal. So, at this point, Queen Victoria herself interceded on the Prince's behalf to protect the reputation of the family and instructed Sir William Gull to intervene.

Gull immediately, in consort with several other doctors conspired to have the young woman declared insane and locked away in a lunatic asylum, where she spent the last remaining 37 years of her life in abject misery, dying in 1906. Ultimately the case was dismissed, saving the Prince and the royals from acute embarrassment and no divorce was granted, not because adultery was unproven but simply because poor Harriet was declared insane.

However, to return to the main story, the matter might have ended there, but for Mary Kelly's greed. Back in Whitechapel, Mary had befriended three other local prostitutes to whom she boasted of her 'royal connections' and in the spring of 1888 the quartet, led by Mary, hatched a plan to demand money from Walter Sickert, threatening to otherwise make the story public. Being a simple girl, she had not fully comprehended the fact that she was in effect also holding-to-ransom a group of psychopathic murderers who would literally stop at nothing and had the means to kill with impunity whilst enjoying the full 'protection' of people in high places.

Sickert immediately passed word to Eddy who informed his father, and the Prince of Wales discussed the threat in the greatest secrecy with trusted fellow masons in the Royal Alpha Lodge. Subsequently, a special meeting was arranged at the Lodge by the royal masons known as the 'Princes of the Blood Royal,' whereby they agreed to form a 'hunting party' to literally hunt-down and kill the hapless girls as punishment for their sheer audacity and significantly, as a masonic blood-sacrifice ritual.

The 'hunting party' was drawn exclusively from the Royal Alpha Masonic Lodge and included Sir William Gull, Eddy's former Cambridge University tutor J. K. (James Kenneth) Stephen and Sir Charles Warren, Commissioner of the Metropolitan Police (who took no active part in the killings but who helped facilitate the plot and expedite the cover-up.) To drive them about their sordid business they recruited a coachman who had previously betrayed Prince Eddy's indiscretions to the royals, one John Netley.

Warren provided what information he could, on the girls' whereabouts using his privileged position in the police force and Sir William Gull prepared grapes injected with opium, which would be offered to the victims to subdue them so that the dastardly deed could take place with a minimum of fuss. It was arranged that John Netley, the coach driver and a particularly nasty character, was to be the 'getaway driver' and the 'lookout' would be J.K. Stephen, a cousin of Virginia Woolf and another freemason with royal links, whilst the murders were planned to occur within Gull's carriage—away from prying eyes.

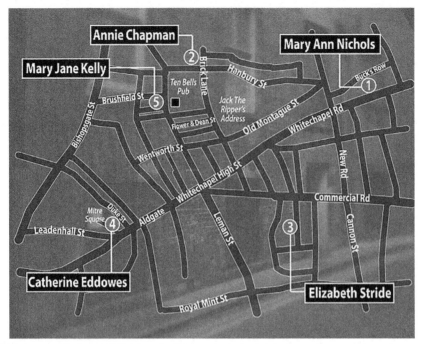

It should be noted that Abberline's diaries confirmed that the modus operandus was not that of one person only and that the murders were planned and performed according to masonic ritual, similar to a fox-hunt. These are facts which were never allowed to come to light.

So, who was the ringleader of this murderous gang? None other than the prominent freemason, Secretary of State for India, the Leader of the House of Commons and the Chancellor of the Exchequer, Lord Randolph Spencer-Churchill, father of the future prime minister, Winston Churchill. Churchill was not only the 'brains' behind the entire operation, but he was also personally responsible for the cutting of masonic emblems and symbols into the bodies of the victims, whilst the skilled surgeon's hands of William Gull performed the organ removals.

The killings and mutilations were not observed by the public simply because four of them were not carried out in the streets where the bodies were found, but in a moving coach, whilst the last was perpetrated *in situ*, in the victim Mary Kelly's own room. The police must have been aware that the bodies had been moved to their resting places due to the lack of blood as the whole pavement area would surely have been awash with blood had the rituals been performed there. Obviously though, this fact was never publicly disclosed by the police.

The assassins set about discovering the blackmailers' whereabouts with 'insider' help from Warren and then systematically plotted their ritualistic executions. The murderous spree began on the 31st August 1888 with Mary Ann Nicholls as their first victim and continued with the killing of Annie Chapman on the 8th September. In turn each woman was lured inside the coach, then killed and mutilated in the ritualistic way that the three 'Juwes,' Jubela, Jubelo and Jubelum, the murderers of Hiram Abiff in King Solomon's Temple, were executed in the old Masonic legend. Their throats were 'cut across,' from left to right, their bodies torn open, their internal organs deftly removed and arranged around the corpses in their final resting places and their entrails 'thrown over' the left shoulder.

On the 30th September there were two further killings but on that night things did not go smoothly. As the murderers were dumping that night's first victim, Lizzie Stride, in Berner Street, they were interrupted and had to abandon her corpse before its ritual mutilation had been completed. More alarming still, the night's second victim, Catherine Eddowes, was, according to Sickert, almost immediately discovered to have been killed in error. It was learnt that poor Catherine had for some time lived with a man called John Kelly, had often used his surname and so had been wrongly identified by the gang's underworld informants as the blackmailer-in-chief, Mary Kelly.

That mistake nearly led to the group's undoing. In the mistaken belief that this was to be the climactic, final episode of their campaign, the group had already arranged Catherine's corpse, more completely mutilated than any of her predecessors, in Mitre Square (significantly masonic) opposite the masonic Temple and close to the Whitechapel Road. They had chalked on a nearby wall a masonic slogan to act as a postscript to the whole sordid affair. Abberline copied it down into his notebook and it said:

The Juwes are the men thatwill notbe blamedfor nothing.

Arriving on the scene suspiciously quickly, Sir Charles Warren, to the acute surprise of his underlings, ordered that the chalked epitaph, presumed by observers to be in the killer's hand, noted by Abberline to be that of an 'educated' man, should be immediately washed down and erased. The reason he gave was that he did not want anti-Jewish sentiment to be inflamed, but Sickert suggested the real reason was that too many insiders would recognise that the message referred not to the 'Jews' but to the 'Juwes' of Masonic legend, and would therefore identify the killers as freemasons.

After this setback there was a pause of more than a month, the longest interval between the killings, whilst the group redoubled their efforts to find the real Mary Kelly who was by this time lying low in fear of her life. Meanwhile, rumours of the killer's associations with freemasonry and with the royal family continued to grow. It was not until the 9th November that Mary Kelly was finally tracked down. To use the coach again was deemed to be too dangerous now, so she was dispatched in her own Dorset Street lodgings, more bloodily mutilated than any of her fellow-conspirators, her throat slashed, her body brutally cut apart and her intestines arranged ritually about the room.

There is in existence a police drawing of the last person to be seen with Mary whilst she was still alive and this bears an uncanny resemblance to no less a person than Lord Randolph Spencer-Churchill himself. Of course, this particular 'lead' was never followed-up by the masonic-controlled and run Metropolitan Police. J.K. Stephen, again according to Abberline's diaries, actually went to the police, made a full confession and surrendered himself in a fit of guilt but of course no arrests were made and Stephen was also released without charge whilst Abberline resigned his position with the force and retired forthwith as a direct result of his disgust at the inaction and cover-up on the part of the police. Indeed there are still files in existence in Scotland Yard that have been sealed forever to prevent the truth from ever being revealed. Stephen himself suffered a complete mental and physical breakdown shortly after the attacks and died a sad, lonely death in a lunatic asylum in Northampton, three years later at the age of only 33.

In the late 1970s, a researcher and author, Stephen Knight, managed to obtain limited access to the 'Ripper' files but discovered that there were many gaps in the records. Despite this, he still managed to unearth new leads and information based upon which he wrote a book *Jack the Ripper—the final solution*. Unfortunately before publication, many of the more incriminating parts were 'stolen' and in those days, before personal computers were commonplace he had no back-ups or copies as protection. After the book was eventually published, minus the more incriminating information, he published another book. *'The Brotherhood'* which exposed the gross corruption and illegality prevalent in the freemasonic movement and shortly afterwards he was dead—allegedly poisoned—but of course no arrests were ever made. No change there then.

When Prince Eddy found out that his wife had been lobotomised he had a nervous breakdown as a result and when he learned the truth about the 'Ripper' murders, he withdrew within himself and was never the same again thereafter.

Sickert fled the country immediately, upon hearing the news of Annie Crook's abduction and took up residence in Dieppe, France in an attempt to protect her child, Alice. When Alice grew up, she and Walter became lovers and in turn had a child themselves who went by the name of Joseph Sickert—the very same man who held Inspector Abberline's diaries after inheriting them from his father.

In the meantime, Prince Eddy, his mental health by now completely shattered, was given into the care of the Earl of Strathmore who owned Glamis Castle in Scotland, until such a time as it had been decided by 'the firm' what was to be done with him. The royal family then blatantly lied to the world and announced that Eddy had sadly passed away at the age of only 28, on the 14th January 1892 due to influenza (that same old story again) but of course Eddy was still alive and being held in Balmoral Castle having not yet made the final move to Glamis.

Balmoral is approximately 1000 feet (300 metres) above sea-level and as such is partly surrounded by steep cliffs. This was the intended site for the planned murder of Eddy, to be undertaken by Randolph Churchill and John Netley the coachman. The prince was pushed from the cliff-top but somehow managed to survive his fall and after the passage of two days had endeavoured to crawl all the way back to Balmoral where he was found at the door by his incredulous hosts. It was decided after this that the best option would be to just incarcerate him at Glamis for the rest of his life and the Earl of Strathmore agreed to undertake this task on behalf of the royals in return for one simple favour. The favour he stipulated was that **one of his daughters be allowed to marry a future king of England.**

Prince Eddy died in 1933, forty one years after his 'official' death date and during this time, his mother visited him only once, but took a photograph of him which she apparently sent to her cousin. This photograph is still in existence and shows a much older Eddy thoughtfully painting a picture which would sadly never be seen by anyone outside the walls of Glamis Castle.

The pact between Strathmore and the royal family was eventually fulfilled in 1923 when Lady Elizabeth Bowes-Lyon (his daughter, b. 1900) married the future King George VI of England after originally being promised to his brother, the heir to the throne and eventually the former King Edward VIII (he of abdication fame.) In 1936 George ascended the throne upon his elder brother's abdication and Elizabeth became his queen consort. Elizabeth of course was more commonly known as the Queen Mother and the mother of the current incumbent of the family firm, Queen Elizabeth the second. She went to her grave in 2002 without ever revealing the secret and thus the world was never aware of this unholy pact.

In a further twist, as revealed in the Duke of Windsor's (the former King Edward VIII's) last known interview, shortly before he died, he revealed to Michael Thornton, the author of *'Royal Feud—The Queen Mother and the Duchess of Windsor,'* that the Queen Mother had been in love with him and not his brother Bertie (who eventually became King George VI.) In fact it was the Queen Mother's treachery that was the reason why the Duke and Duchess of Windsor were banished from England and forced to live out the rest of their lives in France. Here is a transcript from the final interview of the Duke of Windsor (formerly King Edward VIII of England,) with the author Michael Thornton . . .

"'So you're planning to write a book about the Queen Mother,' said the Duke, exchanging a conspiratorial smile with his wife.

'Well, we shall have to be extremely careful what we say on that subject, won't we darling?'

'Why is that, Sir?' I inquired innocently, although I was well aware of the reason.

The Duke, only months away from being diagnosed with inoperable throat cancer, was interrupted by a convulsive spasm of coughing.

He cleared his throat and added, 'I hope your book will tell the truth, instead of all that gush they dish out about her. Behind that great abundance of charm is a shrewd, scheming and extremely ruthless woman.'

He must have noticed my surprised reaction, for he quickly added, with his most charming smile, '. . . but, of course, you cannot quote that.'

The Duchess was less inhibited. 'The Duke would have loved to return to live in the land of his birth, but our way was blocked at every turn. We were never allowed to go back, and we never will be allowed. Not until the day we die. She will never permit it. When we are dead, perhaps she may at last forgive us.'

When I asked her the reason, the Duchess's right arm shot out as if she was taking aim with a gun and she said, 'Jealousy.'

'Jealousy of the Duke?' I wondered. 'No!' cried the Duchess, and for the first time her southern American origins were audible. 'Jealousy of me for having married him.'

The Duke, who appeared vaguely uncomfortable with this topic, murmured, 'Well, it's hard to explain. But, yes, Elizabeth (the Queen Mother) was rather fonder of me than she ought to have been. And after I married Wallis, her attitude towards me changed. My sister-in-law is an arch-intriguer, and she has dedicated herself to making life hell for both of us.'"

Was it intended then that they were introduced with the specific aim of a royal arranged marriage between the two in order to fulfil the promise to Strathmore, her father and then when she was rejected by him (he was a notorious playboy and rebel in his younger days so quite possibly he went against the wishes of his family in the matter) she/they decided she would have to settle for second best in his younger brother? After all it was she who fought tooth and nail to have them disinherited by the royals and banished to France.

And is it then also possible and most intriguingly of all, that Edward VIII was forced into abdication deliberately, by denying him the right to marry Wallis Simpson whilst he was still King, in order that the decades-old promise would come to fruition and that Elizabeth Bowes-Lyon, the daughter of the Earl of Strathmore could become Queen? There was obviously no other way of fulfilling this promise if Edward was determined to marry Mrs Simpson. Had it been expedient for the powers that be, that Edward **was** to marry Mrs Simpson whilst still king, there is no doubt in my mind that this would have been allowed to happen. The rules are changed and manipulated to suit whatever is best for our controllers, after all.

And there is also much irony and even déja vu in the tragic story of the Queen Mother's nieces, Nerissa and Katherine Bowes-Lyon, both born mentally deficient and unable to speak. They were confined in the Royal Earlswood Mental Hospital at Redhill, Surrey in 1941, where they remained for the rest of their lives. Although the Queen Mother (incidentally, the patron of the mental health charity 'Mencap,') knew that the statement in *Burke's Peerage* that both women were dead (published after false information had been supplied by their mother) was untrue, she never visited or ever again acknowledged either of them. How typical.

Then in a strange postscript to the story, in 1973, the BBC produced a truly bizarre investigation into the 'Ripper' mystery featuring, amongst other strange anomalies, fictional television detectives who all attempted to solve the enigma in their own styles. Several researchers were employed to extract all the information they possibly could about all the potential suspects and after speaking with a long-retired, un-named Scotland Yard detective, one researcher was advised to seek the help of a man by the name of Joseph Sickert who apparently knew about the clandestine marriage of Prince Eddy and a poor Catholic girl by the name of Annie Crook. The researchers could find no evidence of the marriage or the man Sickert and so puzzled by this, they went back to their Scotland Yard contact who revealed that the details he had given them were incorrect (apparently to test their intentions, he said.) He then gave them Sickert's real address and phone number no less, and after being tracked down, Sickert willingly told his amazing story as it had been outlined to him by his mother and father many years previously.

Sickert explained that the monarchy had been very vulnerable and unpopular at that time and the news of a royal scandal was likely to cause a revolution. Queen Victoria supposedly handed the matter to Lord Salisbury, her Prime Minister, for resolution and Salisbury ordered a raid on the Cleveland Street apartment and Eddy and Annie were abducted in separate cabs. Her child, a girl by the name of Alice Margaret, had somehow escaped in the care of Walter Sickert who had been one step ahead of the royals all along.

Sir William Gull died shortly after the murders in early 1890, as did JK Stephen, in early 1892 at the extremely early age of 33 and significantly both had been committed to insane asylums immediately prior to death. Randolph Churchill died in 1895 also rumoured to be insane, but it was claimed, as a result of syphilis. Annie Crook also died insane in a workhouse in 1920 as a direct result of a lobotomy and severe mental trauma. Netley was chased by an angry mob after he unsuccessfully tried to run over Alice Margaret with his cab and he was believed to have been drowned in the Thames. There does appear to be an awful lot of insanity and strange deaths around at that time—nothing much ever changes, really.

Sickert also said that his father was fascinated with the murders and bore great guilt over them. Walter Sickert, after all, had been the one who introduced Eddy to Annie and begun the grisly game. To attempt to alleviate his guilt, as he could say nothing safely, he painted clues as to the identity of the murderers into several of his most famous paintings and he later married Alice Margaret.

To say that the BBC researchers were stunned by these revelations would be a gross understatement. In checking the facts, they found that a woman named Annie Crook definitely lived in Cleveland Street at that time and that she did give birth to a daughter at the same time that Sickert said she did. They also believed strongly that this 'theory' was the most feasible one of all (as do I) and they incorporated it into the show. I also traced Annie's death using public records and can confirm that she really did exist, and died in the 'lunatic' ward of Chelsea workhouse as stated.

When it was screened, the BBC production was confusing to many viewers. The ludicrous combination of facts with fictional detectives and what was to many, an outlandish theory involving people who in their beliefs could do no wrong, prompted much questioning of the programme's veracity at the time. Joseph Sickert actually appeared personally in the last episode and verified absolutely everything that had been said. As previously related, it was agreed by all that this version of events was the most likely solution to the mystery.

Stephen Knight, the late author, entered the story a little later. After watching the BBC programme, he asked Joseph Sickert for an interview and after some indecision, Sickert agreed. During the course of their interview, which took place over several meetings, Knight also became convinced that Joseph Sickert believed he was telling the truth. He said that the story had been told to him by his father to explain why his mother always looked so sad and why both she and Joseph were partially deaf (as was Eddy.)

Once familiar with the basics of the plot, Knight then attempted to confirm the theory and eventually, he felt that the story warranted a book. Sickert was upset by this as he had only agreed to a short interview for an article and wanted no further publicity and exposure of his father's role in the story. Undaunted, Knight went ahead with his book anyway but amazingly and contrary to what he had been told by Sickert, attempted to implicate Walter Sickert as the murderer. As a direct result of this action, Joseph Sickert cut off all ties with Knight and immediately publicly denied the whole story—not just simply his father's alleged involvement in it all—saying that he had made it up for sensationalism.

This I find hard to believe. How could the detective, contacted by the BBC have known Sickert's whereabouts or even known who he was or somehow involved if the whole story was concocted? And also if Sickert did make it up for 'sensationalism,' why did he retreat back into obscurity as soon as he realised that Knight was giving him the publicity he allegedly sought in the first place. No smoke without fire I strongly believe and knowing what I know about masonic operations and royal subterfuge down the ages, although there is no categorical proof that this version of events is the correct one, it does 'tick a lot of boxes' and contains more than a smattering of circumstantial evidence.

A further legacy of this sorry affair was that the payoff for the Spencer family, was two terms as prime minister for Lord Randolph's son and two generations later, Lady Diana Spencer became the wife of the future King Charles III and mother to the future King William V and his brother Harry, only to be famously discarded once she had fulfilled her wifely duties in providing her highly-desirable genes to produce a 'heir and a spare,' and eventually being brutally and ritually murdered herself in 1997 in Paris.

This then is the **real** story of Jack the Ripper, straight from the 'horse's mouth' (ie. Joseph Sickert's mouth.) These facts must be known by the Elite but as always, they close ranks to prevent the real truth from becoming known. All of the multiplicity of theories that abound as to the identity of the killer and the many films, documentaries and TV programmes that portray an unending search for the 'truth' are nothing more than elaborate smokescreens, born from the deliberate confusion engendered by the Elite to protect the guilty, as is their usual modus operandus. Yet another tiny example of how easy it is for these psychopaths to provide us all with a completed distorted view of both history and our existing reality.

More Royal Misdemeanours

Winston Churchill always claimed that he was the political heir of his father, the brilliant but maverick Lord Randolph Churchill, but he undoubtedly inherited his indomitability and joie de vivre from his mother. She was born Jennie Jerome in New York in 1854, one of three daughters of the Jewish millionaire, Leonard Jerome. Beautiful, musical and extremely vivacious, she met Lord Randolph, the second son of the seventh Duke of Marlborough, at Cowes in August 1873.

Marrying an American heiress was becoming a common response from impoverished members of the British aristocracy to their financial problems. There was also in this case a strong physical attraction and in this regard, the couple, seemed to have been rather impatient as Winston was born only six months after their wedding in April 1874. However, maybe all is not as it seems to be.

Things, however, soon went wrong. Exiled to Ireland after ostracism by the Prince of Wales (the future King Edward VII,) the couple spent much of their time apart and as a result Winston's younger brother Jack, born in 1880, was almost certainly the son of Lord Falmouth.

For all Lord Randolph's brilliance and his huge popularity among Tory voters, he made enemies among the leadership and indeed 'overplayed his hand' once too often over a misjudged resignation in 1886, and this brought an end to his political career.

Leonard Jerome, her father, also lost most of his money, leaving Jennie with expensive habits but a permanently inadequate income. She was a distant mother to the young Winston, who turned instead to his beloved nanny, Mrs. Everest, but the mother and son's later relationship became a very strong and mutually supportive one. Widowed in 1895, Jennie married again, twice, to handsome men much younger than herself and she clearly also had many affairs, including one with the Prince of Wales.

Researcher Greg Hallett is convinced that Winston Churchill was the son of the Prince of Wales (Edward VII) and Jennie Jerome-Churchill. Why otherwise did the Prince of Wales ostracise the Churchills and send them to Ireland? She was three months pregnant when she married Lord Randolph Churchill and it was noted in many quarters that the young Winston resembled the young Prince of Wales far more than he did his alleged father, Lord Randolph Churchill.

The Triple Entente was the name given to the alliance between Great Britain, France and Russia which was formed during the first decade of the twentieth century and which ultimately led to the outbreak of the First World War. This agreement was the personal creation of King Edward VII of Britain, or more accurately speaking, of his bankster friends. It was King Edward VII who instigated the British alliance with Japan, the Russo-Japanese War, and the 1905 Russian Revolution and it was also he, acting as the autocrat of British foreign policy who engineered the 'Entente Cordiale' between Britain and France in 1903-04 and who then went on to seal the fateful 'British-Russian Entente,' of 1907.

It was also King Edward who 'massaged' Theodore Roosevelt and other American political leaders in order to help bring about the US/UK so-called 'special relationship,' which became extremely strong at the time of his reign. This diplomatic work was masterminded and carried out by Edward personally, with various British military-men, politicians and diplomats merely following in his wake. Edward had a geopolitical vision of brutal simplicity; the encirclement of Germany with a hostile coalition, followed by a war of annihilation in which many of Britain's erstwhile 'allies,' specifically France and Russia would also be decimated and crippled.

Skipping forward slightly again now to 1936 and the strange case of the abdication of King Edward VIII and the accession to the throne of King George VI of the film, '*The Kings Speech*' fame, who had an IQ of only one point above retarded and his consort, Elizabeth Bowes-Lyon. Is it possible that their betrothal and marriage in 1923 were engineered in fulfillment of Edward VII's promise to Elizabeth's father as related in the previous section? Knowing what we do about these people, I would say makes it all eminently possible.

In fact, their first child was actually a severely handicapped epileptic and so was merely left by them to die at the hospital. This resulted in the removal of the mentally subnormal King George VI from his duties as the royal 'sire' and he was (according to Greg Hallett's research) replaced in that role by Winston Churchill who was, if you remember, the illegitimate son of King Edward VII.

Elizabeth Bowes-Lyon was initially destined to be engaged to the future King Edward VIII in their youth and who reigned for just less than one year, in 1936. However, he was a notorious playboy and was not interested in her. She was then given the option to become engaged to the future George VI, Edward VIII's brother but this time it was she that refused.

For this reason it was not actually her that married George, but her 'whipping-boy.' The term 'whipping-boy' traditionally refers to a scapegoat or one who is singled out for blame or punishment.

It may seem very odd to us today that down the ages, the royals kept a substitute simply for the purpose of beating him when a prince (or princess) did wrong, but that was and still is, exactly the case. 'Whipping-boy' was in fact an established position at the English royal court at least from the Tudor and Stuart eras of the 15th and 16th centuries onwards, but probably much, much earlier. However the whipping-boys were not merely hapless street-urchins living a life of torment, but high-born companions to the royal princes. They were educated alongside them, often became best friends and shared many of the privileges of royalty. The downside for them obviously though was that if the prince did misbehave in any way then it was the whipping-boy that bore the consequences. It was also considered a form of punishment to the prince/princess that someone he/she cared about was made to suffer on his/her behalf.

Often the whipping-boy is used as a stand-in for photographs and sometimes there may be two photographs taken, one with the 'real' prince/princess and one with the whipping-boy in order to provide a future historical 'proof' and record of the person's past.

Elizabeth Bowes-Lyon's whipping-boy, obviously a girl in this case, was known to hail from Waterford, in Ireland. The true Elizabeth Bowes-Lyon married someone else and lived in obscurity in France and died in 1950 and it was in fact her whipping-boy that married King George VI.

Then in 1925, Winston Churchill provided the sperm for the artificial insemination of Elizabeth Bowes-Lyons' whipping-boy, resulting in the birth of Princess Elizabeth, who was born in a room above the Coach and Horses pub in Bruton Street in London in 1926. Artificial insemination was already well established and being used covertly by this time.

When King George VI died in 1952, the illegitimate Princess Elizabeth became Queen Elizabeth II of the United Kingdom and inherited all the royal wealth. In 1946, she became engaged to Prince Philip due to the machinations of Lord Louis Mountbatten, before marrying him in 1947.

Born as Seine Durchlaucht Prinz Ludwig von Battenberg (His Serene Highness, Prince Louis of Battenberg), Lord Louis Mountbatten (1900-1979) was a known paedophile, homosexual and sexual pervert. His German titles and name were discarded during WWI, when his family changed their surname from Battenberg to Mountbatten in an effort to distance themselves from their German heritage, whilst at the same time the reigning royal House of Saxe-Coburg and Gotha changed its name to Windsor in a similar attempt to deceive. In truth, the name of the reigning British royal house has changed numerous times over the centuries. At the death of Queen Victoria, her son and successor King Edward VII became the first monarch of the House of Saxe-Coburg and Gotha (being the son of Victoria's husband, Albert of Saxe-Coburg and Gotha.)

Strong anti-German sentiment amongst the people of the British Empire during World War I reached its peak in March 1917, when the Gotha G.IV, a German heavy aircraft capable of crossing the English Channel began bombing London directly. This obviously caused alarm amongst the royals as the aircraft bore the same name as the part of the name of the Royal Family. Additionally, the bombings were synchronous with the abdication of King George's first cousin, Nicholas II, the Tsar of Russia on 15 March 1917, which also raised the possibility of abolition of other monarchies in Europe. Thus King George V, the reigning monarch at the time was finally convinced to abandon all titles held under the German Crown, and to change German titles and house names to anglicised versions.

On 17th July 1917, a Royal Proclamation issued by George V which changed the name of the royal house to Windsor and specified that all descendants in the male line of Queen Victoria who are subjects of these realms, other than female descendants who may marry or may have married, shall bear the said name of Windsor.

The King also decided that his various relatives who were British subjects relinquish use of all German titles and styles, and adopt British-sounding surnames and compensated several of his male relatives by creating them British peers. Thus overnight, his cousin, Prince Louis of Battenberg, who earlier in the war had been forced to resign as First Sea Lord through anti-German feeling, became Louis Mountbatten, 1st Marquess of Milford Haven, while his brother-in-law, the Duke of Teck, became Adolphus Cambridge, 1st Marquess of Cambridge. Other relatives, such as Princess Marie Louise and Princess Helena Victoria of Schleswig-Holstein, simply dropped their territorial designations.

In Letters Patent, documented on 11th December 1917, the King restricted the style 'His (or Her) Royal Highness' and the titular dignity of 'Prince (or Princess) of Great Britain and Ireland' to the children of the Sovereign, the children of the sons of the Sovereign and the eldest living son of the eldest living son of a Prince of Wales. The Letters Patent also stated that … *"the titles of Royal Highness, Highness or Serene Highness, and the titular dignity of Prince and Princess shall cease except those titles already granted and remaining unrevoked."*

Lord Louis Mountbatten was a great-grandson of Queen Victoria and the uncle of Prince Philip (consort of Queen Elizabeth II.) Mountbatten was also a promiscuous bisexual who was famously rumoured to have had an affair with Edward VIII (who was Prince of Wales at the time) when he accompanied him on his Empire tours. It was apparently common knowledge also that Prince Philip and Lord Louis Mountbatten also had sexual relations.

Another 'close' friend was an Irish student whom he met at Cambridge, James Jeremiah Victor Fitzwilliam Murphy, who was known by the name of Peter Murphy, a leading Cambridge homosexual with strong left-wing leanings. He became Mountbatten's closest and constant companion and Mountbatten supported him with an annual allowance of £600 ($1000) until Murphy's death in 1966. The well-known British homosexual playwright and actor Noel Coward was also included among Lord Louis' close circle of friends.

Although Mountbatten married Edwina Ashley, a wealthy socialite, in 1922, this was probably just a marriage of convenience as he had a string of lovers of both sexes and of all social classes. As he himself once succinctly put it, *"Edwina and I spent all our married lives getting into other people's beds."*

His wife also had a torrid affair whilst in India with Pandit Nehru, Prime Minister of India and she, Nehru and Mountbatten were fully engaged in a classic love triangle, but it is generally acknowledged that Nehru was the love of Edwina's life. Indeed all three of them were known by insiders as having bisexual proclivities and Mountbatten himself said that they were a 'happy little threesome.' However, having said that, the Mountbattens fought most of the time and lived apart for much of their lives.

Between affairs Lord Louis took time out from his hectic sexual life and became Admiral of the Fleet in the British Royal Navy, the last Viceroy of India and the first Governor-General of the newly-independent India. Although he was a great friend of Winston Churchill for a long time, after 1948 Churchill never spoke to him again over Mountbatten's role in the independence of Pakistan and India and it was on 15th August 1947, on Mountbatten's 'watch,' that Britain finally relinquished its rights to India.

Mountbatten also forged a close bond with his great-nephew Prince Charles, the Prince of Wales, who was deeply affected by his murder in 1979. Mountbatten had a very strong, some may say, unhealthy influence on Prince Charles, who declared that things would never be the same after the loss of his mentor. Perhaps unsurprisingly given all of above, he was known as 'Dickie' to family and close friends, despite the fact that 'Richard' was not among his given names and equally widely known throughout the military of all ranks as 'Mount-bottom.'

In the book, 'War of the Windsors,' authors Lynn Picknett and Clive Prince, confirmed that Lord Louis Mountbatten had the nickname 'Dickie'… for a very good reason. As the last Viceroy of India, he was a practising homo-paedophile who sexually exploited hundreds of young Indian peasant boys in order to satisfy his exceptionally strong, but warped sex-drive.

In another book, 'The Kincora Scandal,' by Chris Moore, the author connects Mountbatten to a child prostitution vice-ring in Belfast, Ireland. Authorities failed to intervene at the Kincora care home for boys, despite a deluge of reports over the years of endemic child sexual abuse taking place there.

The operators of the Kincora child prostitution ring were eventually convicted in 1981 of the ritual sexual abuse of defenceless young boys, who were in effect traded like prostitutes. No charges were ever brought against the known VIP customers, royals, politicians, lawyers and judges involved. Nothing unsurprising about that really though. The intelligence services are heavily involved in all manner of perverted activities themselves and they protect those in high places that also engage in them, well at least until the time when it becomes expedient to sacrifice or dispose of them. In 1979, Mountbatten was killed by a bomb planted on his boat, allegedly by the IRA, but which act in reality was the work of the British Intelligence service, MI-5.

However his cold-blooded murder was nothing to do with his long association with the endemic sexual abuse of children and adults alike, but because he had become too vocal on issues such as the unification of Ireland, and for his anti-nuclear power stance. In short, he had become a 'loose cannon' in his old age and thus an embarrassment to the establishment and there were too many royal secrets at stake. His killing would now better serve the purposes of his masters and his own legacy, by his being hailed as a martyr to Britain's cause.

However, Mountbatten's many sexual indiscretions paled in comparison to those of his elder brother George, who inherited the title Marquis of Milford Haven on the death of their father. George was also a promiscuous bisexual who was married to another bisexual, Nadeja, Countess of Torbay, who was a niece of Czar Nicholas II. One of George's several claims to infamy was his vast collection of pornography, upon which he lavished considerable amounts of money and carefully bound it into several volumes, each emblazoned with the family crest. Some of the pornography consisted of photos of aristocrats enjoying sex with their servants, but far more disturbing were the pictures of family orgies in which even children were actively involved in sexual acts and even bestiality.

Upon George's death in 1938, the collection was inherited by his son, so part of it is it still in the hands of the Mountbatten family, although the bulk of it was donated to the British Museum. It is not available for public viewing however, for obvious reasons.

It was Louis Mountbatten who introduced the well-known paedophile Jimmy Savile to Prince Charles. They spent a great deal of time together, some of which was under the guise of 'charity events.' On Savile's 80th birthday, Prince Charles sent Jimmy Savile a pair of gold cufflinks, a box of cigars and a note saying, *"No one will ever know what you've done for this country."* I think we do now Charlie boy, I think we do now. There is now an incredible amount of evidence against Savile from the hundreds if not thousands of children that he abused during his lifetime. Did the royals not know what was going on? Of course they did and indeed I would suggest that they were more than happy to be an integral part of it—so long as their involvement could remain a closely-guarded secret.

There is much speculation that Prince Charles is definitely not the father of Prince Harry, his second son and also that Princess Diana had numerous extra-marital relationships because of her knowledge that Prince Charles was not only continuing his long-standing affair with Camilla Parker Bowles, but that Prince Charles was actually a paedophile also.

Whilst in the Royal Navy, Prince Philip was also notorious for getting drunk and then lying face-down so that he could be sodomised. Several of the sailors who sodomised have now come forward and publicly admitted this fact, so there seems little doubt that it is true. In fact not only was Philip a sodomite, he was also a prolific paedophile. On the royal family's extensive Sandringham Estate in Norfolk, many bodies including those of children, have recently been discovered in shallow, unmarked graves. Of course, this in itself is not proof of 'royal murder,' as such, but perhaps the following story is…

"I am a survivor of the Kamloops and Mission Indian residential schools, both run by the Roman Catholic Church.

In September 1964 when I was 12 years old, I was an inmate at the Kamloops school and we were visited by the Queen of England and Prince Phillip. I remember it was strange because they came by themselves, no big fanfare or nothing. But I recognised them, and the school principal told us it was the Queen and we all got given new clothes and good food for the first time in months, the day before she arrived.

The day she got to the school, I was part of a group of kids that went on a picnic with the Queen and her husband and school officials, down to a meadow near Dead Man's Creek. I remember it was weird because we all had to bend down and kiss her foot, a white laced boot. After a while, I saw the Queen leave that picnic with ten children from the school, and those children never returned. We never heard anything more about them and never met them again even when we were older. They were all from around there, but they all vanished.

The group that disappeared was seven boys and three girls, in age from six to fourteen years old. I don't remember their names, just an occasional first name like Cecilia and there was an Edward.

What happened was also witnessed by my friend George Adolph, who was 11 years old at the time and a student there too." William Arnold Combes

William Combes 1952-2011

Shortly after 'going public' with his story, William, at the time 59 years old and in excellent health, died suddenly and quite unexpectedly and seemingly for no reason as researcher Kevin Annett relates . . .

"The aboriginal man who claimed to witness the abduction of ten fellow residential school children by the Queen of England and her husband in October, 1964 at the Catholic school in Kamloops, B.C. has died suddenly at the Catholic-run St. Paul's Hospital in Vancouver.

William Combes, age 59 and in good health, was scheduled to be a primary witness at the opening session of the International Tribunal into Crimes of Church and State (ITCCS) on September 12 in London, England.

I last saw William ten days ago, on the eve of my departure for a European speaking tour, and he looked better than I had seen him in years. According to his partner Mae, William was in stable health and was assigned a new doctor at St. Paul's Hospital this past week. William was then committed to the hospital for 'tests,' and his health began to immediately deteriorate. He died suddenly yesterday of a still-undisclosed cause.

The Vancouver Coroner's Office refuses to comment on William's death.

William was the sole survivor of a group of three aboriginal boys who claim to have witnessed the abduction of ten children during a royal visit to the Kamloops residential school in mid-October 1964, when both the Queen and Prince Philip were in Canada.

I believe that William Combes died of foul play, and that his murder was arranged by those who stood to lose from his speaking out about his witnessing of the child abductions and other crimes of murder and torture at Catholic Indian residential schools.

His murderers have not won. William's videotaped statements, including his witness of the 1964 abductions, have been registered in the archives of our ITCCS, and will be made public at our opening session on September 12, 2011."

Make of that what you will.

Prince Philip is Prince William and Harry's grandfather and the husband of Queen Elizabeth II. He married the Queen in 1947 and changed his German name from Philip Battenberg to Philip Mountbatten to conceal his German ancestry. Both of Philip's sisters married high ranking German officers in the Nazi Party. His sister Sophie married Nazi SS colonel Christoph Von Hesse, chief of Hermann Göring's Secret Intelligence Service.

Prince Philip's German uncle, Lord Louis Mountbatten was a central figure in secret communications between the British royal family and their pro-Hitler cousins in Germany and his mother was Princess Alice Battenberg, granddaughter of Queen Victoria. She was eventually diagnosed as a paranoid-schizophrenic and committed to a mental institution in Switzerland and his German father then absconded with a wealthy mistress which left the boy parentless. Philip's uncle George Mountbatten, the paedophile pornographer, then became his surrogate father and legal guardian.

One of the biggest public-relations hoaxes, among almost countless others, ever perpetrated by the British Crown, is that King Edward VIII, who abdicated the throne in 1936 was a 'black sheep,' due to his support for the Nazis, an aberration in the otherwise unblemished Windsor family. Actually, nothing could be further from the truth. The British monarchy and the City of London's leading Crown banksters, enthusiastically backed Hitler and the Nazis, bankrolled and supported his election and also did everything possible to build the Nazi war machine, in preparation for Britain and her allies' planned geopolitical war between Germany and Russia. Indeed, long after the abdication of Edward VIII, the Windsors maintained their direct Nazi links. So, not only was Philip trained in the Hitler Youth curriculum, but his German brothers-in-law, with whom he lived at the time, all became high-ranking figures in the Nazi Party.

Although Buckingham Palace's rumour-mill has tried to depict this wartime collaboration with the enemy as mere family correspondence, the correspondence apparently included messages from Prince Philip's secret ally, the Duke of Windsor (the abdicated, former Edward VIII). On 20th November 1995, the *Washington Times* reported, based on recently discovered Portuguese Secret Service files first published in the London Observer, that the Duke of Windsor had been in close collaboration with the Nazis in Spain and Portugal to foment a revolution in wartime Britain, that would topple the Churchill government, depose his brother King George VI, and allow him to regain the throne, with his Queen, Wallis Simpson at his side.

Whatever correspondence had been sent from the royals to Germany during the war was said to be hidden in Prince Christoph of Hesse's Kronberg Castle and so in June 1945, King George VI dispatched the former MI-5 officer and now 'Surveyor of the King's Pictures,' Anthony Blunt, to retrieve this incriminating evidence.

Later, Queen Elizabeth II reportedly insisted that there be no interrogation of Blunt about his secret trip to the castle and it is significant that the House of Windsor was absolutely desperate to prevent those documents from Kronberg Castle, from falling into American Army hands during the German 'liberation.' Clearly, it is quite logical to assume that Prince Philip's patron Lord Mountbatten, Mountbatten's sister, Crown

Princess Louise, and Philip's brother-in-law Prince Christoph were not just exchanging family pleasantries.

The Royally-sanctioned Murder of Princess Diana

In their acclaimed book, '*Princess Diana: The Evidence*,' authors Jon King and John Beveridge present evidence that a highly sophisticated assassination technique, known as 'Boston Brakes' was used to cause the Princess's vehicle to crash as it drove through the Pont d'Alma tunnel, Paris, in the early hours of 31 August 1997.

This, they reveal, is the favoured assassination technique currently being employed by the West's intelligence services due to its plausible deniability.

The authors were able to compile a very detailed and compelling case due to information gleaned from their well-placed intelligence and security contacts, mostly former special and elite forces members, mercenaries, royal bodyguards and on occasion, hired assassins. Indeed some of these military employees disclosed details of prior operations in which the 'Boston Brakes' technique had been successfully used. Others, who fought in Angola, one of the locations of Diana's landmines campaign, shed light on the secret oil and diamond wars still raging in central Africa and in particular the dirty, arms-for-oil deals carried out by MI-6, the French DGSE, the CIA and the Bush-Cheney oil syndicate.

By focussing the light of the world's media on Angola, the authors were told, the Princess was in danger of exposing all these dirty deeds and was thus placing herself directly in 'harm's way.' The fact that she was compiling a dossier containing the names of British politicians and high-powered businessmen involved in the deals was also an important factor in the decision to dispose of her.

"From the minute the decoy car left the Ritz to the moment the tail car closed in ... it was obvious what was going down. Anyone who knows what they're talking about will tell you the same." Former Royal bodyguard, Mike Grey.

Grey added ... *"The operation bore all the classic hallmarks of a security service assassination ... I have no doubts whatsoever given my twenty years' experience in various sections of the security industry, that Diana was assassinated. The security service hallmarks are plain to see."*

But it was former SAS officer and world-famous explorer, Sir Ranulph Fiennes, who offered perhaps the most telling revelation of all. The 'Boston Brakes' method of assassination, Fiennes revealed, has been in use since at least the 1980s and deploys a microchip transceiver which takes over the target vehicle's steering, brakes and acceleration capability at the critical moment. The method, he said, was first deployed by the CIA in Boston, Massachusetts, hence the name but has since been adopted by intelligence and security forces the world over, as well as by private 'security firms' and their hit-squads.

One would expect that with the financial means Dodi Fayed and Princess Diana had at their disposal there was absolutely no reason why they should have been expected to use a vehicle that had actually been snatched at gunpoint a few days prior to the fateful night, yet had mysteriously, soon been returned. Yet that is precisely what happened. The car in which the ill-fated couple was travelling, a Mercedes Benz S280, had been stolen some days prior to the crash. This fact on its own was perhaps nothing more than pure coincidence, but the strange element to the story was that the Mercedes had been returned a few days earlier in pristine condition save for one very important aspect… The on-board computer chip was missing from the stolen Mercedes!

This chip controls, amongst other things, the navigation, acceleration, steering and braking of a vehicle. The very fact that the car had had its chip stolen some days earlier (yet nothing else, thus suggesting that the car-snatchers were no ordinary thieves) drags the so-called 'accident' firmly into 'conspiracy' territory.

In fact Fiennes did indeed confirm the relatively common use of this assassination method with particular reference to the death in England of SAS Major Michael Marman, in a 1986 car accident that bears uncanny resemblance to that of Princess Diana, Dodi Fayed and Henri Paul, and which was carried-out by a private hit-squad known simply as 'The Clinic.'

Further instances of the Boston Brakes in action are also cited in King and Beveridge's book, including the death by 'road traffic accident' of Diana's former lover and bodyguard, Barry Mannakee in 1987 and maybe surprisingly to some, the attempted assassination by 'road traffic accident' of Camilla Parker-Bowles, just two months prior to Diana's own fatal crash. According to sources quoted by the authors, the attempt on Camilla Parker-Bowles' life was the result of a 'constitutional crisis' engendered by Prince Charles' desire to marry his long-term lover while Diana was still alive.

So, assuming someone wanted to expedite a very sensitive, high-profile assassination but at the same time create as little fuss as possible, the best way to achieve it is of course, to make it appear to be an accident. With this in mind, the disappearance of the on-board computer chip from the Mercedes then begins to make sense. Steal the car, remove the computer chip, replace the old chip with a new 'doctored' chip that allows a third party to gain remote access to the car's controls and that is all that is needed to stage a very genuine-looking 'accident.'

Furthermore, very suspiciously to my mind, the stolen, recovered Mercedes Benz S280 was the 'only vehicle available' to the Princess and her companions that night. Of course it was, yes. We believe you.

The initial reports 'leaked' to the press suggested that the Mercedes involved in the crash had been travelling at a speed of 120 mph prior to the crash. In the reports, it also clearly stated that the speedometer of the car was stuck on 196 kilometres per hour (122mph) after the impact. If the car had been traveling anywhere near that speed, wearing a seat-belt or not, no-one would have stood even the remotest chance of surviving the crash. In fact the only person to survive the crash was bodyguard, Trevor Rhys-Jones who was sitting in the front, right-hand passenger seat and who is also widely believed by researchers to have been an active agent of the MI-6 or MI-5 branches of the British Secret Service.

Several professional drivers have decried the ridiculous, claimed speed as being nothing short of preposterous and from all the evidence available, declared that the car was travelling at about 60 mph (96km/h) maximum, at the time of the accident. To date, despite its offers of help in solving the riddle, the Mercedes Benz Company and its experts have never been allowed to examine the car. This in itself is also very strange. Why would the powers-that-be not wish to enlist the help of anyone who could shed some light on the real facts, if there was nothing at all to hide and they wished to find the answers?

Why was Trevor Rhys-Jones who was sat, 'seat-belted' in the front passenger seat and thereby in the least survivable position for such an accident, in fact quite contrarily, the only survivor (the front passenger seat is well-known in the car industry as 'the death seat.')

The widespread view, as deliberately propagated by the controlled media is that had Princess Diana and Dodi Fayed been wearing seatbelts, they would likely have survived the crash. However again this stretches credibility to breaking-point and beyond. Diana **did** survive the crash and actually spoke to an off-duty French Doctor (not affiliated with the authorities) who arrived shortly after the incident and administered first aid to her. Interviewed in the following days by the world's media, he stated categorically that *'I thought her life could be saved.'*

Additionally, from my own personal experience of the incident, albeit second-hand, It may or may not be true, but I have heard this from a friend of a friend (who incidentally absolutely swears it to be the truth and I have no reason to disbelieve it) that she was in Paris on the night of the crash and got back to her hotel room after a late night out and switched on the TV in the room. The local 24-hour news channel was airing the first pictures of an appalling car accident in Paris and she was just in time to see the televised images of a young blonde woman, obviously dazed and groggy, but who was nevertheless able to enter the ambulance on foot, albeit with assistance from paramedics on either side of her. She recognised this woman as Princess Diana and went to bed thinking that Diana had 'had a lucky escape.' She was obviously shocked and mystified next day when she awoke to all the reports of the princess's death in the car crash.

Of course those images were never shown or referred-to ever again as is usual in these cases, much like most of the mysteriously disappearing, original news footage whenever there is a suspicious incident of this kind. As a footnote to, and confirmation of this, I have recently seen evidence of the fact that on that fateful night, the BBC news anchor Martyn Lewis in the BBC's first 'newsflash' announced that Dodi had been killed outright, but that Diana had been seen 'walking into an ambulance.'

Whatever the real truth regarding the above may be, this is certainly possible in my view. There was obviously no absolutely fool-proof way to ensure Diana's death, even in a staged crash and so there would have had to be a contingency plan in place in the event of her survival against the odds. If Diana had indeed survived the impact of the crash, then drastic steps would have needed to be undertaken to ensure that she did not survive and maybe this explains why it took the ambulance almost two hours to travel the mere 4km (2½ miles) to the Pitie Salpétriére Hospital. I have not yet heard another credible reason as to why that should have been the case. At one point in the ambulance's journey it apparently parked at the kerb-side for over twenty minutes just 600 metres from the hospital. This has never been satisfactorily explained by those who control what we are meant to see, hear and believe.

Perhaps the reason that Princess Diana was not wearing her seatbelt is because it was mysteriously but very conveniently jammed in such a way as to render it unusable.

Princess Diana was extremely vocal in her criticism of the Royal family. She was outspoken about the issue of land-mines, the environment and many social issues. She certainly knew her life was in danger, as evidenced in the letter she wrote to her butler, Paul Burrell, (below) in October 1993, just ten months after her separation from Prince Charles.

Excerpt from Princess Diana's letter to Paul Burrell, her butler

In July 1997, Dodi Al-Fayed, son of the billionaire Mohamed Al-Fayed, became romantically involved with Diana, Princess of Wales. Dodi was born in Alexandria, Egypt, son of the billionaire Mohamed Al-Fayed, former owner of Harrods department store, and of Fulham Football Club and the Hôtel Ritz in Paris. Dodi was of Egyptian descent from his father and Spanish, Turkish, and Arab descent from his mother and a Muslim by faith.

Whilst still officially engaged to the American model Kelly Fisher, Dodi began his relationship with Diana which of course, as does any news involving a celebrity or 'royal,' created a media feeding-frenzy as the paparazzi tried to capture pictures of them together. In fact the paparazzi were set (or should that be 'set-up') to become the scapegoats for the tragic incident.

Dodi and Diana had broken their journey back to London by stopping off at Paris, after having spent nine days together on holiday in the French and Italian Rivieras abroad the Al-Fayed family yacht and it is believed by several sources, that the pregnant Diana was ready to remove the young princes, William and Harry from the 'clutches' of the Royal Family to start a new life abroad.

An expert on the life of Diana, Alan Power, suggested that she was murdered to spare the establishment the shame and embarrassment she was about to trigger with sensational revelations of the inner-secrets of the monarchy and further claimed that just nine days before her death, the besotted couple had ordered an *Alberto Repossi* engagement ring and planned to marry in October or November the same year. Meanwhile, the monarchy fumed silently at Diana's new-found freedom and happiness and her perceived indiscretions and unacceptably liberal attitudes to her fellow-man—something that caused Diana to be well-loved by all (except them, of course.) This would not 'do' at all.

Power's book, *The Princess Diana Conspiracy* alleges that she was murdered on the orders of Buckingham Palace because she was about to release a shocking dossier chronicling Prince Charles' sordid sex secrets and that she was actually killed by an elite team of SAS and MI-6 operatives, known as '*The Increment*,' acting on direct orders from 'above.'

In 2011, the actor, Keith Allen produced a $5 million documentary called *Unlawful Killing*. Unsurprisingly, this was immediately condemned by both the Royal family and their bankster / establishment friends and even banned from general release in Britain, regardless of the fact that it was made available almost everywhere else.

The documentary relates testimonies from numerous credible sources, all expressing the opinion that her death was murder. Mohamed Al-Fayed, Dodi's father, went even further than this, stating that it was a pre-meditated slaughter by the 'bloody racist' royal family. He believes strongly that the royal family had his son killed because they were too racist to accept a foreign, Muslim step-father or a Muslim half-brother or half-sister for the future king. And the film-maker himself, Keith Allen, pointed out how 'chillingly convenient' it was for the Windsors that the crash happened at that moment in time.

Even the inquest at the Royal Courts of Justice, (justice, what justice?) was widely dismissed in the film as a 'cover up.' The fact that Prince Charles, in spite of being implicated by Diana's letter as trying to kill her exactly the way she died, was not even asked to appear as a witness is extremely 'suspicious' in itself. One law for us and no laws for them. In fact, the Royal Courts of Justice first attempted to conduct the inquest without a jury, a move that was only prevented by the sheer weight of public opinion and pressure. It certainly brings into question the impartiality of an inquest conducted at the Royal Courts of Justice led by a coroner who has sworn his allegiance to the Queen, in a case where members of the royal family should have been among the prime suspects. Perhaps unsurprisingly then, the film-maker concluded that the coroner gave the distinct impression throughout the proceedings, that he had already 'made up his mind' about the outcome, before it had even begun. All of which is totally unsurprising.

The whole point of the inquest was supposedly to examine the suspicious circumstances surrounding the car crash and reach a conclusion based on that. Was it pure coincidence that Diana had told many people that she had been warned by a confidential source in the palace that Prince Philip had planned to deliberately kill her in a car crash, exactly the way she died? Why were the CCTV cameras along the route of the crash car apparently 'not working,' that evening, a 'coincidence' shared with several other comparable incidents, 9/11 and the 7/7 London Tube attacks, for example?

Were the driver's blood samples tampered with, to produce an alcohol and Carbon Monoxide level that would surely have made him 'falling-down drunk,' whilst managing to give the impression to all that he was in fact completely sober? Why were Diana's phone calls being bugged by the American NSA?

Why was Diana's seat belt 'jammed' on the night of the accident, preventing her from—as she normally would—wearing a seat belt, which probably would have saved her life, other circumstances notwithstanding? Why did the police fail to identify the owners or driver of any of the five other vehicles involved in the crash? And why did it take ambulances two hours to transport Diana to the 'nearest' hospital, whilst passing other nearer hospitals on the way there?

According to the film, the many suspicious circumstances did not end there. Even before the end of the medical examination of his body, the French press had already published headlines according to which the driver, Henri Paul was 'as drunk as a pig' and that was in spite of the fact that according to his hotel bill he had drunk only had two small Ricards. Again similar to other suspicious incidents, the site of the crash was almost immediately cleaned and any forensic evidence immediately washed-away. The film points out the similarity to the case of the Pakistani politician Benazir Bhutto, where the site of her murder was hosed down by police almost immediately after the attack. Obviously it is infinitely easier to claim that it was just an unfortunate accident or the facts be twisted to fit the 'official story,' if the evidence is destroyed.

At the conclusion of the inquest, the jury had heard such a vast amount of suspicious information that the coroner dare not take any risks as to whether the 'correct,' desired verdict of 'accidental death' would be returned. And so, in his three day summing-up of the evidence and instructions to the jury, he actually told them to ignore the eye-witness statements and forbade them to even consider the possibility of 'unlawful killing' (in other words, murder.) The sensible, honest jury however, completely disregarded the coroner's instructions, and spent a whole week carefully examining all the evidence for themselves, finally returning a verdict of 'unlawful killing!'

However, this did not prevent the worldwide media from totally misrepresenting the inquest's verdict. In a massive world-wide misinformation campaign led by the BBC (who else?) the story was twisted to imply that the inquest jury had decided that it was the paparazzi who were responsible for the crash but what the inquest actually established was that the other vehicles (those mystery vehicles, not driven by paparazzi) surrounding Diana's car in the tunnel that caused the 'accident.' To this day, most people are unaware of the 'unlawful killing' verdict and believe that the Inquest delivered an 'accidental death' verdict. This in itself demonstrates both the role of, and the ability of, the mainstream, mass-media to manipulate the facts and actually form public opinion.

The film also closely examined the negative attitude of the media 'hacks' towards the inquest, who obviously considered it to be a waste of time. Using a 'mole' and a hidden camera, 'planted' into the media camp, Allen discovered that it was quite common for the journalists observing the inquest to fall asleep, read or simply chit-chat amongst themselves instead of paying attention to the witness statements. They were only interested in information confirming the pre-established consensus, the 'party-line' passed-down through the years since the crash, that Paul's drunk-driving and harassment by the paparazzi had caused the crash, and ignored all the evidence contradicting it.

All views contrary to the official story were regarded as simply 'crazy' or a 'just a conspiracy theory' and part of the problem, according to the film, was the fact that it was the media 'royal correspondents,' not legal journalists who were covering the inquest, in spite of the fact that Diana no longer had 'royal' status at the time of her death. How can for example, the BBC's royal correspondent be totally impartial when it is their job to present the royal family and everything they do or say, in the most favourable light possible. But regardless, they would in any event, not have accepted the detailed contra-evidence presented or acknowledged that the establishment was manipulating information behind the scenes, regarding which and how much evidence they were being made privy to. For example, this is the reason why the media never questioned why the Royal Courts of Justice censored the letters written from Prince Philip to Diana, into abject incomprehensibility.

The Coroner went even so far as to forbid close friends of Diana to relate to the inquest the contents of several extremely hostile letters from Prince Philip written to Diana not long before her death.

The film also describes the accident itself, based on the reports of several witness statements in the inquest. Diana's powerful Mercedes Benz quickly left behind the pursuing paparazzi but when the Mercedes entered the tunnel, they were immediately surrounded and confronted by four motorcycles and a white Fiat Uno which had been waiting on a small feeder road to the tunnel and had emerged in the wake of the Mercedes as it swooped past. Suddenly a very bright flash of light blinded Henri Paul, causing him to lose control and crash head-on into a solid concrete pillar. None of the other vehicles were ever identified and it was verified by no less than the hitherto absolutely compliant French police that none of these vehicles were driven by any of the paparazzi in attendance that night.

Perhaps the most bizarre circumstance of the accident surrounded the behaviour of the paramedics and doctors in attendance at the crash site and during the 'short' trip to hospital. Several ambulances arrived quickly at the scene of the accident and of course, given the time, the early morning shortly after midnight, the streets were virtually empty. And yet, it actually took the ambulance carrying Diana, well over an hour to cover the 3.7 miles to the 'nearest hospital,' whilst maintaining complete radio silence. In actual fact there were even two nearer hospitals than the *Pitie Salpétriére*, where she was taken. It is also remarkable to note that it took the oddly-behaving doctor supervising Diana's treatment, Jean-Marc Martino, a full thirty seven minutes to move the still conscious Princess from the undamaged back of her car into the ambulance. (Notwithstanding the fact that it is almost certain that Diana was fully capable of walking into the ambulance, albeit aided.) Had she received prompt hospital treatment, all the expert witnesses at the inquest agreed that Diana would most likely have survived.

The head of MI-6 made the absolutely laughable statement during the inquest that his agency had never killed or had ordered anyone killed in the past 50 years. Indeed, former MI-6 agent Richard Tomlinson, an inquest witness, whose book '*The Big Breach*' describes how MI-6 had planned to murder the Serbian leader, Milosevic using exactly the same 'Boston Brakes' method and by causing his car to crash in a narrow tunnel by flashing a very bright light into the driver's eyes. The MI-6 chief was quite obviously lying through his teeth, a view supported in the film by another former senior MI-6 agent, Baroness Daphne Park, who clearly stated that she had been involved in murders on behalf of that most shady organisation.

In truth, MI-6 and the other secret service agencies had more reason to want Diana dead than simply just her intention to marry a Muslim. Her involvement with and enthusiastic, high-profile support for the world-wide campaign to ban anti-personnel landmines caused anger and consternation within the armaments industry and the corrupt government officials who facilitated the legality of them—all at a 'price' of course. The then British Minister of Defence, Nicholas Soames even telephoned Diana and warned her, *"Don't meddle in things you don't know anything about. Accidents can happen."* This is as much of an overt threat as it is possible to make I believe, without actually openly using the words 'or we will kill you.'

Her murder took place just three weeks before the Oslo conference to discuss the ban on anti-personnel mines. Without Diana as the most prominent ambassador to the conference, most of the world's media ignored the event and of course without the media spotlight, the conference quietly yet firmly rejected the motion to enforce a ban.

The autopsy of Henri Paul, which stated that he was completely drunk, in spite of having consumed only two Ricards that night and appearing completely sober on the hotel CCTV captured when leaving the hotel, was performed by Professor Dominique Lecomte, a doctor notorious for her involvement in several previous French government cover-ups. Her autopsy was heavily criticised by several other medical experts as being totally incompetent and containing several critical errors, as was the conclusion from the result of the blood test which was highly suspicious and suggested it likely that the sample had been contaminated or more likely, tampered with. Professor Lecomte and Dr. Lepin the blood analyst, both refused to attend the inquest, after being ordered not to by the French government so as to protect 'French state secrets and interests.'

Diana had not only spoken to numerous friends about her ex-husband's family planning to kill her in a car accident and mentioned it in a letter to her butler, she had also written a similar letter to her lawyer who immediately passed it to the police. But in spite of her death in almost exactly in the precise way described in her letter, the Chief of the Metropolitan Police, Paul Condon, concealed the letter for three years, thus knowingly breaking the law by withholding this devastating evidence. However it is unsurprising to note that he was subsequently rewarded handsomely by the Queen by being offered a life-peerage and he has now taken his seat in the House of Lords, like the good little establishment lackey that he surely is.

In spite of no longer being 'Royal' at the time of her death, Diana was embalmed within hours of her death, according to the film, to make it impossible to perform a pregnancy test. Not only were her organs removed and destroyed, but so was the blood sample, taken from her upon her arrival at the Paris hospital.

The Queen's Private Secretary, Sir Robert Fellowes was the highest-ranked representative of the Windsors appearing at the inquest. Under oath, he claimed to have been on holiday (vacation) for the entire period before, during and after the accident and yet the diary of Tony Blair's press secretary Alastair Campbell clearly states that he met Fellowes on several occasions throughout the period during which he claimed to have been away. Diana had mentioned to friends on several occasions that he was one of the three people of whom she was most afraid and firmly believed that Fellowes hated her with a passion and wanted her out of the way of the Royal family. The film strongly suggested that Fellowes had a leading role in the arrangements for her death.

The prime suspect in the cause of the crash was the driver of the Fiat Uno which was seen and reported by several eye-witnesses. Neither the English nor the French police was apparently able to identify him and yet one of the most notorious paparazzi, the Frenchman, James Andanson, with suspected connections to several country's security services, drove a Fiat Uno exactly matching the description of the one involved in the crash. Andanson, who made a living selling pictures of British royalty and other celebrities to the media, lived in France and was known to have followed Diana and Dodi on their holiday together, immediately prior to the accident. He was not part of the paparazzi crowd waiting in front of the Ritz hotel owned by Dodi's father and when interviewed by French police about his whereabouts, made contradictory statements, as did his wife and son who provided his 'alibi.' In spite of all this, the investigation into his involvement was quietly dropped and the search for the 'missing' Fiat Uno soon abandoned. The inquest also made no attempt to establish who was driving the implicated car.

Three years after the crash, in 2000, Andanson was found dead in his burnt-out white Fiat Uno on government-owned land near Montpellier, France. He had no car keys with him and the two firemen who found his body had seen two bullet holes in his skull. The French police however concluded that he had committed suicide but you do not need to be a 'conspiracy theorist' to find it hard to believe that a man shot himself in the head twice before setting fire to his car.

Perhaps the most controversial aspect of the documentary is the interview with leading British clinical psychologist Oliver James, describing Prince Philip as someone with no internal sense of right or wrong. In his expert opinion, Prince Philip exhibits all the symptoms of psychopathy as do many other mass-murderers.

In summary, the film very convincingly posits, that in the light of the long list of suspicious circumstances and cover-ups, it would be far too much of a coincidence that Diana was killed exactly at a time when Western secret services and armament manufacturers were infuriated by her anti-personnel landmine campaign. It was also probably no coincidence that the Windsors were terrified by the thoughts of what Diana would be prepared to reveal about their 'inner secrets.' She had reached the point whereby she felt so badly used by Charles and his family that she would probably have stopped at nothing to get back at them in any way she could. Then of course there was also the far from small issue of the strong possibility of a Muslim step-father and Muslim siblings to the future British King.

'Unlawful Killing' made its industry debut at the Cannes Film festival in May, 2011. This was followed in July, by its public premiere at the Galway Film Festival in Ireland. In both cases, both critic and audience reaction was extremely favourable. However, the Royals, the Establishment and the banksters, were 'not amused.' They set in motion, every legal, financial and propaganda obstacle they could muster in order to prevent its release. From demanding no less than 87 cuts to the film, to publicly smearing its findings, they eventually made it so difficult, that the film was banned in the United Kingdom and France and Fayed had to abandon its proposed release. Even after being made available on the internet, it was removed by the powers that be.

However, having noted all of Mohamed Fayed's outrage and indignation at the murder of his beloved son, I do wonder if there was 'more than meets the eye' to his anger. His own shady background of heavy involvement himself in the arms trade, money laundering etc., not to mention the absolute control he exercised over Dodi and his relationship with Diana, in almost every detail of their daily lives, begs the question, how come his own very extensive, powerful security resources failed to protect them on that day?

Was it just possible that he could have himself been part of the conspiracy, but that his indignation at the incident was due in no small part to the fact that he actually expected his son to be spared the same fate as Diana? There are so many shades of grey in this whole incident, like that of so many other political assassinations where the complexity of the evil inherent within, is almost endless.

A British pro-establishment journalist, Sue Reid of the *Daily Mail* wrote on 30th August 2013, that . . .

"The final, haunting photo of Princess Diana, taken on the night she died, shows her sitting with her boyfriend Dodi Fayed in the back of a Mercedes car as it roars away from the rear entrance of the Paris Ritz Hotel, heading for the couple's secret love-nest near the Champs-Elysees.

Diana is twisting her head to peer out of the Mercedes' rear window, anxiously looking to see if her car is being chased by the paparazzi who had besieged her and Dodi since their arrival in the French capital from a Mediterranean holiday eight hours earlier.

At the wheel is chauffeur, Henri Paul. Dodi's bodyguard Trevor Rees-Jones is in the front passenger seat. What happened over the next two minutes is central to a new probe by Scotland Yard into an astonishing claim from a Special Air Services (SAS) sniper, known as 'Soldier N,' that members of his elite British army regiment assassinated Diana seconds after the Mercedes sped at 63mph into the notoriously dangerous Pont d'Alma road tunnel.

Many will dismiss Soldier N's claims as yet another conspiracy theory. After all, millions of words have been written about Diana's death at 12.20am on Sunday, August 31, 1997. The world was led to believe the blame lay with the grossly negligent driving of an intoxicated Mr. Paul and the pursuing paparazzi. But — however unlikely they may seem at first glance — I am convinced there is something in Soldier N's claims.

Ever since Diana's death at the age of 36, I have investigated forensically the events that led up to the crash and what happened afterwards. I have spoken to eye-witnesses, French and British intelligence officers, SAS soldiers and to friends of Diana and Dodi. And I have interviewed the Brittany-based parents of the 41-year-old chauffeur Henri Paul. They told me, with tears in their eyes, that their son was not a heavy drinker: his chosen potion was a bottle of beer or the occasional Ricard, a liquorice-flavored aperitif.

The fact is that too many of these accounts suggest that Diana's death was no accident. Crucially, my investigations show that the paparazzi who supposedly hounded Diana to her death were not even in the Pont d'Alma tunnel at the time of the car crash. They also reveal how a high-powered black motorbike — which did not belong to any of the paparazzi — shot past Diana's Mercedes in the tunnel. Eyewitnesses say its rider and pillion passenger deliberately caused the car to crash.

In addition, my inquiries unearthed the existence of a shadowy SAS unit that answers to MI-6, as well as the names of two MI-6 officers who were linked by a number of sources to Diana's death.

Could the Establishment really have turned Henri Paul and the paparazzi into scapegoats? Could there have been a skilful cover-up by people in powerful places to hide exactly what did happen?

There is little doubt that Diana, recently divorced from Prince Charles, was a thorn in the side of the Royal Family. Her romance with Dodi, though only six weeks old, was serious. The Princess had given her lover her 'most precious possession' — a pair of her deceased father's cufflinks — and phoned friends, saying she had a 'big surprise' for them when she returned from Paris.

Dodi had slipped out of the Ritz Hotel, as Diana was having her hair done, to collect a jewel-encrusted ring adorned with the words 'Tell Me Yes,' from a swanky Paris jeweller. It came from a collection of engagement rings.

Rumours were circulating, too, that the Princess was pregnant. Photographs of her in a leopard-print swimsuit, on holiday in the South of France 14 days earlier, show an unmistakable bump around her waistline. And, as the Mail revealed after Diana's death, she had visited — in the strictest secrecy — a leading London hospital for a pregnancy scan just before that photo was snapped.

To add to the disquiet, the mother of a future King of England and head of the Church of England was threatening to move abroad with her Muslim boyfriend and take the royal Princes, William and Harry, with her.

Dodi had bought an estate, once owned by film star Julie Andrews, by the beach in Malibu, California, and shown Diana a video of it. He told her the sumptuous house was where they would spend their married life. Ostracised by the Royal Family and stripped of her HRH title, Diana was said to be excited by the prospect.

Dodi's father, Mohamed Al Fayed, the multi-millionaire former owner of Harrods, insists Diana was pregnant by his son and preparing to tell the young Princes about her forthcoming marriage when she returned to Britain on September 1 — the day after the crash — before they went back to boarding school.

However far-fetched it sounds, all the Establishment concerns about Diana were genuine. But could this really have led to her assassination? And if so, how could it have been carried out?

These questions are partially answered by the compelling testimony of 14 independent eye-witnesses near the crash scene that night. They say Diana's car was surrounded at the entrance to the Alma tunnel by a phalanx of cars and motorcycles, which sped after the Mercedes.

The assumption has always been that the cars and bikes were carrying the paparazzi. By the Monday morning after the crash, outside the Alma tunnel, a huge message had appeared. 'Killer paparazzi' had been sprayed in gold paint on the walls.

No-one, to this day, knows who put it there — or why they were not stopped by the French authorities from doing so. Yet the paparazzi following Diana did not reach the Pont d'Alma tunnel until at least one minute after the crash, so they cannot be to blame. Indeed, two years later they were cleared of manslaughter charges after the French state prosecutor said there was 'insufficient evidence' of their involvement in Diana's death.

What happened is that the paparazzi had been deceived. In a clever ploy devised by Henri Paul, the Ritz had placed a decoy Mercedes at the front of the hotel to confuse the photographers, which allowed the lovers to slip out of the back door into a similar car. The last picture of Diana peering from the rear window was taken by a France-based photographer who had seen through the ruse and was standing on the pavement by the hotel's rear entrance watching as the 'real' Mercedes sped off.

Yet that Mercedes was definitely being hotly pursued when in the tunnel. The independent witnesses insist it was being followed not only by the black motorbike, but by two speeding cars, a dark saloon and a white turbo Fiat Uno.

There is no evidence to link these cars or the motorcycle to the paparazzi who had been waiting at the Ritz. The saloon tail-gated the Mercedes, which made the chauffeur — thinking, wrongly, he was being pursued by paparazzi — drive even faster and more erratically. Meanwhile, the Uno accelerated, clipping the side of the Mercedes to push it to one side.

This manoeuver allowed the black motorbike to speed past Diana's car, with its two riders *wearing helmets that hid their faces. Witnesses claim that when the bike was about 15ft in front of the car, there was a fierce flash of white light from the motorbike. The suggestion is that this came from a laser beam (dazzler laser) carried by the pillion passenger and directed at the car.*

The witnesses' view is that the flash of light blinded Henri Paul temporarily. It was followed by a loud bang as the limousine swerved violently before slamming into the 13th pillar in the tunnel and being reduced to a mass of wrecked metal. One of those eyewitnesses, a French harbour pilot driving ahead of the Mercedes through the tunnel, watched the scene in his rear-view mirror.

Chillingly, he recalls the black motorbike stopping after the crash and one of the riders jumping off the bike before going to peer in the Mercedes window at the passengers. The rider, who kept his helmet on, then turned to his compatriot on the bike and gave a gesture used informally in the military (where both arms are crossed over the body and then thrown out straight to each side) to indicate 'mission accomplished.' Afterwards, he climbed back on the motorcycle, which raced off out of the tunnel. The riders on the bike, and the vehicle itself, have never been identified.

The harbour pilot, whose wife was with him in the car, has described the horrifying scenario as resembling a 'terrorist attack.' So, who could have been driving the bike and the other vehicles that did follow Diana's car into the Alma tunnel that night? Could they really have been part of the plot to get rid of Diana and her lover — a plot orchestrated by MI-6 or the SAS regiment, as the latest sensational claims suggest?

After Diana's death, I received a nine-line note in the post containing the names of two MI-6 men who have spent their entire careers working at the heart of the British Establishment, representing the Government as senior diplomats, whom I will call X and Y. Written in blue felt-tip pen on a flimsy piece of paper ripped from an A4 exercise book, the note said: 'If you are brave enough, dig deeper to learn about X and Y. Both were MI-6. Both were involved at the highest level in the murder of the Princess.' It signed off with the words: 'Good luck.'

Of course, an unsigned note does not provide firm evidence, or anything like it, that MI-6 spies were operating in Paris that evening or were connected with Diana's death. Yet their names came up again when I received a call from a well-placed source within the intelligence services. He named the same two men, X and Y, who had overseen the 'Paris operation' and said the crash was designed to frighten Diana into halting her romance with Dodi because he was considered an unsuitable partner.

'We hoped to break her arm or cause a minor injury,' said my informant. 'The operation was also overseen by a top MI-6 officer known as 'the tall man,' who is now retired and living on the Continent. He admits it went wrong. No-one in MI-6 wanted Diana to be killed.'

And this week the men's names were mentioned again, this time by Moscow intelligence. According to the author of a new book, the Russian Foreign Intelligence Service, the SVR, knew that X and Y were in Paris on the night Diana died. And after the car crash the SVR set out to find out why. Gennady Sokolov, whose book 'The Kremlin vs. The Windsors' will be published next year, told me this week: 'Of course our people were following your agents.'

They were senior MI-6 officers operating secretly in Paris that night, without the knowledge of even French counter-intelligence. They left again after she was dead.

Her relationship and possible marriage to Dodi was deeply worrying to senior royals in Britain. The Princess's phone was constantly listened-to and she was followed all the time. After the crash, public opinion was deliberately led astray. Scapegoats were created, such as the paparazzi and the drunk driver. There was a dance around Henri Paul, saying he was an alcohol addict, a virtual kamikaze, who helped to destroy them all. It is total nonsense.

From the very beginning, it was clear to me it was not just an accident. My sources in the SVR and other Russian secret services are sure it was a very English murder. They have talked to me about an SAS squad called The Increment, which is attached to MI-6, being involved in the assassination. These guys work on the top level without leaving a single trace, and — perhaps — one was on the motorbike following Diana's car.'

But why did none of this extraordinary story come out at the inquest into Diana's death, which should have been the final word on it? It's true that 14 tunnel witnesses were at least allowed to appear or send their testimonies. But much of their vital information was completely submerged by the sheer volume of evidence presented over the six months of the hearing.

We heard that chauffeur Henri Paul and Dodi Fayed were killed instantly; that the sole survivor was the bodyguard Trevor Rees Jones, who suffered such devastating facial injuries he has no memory of events in the tunnel, and that with the pulmonary vein in her chest torn, Diana died nearly four hours later of heart failure and blood loss at Paris' Pitié Salpétriére hospital.

But we also know that the inquest never unraveled the full truth. More than 170 important witnesses, including the doctor who embalmed Diana's body (a process that camouflages pregnancy in post-mortem blood tests) were never called to the inquest.

One radiologist from Pitié Salpétriére hospital, who said that she had seen a small foetus of perhaps six to ten weeks in the Princess's womb during an X-ray and a later sonogram of her body, was not questioned. Instead, she was allowed by the judge heading the inquest, Lord Justice Scott Baker, to send a statement giving her current address in America and no more details.

Crucially, the hearing was cruelly unfair to chauffeur Henri Paul, who was vilified from the beginning.

On the day after the crash, French authorities insisted that he was an alcoholic and 'drunk as a pig' when he left the Ritz that night to drive the lovers to Dodi's Paris apartment near the Champs-Elysees.

It has since emerged that the blood tests on Paul's body had not been completed when they made the announcement to journalists. Furthermore, the chauffeur had passed an intensive medical examination for flying lessons three days before the crash — his liver showed no sign of alcohol abuse. A string of witnesses at the Ritz say Paul drank two shots of his favorite Ricard at the bar before taking to the wheel, which was confirmed by bar receipts at the hotel.

However, after a shambolic mix- up over his blood samples (deliberate or otherwise,) it was pronounced by a medical expert at the inquest that Paul had downed ten of the aperitifs, was twice over the British driving limit and three times over the French one, when he drove the Mercedes that night."

But for all the endless cover-ups and lies, Princess Diana survived the Crown-sanctioned assassination attempt in the car and like so many before her and since, Diana finally fell victim to a 'doctor-assisted assassination,' by the Crown/bankster 'backup' team in the ambulance.

Diana's ancestry

In Tina Brown's book '*The Diana Chronicles*,' the author claims that Princess Diana's mother Frances Shand Kydd had a long-running affair with Sir James Goldsmith during her marriage to Earl Spencer. She suggests that Diana who was born in 1961, was Goldsmith's love-child and not Spencer's daughter.

The late Sir James Goldsmith, a Jewish bankster and publisher, was a cousin of the Rothschilds. James Goldsmith's grandfather, Adolphe Goldschmidt came to London as a multi-millionaire in 1895 and changed the family name from the German, 'Goldschmidt' to the Anglicised 'Goldsmith.' There is no denying that the affair took place at a time when Frances was deeply unhappy in her marriage to the Earl Spencer, who was 'drinking heavily' and 'being beastly towards her.' She eventually divorced him and remarried in 1969. However, Diana was not only similar to James Goldsmith in looks, 'but also in her charisma and her sexual appetites . . . ' She also shared a striking physical resemblance to the children of Sir James Goldsmith—Zak Goldsmith, Ben Goldsmith and Jemima Goldsmith. They are all allegedly Diana's half-brothers and sister.

News reports that both Diana and Jemima were fathered by swashbuckling tycoon Sir James Goldsmith caused controversy throughout Australia and Britain and the plain facts are that during Diana's unhappy marriage to Charles, she did not seek and nor was she offered, solace by the Spencers. She sought solace from her surrogate family, the Goldsmiths. Following the Rothschild protocol of interbreeding to keep the power and wealth all-in-the-family, Diana's alleged half-brother Ben Goldsmith married Kate Rothschild in 2003.

The *original and current* definition of a Jew, is someone whose mother is Jewish. Judaism is passed down through the matriarchal lineage. Prince William's mother, Princess Diana, had a Jewish mother (Frances Ruth Burke Roche) and she also likely had a Jewish father which would make Princes William and Harry, both Jewish too.

The Jewish holy book the Torah, forbids a Jewish man from marrying a Gentile woman otherwise his children to that woman will not be regarded as Jewish. Interestingly, Prince William's in-laws are believed to be Jewish too, which means that not only are Kate and William, the future King and Queen, Jewish but also all their offspring too.

One law for us, no laws for them . . .

As the head of the Crown, (the banksters main front,) the British monarch cannot be charged with a crime, arrested, sued, or even be required to testify in court as long as she or he reigns over the United Kingdom and Commonwealth. In other words she has total diplomatic immunity, a free rein to do whatever she will and if she decided to assassinate passers-by in The Mall, from the Buckingham Palace balcony with a high-powered rifle, even this would not be enough for the monarch to be indicted.

And for added protection and for the ultimate insult . . . Members of Parliament, Lords, Judges, Police, Military, and even the Scouts and girl guides, all swear an *Oath of Allegiance* to the Monarch. An oath of loyalty and devotion, that is not to the country, not to the British government or people but to the royal-criminal cabal. MPs are prevented from even raising the subject of the abolition of the monarchy, because of this sworn oath of loyalty.

Another entity that swears total allegiance to the Queen and therefore to the Crown, is the intelligence community. MI-5 is Britain's domestic military intelligence division whilst MI-6 is the foreign military intelligence division. Although officially described as 'services,' they are a hybrid of government departments and 'plain-clothes' military units, in effect, operationally-controlled foreign powers.

Known as *The Secret State* and nicknamed *The Permanent Government* in Robin Ramsey and Stephen Dorril's book *'Smear! Wilson and the Secret State,'* they operate as a 'state within a state,' being subject to only token democratic accountability. They go to great lengths, including lying to elected-ministers and use of the archaic 'Official Secrets Act' in order to ward-off embarrassing revelations about what a waste of our public money many of their operations are . . . and also to deflect any scrutiny of their activities. The IOPS (Information Operations Planning System) department of MI-6 often 'plants' stories beneficial to the *Secret State* to gullible journalists in order to facilitate this.

In her 64 years (at time of writing) as unelected head of state, and head of the Church of England, many international crimes have been committed by the Crown's security services and thus by implication, Elizabeth herself. Through the never-ending quest for profit at any cost through oil, gold, diamonds or drugs, the Queen has provided the banksters, the Rothschilds, the perfect front for a plethora of crimes, at both domestically and abroad . . .

Foreign Crimes *during* the reign of the current Monarch

Kenya, 1952-1956

A liberation campaign was launched by the Mau Mau (native Kenyans) and the

British response was to immediately close the 149 schools of the Kikuyu Independent Schools Association, 21 schools of the Kikuyu Karinga Education Association, and 14 other independent schools in the country. They were, wrote historian Walter Rodney, *"...considered training grounds for rebellion."* The British then imposed a state of emergency and brutally suppressed the Mau Mau freedom fighters. British forces committed many atrocities, established concentration camps and 'resettled' hundreds of thousands of people in 'protected villages,' resulting in the deaths of around 150,000 Africans.

Guyana, 1953

In October of 1953, Britain suspended Guyana's constitution. The People's Progressive Party, (PPP) was the first truly democratic political party in Guyana and was also multi-racial. It was at that time the only party in the Caribbean with a mandate to protect the lower or underclasses of society from the rich predators and bankers who saw the country and its people as yet another resource to be exploited for their own ends. Predictably, the PPP came into conflict with its British imperialist masters and so Britain immediately dispatched troops and installed an interim administration after the 'democratic process' had not produced a result to meet with its approval.

Libya, 1953

On 7th December Britain established military bases in Libya for a period of 20 years, ostensibly in return for economic subsidies, which never actually reached 'the people' but instead served to maintain a puppet government, friendly to British financial, commercial and military interests.

Egypt, 1956-1957

President Gamel Abdel Nasser unilaterally decided to 'nationalise' the Suez Canal causing conflict with Britain whose trade with the Middle and Far East would be severely restricted as a result. According to the historian J.M. Roberts, *"The British, French, and Israelis conspired to overthrow [Nasser] in the Suez adventure, the last fling of old-style imperialism."* The incident is notable also for the fact that in the inordinate rush to dispatch troops to Egypt, the British Prime Minister still had to obtain the signed approval of the Queen. According to historian Ben Pimlott, *"...the hastily prepared Proclamation..."* was passed to her for signature whilst she was at a horse race meeting and, *"...Her approval was required before it could be read-out in the House of Commons the same afternoon."* In the wake of the failed Suez invasion, MI-6 planned and carried-out several assassination attempts against President Nasser. The US were also involved, recruiting the Saudis and Iraqis to assist them. In fact, Britain had already made plans to assassinate Nasser, even before he had nationalised the Suez Canal.

Yemen, 1959

The Federation of Arab Emirates of the South was created as an autonomous territory under British 'protection.' Britain had previously occupied parts of Yemen in 1837, the year Victoria became Queen.

Kenya, 1961

Britain was forced to introduce a new policy which allowed Africans to buy property and farms in the White Highlands and Kenya's first pre-independence general elections were held.

By the sale of over-priced land previously seized by the white settlers, not only did the settlers make a great deal of money, but it was also ensured that the land would pass into the hands of either wealthy individuals who would protect European bankster and business interests or people trapped by the debts they incurred in borrowing money to buy the land.

Guyana, 1962

The US concluded that PPP leader Dr. Jagan was a 'communist' and although all alternatives to him were unacceptable to the people or downright crooked, the US nevertheless backed Jagan's opponents under an 'independent,' British Guyana which would cause the US money interests far fewer problems than the existing, elected government. Jagan announced a budget which was widely praised by international commentators, but the US/British controlled opposition condemned it and used it as an excuse to instigate violent protests. The opposition was supported by local labour organisations who received support from certain US union groups, funded by the CIA.

The British Governor-General initially refused to send troops to quell the disturbances, but eventually did so under pressure after the arson, looting and deaths in the capital began to spiral out of control. Jagan was forced to withdraw his controversial, unacceptable budget plan.

Yemen, 1962

MI-6 began covertly providing arms, funding and logistical support to pro-British 'rebels' in a dirty war against pro-Egyptian republican forces. The British Government secretly colluded with Israel's Mossad and the Saudi regime and around 200,000 innocents died in the war.

Then in 1963, Britain rejected a UN call for it to withdraw and permit self-determination.

Australia, 1975

The government of Prime Minister Gough Whitlam was beset by resignations and the blocking of its budget by the upper house of the Parliament and in an unprecedented move, the UK governor-general, the official, unelected representative of the Monarchy, summarily dismissed Whitlam and his government. A caretaker administration was installed and the speaker of the Australian House of Commons wrote to the Queen to ask her to restore Whitlam to office, but she declined to intervene, stating that it would not be 'proper' for her to do so.

It later transpired that the CIA had apparently vigorously lobbied Kerr to dismiss Whitlam, because he was raising awareness of and questioning the fact that the US was running a clandestine outpost of the CIA and a centre for spy satellites in the Australian outback.

Falkland Islands, 1982

Even after the UK proclaimed sovereignty over the islands in 1833, Argentina contested the move and had long sought to wrest them back under her control. Then in 1982, the military junta of Argentina seized the islands—which lay just off its coast—prompting the British to send in warships and troops to wage a 74-day battle for control in order to protect their strategic interests in the region. They eventually re-took the islands, but to this day, Argentina still disputes their ownership. A comparable situation would be if Argentina 'owned' the Orkney Islands and used them as a base for extracting the North Sea Oil reserves, under British noses.

Ireland, 1500-date

The Pope at the time, 'gave' Ireland to King Henry VII but his successor then attempted to take it back again when Henry's son, Henry VIII broke away from the Roman Catholic Church. Nevertheless, the UK has held all or part of the island ever since the late 15th century. Since that time there has been an ongoing catalogue of conflicts, uprisings and bloody disputes between the two nations, culminating in the latest conflict (of the 1970s to the 1990s) instigated and perpetuated by the British government-controlled and so-called, 'Irish Republican Army' (IRA,) which is in reality just a fabricated construct of the British security services.

The steady decline of British ability to influence foreign affairs now corresponds to Britain's ever-diminishing stature as an imperial power.

However, even in an age of increasing indifference to the Monarchy and the less than deferential regard for our 'masters,' what has certainly not declined is the ongoing, unacceptably deferential treatment of the British Monarchy, by the establishment and media. The International Criminal Court readily indicts those deemed to be 'rogue' leaders from the Middle East and Africa and the third world in general, but there is nary a word of condemnation forthcoming, of British, US or Israeli crimes or their officials, from the Queen downwards.

Next we will scrutinise the role of the British Royals and the Crown in the reconfiguring of the world through the medium of war, for their own nefarious purposes and those of their bankster friends . . .

Chapter 6
Bankster War Crimes—World War I

He's five foot two and he's six feet four
He fights with missiles and with spears
He's all of thirty-one and he's only seventeen
Been a soldier for a thousand years

He's a Catholic, a Hindu, an Atheist, a Jain
A Buddhist and a Baptist and a Jew
And he knows he shouldn't kill and he knows he always will
Kill you for me my friend and me for you

And he's fighting for Canada
He's fighting for France, he's fighting for the USA
And he's fighting for the Russians
And he's fighting for Japan
And he thinks we'll put an end to war this way

And he's fighting for Democracy, he's fighting for the Reds
He says 'It's for the peace of all'
He's the one who must decide, who's to live and who's to die
And he never sees the writing on the wall

But without him
How would Hitler have condemned him at Labau?
Without him Caesar would have stood alone
He's the one who gives his body as a weapon of the war
And without him all this killing can't go on

He's the Universal Soldier and he really is to blame
His orders come from far away no more
They come from here and there and you and me
And brothers can't you see
This is not the way we put an end to war.

'The Universal Soldier,' Buffy Sainte-Marie

Thus far, it has hopefully already been made apparent that the banksters certainly love war and the massive debts it creates for nations and thus by extension therefore, the correspondingly massive profits it makes for them. Indeed, their insatiable lust for these profits knows no bounds. The establishment of the banksters' Federal Reserve Bank in the United States in 1913, coupled with their numerous other central banks throughout the world and the control they exert over the media in all forms, provided them with the unchallenged ability to rob from virtually every human being on the planet with absolute impunity and without regard to consequences.

In order to counter any question, debate or opposition to the Zionist banksters' crimes, they simply made it a hate-crime or deemed it 'racist,' to even discuss them. In fact, they pre-empted the whole issue by creating the *Anti-Defamation League of B'Nai B'rith* (ADL) in the months prior to the launch of the Federal Reserve Bank and in order to intimidate and condemn anyone speaking out against the Zionists. Anyone deemed to be a threat is thereby automatically regarded by the masses as someone who is attacking and threatening ALL Jewish people. 'Anti-Semite,' is the accusation and this is the perfect alibi and the perfect defence against criticism of any kind.

The ADL was founded by a Chicago lawyer, Sigmund Livingston in response to the 1913 murder/rape trial of Leo Frank a middle-class Jewish manager of a sweat-shop in Georgia who raped and murdered a thirteen year old, lower-class Gentile (non-Jewish) child worker. The prominent Jews who even at that time in American history were preparing for the total domination of American society by their own kind, were incensed that the goyim (a derogatory Jewish term for non-Jews) had the audacity to indict one of their own, for the crime despite that the fact that there a was a mass of evidence pointing to Frank's guilt.

Considered one of the most sensational trials of the early 20th century, the Frank case seemed to tick every controversial box of the time, North vs. South, black vs. white, Jew vs. Christian, industrial vs. agrarian etc. During the century that has passed since, it has inspired numerous books and films, TV documentaries, plays, musicals and songs and has fueled legal debates, spawned a travelling exhibition and driven public forums.

It all began on Sunday, 27th April 1913, when the body of Mary Phagan, was discovered in the basement of her workplace, the National Pencil Company factory in Marietta, Georgia. Leo Frank, the northern US-born factory superintendent, was president of the Atlanta chapter of the Jewish secret society, B'nai B'rith. He was also a bisexual paedophile and a drug addict, who managed the factory and all evidence points to the fact that he demanded sex from 13-year old Mary and then when she resisted, he brutally raped and murdered her.

Leo Frank Mary Phagan

Frank and an illiterate black handyman, dragged the body to the basement where they were going to burn it in the factory furnace the next day, but that same night a watchman discovered the body, called the police and after questioning, Frank was arrested, found guilty and sentenced to hang.

However, the governor of Georgia, John Slaton (who purely coincidentally, I'm sure, was the owner of the law firm that represented Frank) commuted his sentence. And so on 16th August 1915, twenty five men abducted him from his bed in a minimum security prison and lynched him in the early hours of the next day.

"Some viewed the commutation by Slaton as a conflict of interest, as Slaton was a law partner of Frank's lead defense counsel. Slaton's actions led to threats of mob violence against the governor, and the Georgia National Guard and local police were enlisted for protection. Fear of retaliation prompted Slaton and his wife to move out of Georgia after his term as governor ended. They did not return to the state for a decade." Wikipedia™

In the aftermath of Frank's murder, the Anti-Defamation League was formed and campaigned vigorously for a posthumous pardon. This was finally granted on a technicality, without establishing either his guilt or innocence in 1986.

The lynching of Leo Frank

The Zionist ADL continues to exploit this incident to the maximum, to this day and Zionist-controlled Hollywood even produced a film in the 1980s, *'The Murder of Mary Phagan,'* starring Jack Lemmon and a young Kevin Spacey, which presented a completely one-sided account of the incident, totally sympathetic to Frank's innocence.

In those days lynchings were not uncommon, not just of blacks as we are deceptively led to believe, but also of whites too (mostly for rape.) However, Leo Frank still remains the only Jew ever known to have been lynched in America and indeed he was the first white man to be brought to trial in the Deep South on a capital charge, solely on the word of a Negro.

What was never revealed at the trial was that Leo Frank had 'previous.' One year before Mary Phagan was raped and killed, Frank raped and in the process, viciously bit another one of his child employees who conceived a child by him and was despatched to a home for unmarried mothers as a result of their brief but illegal and one-sided liaison. So, Frank was actually a sadistic paedophile whose case has been used as a stick for more than a century to attack, defame, slander, libel and generally hold to ransom, ordinary American non-Jewish 'white' citizens. This is the man that the Jewish community lied-about and is used by the Zionists, as their 'martyr' to anti-Semitism.

The conviction of Leo Frank was the impetus for the formation of the Anti-Defamation League of B'nai B'rith in October 1913, after the 500 member strong Atlanta branch of B'nai B'rith voted unanimously on 24th September 1913, to re-elect their 'wrongfully imprisoned' President, Leo Frank to a second term as their leader. Frank ran the affairs of this B'nai B'rith chapter behind bars until September of 1914 but was not re-elected for a third term.

Ever since this sad incident, the ADL has been at the very forefront of perpetuating the hate-crime hoax by falsely claiming that people were shouting and chanting 'hang the Jew' and 'kill the Jew,' outside the open windows of the Leo Frank trial courtroom.

The charter of the ADL states that *"The immediate object of the League is to stop, by appeals to reason and conscience and, if necessary, by appeals to law, the defamation of the Jewish people. Its ultimate purpose is to secure justice and fair treatment to all citizens alike and to put an end forever to unjust and unfair discrimination against and ridicule of any sect, or body of citizens."*

In fact the ADL's true purpose is to protect the Rothschilds and the other banksters' criminal network from exposure. Anyone who dares to call attention to the workings of the New World Order, or The Federal Reserve Bank, will immediately be denounced by the ADL as 'anti-Semitic' or 'Jew haters.' It is the 'enforcement' arm of the totally Zionist/bankster front organisation the B'nai B'rith, which was founded in 1843. B'nai B'rith in Hebrew means 'Sons of the Covenant,' and the covenant that God made with Abraham, the first Jew and afterward renewed with Moses, is the central theme and constitution of Judaism.

As you may remember from a previous chapter, Albert Pike predicted that there would have to be 'Three World Wars' in order to bring to fruition the bankster/Illuminati plans for the so-called New World Order (NWO.) A chain of events therefore had to be created to set the scene for all the unnecessary death and destruction that was to follow.

In June 1914, the first steps in bringing about the long awaited, pre-planned World War was through the use of 'Serbian Nationalists.' It was an NWO secret society known as the 'Black Hand,' possibly working in tandem with the 'Young Turks,' that plotted the murder of the ruler of Austro-Hungary, the Archduke Franz Ferdinand. Serbia at this time was an independent, orthodox Christian nation under the protection of Czarist Russia but many Serbians also lived under Austro-Hungarian rule (in Bosnia)

instead of under Serbian or Russian rule. This arrangement had always been controversial and caused incessant friction, both within Austro-Hungary, and also *between* Russia and Austro-Hungary.

Franz Ferdinand (1863-1914) was heir to the Hapsburg family throne of Austro-Hungary and whilst travelling through the Bosnian city of Sarajevo on an official visit with his wife Sophie, a bomb was thrown at the Archduke's open car. However, he deflected the bomb with his arm and it exploded behind him, injuring several onlookers. Then, contrary to all advice, the royal couple insisted on visiting the injured at the hospital.

However, during the return trip to the palace, their driver turned onto a side street, where a young member of the Serbian sect, the 'Black Hand,' Gavril Princip opened fire on them. Sophie was mortally wounded in the stomach and Franz, in the neck. Franz was still alive when witnesses arrived to give aid and his dying words to Sophie were *"Don't die darling. Live for our children."* They both died shortly afterwards.

By the 29th June 1914, anti-Serbian riots had begun to erupt in the Austro-Hungarian city of Sarajevo (now Bosnia,) no doubt instigated by the agents of those whose best interests would be served by the world becoming involved in a bloody conflict and its ensuing profit opportunities. However profit, whilst a strong motivator was not the prime mover in this case. The banksters wanted more than anything else to re-order the world map, particularly in Europe and in the process destroy the 'upstart,' nation of Germany and Czarist Russia in order to fulfil the Rothschild's threat to the Romanov dynasty, a century previously.

On the 7th July 1914, Austro-Hungary convened a council to discuss the Serbian situation which was now getting out of hand and later that month the Zionist-bankster-controlled, Austro-Hungarian press began to add propagandistic fuel to the fire of escalating anti-Serbian sentiment. False reports of a Serbian conspiracy against Austro-Hungary began to circulate but in an attempt to calm the situation, Kaiser Wilhelm II of Germany encouraged his ally, Austro-Hungary, to try to settle the matter using diplomacy.

But as is often the case, blind patriotic fervour and propaganda won the day and so on 28th July 1914, Austro-Hungary totally succumbed to the prevalent, totally manufactured hysteria and declared war on Serbia, closely followed, the very next day by Russia mobilising its armed forces in solidarity with its ally, Serbia. Then, as planned, the giant dominoes began to topple all across Europe as treaties were invoked and five weeks after Franz Ferdinand's death, the world was thrown into complete turmoil as the bankster's largely conscripted armies prepared to face each other on the battlefields of Europe to act out yet another deadly game initiated by the banksters for their own devious ends.

On 3rd August, now confronted by threats from two fronts, engineered by both France and England, Germany quickly advanced towards France through Belgium while simultaneously confronting Russia in the east. Great Britain then entered the war on the side of its allies, France and Russia and the 'Triple Entente' members France, Russia and Britain agreed that no member would make peace separately with Germany or Austro-Hungary.

Finally, the jigsaw was complete when on 28th October, Russia's southern rival, the Ottoman Turkish Empire, entered the war on the side of Austro-Hungary and Germany.

It is apparent now that there would have been no World War without the banksters' Federal Reserve System. A 'strange' sequence of events, none of which of course were accidental, had occurred. Without Theodore Roosevelt's 'Bull Moose' candidacy, the popular President Taft would have been re-elected and Woodrow Wilson would have returned to the obscurity from whence he had sprung. There would therefore have been no Federal Reserve Act at this time and WWI could not have been financed.

The major European nations had all been induced to maintain large standing armies as a policy of the central banks which dictated their governments' decisions and from 1887 to 1914, this precarious system of heavily-armed but bankrupt European nations endured, whilst the United States continued to be a debtor nation, borrowing money from abroad, but making few international loans, because it had no central bank. The system of national loans developed by the Rothschilds and their fellow banksters served to finance European struggles during the nineteenth century because they were distributed over Rothschild branches in several countries. But by 1900, it was obvious that Europe could not afford a major war. Most had large armies, universal military service and 'state of the art' modern weapons but their economies could not support the enormous expenditures required to maintain them on a permanent basis.

The Federal Reserve System began operating in early 1914 and coerced the American government to lend the European Allies twenty five billion dollars which was never repaid, although of course, a considerable sum in interest was repaid to the banksters themselves. The US was ultimately induced to declare war on Germany, with whom they had no conceivable political or economic quarrel and also despite the fact that the United States possessed the largest number of people of German origin of any country in the world. Almost half of its citizens were of German descent and it was only by the narrowest of margins that German had lost out in the voting for the national language of the USA.

The banksters had been waiting impatiently since 1887 for the United States to enact a central bank policy in order to enable them to finance a major European war among the nations they had already bankrupted with armament and 'defence' programs. The most important element of any central bank mechanism of course is war finance.

The background of the notorious banksters, *Kuhn, Loeb and Company* had been exposed in *Truth Magazine* in 1912…

"Mr. Schiff is head of the great private banking house of Kuhn, Loeb and Co., which represents the Rothschild interest on this side of the Atlantic. He has been described as a financial strategist and has been for years the financial minister to the great impersonal power known as Standard Oil. He was hand-in-glove with the Harrimans, the Goulds and the Rockefellers, in all their railroad enterprises and has become the dominant power in the railroad and financial world in America. Louis Brandeis, because of his great ability as a lawyer and for other reasons which will appear later, was selected by Schiff as the instrument through which Schiff hoped to achieve his ambition in New England. His job was to carry on an agitation which would undermine public confidence in the New Haven system and cause a decrease in the price of its securities, thus forcing them on the market for the wreckers to buy."

Schiff's lawyer, Brandeis is worthy of mention as the first available appointment on the Supreme Court of the United States which Woodrow Wilson was allowed to fill.

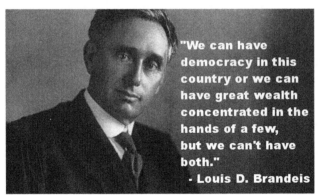

Between 1901 and 1913 the House of Morgan and the House of Rockefeller formed close alliances with the Duke and the Mellon families. This group consolidated their power and came to dominate other Wall Street, bankster powers including those of, Carnegie, Whitney, Vanderbilt, Brown-Harriman, and Dillon-Reed. The powerful interests of the *Round Table Group* however wished to control the people further by having the government impose an 'income' tax and deposit the proceeds into the central bank. The group would thereafter assume control of the bank and thereby control the money and subsequently, virtually everything else by dint of its colossal wealth. Indeed, the *Round Table* went on to take control of the US State Department and formulate government policy, which would determine how the money was to be spent and also control the CIA which would gather information, script and produce psycho-political operations focussed upon the unsuspecting masses in order to influence them into acting and thinking in accord with *Round Table* controlled, State Department policy decisions.

It was also the intention of the *Round Table* to consolidate all the nations of the world into a single nation, with a single central bank under their control, and a single international security system; the much-vaunted 'New World Order.'

And so as previously related, it transpired that amongst the first legislation introduced by the Wilson administration was the institution of the illegally sanctioned graduated income tax in 1913 and the creation of a central bank, the Federal Reserve. An inheritance tax was also instituted and these tax laws were utilised to rationalise the need for legislation that allowed the establishment of tax-exempt foundations. The tax-exempt foundations became the link between the Group members' personal, private corporations and the national University system. The Group would control the Universities by controlling the sources of their funding which was derived mainly from money, sheltered from taxes and subsequently being channeled into projects that would help achieve *Round Table Group* aims.

And so, to return to the main thrust of this chapter, Europe, with the rest of the world following swiftly in its wake, exploded into violence in August 1914, with the banksters now all-set to finance and arm both sides of the conflict and thereby reap their expected massive profits, whilst also waiting for all their insidious, highly manipulative geo-political goals to be fulfilled.

World War I Begins in Earnest

After Germany's initial, westward onslaught towards Paris was brought to a halt, the Western Front settled-down into a bloody stalemate with trench lines that would change little until 1918, and stretching from the North Sea coast to the Swiss Alps. In the East, the Russian army successfully engaged the Austro-Hungarian forces but was soon forced to retreat by the German army. Additional fronts were then opened in Eastern Europe and Asia Minor when the Ottoman Empire (Turkey) joined the war on Germany's side in late 1914. However this was balanced by Italy's switching of sides and joining the Entente powers in 1915.

At sea, the British Navy blockaded Germany whilst her U-boats attempted to counter the blockade by sinking many British merchant ships carrying arms and other war supplies.

The Zionist banksters on both sides of the Atlantic were desperate to drag the US into the war against Germany and Lord of the Admiralty, Winston Churchill and President Wilson's Marxist advisor, Edward Mandel House colluding together believed that if the Germans could be enticed into sinking a British ship with Americans on board, the resulting public outcry would be such that Wilson's promise not to involve the US in any European war would be forgotten and thus America would be drawn 'against her will' into the war. Another classic Hegelian Dialectic, (problem, reaction, solution.)

So it transpired that Churchill and Woodrow Wilson in an operation totally financed by the banksters, arranged for a large, illegal shipment of weapons (it was against US law to place weapons or ammunition on a passenger ship travelling to Britain or Germany) on the *Lusitania* in May of 1915.

The *Lusitania* was a luxury ocean liner, owned by the *British Cunard Steamship Line* and officially part of the British auxiliary navy. She had been commandeered by the British Government for war use for which the ship's owners were paid £218,000 a year. As an auxiliary naval ship, the *Lusitania* was under orders from the British Admiralty to ram any German ship seeking to inspect her cargo.

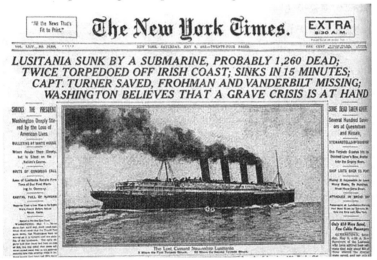
Contemporary newspaper report of the sinking

Three German spies attempted to confirm that the 'ninety tons of unrefrigerated butter' destined for a British naval base were weapons and ammunition, however they were discovered and detained on the ship to prevent word getting out, but the weapons were seen by ethnic German dock-workers as they were being loaded onto the *Lusitania* and they reported this to the German Embassy.

So in order to warn would-be American passengers about the weapons shipment being carried, thus making the *Lusitania* a legitimate target for its U-boats, the Imperial German Embassy attempted to place an advertisement in 50 US east coast newspapers. These ads were to be printed with a date of 22nd April 1915, but the US State Department managed to block them all—significantly, except one and this is the reason that we know that all this is a true representation of the events.

George Viereck, from the German embassy, protested to the US State Department on 26th April that the ads were being withheld from publication and he even met with Secretary of State, William Jennings Bryan and produced copies of the *Lusitania's* supplementary manifests. Bryan, previously unaware of the 'plot' and impressed by this evidence of the plan to ship illegal weapons on *Lusitania,* immediately sanctioned publication of the warning. However, someone superior to the Secretary of State, likely Colonel House and/or President Wilson, overruled Bryan.

Significantly, Captain Dow, the previous captain of the *Lusitania*, had resigned on 8th March 1915 because he was no longer willing 'to carry the responsibility of mixing passengers with munitions or contraband.' He had had a 'close call' just two days previously and was aware that the rules of naval warfare had changed in October 1914, when Churchill had issued orders that British merchant ships with munitions or contraband, must ram U-boats.

Prior to this change by Churchill, both England and Germany adhered to Cruiser Rules. The Cruiser Rules enabled crews and passengers to escape in lifeboats before being the ships were fired upon but with the advent of the new Churchill ram rules, German U-boats could no longer risk surfacing to issue a warning and therefore attacked while still submerged.

The single ad that slipped past the government censors appeared in the *'Des Moines Register'* of 22nd April 1915 and is reproduced below…

> **NOTICE!**
> TRAVELLERS intending to embark on the Atlantic voyage are reminded that a state of war exists between Germany and her allies and GreatBritian and her allies; that the zone of war includes the waters adjacent to the British Isles; that in accordance with formal notice given by the Imperial German Government, vessels flying the flag of Great Britian, or of any of her allies, are liable to destruction in those waters and that travellers sailing in the war zone on ships of Great Britian or her allies do so at their own risk.
> **IMPERIAL GERMAN EMBASSY,**
> WASHINGTON, D. C., APRIL 22, 1915.

RMS Lusitania was the most famous ship in the world at this time, the *Cunard Line's* crown jewel. She was the ship of choice for any discerning traveller's Atlantic crossing and had a capacity of about 2,200 passengers and 850 crew members. She could cruise at an average speed of around 25 knots with a top speed of 27 knots, slightly over 30 mph. Her first-class accommodations were the equal of those of the *White Star line's* giant *RMS Olympic*, and all classes enjoyed a highly comfortable voyage across the Atlantic Ocean.

However, of course the rest of the story is 'history,' as they say. On 7th May 1915, just off the southern coast of Ireland RMS Lusitania was sunk by the U-20, a German submarine under the command of Captain Walter Schwieger, or was it?

The 1st May is a 'special date' in Illuminati circles, well-known as the day of Baal/Beltane, the devil's day. This day also has significance as the day chosen to 'celebrate' Communist Russia's revolution, by its founders, the same bankster cartels that funded American and British war efforts.

The following is from a 2004 article, from one of the most reliable former intelligence sources, Anthony Thomas Trevor-Stokes, known to all *truth-seekers* as simply 'T Stokes,' now sadly deceased…

"I first heard this story version many years ago from a senior Freemason in London at the Hackney retired Seamen's Mission. This man's father was present at Churchill's initiation at age 26 and much other relevant info was given in exchange for a large bottle of Scotch whisky. My many years of research, says to me that this is true.

The Lusitania's sinking created outrage, that a passenger ship would be sunk, and was a determining factor in bringing in the USA onto Britain's side in WW1. Both Pearl Harbor and 9/11 were staged 'theatre pieces,' and so was the Lusitania sunk with the same bankster/Illuminati game plan.

The ship's Captain, William Turner had shown himself to be fearless, rescuing a man and a boy from a sinking ship and other acts of heroism, he could also obey orders to the letter, but he was not a popular figure with Cunard Shipping, who felt that a ship's captain should also have 'people skills' to entertain the passengers in route. Capt. Turner was the son of a sea captain, yet lacked these skills, and was uncomfortable and silent, and would avoid travelling company.

Poorly educated and leaving school aged 8, his family wanted him to enter the church because he was a superstitious man who bought a brand new bowler hat before each voyage, and was jokingly referred to as 'Captain Bowler.'

The ship Lusitania was sunk off the Irish coast on 7th May 1915, the inquest damned the experienced pilot of the Lusitania, Captain William Turner, for not following the established defensive custom of avoiding the U-Boats that gathered in the shallow waters off the Irish coast, in fact he almost ran into them, despite knowing in advance where they lay.

The inquest also stated that although the Lusitania could outrun the subs, it was going at a much slower pace and not zig-zagging as Admiralty practice dictated in its orders, especially as the destroyer escort HMS Juno had been strangely instructed to abandon the Lusitania some while previously.

Winston Churchill was in charge at the Admiralty, the intelligence received by him and Lord Rothschild his mentor and financial benefactor, also had access to all the admiralty documentation and his war team pointed to the fact that the many German émigrés to America had been effective in keeping America out of the war.

The worry to Churchill was simply that the US would remain an isolationist or worse, although America could swing either way, it may yet support Germany. So a plot was hatched by Churchill a 33rd degree mason, in the naval Masonic lodge, and Admiralty HQ with the bosses of Cunard, and the War Dept. to sacrifice Capt. William Turner, the Lusitania, and 1,198 crew and passengers.

The passenger ship that was barred from carrying any armaments, would be loaded with both heavy and light armaments and ammunition, within sight of the many German dock workers. This plan to load weaponry was known to be reported back to the German embassy, which it was. The German reply was to place advertisements in the newspapers of the USA and repeat the warnings to both governments of the ships vulnerability and that any ships carrying weapons would be classed as warships, British and U.S forces officially dismissed this as scaremongering.

Churchill planned the sinking of several ships, among them the HMS Hampshire and the Lusitania, counting on American feelings being high, yet the US authorities were in on it, but like Pearl Harbor and 9/11 it suited their purposes to turn a blind eye.

So Captain William Turner was under orders to continue with the voyage, even though the destroyer escort was recalled, he was told to go slow, his path was plotted by the Admiralty to put the ship 'in direct danger' is the word used in Admiralty documents.

Naval apologists have suggested that the captain may not have known of the weapons on board, but the first mate not only knew, but was issued with a side arm, so if he knew, why not captain William Turner?

Certainly statements by a New York celebrity, Mrs. E. Jacobs say many in the Jewish community knew that it contained weapons and would be sunk. The single page cargo manifest was signed by Capt. Turner, but a supplementary cargo manifest 24 pages long was produced after sailing time, this caused a row with the harbourmaster. This 24 page cargo manifest was destroyed in the mass culling of incriminating war documents pulled together from various sources in the 1960s.

Much other incriminating documentation was shredded... on the orders of Tony Blair, be assured it contained a list of light to very heavy weaponry.

The ship went down in under 18 minutes from one German torpedo, one torpedo was seen as giving long enough for the passengers and crew to reach the lifeboats, yet we are told from the very few survivors that after impact, a huge explosion occurred on board, away from the point of impact.

It was always the intention of the Churchill/Rothschild/bankster alliance that the Lusitania would be a sacrifice to bring in the USA to join the British war effort against Germany.

Underwater explorer and investigator, the highly reputable Robert Ballard is alleged to have told a reporter with intelligence back-grounding, that the shipwreck he saw on the seabed, had a small torpedo entry hole, but significant and unconnected explosive damage which had sunk the ship. The inference from this and other info, being controlled explosions on board was designed to ensure the ship sunk...

Lord Rothschild, whose banks loaned the British the finances for all wars at colossal interest rates, was part of a syndicate with J.P Morgan who was threatening to buy up all the North Atlantic shipping lines including Britain's White Star, so the Lusitania would have been rendered useless anyway.

In 1903 Cunard boss Lord Inverclyde took the threats seriously and lobbied the Balfour administration for a £2.6 million loan to build the Lusitania and the Mauritania.

Rothschild lobbied against Germany for some considerable time previously, while Nathan Rothschild plotted the downfall of the Russian royal family and the revolution, confiscating the Romanov wealth and bank accounts, critics have said that Rothschild representatives planned the war to bring about their plans for profit and world government.

Rothschild would have followed the rule that 'profit is all,' the same Hebrew root word is behind the terms for both money and God—'shekels and Shekinah' which explains the money worship.

Churchill and the Rothschild syndicate, planned to push the German authorities in every way into sinking the Lusitania. This tactic is known in intelligence circles slang as a 'dangle'"

The U-20 fired a single torpedo and its warhead's 300 pounds of explosives detonated upon contact with the *Lusitania*. Captain Turner reported that the first explosion sounded *"like a heavy door being slammed shut,"* and was followed by a much larger explosion that rocked the ship. Turner wrote in the ship's log . . . *". . . an unusually heavy detonation,"* and the *Lusitania* sank within twenty minutes.

On 28th May 1915, Germany's official response to the US government's protest stated that the German government had no intention of attacking US vessels which were not guilty of hostile acts, but that the Lusitania . . .

". . . *was one of the largest and fastest English commerce steamers, constructed with government funds as auxiliary cruisers and is expressly included in the navy list published by the British Admiralty. It is, moreover, known to the Imperial government from reliable information furnished by its officials and neutral passengers that for some time practically all the more valuable English merchant vessels have been provided with guns, ammunition and other weapons, and reinforced with a crew specially practiced in manning guns. According to reports at hand here, the Lusitania when she left New York undoubtedly had guns on board which were mounted under decks and masked.*"

The official letter from the German government also spelled-out that the Lusitania had 5,400 cases of ammunition that would be used to kill German soldiers and another noteworthy section of the letter stated that British merchant marine ships received secret instructions from the British Admiralty in February 1915 to seek protection behind neutral flags and when so disguised, attack German submarines by ramming them.

The German official response that illegal weapons and explosives were on board, explains the second explosion. For decades, the British and American governments denied that there were weapons on the Lusitania and the wreck-site was even declared a 'protected zone,' denying access to divers. And also, in order to further frustrate the ability to determine what the *Lusitania* carried, since 1946 the British Royal Navy has repeatedly dropped depth charges on to the wreck in what was described as 'target practice.'

In 1968, in a blatant attempt to keep the truth secret, the British Secret Service unsuccessfully attempted to buy the salvage rights to the *Lusitania* and in 1993 *PBS Online* visited the wreck and reported that previous visitors had tampered with the evidence.

But whilst the British government continually worked aggressively to distort the truth, weapons were confirmed as being present in the wreckage in July 2006 when Victor Quirke of the Cork Sub Aqua Club found 15,000 rounds of WWI issue, .303 bullets in the bow section of the ship.

On 2nd April 2007, *Cyber Diver News Network* reported that the American owner of the *Lusitania* wreck-site, F. Gregg Bemis, Jr., won the case to conduct salvage operations almost a century after the sinking. Interestingly, the Arts and Heritage Ministry did not protest the use of the *Lusitania* in depth-charge target-practice operations but unsurprisingly did 'help to respect the sanctity of the site,' by totally opposing salvage operations.

Many authors have written in the intervening century since the incident that 1,201 people were sacrificed on the *Lusitania* to create a reason for the US to enter World War I, so this is by no means a new revelation. The reason you may never have heard of this slant on the incident before, is an obvious one really and that is that the powers-that-be wish as few people as possible to know the real truth so that they can maintain their 'romantic' myths about WWI and indeed WWII and their fairy tales of German brutality and aggression in both conflicts.

Historian Howard Zinn wrote in '*A People's History of the United States*,' that *Lusitania* carried 1,248 cases of 3-inch shells, 4,927 boxes of cartridges (1,000 rounds in each box), and 2,000 more cases of small-arms ammunition. Colin Simpson also claims that Churchill and others conspired to deliberately place the ship in harm's way with the hope of sparking an incident that would bring America into World War I, by the manipulation of public opinion against Germany. Historian Patrick Beesely also supports Simpson's assessment.

Christopher Hitchens' book, '*Blood, Class and Nostalgia*,' further proves the responsibility of First Lord of the Admiralty, Winston Churchill in a deliberate action to coerce America into World War I on the British side and history professor Ralph Raico, senior scholar of the *Ludwig von Mises Institute* notes that Churchill wrote the week prior to the *Lusitania* sinking that it was *"most important to attract neutral shipping to our shores, in the hopes especially of embroiling the United States with Germany."*

So, in conclusion, the *Lusitania* incident played a vital role in turning American sentiment against Germany, but still it was not quite yet time for America to enter the war. The Zionist banksters were biding their time in order to achieve maximum leverage whilst simultaneously prolonging the conflict, before eventually ordering President Wilson to commit to war. For the time being, Wilson and his puppet-masters were content to merely verbally condemn the sinking, whilst still refraining from entering the conflict.

The British were of course, disappointed at the lack of immediate effect that the incident evoked. Politicians, journalists, and even the insane Teddy Roosevelt, all mocked Wilson as being timid and indecisive. So, in a blatant effort to keep US passions inflamed, the British fabricated a story about German school children being given a holiday to celebrate the sinking of the *Lusitania*. This fantasy took its rightful place alongside other such anti-German propaganda as those that told of German soldiers nailing live babies to church doors in Belgium, issuing poison sweets (candy) to children and raping nuns. The British knew that they *would* eventually need US help if they were to gain the advantage over The Triple Alliance powers and the Zionists knew this too, but they were biding their time, setting-up the UK and the US for the right moment... **and the right deal!**

The sudden death of Lord Kitchener on 5th June 1916, caused as great an international stir at that time, as the sudden deaths of President Kennedy and Princess Diana would in later years, and just as everyone remembers where they were when the news was announced of their deaths, so it was with Kitchener's demise.

At the outset of World War I, Horatio Herbert Kitchener was recalled home from Cairo, Egypt to become Minister of War. Being widely regarded as a hero of the British Empire, winner of battles in the Sudan, India and the Boer war, children would chant in the street, *"Come home Kitchener of Khartoum,"* and he was said to be more popular than the king himself.

Kitchener was on board the armoured cruiser, *HMS Hampshire* which incidentally was carrying gold meant for the use of 'White' Russians to resist Rothschild's planned communist uprising. But after encountering a severe storm, the *Hampshire's* escort ships were ordered by the Admiralty to return home, leaving the beleaguered ship to find its way through a minefield alone, on its journey to the port of Archangel, in Russia.

The Admiralty was certainly aware that there was a minefield in this location because, the *Laurel Crown* had been sunk there three days earlier by mines laid on the 29th May by U-Boat U-75. This fact was confirmed by intercepted radio traffic.

It was ascertained from witness statements, that the Hampshire with 655 men on board hit one mine, but 'several more explosions' then sank the ship. The lifeboats were said to have been 'un-launch-able' and apparently, instructions were given to the British home guard to shoot the twelve people who somehow survived and who made it ashore. The War Office later claimed that it was believed that the ship was German and wanted no prisoners. A likely story indeed.

So, was this a case of incompetence on a colossal scale or indeed something more sinister and if so, what could have been the reason for the cover-up?

Lord Kitchener was a cult figure, an icon of his time and in spite of his allegedly being a great student and exponent of battle strategy, he had recently refused the recommendations of his front-line advisors to deploy high explosive shells and instead ordered the use of shrapnel shells, which in the 'intimacy' of the trenches, killed as many of his own men as the enemy.

He had also advocated 'bully-boy' press-gang tactics, ensuring that a 'blind-eye' was turned to boys as young as 14 being recruited to the army whilst the legal age to fight in France was 19. He also instigated and widely encouraged the practice of women issuing 'white feathers' of cowardice to young lads, not much more than children outside schools and who had not yet joined the armed forces voluntarily. The War Office, under Kitchener's command also shot young soldiers, some as young as 16, for cowardice whilst knowing fully that they were under-age. Although no accurate government figures are available for child soldiers, the Red Cross and other organisations stated that approximately 80,000 battle casualties were minors.

Kitchener was actually a predatory homosexual, whose appetite for these boys was unquenchable and cruel in the extreme and at the time there were many stories abounding of his 'exploits,' similar in nature to those now circulating regarding the paedophile priests of the Catholic Church of today.

It is also maybe a significant fact that Winston Churchill despised both Kitchener—and especially his popularity.

Many years later, a senior intelligence officer well-known to researcher and 'truth-seeker,' Anthony Thomas Trevor-Stokes (T Stokes,) confided to him on his death-bed …

"Myself and my C.O. went on board the Hampshire, I was told to keep watch outside while he went into Kitchener's cabin, I put my ear to the door, and heard the C.O. say, 'I am going to leave you my pistol with one bullet, I will wait outside and you will do the honourable thing.' We heard a shot, the C.O. went in and retrieved the pistol, and we hurriedly left the ship"

He also claimed that the sinking of the Hampshire with the loss of 643 men was a British cover-up operation, as Kitchener had been directly approached by the Germans seeking peace discussions and his commitment to the war was wavering, whilst of course the establishment and their bankster backers and puppet-masters were still desperate for its continuance.

Indeed, in support of these seemingly 'outrageous' claims, recent dives to the shipwreck have proved that it is possible that the 'several explosions' were *inside* and not outside the ship, as the ripped metalwork protrudes outwards not inwards. As always, we will probably never know the absolute truth of the matter.

Meanwhile, back on the 'Western Front,' the Battle of Verdun raged-on for ten months, from the 21st February until the 18th December 1916, resulting in 306,000 battlefield deaths *(163,000 French and 143,000 German)* plus at least half a million wounded. This represents an average of 30,000 deaths for *each* of the ten months of the battle.

Verdun was the longest and most devastating battle in the Great War, even surpassing the Battle of the Somme for that dubious honour. By the end of the battle, the Germans had almost completely defeated the beleaguered French forces but nevertheless it transpired that in December 1916, Kaiser Wilhelm offered to negotiate a generous peace settlement with the Entente powers. But despite this offer, Britain and France deliberately made impossible demands upon Germany as a condition for even negotiating.

Due to the fact that is always the victors in any conflict who get to write the histories, most people are unaware of the fact that by December 1916, in the third year of the so-called 'Great War,' Germany was all-but victorious. Their U-Boats had swept all the British convoys from the Atlantic Ocean, leaving Britain without ammunition and food for both her soldiers, and her people whilst France was virtually bankrupt and its soldiers were mutinying on the Western Front. They had lost 600,000 of their young men in the defence of Verdun. Germany and Austria-Hungary were sweeping into Russia in the east, and Russia itself was nearing collapse. Turkey was holding its own in the Middle East and Italy was second-best in its battles against Austria Hungary.

It is also significant to note that not a single Entente soldier had set foot on German soil and yet Germany offered France and Britain generous peace terms. They offered a negotiated peace on what is legally referred-to as a 'status quo ante' basis which put simply, means... *'Let the war end now and everything return to as it was previously.'*

Diplomatic messages were sent by Germany to England petitioning for an end to the war, with peace terms proposing an end to hostilities and a restoration of pre-1914 boundaries everywhere on the European continent. This fact has always somehow been excluded from our so called 'history' books in order to maintain the banksters' myths and perpetuate the denigration of the German nation.

However, Britain seriously considered Germany's peace terms as they were faced with little other choice. It seemed to be a case of either accepting the negotiated peace that Germany offered or continuing with the war and being totally annihilated. But the Zionists, led by Chaim Weitzman, who later became the President of Israel, approached the British War Cabinet and said, *"Do not capitulate to Germany. You can still win this war if the United States enters as your ally. We can arrange this, but in return, you must promise us Palestine as a Jewish homeland, once the tide turns in your favour."*

Chaim Weitzman was a Russian-born chemist who moved to England in 1904. By 1915, Weitzman had developed a chemical process of producing acetone from maize. Acetone was a vital ingredient in the production of artillery shells, of which Britain and her allies were in short supply at the beginning of World War I. But it was during this period that Weitzman, through the mediation of Walter Rothschild (who else?) met Sir Arthur Balfour, the First Lord of the Admiralty, and David Lloyd-George, Britain's Minister of Munitions.

The Zionists had been biding their time waiting for just such an opportunity. As they were inextricably linked to the Zionist banksters in the US who totally controlled that nation's foreign policy, they knew that a simple word from them would speedily drag the USA into the war.

Both Balfour and Lloyd-George were under the influence of the Rothschild bankster dynasty, of which the Zionist Jew, Walter Rothschild, was the head and it was definitely not detrimental to Weitzman's goals when in 1916, Lloyd George became the British Prime Minister and Arthur Balfour the Foreign Secretary.

The Rothschilds and their Zionist minions had in fact financed both sides to the point that by mid-1916, almost all the European belligerents were approaching bankruptcy. It costs an absolute fortune to finance a war, and war is therefore extremely profitable to the banksters. So, introducing the United States into the war on the side of Great Britain and France, and with the bankster money and manpower (cannon-fodder) available to the Americans, Germany would be easily defeated and crushed... and importantly (for them) in return, the Zionists demanded a written guarantee that they would be given Palestine at the end of the war.

Although the official declaration of British support for a Jewish homeland was not made public until November 1917 (the Balfour Declaration), *the agreement was in fact reached in December of 1916* and soon after that, the Zionist-agitated anti-German propaganda was unleashed in the US, while the Zionists and Marxists of Germany also begin to undermine Germany's war effort from within.

On the 31st October 1917, General Allenby and 150,000 of his soldiers attacked and wiped out the Turkish garrison in the town of Beer Sheba, in the Negev desert in Palestine (what is now southern Israel.) It has been suggested that they were deliberately diverted from the trench-war in France/Belgium to prevent another very costly attack against the German machine-guns of the Western Front.

The British Government was informed by telegram the next day and on 2nd November 1917 the previously prepared Balfour Declaration was issued. It had already been submitted to and approved by President Woodrow Wilson, and France and Italy publicly endorsed it on the 14th February and 9th May 1918, respectively.

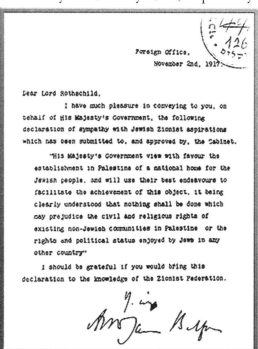

The Balfour Declaration

The name of 'Rothschild' is strongly linked to the pre-Zionist colonisation of Palestine, Baron Edmond Benjamin James de Rothschild having funded and actively managed

Jewish settlements in Palestine since 1882. This is several years before Theodore Herzl is commonly said to have 'invented' Zionism in 1895 (although the word itself apparently dates from 1891.) However, Edmond Rothschild was French and his interests were not shared by the English Rothschilds, such as 2nd Baron, Walter Rothschild, recipient of the Balfour letter. Edmond's Palestine enterprises were based upon Arab labour with Jewish management, quite different from the intention and policies of the Zionists, who sought to replace Arabs with their own countrymen wherever possible, violently if necessary. The rest of the French Rothschild family seems to have had even less interest in Palestine, Edmond's brothers being openly opposed to his involvement in the 'colonies.'

Furthermore, despite the Balfour Declaration being addressed to the 2nd Baron Rothschild (Walter, ennobled 1915) there seems to be no evidence that he was personally interested in either Zionism or Palestine.

It is a fact that most (probably all) prominent British Jews were strongly opposed to Zionism from 1895 to 1917. As the *Boston Globe* put it in 2006, "*When Weizmann secured his goal in 1917, some of the eminences of British Jewry were horrified. David Alexander and Claude Montefiore, presidents respectively of the Board of Deputies of British Jews and of the Anglo-Jewish Association, thought the Balfour Declaration a veritable calamity for the whole Jewish people which must have the effect throughout the world of stamping the Jews as strangers in their native lands, and of undermining their hard-won position as citizens and nationals of those lands.*"

Similarly, the one Jew in the British Government in 1917, Edwin Montague, was most hostile to the idea of a Jewish homeland. One of his three memos on the subject was entitled '*Memorandum on the Anti-Semitism of the British Government*' and was submitted to the Cabinet on 23rd August 1917. The memo stated...

"*At the very time when these Jews [referring to Jews in Russia] have been acknowledged as Jewish Russians and given all liberties, it seems to be inconceivable that Zionism should be officially recognised by the British Government, and that Mr. Balfour should be authorised to say that Palestine was to be reconstituted as the 'national home of the Jewish people.' I do not know what this involves, but I assume that it means that Mohammedans and Christians are to make way for the Jews, and that the Jews should be put in all positions of preference and should be peculiarly associated with Palestine in the same way that England is with the English or France with the French, that Turks and other Mahommedans in Palestine will be regarded as foreigners, just in the same way as Jews will hereafter be treated as foreigners in every country but Palestine.*"

In February 1917, as the Russian economy rapidly deteriorated due to escalating war costs, and the war became 'unpopular,' the 'February Revolution' began in Russia. A combination of Communists, progressive Socialists and disaffected soldiers further destabilised the already weakened reign of Czar Nicholas II. The Czar was forced to abdicate and placed under house arrest pending exile. A 'centre-left' coalition government consisting mainly of Socialists and Communists was established and a power-struggle between the moderate socialist faction and the hard-core Communist (Soviet-Bolshevik) faction ensued.

During the 90 days following the Zionist-British covert 'deal' to appropriate Palestine, the Zionists fulfilled their side of the bargain. An intense propaganda campaign was unleashed in the US, the *Lusitania* incident of two years previously was resurrected along with all the hyperbole surrounding German U-boat warfare.

Then, on 2nd April 1917 the bankster / Zionist puppet, 'pacifist' President Woodrow Wilson *(who remember, was still being blackmailed over the extra-marital affair he had when he was a Princeton professor,)* asked the US Congress for a mandate for a declaration of war and the complicit Congress duly declared war on Germany four days later on the 6th April 1917. Regular armed-forces of the small US military soon began arriving in Europe, but it was not until several months later that the full, mighty force of drafted American manpower was deployed.

According to Under-Secretary of the Navy at the time, Franklin D. Roosevelt, America's heavy industry had been preparing for war for over a year. Both the Army and Navy Departments had been purchasing war supplies in large amounts since early in 1916.

During 1915 and 1916, Wilson had kept faith with the banksters who had installed him in the White House, by continuing to make illegal loans to the Allies. His Secretary of State, William Jennings Bryan, protested constantly, famously and pointedly stating that *"Money is the worst of all contraband."* In fact, by 1917 the Morgans and the Kuhn, Loeb Company had floated $1.5bn in loans to the Allies. The banksters had also financed a plethora of Orwellian-named 'peace' organisations which worked tirelessly to promote the entry of the US into the war. The *Commission for Relief in Belgium* routinely and regularly manufactured German atrocity stories whilst a Carnegie organisation, *The League to Enforce Peace*, also agitated in Washington for entry into war. This later became the *Carnegie Endowment for International Peace,* which during the 1940s was headed by Alger Hiss. One writer at the time stated that he had never seen any so-called 'peace movement' which did not promote war. How true.

The US Ambassador to Britain, Walter Hines Page, complained that he could not afford to take-up the position, and so was given twenty-five thousand dollars a year 'spending money' by Cleveland H. Dodge, president of the *National City Bank.* H.L. Mencken openly accused Page in 1916 of being a British agent, which was unfair, really. Page was actually a banksters' agent.

Cordell Hull remarked in his 'Memoirs' …

"The conflict [World War I] forced the further development of the income-tax principle. Aiming as it did, at the one great untaxed source of revenue, the income-tax law had been enacted in the nick of time to meet the demands of the war. And the conflict also assisted the putting into effect of the Federal Reserve System, likewise in the nick of time."

In Wilson's 'war message' in 1917, he included a despicable tribute to the Russian Communists who were eagerly slaughtering the middle-classes and Christians in that unfortunate country... "*...Assurance has been added to our hope for the future peace of the world by the wonderful and heartening things that have been happening in the last few weeks in Russia. Here is a fit partner for a League of Honor.*"

Wilson's tribute to a bloodthirsty regime which murdered around one-hundred million of its inhabitants in the most barbarous manner, reveals his true sympathies and his true backers, the Zionist banksters who had financed the blood-purge in Russia. At one stage, when the Communist Revolution appeared to be faltering, Wilson sent his personal emissary, Elihu Root, to Russia with $100 million from his 'Special Emergency War Fund' to save the struggling Bolshevik regime.

Nothing could more forcefully illustrate the duplicity of Woodrow Wilson's nature than his nationwide campaign on the slogan, 'He kept us out of war,' when he had pledged ten months earlier to involve the US in the war on the side of England and France. This explains why he was regarded with such contempt by those who learned the true facts of his career. H.L. Mencken wrote that Wilson was 'the perfect model of the Christian cad,' and that we ought 'to dig up his bones and make dice of them.'

After the US entry into World War I, Woodrow Wilson turned the government of the United States over to a trio of his campaign financial backers, the banksters, Paul Warburg, Bernard Baruch and Eugene Meyer. Baruch was appointed head of the *War Industries Board,* with life and death powers over every factory in the United States whilst Eugene Meyer was appointed head of the War Finance Corporation, in charge of the loan programme which financed the war. At this time, Paul Warburg was in total control of the nation's banking system.

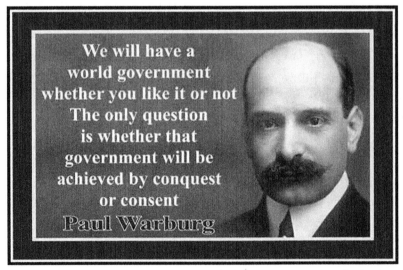

Knowing that the overwhelming sentiment of the American people during 1915 and 1916 had been anti-British and pro-German, the British viewed the prominence of Paul Warburg and *Kuhn, Loeb Company* in the prosecution of the war, with more than a little trepidation. They were uneasy about Warburg's prominent position in the Administration because his brother, Max Warburg, was at that time serving as head of the German Secret Service. A conflict of interest? Certainly not for the banksters.

On the 12th December 1918, the United States Naval Secret Service report on Warburg read as follows...

"WARBURG, PAUL: New York City. German, naturalized citizen, 1911. Was decorated by the Kaiser in 1912, was vice chairman of the Federal Reserve Board. Handled large sums furnished by Germany for Lenin and Trotsky. Has a brother who is leader of the espionage system of Germany."

Strangely enough, this report, which was probably compiled much earlier, while the war with Germany still raged, is not dated until 12th December 1918, significantly after the signing of the Armistice. It does not refer to the fact that Paul Warburg resigned from the Federal Reserve Board in May, 1918, which strongly suggests that it was compiled before May, 1918, when Paul Warburg would theoretically have been open to a charge of treason because of his brother's control of Germany's Secret Service. But of course that would never have happened because it would not have been in the best interests of the banksters at all.

The 1920 obituary of Jacob Schiff revealed for the first time that Schiff, like the Warburgs, also had two brothers in Germany during World War I, Philip and Ludwig, of Frankfurt-on-Main, who also were active as bankers to the German Government. This was not a situation to be taken lightly, as on neither side of the Atlantic were the said bankers obscure individuals who had no influence in the conduct of the war. On the contrary, the Kuhn, Loeb partners held extremely prominent governmental posts in the United States during World War I, whilst in Germany, Max and Fritz Warburg and Philip and Ludwig Schiff, also moved in the highest circles of government.

According to *The New York Times*, Paul Warburg's letter of resignation stated that some objection had been made because he had a brother in the 'Swiss Secret Service.' The *New York Times* has never corrected this blatant falsehood, perhaps because Kuhn, Loeb Company owned a controlling interest in its stock. Max Warburg was certainly not 'Swiss,' and although he had probably come into contact with the Swiss Secret Service during his term of office as head of the German Secret Service, no responsible editor at *The New York Times* could have been unaware of the fact that Max Warburg was definitely as German as the Kaiser, that his family's banking house was in Hamburg, Germany and that he held a number of influential positions in the German Government.

Indeed he represented German interests (allegedly) at the Versailles Peace Conference and remained in Germany until 1939, during a period when persons of his religion were being discriminated against. In order to avoid any personal misfortune during the approaching war, Max Warburg was allowed to sail to New York in 1939, with no confiscation of his immense personal fortune.

It would seem strange (all other things being equal) to reflect that Woodrow Wilson decided to place the fate of the entire USA into the hands of three men whose personal history was one of ruthless speculation and the quest for personal gain, (Paul Warburg, Bernard Baruch and Eugene Meyer) or that during war with Germany, he placed supreme trust in a German immigrant naturalised in 1911, the son of an immigrant from Poland, and the son of an immigrant from France.

Bernard Baruch first came to prominence on Wall Street in 1890 whilst employed by *A.A. Housman and Co*. In 1896 he merged the six principal tobacco companies of the United States into the Consolidated Tobacco Company, thereby forcing James Duke and the *American Tobacco Trust* to enter into this combination. The second great trust set up by Baruch brought the copper industry into the hands of the Guggenheim family, who significantly have controlled it ever since. Baruch also worked with Edward H. Harriman, who was Schiff's 'front man' in the control of America's railway system for the Rothschild bankster family. Baruch and Harriman also combined their 'talents' to gain control over the New York City transit system.

In 1901, Baruch formed the firm of Baruch Brothers, with his brother Herman, in New York and then in 1917, when Baruch was appointed Chairman of the War Industries Board, the name was changed to *Hentz Brothers*.

Testifying before the *Nye Committee* on 13th September 1937, Baruch stated that, *"All wars are economic in their origin."* So 'straight from the horse's mouth,' that belies the usual claim that wars are caused by religious and political disagreements.

A 'profile' of Baruch in the *New Yorker* magazine reported that he made a profit of $750,000 in one day during World War I, after a fake 'peace rumour' was planted in Washington. In *Who's Who*, Baruch mentioned that he was a member of the Commission which handled all purchasing for the Allies during World War I but in fact, Baruch WAS the Commission. He spent the American taxpayer's money at the rate of $10 billion dollars a year and was also the dominant member of the *Munitions Price-Fixing Committee*. He set the prices at which the Government bought war materials and given the track record of these people it would be gross naivety to presume that the orders did not go to firms in which he and his associates had more than just a passing interest.

Some members of Congress were curious about Baruch's qualifications to exercise life and death powers over almost all American industry in time of war. He was not a manufacturer and had never even set foot in a factory. When called before a Congressional Committee, he glibly stated that his profession was 'speculator.' Thus, a self-confessed 'Wall Street gambler' had been made the 'overlord' of American war-time industry.

Baruch's erstwhile partner, Eugene Meyer (*Alaska-Juneau Gold Mining Co.,*) later claimed that Baruch was a 'nitwit,' and that Meyer, with his family bankster connections (*Lazard Freres,*) had guided Baruch's investment career. These claims appeared in the fiftieth anniversary edition of *The Washington Post*, editorial page, 4th June 1983, with a parting shot from Meyer's editor, Al Friendly... *"Every journalist in Washington, Meyer included, knew that Bernard M. Baruch was a self-aggrandizing phony."* In his position as head of the *War Industries Board*, it is believed that Bernard Baruch made a personal profit of some $200 million from the mayhem, death and destruction of WWI. He would go on to 'advise' US Presidents for a further fifty years.

Eugene Meyer (1875-1959,) was son of the partner in the international banking house of *Lazard Freres*, of Paris and New York. In '*My Own Story*,' Baruch explains how Meyer became head of the War Finance Corporation... *"At the outset of World War One, I sought out Eugene Meyer, Jr... who was a man of the highest integrity with a keen desire to be of public service."*

Eugene Meyer's stewardship of the *War Finance Corporation* comprised one of the most amazing financial operations ever partially recorded. I say 'partially recorded,' because subsequent Congressional investigations revealed that each night, the accountancy books were being altered before being subject to the next day's investigations. Louis McFadden, Chairman of the *House Banking and Currency Committee*, figured prominently in two investigations of Meyer, in 1925 and again in 1930, when Meyer was proposed as Governor of the *Federal Reserve Board*. The *Select Committee to Investigate the Destruction of Government Bonds*, submitted, on 2nd March 1925...

"Preparation and Destruction of Government Bonds—68th Congress, 2nd Session, Report No. 1635: p.2. Duplicate bonds amounting to 2314 pairs and duplicate coupons amounting to 4698 pairs ranging in denominations from $50 to $10,000 have been redeemed to July 1, 1924. Some of these duplications have resulted from error and some from fraud."

These investigations may explain why, at the end of World War One, Eugene Meyer was able to buy control of *Allied Chemical and Dye Corporation* and later, the nation's most influential newspaper, *The Washington Post*. The duplication of bonds, 'one for the government, one for me' in denominations to the amount of $10,000 each, resulted in misappropriation of a vast sum of money.

It was Eugene Meyer's *Washington Post*, under the direction of his daughter, Katherine Graham, which was later to play a crucial part in driving Richard Nixon, from the White House, on the grounds of... well, the 'real story' will be related in a later chapter.

The *Liberty Loans* scheme, which sold war bonds to US citizens, were nominally in the jurisdiction of the United States Treasury, under the leadership of Wilson's Secretary of the Treasury, William G. McAdoo, whom *Kuhn, Loeb Co.* had placed in charge of the Hudson-Manhattan Railway Co. in 1902. Paul Warburg had most of the senior management of the *Kuhn Loeb Co.* firm by his side in Washington during the war.

Jerome Hanauer, partner in *Kuhn, Loeb Co.*, was Assistant Secretary of the Treasury in charge of Liberty Loans. The two under-secretaries of the Treasury during the War were S. Parker Gilbert and Roscoe C. Leffingwell. Both Gilbert and Leffingwell came to the Treasury from the law firm of *Cravath and Henderson,* and returned to that firm when they had fulfilled their mission for *Kuhn, Loeb Co.* in the Treasury. Cravath and Henderson were the lawyers for *Kuhn Loeb Co.* Gilbert and Leffingwell subsequently received partnerships in *J.P. Morgan Co.*

Kuhn, Loeb Company, the nation's largest owners of railroad properties in The US and also Mexico, protected their interests during the World War One by enticing Woodrow Wilson to create the *United States Railroad Administration*. The Director-General was William McAdoo, Comptroller of the Currency and Warburg replaced this set-up in

1918 with a tighter organisation which he named the *Federal Transportation Council*. The purpose of both of these organisations was to prevent strikes against *Kuhn, Loeb Company* during the war, in case the railroad workers should try to obtain in wages, some of the millions of dollars in wartime profits which *Kuhn, Loeb* received from the United States Government.

Among the important bankers present in Washington during the War was Herbert Lehman (1878-1963), of the rapidly rising firm of *Lehman Brothers*, banksters of New York. Lehman was promptly placed on the General Staff of the Army, and awarded the rank of Colonel. The Lehmans had had prior experience in 'taking the profits out of war,' a double entendre and one of Baruch's favourite phrases. In his book, *'Men Who Rule America,'* Arthur D. Howden-Smith wrote of the Lehmans, during the American Civil War...

"They were often agents, fixers for both sides, intermediaries for confidential communications and handlers of the many illicit transactions in cotton and drugs for the Confederacy, purveyors of information for the North. The Lehmans, with Mayer in Montgomery, the first capital of the Confederacy, Henry in New Orleans and Emanuel in New York were ideally situated to take advantage of every opportunity for profit which appeared. They seem to have missed few chances."

Other appointments during the First World War were as follows...J.W. McIntosh, director of the *Armor* meat-packing trust, who was made Chief of Subsistence for the United States Army in 1918. He later became Comptroller of the Currency during Calvin Coolidge's Administration and ex-officio member of the Federal Reserve Board. During the Harding Administration, he was director of finance for the *United States Shipping Board* when the Board sold ships to the *Dollar Lines* for a hundredth of their cost and then allowed the *Dollar Line* to default on its payments. After leaving public service, J.W. McIntosh became a partner in *J.W. Wollman Co.,* New York Stockbrokers.

Henry P. Davison, senior partner in *J.P. Morgan Co.*, was appointed head of the *American Red Cross* in 1917 in order to wrest control of the $370 million cash which was collected from the American people in donations. A practice which incidentally, is still ongoing today.

The Intelligence Services

It is an undisputable fact that the world's 'intelligence' services were created to serve the 'Crown,' aka the banksters and not the nation to which they purportedly belong. Their loyalty therefore is to their bankster masters and their compadres and **not** their countries.

For example, Sir William Wiseman, Jewish / Zionist chief of the British Secret Service in the USA during WWI, was a partner of *Kuhn, Loeb and Company*. He worked most closely with Woodrow Wilson's afore-mentioned alter-ego, Colonel Edward Mandel House and was also friendly with Max Warburg, the Jewish head of German intelligence. How bizarre.

Britain's espionage service originated during the reign of Queen Elizabeth I—and it was legendary. Their ciphers were so sophisticated and difficult to 'crack' that the Spanish accused the British of using witchcraft to compose them. Credit for creating the first English secret service usually goes to Elizabeth I's spy master, Sir Francis Walsingham who faced a predicament shared by many of his successors, the need to combat both external and internal threats and the collaboration of the two factions. In the case of the Protestant, Walsingham and his Protestant Queen, the unifying characteristic of their enemies was Catholicism. Walsingham battled this 'menace' by recruiting agents at home and abroad and waging an aggressive campaign of counter-subversion.

His most successful weapon was the agent-provocateur who was tasked with penetrating and compromising hostile conspiracies and known anti-Elizabethan factions. He also followed the maxim that England's enemy's enemy was her friend, or at very least an exploitable tool. In addition to Protestant sympathisers and dissident Catholics, he is also known to have enlisted the help of witches, sorcerers and atheists in England's cause.

The Vatican also has a sophisticated spy-network known as the 'Confessional' and dating-back over a thousand years. With the loss of the Papal States in 1870, the Vatican no longer had *secure communications,* even though the *'Confessional'* was still the most sophisticated spying service in the world.

The British monarchs still bore the pompous title of *Defender of the Faith* and the time to *earn* that title by full co-operation with the Vatican espionage system was ripe by the early twentieth century. This necessitated a *merger* with the Vatican's service and the newly created *British* spy agency, MI-6. The infamous departments of both MI-5 and MI-6 came 'out of the closet' in 1908, MI-5 being formed to concentrate on *domestic* spying while MI-6 was *international in its scope.*

About that time, a series of novels began to appear, written by a man named William Le Queux, one of which was *'The Invasion of 1910,'* written in 1906, warning the British nation about the alleged threat of a German invasion. In Britain's past history, it had always been the Spanish or French who were plotting to invade and indeed, in 1588, England had been saved from invasion because the mighty Spanish Armada was defeated by a combination of the much smaller English navy and the unseasonal, inclement weather in the English Channel that late summer. But a very short time later and up to the advent of WWI, Great Britain had the most powerful navy in the world and the popular saying decreed that *'Britannia rules the waves.'*

William Le Queux pronounced 'Q' was a Jesuit and bestselling propaganda writer, the forerunner of the *James Bond* author Ian Fleming in many ways. His overt 'in your face' style of propaganda sparked an anti-German mood and contributed to the formation of MI-5 and MI-6. The famous novel *'The Thirty Nine Steps'* by John Buchan first published in 1915 also takes a similar stance, continuing on from the example of *'The Invasion of 1910.'*

"In reality, it was Germany that was totally infiltrated by the British MI-6 and they helped the Kaiser with the invasion of Belgium and France in August 1914. The Germans did not constitute anything like a major threat and the spy scare that swept Britain in the early 1900s was in fact out of all proportion to the reality. It was stoked, even orchestrated, by the author William Le Queux, who produced a series of best-selling books—with titles like 'Spies of the Kaiser: Plotting the Downfall of England' and 'The Invasion of 1910'—that deliberately set out to blur the lines between fact and fiction.

Le Queux protested vigorously to anyone who would listen, and many influential people did, that the authorities were negligently ignoring the German threat. Lord Northcliffe, proprietor of the Daily Mail, serialised The Invasion of 1910 in his newspaper, carefully rerouting the hypothetical marauding Hun troops through towns and villages where the circulation was at its highest." Smith, 'MI-6. The Real James Bonds,' p. 1.)

Le Queux compared the Franco-Prussian War of 1870 to the forthcoming invasion of England in 1910 and what MI-6 really had in mind was a repeat of that war, with a united Germany invading France, restoring the monarchy, and as a bonus restoring the Papal States. However, the rapid Prussian victory of the Franco-Prussian war was not repeated, as World War I became a stalemate of bloody trench warfare.

With the stalemate and thousands dying daily, MI-6 pulled off another *diabolical plot in an attempt* to get the United States embroiled in the war. It had been a telegram that had led to the start of the Franco Prussian war, so why not use a telegram to get the US involved in WWI too? That was the reasoning of MI-6, as their agent in Germany sent a telegram to the German ambassador in Mexico, promising German help to recover the territories that Mexico had lost in the Mexican-American War.

Sir William Wiseman (who else?) was the MI-6 agent charged with getting the US involved in WWI and his counterpart in Germany was Arthur Zimmermann. Zimmermann was the author of the infamous Zimmermann telegram which contributed significantly to President Wilson's declaration of war on Germany.

At the very beginning of the war, the English cable ship *Telconia* destroyed five of the undersea Atlantic cables connecting Germany with the Americas after which only one cable remained open to Germany. Owned by the US, it ran from West Africa to Brazil. Apart from the West Africa-Brazil cable, all German communications to the States had to be made via unsecure radio.

Zimmermann's telegram said . . .

"We intend to begin on the first of February, unrestricted submarine warfare. We shall endeavour in spite of this to keep the United States of America neutral. In the event of this not succeeding, we make Mexico a proposal of alliance on the following basis: make war

together, make peace together, generous financial support and an understanding on our part that Mexico is to reconquer the lost territory in Texas, New Mexico, and Arizona. The settlement in detail is left to you. You will inform the President of the above most secretly as soon as the outbreak of war with the United States of America is certain and add the suggestion that he should, on his own initiative, invite Japan to immediate adherence and at the same time mediate between Japan and ourselves. Please call the President's attention to the fact that the ruthless employment of our submarines now offers the prospect of compelling England in a few months to make peace. Zimmermann."

The telegram was deliberately *leaked* to the press by Wilson on 1st March 1917 and it created a sensation. Many people however were highly sceptical and suspected British treachery. But then, to the utter amazement of all, Zimmermann admitted that *he* had sent the telegram ...

"*If, on top of these denials, Zimmermann challenged the United States to prove the authenticity of the telegram, the American government, restricted by its pledge of secrecy to Great Britain, would be unable to do it. The Cabinet could only agree to assert emphatically that they possessed conclusive evidence, and unhappily disperse.*

Unbelievably, next morning, to the 'profound amazement and relief,' in Lansing's words, of everyone concerned, Zimmermann inexplicably admitted his authorship. It was a second blunder, wrote Lansing, almost bemused with relief, of a most astounding kind.

He thought it showed Zimmermann to be not at all astute and resourceful, for in admitting the truth he not only settled the question in American minds but threw away an opportunity to find out how we had obtained the message. What led Zimmermann, who, despite Lansing, was both astute and resourceful, to commit this historic boner, is not known. That he was too stunned to think clearly is unlikely, for the Germans had had two days to consider their answer and Germans do not issue official statements off the cuff. Probably he reasoned that since the Americans had somehow acquired a true version of the message they were likely also to have acquired some documentary proof of its authorship; therefore denial could only make him look foolish. This was logical but as not infrequent with logic, wrong. Tuckman, *The Zimmermann Telegram*, p. 183.

As illogical as Zimmermann's admission may seem, it all makes perfect sense when we understand that it was the two country's respective intelligence communities colluding together and Zimmerman was just one of hundreds of MI-6 agents working in Germany, albeit a very senior one.

President Woodrow Wilson's real name was 'Wolfson' and his father was a Khazarian Jew from Germany and thanks to the 'miracle' of the Zimmermann telegram, Wilson was now free, backed by the majority of public opinion to declare war on Germany on the 2nd April 1917. With the unlimited resources of the United States, the British were able to withdraw soldiers from the Western Front, and deploy them to Palestine to fight the Turks.

T. E. Lawrence, better known as 'Lawrence of Arabia,' was just one of the many MI-6 agents in the Middle East. He worked closely with Harry St. John Bridger Philby (father of future Soviet spy Kim Philby) to expel the Turks and create a Khazarian 'Jewish' state in the region. Out of the ruins of the defeated Turkish Empire and Saudi Arabia, the state of 'Israel' was to be created. However, I will return to 'Lawrence of Arabia' later.

The *J. Henry Schroder Banking Company* is listed as one of the seventeen merchant bankers who make up the exclusive *Accepting Houses Committee* in London. Although it is virtually unknown in the United States, it has played a large part in its history. And as did the others on this list, it firstly had to be approved by the Bank of England. At the turn of the nineteenth century, in 1900, Baron Bruno von Schroder established the London branch of the firm and was soon joined by Frank Cyril Tiarks, in 1902. Tiarks married Emma Franziska of Hamburg, and was a director of the Bank of England from 1912 to 1945.

During World War I, the *J. Henry Schroder Banking Company* played an important role behind the scenes. No mainstream historian has ever offered anything approaching a reasonable explanation as to how World War I started, other than to parrot the usual 'assassination of Archduke Ferdinand was assassinated at Sarajevo by Gavril Princip,' scenario. This is usually followed by, 'Austria then demanded an apology from Serbia and Serbia sent a note of apology but despite this, Austria declared war anyway and soon the other nations of Europe joined the fray as treaties were invoked.'

In fact, once the war had started, it was quite difficult to keep it going—rather like trying to start a fire with damp wood, such was the weakness of the premise upon which it had been artificially provoked. The principal problem was that Germany was desperately short of food and coal and without Germany, the war could not go on. John Hamill in '*The Strange Career of Mr. Hoover,*' explains how the problem was solved. He quoted from '*Nordeutsche Allegmeine Zeitung,*' 4th March 1915 . . .

"*Justice, however, demands that publicity should be given to the pre-eminent part taken by the German authorities in Belgium in the solution of this problem. The initiative came from them and it was only due to their continuous relations with the American Relief Committee that the provisioning question was solved.*" Hamill points out "*That is what the Belgian Relief Committee was organized for—to keep Germany in food.*"

The *Belgian Relief Commission* was organised by Emile Francqui (1863-1935,) director of a large Belgian bank, *Societe Generale*, and a London mining promoter, an American named Herbert Hoover, who had been associated with Francqui in a number of scandals which had become celebrated court cases, notably the *Kaiping Coal Company* scandal in China, said to have sparked the infamous Boxer Rebellion of 1900, whose goal was the expulsion of all foreign businessmen from China.

Hoover had been barred from dealing on the London Stock Exchange because of one judgement against him and his associate, Stanley Rowe had been sent to prison for ten years. With this background, Hoover was obviously regarded as an ideal choice for a career in humanitarian work.

Hoover had also carried out a number of mining promotions in various parts of the world as a secret agent for the Rothschild bankster dynasty and had been rewarded with a directorship in one of the principal Rothschild enterprises, the *Rio Tinto* mines in Spain and Bolivia. Francqui and Hoover threw themselves into the seemingly impossible task of provisioning Germany during the First World War.

Their success was noted in the '*Nordeutsche Allgemeine Zeitung*,' of 13th March 1915, which noted that large quantities of food were now arriving from Belgium by rail. *Schmoller's Yearbook for Legislation, Administration and Political Economy* for 1916, shows that one billion pounds of meat, one and a half billion pounds of potatoes, one and a half billion pounds of bread, and one hundred and twenty-one millions pounds of butter had been shipped from Belgium to Germany in that year alone. A patriotic British woman who had operated a small hospital in Belgium for several years, Edith Cavell, wrote to the *Nursing Mirror* in London in April 1915, complaining that the … *"Belgian Relief supplies were being shipped to Germany to feed the German army."*

The Germans considered Miss Cavell to be of no importance, and paid no attention to her, but the British Intelligence Service in London was appalled by Miss Cavell's discovery, and demanded that the Germans arrest her as a spy. Sir William Wiseman, head of British Intelligence, and partner of *Kuhn Loeb Company*, feared that the continuance of the war was under threat and secretly notified the Germans that Miss Cavell must be executed. The Germans reluctantly, duly arrested her and charged her with aiding prisoners of war to escape. The usual penalty for this offence was three months imprisonment, but the German authorities meekly bowed to Sir William Wiseman's demands and executed Edith Cavell by firing squad, thereby creating one of WWI's principal martyrs.

Of course the British propaganda machine now had enough material to boost anti-German sentiment even further, for many months to come.

With Edith Cavell no longer a threat to their 'little game,' the 'Belgian Relief' operation continued unabated, although in 1916, German emissaries again approached London officials with the information that they did not believe Germany could continue military operations, not only because of food shortages, but because of financial problems. More 'emergency relief' was therefore sent, enabling Germany to continue in the war until November, 1918, by which time the war had finally lost its impetus and came to an abrupt end.

This is all meticulously documented in a book entitled, '*The Triumph of Unarmed Forces 1914-1918*' (1923) by Rear Admiral M.W.W.P. Consett, who was the British Naval Attaché in Sweden. His job was to keep track of the movement of supplies, in other words the aforesaid 'unarmed forces' necessary for the continuation of the conflict. For example, Scandinavia was completely dependent on British coal. This had the effect of ensuring that the Swedish iron ore that was manufactured into the U-Boats that sank Allied shipping, reached Germany on vessels powered by British coal.

Germany desperately needed glycerine for the manufacture of explosives but England had no trouble securing this substance because it controlled the seas. However, after the war began, the demand for these products from neutral countries 'exploded' and the British continued to fill these orders. Of course, the same applied to copper, zinc, nickel, tin, and many other essential products. Consett believed that if they had been embargoed, the war would have been over by 1915.

The trade of tea, coffee and cocoa to neutral countries also increased dramatically but these products were often unavailable there. Instead, they were all redirected to Germany, making huge profits in the process. Consett's protestations of course, were unheeded. The Minister of Blockades was Robert Cecil, a member of the *Round Table*, in other words another puppet of the banksters.

Similarly, the banksters financed the German side through their Scandinavian banks to the tune of £45 million sterling thereby making both sides of the conflict their 'debt slaves.'

"Despite the huge revenues raised from taxation, the British national debt rose tenfold. The government failed to use its bargaining power as the only really massive borrower in wartime to get money at low rates of interest and the French national debt rose from 28 billion to 151 billion francs." Davies, *'The History of Money'*

World War I profits

Commodity	Years	Average profit	Years	Average Profit	% Increase
Gunpowder	1910-14	$6m	1914-18	$58m	1,000%
Bethlehem Steel	1910-14	$6m	1914-18	$49m	800%
US Steel	1909-14	$105m	1914-18	$240m	230%
Anaconda Copper	1910-14	$10m	1914-18	$34m	340%
Utah Copper	1910-14	$5m	1914-18	$21m	425%
Central Leather Co.	1911-14	$1.1m	1916	$15m	1,100%
General Chemicals	1911-14	$0.8m	1917-18	$12m	1,500%
Int. Nickel Co.	1911-14	$4m	1917-18	$73m	1,700%
American Sugar	1911-14	$2m	1916	$6m	300%

"World War I was waged by 27 nations; it mobilised 66,103,164 men of whom 37,494,186 became casualties (around 7 million dead.) Its direct costs were estimated at $208,000,000,000, its indirect costs at $151,000,000,000. And these figures do not include the additional billions in interest payments, veterans' care and pensions, and similar expenses..." '*The Merchants of Death*'

As a result of WWI, the banksters reconfigured Europe in preparation for the next predicted world war and in the process and exactly as planned, the 'old order' was destroyed. Four empires (the Russian, German, Austro-Hungarian and Ottoman) lay in ruins and as an added bonus, the banksters had set-up their Bolshevik friends in Russia as a way of acquiring even more 'property' and territory And not least of all, they had ensured that Palestine would eventually, if not immediately become a 'Jewish' state under their control which as 'Israel' would be a perennial source of new conflict in the Middle East.

Modern history is in reality the account of how the banksters convert credit monopoly into a monopoly of power. This entails destroying our connection with nation, religion, race and family. It means substituting objective truth (God, nature) with their own dictats of political correctness, modernism, diversity, globalisation, feminism and the homo-sexualisation of society.

In 1918 when the deceptively named 'war to end all wars,' a war between the richest and most powerful nations on earth ended, it was the greatest, bloodiest, most expensive, most disruptive, most damaging and most traumatising war the world had ever seen. It left millions dead, maimed, shell-shocked, dispossessed, impoverished, starving and bitter. It deprived families of their bread-winners, wives of husbands and children of their fathers on a scale never before witnessed. Victory brought a sense of relief rather than elation or sorrow and in the aftermath, the world's great powers, aka the banksters, were already gearing-themselves for episode two. This was indeed a war that had crushed people's hopes, destroyed countless lives, brought down empires and at its conclusion sowed the seeds of further conflict and suffering. The extent to which it achieved all these things, made the First World War a war the likes of which the world had never seen before.

Once known as 'The Great War,' or as 'The War to End All Wars' or even 'The World War' until its sequel got underway, even the final resolution of the war was soon to be dubbed 'the peace to end all peaces.'

The Treaty of Versailles

Apart from a brief, final rally in the autumn of 1918, the German forces were well beaten, surrendered unconditionally and the Armistice was duly signed which ended the war on the 11th November 1918 at 11.00 am, thus bringing to an end four years of horrific, unspeakable bloodshed. Now all that remained was the Treaty of Versailles, which the Germans genuinely believed would be a fair and just settlement of post-war reparations for a nation that had been absolutely shattered beyond the point of recognition, by the privations and horrors of the war. In this they were to be bitterly disappointed. In fact the terms of the treaty were so inordinately destructive to the German nation that it not only lost much of its territory but it did not actually make the final reparations payment until 2009! This in fact led directly to the economic conditions that set the scene for the rise of Hitler and ultimately to World War II. All as pre-planned, by our anti-heroes, the banksters, of course.

The treaty that officially ended WWI was the 'Treaty of Versailles' in 1919. This is the reason why the dates of this war are sometimes recorded as 1914-19. Although it has to be said that it has now been recently surreptitiously announced that WWI has now 'officially' ended due to Germany's final reparation payment having been made, 90 years after the event.

Several interesting personalities attended these meetings. In the British delegation was the British economist John Maynard Keynes and representing the American bankster interests was Paul Warburg, the Chairman of the *Federal Reserve*. His brother Max, the head of the German bankster firm of *M.M. Warburg and Company*, of Hamburg, Germany and who was not only in charge of Germany's finances but as a leader of the German espionage network, was there as a representative of the German government. Do we need any more proof of collusion between the two sides to achieve maximum impact on the welfare of ordinary Germans?

The Treaty was purportedly written to end the war, but another delegate to the conference, Lord Curzon of England, the British Foreign Secretary, saw through what the actual intent was and said ... *"This is no peace; this is only a truce for twenty years."* Lord Curzon felt that the terms of the Treaty were setting the stage for a second world war and what is even more interesting, he had even correctly predicted the year it would start as 1939.

One of the major tenets of the Treaty, specified swingeing war reparations to be paid to the victorious nations by the German government. It was this factor alone that precipitated three events. The 'hyperinflation' of the German Mark between 1920 and 1923, causing untold suffering to the ordinary German people which also led to the virtual destruction of the middle classes and last but by no means least, facilitated the rise to power of someone who would rightly or wrongly be seen as a saviour, a messiah to the German people, Adolf Hitler.

Thus were deliberately sown the seeds of World War II, setting in motion an unstoppable chain of events that would eventually, finally lead to the establishment of the Jewish homeland and to all the complex, inter-related actions that have shaped the world of the early twenty-first century, in which we all live today.

The extent of the war reparations were decided upon by another banksters' stooge John Foster Dulles, one of the founders of the Council on Foreign Relations, and later the Secretary of State to President Dwight D. Eisenhower. Even Keynes himself, not known for his liberal views, was so disturbed by the extent to which the Treaty had been slanted towards the impossibility of fulfilling the terms and therefore presaging the destruction of Germany (one of the objects of the war in the first place) that he wrote, *"The peace is outrageous and impossible and can bring nothing but misfortune behind it."*

In addition to penning the Treaty of Versailles, the victors also proposed and propounded the Charter of the League of Nations, the hoped-for preliminary to the bankster and New World Order's one-world government, ratified on the 10th January 1920, and signed by President Wilson for the American government. Wilson brought the treaty back to the United States and requested that the Senate ratify it. The Senate, for once remembering George Washington's advice to avoid foreign entanglements and reflecting the views of the American people who did not wish to enter the League, refused to ratify the treaty.

With the benefit of hindsight it has become apparent that Wilson intended to head the planned world government it was hoped to bring along by the imposition of the League of Nations upon the world. Unsurprisingly he was devastated when the Treaty was not ratified as he fully expected to become the first President of the World, only to have it taken away by the actions of the Senate of the United States. Of course, we are still to this day awaiting the dawn of world government but the Elite are nothing if not patient and they firmly believe that their efforts in this direction will be fully rewarded before much more time has elapsed, although they are not quite 'counting their chickens' just yet...

"As the World plummets into a contrived financial meltdown, those who believe themselves to be the rightful rulers of a planetary fiefdom [the banksters—JH] are convinced that they have a very short window of opportunity to establish their One World Government. Their vision is for total control of all planetary resources including human resources, which will be reduced to the chosen 500,000,000. However, things are not going entirely to plan. Obama's mentor, Zbigniew Brzezinski recently identified 'the rapid political awakening amongst the masses' as the biggest obstacle to establishing a One World Government. In 1970 Brzezinski observed that the challenge for Western governments will be to keep their people locked into consumerist materialism...preventing them from realising who they truly are!" Ian R Crane, geo-political researcher, February 2011

One of the by-products of this devastating conflict was to provide an unparalleled opportunity for the Elite families to generate huge profits at the expense of governments and thus the public in the form of war supplies and armaments. These super-rich families, not only desired that the war be won, but they made sure that the victory was expensive to the common taxpayers and beneficial to their own finances. Indeed, one of the families who reaped the exorbitant profits were our old friends, the Rockefellers, who were for obvious reasons, very eager for the United States to enter World War I and who made more than $200m from the conflict which incidentally is $16bn in today's values.

However, support for the League of Nations continued. The Grand Orient Lodge of Freemasonry of France was one which advised all of its members, *"It is the duty of universal Freemasonry to give its full support to the League of Nations...."* Predictably, the League of Nations became a major issue during the Presidential election of 1920 when the Republican candidate Warren G. Harding was on record as opposing the League and further attempts to ratify the charter, saying, *"It will avail nothing to discuss in detail the League covenant, which was conceived for world super-government In the existing League of Nations, world governing with its super-powers, this Republic will have no part."*

He was opposed in the Republican primaries by General Leonard Wood, one of the Republican 'hawks,' who was backed by a powerful group of rich men who hoped to install a military man in the White House. The American people, once again manifesting their disapproval of the League, voted for Harding as evidence of that distrust and concern and Harding beat the opposition by a greater margin than did President

Wilson during the election of 1916. Wilson only managed to get fifty-two percent of the vote, whilst Harding achieved sixty-four percent.

Harding was a supporter of William Howard Taft, the President who opposed the bankers and their Federal Reserve Bill. After his election, he named Harry M. Daugherty, Taft's campaign manager, as his Attorney General. His other Cabinet appointments were not as wise however, as he 'inexplicably' surrounded himself with men representing the oil industry. His chosen Secretary of State was Charles Evans Hughes, an attorney of Standard Oil; his Secretary of the Treasury was Andrew Mellon, owner of Gulf Oil; his Postmaster General was Will Hays, an attorney for Sinclair Oil; and his Secretary of the Interior was Albert Fall, a protégé of the oil men.

It was the aptly named Fall, who was indeed to be Harding's downfall as he later accepted a bribe from Harry Sinclair in exchange for a lease of the Navy's oil reserves in Teapot Dome, Wyoming. There are many who believe that the scandal was intended to discredit the Harding administration in an attempt to remove him from office for two very important reasons. Harding was consistently vocal against the League of Nations, and there was still a chance that its supporters could get the United States to join, as the League had survived the Senate's prior refusal to ratify the treaty and Attorney General Daugherty had been prosecuting the oil trusts under the Sherman anti-trust laws.

These activities did not please the oil interests who had created the Teapot Dome scandal. But Harding perhaps unsurprisingly as is often the case, unfortunately did not live to see the full repercussions of the artificial scandal, as he died on the 2nd August 1923, before the story completely surfaced. Indeed, there are many who believe that there were some who could not wait for the Teapot Dome scandal to remove President Harding and that he was poisoned as were several of his predecessors.

Nevertheless the oil barons allowed it to completely play its course as a warning to future Presidents of the United States not to oppose the oil interests or indeed any other powerful, vested, corporate interests and to date, with one or two notable exceptions, the warning has been generally heeded. Not many have chosen to contend with the true rulers of the United States—certainly not and lived to tell the tale anyway, eh Mr. Kennedy?

Chapter 7
The Red, Zionist Menace

As if the horrendous, massive death and misery of World War I, was not enough to satisfy the banksters' overwhelming greed and their evil plans for total world denomination, what was about to follow as a direct consequence of their creation of Communism, was guaranteed to split the world apart, even further.

So what exactly is Communism? We all *think* we know what it is, but let us examine it for a moment.

Sadly, many people ignorantly think that it died with the Soviet Union. In fact, nothing could be further from the truth. Communism is still alive and kicking but not just in Russia or China anymore.

Communism is...

"A theory or system of social organization based on the holding of all property and means of production in common, actual ownership being ascribed to the community as a whole or to the state; A system of social organization in which all economic and social activity is controlled by a totalitarian state—dominated by a single and self-perpetuating political party." Dictionary.com

Let me be generous and take only a couple of excerpts from that as an illustration...

'**...in which all economic and social activity is controlled by a totalitarian state.**' Would today's society come close to that by any chance? We now have 'governments' with many unelected and unaccountable 'Quangos' and 'Czars' currently dictating business practices, profit margins and pay scales. And worst of all, in Europe at least, we now have the totally unelected and unaccountable leaders of the EU dictating to the governments of its member states exactly what laws it can or cannot pass and even imposing its own laws upon them whilst extracting gigantic payments from them, totally disproportionate to any benefits that may accrue from membership.

'**...dominated by a single and self-perpetuating political party.**' In America today the incumbent Democrat Party, operates a virtual dictatorship, bypassing the other two branches of 'equal government' by the expedient of the longest list of presidential 'executive orders' issued in US history, self-perpetuated by the flow of massive funds from the Party to labour unions to government employees, entertainers, sportspeople, journalists and welfare recipients, back to the unions who in turn fund the Democrat Party or support it directly. Whilst most other so-called 'democratic' nations operate a virtually closed two or three party system that absolutely precludes any views or policies outside the status quo, from permeating the general citizenry's awareness or consciousness.

So when did this diluted version of Communism that we now have within our 'western nations' replace the 'freedom and liberty' we all previously enjoyed? Was it the slow, incremental process, as designed by the banksters and their puppet politicians, that they will have you believe is 'progress?' In fact it has been evolving painfully slowly from the very first spark of civilisation, whilst no-one was paying attention.

In the US, lawyers and judges first started trying to dismantle the Constitution, almost before the ink was dry on the page. And in addition, the banksters were also attempting from the very beginning of 'independence,' to impose a permanent central bank on the US people. So, in truth, freedom and liberty have been under assault from the very dawn of the nation, in America.

" *...a subtle corps of sappers and miners constantly worked underground to undermine our Constitution from a co-ordinate of a general and special government to a general supreme one alone.*" Thomas Jefferson

Let us now also examine... '*...the holding of all property and means of production in common, actual ownership being ascribed to the community as a whole or to the state.*' This definition has it exactly right, except for the fact that the property and means of production in question ALL belong to the bankster families.

Communism—in the beginning

Georg Wilhelm Friedrich Hegel (1770-1831) was a 19th Century German philosopher and theologian who wrote *'The Science of Logic,'* in 1812. In the view of many historians, Hegel is probably the greatest of the German idealist philosophers.

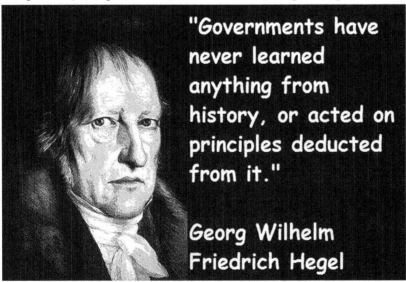

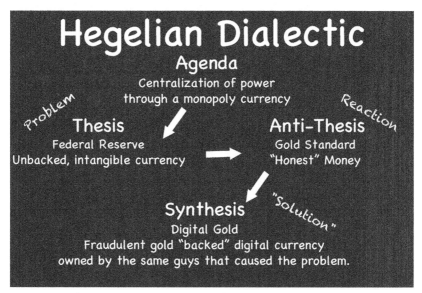

In 1847 the *London Communist League,* whose most prominent members were Karl Marx and Friedrich Engels, used Hegel's dialectic theory to back up their economic theory of Communism. Now, in the 21st century, Hegelian-Marxist thinking affects our entire social and political structure. The *Hegelian Dialectic* is the framework for guiding our thoughts and actions into conflicts that lead us to a predetermined solution. If we do not understand how the Hegelian Dialectic shapes our perceptions of the world, then we do not know how we are helping to implement the banksters' vision for the future.

Hegel's dialectic is the tool which manipulates us into a circular pattern of thought and action. Every time we fight for, or defend against an ideology we are playing a necessary role in Marx and Engels' grand design to advance humanity into a dictatorship of the proletariat, otherwise referred to commonly as The New World Order. The synthetic Hegelian 'solution' to all these conflicts cannot be introduced unless we all take sides and thereby advance the agenda, which is of course our natural inclination.

The Marxist (bankster) global agenda is moving along at breakneck speed and the only way to prevent international land-grabs, privacy invasions, expanded domestic police powers, insane so-called 'wars' against inanimate objects (cancer, drugs, terrorism etc.) and transient verbs, covert actions, and outright assaults on individual liberty, is to metaphorically step outside the dialectic. Only then can we be released from the limitations of controlled and guided thought.

When we understand what motivated Hegel, we can see his influence on all of our destinies. Then we will become real players in the very real game that has been going on for at least 240 years (since 1776.)

Hegelian conflicts steer every political arena on the planet, from the United Nations to the major political parties, all the way down to local education boards and community and local councils. Dialogues and consensus-building are primary tools of the dialectic, but fear and intimidation are also acceptable formats for obtaining the goal. Focussing on Hegel's and Engel's ultimate agenda and avoiding being entrapped in their impenetrable theories of social evolution, gives us the opportunity to think and act our way towards freedom, justice and *genuine* liberty for all.

Today the dialectic is active in every political issue that encourages and promotes the taking of sides. We may see it in action in environmentalists instigating conflicts against private property owners, in Democrats against Republicans or Labour against Conservative, in 'greens' against libertarians, in Communists against socialists, in 'neo-cons' against traditional conservatives, in community activists against individuals, in pro-choice versus pro-life, in Christians against Muslims, in isolationists versus interventionists and in peace activists against the war hawks.

No matter what the issue, the invisible dialectic aims to control both the conflict and the resolution of differences, and leads everyone involved into a new cycle of conflicts and Communism is just one of the vehicles that the banksters use to divide us, before conquering us.

Communism—the Rise

In 1793, Poland was divided between Prussia and Russia. This was of paramount significance to Russia because she thereby, instantly acquired the world's largest Jewish population, the former Khazarian 'Jews' that is. Russia had always had an Imperial or Royal Head of State with a Czar (monarch) as its supreme ruler and the Czar had decreed in 1772 that Jews *could* settle in Greater Russia but only in the vast area known as the 'Pale of Settlement.'

This 'Pale' extended from the Crimea, almost to the Baltic Sea, encompassing an area half as great as Western Europe. Because Jews had always maintained their own distinct and separate community within Christian societies, the Pale could not be described as discriminatory. It not only protected Russians from Jewish influence, but protected Jews from their Christian hosts too, as Jewish influence was often despised by the Christian community.

Under Czar Alexander I, many restrictions against residence 'beyond the Pale' were relaxed and by 1881, the Jews had greatly prospered and achieved a virtual monopoly in the liquor, tobacco, and retail industries. But, the Jews, in the process, made sure that the Gentiles were excluded in every possible way and from this Hegelian conflict of Jews against Christians, the twin evils of Zionism and Communism were born.

The Polish surname, Trotsky was not the one with which the infamous revolutionary was born. His true name was Levi Davidovich Bronstein and he was born in 1879 into a wealthy family of Jewish landowners in southern Ukraine (ie. within 'the Pale.')

In the autumn (fall) of 1888, at the age of 9, Bronstein moved from the family estate to the coastal resort of Odessa, where he lived with his mother's nephew, Moses Filipovich Spentzer, a liberal, Jewish publisher and after attending high school in Odessa, he went on to college at Nikolayev, where he became involved with a group of Jewish 'socialists.' From this early exposure to socialism, he began to read Marx and soon became an agitator within the fledgling trade-union organisations in the area. Eventually he was arrested and jailed and it was at this point in his career that he decided to adopt the pseudonym by which he became popularly known. With more than a hint of irony, he adopted the name of his Polish prison warden, Trotsky, thus disguising his Jewish origins.

In late 1899 he was transferred to a prison in Moscow, and was sent for trial early in the following year and sentenced to four years exile in Siberia. However, before the sentence could be expedited, Trotsky decided to marry one of his fellow Jewish agitators, Alexandra Lyovna Sokolovskaya and they were married in the jail before being sent to their exile in Siberia.

Despite the rigours of the Siberian climate and the privations he endured, Trotsky was able to contribute prolifically to the local, Irkutsk newspaper and to study Marxist books and philosophy and it was around this time that he heard the name of 'Lenin,' a fellow-Communist agitator, and the two began corresponding. Lenin suggested that Trotsky should abandon his Siberian exile and go and live in a foreign country. In this task, Lenin assured him that his 'friends' would assist, so eventually Trotsky arrived in Vienna, where he was aided by his fellow Jewish Communist, Victor Adler before moving on to Zurich, where another Jewish Communist, Paul Axelrod, was his contact. Trotsky's wife and children were left behind in Siberia.

Trotsky finally met Lenin at a 'rooming house' at 30 Holford Square, King's Cross, London and was almost immediately appointed editor of *The Spark*, an 'underground'

Communist newspaper which was principally directed at Russian agitation. Trotsky also presented several Marxist lectures in London's predominantly Jewish, Whitechapel district.

After establishing strategy at various conferences in London, Brussels and Paris, Trotsky, using a fake passport, returned to Russia in 1905 in order to launch the long-planned revolution. After several months of agitation, Trotsky was again arrested and sentenced to jail at the Peter-Paul prison in St. Petersburg, along with two other Jewish Marxist agitators, Leon Deutsch and Alexander 'Parvus' Helphand. After being sentenced to exile in Siberia once more, Trotsky merely caught another train going in the opposite direction and ended-up in Finland.

After several more years agitating around various countries in Western Europe, Trotsky arrived in New York, where he worked as a journalist on the Russian Communist newspaper *Novy Mir*, from its offices at 177, St. Mark's Place on the Lower East Side, in the very heart of the Jewish section of Manhattan. *Novy Mir* (New World) was owned by two Communist Jews by the name of Weinstein and Brailovsky but according to the New York police, who closely monitored Trotsky's activities, his main associates during this period were Emma Goldman and Alexander Berman.

By the beginning of 1917, the build-up to the Russian revolution was gaining momentum and Trotsky sensed that the time was ripe for another Soviet takeover bid, following the failed attempt in 1905 but which had nevertheless served to destabilise the monarchy. But finance for the revolution was desperately needed and strangely (or maybe not) these so-called 'sworn enemies of Capitalism' had no difficulty whatsoever in raising vast amounts of funding from Jewish banksters on both sides of the Atlantic.

Jacob H. Schiff supplied $20 million of *Kuhn Loeb* money for the proposed Bolshevik takeover of Russia and Parvus, Trotsky's cell-mate in the Peter-Paul prison, was now himself a wealthy coal broker and he was also away in the Balkans making deals on behalf of the Imperial German government. Parvus had been instrumental in guiding the ideology of Leon Trotsky as well as the half-Jewish, Vladimir Lenin (real name, Vladimir Ilyich Ulyanov.) The main 'lesson' that Trotsky had learned from his mentor, Parvus was that Jewish people are their own collective Messiah and would attain dominance over all others through the mixing and therefore diluting of the other races (multi-culturalism and mass-immigration) and the elimination of all national boundaries.

By 1917, the Jewish/Zionist desire to destroy the Czar had turned almost the entire urban population of Russia against the monarchy and WWI had caused severe food shortages, breakdowns in transportation, and factory closings due to material shortages, thus contributing to the general unrest.

Lower-level Jewish revolutionaries, their leaders being at that time out of the country, fanned the flames of dissent and on 10th March 1917 an American photographer, Donald Thompson, reported that a rich man who tried to pass through the growing mob ... "*...was dragged out of his sleigh and beaten. He took refuge in a stalled streetcar* *where he was followed by the working men. One of them took a small iron bar and beat his head to a pulp. Many of the men carried red flags . . ."*

At this time the only thing holding the angry mob at bay was the St. Petersburg police and so the mob turned-on the police who were forced to barricade themselves in their police stations. Here they were slaughtered almost to the last man and the prisons were emptied of their entire populations, including serious criminals of every category. Czar Nicholas II was not in St. Petersburg at the time, but after hearing the details and misunderstanding the situation, he sent a message requesting that the Duma (parliament) be dissolved. The Czar abdicated his throne five days later.

Two governing bodies ruled Russian jointly for the next eight months commencing 12th March 1917. The 'Provisional Government' and the 'Petersburg Soviet.' The Provisional Government immediately allowed all exiled political prisoners to return from Siberia and at least ninety thousand streamed back into Russia in late April, May, June, and July.

On the 26th March, Trotsky left New York, for Russia. He was accompanied by many Jewish-Marxist soldiers-of-fortune from the Lower East Side, plus $20m of gold courtesy of Jacob Schiff. However, when his ship called at Halifax, Nova Scotia, Trotsky was arrested by the British authorities, on the sound rationale that he was heading for Russia in order to take Russia out of the Great War and thereby increase the Germans' chances of ultimately winning the war. But, in a stunning reversal of fortune, the American President, Woodrow Wilson intervened, threatening not to enter the war unless Trotsky was allowed to continue on his way, unimpeded.

By the time Trotsky reached Russia, the revolution had already taken place, the Czar had been deposed and a replacement, democratic government installed. But being a good Communist, Trotsky wanted to have things his own way. However the democrats, under Kerensky, were wise to these ambitions and warrants were issued for the arrest of both Trotsky and Lenin on the basis that they were agents of the Imperial German government, a not unreasonable assumption since Lenin had been sent back into Russia on a diplomatically-sealed German train and Trotsky had been sent by Jacob Schiff, a cousin of the German Minister of the Interior, Felix Warburg.

The 90,000 returning exiles mentioned previously were the heart and soul of the Bolshevik revolution. They were almost exclusively Jewish and hungry for power and Trotsky immediately joined the Bolsheviks on his return from New York.

By October 1917 the Socialist Prime Minister, Kerensky was struggling to keep a bad economy afloat, an unstable coalition government together and a tired Russian nation in the world war. The time was now ripe for the Reds to stage another violent coup, but this time, Trotsky, Lenin and their evil gang succeeded. With backing from the Red army *(many of which had been brainwashed in 1905 Japanese POW camps by Jacob Schiff's reading materials,)* the Capital City of St. Petersburg was seized during the ensuing 'October Revolution,' aka 'Red October.'

Kerensky fled for his life and the new Soviet regime immediately moved to withdraw

Russian troops from the war. Outside of St. Petersburg (by now renamed Petrograd,) the predominantly Jewish, Red government was not recognised as legitimate but a bloody civil war between the Jewish-led 'Reds' and the opposing Christian 'Whites' was now imminent.

"The Bolshevik leaders here (Russia,) most of whom are Jews and 90 percent of whom are returned exiles, care little for Russia or any other country but are internationalists and they are trying to start a world-wide social revolution." David R. Francis, US Ambassador to Russia, January 1918

After the fall of St. Petersburg to the Reds, the counter-revolutionary civil war against the 'whites' tore Russia apart for three more years. The various opponents of the 'Reds' were collectively referred to as the 'Whites.'

When it quickly became apparent that the Red revolutionary army composed solely of workers and a few Jewish, ex-Czarist troops was far too small to quell the White counter-revolution, Trotsky instituted a mandatory conscription of the rural peasantry into the Red Army. Any opposition of the semi-literate, rural Russians to Red Army conscription was overcome by brute force and terror tactics and hostages and their families were simply tortured and killed when necessary, in order to force compliance.

In the spring of 1918, the Russian Reds had realised that they were unable to fight a civil war at home and an external war against Germany at the same time, so Lenin and Trotsky had no choice but to take Russia out of the war and bring home the troops to fight their internal enemy. This enabled Germany to divert its forces from the east and stage a major western offensive before the arrival of the majority of the American army.

Their counter-offensive operation, known now to history as the 'Spring Offensive,' commenced on 21st March 1918 with an attack on British forces in northern France and was so effective that the Germans achieved a previously unprecedented advance of forty miles. With Paris now a mere seventy-five miles away, the Germans believed that victory was theirs and Kaiser Wilhelm II even declared a national holiday in celebration. However, at just this critical moment, Jewish-Marxist and Zionist leaders in Germany betrayed their own country.

The Marxist trade-union leaders ordered factory strikes which deprived German troops of critical supplies and the Jewish-owned press, which had enthusiastically espoused war in 1914, suddenly performed a U-turn and began decrying the German military. German morale quickly began to deteriorate, as did essential industrial output and new recruits arrived at the front-line with a defeatist attitude as anti-war protests and general discontent spread rapidly, all throughout Germany.

The Spring Offensive ground to a halt as the first Americans began to arrive on the battlefields of France. In the light of the sudden announcement of the Balfour Declaration, German Zionists began betraying Germany so that Palestine could be prised from Germany's Turkish ally and given to the Jews. German-Jewish Marxists and 'democratic Socialists' also regarded a German defeat as a means to destabilise the nation and stage a revolution.

After the war, the treasonous betrayal of 1918 became known as 'The Stab-in-the-Back' although modern, brain-washed mainstream 'historians' dismiss this as a 'legend.' But in reality, there was nothing mythical about it and the plain, simple truth is that on the brink of final victory, Germany was betrayed from within.

Czar Nicholas II had hoped to be exiled to Great Britain while Kerensky was in power, but his British relatives, the Royal family, refused to allow him and his family into the country and so the Bolsheviks held Nicholas, his wife Alexandra, his four daughters, and young son under house arrest in a remote location. As a boy, Nicholas had witnessed the murder of his grandfather, Alexander II, in 1881. His 'timidity' had been demonstrated when he failed to execute Red leaders such as Lenin and Trotsky after the failed 1905 revolution but his misguided mercy would come back to haunt both him and his family as they were all denied similar compassion.

In the early hours of the 17th July 1918, the Romanov Family was awakened, ordered to dress and then herded into the cellar of the house in which they were being held. Moments later, Jewish-Red assassins stormed-in and gunned-down the entire family, their doctor and three servants in cold-blood. Some of the Romanov daughters were stabbed and clubbed to death when the gunfire failed to kill them outright. News of the brutal murder of the Romanovs sent shock-waves throughout Russia and all of Christian Europe.

With the Russian Civil War raging, the *Communist International*, known as the '*Comintern*,' was established in Moscow. The Comintern stated *openly* that its intention is to fight ...

"*... by all available means, including armed force, for the overthrow of the international 'bourgeoisie,' the entrepreneurial class and for the creation of an international Soviet republic, Communist world government—aka the New World Order.*"

From 1918-1922, Comintern-affiliated Communist parties formed in France, Italy, China, Germany, Spain, Belgium, the UK, the US and many other nations. All Communists operated under the control and direction of the Moscow Reds, who are themselves financed by the same Globalist-Zionist international banksters and world masters that created the Federal Reserve and brought about the Great War. However the vast majority of these 'satellite' Communist groups had no real idea of what Communism really represented, they simply believed that they were fighting for the freedom and for the benefit of the ordinary men and women of the world, against their Elite oppressors. And this fallacy was of course maintained by the Communist hierarchy, in order to keep its millions of new adherents, onside.

Then in September 1918, the Russian Reds planned to commence a reign of terror strategically to intimidate their White adversaries into submission. On orders from Lenin and Trotsky, the '*Red Terror*' was announced by Yakov Sverlov. This was marked by mass arrests, often in the middle of the night, executions, and horrendous tortures. As many as 100,000 Russians were murdered in the Red Terror, carried out by the Jewish-run Cheka (secret police.)

Among the verifiable atrocities committed, often in view of the victim's family members, were:

- 40,000 'White' prisoners publicly hanged in the Ukraine
- Burning coals inserted in women's vaginas
- Crucifixions
- Rapes
- Victims submerged in boiling oil or tar
- Victims nailed into coffins filled with hungry rats
- Victims soaked with water, and left to turn into human ice-cubes in the winter weather.
- Priests, monks and nuns had molten lead poured down their throats and were burned alive.

The demoralising terror takes a heavy psychological toll on the terrified Russian people and by 1922, many were broken into total submission to the Red monsters of the dreaded Cheka.

By the advent of the Red Terror in late 1918, back in France, it was now apparent that Germany could not now win the Great War but nevertheless, as he had in 1916, the Kaiser again offered to negotiate peace on terms favourable to all parties. Although Germany was no longer in a position to win the war, the Allies were struggling too. Germany's Eastern front with Russia was closed, there were no Allied troops on German soil, the capital city, Berlin was 900 miles distant from the current Western front and the German military was still entirely capable of defending the German homeland from an Allied invasion.

But despite this, the home-front was collapsing. As related previously, treasonous socialist politicians, Marxist trade-union leaders, and Zionist media moguls, had combined to demoralise the population and destabilise Germany. The Kaiser was forced to abdicate and enter exile in Holland whilst expressing his regrets for his past 'liberalism' and denouncing the *"Jewish influence that has ruined Germany."*

On 11th November 1918, representatives of the newly formed 'Weimar Republic' (formed in the city of Weimar) signed an armistice with the Allies to end the war. And so it transpired that incredibly, at a time when the Allies had still been unable to invade Germany, the German military was ordered to lay-down its arms and withdraw from the front lines. Based on Woodrow Wilson's empty promise of 'peace without victory,' leaders of Germany had suddenly placed their nation at the complete mercy of the New World Order.

As a 25-year-old 'starving' artist from Austria, the young Adolf Hitler had volunteered to serve in the Austrian Army in 1914. Afflicted with tuberculosis during his youth, he was initially rejected for military service. However he was later accepted and served in the German armed forces with distinction and bravery. In August of 1918, Hitler was awarded the prestigious German Iron Cross 1st Class, and was promoted to Lance

Corporal and in October 1918, was temporarily blinded in a British poison gas attack. While recovering his eyesight, Hitler heard of Germany's inexplicable and complete unconditional surrender and as were many other Germans, was confused and outraged. It seemed to him and his compatriots that the sacrifice and suffering that the German soldiers and nation in general had endured for so long, had been for nothing.

Lance Corporal Adolf Hitler

Unsurprisingly, along with many others, Hitler wanted answers, and he determined that he would not rest until the 'November criminals' (his term) were exposed and Germany's honour restored.

The Armistice on 11th November released the German troops from the horror they had endured, as indeed both sides had, on the Western Front, and they began to wearily trudge home. As the Armistice was strictly speaking an agreement to cease the hostilities and *not* a surrender, these troops still had their weapons. The active troops remained under the command of the *Oberste Heeresleitung*, and therefore of General Groener, but the others organised locally into several hundred local *Freikorps*, each varying from a few hundred men to brigade size. The German veterans known as '*Freikorps*' were originally militia, very similar to their British counterparts, the 'Home Guard' but in 1918 they became anything from homes-away-from-home for returning soldiers who felt alienated from German society and its rapid dislocations, up to fully-fledged and well-armed paramilitary organisations. On occasions, fighting between the *Freikorps* and the Army broke-out, particularly during an Army mutiny in Berlin in late November but in the main, both Army and *Freikorps* were united and fought the Communist and Spartacist League attempts to control German cities and to suppress uprisings by Polish separatists in the east.

In 1915, the Jewish Reds, Karl Liebknecht and Rosa Luxemburg founded the '*Spartacus League*' (named after Illuminati founder Adam Weishaupt's code name of 'Spartacus.') and on 1st January 1919, the group became known as the 'Communist Party of Germany.' That same month, the Sparticists, aided by Jewish-Hungarian Communist Bela Kun, took advantage of the German surrender and post-war chaos, by staging a revolutionary coup in Berlin. But the attempted Communist takeover of Berlin was short-lived as the Freikorps units soon reclaimed control from the Jewish Reds and their followers. Luxemburg, Liebknecht and some of their supporters were duly captured and executed and thus had the Freikorps saved Germany from the same deadly fate that had befallen Russia. However, the new 'democratic socialist' Germany was soon to face other serious problems.

At roughly the same time as the suppression of the Spartacist uprising in Berlin, in January 1919, a general election was held for members of the constituent assembly which would form the core of the government of the new German Republic. Then in February, in an attempt to avoid the ongoing hostilities in Berlin, the constituent assembly moved to Weimar, some one hundred miles to the southwest and in February elected Ebert, the Republic's first *Reichspräsident*. Meanwhile, another coup was attempted in Munich, but this was also suppressed by both the *Freikorps* and the regular Army, and almost one thousand Communists were detained and shot.

But this was far from the end of the Reds' attempted power-grab and just as did the hard-core Reds of Russia, the Reds of Germany continued trying to wrest power from the democratic socialists.

The Paris Peace Conference was the meeting of the Allied victors to determine the new international borders in Europe and punishments for the defeated nations, in-line with the wishes of the Zionist banksters' designs on a New World Order. The budding Global-Zionist World Government devised a whole series of treaties that would re-model Europe and indeed the world, to their own designs. At its centre were the leaders of the three 'Superpowers,' Woodrow Wilson (US,) Prime Ministers David Lloyd-George (UK) and Georges Clemenceau (France.) Germany was not invited and was to have no say in the final decisions.

The Paris Peace Conference resulted in the Treaties of 'St. Germain' (with Austria,) 'Trianon' (with Hungary,) 'Neuilly' (with Bulgaria,) 'Sevres' (the Ottoman Empire/ Turkey) and Versailles (with Germany.) The 'Treaty of Sevres,' signed by the Sultan in August 1920, was an almost immediate failure. Mustapha Kemal deposed and exiled the Sultan by 1922 and immediately began re-conquering territories which had been ceded by the Sultan's signature on the Treaty. The Allies hastily compiled a new treaty with the surprisingly formidable Kemal, the 'Treaty of Lausanne,' which he signed in 1923. As a 'voluntary' treaty drawn up between approximate equals, it became the only relatively successful treaty of the batch.

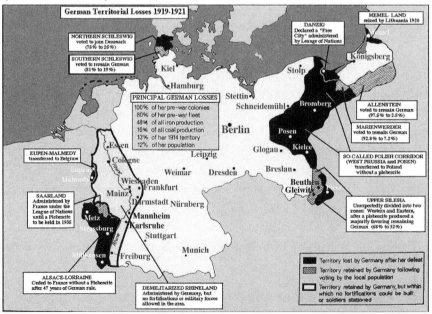

German territorial losses 1919-21 as a result of the Treaty of Versailles

In contrast, Germany had no-one who was prepared to negotiate with the vigorousness that Kemal had exhibited and had no soldiers available to despatch to a reopened war on the Western Front. In fact, all Germany's troops were engaged in fighting Communists or on the eastern frontiers fighting the resurgent Poles. The British Royal Navy's wartime blockade, still in force, had rendered the German position even more perilous and so Germany signed the Treaty of Versailles in June 1919 with little protest. This had two important effects; firstly, it officially ended the hostilities between Germany and the Allied powers and secondly, it convinced the German voters that their brief experiment with political moderation had been a failure. They felt strongly that Germany had not been treated as a 'reasonable' country by the terms of the Treaty of Versailles and the obvious conclusion was that moderation as a political philosophy was ineffective and German politics subsequently split into the *perceived* extremes of 'far Left' and 'far Right.'

The German government at Weimar, therefore, drawing-up a constitution for the new German Republic, had to construct an equitable formula which would include parties and factions from the diametrical extremes of the political spectrum, from outright Bolsheviks to raving Monarchists. *Reichspräsident* Ebert signed the new constitution into law in August 1920 and the new Weimar constitution was a model of democratic government, guaranteed to include members of every political shade.

Unfortunately, as Constitutions go, its liberalism was regarded by some as its weakness and never more so than in the way the that National Socialist German Worker's Party (or NSDAP,) was able to, by entirely legal and democratic means, turn a minority mandate into effective control of the government, thus making the world familiar with a new word, *Nationalsozialistische*, or Nazi.

It is a moot point really. The Nazi German government, over the course of its actual thirteen year reign and prior to its utter, bloody annihilation, was set to become the most vilified, misrepresented and detested regime in the history of the civilised world. The mere mention of the words 'swastika,' 'Nazi,' 'Hitler,' etc. invoke instant and often highly indignant revulsion amongst many people. But, is all the bile and vociferous outrage directed at all-things Nazi, its many adherents and Adolf Hitler himself, totally justified or is there, maybe an agenda at work? An insidious bankster-driven agenda, no less? We shall see.

But for now let us return once again to the 1920s where we left-off, and indeed long before that particularly dire turn of events. Back in 1919-1920, the Weimar government followed a progressive, liberal agenda, enacting universal suffrage, an 8-hour workday, agricultural labour reform, and other hallmarks of a modern state.

Finally, by November 1919 the cumulative damage caused to the *Reichstag* building by all the revolts was repaired and the Republican government moved from Weimar back home to Berlin. After the ratification of the Treaty of Versailles by the newly-formed *League of Nations* in January 1920, the new regular German military force, the *Reichswehr* had to be reduced to no more than 100,000 men, such, at least, was the Allied plan. But at that time the *Reichswehr* consisted of some 350,000 men including the various *Freikorps* that totalled in excess of 250,000. Obviously, the *Freikorps* would have to go and the government began to tackle that job in 1920.

In March 1920, it ordered the disbandment of one of the *Freikorps* units, the *Marinebrigade Ehrhardt*. Although only a modest cadre of some 6000 men, the *Marinebrigade Ehrhardt* had had a colourful history, participating in the fighting to retake the northwest ports of Bremen, Cuxhaven and Wilhelmshaven from local revolutionaries in early 1919. Afterwards it was deployed to central Germany to combat local communist uprisings there and it was also among the *Freikorps* which suppressed the Communist uprising in Munich. Then in August, the *Brigade Ehrhardt* crushed Polish separatists in Upper Silesia and so perhaps unsurprisingly, when ordered to disband, the *Marinebrigade Ehrhardt* resisted the command. It appealed to the commander of the Berlin *Reichswehr*, General Lüttwitz, who after failing to enlist the co-operation of *Reichspräsident* Ebert, ordered the Brigade to march on Berlin, which was occupied by them in mid-March. The head of the *Heeresleitung*, General Hans von Seeckt, when ordered by the government to suppress this putsch, refused to fight what he considered a fellow *Reichswehr* unit, although he conspicuously refused to support it, either.

This occupation of Berlin coincided, perhaps by design, with an attempt by Dr. Wolfgang Kapp, a former president of East Prussia, to declare the Ebert government in violation of the new constitution. Kapp had a valid point, as the constituent assembly had elected Ebert president of the German Republic in 1919. Ebert signed the new Weimar constitution into law in August of 1920 but the constitution provided for the president to be elected by a national election and not by the constituent assembly. So Kapp's actual motives were probably more sinister than merely pointing-out a procedural nicety and while the Ebert government decamped to Dresden, Kapp used the occupation of Berlin by the *Marinebrigade Ehrhardt* to declare the presidency of Ebert null and void and announced that he himself would serve as Imperial chancellor until new elections could be organised.

The Ebert government in absentia, called for a general strike by German workers, emphasising, possibly correctly, that the reactionaries who had seized Berlin, were intent on restoring the ex-Kaiser who was at that time safely ensconced in the Netherlands, where Queen Wilhelmina had given him a modest castle and resolutely rejected Allied demands for his extradition. German workers responded to this threat with enthusiasm and their strike effectively paralysed Berlin, as well as much of the rest of the country.

But to return to the Treaty of Versailles... According to Part V of the Treaty, the size of the army, the number of War Ministry staff and numbers of customs agents, forest rangers, coastguards, and police were all limited. The total numbers of guns (artillery,) machine guns, trench-mortars, rifles and munitions stockpiles available to Germany were also restricted and no imports or exports of arms and munitions were permitted.

Neither was Germany allowed to have poison gas, tanks, armoured cars, submarines, dirigibles, a military air force or its traditional General Staff. Numbers and sizes of warships were also limited and all forts in western Germany were to be dismantled. Gun clubs were allowed so long as they had no connection whatsoever with the military.

The Treaty specified the minimum enlistment period in the army as 12 years for privates and NCOs, and 25 years for officers. This was to prevent Germany from using the system followed by all major WWI belligerents (except the US,) which allowed them to put millions of trained and equipped men in the field in a matter of weeks. The idea was that all able-bodied men would undergo basic military training and then be demobilised and returned to civilian life. Upon mobilisation or the outbreak of war, they could be called-up immediately, issued with equipment and packed into trains bound for the front.

There was much, much more too, Versailles was a lengthy treaty. But for our purposes, the noteworthy fact is that it was concerned with grand objectives, such as who was going to pay for the near-total destruction of Belgium and much of northern France, where exactly to draw the borders of Poland and how to give Danzig access to the Baltic Sea when East Prussia happened to be in the way.

The power-mad bankster-globalists believe it is their right or prerogative to dismantle existing nations and create new ones as they see fit and to hell with the wishes or needs of the populace whose heritage, traditions and lives they may shatter in the course of their evil machinations. The Austro-Hungarian and Ottoman Empires almost instantly ceased to exist and their disparate peoples were simply assigned to other states in whatever way it suited them. The Paris Conference, as well as formulating the various treaties, also established the framework for the banksters' fledgling, future One-World Government, 'The League of Nations.'

A strong Zionist delegation was also present at the Conference. They had engineered the entry of America into the war by their chicanery and now it was time for them to collect payment for the 'services rendered' to Britain. The former Arab territories of the Ottoman Empire were separated from Turkish rule and broken up into smaller states, Palestine being destined to become a British protectorate. The Zionist mandate, the Balfour Declaration, supposedly established the Jewish people's entitlement to Palestine, to be re-named 'Israel' as guaranteed by the League of Nations *(exactly as Herzl had predicted in 1897!) and* Jews from all over the world would now be allowed to immigrate there. The Arabs of Palestine were never consulted about this and they were of course, quite rightly upset and angry. Britain promising Palestine to the Jews is almost like China promising Wales to Russia. What right would they have to do it? None whatsoever of course, using the logic that we believe prevails, but of course the bankster masters of the universe operate in a totally different sphere and with rules that only apply, whenever they may see fit.

The abject unfairness, cruelty even, of the Treaty of Versailles is still recognised today—even by liberal, establishment historians. With Germany disarmed by its new government, *and with no German representatives present,* the Zionist banksters proceeded to rape the German nation, whose Kaiser did not want war, had tried his best to avert war and offered more than once to make peace after the war had begun. (We will see later how history would repeat itself in this regard.)

The Treaty contained 440 clauses in total, 414 of which were dedicated towards punishing Germany. To summarise, the key provisions that Germany was forced to accept were:

1. Germany accepts 100% responsibility for the war
2. German armed forces were to be restricted to 100,000 men
3. The industrial German Rhineland would be occupied by French troops for the next 15 years
4. Kaiser Wilhelm was to be tried for 'offences against international morality'
5. The German region of West Prussia was to be sliced-up and given to the new nation of Poland. (As a result, millions of West Prussians were forcefully expelled from their homes and East Prussia was isolated from the rest of the German mainland)
6. The German Sudetenland region was stripped away and given to the newly created nation of Czechoslovakia
7. The newly formed state of Austria was forbidden from uniting with their German-speaking brethren in Germany
8. Germany was stripped of her African colonies. Britain, France and Belgium take them over
9. The coal-rich Saar region of Germany was placed under League of Nations control for 15 years (During this time, its coal was to be shipped to France)
10. The strategic Baltic Sea port city of Danzig was to be separated from Germany and declared a 'free city'
11. Germany was ordered to pay massive war reparations in the form of money and natural resources. The crushing burden of the payments (equal to almost 1 trillion dollars in modern US currency) would devastate the German economy and later cause a hyperinflationary monetary collapse

Unsurprisingly, the inhumane, unjust Treaty of Versailles breeds resentment and anger in Germany for many years to come and is indeed largely responsible for the conditions that created WWII, twenty years later—as was its intent.

During the Russian Civil War, the Jewish-Hungarian Bela Kun fought for the Communists and as a commander, ordered the killings of many thousands of anti-Communists (Whites.) Then, upon the collapse of the Austro-Hungarian Empire, Kun saw an opportunity to impose Communism in Hungary and in November 1918, he and several hundred other Hungarian Reds returned to Hungary with funds provided by the Soviets and with which he rapidly founded the Hungarian Communist Party on 4th November 1918. Following this, the Hungarian Soviet Republic was soon established and Kun as leader, reported directly to Lenin and was the dominant personality in the government during its brief existence. The first act of his government was to 'nationalise,' a euphemism for 'confiscate,' all private property.

After an anti-Communist coup attempt in Hungary in June 1919, Kun organised a response in the form of another 'Red Terror,' this time in Hungary and carried out by secret police and mostly Jewish, irregular army units. The 'Red Tribunals' condemned 600 prominent Hungarians to death.

However, Kun's Communist reign of terror was relatively short-lived and he and his henchmen were soon removed from power following an invasion by Romania. Kun immediately fled to the USSR.

What modern day historians mockingly refer to as 'The First Red Scare,' came about just eighteen years after the Reds murdered US President McKinley in 1901. The 1919 'Red Scare' is marked by a campaign of Communist terror and radical political agitation in America, set against the backdrop of Lenin's ongoing bloodbath and Woodrow Wilson's ever-weakening economy.

In April 1919, booby-trap mail bombs were sent to several prominent Americans. But after the first bomb fizzles and the second one injures the wife of a US Senator, the remaining 28 are quickly intercepted by the postal authorities. On 1st May (May Day,) the Reds staged huge rallies that led to violence in Boston, New York and Cleveland. Two die and forty people were injured as patriotic Americans clash with mostly foreign-born Reds.

Then, in June, an additional eight bombs were mailed, killing two innocent people and in September, Marxist Union leaders organised steel strikes, followed by coal strikes in November.

The Zionist-Globalist pressure on Woodrow Wilson became too much for the weak-willed president to handle by November 1919. His *New World Order* masters had driven their blackmailed-puppet very hard since 1912 and Wilson was ordered to undertake an intense, year-long cross-country campaign to win public support for US entry into the world government blueprint known as The League of Nations, which was established at the Paris Peace Conference.

During his gruelling propaganda tour, the stress became too much for Wilson and he suffered a massive stroke that left him severely paralysed. For the next seventeen months, the enfeebled President lay in his bed on the brink of death, barely able to write his own name, but *the outside world was never told of Wilson's illness. He was still too valuable to the banksters and all subsequent communication with him was through his wife, Edith.*

Fortunately for the world, after an intense, year-long campaign to win support for entry into the League of Nations, the paralysed President Wilson and his Globalist bankster masters were dealt a devastating blow to their plans for world domination, when the Senate failed to approve US membership. Bankster pressure actually forced the Senate to vote three times, but the necessary two-thirds majority still could not be achieved. Leading the opposition to membership in the infant World Government were Senators Henry Cabot Lodge, Warren Harding, and William Borah, all Republicans.

"I would sooner lose in a right cause than win in a wrong cause. As long as I can distinguish between right and wrong, I shall do what I believe to be right—whatever the consequences."
William Edgar Borah

This was actually the death-knell of the League of Nations. Without American support, the plans just fell-apart and the scheme was soon abandoned as a lost cause. However, the banksters are nothing if not patient. Patient AND persistent.

Many of the American people had now realised that the very strange war in which they had just taken part, served no American interest at all. They wanted to be involved in Europe's affairs no longer and simply wished to 'return to normality.' But the Globalist/Marxist bankers carried-on scheming against the people until they finally got their 'foot in the door' of their much-vaunted, New World Order.

The efforts of Attorney General A. Mitchell Palmer weakened the Reds power greatly. Though opposed by the Communist-loving ACLU and undermined by many of the Wilson Cabinet, Palmer pressed-on regardless with his roundups, purges and investigations of the Reds. During the ongoing interrogations of suspects, Palmer's Federal Agent thugs were not shy of beating-up the foreign Reds, including many Russian-Jewish radicals, as well as Italian and East European Anarchists, in the investigation process.

Palmer deported 249 foreign Reds, including leaders such as 'Red Emma' Goldman, who inspired and praised the 1901 McKinley murder and then he focussed on the Marxist labour strikes, leaving his young assistant, J. Edgar Hoover, to deal with the foreigners. Hoover rounded-up 3000 more foreign radicals and in total, 5000 radicals were arrested and 556 violent Reds were summarily deported from America.

Also in 1919, in parallel to all the shenanigans in the rest of Europe and the USA, Adolf Hitler joined the tiny German Workers Party (DAP,) becoming member number 7. (There were obviously only six other members of the nationalist group.)

The 30-year old self-educated artist from Austria was penniless and had no political connections but his oratory, organisational and marketing skills and his charisma, quickly propelled him to leadership of the tiny group. His passionate, mesmerising beer-hall speeches stopped onlookers in their tracks and his audience, growing larger and larger every day, was utterly captivated by his oratory. He denounced the Versailles Treaty, the Allied occupation, his 'November Criminals,' the Marxists, the Jewish press, and the international banksters alike.

DAP membership rapidly increased, being recruited heavily from unemployed young men and disgruntled ex-soldiers who felt betrayed by the government after the 'strange' end to the war. Hitler had an already partially-converted, ready-made audience and in addition he appealed to veterans because he himself had been a frontline soldier, twice decorated for serious injuries sustained and twice more for conspicuous bravery.

To entice recruits away from *both* the rival 'right' Nationalist and 'left' Socialist parties, Hitler simply added the words 'National' and 'Socialist' into the party's name, making it **NS**DAP. They never referred to themselves as 'Nazis,' this was a later, derogatory shortening of the organisation's full title.

Back in England, in 1920, the *First Lord of the Admiralty* and war-criminal, Winston Churchill became a staunch supporter of Zionism, but nevertheless claimed to be an opponent of Jewish Communism. Although this was probably more to do with his bank balance, than his conscience (did he actually have one?) It is known that from being in constant debt, he suddenly acquired a large sum of money, enough to fund his extravagant lifestyle—and strange penchant for extremely expensive ladies underwear—although that is another story for another time, maybe.

Although both, primarily Jewish movements traced their roots back to the same Rothschild bankster-crime family, they sometimes appeared to contradict and conflict with each other. In an editorial appearing in the *Illustrated Sunday Herald* entitled 'Zionism vs. Bolshevism,' Churchill argued that Jews should support Zionism as a preferable alternative to Communism, entirely missing the point that both movements emanated from precisely the same source and were/are inextricably linked.

"This movement among the Jews is not new. From the days of Weishaupt to those of Karl Marx, and down to Trotsky (Russia,) Bela Kun (Hungary,) Rosa Luxemburg (Germany,) and Emma Goldman (United States,) this worldwide conspiracy for the overthrow of civilisation and for the reconstitution of society on the basis of arrested development, envious malevolence, and impossible equality, has been steadily growing. It played, as a modern writer, Mrs. Webster, has so ably shown, a definitely recognisable part in the tragedy of the French Revolution.

It has been the mainspring of every subversive movement during the Nineteenth Century; and now at last this band of extraordinary personalities from the underworld of the great cities of Europe and America have gripped the Russian people by the hair of their heads and have become practically the undisputed masters of that enormous empire." Winston Churchill

At the Paris Peace Conference, the bankster-globalists from both the US and UK agreed to establish twin, so-called 'think tanks' that were to dominate the political affairs of both nations for the next century. Firstly in 1920, the Fabian Society dominated, *Royal Institute of International Affairs* (RIIA) (now *Chatham House)* was created in London, followed in 1921 by the *Council on Foreign Relations* (CFR) in New York with prominent bankster and 'father of the Fed,' Paul Warburg serving as its first Director.

'Chatham House Rules' of secrecy govern the members of both organisations. Membership is by invitation only and although members may discuss the generalities of group meetings, they are expected to remain discreet regarding who attends the meetings and specifically what is discussed and agreed. Isn't 'Democracy at work,' a wonderful thing to behold?

Through the decades of their existence, the membership of both the CFR and Chatham have included prominent names from politics, the media, banking, industry and academia whilst politically-speaking, the members have also included a mixed bag of

Globalists, Communists, Zionists, ambitious careerists and many well-meaning dupes. The chosen few recruited by the influential one-world government banksters often find themselves on a fast-track to greater fame and fortune, provided they play by the rules and are openly seen to support and promote the agenda.

By 1921, Lenin's cruel and persistent oppression of the Russian people had broken both their nerves and their will to resist and the Famine of 1921 that, partly due to governmental incompetence, and partially a deliberate effort to kill off any Russians still not willing to support the Red takeover, was a further, massive blow to their efforts to survive against all odds.

The Communists ran the money-printing presses to finance their civil war and welfare schemes and when inflation followed, as it was certain to, they imposed rigid price controls, causing farmers to lose their livelihoods. The Communists then seized all seeds and food and placed it under their control, thereby greatly compounding the shortages. The resulting, horrific famine is then used to selectively feed those regions submissive to the Reds, and as a weapon to starve those loyal to the Whites.

Starving Russians and Ukrainians resorted to eating grass and even cannibalism and the horror escalated even further when Lenin deliberately blocked foreign relief food supplies from reaching their intended recipients. When the famine death toll reached ten million, Lenin finally allowed food to be distributed to the starving populace but were it not for the foreign aid, the death toll for Lenin's cruel actions would surely have doubled or even tripled.

At the conclusion of the Red Terror, Red Famine, and Red-White Civil War, in 1922, Lenin and Trotsky formally established the Soviet Union with its new capital, of Moscow. The former Russian Empire was henceforth to be known as the USSR (Union of Soviet Socialist Republics.) This huge 'new' country straddled both the European and Asian landmass but of its constituent republics, Russia itself was by far the largest and most populated.

The well-documented criminal brutality of the Soviets totally shocked the world, as did the Communist's openly declared intention to overthrow all other nations' governments and replace them with their own kind. For this reason, three consecutive US Republican Presidents (Harding, Coolidge and Hoover,) categorically refused to diplomatically recognise the Soviet Union.

Then in order to counter the Soviet promotion of Zionist-Communism and promote the Hegelian dialectic worldwide, the banksters created a form of 'anti-Communism' which would be named 'Fascism.' The engineered economic depression that followed World War I gave the Reds and socialists an opportunity to agitate in post-war Italy but Benito Mussolini and his newly-formed Fascist Party decided to act quickly before the Communists could gain absolute power. Unfortunately for the banksters though, their plan backfired somewhat and Fascism, in the hands of Mussolini (and later Hitler) mutated into a form of defiance of bankster power—as we will see.

In the October of 1922, in the presence of 60,000 people at the Fascist Congress in Naples, Mussolini declared that... *"Our programme, is simple: we want to rule Italy."*

His Fascist 'Blackshirts' quickly gained the support and momentum required to capture the strategic cities of Italy and Mussolini then personally led a march of 30,000 men on the capital city, Rome. On 28th October, the sympathetic King Victor Emmanuel III, whose father had been murdered by a Communist in 1900, simply, with no fuss, ceded political power to Mussolini and his 'fascisti,' who were strongly supported by most Italian war veterans and the middle classes.

The corrupt Communist and left-wing political parties were systematically shut-down and under the leadership of Mussolini, the pro-business Fascist Party assumed control of the country and quickly restored order to the formerly chaotic Italy.

It is perhaps important to consider the tenets of true Fascism at this juncture. Fascism combines an honest and sound monetary system controlled by the government and significantly NOT central banksters, with a modicum of free enterprise and state-regulated corporatism. I say 'significantly' because we are now getting to the crux of why Fascism as a system is so vilified as 'evil,' today by our Zionist-Communist central bankster overlords. It may also bring us closer to understanding how and why Hitler, Mussolini and the German and Italian states had to be destroyed and furthermore why ever since the end of WWII, their 'reputations' have had to be absolutely shattered into tiny pieces and their very names engineered into the evocation of pure evil and hatred in our minds.

There are so many examples of this in action and we really do have to struggle hard to suspend our cognitive dissonance, in order that we can actually take all this on-board, such is the overwhelming might of anti-Hitler and anti-Fascist propaganda to which we have been subjected all our lives. I realise that for some, this may well be impossible, indeed I admit that it did take me a long time before I could even begin to accept and comprehend the staggering scale of the deception and propaganda, which of course is still ongoing. The banksters still cannot allow any semblance of sympathy for the Fascist system to permeate our consciousness as it poses the gravest danger imaginable to their sordid empire. And so the attacks and vilifications continue on and on. I personally counted on my Satellite TV channels, taking one week in October 2015 at random, more than sixty programmes—in one week, sixty (!), that were still denigrating the twin evils of fascism and Hitler and his many cohorts or reminding us of the utter horrors of the so-called 'holocaust.' Had I performed the same exercise in April or May 2015 though, I suspect that number would have been well into the hundreds due to that being the 70th anniversary of the war's end, in the European theatre at least. And what is more, these programmes are continually re-cycled ad nauseum, 'lest we forget.' Not that we are ever likely to forget—the bankster-controlled media would never let that happen.

Was the above campaign a success, in hindsight do you think? Maybe, but those 'indestructible weeds' are growing pretty wild and prolifically right here and now.

I am NOT a fascist and nor am I particularly a Hitler 'fan,' either. My point here is that although he was certainly no angel (name me one politician ever, who was) and Fascism is not some cosy, benevolent and caring system of governance, but neither is it the utter abomination it is made-out to be by the might of all the banksters' many vested interests. And nor was Hitler, 'evil personified' either, as we shall see later. But for now, back to the story...

"Atrocity propaganda is how we won the war. And we're only really beginning with it now! We will continue this atrocity propaganda, we will escalate it until nobody will accept even a good word from the Germans, until all the sympathy they may still have abroad will have been destroyed and they themselves will be so confused that they will no longer know what they are doing. Once that has been achieved, once they begin to run down their own country and their own people, not reluctantly but with eagerness to please the victors, only then will our victory be complete. It will never be final.

Re-education needs careful tending, like an English lawn. Even one moment of negligence, and the weeds crop up again - those indestructible weeds of historical truth."

Sefton Delmer (1904-1979), former British Chief of `Black propaganda': Said after the German surrender in 1945, in a conversation with the German professor of International Law, Dr. Friedrich Grimm.

Yes Mr. Delmer, the truth is very resilient! It is here and it is growing fast ---> justice4germans.wordpress.com

By January 1923, more than four years had passed since Germany's complete and total surrender at the end of the Great War. The poverty and hunger-stricken German nation was by this time having severe difficulty in making the massive, extortionate reparations payments imposed by The Treaty of Versailles and so, having already destroyed the value of Germany's currency, the Allies demanded to be paid in timber and coal.

Then in a further humiliation of already occupied Germany, 60,000 troops from Belgium, France, and the French, African colonies expanded the occupation from the Rhineland into the defenceless, industrial Ruhr region and whilst innocent German children were starving, the Allies collected their stolen booty of German commodities. Machine gun posts were set-up in the streets in order to deter resistance as Allied troops openly steal food and supplies from German shopkeepers.

Other than to stage peaceful, passive demonstrations, there was nothing that the disarmed, humiliated, hungry and helpless German people could do about this latest outrage. However, worse, much worse was still to come for the beleaguered German nation. With Allied troops occupying the Ruhr and the German Mark losing its value to inflation, Germany was suddenly plunged into a horrific hyperinflationary, downward spiral. The socialist Weimar government and the Warburg/Rothschild central,

Reichsbank had resorted to massively expanding the money supply and flooding the economy with their worthless fiat, non-commodity-backed paper money, mostly to cover the crushing debt imposed by the Versailles Treaty, and also to keep the Weimar Republic's socialist welfare state afloat—all with disastrous consequences.

The true facts of this financial disaster do not appear in any mainstream history textbooks today. Today's history uses this inflation to twist the truth into its opposite. It cites the radical devaluation of the German mark as an example of the dire consequences that ensue when governments print their own money, rather than borrow it from the private cartels run by the banksters. In reality the exact opposite is the truth, as with so much of our accepted historical 'wisdom' today.

As stated, the Weimar financial crisis actually began with the impossible reparations payments imposed at the Treaty of Versailles. Hjalmar Schacht (who was never a Nazi Party member and now it appears clear why that was the case,) the Rothschild agent who was currency commissioner for the Republic, opposed letting the German government print its own money...

"The Treaty of Versailles is a model of ingenious measures for the economic destruction of Germany. Germany could not find any way of holding its head above the water, other than by the inflationary expedient of printing bank notes."

Schacht echoes the history books' deception that Weimar inflation was caused when the German government printed its own money; however, in his 1967 book '*The Magic of Money,*' Schacht revealed that it was the privately owned '*Reichsbank*', not the German government that was injecting new money into the economy. Thus, it was that this bankster-owned and run private bank caused the Weimar hyperinflation.

Like the US Federal Reserve, the Reichsbank was overseen by appointed government officials, but was operated for private gain. What drove the wartime inflation into hyperinflation was speculation by foreign investors, who sold the German Mark short, betting on its decreasing value. Using the manipulative device known as the 'short sell,' speculators borrow something they do not own, sell it and then 'cover' by buying it back at the lower price.

Speculation in the German Mark was made possible because the privately owned Reichsbank (not yet under Nazi control) made massive amounts of currency available for borrowing. This currency, like all first-world currency today, was created with accounting entries in the bank's books and then this 'magic' money was lent at compound interest. When the Reichsbank could not keep up with the voracious demand for Marks, other private banks were then allowed to also create Marks out of nothing and to lend them at interest. The result was runaway debt and inflation.

On the 24th June 1922, right-wing fanatics assassinated Walter Rathenau, the moderate German foreign minister. Rathenau was a charismatic figure and the idea that a popular, wealthy and glamorous government minister could be shot in a law-abiding society shattered the faith of the German people, who needed to believe that the country was in safe hands after the trauma of the previous decade. The wealthier, by now extremely nervous citizens were already taking their money out of banks and investing it into 'real goods' such as diamonds, works of art and safe real-estate, with true intrinsic values, unlike currency, which the banksters manipulate up or downwards to suit their own agendas. Eventually, the ordinary German citizens also began to trade their Marks for real commodities.

The British historian Adam Fergusson noted that pianos were being bought, even by non-musical families. Sellers held back because the Mark was worth less every day and as prices soared, the amounts of currency demanded became greater and greater and the German Central Bank responded to these demands through the printing of more, increasingly worthless paper. Yet still the ruling authorities did not acknowledge that there was anything amiss.

Why did the German government not act sooner to halt the inflation? The problem was partly that it was a shaky, fragile government, especially after the assassination of Rathenau. The vengeful French had sent their army into the Ruhr to enforce their demands for reparations due under the Versailles Treaty and the Germans were powerless to resist due to the virtual disbandment of their armed forces and they feared unemployment far more than inflation.

And so the printing presses continued on and on, producing the ever-decreasing in value Mark and once they began to run, they were impossible to stop. The price increases became unmanageable. Menus in cafes could not be revised quickly enough to keep up with the speed of the inflation. A student at Freiburg University ordered a cup of coffee at a café and the price on the menu was 5,000 Marks per cup. He had two cups but when the bill arrived, it was for 14,000 Marks. *"If you wanted to save money and you want two cups of coffee, you should have ordered them both at the same time,"* he was told by the proprietor.

Things became so bad that people would not even bother to bend down to pick up a one hundred million Mark note carelessly discarded by a passer-by as by that time it had become worth less than the paper upon which it was printed. There was a famous case of a man walking along a street on a shopping trip to buy bread, carrying his money in a large wicker basket, such was the quantity and bulk of the notes he needed to carry. Upon unsuccessfully attempting to enter a particularly busy shop, he reasoned that he could quite safely leave most of his money outside in the basket as no-one would bother to risk stealing such a bulky yet paltry amount of money. He was absolutely correct. When he returned, he found his money was all still there on the ground, but someone had stolen his basket!

The presses of the Reichsbank could not keep up to demand, even though they ran through the night. A factory worker described payday, which was every day at 11 am . . . *"At 11.00 in the morning a siren sounded, and everyone gathered in the factory forecourt, where a five-ton lorry was drawn up loaded to overflowing with paper money. The chief cashier and his assistants climbed up on top. They read out names and just threw out bundles of notes. As soon as you had caught one you made a dash for the nearest shop and bought just anything that was going."* Teachers, paid at 10 am, took their money into the playground to meet relatives who took the bundles and hurried off with them. Banks closed at 11 am as by this time they had invariably run out of cash anyway.

When the 1,000-billion Mark note was first issued in mid-1923, few bothered to collect the change when they spent it. But by November 1923, with one US dollar equal to one trillion Marks, the breakdown was complete and the German economy had become one of barter only. The currency had completely lost its value—and its meaning.

Then, a new president took over the Reichsbank, Horace Greeley Hjalmar Schacht, who came by his first two names because of his father's admiration for an editor of the *New York Tribune*. The *Rentenmark* was not Schacht's idea, but he executed it and as the Reichsbank president, he received all the credit for it. For decades afterward he was able to maintain a reputation for financial wizardry and he became the architect of the financial prosperity brought by the Nazi party.

Obviously, although the currency was worthless, Germany was still a relatively commodity-rich country with mines, farms, factories, and natural resources aplenty. The backing for the Rentenmark was mortgages on the land and bonds on the factories, but that backing was a fiction; the factories and land could not be turned into cash or used abroad. Nine zeros were struck from the currency, that is, one Rentenmark was equal to one billion old Marks. The Germans wanted desperately to believe in the Rentenmark, and so they simply did just that.

But although the country slowly began to function almost normally again, the savings of the middle-classes were never restored, nor were the values of hard work and decency that had accompanied the savings. All those assets were literally subsumed into the banksters' considerable coffers and with the currency went many of the lifetime plans of average, ordinary citizens. It was the custom in Germany for the bride to bring some money to a marriage (a dowry) and as a result, many marriages were cancelled and many war widows (and these were present in large numbers) dependent on insurance, found themselves destitute. People who had worked for a lifetime and built up a sizeable pension fund, found that their pensions would not even buy a cup of coffee. Such are the ways that the ordinary citizens of the world are cheated out of the money by these vultures.

"The cities were still there, the houses not yet bombed and in ruins, but the victims were millions of people. They had lost their fortunes, their savings; they were dazed and inflation-shocked and did not understand how it had happened to them and who the foe was who had defeated them. Yet they had lost their self-assurance, their feeling that they themselves could be the masters of their own lives if only they worked hard enough; and lost, too, were the old values of morals, of ethics, of decency." Pearl Buck, American author

Thus, according to Schacht himself, the German government did not cause the Weimar hyperinflation. On the contrary, the government brought hyperinflation under control. It placed the Reichsbank under strict government regulation and took prompt corrective measures to eliminate foreign speculation. One of those measures was to eliminate easy access to loans from private banks and eventually Hitler regained Germany's financial stability through the issuance of Government Treasury Certificates.

What really causes hyperinflation is uncontrolled speculation. When speculation is coupled with debt (owed to private banking cartels) the result is always disaster. On the other hand, when a government issues currency in carefully measured ways, it causes supply and demand to increase together, leaving prices unaffected. Hence there is no inflation, no debt, no unemployment and no need for income taxes.

Naturally this terrifies the banksters, it eliminates their powers, since their control of banking allows them to buy the media, the government and everything else. Were the nations of the world to revert to Government-only money issuance, then the world financial crisis would be solved overnight, as would much of the ever-increasing wars, poverty and suffering we are currently witnessing.

Significantly, it was in the midst of this financial carnage that further devastated an already prostrated nation, that an unobtrusive, former army corporal was thrust into the spotlight and promoted as a great 'leader of men.' The prevailing conditions of the time providing a perfect stage for anyone with any aspirations of greatness and the ability to 'mesmerise' his audiences with nationalist, patriotic rhetoric. And thus the world was introduced to the soon-to-be world public enemy number one, Adolf Hitler...

On the 8th of November 1923, as the German people seethed with anger over the hyperinflation and the French occupation, Hitler decided that the time was right to seize power from the local government in Munich. Hoping that former members of the German military would join the uprising and then move against the national government in Berlin, Hitler used a political rally in a Munich Beer Hall to launch a putsch (coup,) which would later become known as the famous, *'Munich Beer Hall Putsch.'*

The local uprising was ignited by Hitler's moving speech, but failed to sustain itself as was hoped. Troops opened fire on the nationalist rebels, killing sixteen of them and Hitler and others were arrested and tried for treason. At his trial, Hitler took advantage of the opportunity to share his ideology, which was then published in the newspapers. The judge was impressed with both his eloquence and his views and issued a lenient sentence for him and his colleagues. Although the Munich coup had failed, the legend of the great orator grew exponentially, attracting many new followers and membership in Hitler's NSDAP had attained about 20,000 by the end of 1923.

Having pledged a 'return to normalcy,' Warren Harding was elected the 29th US President in 1920. An vocal opponent of entry into the League of Nations, his victory over James Cox and his VP running-mate, Franklin D Roosevelt (Theodore Roosevelt's cousin), constituted the largest Presidential election landslide in America's history (60%-34%.)

Harding inherited an economic depression and quickly moved to reduce income taxes and cut government spending by 50%. With the private economy now freed from the parasitic dead weight of bankster-controlled 'big government,' an historic economic boom soon ensued and the 'Roaring Twenties' were indeed a period of great prosperity and happiness for the American people. Harding was systematically unravelling the damage to the economy done by Woodrow Wilson and his puppet-masters and gradually returning the country to the halcyon days of William Howard Taft, whom he named as his Chief Justice of the Supreme Court.

Harding's support for free-markets, limited government, low taxes, neutral foreign policy and his refusal to grant diplomatic recognition to the appalling and murderous Soviet Union, all went strongly against the banksters' wishes and so right on cue, they unleashed an intense media smear-campaign regarding 'scandals' in Harding's administration, against the highly-popular President.

In 1922, Interior Secretary Albert B. Fall accepted a bribe of over $400,000 from *Mammoth Oil* and *Pan America Petroleum* to obtain the leasing rights to the oil reserves at Teapot Dome in Wyoming. Unfortunately for the aptly-named Fall, the press were notified and he was exposed. Prior to Watergate this was considered the 'greatest and most sensational scandal in the history of American politics.' Some elements of the Eastern, bankster-controlled press were unrelenting in their attacks upon Harding but despite this, the American public were unconvinced by the propaganda and so Harding, and his policies, remained popular. As with so many other Presidents, Czars and other leaders before him, the Zionist banksters therefore decided to remove Warren Harding from office.

Whilst recovering from a strange sickness that had stricken him in San Francisco, President Harding died suddenly on the 2nd August 1923, during the middle of a conversation with his wife and doctors could not agree on the cause of his strange death. However, despite this, within an hour of his demise, Harding's body was embalmed and placed in a casket and the following morning, the body was on a train, headed back to Washington. Incredibly, *no autopsy was ever performed* and the strong suspicions of a deliberate, poisoning (the banksters' assassination method of choice, through the years) spread throughout America. The sudden death of the 57-year-old statesman, who successfully reversed most of Wilson's damage in just 29 months, remains a mystery to this day. Unsurprisingly, mainstream historians now rate Harding as 'the worst President ever.'

Harding was immediately replaced in office by his Vice President, Calvin Coolidge, according to the tenets of the Constitution, but after Harding's apparent assassination, America was unsure what to make of Calvin Coolidge the little-known new President. It was widely believed that Coolidge would serve the remaining 19 months of Harding's term, and then be replaced at the Republican Convention in 1924 but after continuing Harding's policies, Coolidge became very popular himself and so was nominated to run against the Democrat, John Davis.

The banksters then promoted their own place-man Robert La Follette, the 'Progressive Party' nominee but on Election Day 1924, Coolidge won 35 states, Davis 12, and La Follette only his home state!

And so a brief period of peace and prosperity settled over the United States, with the banksters' insidious political influence severely depleted. Obviously it was unlikely that they would allow that to continue without a struggle, and so it proved. They realised that they could not simply just keep-on killing Presidents and so the 'Fed' began laying a financial 'bomb' beneath the nation's prosperity and when that bomb was finally detonated in 1929, the era of Constitutional Republicanism was to be swept away for good.

When Lenin died in 1924, Joseph Stalin the General Secretary of the Communist Party Central Committee, skilfully outmanoeuvred the Red Army leader, Trotsky to seize leadership of the USSR. Stalin eventually expelled Trotsky from the Communist Party and then from the USSR itself before finally ordering his assassination to be expedited by a Soviet agent in Mexico, sixteen years later.

Stalin's immediate brutality instilled fear not only into the hopelessly enslaved people of the Soviet Union, but also into the hearts of fellow Communists that the extremely paranoid Stalin believed may challenge his leadership. The egomaniac even renamed the city of Tsaritsyn after himself; Stalingrad (now Volgograd since 1961) and ordered the erection of statues of himself in town squares.

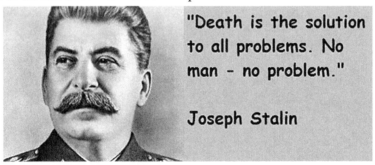

From time to time, the smiling, psychopathic mass-murderer enjoyed a purge of many of his own Communist allies as well as his perceived enemies. He soon disposed of his first wife and then drove his second wife as well as one of his sons, to suicide. And so in the years to follow, Stalin's chillingly extensive crimes against humanity would make Lenin's Red Terror and Red Famine seem like a summer Sunday afternoon picnic, by comparison.

Also in 1924, a restructuring of Germany's reparations debt, (the 'Dawes Plan') as well as the Allied debt to the US Treasury (which in turn is payable to the banksters) was instituted. The terms were still very harsh, but at least it had the effect of temporarily stabilising the German economy and its currency.

However, five years later the Dawes plan also failed and was replaced by the 'Young Plan.' The reality of the Dawes Plan, named after US Vice-President Charles Dawes, was that Dawes himself had little to do with it and it was in fact the Zionist-Globalist banksters who were imposing the new plan.

"The international bankers dictated the Dawes reparations settlement. The protocol, which was signed between the allies and Germany, is the triumph of the international financier. Agreement would never have been reached without the brutal intervention of the

international bankers. They swept statesman, politicians, and journalists aside, and issued their orders with the imperiousness of absolute Monarchs, who knew there was no appeal from their ruthless decrees. The Dawes report was fashioned by the Money Kings." Former UK Prime Minister, David Lloyd-George

During his eight-month imprisonment of 1924, Hitler had dictated his now famous book, *'Mein Kampf* (My Struggle.) whilst his close associate, Rudolf Hess, imprisoned with Hitler, faithfully committed all Hitler's ideas to paper in readiness for its publication which was to take place the following year, 1925. In this sensational work, Hitler unambiguously and vociferously placed the blame for Germany's sorry state (accurately) upon the global bankster conspiracy of Marxists and finance capitalists and their covert domination of everything. Are you now beginning to see how history was about to unfold, a little more clearly now, dear reader!?

According to Hitler, this global conspiracy, directed by the Zionist-Jewish bankers, engineered Germany's loss of World War I, the Russian revolution, the Versailles Treaty, and the resulting hyperinflation that devastated Germany, all for personal financial gain. He accused the elite, Marxist Jews of Germany of controlling newspapers and banking, fomenting wars, and corrupting the art, culture and morality of all Europe. Was he possibly correct in these oft-denigrated and ridiculed insinuations, after all?

Mein Kampf combined elements of a political manifesto and an autobiography, along with discussions of history, philosophy and economics. Originally written for the followers of National Socialism, *Mein Kampf* quickly grew in popularity, making Hitler a very wealthy man.

But back in Russia, as part of Stalin's first '5 Year Plan,' the small farmers of the Soviet Union were forced into a typically Communist, collectivisation scheme whereby the government and not 'the market,' controlled output and set prices. Land, livestock, and equipment became the property of 'the people,' which is in fact a euphemism for the State and those who control it. Reluctant farmers were smeared in the State-owned Soviet press as 'greedy capitalists,' and those who continued to resist the state's directives were cold-bloodedly murdered or imprisoned without trial.

Thousands of private farmers were killed, but the really significant death tolls began to rack-up in the early 1930s. Like all centrally-planned economic schemes, in which 'intellectuals' believe that they know better than the actual farmer, Stalin's collectivisation and other subsequent '5-Year Plans,' yielded only extremely low living standards for the Soviet people. In fact the average citizen was far worse-off materially under the Communists than they had been under the Czarist rulers. But of course that was all as planned.

The 340 feet (100 metre) tall Cathedral of Christ the Saviour was the grandest Orthodox Christian Church in the world. Completed in 1883, it had taken nearly 20 years to build, and another 20 years to decoratively paint its marble, granite, and gold plated interior. After Lenin's death, the Christian-hating Soviet Marxist-Jews chose the location of the Cathedral to be the site of a monument to Lenin and Communism, known as the Palace of the Soviets and so on the 5th December 1931, by order of Stalin's minister and Jewish brother-in-law, Lazar Kaganovich the Cathedral was dynamited and reduced to rubble, whilst Jewish Reds watched and laughed as horrified Christians grieved in terrified silence over the cruel destruction of their religious and cultural icon.

Ironically, due to poor planning and lack of funds, the Palace of the Soviets never even materialised. The site was turned into a huge public swimming pool instead and in 1990, after *Glasnost*, the Russian Orthodox Church received permission, from what was by this time a more 'open' Government, to rebuild the Cathedral of Christ the Saviour. Although the interior was not as elaborate as the original, it is still and remains to this day, a magnificent structure once again.

The next in the long line of calamitous events to overtake the ordinary Russian citizens was what became known as the '*Holodomor*' (Ukrainian translation, *Killing by hunger.*) This was another engineered famine, occurring mainly in the Ukrainian Republic of the Soviet Union during 1932-33. It was caused partly by the sheer folly of Stalin's latest socialist scheme and partly by a deliberate, strategic terror-plan (another one) engineered by Stalin's powerful, psychopathic Jewish brother-in-law, Lazar Kaganovich.

The evil, mass murderer Lazar Kaganovich, would live to the ripe old age of 98, finally dying in 1991.

In 1911 he had joined the Jewish-founded Communist Party and became involved with the Bolsheviks (Lower East Side, New York Zionists) who, financed by the banksters, *Kuehn Loeb* took an active part in the 1917 takeover of Christian Russia by Communist Jews and rose rapidly through the Party hierarchy.

From 1925 to 1928, he was first secretary of the party organisation in Ukraine and by 1930 was a full-member of the Politburo. Kaganovich was one of a small group of Stalin's top sadists pushing for very high rates of collectivisation after 1929. He became Stalin's premier butcher of Christian Russians during the late 1920s and early 1930s when the Kremlin Zionists launched their assault against the kulaks (Christian, small landowners) and implemented a ruthless policy of land collectivisation.

By any standards, Kaganovich was one of the most prolific mass-murderers in history and it is small wonder that during World War II, large numbers of Ukrainians greeted the invading Germans as liberators, with many joining the Waffen-SS in an effort to keep Communism-Zionism from enslaving all of Europe.

Encyclopaedia Britannica estimates that 7-8 million people, 5 million of them Ukrainian, were starved to death by Stalin's famine but some estimates were as high as 10 million. The famine-genocide was aimed at stamping-out Ukrainian nationalism as well as starving anti-communist peasants in Belarus, Kazakhstan and Russia itself.

Despite Soviet denials of the famine and a strict news blackout in most of the US Zionist/Globalist press, the truth of the Holodomor was indeed known to the West, even at the time. Unlike Lenin's terror famine of 1921, this time no outside assistance whatsoever, was permitted in the Soviet Union. Millions died a slow, distressing death and some people even resorted to cannibalism of the already dead in order to survive. Throughout this famine, Stalin and his henchmen destroyed any last lingering, remaining resistance to the Red Revolution.

The harvest of 1932 was only 12 per cent less than the average of 1926-1930. However, the authorities continued with the systematic confiscation of grain from peasants while Stalin upped the grain quota by 44 per cent. Death or ten years at labour camps was announced as a punishment for those who did not contribute to the state's grain collection. Robert Conquest notes that even though there is no direct proof that the famine was planned by Stalin beforehand, his policies show that he considered it as an effective way to punish Ukrainian peasantry for their resistance to collectivisation.

A special law was passed in Moscow prohibiting the distribution of grain to peasants before the state plan was fully executed. Special commissions were searching for grain and even those who were dying of hunger were not allowed to keep anything. Peasants had to resort to eating cats, dogs, rats, leaves, and even cases of cannibalism were not uncommon. Nevertheless, while the villages were dying of hunger, the party activists kept collecting grain.

The 1930s are known in Soviet history as the time of Great Terror. Ukraine suffered heavily under Soviet mass repressions and in 1929-1930 45 leading scientists, scholars and writers were arrested for belonging to the fictitious 'Union for Ukraine's Liberation.' This fake organisation invented by the Soviet authorities was declared to be planning Stalin's assassination and the separation of Ukraine from the USSR.

In 1933, the repression of Ukrainian Communist party members began. They were excluded from the party for 'ideological mistakes' another Communist euphemism for disagreement with Stalin's ideas and policies. Those who spearheaded the 'Ukrainisation' policy in the 1920s were accused of supporting 'cultural counter-revolution' and 'isolating Ukrainian workers from the beneficial influence of Russian culture.' Hilarious stuff indeed but not so funny I suppose, to be on the receiving-end.

Thousands of members of the new Soviet intelligentsia were sent to labour camps or executed and of 240 well-known Ukrainian writers, 200 'disappeared,' never to be seen again and of 85 linguists, at least 62 were killed.

The terror was indeed widespread. Suspicion and fear became the realities of the time and in 1937, Stalin decided to eliminate the Ukrainian Communist Party's leadership as well as the Ukrainian Soviet government. Three of Stalin's representatives, Vyacheslav

Molotov, Nikolay Yezhov and Nikita Khrushchev, were dispatched to Kiev to carry out the 'purge.' By June 1938, 17 ministers of the Ukrainian government and almost all members of the Central Committee had been arrested and executed.

Overall, the repressions affected 37 per cent of Ukrainian Communist Party members, i.e. about 170,000 people.

"It can seem a paradox that they were executing their 'own men'—the leading activists of the party and state, famous military commanders," noted Vasily Zaitsev, a 'Hero of the Soviet Union' and further explained that, *"...there was nothing strange about it because 'old activists' who had survived conspiracy and Czarist repressions and civil war and believed in the ideals of the revolution were not fit for the ruling class, whilst being 'fathers of nation' at the top of the bureaucratic pyramid. They had to be eliminated to assign the new bureaucracy that entered the party after the revolution and did not have old-fashioned revolutionary fantasies and would be faithful to the leader."*

Soviet authorities attempted to cover up the events of 1932-33, denying that the famine had occurred until the last days of the Soviet Union. Only after Ukraine became an independent state again in the early 1990s, was the Holodomor famine admitted-to. In 2006 the independent Ukrainian parliament formally recognised that the famine was a genocide against the Ukrainian nation, although it is still disputed by some bankster-controlled or duped historians as to whether or not it can be defined as a genocide. Regardless of this controversy however, 26 countries have recognised the Holodomor as such.

Josef Stalin had the census figures altered to hide the millions of famine deaths when the Ukraine and northern Caucasus region had an extremely poor harvest in 1932, just as Stalin was demanding heavy requisitions of grain to sell abroad to finance his industrialisation program which was in addition to the enforced collective farming of 1929.

Stalin is conservatively estimated to have been responsible for the murder and/or starvation of between 40-60 million Russians and Ukrainians during his reign of terror, while the total deaths resulting from the kulak purges and famine, at the bloody hands of Kaganovich, may be conservatively estimated at about 15 million. The exact figures will never be known.

But now, please be prepared for an introduction to even more crazed, sadist, Zionist mass-murderers, a little later...

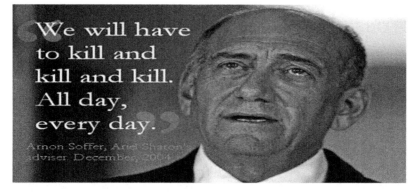

Chapter 8
The Depths of Depression

After the years of unimaginable madness and death, courtesy of World War I and the so-called Spanish Flu, came an era known as the 'Roaring Twenties.' It was a time of unheard-of prosperity for the majority, of a new decadence, reckless abandon, radio and mass entertainment.

"In 1929, as the dizzy decade nears its end, the country is stock market crazy. The great and the humble, the rich man and the working man, the housewife and the shop girl, all take their daily flyer in the market, and no-one seems to lose. Then like a bombshell, comes that never to be forgotten Black Tuesday, October 29th ... Confusion spreads through the canyons of New York City's financial district, and men stare wild eyed at the spectacle of complete ruin. More than 16.5 million shares change hands in a single day of frenzied selling. The paper fortunes built up over the past few years, crumble into nothing before this disaster, which is to touch every man, woman and child in America!"

From the screenplay of *'The Roaring Twenties,'* Warner Bros. 1939

The Wall Street stock market crash impacted the whole world. The banksters certainly made sure of that. As per usual, they drew-in the wealth of the masses and then, rapidly 'pulled the plug' on them in order to appropriate all the huge amounts of capital that had been injected into stock and share values.

The combatant nations in World War I had amassed huge debts (to the banksters) and their peoples had experienced great suffering, followed in 1918 by a severe pandemic 'flu' that worldwide killed almost as many as had the war itself. The aftermath of World War I saw drastic political, cultural and social change across Europe, Asia and Africa and even in areas outside of those that were directly involved in the war.

But by the 1920s, the war was rapidly becoming a bad memory, and a period of relentless global optimism stoked by the hope that the destruction and privations of global war would never happen again, had prevailed. The masses now firmly believed that through determination and perseverance, the energies of mankind could be harnessed toward the creative, rather than the destruction that warfare wreaked.

In the 'first' world, mass-produced consumer goods, radios, cars, vacuum cleaners, fridges, canned food, telephones and much more, all became widely available for the first time and a new wave of industrialist entrepreneurs accrued great wealth. These new technologies instigated huge social change, for example, mass-produced vehicles became common throughout America and Europe and the fledgling car industry's effects were widespread and profound, contributing to the development of the highway system, motels, service stations, used car dealerships and suburban housing developments.

The mass electrification of towns and cities progressed apace as more and more of the world was added to the electricity grid. New power plants were constructed and electricity production and consumption increased exponentially. Telephone lines were also being deployed across vast tracts of the world and indoor plumbing and modern sewage systems were installed for the first time in many areas.

All of these new, beneficial technologies and infrastructures also contributed to the general, exuberant mood reflected in a commensurate growth in the stock exchange. Stock and share prices moved both up and down throughout 1925 and 1926, followed by the beginnings of a strong upward trend in 1927. But by 1928, stocks and shares had become the talk of the masses and discussions about stocks could be heard in offices and factories everywhere. Newspapers reported stories of 'ordinary' people such as chauffeurs, maids and blue-collar workers making fortunes in the stock market. Yet very few people studied or understood the finances and underlying businesses of the companies in which they invested and thousands of fraudulent companies were formed that entrapped incautious investors. Many small investors never even realised that a crash or even a downturn was possible because in their over-confident, short experience, the prices of stocks had only ever gone one way.

Yet stock growth far exceeded growth in the underlying industrial economy and worse still, the over-confident growth was debt-fuelled. Those insisting that stock prices would continue to rise were not simply just gambling with their own funds, they were often leveraging other's money, including commercial banks betting with customers' funds sometimes at a ratio of ten or twenty-to-one. As stock prices moved higher and higher, more and more individuals were inexorably drawn into the system, using their life savings or meagre pensions to in effect gamble-away their future financial security, although of course they were never made aware of this fact. Please stop me if you have heard this story before somewhere, much more recently!

Then, as the end of the decade approached, the Federal Reserve's policy of 'easy money' had made it profitable for investors to borrow money at artificially low interest rates and then purchase stocks with the money. This in effect, is akin to taking out a mortgage in order to place the money on a racehorse, but of course the public's unrealistic optimism was never tempered by words of caution from those who knew better. And just like two conmen working the same 'mug,' the Zionist Federal Reserve doled-out massive amounts of credit whilst their brethren in arms, the Zionist press hyped-up the Stock Market 'bubble' and drew more and more 'investments' into it with their fake enthusiasm for the bubble's 'unlimited growth potential.' With hindsight of course, it is patently obvious that any bubble has a finite life and when it reaches its maximum sustainable size, as all bubbles do, it would disappear into thin air in the blink of a bankster's greedy eye.

In April 1929, with the stock market at an all-time high, Paul Warburg sent out a secret warning to his bankster friends that a collapse and nationwide depression had been planned for later that year. It was certainly no coincidence that according to the biographies of all the Wall Street bankster giants of that era; John D. Rockefeller, J. P. Morgan jr., Joseph Kennedy, Bernard Baruch et al, that they all 'fortunately' managed to withdraw from the stock market completely, just before the crash and convert their assets into cash or gold.

So as planned, in August of that year, the Federal Reserve began to tighten the money supply. Slowly, slowly at first in order to give plenty of warning to their compadres and then, quite suddenly and without general warning, on 24th October, the banksters called-in their 24-hour broker call-loans. This meant that both the stockbrokers and their customers had to sell their stocks in order to cover their loans, irrespective of the price they could get for them. As a result of this action, the stock market crashed on a day that would go down in history as, 'Black Thursday.'

The crash would later be defined into three phases, Black Thursday, Black Monday and Black Tuesday.

Black Thursday came first, on 24th October 1929. The market finally turned steeply downwards due to the actions of the banksters as related above and investors began to panic. Then, on Black Monday, even more investors decided to exit the market, causing stock prices to slide even further with a record loss in the Dow-Jones Index on that one day alone of 13%. On Black Tuesday, amidst rumours that President Herbert Hoover would not veto the pending tariff bill, the stock market plummeted even further. Approximately 16 million shares were traded that day, another record, and the Dow lost another 12% that day, $14 billion in value, bringing the week's total losses to $30 billion, ten times more than the US annual budget and more than the US had spent in all of World War I, just to put the scale of the disaster in perspective.

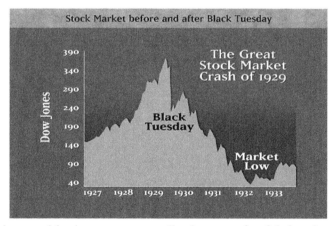

Many people then suddenly, quite naturally, became fearful for their money in the banks but when they arrived at the banks' doors in huge throngs to withdraw their money, the banks, who obviously operated under the odious fractional reserve lending requirements, owed far more money than they actually had in their possession and were unable to pay their depositors. Banks then began to fail by the thousands. By 1933, 11,000 had disappeared, thus consolidating and sustaining the 'Great Depression.'

This was the first truly global crash. The falls in share prices on the 24th and 29th October 1929 were practically instantaneous in all financial markets, except Japan and the depression that ensued was the first truly world-wide such event. The problems of excessive leverage, over-optimism and over-speculation was evident deep within the global economy before the crash and spilled over into economic, social and political chaos afterward.

Between 1929 and 1933, the banksters reduced the money supply by an additional 33%. Only a few weeks after the crash, $3bn of wealth had 'vanished' and within a year this had grown to astonishing $40 billion of wealth that had apparently disappeared, according to the lying, predominantly Zionist media.

But of course, this absolute fortune had not really 'vanished,' it had simply been 're-distributed' from the hands of the unsuspecting masses, the millions of small-time investors, to become consolidated in much fewer hands, as was pre-planned. I do not think I need to spell-out in large letters into whose hands this vast fortune passed, I presume? Indeed, this is the reason why booms and depressions are artificially created, whilst the banksters' many apologists offer lame excuses about 'market-forces' or 'business-cycles.'

Republican Representative Louis T. McFadden of Pennsylvania, the Former Chairman of the *House Banking and Currency Commission*, stated on the 10th June 1932, that...

"We have in this country one of the most corrupt institutions the world has ever known. I refer to the Federal Reserve Board... This evil institution has impoverished... the people of the United States... and has practically bankrupted our government. It has done this through... the corrupt practices of the moneyed vultures who control it.

It was not accidental. It was a carefully contrived occurrence... The international bankers sought to bring about a condition of despair here so that they might emerge as rulers of us all.

When the Federal Reserve Act was passed, the people of these United States did not perceive that a world banking system was being set up here. A super-state controlled by international bankers and industrialists acting together to enslave the world. Every effort has been made by the Fed to conceal its powers but the truth is the Fed has usurped the government."

How very true. McFadden also warned Congress, that Americans were paying for Hitler's rise to power...

"After WWI, Germany fell into the hands of the German international bankers. Those bankers bought her and they now own her, lock, stock, and barrel. They have purchased her industries, they have mortgages on her soil, they control her productions and they control all her public utilities. The international German bankers have subsidised the present Government of Germany and they have also supplied every dollar of the money Adolf Hitler had used in his lavish campaign to build up a threat to the government of Bruening. When Bruening fails to obey the orders of the German International Bankers, Hitler is brought forth to scare the Germans into submission.

Through the Federal Reserve Board over $30 billion of American money has been pumped into Germany. You have all heard of the spending that has taken place in Germany, modernistic dwellings, her great planetariums, her gymnasiums, her swimming pools, her fine public highways, her perfect factories. All this was done on our money. All this was given to Germany through the Federal Reserve Board. The Federal Reserve has pumped so many billions into Germany that they dare not name the total."

After he unsurprisingly lost his congressional seat in 1934, McFadden remained in the public eye as a vigorous opponent of the Federal Reserve and a thorn in the side of the banksters until his sudden death on 3rd October 1936. There had been two previous attempts on his life. Two bullets were fired at him on one occasion, and later he was poisoned at a banquet. (That popular method of choice again) But, on the third attempt, the assassins succeeded and the most articulate and vociferous critic of the Federal Reserve and the banksters' covert control of the nation was finally silenced forever.

"Britain is the slave of an international financial bloc." Former British Prime Minister, David Lloyd-George

"Democracy has no more persistent and insidious foe than money power . . . questions regarding the Bank of England, its conduct and its objects are not allowed, by the Speaker of the House of Commons." Lord Bryce

With the crash of the stock market, the nation's 'independent' banks (those outside the Federal Reserve System) suffered significant losses, due in part to the loss of investments. These losses were then of course immediately passed-on to their customers and investors that had survived the worst of the crash. Mortgages on houses and other properties were foreclosed and many people became homeless as result. Businesses, both large and small, were not immune from this disaster either, they also closed down in their multitudes, creating mass unemployment as a by-product. So, citizens that had invested money in the market found themselves completely penniless and without a prospect of any income—there were no jobs to be had. An estimated $140 billion was lost by people that had deposited their money in banks by 1933.

So, with the world and American economy completely collapsed, the American mid-West then suffered a further economic and ecologically-catastrophic event. Beginning around 1931, the farms of Kansas, Oklahoma, Texas, Colorado, and New Mexico suffered a decade of drought, dust, disease and death, referred to by history as the 'Dust Bowl.' Farmers of the region had in desperation, attempted to counter the economic devastation of the Depression by increasing their crop yields and to expedite this, they ploughed and planted land which should have remained 'fallow' for a year or two in order to allow its nutrients to be naturally replenished. This over-ploughing resulted in the destruction of the native and drought-resistant prairie grass which helped to bind the soil together and this combined with the land mismanagement, extreme drought conditions and high-winds, resulted in great dust storms, also known as *Black Blizzards*, as the soil lost all of its 'substance' and simply 'blew away.' These dust storms were so immense and frightening that the farmers thought Armageddon had arrived early. Black Blizzards would rapidly turn day into night and cover areas the size of states, burying houses, cars, and farm equipment. It was believed that an average of about 2-3 feet of topsoil eroded away, destroying all the farmers crops and rendering the land unsuitable for future planting.

Scenes from the mid-West 'Dust Bowl' of the 1930s

The dust storms were devastating to the farmers, the nation's and indeed the world's food supplies and the US economy. In 1935, the *Black Blizzard* blew for 26 days consecutive days, greatly affecting the farmers and their family's health.

During the catastrophe, the bankruptcy of mid-West farmers increased by almost sixty-six percent and approximately 750,000 farms were re-possessed by the banksters. Socially the family unit was affected; marriage and therefore birth rates declined and farmers were unable to feed their families. Over one million women were abandoned by their husbands through the necessity of travelling to find work and many would never return. These extreme conditions eventually led to mass migration from the vast farmlands and tens of thousands of families just abandoned their farms and headed west to California and Oregon, since farming conditions there were more amenable. This catastrophe and its social impact is well-documented in the novel, '*The Grapes of Wrath*,' by John Steinbeck.

So how bad was the Great Depression? During the four years from 1929 to 1933, production in US factories, mines and utilities fell by more than half and disposable incomes dropped 28 percent. Stock prices collapsed to one-tenth of their pre-crash height and the number of unemployed rose from 1.6 million in 1929 to a staggering 12.8 million in 1933, a figure that represented 25% of the workforce. Quite understandably, ugly rumours of revolution simmered for the first time in living memory.

To properly understand the events of the time, it is necessary to view the Great Depression as not one, but four consecutive phases making up the whole. Professor Hans Sennholz labelled these four phases . . .

- The business cycle
- The disintegration of the world economy
- The New Deal
- The Wagner Act.

The first phase explained how and why the crash of 1929 happened in the first place, whilst the other three demonstrated how government intervention kept the economy artificially suppressed for over a decade, unnecessarily prolonging the pain, which was part of the banksters' plan all along.

During his last year in office (1932) President Hoover introduced a desperate plan to bail out the failing banks, but he needed support from the Democratic Congress, which was not forthcoming. That same year Franklin D. Roosevelt was elected in the 1932 presidential election and in 1933 he announced sweeping emergency banking measures and only then did the Fed begin to inject money into the economy and thus began the long process of recovery.

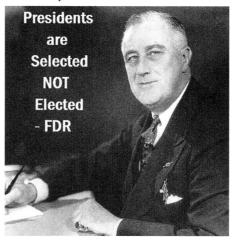

Franklin Delano Roosevelt's roots extend back into the 17th Century when the wealthy Dutch Delano and Roosevelt (Rosenfeldt) families arrived in New Amsterdam (Manhattan.) By the 1880s, these families were a well-established part of New York's financial, political and social hierarchy. FDR (born 30th January 1882,) of course had all of the benefits that come with being born into a patrician family; money, education, and connections.

Until the age of 14, young Roosevelt was home-schooled, before graduating from Harvard with mediocre grades. He used his many connections to find employment as a lawyer on Wall Street in 1908 and his political ambitions were fulfilled when he was elected Senator for New York State in 1911. FDR's support network was greatly enhanced after October 1911, when he was initiated into Freemasonry at Holland Lodge #8 in New York. He would later rise to become a 32nd degree Mason and Shriner, according to Professor Johan von Leers, in 'The Power Behind the President,' Stockholm, 1941, page 148

When Woodrow Wilson took office, he appointed FDR Assistant US Secretary to the Navy. FDR would hold this position throughout World War I and until the end of Wilson's presidency. His connections would prove to be advantageous when he was rebuked by Congress for his part in the Newport, US Navy homosexual entrapment scandal in the spring of 1920. A Senate subcommittee concluded that FDR had committed perjury before a Naval Court of Inquiry about his investigation of a homosexual corruption ring at the Newport, Rhode Island, Naval Station. FDR, as Assistant Secretary of the Navy, had approved the use of decoys to entrap homosexuals (young sailors were instructed-in and ordered by FDR's lackeys to perform indecent homosexual acts but further details are truly unprintable.) To be frank I could not even bring myself to write them down.

But FDR escaped relatively unscathed, as later that same year he was still the Democratic

Party's Vice-Presidential candidate, on the ticket with Presidential candidate Ohio Governor James Cox, who eventually lost-out to Republicans Warren Harding and Calvin Coolidge.

FDR contracted polio in 1921. Withholding this disability from the public has been referred-to as a 'splendid deception.' However, the voters were deprived of important information about a candidate for the highest office. In May 1944 after he had suffered a heart attack, doctors told FDR that if he wanted to avert death, he could not work more than four-hour days but nevertheless even after this, FDR still decided to run for a fourth term. In 1944 he spent 200 days away from the White House in rest or recuperative travel and whilst from his own perspective this was simply a self-serving deception, it was effectively a fraud on the people and it damaged the country. He was utterly unfit for his high office long before the election. The lives of millions depended on the judgment of a man whose mind was warped by arteriosclerosis and the strong medication, digitalis. He had also contracted cancer.

Until he became President, FDR despite his family wealth had always personally struggled financially. He never made more than $25,000 a year as a lawyer, an occupation he had to relinquish in early 1923 because of his polio and his only business was his Warm Springs resort, bought with his mother's money, which he ran as a health spa. But then as a condition of running for governor in 1928 his Democratic 'kingmaker,' John Jakob Raskob paid-off his $250,000 debts.

Raskob's rise through the ranks of the *DuPont* weapons/chemical industry began in 1900, when Pierre du Pont hired him as a bookkeeper for his steel and railway businesses. Raskob then became Pierre's private secretary, his assistant in 1902, assistant treasurer 1911 and treasurer on the Executive Committee in 1914.

By 1915, *DuPont* was beginning to absorb *General Motors*. With 3,000 shares, Pierre du Pont was GM's largest minority stockholder and eventually became GM's chairman and put Raskob on the board. Their goal was to have all GM cars use paint, varnish, lacquer and artificial leather from *DuPont*. By 1918, Raskob was GM's vice president and chaired its Finance Committee and in 1919, Pierre placed family 'friends' onto GM's board, Nobel, their European gunpowder ally and J.P. Morgan and the following year, with financial trickery and $35 million of Morgan's money, du Pont's empire now owned GM.

Raskob, by 1928 now dubbed the 'Wizard of Wall Street,' informed the bankster-controlled press that GM's value would skyrocket. This falsely boosted the stock by almost $50 million, to $3.3 billion, the highest yet reached by any US industrial stock. A few weeks later, its fall caused a panic, the 'bull market' collapsed and Raskob, resigned as du Pont's treasurer.

During the Roaring Twenties, insider trading was not yet illegal. Some brokerages, including *J.P. Morgan* and *Kuhn Loeb*, sold shares to 'preferred' clients, at below current prices. Of course, this scam removed money from small investors and made the rich, richer. Raskob was himself on J.P. Morgan's 'preferred list' and in 1929, he used this advantage to unfairly profit on *Standard Brands* and *United Corporation* stocks.

Raskob was also instrumental in persuading ordinary Americans to trust Wall Street. Just before the 1929 Crash, the *New York Times* had quoted him as saying... *"Prudent investors are now buying stocks in huge quantities and will profit handsomely when this hysteria is over."* That same year, his famous article 'Everybody Ought to be Rich' in the *Ladies Home Journal*, said that investments of $15 a month, would yield $80,000 in 20 years and meanwhile, his millionaire, bankster friends were busily selling stocks to get out of the market before the Crash.

Raskob also strongly promoted the 40-hour, five-day working week policy. In 'What Next in America' (*North American Review*, November 1929), he justified this policy not through any concern for the welfare of the workers, but as a 'good business move,' in order to... *"...give workers additional time...to function as consumers of what they produce. We have got production geared up to such speed...that we are faced with...the problem of getting the goods...consumed. Every manufacturer, every capitalist concerned with financing industry, knows this.... If we add a full Saturday holiday...there will be an immediate and tremendous increase in...consumption of automobiles, tires, gasoline, oil and roads."*

Of course the plan succeeded. Workers did spend more, thus funnelling their earnings directly back to the back to the bankster-industrialists from whence they had just come. But the ongoing Depression soon stopped their spending as the economy ground to a full stop.

Despite all the atrocities occurring at Stalin's behest and well-known as they were to the Americans, on 17th November 1933, FDR became the first United States President to formally recognise the Communist Soviet Union as a legitimate nation, thereby legitimising the already ongoing trade and commerce with the Soviets. This recognition acknowledged the actual situation whereby Ukrainian grain and other raw materials were being sold in exchange for British and American machinery.

FDR imposed central planning through his 'New Deal,' regulations and programmes. His close advisor Douglas said that... *"The present pseudo-planned economy leads relentlessly into the complete autocracy and tyranny of the Collectivist State."* But FDR broke every campaign promise he had made and the New Deal was exactly the opposite of what he had promised. He had promised... *"I propose to you that the government, big and little, be made solvent and that the example be set by the President of the United States and his cabinet...Stop the deficits! Stop the deficits!"* He also falsely promised to *"...reduce the cost of government operations by 25 percent"* and called for a sound gold-based currency. Instead, Roosevelt engaged in a huge spending-spree and implemented the first twelve planks of the Socialist Party platform, which in substance, was the New Deal. Of course, the New Deal was not his idea—it was the will of his hidden masters, the Marxist-Zionist banksters.

From 1933 to 1936, government expenditures increased by more than 83 percent and he closed many non-Federal Reserve banks with no intention or thought of ever re-opening them (only central banks are needed in Marxist economics.) But after two years the New Deal was such a failure through waste, mismanagement and outright corruption that FDR had to introduce a 'New, New Deal." The New Deal has been called 'a study in economic confusion.' Herbert Hoover, the 1928 Democrat Presidential Nominee, Alfred E. Smith and the 1924 Democrat Presidential Nominee, John Davis, all dubbed the New Deal 'communistic.'

Gottfried Haberler, Professor of Economics at Harvard and President of the *American Economic Association* and (allegedly) the world's leading authority on economic depressions, called the failure of the New Deal a policy disaster *"...unparalleled in other countries."* And Winston Churchill said in 1937 that *"The Washington administration has waged so ruthless a war on private enterprise that the US...is actually...leading the world back into the trough of depression."* The New Deal was repudiated by the voters in 1938 and the Republicans took effective control of Congress. FDR had made the depression worse and prolonged it at his controller's behest and all exactly as planned.

When he was elected there were 11,586,000 unemployed and in 1939, seven years later, there were still 11,369,000 unemployed. In 1932 there were 16,620,000 on relief and in 1939, after seven years there were 19,648,000 on relief.

FDR supporter Merle Thorpe wrote in 1935, *"We have given legislative status, either in whole or in part, to eight of the ten points of the Communist Manifesto of 1848; and, as some point out, done a better job of implementation than Russia."*

Religious leader, Colonel Eugene N. Sanctuary's pamphlet '*Is the New Deal Communist?*' made a point-by-point comparison of it, to Marx's 1848 programme. Indeed, every aspect of the New Deal, whether it was one that encouraged recovery or not, was a choice unerringly true to the essential design of totalitarian, Communist government...

1. To extend the power of executive government, to rule by decrees and rules and regulations of its own making (between 1933 and 1943 FDR issued 3,556 Executive orders)
2. To strengthen its hold on the economic life of the nation
3. To extend power over the individual—the domestication of individuality
4. To degrade the parliamentary principle
5. To impair the independent Constitutional judicial power
6. To weaken all other powers—private enterprise and finance, state and local government

It is almost amusing that FDR built a cult of personality just as Stalin had (it is necessary in a tyranny because in rule by men, loyalty is not to law or country but to a person. Power then depends on such a cult.)

In early April 1933, in a move which mimicked that of Lenin's 1917 decree, FDR confiscated the gold holdings of private US citizens at a price of $20.67 per ounce on the grounds of 'national emergency.' Any citizens who did not comply with this unconstitutional 'law' were subject to $10,000 fines and / or imprisonment. Then less than one year later in January 1934, FDR suddenly set the value of an ounce of gold at $35 per ounce, and a few months later he also doubled the price of silver. In effect, these actions were an outright theft from the US middle classes, whilst larger holders and hoarders of gold and silver who kept their assets in foreign accounts, in other words, the banksters, made an instant 70% return on their holdings.

In January 1933, bankster Bernard Baruch had told FDR's son-in-law, Curtis Dall, that he personally held almost one third of the entire world's silver. Thus Baruch and many others of his ilk made a huge fortune when the price of silver was raised, whilst as usual, all American small businessmen and farmers suffered.

This gold confiscation legislation / advice derived from the insidious *Council on Foreign Relations* and the Federal Reserve Bank Board and in implementing this policy in his first year in office, FDR showed where his real loyalties lay, and that was to the international banksters.

In 1933, both Stalin and Roosevelt consolidated their leadership positions in their respective countries and for the next twelve years they autocratically dictated global geo-political decisions although they were not League of Nations members.

"There is in Chicago and in a very large part of the country, more suffering than there was in 1933 when the President came into office. It is a common sight to see children salvaging food from garbage cans." Grace Abbot, 1936

"Mr. Roosevelt made depression and unemployment a chronic fact in American life." Labour leader, John L. Lewis

"The story that Wall Street bankers planned to overthrow FDR in 1933 still makes the rounds in 2007. Recently, the BBC named George W. Bush's grandfather, Prescott Bush as one of the conspirators. The NWO apparently still considers Roosevelt and the New Deal as propaganda assets. They want us to think the bankers don't run the government...

The Illuminati bankers staged the coup to give FDR credibility as Wall Street's nemesis. As I will show, they routinely used such tricks to build up their Presidential puppet. The conspirators (members of the American Liberty League) approached retired Major General Smedley Darlington Butler to use 500,000 veterans to remove FDR and become a Mussolini-like figure.

Butler was absolutely the LAST man you would ask if you were serious. The most decorated Marine in history; Gen. Smedley Butler recently had been forced to resign by Herbert Hoover for calling Mussolini a 'mad dog' and warning that his fascist cohorts 'were about to break loose in Europe.' Butler refused to retract his remarks and thus became a national hero overnight.

However, if you wanted someone to expose your coup (as he did; thought it 'smacked of treason,') Butler was the 'go-to' person. Nor was Butler fond of Wall Street. He was touring the

nation with a speech stating that the bankers used the US army as 'gangsters for capitalism,' thugs and debt collectors. 'Looking back on it, I feel that I could have given Al Capone a few hints,' Butler said. 'The best he could do was ... operate his racket in three districts. I operated on three continents.' ('War is a Racket,' 1933)

'There was definitely something crazy about the whole affair,' remarked Curt Gentry. 'Butler who had gained prominence for speaking out against fascism, being asked to become an American Duce.' ('J. Edgar Hoover' p. 203)

Nevertheless, Gentry and most other historians accepted the tale, indicating their function as highly paid flacks. The story received its widest currency in Jules Archer's book 'The Plot to Seize the White House' (1973). Judging from Archer's other works, he is either the Illuminati's best propagandist or biggest dupe (or both.)

Who was FDR?

For the answer, we are indebted to a book by a courageous honest, public-spirited New York doctor, Emmanuel Josephson: 'The Strange Death of Franklin D. Roosevelt' (1948)

FDR was the scion of two Illuminati families, the Delanos, and the Roosevelts. He was related to a dozen US Presidents: four on the Roosevelt side and eight on the Delano side. He was a third cousin of King George VI and Queen Elizabeth.

These families have some Jewish antecedents but they also have Dutch, German, Swedish and principally English blood. FDR's mother's father, Warren Delano made a fortune in the opium trade. His father James Roosevelt was Vice President of a railway and director of several companies.

FDR was a spoiled brat who always changed the rules to suit his whims. He was tutored privately, and failed law school but allowed to enter the bar anyway. He never held a real job. In the 1920's, he helped float some stock market scams. As Governor and later President, he was extremely suggestible, evasive and shifty.

Louis Howe created his public persona and did his thinking for him. Howe was FDR's 'alter and wiser ego.' FDR had a small army of speech writers and sometimes there were screwups. For his Democratic nomination acceptance in 1932, he was handed two speeches with diametrically opposed views and read them both.

After his attack of encephalomyelitis, the Rockefellers gave him a health spa at Warm Springs, Georgia. They subsequently funnelled millions of dollars to FDR in the guise of charitable contributions to his 'foundation.' (Dr. Josephson found that the institution did not accept charity cases and didn't issue financial statements.) In Josephson's words, 'Roosevelt was magnificently bribed to run for office. By the end of 1930, some $700,000 was poured into the coffers of the foundation ... [FDR] was the pathetic puppet of conspirators scheming the destruction of democracy and the establishment of an American monarchy.'

In return, the US Treasury under FDR spent hundreds of millions bribing Saudi King Ibn Saud and building oil infrastructure in Saudi Arabia to benefit Standard Oil. Josephson said the basic doctrines of the Rockefeller Empire are 'feudalistic monarchic *government'... 'monopoly of every necessity of life and of national existence, and absolute dictatorship...'*

The rich must 'divide and rule': 'The people must be dealt with not as Americans but as minorities set at each other's throats, Labour vs. Capital, Black vs. White, Catholic vs. Protestant, Christian vs. Jew for e.g.' He could have added male vs. female and gay vs. straight.

Rich degenerate inbreeds running for President naturally pretend to defend the public good. Naturally their banker-sponsors are willing to feign displeasure and opposition.

FDR learned the game from his cousin Theodore Roosevelt who pretended to be a 'trust buster' whilst remaining a creation of the trusts and giving the country to them. The contributors to FDR's 1932 campaign include a 'Who's Who' of the US business elite, the same people who supposedly tried to overthrow him a year later: Hearst, Rockefeller, Morgan, Baruch, Du Pont and Astor. In 1933, a group of 'publicity men' advised that fascism was becoming unpopular in America and FDR could score points by opposing the Nazis. 'They suggested that Hearst and his publications launch a sham attack on Roosevelt and at the same time pretend to support Nazism and Fascism, thus throwing the Anti-Nazis and Anti-Fascists into the Roosevelt camp.'

'As the perverter's of public opinion expected, the gullible public raged at Hearst and flocked to the standards of Roosevelt, blind to the fact that he was giving them another of the same brand of dictatorship.'

The antagonism was an utter sham. Hearst employed FDR's son Elliot, his daughter and her husband! Similarly the public enmity of the munitions manufacturing DuPonts was also a sham. Ethel Du Pont married FDR Jr.

'The Liberty League was then set up for the ostensible purpose of attacking Roosevelt and fighting his re-election. This served to throw the entire pacifist vote into Roosevelt's camp and helped reassure his re-election.' Clearly the 'Fascist Coup' was just another clever ploy invented by the 'publicity men.'

Curtis Dall was a banker and FDR's son-in-law. He portrays the President not as a leader but as a 'quarterback' with little actual power. The 'coaching staff' consisted of a coterie of handlers ('advisers' like Louis Howe, Bernard Baruch and Harry Hopkins) who represented the international banking cartel. For Dall, FDR ultimately was a traitor manipulated by 'World Money' and motivated by conceit and personal ambition. (Dall, FDR: My Exploited Father-In-Law 1970)

The 1933 'Banker's Coup' is indicative of the trouble the financial elite takes, to deceive the public." henrymakow.com

In 1934, the 32nd degree Mason Henry Wallace, FDR's Secretary of Agriculture, Vice President and the 1948 US Communist party-endorsed Presidential candidate, submitted a proposal to the President to mint a coin depicting Illuminati / Masonic symbology on the obverse and reverse. Roosevelt, approved of the idea but opted instead to place it on the dollar bill.

"...the Latin phrase Novus Ordo Seclorum impressed me as meaning the 'New Deal' of the Ages. Roosevelt as he looked at the coloured reproduction of the Seal was first struck with the representation of the 'All-Seeing Eye,' a Masonic representation of the Great Architect of the Universe. Next he was impressed with the idea that the foundation for the new order of the ages had been laid in 1776 (May 1st, 1776, founding of the Illuminati) but would be completed only under the eye of the Great Architect. Roosevelt like myself was a 32nd degree Mason. He suggested that the Seal be put on the dollar bill rather than a coin." Henry Wallace, in a letter dated 6th February 1951

Illuminati symbology on American currency

Once freed from the worst excesses of the New Deal, the economy showed some signs of life once more. Unemployment dropped to 18 percent in 1935, 14 percent in 1936, and even lower in 1937 but by 1938, it was back up to 20 percent as the economy slumped again. The stock market crashed again, nearly 50 percent between August 1937 and March 1938 and the 'economic stimulus' of Roosevelt's New Deal had achieved a real 'first,' a depression within a depression.

FDR's political views were shaped by a British MI-6 agent named Louis Howe whom he first encountered in 1912 and who was always very secretive about his political beliefs. Howe saw in FDR an ambitious, ruthless young man with no moral compass or real ideas of his own. Over years of conversations, and speech writing and agenda planning, and especially during the onset of FDR's polio when Howe lived with them and they depended on him, Howe shaped both FDR and Eleanor.

He was their brain and they were his disciples. He taught them an ideology and they thus became ideologues. In a *Cosmopolitan* article in April 1934, Howe wrote quoting his protégé FDR, that *"...the time has arrived to build a new kind of government founded on the doctrine of the good neighbour and not the cruel doctrine of 'rugged individualism.'"* In other words, FDR stood for the obliteration of individualism at the hands of a ruthless, all powerful state—aka communism.

In August, 1935, Huey Long announced his Presidential campaign. He recognised that wealth was being rapidly transferred from ordinary, working Americans to the banksters and so Long proposed the 'Share our Wealth' programme which decreed that no individual family could hold more than $5 million in wealth and receive more than $1 million in annual income. An accomplished orator and statesman, Long had pointed out many of the fallacies of Roosevelt and the New (Zionist bankster) Deal and many people were now taking notice. The banksters were also taking notice and were become concerned by Huey Long, as the Great Depression threatened to thrust Long into the Presidency.

In March of 1935, Huey Long made a broadcast and had it placed in the Congressional record. But as we know, FDR was totally controlled by the banksters, and their agents and there was no way that were going to let some upstart, 'firebrand Southerner' become President at this critical juncture. On Sunday, 8th September 1935, Huey Long was at the Capital building in Baton Rouge, Louisiana, attending a session called by Judge Benjamin Pavy, one of Long's political enemies. As Long, walked along a corridor in the building, a Dr. Carl Weiss (actually Pavy's son in law) calmly walked-up to him and shot him in the abdomen. In response, Long's bodyguards shot the Jewish doctor over thirty times, killing him outright (unsurprisingly.)

Huey Long's wound was not life threatening as such, but the bullet had hit a kidney, and that caused blood poisoning. Two surgeons were despatched from New Orleans, but Dr Arthur Vidrine, a Jewish physician had other ideas. He declared that he would have to perform emergency surgery before they had a chance to arrive and when the two surgeons arrived they were appalled at Vidrine's obvious and calculatingly incompetent job. They went so far as to openly state that he was an accomplice of the attacker. Long never recovered from the operation, dying almost immediately. His funeral was attended by well over 100,000 mourners.

Huey Long was remembered as Louisiana's greatest governor. His state tax system basically used the wealthy to pay for Louisiana schools. He reduced Louisiana's illiteracy rate from 22%, down to 5% and the road system went from 300 miles to 3200 miles of paved roads. Among his Presidential promises whilst campaigning, was the restriction of the power of the Federal Reserve and to tax the wealthy and the corporations appropriately. His life mission was to redistribute the wealth away from the banksters.

Huey Long without doubt, had been a problem for the banksters and a barrier to FDR's re-election. His death was, without doubt, very convenient for them, and very timely. Notes and recordings found by Mimi L. Eustis, written by her father Samuel Todd Churchill, who was a highly regarded member of a New Orleans secret society called the 'Mystick Krewe of Comus,' provide even more compelling details of an assassination conspiracy.

However let us now leave the United States for the time being and concentrate on events taking place across the Atlantic Ocean, most specifically in Germany.

The German elections of 1932 were held with the ever-present threat of open violence. The 'far right' and 'far left' factions were nowhere near the resolution of their differences and violent squabbles had become a regular occurrence. Neither side would ever admit to being the instigators of the violence and whichever faction you believe to be the initial aggressor, we only need to look at the track-record of the Soviet Communists in this regard to get some inkling of a clue as to where the majority of the blame lay, in my view. Anyway, regardless of the direction of blame, Red paramilitaries frequently clashed openly in the streets with NSDAP 'brown shirts,' but this apart, it was Hitler's

NSDAP that recorded major gains, winning 230 Reichstag seats. It was now the largest political party, but nevertheless still had no outright majority in the 608 member body.

However, political deadlock meant that another election became a necessity in November that same year resulting in a house composed of, NSDAP: 196, Social Democrats: 121, Communists: 100, Centre Party: 70, and 9 other minor parties split about 100 seats. Germany's chaotic political scene was bitterly divided.

The brutal 'austerity' measures of Chancellor Heinrich Brüning had shrunk the national economy by about 25%, but still did not prevent the German budget deficit from growing and unemployment exceeded 30% as 250,000 desperate Germans committed suicide from 1930-1932.

In addition to a Parliamentary Reichstag and a Chancellor, Germany also had a President with unique powers. President Paul von Hindenburg was a World War I Field Marshall and a national hero and politically, he was a non-Party 'independent.' On the basis of NSDAP's 196 seats and in order to end the deadlock, Hitler petitioned Hindenburg to appoint him as Chancellor, but Hindenburg refused the request.

So, after two parliamentary elections in 1932, Germany remained virtually ungovernable as the Socialist and Communist Parties continue to confront the NSDAP, often with violence. President Hindenburg gradually became extremely concerned that the Communists would exploit the chaos and attempt another revolution, but he eventually came to the conclusion that Hitler and the NSDAP were the only way to prevent this undesirable situation.

And so, in order to protect Germany from Communism, on 30th January 1933, Hindenburg finally relented and appointed Hitler as Chancellor of Germany. Hitler's powers were fairly limited at this stage, but the NSDAP now had predominance in what was still a very unstable situation. But the Communists did not give-u that easily and were constantly trying to destabilise Hitler's government, calling for massive country-wide strikes. Meanwhile in the US, the Zionist, Sulzberger-owned *New York Times* began an anti-Hitler campaign on its front page of 31st January 1933 and Zionist Sarnoff's *NBC* and Zionist Paley's *CBS* soon followed suit.

Four weeks after Hitler's appointment as Chancellor, Communist agitators burned-down the Reichstag. The police caught a Dutch Communist named Marinus van der Lubbe who had recently arrived in Germany, in the act. The fire was meant to have been the catalyst for a Red-instigated and Russian-funded civil war, aimed at toppling the crumbling Weimar state before Hitler and NSDAP could become established. Whilst evidence would now tend to favour the premise that van der Lubbe was a renegade member of an insignificant Dutch Communist group, this did not stop Hitler from attempting to make great capital out of the event. He immediately accused the German Communist party of a 'conspiracy' to destroy his new government and used it to fuel a massive propaganda campaign and clamp-down on them in any way he could.

So loud, long and disproportionate were the NSDAP protestations that it soon began to sound as though '...*the lady doth protest too much.*' This actually back-fired on

Hitler when the world began to suspect that it was all a 'false flag' operation and committed by Hitler's own henchmen in order to generate an excuse for the backlash against the Communists—but this was not the case despite Hitler's 'own goal.' However the bankster-dominated world's press had plenty to say about it all and of course they lost no time in heavily promoting the fiction that it was Hitler, Goebbels et al that had performed a 'self-inflicted wound' for political gain.

"…Author in chief of the 'Hitler, Göring and Goebbels did it' fiction, was Willy Münzenberg, the propaganda genius of the German Communist Party. He had managed to escape the German police roundup on February 28th and to flee to Paris. Willy, a dynamic little fellow full of charm and imagination, whom I was later to meet frequently in Paris, soon set up a workshop in the student quarter on the left bank. Then, with the help of a small team of collaborators he proceeded to fake up a number of stories all going to show that the Reichstag fire was a Nazi conspiracy. Every little bit of fact that came the way of the team was seized, twisted and embellished to make up the 'dossier' which was promptly published in two 'Brown Books.'

The recipe by which they worked was simple enough. For instance when Walter Gempp, the Berlin Fire chief who had personally directed the operations in the burning Reichstag, was dismissed because he had accepted extensive bribes from a fire extinguisher concern, Willy Münzenberg and his merry men immediately turned him into a brave anti-Nazi martyr. Gempp, they said, had been got rid of because he knew too much about the fire's Nazi origin, and because he had complained publicly that he had been hindered by the Nazis in his firefighting. He had complained, they alleged, that when his firemen got into the Reichstag they found at least twenty Storm troopers already there. A brilliant invention. I can vouch myself, that when I went round the burning building, we met only police officers, no Storm troopers. But it was universally accepted as the truth.

On May 8, 1933, Ernst Oberfohren, the deputy chief of the nationalist Party and a bitter opponent of his leader Hugenberg's alliance with Hitler, committed suicide out of chagrin over the way things were going in Germany.

Münzenberg at once faked up a secret document which, he alleged, Oberfohren had left behind telling the inside history of the fire. It too proved wonderfully effective. My colleague at the Manchester Guardian fell for the fake and sent a long dispatch, citing it as proof of the Nazi's guilt.

My editor immediately wanted to know why I had not done the same. So I pointed out that apart from other improbabilities contained in the alleged Oberfohren document, I was particularly doubtful concerning the validity of one of the ten points it put forward as proof of the Nazi guilt. This 'point' was not in the Manchester Guardian version but it was contained in the copy of the document I had seen. 'I think you will agree that it rather undermines the credibility of Herr Oberfohren's alleged revelations—if indeed he was their author. Listen to this!' And then I read him the passage … 'Hitler's constant companion and friend, the English journalist Delmer,' it said, 'telegraphed full details of the fire to his newspaper before it was discovered, and the name of van der Lubbe as being the culprit.'

The Editor agreed that perhaps we had not been scooped after all. Münzenberg and his team freely seasoned their inventions with Nazi names to give them the stamp of authenticity. Heines the Stormtrooper's leader they said, had led a posse of his men into the Reichstag, through the subterranean passage connecting it with Göring's palace. There they had then poured petrol over the benches in the assembly hall. The story was believed all the world over. The fact that Heines was four hundred miles away at Gleiwitz in Silesia, when this was supposed to be happening, did not detract from it at all.

The Münzenberg team declared that the protocol drawn up by Commissary Heisig and Commissary Zirpins during their interrogation of van der Lubbe and signed by him had been destroyed because in it van der Lubbe said that he had not laid the fire in the debating chamber. 'Someone else' he was alleged to have said, 'must have done that.' He had only set fires in the restaurant and the corridors. In fact the protocol was never destroyed. It still exists today and extracts from it were recently published. In it—as I have already stated—van der Lubbe states that he was responsible for all the fires in the building and had no helpers. And he continued to protest his sole responsibility for the fire at the trial—right up to the last.

When the Nazis tried to contradict the 'Brown Book's' accusations they were too late. The world, shocked by their appalling crimes against the Jews and horrified by the lawlessness of the Storm troopers, was only too ready to believe that the fire was their work.

The legend first sponsored by Münzenberg grew and grew. After the collapse of Hitler, it became standard practice for former Nazi high-ups to alibi themselves with some new piece of 'evidence' proving that the Nazis fired the Reichstag. But in almost all instances they merely elaborated some point in Willy Münzenberg's ingenious myth. Even today, when the 'Hitler, Göring and Goebbels did it' legend has been thoroughly exploded as a result of the meticulous and painstaking historical investigation done by the German writer Fritz Tobias, I fear it will still live on among the historical lumber filling the minds of most people. But not, I hope, the minds of those who read this book." Sefton Delmer, British journalist and author, *'Trail Sinister,' 1961*

Within hours, Hitler and his staff had orchestrated raids on the homes of around 400 suspected Communist sympathisers and the next morning, Hitler forced the institution of the Reichstag Fire Decree and the implementing of Article 48 of the Weimar Constitution, which authorised President Hindenburg, who by that time did whatever Hitler commanded, to completely suspend civil liberties in this time of 'national emergency.'

Article 48 was meant to be a temporary measure, to be revoked once the emergency was over, but it was never revoked and overnight, German citizens lost the rights to free expression, assembly, form groups, due process of law, and left them subject to complete government control over their homes, property, companies and several search and seizure options. Hitler from that point on, then became a dictator.

Then, Hitler arranged another election, scheduled for only five days later and as a result of the anti-Communist fervour generated in the aftermath of the fire, the Nazis cruised to a crushing victory. Goebbels was installed as the Reich Minister of Public

Enlightenment and Propaganda and Göring created the infamous Gestapo in November of 1933. Van der Lubbe was tried, found guilty and in 1934, beheaded.

The newspaper headline below depicts what really happened in March of 1933. World Jewry or Judea (actually Zionism and not the Jewish people) declared war on Germany—and not the other way around as is disingenuously portrayed to be the case. At this point in time, there had been no German pogroms against the Jews, no excessively anti-Jewish feelings manifest and no legislation discriminating against them; indeed the Jewish element of the German economy was regarded as being an essential component of the hoped-for wider economic recovery and prosperity of the country, its economy being as stagnant as it was, in this period prior to Hitler's mass re-armament of the German forces.

The headline of the British Daily Express, 24th March 1933

Jewish Zionist leaders were quoted as calling for 'Holy War' against the entire German people. The article reveals that... "...*the Jewish wholesaler will quit his house, the banker his stock exchange, the merchant his business and the beggar his humble hut, in order to join the holy war against Hitler's people. ....Germany is now confronted with an international boycott of its trade, its finances, and its industry."*

"The war against Germany will be waged by all Jewish communities, conferences, congresses ... by every individual Jew. Thereby the war against Germany will ideologically enliven and promote our interests, which require that Germany be wholly destroyed. The danger for us Jews lies in the whole German people, in Germany as a whole as well as individually. It must be rendered harmless for all time .... In this war we Jews have to participate, and this with all the strength and might we have at our disposal." The Jewish newspaper, *'Natscha Retsch'*, 1933

Germany responded to the International Jewish-Zionist boycott by themselves boycotting Jewish stores and a few days later, Hitler responded to the charges being made against the new Germany, stating on the 28th March that... "*Lies and slander of positively hair-raising perversity are being launched against Germany.*"

Growing 'anti-Semitism' in Germany and by the German government in response to the boycott played right into the hands of the Elite Zionist leaders as indeed they had hoped it would. Prior to the escalation of anti-Semitism as a result of the boycott, the majority of German Jews had little sympathy for the Zionist cause of promoting the immigration of world Jewry to Palestine. Making the situation in Germany as uncomfortable for the Jews as possible, in cooperation with German National Socialism, was part of the Zionist plan to achieve their goal of populating Palestine with a Jewish majority.

"For all intents and purposes, the National Socialist government was the best thing to happen to Zionism in its history, for it 'proved' to many Jews that Europeans were irredeemably anti-Jewish and that Palestine was the only answer: Zionism came to represent the overwhelming majority of Jews solely by trickery and cooperation with Adolf Hitler." www.jewwatch.com

Like FDR, Hitler assumed *authoritative* power in March 1933 and as did FDR, Hitler inherited an economic disaster, but there the similarities ended. Whereas FDR implemented all of the bankster-Globalists' economic and foreign policy plans, Hitler by contrast, openly defied the architects of the New World Order by implementing the following policies:

- Withdrew Germany from the League of Nations
- Banned the Communist Party and arrested its leaders
- Replaced the national Marxist Trade Unions with company unions.
- Established the NSDAP as Germany's only political Party
- Refused to make any more reparations payments of the Versailles Treaty/ Dawes Plan
- Removed control of Germany's Reichsbank away from Warburg/Rothschild banksters and *issued his own debt free currency*
- Restricted Jewish ownership of radio and newspapers
- Cut taxes and provided tax incentives for mothers to stay at home and raise their children
- Rebuilt German infrastructure and initiated projects like the Autobahn Highway system, financed by debt-free notes paid to the workers.

On the 1st June 1933, The *Washington Post* was one of many businesses to go bankrupt during the Great Depression. Its owner Ned McLean sold the newspaper at a bankruptcy auction and the buyer was the Zionist, former Federal Reserve Chairman and active member of the CFR, Eugene Meyer. Meyer immediately changed The Post's editorial policy, transforming the influential newspaper into a pro-FDR, anti-Germany and soft-on-Stalin, Communist-sympathising propaganda sheet. He then almost immediately fired the current editor for refusing to endorse diplomatic recognition of the Soviet Union.

In fact the *Post* continued to run at a loss for the next twenty years but Meyer did not care. He had bought the Post for influence, not profit.

In fact the Zionist ownership of American media began years earlier. David Sarnoff was born in a small Jewish village in Czarist Russia and immigrated to New York in 1900 but by 1919, Sarnoff was General Manager of *RCA Radio*. In 1926, Sarnoff's *RCA* formed *NBC*, the first major broadcast network in the United States and indeed it was Sarnoff who was instrumental in building the AM broadcasting radio business which became the pre-eminent public radio standard for the majority of the 20th century. During World War II, Sarnoff (who had no military experience) served under General Eisenhower as a Brigadier General and 'Communications Consultant.'

When television in America was born, under the auspices of the National Broadcast Corporation, the first TV show aired at the New York World's Fair and was introduced by Sarnoff himself. Leadership of RCA-NBC eventually passed-down to Sarnoff's eldest son, Robert, one of the husbands of Felicia Schiff-Warburg of the two prominent bankster families. Franklin Roosevelt Jr. (son of FDR) was incidentally, also an ex-husband of Felicia Schiff-Warburg. The Sarnoff Family in fact controlled RCA-NBC TV for more than 60 years.

William S. Paley (Paloff) was the son of Jewish immigrants who came from the Ukraine region of the Czarist Russian Empire and in 1928, the 27-year old businessman secured the majority ownership of the *CBS Radio* network (of which his father Samuel Paloff had been part-owner.) Within the next decade, Paley expanded *CBS* into a national institution with 114 affiliate stations. During World War II, Paley, like Sarnoff of *NBC*, served under General Eisenhower as a colonel in the *Psychological Warfare* branch of the Office of War Information.

As the absolute ruler of the *CBS radio* (and later TV) empire, Paley is without question, one of the most powerful figures of the 20th Century and with David Sarnoff controlling RCA-NBC, and Paley in control of CBS, the pre-TV medium of radio had rapidly fallen under absolute Zionist control.

Albert Voegler, Gustav Krupp, Alfred Krupp, Fritz Thyssen and Emile Kirdorf who had provided some of the funds for rise of Nazism, began complaining that one of Hitler's early supporters, Ernst Roehm and several other leaders of the SA were homosexuals. Ernst Roehm had been with Hitler since the DAP days of 1919. He rose to SA Chief of Staff, transforming the Brown Shirt militia from a handful of hardened thugs and embittered ex-soldiers into an effective fighting force, five-hundred thousand strong, in fact the chief instrument of Nazi enforcement. Hitler needed Rohm's military skill and could rely on his personal loyalty but Hitler as Fuehrer (leader) had become wary of Roehm's huge, loyal power-base within the Party and Roehm's blatant homosexuality, ignored by Hitler for over a decade was increasingly being seen as a detriment to the image of the *NSDAP*.

So, on 29th June 1934, during what would become known as the 'Night of the Long Knives,' Hitler had Ernst Roehm arrested. Around 200 other senior SA officers were also arrested and many were shot as soon as they were captured. Hitler wanted to pardon Roehm because of his long service to the Party, but under pressure from Goering and Himmler, Hitler agreed to eliminate him. He insisted that Roehm be allowed to commit suicide, but when he refused, two SS men shot him. This drastically reduced the power of the SA and they were in fact replaced by the SS as the dominant force in Germany.

Following the 'Night of the Long Knives,' nothing stood between Hitler and absolute power in Germany, except the 86-year-old German President, Paul von Hindenburg, who now lay close to death at his country estate in East Prussia. Although Hindenburg was in increasingly bad health, the Nazis ensured that whenever Hindenburg appeared in public, it was always in Hitler's company.

During these appearances, Hitler made a great show of the utmost respect and reverence for the President but in private, continued to detest Hindenburg and expressed the hope that *the old reactionary* would die as soon as possible, so that Hitler could merge the offices of Chancellor and President into one.

Hitler was always very conscious of the fact that the President was the Supreme Commander-In-Chief of the German armed forces, and that as Hindenburg was still a revered figure in the German Army, if the President decided to sack Hitler as Chancellor, there was little doubt that the *Reichswehr* would side with Hindenburg. Thus, as long as Hindenburg lived, Hitler was always very careful to avoid offending him. In fact Hindenburg remained in office until his death from lung cancer at his home in East Prussia in August 1934, and as far as Hitler was concerned, Hindenburg's demise could not have been timed any better. He had just broken the grip of the unruly SA and cemented the support of the Army's General Staff and now he just needed to resolve the issue of who would succeed Hindenburg as president.

Hitler, of course decided that it was he that should succeed Hindenburg, but not as President, but instead as 'Führer' (leader) of the German people. However, there were still a few influential old-time conservatives in Germany who hoped for a return of the monarchy or perhaps some kind of non-Nazi nationalist government after Hindenburg's death. Although they loathed democracy, they also loathed the excesses of the Hitler regime. These were proud men from the 1800s reared in the days of Princes and Kings and ancient codes of honour.

Among those conservatives was Franz von Papen, Germany's Vice Chancellor, who was a confidant of President Hindenburg. Just before the Night of the Long Knives, Hindenburg had told him, *"Papen, things are going badly. See what you can do."* But Papen had been unable to do anything except to barely escape with his own life. However, he had one last 'trick up his sleeve.' In April 1934 he almost convinced Hindenburg to declare in his will that Germany should return to a constitutional monarchy upon his death. Hindenburg at first agreed to insert it in his will, but then changed his mind and instead put it in the form of a personal letter to Hitler, to be delivered after his death. However, for Hitler and his followers, the idea of returning to a monarchy at this point was utterly laughable. Hitler had the Reichstag completely in his control and exercised his power to prevent any such thing from ever happening. He simply had a law drafted abolishing the office of President and proclaiming himself as Führer.

Within hours of Hindenburg's death, the Reichstag announced the following law, back-dated to 1st August:

"The Reich Government has enacted the following law which is hereby promulgated:

Section 1. The office of Reich President will be combined with that of Reich Chancellor. The existing authority of the Reich President will consequently be transferred to the Führer and Reich Chancellor, Adolf Hitler. He will select his deputy.

Section 2. This law is effective as of the time of the death of Reich President von Hindenburg."

The law was technically illegal since it violated provisions of the German constitution concerning Presidential succession as well as the Enabling Act of 1933 which forbade Hitler from altering the presidency. But that did not matter much anymore and unsurprisingly, no-one raised any objections.

In September, 1934, at the annual Nuremberg Nazi Party rallies, a euphoric Hitler proclaimed, *"The German form of life is definitely determined for the next thousand years. The 'Age of Nerves' of the nineteenth century has found its close with us. There will be no revolution in Germany for the next thousand years."*

His much-vaunted 'Thousand Year Reich,' had just begun—or so he believed. However, the banksters had other ideas.

By 1936, Hitler's economic recovery, based on his own debt-free currency had become the most stunning economic revival in world history. While the rest of the world remained in the vice-like grip of the banksters' great depression, Germany boomed. This however had by no means gone unnoticed by the banksters.

Unemployment, which had been at 30% a few years earlier, was now under 5%. Productivity was up exponentially, as were wages, and by freeing Germany from the heavy taxation of the Weimar Republic, the cruel burden of the Versailles Treaty, and the perpetual interest costs of Weimar's debt-based Central Bank currency, Hitler had unleashed the private economy whilst using the public sector wisely.

Unlike FDR's wasteful and useless, sham public works programmes, Hitler's public works were useful investments, improving the lives of the German people beyond all recognition. Low taxes, lean government, *debt-free currency* and a business-friendly environment were the 'secrets' of Hitler's economic miracle, and of his universal popularity amongst the grateful German people.

Along with the stunning economic rebound, freed from the clutches of the banksters, the re-born Germany also experienced a cultural and moral rebirth. The NSDAP, whose membership was open to all Germans of sound moral character, swept-away all the pornography and degeneracy and debauchery that had thrived under the Weimar State. Classical art made a strong comeback and so-called 'modern art' was relegated to its proper place—as an object of ridicule. The future looked extremely bright for Germany.

Now back to the USA again to examine more closely, the events of the 6th May 1937.

For some strange reason, there were twenty-two photographers present at 7 pm to film the arrival of the German airship, the *Hindenburg* in a New Jersey airfield. This would seem quite excessive for an event which had already occurred twenty times in the previous year at the same field, without incident so why would this event require so many photographers, five of whom were newsreel photographers?

The *Hindenburg* was behind schedule by exactly 12 hours, it had been supposed to land at 7 am. Both the captain and first officer admitted they were wary of a possible bomb attempt because of the current tensions with Germany and sabotage was maybe a serious possibility, yet it was strictly not to be mentioned by the compliant press after the 'accident.'

Everyone knows what supposedly happened next, but not one of the photographers caught the actual 'spark' that allegedly led to the 'explosion.' There was plenty of footage of a large fireball above the airship with a portion of the outer skin opened up and there was footage of the poor souls trying to escape the burning wreckage, but no one caught the spark on film. Strange that with twenty-two photographers present, all of whom would be vying for a potential 'scoop,' that nothing of that sort was recorded.

The most serious problem with the mainstream version of the Hindenburg 'explosion' scenario is the fact that Hydrogen, by itself, separated from oxygen in a sealed gas cell (*Hindenburg* had 16 separate cells,) does not burn. Hydrogen and oxygen need to be combined stoichiometrically for this to happen, but there was only pure hydrogen in the *Hindenburg*. Even striking a match inside a hydrogen fuel cell would do nothing at all except immediately extinguish the flame as soon as the oxygen, in solid oxide form, contained within the match-head powder was exhausted. If a static spark ignited Hindenburg, it would have started burning on the outside of the ship's skin where air containing oxygen could have mixed with the hydrogen escaping from a small leak and even if there was a static electricity spark, as had never yet occurred in 30 years of successful operation, how would a flame requiring oxygen, burn its way inside the gas cell where there is no oxygen? It is all an impossibility.

Hindenburg had instruments that would have detected and transmitted the slightest changes in gas pressure to the bridge, so any sizable leak would have caused a pressure-drop almost immediately and would have been detected and the pilots would have then sought to correct the problem. If a spark had then occurred in this split section time window, a small flame on the outside skin would have been visible, burning like the head of a small gas torch where the hole was. But there was no way that the flame could have entered the cell, and no way were there any signs of a bomb or explosion there.

Over a period of seven years, the *Graf Zeppelin* logged more than 1,000,000 miles, carried 18,000 passengers in safety and comfort and made 144 successful Atlantic crossings using only hydrogen as the buoyancy material. Airships are a simple form of anti-gravitation device. They are much more efficient for transporting people and cargo than piston driven and modern day aircraft which have to lift such heavy fuel loads and plough through the air by sheer force in order to keep them aloft. Upon reaching a height of about 500 feet, the engines are started and away they go, like a ship floating in water.

Airship use should have been expanded and continued, but of course it was shut down in favour of inefficient propeller and now jet-driven aircraft, which today consume incredibly large amounts of kerosene, otherwise known as expensive jet fuel, which is also detrimental to the environment.

One of the rare sources of 'alternative' news and information before the advent and growth of the Internet, was an irregular newsletter compiled and distributed by Hilaire du Berrier, who had served in the OSS during World War II. After the war, the OSS, *'Office of Strategic Services,'* changed its name to the CIA, *'Central Intelligence Agency'* and 'downsized,' a euphemism for eliminating the anti-Communists within its ranks. Du Berrier maintained numerous international espionage contacts and ran his 'intelligence' newsletter out of Monaco from 1958 to 2001. His very last report ironically was on 9/11/2001 at age 96. No doubt he would have had an absolute 'field-day,' with that particular subject matter!

Anyway, according to du Berrier, the man behind the Hindenburg disaster was Moe Berg -- a major league baseball player, master of languages, a Zionist, and like du Berrier an undercover OSS agent. Du Berrier's source was Tim McAuliffe, a legend of the Boston sports equipment industry . . .

McAuliffe became the friend, adviser and 'uncle' to many of the young athletes in the Boston area and the Red Sox baseball team made his apartment their 'hang-out.' Moe Berg, the catcher, told him that . . .

"We had to do something that would make that maniac (Hitler) attack us."

All McAuliffe could think of to say was, "Moe, surely you didn't kill twenty-five people just for that?" But he was too upset to say any more and finished his meal in silence whilst Berg went on talking.

"I couldn't be there myself," he said, "I was scheduled for a game, but I did the planning and four of my men carried it out."

According to Berg, they used a rifle with a telescopic sight, although the sight was totally unnecessary with a target that big. When the ship approached, the men were hiding in the bushes at Lakehurst and the first shot with an incendiary bullet set the after-end on fire.

McAuliffe lay awake that night, looking at the ceiling and thinking about Berg's 'confession.' He was too scared to tell his story to the FBI in case they charged him with being an accomplice. The more he thought about it, the more he realised it was not the work of a single man. There was teamwork involved for sure, but McAuliffe had no way of knowing how deep it ran. It was at the height of the depression and he was afraid he might lose his job.

It was some years before he started besieging editors and government officials with his story and when he did no one would listen to him. Some editors were afraid of being accused of 'anti-Semitism.' Then, when he offered to testify before a government committee, Secret Service men descended on his apartment. A man named Kent Tyler had seen the shots fired but Tyler was silenced by the government. Herb Morrison, who covered the disaster for NBC, never answered his letters."

Du Berrier further reported that 'both Washington and Berlin wanted the affair dropped.' Herman Goering in fact, ordered German intelligence to compile a report but suppressed its findings 'lest passions be aroused in Germany and around the world.' This action, I believe demonstrates that the Germans were not the bloodthirsty gang of cut-throats determined at any cost to drag the world kicking and screaming headlong into another conflagration, as they are always, constantly portrayed by the Zionist bankster's media.

Du Berrier was certainly not a man to invent things and McAuliffe, as a sports equipment dealer, was not a 'political' person and would have had no reason to invent the story about Berg, who did not become publicly known as a spy until the first book was published about him some 40 years later. And it is simply too much of a coincidence to suggest that the *Hindenburg* simply exploded, from the accepted explanation of 'static electricity,' just as she was docking, when no such discharge had ever occurred during the course of her many other trips. An incendiary bullet, fired under the cover of darkness, would have been the perfect tool to set the airship ablaze.

Moe Berg had a reputation as 'the brainiest guy in baseball.' At Princeton, where he studied seven languages, he communicated in Latin with the college's second baseman and he later attended Columbia Law School and the Sorbonne. After fifteen undistinguished seasons as a professional baseball player, he became a spy with the OSS during World War II, parachuting into Yugoslavia and interrogating Italian physicists about the German nuclear programme. Apparently, his is the only baseball card on display at CIA headquarters.

On the eve of World War II, the German chemical complex of *I.G. Farben* was the largest chemical manufacturing enterprise in the world, with extraordinary political and economic power and influence within the Nazi state. Farben has been aptly described as 'a state within a state.' The Farben cartel dated from 1925, when Hermann Schmitz (with Wall Street financial assistance) created the super-giant chemical enterprise out of six already huge German chemical companies Badische Anilin, Bayer, Agfa, Hoechst, Weiler-ter-Meer, and Griesheim-Elektron. These companies were merged to become *Internationale Gesellschaft Farbenindustrie A.G.* or *IG Farben* for short.

The declared goal of this cartel, as is the case with all giant corporations, almost without exception, was to obtain control of the global markets in their key industrial sectors of chemistry, pharmaceuticals and petrochemicals and in 1925 when this cartel was founded, its corporate value already surpassed 11 billion Reichsmarks and it employed more than 80,000 people.

Without the capital supplied by the banksters, from the City of London and Wall

Street, there would have been no *IG Farben* in the first place and almost certainly no World War II. But of course, we now know that this was all part of the ongoing, long-range evil scheme anyway.

German banksters on the Farben Board of Directors in the late 1920s included the Hamburg bankster Max Warburg, whose brother Paul Warburg was a founder of the Federal Reserve System in the United States. Probably not coincidentally, Paul Warburg was also on the board of *IG Farben's* wholly owned US subsidiary.

Hermann Schmitz, the organiser of *IG Farben* in 1925, became a prominent early Nazi and supporter of Hitler, as well as chairman of the Swiss *IG Chemic* and president of the American *IG Farben*. The Farben complex both in Germany and the United States then developed into an integral part of the formation and operation of the Nazi state machine, the Wehrmacht and the SS.

One of the strategic industries for which *IG Farben* sought global control was the pharmaceutical 'investment business.' They knew that the pharmaceutical industry is not primarily a health industry as it purports to be, but merely an investment business that defines the human body as its marketplace. Whilst presenting itself as the purveyor of health, the entire existence of this investment industry has always been based on the continuation and expansion of diseases as multi-billion dollar markets for their patented drugs. The precondition for establishing a global monopoly for this investment business with patented drugs, as it indeed still is to this day, was the attempt to systematically eliminate all non-patentable, and therefore non-profitable, natural therapies.

Several researchers have argued that Germany could not have gone to war in 1939 without *IG Farben.* Between 1927 and the beginning of World War II, Farben doubled in size, an expansion made possible in great part by American technical assistance and by American bond issues, such as the one for $30 million offered by *National City Bank*. By 1939 Farben had acquired a participation and managerial influence in almost 400 other German companies and over 500 foreign firms. Farben owned its own coal mines, its own electric power plants, iron and steel units, banks, research units, and numerous commercial enterprises. There were over 2,000 cartel agreements between Farben and foreign firms, including *Standard Oil of New Jersey, DuPont, Alcoa, Dow Chemical,* and others in the United States.

However, the *full* story of *IG Farben* and its world-wide activities before World War II will never be known, as key German records were destroyed in 1945 in anticipation of the Allied victory. However, one post-war investigation by the US War Department concluded that...

"Without I. G.'s immense productive facilities, its intense research, and vast international affiliations, Germany's prosecution of the war would have been unthinkable and impossible; Farben not only directed its energies toward arming Germany, but concentrated on weakening her intended victims, and this double-barrelled attempt to expand the German industrial potential for war and to restrict that of the rest of the world was not conceived and executed 'in the normal course of business.' The proof is overwhelming that I. G. Farben

officials had full prior knowledge of Germany's plan for world conquest and of each specific aggressive act later undertaken . . . ."

Directors of Farben companies of course were not only Germans but also prominent American financiers, but the final sentence above is yet more anti-German propaganda, unfortunately. I will shortly provide ample proof that not only did Hitler and Germany NOT intend 'world conquest' but also that Hitler, in the months and weeks leading up to the outbreak of the war and indeed in the early months of the war, before he finally realised the hopelessness of his task, actually fought an eloquent battle of words with both England and the US in an attempt to avert conflict. Indeed it was the allies, backed by a massive propaganda campaign that wanted war and the ultimate destruction of Germany—exactly as they had prior to the earlier conflict.

This 1945 US War Department report also concluded that Farben's instructions from Hitler in the pre-war period was to enable German self-sufficiency in rubber, petroleum, lubricating oils, magnesium, fibres, tanning agents, fats and explosives. To fulfil this critical task, the War Department claimed, vast sums were spent on processes to extract these war materials from indigenous German raw materials, in particular the plentiful German coal resources. This however, was simply more deception, designed to promote the myth that Germany, under Hitler was making long-term plans for the war at this time.

It is a known fact that much of the bankster-controlled financial and industrial complex in the US and Britain were complicit in the assistance in the re-building of German industrial might in the 1930s and whilst this may seem like a contradiction, there were two main reasons for this . . .

Number one was the great god of 'profit,' a subject always close to the banksters' hearts and at the forefront of virtually all of their machinations and activities, both overt and covert. But the spin-off from all these investments and joint-projects was that it was actually deliberately building-up Germany's war machine in order to provide a viable adversary to oppose in a major war. By this I mean that had Britain, France and the US decided to prosecute the war in 1931, for example, then it would have been a very short one indeed. At this juncture, there was no Hitler, the cartoon-like bogeyman to hold up as a figure of hate, no German war machine and no industrial infrastructure with which to successfully feed a war economy. In short, the allies needed a powerful enemy to oppose them and so basically decided to construct a viable one for themselves! A perfect, win-win solution.

For example, the *Standard Oil* group of companies, of which the Rockefeller bankster family owned a one-quarter (and controlling) interest, was of critical assistance in helping Germany prepare for World War II. This assistance in military preparation transpired because Germany's relatively insignificant supplies of crude petroleum were quite insufficient for modern mechanised warfare. In 1934 for instance, about 85 percent of German finished petroleum products were imported and so the solution adopted was to manufacture synthetic gasoline from its plentiful domestic coal supplies. It was this hydrogenation process of producing synthetic gasoline and iso-octane properties in gasoline that enabled Germany to go to war and this process was developed and financed by the *Standard Oil* laboratories in the United States in partnership with *IG Farben*.

IG Farben owned half of Standard Oil, and Standard owned half of Farben and the Rockefeller family owned a quarter of the whole package. It was a 'marriage made in hell,' with shysters John Foster and Allen Dulles eagerly serving and receiving their fees of course, as midwives at the birth. *Standard-Farben*, together operated more than forty concentration camps in Germany and Nazi-occupied countries, including Auschwitz, to provide an endless stream of slave labour to the American corporations operating in Germany.

Standard also supplied enormous amounts of conventional oil to the Germans. Rockefeller vessels deceptively operating under the Panamanian flag, shuttled between Mexico and Tenerife in the Canary Islands, ostensibly to supply the Spanish refinery there, but in reality, supplying the German U-boats attempting to starve Britain into submission.

The American-owned multi-national giant, *General Electric* also, incidentally, had an unparalleled role in twentieth-century history. GE electrified the Soviet Union in the 1920s and 1930s, and generously fulfilled for the Soviets, Lenin's dictat that 'Socialism = electrification.'

Indeed, *General Electric* directors were found to be enmeshed in each of these three distinct historical events; the development of the Soviet Union, the creation of Roosevelt's New Deal and the rise of pre-war Germany, which also suggests that 'Big Business,' all bankster-controlled and run of course, are keenly interested in the 'socialisation' of the world, for their own purposes and objectives, rather than the maintenance of a fair market-place in a 'free' society. *General Electric* in fact, profited handsomely from Bolshevism, from Roosevelt's New Deal socialism, and from National Socialism in Hitler's Germany.

Henry Ford was often seen as an enigma amongst the Wall Street elite. For many years in the 1920s and 30s, Ford was popularly known as an enemy of the financial establishment. He accused JP Morgan and others of using war and revolution as a road to profit and their influence in social systems as a means of personal advancement and by 1938, Henry Ford had divided financiers into two classes; those who profited from war and used their influence to bring about war for profit, and the 'constructive' financiers. Among the latter group he included the House of Morgan.

Nevertheless, Henry Ford was also one of the most famous of Hitler's foreign backers and he was rewarded in 1938 for this long-lasting support with the highest Nazi decoration for distinguished foreigners, the 'Grand Cross of the German Eagle.' The *New York Times* reported that it was the first time the Grand Cross had been awarded in the United States and was to celebrate Henry Ford's 75th birthday. Predictably, this Nazi 'award' aroused a storm of controversy in the United States and ultimately degenerated into an exchange of diplomatic notes between the German Government and the US State Department. Whilst Ford publicly protested that he was not in favour of totalitarian governments, he knowingly profited from both sides of World War II, from French and German plants producing vehicles at a profit for the Wehrmacht, and from US plants building vehicles at a profit for the US Army.

Despite the fact that Ford's plants also supplied the Germans with thousands of engines for their warplanes, Henry Ford refused to allow Ford to supply England with airplane engines.

It is also a fact that *General Motors* manufactured thousands of German military trucks and Panzer tanks using concentration camp slave labour and both *Ford* and *General Motors*, whilst converting their factories in Germany to the production of armaments for the German war-machine, refused requests from the US government to increase military production at their plants in the United States.

Henry Ford had previously shown his true colours when dealing with the *United Auto Workers* (UAW) union. Trade-unions were established to 'fight' for the rights of workers against the often all-powerful might of large corporations, more often than not on picket lines, in contract negotiations, and through media coverage rather than literally. However, violence and intimidation of union organisers and members has a long, sordid history and the events of 26th May 1937 was one of the most significant examples of that. It was a battle that ultimately cost the capitalists their cover-up of lies and deception.

This battle took place outside Detroit at the Ford Motor company's Rouge Complex, a huge Dearborn industrial park on the Detroit River. Walter Reuther and other UAW organisers were present in order to show their solidarity with Ford workers as they attempted to negotiate for better pay and shorter working hours. A leaflet campaign had been prepared, and the press arrived to cover the event. What happened next, unfortunately for Henry Ford, was captured on film by a *Detroit News* photographer.

The infamous Harry Bennett was 'head of security' for Ford and he was, essentially, Henry Ford's 'fixer,' a tough, uncompromising former boxer whom Ford had hired after asking him a single question, *"Can you shoot?"* Although Bennett was tough, he was also paranoid. He had built himself a home on the Detroit River that was a veritable fortress with hidden tunnels, an interior stairway that led directly to a dock under the house, complete with getaway motor boat and a moat ringed with explosives ready to be triggered.

Bennett had begun his career at Ford as a clerk in the parts department but quickly rose to prominence as perhaps America's most famous 'corporate thug.' He soon ingratiated himself with Henry Ford, becoming his 'right-hand man' in the 1920s. Other than Ford's wife Clara, Bennett was perhaps the person closest to his boss during the final decades of Ford's life. Bennett headed-up Ford's notorious Security Department, with a large staff of often brutal, thugs and in addition there was a spy service made-up of thousands more, who would willingly snitch on their fellow employees. Together they monitored Ford employees, intimidated union organisers, delivered punishments and guarded Ford and his family.

Bennett's security force were known as 'service men,' and it was composed of former athletes, Detroit gang-members, and ex-convicts and it was this security 'army' that had shot at Ford workers, alongside the police during the 'Ford Hunger March' in 1932, killing five and wounding 60.

Henry Ford sought the media's sympathy in his fight against the workers that were asking for an 'extravagant' two dollars more per day in pay, so Bennett hosted a lavish feast for them at the beginning of May and indeed many of those same reporters and photographers turned up to cover the UAW presence at the Rouge Complex on 26th May.

As the UAW organisers posed for press *photographs* on a pedestrian overpass that led from the plant to the parking lot, Bennett arrived with 40 of his security force. The 'service men' immediately attacked the union negotiators. One of them was thrown down a flight of stairs on the overpass bridge, kicked and punched, and then thrown down a second flight of stairs. Another's jacket was pulled up over his head and he was savagely beaten and yet another was thrown off the overpass and landed on concrete 30 feet below, breaking his back.

Members of the Ford women's auxiliary had also arrived to distribute leaflets to other workers as they came-off shift and these women were also attacked and beaten whilst Dearborn police officers stood by and watched. Later they explained that Bennett's security forces were 'defending private property' and they did not want to interfere.

Bennett's attacking security officers then rounded-on the members of the press who had attended the event. Reporters had notes ripped from them, cameras were smashed, film was confiscated and burned and one reporter was even chased by a group of 'service men' for five miles before he finally sought sanctuary in a police station. However, one of the photographers escaped and managed to protect the glass-plate negatives of his photographs. He hid the real negatives in his back seat and surrendered some blank ones to Ford security before making his getaway.

Bennett later declared to the media, *"The affair was deliberately provoked by union officials...I know definitely no Ford service man or plant police were involved in any way in the fight."* But the smuggled photographs, however, told a different story.

The outcome of the 'Battle of the Overpass' was the negative attention it brought to Henry Ford and the way he treated his workers. Called before the National Labor Relations Board, Ford had to answer charges involving dozens of unfair labour practices in violation of the Wagner Act. Prior to the hearing, Ford tried to forestall the bad publicity by raising worker's pay by $1.50 a day, an announcement he made immediately after the 'battle' ended, but the opinion of both the National Labor Relations Board as well as the entire country went against him and forced him, three years later, to sign a UAW contract, permitting them to represent all Ford workers in future.

Back to the main thrust of the story again, though. American-owned companies by the hundred, became involved in the manufacture of Panzer tanks and other military vehicles, warplane engines, navigational equipment for Luftwaffe bombers, radar, high explosives, aircraft aluminium, bomb parts and many other types of vital war material for the German war effort.

Ford, General Motors, Standard Oil, DuPont, Remington Arms, Alcoa and many others had joint ventures in Germany and cartel agreements with *IG Farben*. And as well as building radar for Germany, General Electric entered into a cartel agreement with armaments manufacturer, *Krupp*, to restrict the production of tungsten carbide, a vital war material, in the United States.

IT&T obligingly created the German military's communications systems and provided vital bomb components for their friends in the Third Reich and the company also produced thirty thousand fuses a month for shells to be used against American and Allied troops. During 1944 and 1945, *IT&T* also supplied the Germans with guidance components for the deadly V1 and V2 rockets which rained down on London's helpless populace.

IT&T also made its South American subsidiaries available for German intelligence operations and also the capital to German aircraft manufacturers building bombers for the Luftwaffe. Ultimately, *IT&T* owned 28% of Focke-Wulfe, one of the leading producers of warplanes.

Prescott Bush was the founder of the Bush political dynasty and was once considered a potential presidential candidate himself. Like his son, George, and grandson, George W, he went to Yale where he was, again like his descendants, a member of the secretive and influential Skull and Bones student society. He was an artillery captain in the First World War and married Dorothy Walker, the daughter of George Herbert Walker in 1921.

Other US corporations with major ties to the Nazis included *Eastman Kodak, Chrysler, Bendix, Sperry Gyroscope,* the Mellon family's *Alcoa*, the Rockefellers' *Chase National Bank* and *International Harvester*. The profits of the American companies are kept, for the most part, within Germany where they are used to finance the war effort.

The following is from an article by Ben Aris and Duncan Campbell for the British establishment newspaper, *The Guardian*, 25th September 2004 …

"George Bush's grandfather, the late US senator Prescott Bush, was a director and shareholder of companies that profited from their involvement with the financial backers of Nazi Germany... The Guardian has obtained confirmation from newly discovered files in the US National Archives that a firm of which Prescott Bush was a director was involved with the financial architects of Nazism. His business dealings, which continued until his company's assets were seized in 1942 under the Trading with the Enemy Act, has led more than 60 years later to a civil action for damages being brought in Germany against the Bush family by two former slave laborers at Auschwitz and to a hum of pre-election controversy.

The evidence has also prompted one former US Nazi war crimes prosecutor to argue that the late senator's action should have been grounds for prosecution for giving aid and comfort to the enemy. The debate over Prescott Bush's behavior has been bubbling under the surface for some time. There has been a steady, internet chatter about the 'Bush/Nazi' connection, much of it inaccurate and unfair.

But the new documents, many of which were only declassified last year, show that even after America had entered the war and when there was already significant information about the Nazi's plans and policies, he worked for and profited from companies closely involved with the very German businesses that financed Hitler's rise to power. It has also been suggested that the money he made from these dealings helped to establish the Bush family fortune and set up its political dynasty.

Remarkably, little of Bush's dealings with Germany has received public scrutiny, partly because of the secret status of the documentation involving him. But now the multibillion dollar legal action for damages by two Holocaust survivors against the Bush family, and the imminent publication of three books on the subject are threatening to make Prescott Bush's business history an uncomfortable issue for his grandson, George W, as he seeks re-election.

While there is no suggestion that Prescott Bush was sympathetic to the Nazi cause, the documents reveal that the firm he worked for, Brown Brothers Harriman (BBH), acted as a US base for the German industrialist, Fritz Thyssen, who helped finance Hitler in the 1930s before falling out with him at the end of the decade.

The Guardian has seen evidence that shows Bush was the director of the New York-based Union Banking Corporation (UBC) that represented Thyssen's US interests and he continued to work for the bank after America entered the war.

Bush was also on the board of at least one of the companies that formed part of a multinational network of front companies to allow Thyssen to move assets around the world. Thyssen owned the largest steel and coal company in Germany and grew rich from Hitler's efforts to re-arm between the two world wars. One of the pillars in Thyssen's international corporate web, UBC, worked exclusively for, and was owned by, a Thyssen-controlled bank in the Netherlands. More tantalising are Bush's links to the Consolidated Silesian Steel Company (CSSC), based in mineral rich Silesia on the German-Polish border. During the war, the company made use of Nazi slave labour from the concentration camps, including Auschwitz. The ownership of CSSC changed hands several times in the 1930s, but documents from the US National Archive declassified last year link Bush to CSSC, although it is not clear if he and UBC were still involved in the company when Thyssen's American assets were seized in 1942.

Three sets of archives spell out Prescott Bush's involvement. All three are readily available, thanks to the efficient US archive system and a helpful and dedicated staff at both the Library of Congress in Washington and the National Archives at the University of Maryland. The first set of files, the Harriman papers in the Library of Congress, show that Prescott Bush was a director and shareholder of a number of companies involved with Thyssen.

The second set of papers, which are in the National Archives, are contained in vesting order number 248 which records the seizure of the company assets. What these files show is that on October 20 1942 the alien property custodian seized the assets of the UBC, of which Prescott Bush was a director.

Having gone through the books of the bank, further seizures were made against two affiliates, the Holland-American Trading Corporation and the Seamless Steel Equipment Corporation. By November, the Silesian-American Company, another of Prescott Bush's ventures, had also been seized.

The third set of documents, also at the National Archives, are contained in the files on IG Farben, who was prosecuted for war crimes. A report issued by the Office of Alien Property Custodian in 1942 stated of the companies that "since 1939, these (steel and mining) properties have been in possession of and have been operated by the German government and have undoubtedly been of considerable assistance to that country's war effort."

"If the Nazis won, some of these 'business realists' would have been impeccably Nazi. If the Nazis lost, the same businessmen were impeccably American." William Stephenson, Head of British Security Coordination

All of the above examples totally support the premise that the banksters and their related industrial conglomerates took no sides during the war. Their lust for profits was not diminished or deterred by any thoughts of illegally 'trading with the enemy,' whatsoever. It further strongly supports the notion that these bankster-elites recognise no borders, have no allegiance to any particular country, even their own, and their only concerns are the consolidation and increase of their ongoing mega-profits and their quest to subjugate the entire population of the world in order that the poor get poorer and the already rich (themselves) get even richer.

After the outbreak of the Spanish Civil War in 1936, The Russian controlled *Comintern* sent Red volunteers from all over the world to fight for their cause against the Spanish regime. As always, the Communists were involved in sickening atrocities against civilians, such as setting fire to the wives and children of Nationalist officers after dousing them with petrol. The Zionist Reds were determined to stamp out Christianity in Spain too, and to this end they raped nuns, tortured priests and set fire to churches with the worshippers locked inside.

But despite the Communists' best efforts, the Spanish Civil War ended in victory for General Franco's Nationalists, but the war between Red Globalism and European

Nationalism was only just beginning to ignite. On the 25th November 1937, Germany and Japan agreed to the *Anti-Comintern Pact*, a mutual defence treaty directed at the Soviet-controlled *Communist International*. The pact stated that…

"Recognising that the aim of the Communist International, known as the Comintern, is to disintegrate and subdue existing States by all the means at its command; convinced that the toleration of interference by the Communist International in the internal affairs of the nations not only endangers their internal peace and social wellbeing, but is also a menace to the peace of the world desirous of cooperating in the defence against Communist subversive activities."

In case of an attack by the Soviet Union against Germany or Japan, the two countries agreed to take measures *"… to safeguard their common interests."* Mussolini's Italy also joined the Anti-Comintern and several other nations also joined subsequently and Germany even invited Britain and Poland to join the Anti-Comintern, but they declined. No surprises there, then.

In 1938, mounting pressure on both sides of the border between the two nations, resulted in the *'Anschluss,'* the voluntary incorporation of Austria into the German Reich which was supported by 99% of Austrians, but opposed by the puppet, Austrian government instituted by the Allies after World War I.

The Versailles Treaty had broken-up the Austro-Hungarian Empire and forbade Austria from uniting with Germany, but after witnessing the miraculous recovery of Germany throughout the early 1930s due to their the freedom from the economic straitjacket of the banksters, and the incredible enhancements in the German living standards, there was a great desire in Austria to unite with their ecstatic, Teutonic brothers and sisters. So, without a single shot being fired, German forces moved-in unopposed and were greeted as liberators by the overjoyed Austrians.

And when Hitler himself arrived in the land of his birth, he was given a hero's welcome by the frenzied Austrian crowds. Unsurprisingly, the world's Zionist media portrayed the joyful unification as 'Germany conquers Austria.'

When the Treaty of Versailles dismantled the Austro-Hungarian Empire, it forced Czechs, Slovaks and Germans into the artificially-created state of Czechoslovakia. The German region, the Sudetenland, lay southeast of Germany, had three million German inhabitants and similarly to the Austrians, the Sudetenlanders also wished to unite with their homeland, the German Reich. However, Czechoslovakia and its Communist President, Edward Benes, would not allow them the right to self-determination and the Sudetenland Germans were instead persecuted by the Globalist-owned state of Czechoslovakia.

Understandably, Hitler and the German people were becoming angered by the Czech abuse of their brethren and he declared that he would no longer tolerate any Czech mistreatment of the Sudeten-German community in Bohemia, and as a result of the growing tensions between Germany and the Czechs and also Germany having to endure constant Polish incursions and sabre-rattling on its territories, it was difficult to see how a general European war could now be avoided. The Czechs had a modern army of twenty-five divisions, and if the German army crossed the border, the Czechs would no doubt give a good account of themselves. The French and Russians had promised their full support if that happened, and the British would also join the anti-German coalition.

At the last moment however, Neville Chamberlain, the British Prime Minister, made a personal intervention and in order to resolve the matter peacefully, Hitler called for an international conference in Munich, attended by England, France, and Italy.

Chamberlain at heart, was a man of peace and did not wish Europe to descend into another state of war and chaos again so soon after the World War had wreaked such utter havoc and destruction, but he had reckoned without the war-mongering banksters' demented obsession. He also recognised that Germany had genuine grievances and persuaded himself that if these were met quickly, that a repeat of the 1914-18 war could be avoided. Quoting his personal motto, 'Peace at any price,' he flew to Munich and persuaded Hitler into calling-off his attack in return for German re-possession of the Sudetenland. The French were relieved to let Chamberlain defuse tensions; the Russians said nothing and the Czechs, knowing that they could not fight alone, were also secretly relieved and signed the agreement.

Once the artificial Czechoslovakian state had been successfully dissolved, Germany established autonomous protectorates over what remained (Bohemia and Moravia) and again, with no violence whatsoever or even a single drop of blood being shed, the ethnic Germans were welcomed back into the Reich whilst the other ethnic groups were given their own states; a 'win-win' for everyone. In scenes echoing his Austrian reception, Hitler also received a delirious welcome upon visiting the Sudetenland.

However, as alluded-to, the banksters were not happy with this turn of events and now had to find another way to create the spark that would set Europe ablaze once again. Furthermore, contrary to what you may have 'learned' in modern history lessons at school, college or University, read in articles or books or watched in fictional films and so-called 'factual documentaries' about the catalyst of the start of hostilities in 1939, the conflict was absolutely not initiated by Germany. In collusion with the elite, bankster-controlled networks in Europe, primarily Britain, Poland had constantly violated Germany's borders without provocation.

At the risk of repetition, it is extremely important that everyone should understand that Hitler DID NOT want war of any kind, let alone to conquer the world or even Europe, as is the constant claim of the Zionist-globalist banksters and their legions of apologists.

He was however, backed into a corner by the deceitful allies and put into a position where Germany had absolutely no option but to defend themselves, if necessary by pre-emptive strikes.

"Germany is too strong. We must destroy her." Winston Churchill, November 1936

"The war was not just a matter of the elimination of Fascism in Germany, but rather of obtaining German sales markets." Winston Churchill, March 1946

"Britain was taking advantage of the situation to go to war against Germany because the Reich had become too strong and had upset the European economic balance." Ralph F. Keeling, Institute of American Economics

"I believe now that Hitler and the German people did not want war. But we declared war on Germany, intent on destroying it, in accordance with our principle of balance of power and we were encouraged by the Americans around Roosevelt. We ignored Hitler's pleadings not to enter into war. Now we are forced to realise that Hitler was right." Former UK Attorney General, Sir Hartley Shawcross, 16th March 1984

"The last thing Hitler wanted was to produce another great war." Sir Basil Liddell-Hart, historian

"I see no reason why this war must go on. I am grieved to think of the sacrifices which it will claim. I would like to avert them." Adolf Hitler, July 1940

"We entered the war of our own free will, without ourselves being directly assaulted." Winston Churchill in a Guild Hall speech, July 1943

"The state of German armament in 1939 gives the decisive proof that Hitler was not contemplating general war, and probably not intending war at all." (p.267) and *"Even in 1939 the German army was not equipped for a prolonged war; and in 1940 the German land forces were inferior to the French in everything except leadership."* British historian, Professor A.J.P. Taylor, 'The Origins of the Second World War' (p104-105)

In March 1939, Poland, already occupying German territory legally 'acquired' in 1919 at Versailles, invaded Czechoslovakia and during the months preceding the outbreak of war, Polish armed forces repeatedly violated German borders. On the 31st August 1939 Polish irregular armed forces launched a full scale attack on the German border town of Gleiwitz (significantly now Gliwice, in Poland.)

Within hours Germany retaliated by launching an attack on Poland, resulting in Britain and France's declarations of war on the German nation on 3rd September 1939. In Britain's case this declaration of war was constitutionally illegal as it was never ratified by Parliament. Of course the allied propaganda machine churned out the untrue story that the attack on Germany's border had been carried-out by German soldiers dressed in Polish uniforms, in a false-flag operation. Indeed to this day, mainstream history holds this version of events to be true, but it is not.

Despite her borders being constantly attacked by the numerically superior armies of France and England and economically strangled by Elite financial interests, Germany refused to be drawn into action against Britain, repeatedly negotiated for peace and undertook no overt offensive strategies for around nine months. This period was known as the 'phony war.' However, Germany did carry-out a full-blooded, pre-emptive strike, the Blitzkrieg (lightening war) on Northern Europe, but only after it discovered that

England intended to broaden the western front by occupying the Benelux countries and Norway, thus directly threatening Germany's borders.

A few days after Britain declared war on Germany, the bootlegger, Mafia asset, chronic adulterer, devout coward, investor in Nazi industry and US Ambassador to the United Kingdom, Joseph Kennedy held a farewell dinner for his nine children before sending them back to the US where they would be safe from the anticipated, German bombing raids on London.

World War Two had now begun in earnest and another six appalling years of darkness, bloodshed and misery was about to descend on Europe, for the second time in only twenty years ...

Chapter 9
World War Two—The Problem

"There are two world histories. One is the official and full of lies, destined to be taught in schools, the other is the secret history, which harbours the true causes and occurrences."
Honore de Balzac

"In war, truth is the first casualty." Aeschylus, Greek tragic dramatist (525 BC—456 BC)

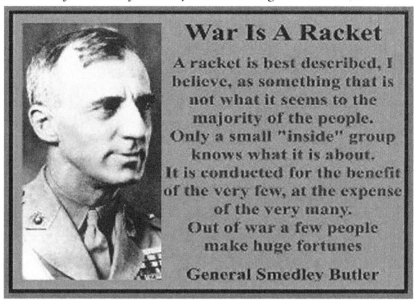

Throughout history, various men of military standing have spoken-out against the actions of the military hierarchy. Some have exposed the atrocities that have been covered-up, whilst others have revealed the deceptions that have been used against the public or actions that have been taken that are contrary to what they view as moral principles. Major-General Smedley Darlington Butler is one of the most prominent, high-ranking servicemen who has publicly opposed the actions of the military in which he formerly served.

Marine General Butler is also one of the most highly-decorated military men from the pre-World War II era. Twice a US *Medal of Honor* recipient, he served from 1898 to 1931 and saw action all over the world. Eventually he became a prominent political figure and was one of America's most important leaders of the liberal movement of the 1930s. Butler advocated military isolationism and was totally against American involvement in World War II. His isolationist views are certainly unpopular today and in fact are incompatible with the current geopolitical 'norm' and were developed from his 33 years of service as what he referred-to as *"…a gangster for capitalism."*

In total, Butler delivered over 1,200 speeches in over 700 cities during his speaking tour of the United States and in 1935 published his pamphlet '*War is a Racket,*' which divided opinion hugely at the time of its publication, as it still does to this day. The foreword by Lowell Thomas spoke of Butler's *"moral as well as physical courage"* and noted that *"Even his opponents concede that in his stand on public questions, General Butler has been motivated by the same fiery integrity and loyal patriotism which has distinguished his service in countless Marine campaigns."*

What Butler fought so hard for was to take the focus off of moral and ideological arguments for war and concentrate on the geo-political factors that actually motivated war. He tried to raise awareness of what the real motivating factors of war were, as well as its usual dire consequences and indeed was one of the first soldiers to really bring the economic implications of war to the forefront of the public conscience.

In *War is a Racket,* (which by the way is still in print and available to buy on the internet,) Butler exposes in wonderfully blunt detail how the American 'military machine' was used exclusively to the benefit of wealthy American industrialists and banksters. He noted how proponents of war typically call on God as a supporter of the cause and how they embellish the mission as one of liberation and the spreading of freedom, but that these people tend to shy away from discussing the economic details of military ventures.

The following is an excerpt from a speech he made in 1933...

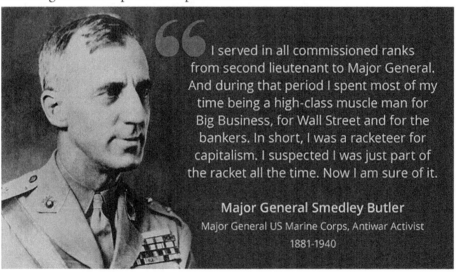

"War is just a racket. A racket is best described, I believe, as something that is not what it seems to the majority of people. Only a small inside group knows what it is about. It is conducted for the benefit of the very few at the expense of the masses.

I believe in adequate defence at the coastline and nothing else. If a nation comes over here to fight, then we'll fight. The trouble with America is that when the dollar only earns 6 percent over here, then it gets restless and goes overseas to get 100 percent. Then the flag follows the dollar and the soldiers follow the flag.

I wouldn't go to war again as I have done to protect some lousy investment of the bankers. There are only two things we should fight for. One is the defence of our homes and the other is the Bill of Rights. War for any other reason is simply a racket.

There isn't a trick in the racketeering bag that the military gang is blind to. It has its 'finger-men' to point out enemies, its 'muscle-men' to destroy enemies, its 'brain-men' to plan war preparations, and a 'Big Boss,' Super-Nationalistic-Capitalism.

It may seem odd for me, a military man to adopt such a comparison. Truthfulness compels me to. I spent thirty-three years and four months in active military service as a member of this country's most agile military force, the Marine Corps. I served in all commissioned ranks from Second Lieutenant to Major-General and during that period, I spent most of my time being a high class muscle-man for Big Business, for Wall Street and for the Bankers. In short, I was a racketeer, a gangster for capitalism.

I suspected I was just part of a racket at the time. Now I am sure of it. Like all the members of the military profession, I never had a thought of my own until I left the service. My mental faculties remained in suspended animation while I obeyed the orders of higher-ups. This is typical with everyone in the military service.

I helped make Mexico, especially Tampico, safe for American oil interests in 1914. I helped make Haiti and Cuba a decent place for the National City Bank boys to collect revenues in. I helped in the raping of half a dozen Central American republics for the benefits of Wall Street.

The record of racketeering is long. I helped purify Nicaragua for the international banking house of Brown Brothers in 1909-1912. I brought light to the Dominican Republic for American sugar interests in 1916. In China I helped to see to it that Standard Oil went its way unmolested.

During those years, I had, as the boys in the back room would say, a swell racket. Looking back on it, I feel that I could have given Al Capone a few hints. The best he could do was to operate his racket in three districts. I operated on three continents."

The following is a quotation is from the acclaimed British Intelligence operative Anthony Thomas Trevor-Stokes, better known to truth-seekers everywhere as 'T. Stokes . . .'

"Winston Churchill, who led Britain into both World Wars with his famous 'victory' salute, is still revered by many people and was in a recent, rigged newspaper poll voted Britain's greatest Englishman.

Churchill has been exposed as a long term Zionist/bankster puppet, and served their interest before that of Britain, and whom has been shown to be from documental research and Humint, (human intelligence) to have been a Druid priest, a one-time fringe spiritualist and member of the 'Golden Dawn,' and most damning of all, a 33rd degree mason. Masonry is universally accepted as a racist, anti-Christian and a secretly, elitist anti-democratic organisation.

This establishes his interest in the occult from day one, and he himself has said on record that he escaped capture in the Boer war, by his psychic ability to choose to knock on the one door that would give him shelter, his statement here is questionable from archive material research but let's leave this for now.

His 'V' salute is a recognised greeting of the horned god, the symbol of the Devil worshipping Illuminati, as demonstrated in 'Skull and Bones' initiates.

The version of the 'V' salute as shown in the Star Trek TV show by Spock, is a greeting by Rabbis in the Hebrew tradition, the hand split down the centre represents the 2 fingers on each side of the 'V' in deVil, as the initials DE and IL represent the fingers.. The initial 'V' is the 22nd letter in the alphabet, a sacred number in Hebrew numerology, and corresponds in the tarot pack to the major arcana.

Winston changed sides in his political career four times, and his skills were on offer on several more occasions for the right price, this meant he was known in the House of Commons as 'The Shithouse' from his initials 'WC.' He accepted £150,000 to bring Britain into World War II for the Rothschild bankers against Germany, and to latterly drag in the USA.

Archbishop Lang the Church of England expert on occult subjects, prior to WWII was privy to Churchill's putting together of the 'Black Team' those wartime astrologers, dowsers and ritual magicians, under the stewardship of Louis de Whol, Dennis Wheatley, Dion Fortune, Dr Alexander Cannon and Ian Fleming both claimed that Churchill had wartime dealings with Aleister Crowley, advertised as the world's 'wickedest man,' and the famous East-end spirit medium Joe Benjamin, who was often advertised in the sixties as, Winston's favourite medium.

Sefton Delmer the journalist and black propaganda and psy-ops leader confirmed that 33rd degree masons Churchill and Aleister Crowley were involved in wartime sacrifices at the Devils Chimney on England's south coast. Churchill wanted occult advice on all wartime events, even insisting on mass, fake astrological pamphlet drops, and other hate propaganda leaflets being dropped from British aircraft over Germany.

The master-spy, Rothschild operative and traitor, Sir Anthony Blunt has said on record, Hitler was negotiating for peace right through the war, and sent his deputy Rudolph Hess to Britain to pursue an honourable peace which Churchill continually refused, following Rothschild advice for total destruction as shown in his needless firebombing of German dormitory cities, this can be seen as the typical 'Satanic Sacrifice' as recorded in the Old Testament as a 'burnt offering' and in the biblical burning of witches. Sir Anthony Blunt put on record his distaste at Churchill's support of the Soviet rape squads sent in to defile the women and children in the last days of the Third Reich, disrupting the racial purity of the eugenics tables, and the sacrificial fire-bombing was only equalled by Churchill's refusal to Leo Amery who begged help for India in the 1943 famine disasters, while Churchill sent food and arms to Russia, this surely is Satanism at its worst?

Patrick Kinna (Churchill's secretary) tells us we were reading the German Enigma codes so knew which ships would be sunk, and we sent out decoy ships to keep the U-Boats away from those ships we wanted kept safe, we knew the town of Coventry would be bombed but Churchill did not evacuate and left the people to their fate.

Britain's intelligence services had saturation coverage of the Third Reich up to and through WWII and told us the Germans were a threat to Russia—not Britain, so Churchill formed his own people called the S.O.E. and these were recruited from leftie rabble rousers and socialist sympathisers, and were told to, 'set Europe ablaze,' the purpose was to sacrifice Europe for Churchill's ambitions, and to insure Germany would clamp down on them, which was exactly what happened.

It was suggested to me some years ago, that Churchill was blackmailed over a homosexual affair with his secretary into a pro-Zionist stance, in a similar fashion to what happened with the Prime minister Edward Heath with the 'sailor boy' activities, and the Tony Blair / Lord Levy 'Miranda revelations.' Churchill's biographer, Sir Martin Gilbert discussed with several people and argued with Churchill's doctor Lord Moran over the many alleged visits to the teenage 'bum-boy' dens of Morocco.

Soviet spy Eugene Ivanov was just one who documented Churchill's alcoholism and mental instability, all now in G.R.U archives. Churchill accepted secret bribes in WW I under the name of Colonel Arden, and one of his bank accounts in WW II was alleged to be in the name of 'A Connolly.'

Britain in the 1930s had a posture that assisted Germany in its anti-Russia stance, yet Churchill on his own, in pure Tony Blair fashion, turns the tables and decides Germany is the enemy and took us to war.

Hitler had a thing about the Anglo Saxon race, that is, Germany, Britain and the U.S.A and did not want war with us. If we had listened to our intelligence services we would have let Russia and Germany fight it out, and we could have easily dealt with the weakened winner, and World war two and the Cold war would never have happened, but Churchill had Vernon Kell reputedly the world best intelligence chief retired off and murdered, and naval intel head, Admiral Sir Barry Domville incarcerated for the wars duration for their opposition to Churchill's plans."

So, Winston Churchill sold out to the banksters against the welfare of his own nation, to line his own pockets in the manner of a modern Judas. How very unsurprising.

"Ponder on this . . . on April 20th Hitler's birthday, because his war with the usurers, asset strippers and bankers, brought Russia to threaten both Germany and England, Churchill took us into WWII, Poland was just the excuse, the same as in all the wars now we fight them for the bankers." Admiral Sir Barry Edward Domville KBE (Knight Commander, Order of the British Empire), CB (Companion, Order of the Bath), CMG (Commander, Order of St Michael and St George) assistant secretary to the Imperial Defence Committee, Director of Naval Intelligence (1927-30) and President of the Royal Naval College (1932-34)

Conventional, mainstream 'history,' an adjunct of the corrupt, ruling orthodoxy, records that Admiral Sir Barry Edward Domville was a distinguished Royal Navy officer who blighted his illustrious career by developing 'extreme right-wing political views' and becoming a 'leading British fascist.' Domville visited Nazi Germany in 1935 and was invited to attend the Nuremberg Rally of September 1936 as a guest of the German Ambassador, Joachim von Ribbentrop. His fondness for Germany and her people led him to establish a pro-German organisation, the Anglo-German Link, whose membership peaked at around 4,300. It was an 'independent non-party organisation to promote Anglo-German friendship' whose intended purpose was... "*To foster the mutual knowledge and understanding between the British and German peoples, and to counteract the flood of lies with which our people were being regaled in their daily papers.*"

The war hysteria being ratcheted-up by the propaganda fed through the media in all its forms ensured that despotic, un-constitutional legislation was passed without any undue delay or debate in the British Parliament, endowing the Home Secretary with the right to imprison without trial, anyone he believed likely to 'endanger the safety of the realm.' In other words, anyone whom the Government saw fit. Consequently, a Defence Regulation Order, the infamous 'Regulation 18b,' was passed by the 'mother of all Parliaments,' that was a useful tool for those wishing to silence the dissenting voices to the unfolding nightmare, the totally avoidable carnage, that is usually referred-to as the Second World War. Regulation 18b was ruthlessly enforced and hundreds of gallant servicemen (and some of their wives) who had fought with great distinction in World War I and received many decorations, but who, only because they opposed the new war with Germany, on moral grounds and not because of any crime they had committed, were imprisoned without charge or trial throughout most of the Second World War. Some were well known, such as Oswald Mosley and some were very distinguished, such as Admiral Sir Barry Domville.

Indeed, nearly two thousand less well-known men and women were also imprisoned by the Home Secretary, Herbert Morrison and Prime Minister, Winston Churchill. Although Domville, when visiting Nazi Germany with Link members, had always been very careful to keep clear of excessive contact with 'official Nazidom,' his leadership of the Link was sufficient to secure his imprisonment without trial under the infamous, unlawful regulation. And, for the next three years, 'home' for this honourable man was to be a prison cell, with a plank-bed two inches from the floor, a table, chair and washstand. Domville's autobiography, '*From Admiral to Cabin Boy,*' was written during this imprisonment and published in 1947.

So why did the self-styled guardians of 'liberty and freedom,' those very traitors who exhorted the British people to make the ultimate sacrifice for 'democracy and freedom,' seek to imprison Domville? Was this most unfair punishment meted-out to him by those who despised his admiration for Germany and Germans or was it something more sinister? Could it have been that Domville's enemies sought revenge for his embarrassingly accurate views and intimate knowledge of the inner workings of government and also wished to deny him a platform upon which to expose the treasonous activities of the few that were knowingly bringing the British Empire to its knees?

Before the First World War, Domville, by virtue of his rank and position, began to gain knowledge of the dark secrets of high government and the secret treachery of the British establishment. Furthermore, after World War I, Domville attended numerous peace conferences and knew both Lloyd-George and Churchill and was as well-informed on geo-politics and of the workings of the human heart and mind as one would expect of a future Director of Naval Intelligence. His general impression from these experiences was one of alarm that venal politicians and faceless bureaucrats possessed an unerring knack of prosecuting policies that repeatedly saw the 'betrayal of all true British interests.' Moreover, he realised that successive British governments made seemingly stupid or even near-suicidal decisions, (as indeed they still do today) which made no sense whatever in purely logical terms.

In short, Domville realised that the terrible betrayal of Britain and her people by the ruling establishment was so appalling and wholly avoidable, that it could not have been happening by accident and another, hidden force with its own agenda whose objectives were at odds with proper, rational government, was obviously at work. Domville wrote of this epiphany in his autobiography...

"From that time onwards I had a strong suspicion that there was some mysterious power at work behind the scenes controlling the actions of the figures visibly taking part in the Government of the country. I had not the least idea whence this power emanated, nor could I gauge the strength of its influence, I was in far too humble a position to make such lofty discoveries. Still the feeling persisted. We always vaguely referred to this hidden control amongst ourselves as 'the Treasury'... This mysterious power...I christened Judmas, because, as I discovered at a much later date, its source is the Judaeo-Masonic combination, which has wielded such a baneful influence in world history for many centuries."

Domville's conclusions are in no sense the product of 'hate' or so-called 'anti-Semitism' as Zionist apologists would have us all believe, but rather of common-sense and acute observation from an honourable, pragmatic man who witnessed the apparent absurdities and injustices of high politics but could not quite account for them. In fact, he viewed with utter contempt the complacent, self-seeking, corrupt and seemingly 'foolish,' British Liberal Establishment that repeatedly betrayed the British people on all levels and in all spheres of endeavour. He further understood very well that 'the puppets dance, whilst hidden forces pull the strings from behind the scenes' but he did not fully understand what these hidden forces actually were. He was prescient enough to recognise though that these 'hidden forces' desired what we now call globalisation, or the 'New World Order' and whose architects, these 'globalisers,' were.

Recently de-classified documents now in the National archives such as the 1939 MI-5 file on MP Sir Archibald Maule-Ramsey and the 224 members of one important anti-war group, prove beyond doubt that Winston Churchill was part of the Zionist banksters' plot to replace Neville Chamberlain and drag Britain into war.

Sir Archibald Maule-Ramsay (1894-1955) was the main critic in the House of Commons of having Jews in the government, and in 1938 he began a campaign to have War Minister Leslie Hore-Belisha, fired. In one speech on the 27th April of that year he warned that Hore-Belisha, *"would lead us to war with our blood brothers of the Nordic race to make way for a Bolshevised Europe, as openly wanted by Sir Herbert Morrison and the Jewish pressure groups."*

Maule-Ramsey also petitioned in the House of Commons to have Winston Churchill de-selected as MP for Epping for his constant warmongering and links to unelected forces, and also sought direct guarantees of peace from Hitler and Mussolini. An agent for Lord Victor Rothschild's pro-Jewish banker group named Flora Solomons, confessed in an interview that war with Germany was considered vital in order to restore the banksters' control.

Interestingly, Churchill was also accused of murder in some quarters. A senior member of MI-5 through the war named Sorrell, kept copies of the documentation of Churchill's alleged murders and treachery, and was one of several intelligence officers secretly informing the magazine *'Truth.'*

And Churchill, according to new research, was guilty of at least three murders; his mother Lady Jennie Churchill between 11th and 29th June 1921, spymaster and the first head of the British Secret Service George M. Smith-Cumming at his house, 1 Melbury Road, Kensington on the 14th June 1923 and T.E. Lawrence better known as *Lawrence of Arabia* between 13th and 19th May 1935. There was no question of Churchill killing with his own hands—he was far too careful and squeamish for such things. But he *was* the man who issued the orders to kill and as such is equally guilty as those that carried out his orders. These were not political murders by the State but the acts of a man hell-bent on revenge on his mother, she having cheated him out of his inheritance and then ensuring he would not be caught and as a consequence, disgrace the name he carried. He achieved this latter goal by killing the two men that knew what he had done to his mother.

[Those who wish to pursue this matter further will find plenty of good information on the internet, however this is not really relevant to the contents of this book as such. It is merely mentioned here to illustrate the type of man that Churchill indeed was—JH]

Many people today question why the foremost 'seats of learning,' such as Oxford and Cambridge University, actively encouraged and promoted Russian 'Socialism/Communism' in the 1930s. In Russia, Communists had destroyed democracy in all the Universities, the mines, the factories, much of the armed services and even the church was infected with the disease of socialism in its many guises. But all of society was under attack, from almost every direction and such was and is the overwhelming power of these forces of evil, that virtually nothing or no-one could stand in their way.

But there were some pockets of resistance and one of those to stand against the creeping, insidious Communist menace as espoused by the banksters was Adolf Hitler in Germany. He successfully extinguished the Communist threat by creating almost full employment, making it possible for 'ordinary' working people to enjoy car ownership through the 'people's car' or Volkswagen. He also undertook a massive programme of public works, building motorways and public leisure facilities, free holidays for all workers and their families at purpose-built holiday resorts and even on cruise ships. However, he committed the cardinal sin of removing the power to create and issue money, away from the international banksters, those predatory financiers, exploiters, asset-strippers and 'money changers'—and this led to his ultimate downfall.

However, it was Lord Victor Rothschild, bankster-supreme and later exposed as the infamous 'fifth man' in the Cambridge spy-scandal, who wrote the letters of introduction for all the 'Cambridge traitors,' Anthony Blunt, Donald Maclean, Kim Philby and Guy Burgess among others, to the Intelligence services, and he also protected them at every turn. Rothschild's 'Apostles' were above the law and all were allowed to get away and even George Blake who was sentenced to 42 years was allowed to escape to Russia in a Royal Navy ship, despite his escape officially being blamed on 'peace activists.'

Rothschild and his organisation was behind the loans for the British war effort in WWII, whilst his bank also loaned money for German re-armament, and the building of at least two concentration camps.

Winston Churchill's loyalties were to say the least, 'flexible' and he changed parties, four times during the course of his political career. He was absolutely not averse either, to a little bribery and corruption. His propensity for the acceptance of surreptitious 'gifts' in large brown envelopes was well-known and often commented-upon. Obviously the banksters too, were well aware of this fact and saw Churchill as a possible asset. In fact, it was Ernst Cassels the Rothschild agent, who 'bought' Churchill's loyalty to the Zionist cause and to actively lobby for war with Germany, for the princely sum of £150,000. Churchill, Rothschild's Judas, was on the verge of losing his home at this time due to massive debts and his bodyguard, Walter Thompson said that his fortnightly bill for alcohol, gambling and prostitutes, was equal to what a working-man earned in a year.

In his book '*Spycatcher*,' an exposure of the British Intelligence services, Peter Wright made it clear that there was a high-level traitor present in the Service, right through WWII and into the Cold War and that this had virtually torn-apart British intelligence, and had thoroughly compromised almost every single operation between 1938 and 1964. As previously stated, bankster Nathaniel Mayer Victor (Lord) Rothschild, was eventually identified as that high-level traitor, and of course he was the man who controlled Winston Churchill.

This leads us to a pertinent question at this point. Which of the two scenarios is most plausible? That one of the richest men in the world, Victor Rothschild (and many others such as he) espoused Communist ideals so that his own fabulous wealth and position could be taken away in the alleged Communistic trait of wealth-sharing? Or is it more likely that Communism was and still is in fact, a subtle bankster deception, designed to curb the wealth and especially the freedoms of the ordinary citizens under the false pretence of bestowing 'equality' upon the masses?

Unfortunately millions if not billions of otherwise well-meaning individuals have been duped into believing-in and fighting-for this clever deception, by those of zero-conscience.

In 1942, Sir Mark Oliphant, a leading British physicist was shocked when a messenger delivered a part from his new 'magnetron technology,' with a warning from MI-5 Security Inspector Victor Rothschild to 'tighten up your security.'

A few days earlier Rothschild had visited Oliphant's Birmingham University lab, quizzed him on his research, and surreptitiously pocketed the three-inch diameter magnetron. Rothschild, the Soviet agent, had transmitted detailed drawings to Moscow before returning the magnetron, a fact later confirmed by his KGB handlers. Oliphant related this story in 1994 to Roland Perry, the Australian author of '*The Fifth Man.*' In 1993, after the dissolution of the Soviet Union, six retired KGB Colonels in Moscow confirmed Rothschild's identity as the 'fifth man' to Roland Perry. Colonel Yuri Modin, the spy ring's handler, said . . .

"Rothschild was the key to most of the Cambridge ring's penetration of British intelligence . . . He had the contacts, he was able to introduce Burgess, Blunt and others to important figures in Intelligence such as Stewart Menzies, Dick White and Robert Vansittart in the Foreign Office, who controlled MI-6." Roland Perry, '*The Fifth Man*'

The Rothschilds are undoubtedly the largest shareholders and de facto controllers of the world's network of central banking systems and Victor Rothschild's career as a Soviet agent confirms that these London-based banksters plan to translate their monopoly on credit into a monopoly on everything else too, using government as their instrument and if they get their way, ultimately a 'world government' dictatorship akin to Communism. In other words, the 'New World Order.'

Rothschild had studied Zoology at Cambridge where Anthony Blunt recruited him for the KGB in 1936. (Blunt later said it was Rothschild who recruited him.) Rothschild also joined MI-5 and was in charge of counter-sabotage, instructing the military on how to recognise various types of bombs and defuse them.

After the induction of Winston Churchill into Rothschild's criminal 'circle,' Perry writes . . .

"The two socialised often, during the war years. Rothschild used his wealth and position to invite the prime minister to private parties. His entree to the wartime leader, plus access to all the key intelligence information, every major weapons development and his command of counter-sabotage operations in Britain, made Rothschild a secretly powerful figure during the war years . . . The result was that Stalin knew as much as Churchill about vital information, often before the British High Command was informed."

Rothschild also helped neutralise enemies of the Soviet Union who approached the British for support. For example, he was involved in the cover-up of the assassination of Polish war leader and British ally Wladyslaw Sikorski, whose plane was blown-up in July 1944. Sikorski had become a threat to Stalin and therefore the British/Soviet relationship after he discovered that the KGB had cold-bloodedly massacred around

20,000 Polish officers in the Katyn Woods in 1940. This was the infamous 'Katyn Massacre' which for decades after the war had been blamed on Germany by the allied powers, until the real truth eventually seeped-out in the aftermath of the fall of the Soviet Union.

Many, many war crimes and atrocities were committed by the Soviets, in other words the Bolshevik Jews under the command of the Jew, Stalin. But of course, as allies in the cause of the New World Order the Soviets were never even accused of, let alone prosecuted or convicted of 'war crimes.' And please do not make the mistake of blaming the 'Russians' in general, for the actions of the Bolsheviks, many millions of innocent Russians suffered and were murdered to at the hands of these unspeakable barbarians. In fact, Alexandr Solzhenitzyn estimated that the Bolsheviks murdered 66 million Russians over the decades.

On the 13th April 1943, Germany announced the discovery of mass graves in the Katyn forest near Smolensk, Russia. The bodies of several thousand men, whose hands had been bound and who had been shot from behind, were found buried there and many more thousands were slaughtered elsewhere, the dead being mostly Polish officers. The Germans realised that the Soviet Union was responsible for the massacre and attempted to use this knowledge to their advantage. They hoped that the revelation would alienate the USSR from its allies, Great Britain, the United States and Poland.

When the news broke about the German discovery, the Polish government-in-exile in England, asked the International Red Cross to conduct an independent investigation and Red Cross findings later indicated that the Soviets were responsible for the massacre. But the Soviets denied culpability and blamed the killings on German forces that had overrun the region in 1941 and subsequently broke diplomatic relations with the Polish government. The 19th April 1943, edition of *Pravda*, the official newspaper of the Communist Party's Central Committee, accused the Polish government of striking a treacherous blow against the USSR. The Soviets also organised their own 'investigation' of the tragedy and determined that the fault lay with Germany but Katyn residents knew differently.

"The stench was bad. When we came, the Germans were removing a layer of earth about a meter thick and then there were coats, bodies and coats, lying there in a row. And they were feeling these bodies, checking the pockets, removing flasks, removing watches, and the Germans set up a museum further out. The Germans wanted witnesses. They wanted us to act as witnesses for history." Dmitry Khudykh, Katyn resident

Neither the British nor the American governments wished to know too much about the mass-graves. If their ally, Joseph Stalin, had ordered the murders, they preferred not to know and to keep it as quiet as possible. For example, when a British diplomat in London wrote a report suggesting that the Soviet Union had been responsible for the massacre, Churchill addressed the issue in a confidential note, stating that . . . *". . . there is no use prowling morbidly round the three year old graves of Smolensk."*

Then in late 1943, as the Red Army began to recapture territory in eastern Poland, the Soviet secret police, the NKVD, cordoned-off the Katyn forest to enable them to create one of the most elaborate cover-ups of the war. After exhuming the bodies from the graves that the Germans had previously uncovered, the NKVD had documents forged to suggest that the Germans had committed the crime. They planted the false documents on the newly exhumed bodies and worked to persuade local people who had witnessed the Soviet crimes to change their stories.

It has been suggested that Stalin wanted as many as possible of the Polish Catholic intelligentsia eliminated at Katyn, as almost all senior Soviets were Jews and detested Christianity.

In 1944, Blunt, Burgess and Philby all stayed with Rothschild at his mansion in Paris. Rothschild was briefly in charge of Allied intelligence in Paris and interrogated many prisoners there. After the war Rothschild spent time in the US overseeing attempts to learn the atom bomb secrets in order no doubt, to pass-on the intelligence gathered, to his Soviet 'friends.' It was due in part to the 'Cambridge Five,' Perry says, that *"...the Russians knew about every major intelligence operation run against them in the years 1945 to 1963."*

Victor Rothschild held many jobs that served to disguise his true role which was probably that of a member of the Illuminati Grand Council. He was in fact an extremely powerful force and no doubt issued orders to Churchill, FDR and Stalin. For example, he ensured that the USSR supported the establishment of the State of Israel. *"He knew the proper back-channels to reach decision-makers in Moscow,"* a KGB Colonel told Perry. *"Let us just say, he got things done. You only did that if you had reached the top. He was very persuasive."*

The fact that Rothschild was protected until his death suggests that this is a conspiracy perpetrated by and for the upper echelons of society, by the Royal/Masonic/Bankster/Illuminati conglomerate.

In fact, Rothschild freely admitted to many friends and acquaintances that there were 'plans in place' for the world map to be re-drawn, that a world-wide 'socialist' government was coming and that those that contributed to the cause would be given positions of great power in this coming 'New World Order.' He would later also pass prime secrets, referred to in the *Spycatcher* book as the 'Crown Jewels,' to the Israelis.

It has lately become a popular myth in 'truth-seeker' circles to conclude that Hitler was a 'British Agent.' As Hitler was known to be in Britain during 1912—13, ostensibly visiting his sister who had married an Englishman, stating that 'Hitler was a British Agent' is a useful paradigm that is claimed by many to clarify many improbable, seemingly illogical events, such as . . .

Why the German war machine was financed and built by the Bank of England and the US Federal Reserve.

Why Hitler was able to expand into the Rhineland without fear of retaliation.

Why Hitler let 335,000 Allied soldiers escape at Dunkirk.

Why Hitler attacked Russia before England was invaded or conquered.

Why the Germans never realised that their communications were compromised.

Why Hitler never sealed the Mediterranean at Gibraltar.

Why Hitler failed to conquer the oil fields of Russia and the Middle East.

Why Hitler gave his racial policies priority over actually winning the war.

Why IG Farben was never bombed, and became the CIA headquarters in Frankfurt after WWII.

…And the biggest improbability of all is said to be that an unknown, working-class, Austrian ex-NCO could ever become the Chancellor of Germany. However this is easily refutable as being 'improbable.' Hitler's rise to power is documented in minute detail and it all makes perfect logical sense. It was no sudden rising from the ranks of obscurity, as has often been the case with other bankster-puppets, some of whose improbable meteoric rises are detailed in this book. It took him over ten years of struggle and manipulation to achieve ultimate power.

Firstly, had Hitler been 'groomed' for power from the time of his visit to Britain in 1912, then his thrusting into the trenches of World War I, as a Private soldier and subsequently a lowly Lance-Corporal, would have been an extremely risky strategy on the part of the banksters and I know for an absolute fact that they would not have risked the safety of their alleged 'protégé' in this way. Furthermore, Hitler was not just an 'ordinary' soldier who literally 'kept his head below the parapet,' keeping himself as safe as possible until the war ended, he was a war hero who put his life on the line on several occasions, being highly decorated in the process. This fact in itself belies that aspect of the wild claims being made.

And with regard to the so-called 'illogical' tactical mistakes he made during the war, well where do I start?

The most obvious reason for building-up Hitler's war capabilities was to render the banksters' proposed war sustainable. Had Hitler and Germany not possessed the wherewithal to fight a war on more or less equitable terms, then they would have been defeated in a week and the banksters' carefully-laid plans for WWII would have been in shreds.

Hitler appeared to make tactical mistakes or errors of judgement, not because he was doing the British a favour, but as is well documented by many, even mainstream historians, this is explainable by the fact that he simply did not want war. At this point in history, he was still hoping to avert further bloodshed and he knew that had he prevented the escape of those trapped at Dunkirk, or worse still annihilated them, then his own fate would have been sealed. He knew that he could not successfully fight a multi-front war, given his existing resources. In fact, he was still desperately seeking a way out and still absolutely believed that the British really did not want a war with Germany. Furthermore, he genuinely believed that Britain and Germany's common enemy was the Zionist bankster-controlled Soviet Union and that the British people were Germany's ethnic 'brothers' with whom there should have been no dispute. It was only when he was finally backed into a corner by the chicanery of Churchill and others that he was forced to adopt the strategy of the 'best form of defence is attack.'

"The last thing Hitler wanted was to produce another great war." Sir Basil Liddell-Hart, British historian

"I see no reason why this war must go on. I am grieved to think of the sacrifices which it will claim. I would like to avert them." Adolf Hitler, July 1940

"Hitler wanted nothing from Britain or her empire, and all the German records uncovered in the last fifty years have confirmed this grim conclusion. Others now echo our view that Churchill knew from code-breaking that Hitler was only bluffing; but for reasons of domestic politics Churchill fostered the fiction in his public speeches ('We shall fight them on the beaches') and he did the same in his private telegrams to President Roosevelt." David Irving, 'Churchill's War'

"The state of German armament in 1939 gives the decisive proof that Hitler was not contemplating general war, and probably not intending war at all. Even in 1939 the German army was not equipped for a prolonged war; and in 1940 the German land forces were inferior to the French in everything except leadership." British historian, Professor A.J.P. Taylor, 'The Origins of the Second World War' (p104-105)

"At the time we believed that the repulse of the Luftwaffe in the 'Battle of Britain' had saved her. That is only part of the explanation, the last part of it. The original cause, which goes much deeper, is that Hitler did not want to conquer England. He took little interest in the invasion preparations and for weeks did nothing to spur them on; then, after a brief impulse to invade, he veered around again and suspended the preparations. He was preparing, instead, to invade Russia." Sir Basil Liddell-Hart, British historian

In April 1939, there was an exchange of documents and dialogue between US President Roosevelt (FDR) and Adolf Hitler, as well as between the Polish and German governments. On 15th April, FDR sent a telegram to Hitler decrying Germany's aggression and demanding assurances of non-aggression. Apparently, Hitler saw this as a last-minute chance to avoid open hostilities in Central Europe, thus avoiding another terrible conflagration. He used this opportunity to openly and honestly address all nations, but especially those most directly involved. On 28th April he called a special session of the Reichstag and through German radio and relayed broadcasts, was heard by much of the world. Yet this important address, an honest and sincere effort to avoid war, is today ignored and air-brushed from history as it does not fit with the widely-accepted, yet inaccurate version of history. Upon reading the selections below, one may clearly see why the banksters chose to isolate and pay no heed to these writings. Indeed, one may even notice parallels with current events.

"Adolf Hitler took a last minute opportunity to speak, not only to the USA, but to the

whole world, just as dark war clouds were surely and certainly on the horizon. He not only addressed the topics in FDR's wire transmission, but spoke clearly on other problematic key issues of the day such as the Versailles debacle, the Anglo-German Naval Treaty, the Munich Agreements, etc. He told the truth about what had been and what was going on in Europe, exhaustively responding to each point raised by the American leader. After a thorough reading, what did I conclude? For one thing, it is quite evident that Germany invited continuing dialogue, not war. Even the casual reader can see this. While the Chancellor speaks strongly and straightforwardly, there are no threats, no aggressive language or provocations. Interestingly, and contradicting the popular image of the 'anti-Semitic Jew baiter,' he says little other than to assign them much of the blame for the financial failures of the post-war era and for the rise of Bolshevism; and this in just a few sentences.

His talk logically progresses into a longer, more detailed examination of how the opportunities following WWI were squandered, hijacked and sabotaged. He asked that Woodrow Wilson's 'Fourteen Points' be fully and equally implemented for all the nations, including Germany. And, he fully recognised Poland's right to the sea, but maintaining Danzig as a German ethnic area. Several sections recount the various efforts to secure fair and lasting agreements with Poland, but all were summarily rejected by the oppressive and recalcitrant military dictatorship that ruled the newly emerged state. And, there is more, but explore the selections below.

This fascinating manuscript is quietly suppressed by simply ignoring it. As said, the very limited partial translation does not do it justice, revealing very little of the real content of this timely foreign policy address by a major world leader. We cover sections which readers may, hopefully, find educational and enlightening. As said, almost all of the quotations herein seem to be unavailable anywhere else. The introductory headings are from those appearing in the margins of the booklet pages. Since the ill-fated Versailles Treaty was central to many of Europe's problems, we begin with that." Dr. Harrell Rhome

Hitler responded to Roosevelt's accusations thus … "*… But the millions were cheated of peace; for not only did the German people or the other peoples fighting on our side suffer through the peace treaties, but these treaties had a devastating effect on the victor countries as well.*

That politics should be controlled by men who had not fought in the war was recognised for the first time as a misfortune. Hatred was unknown to the soldiers, but not to those elderly politicians who had carefully preserved their own precious lives from the horrors of war and who now descended upon humanity as in the guise of insane spirits of revenge.

Hatred, malice and unreason were the intellectual forebears of the Treaty of Versailles. Territories and states with a history going back a thousand years were arbitrarily broken up and dissolved. Men who had belonged together since time immemorial were torn asunder.

No one knows this [the burdens of Versailles] better than the German people. For the Peace Treaty imposed burdens on the German people, which could not have been paid off in a hundred years, although it has been proved conclusively by American teachers of constitutional law, historians and professors of history that Germany was no more to blame for the outbreak of the war than any other nation. It is hard to imagine a clearer and more concise summary of the massive errors at the end of the war, setting the stage for the next one.

The resultant misery and continuous want [after the war] began to bring our nation to political despair. The decent and industrious people of Central Europe thought they could see the possibility of deliverance in the complete destruction of the old order, which to them represented a curse.

Jewish parasites, on the other hand, plundered the nation ruthlessly, and on the other hand, incited the people, reduced as it was to misery. As the misfortune of our nation became the only aim and object of this race, it was possible to breed among the growing army of unemployed suitable elements suitable elements for the Bolshevik revolution. The decay of political order and the confusion of public opinion by the irresponsible Jewish press led to ever stronger shocks to economic life and consequently to increasing misery and to greater readiness to absorb subversive Bolshevik ideas. The army of the Jewish world revolution as the army of the unemployed were called, finally rose to almost seven million. Germany had never known this state of affairs before.

As a matter of fact, these democratic peace dictators destroyed the whole world economy with their Versailles madness.

They [the Western powers] declared at the time that Germany intended to establish herself in Spain, taking Spanish colonies. In a few weeks from now, the victorious hero of Nationalist Spain [Generalissimo Franco] will celebrate his festive entry into the capital of his country. The Spanish people will acclaim him as their deliverer from unspeakable horrors as the liberator from bands of incendiaries, of whom it is estimated that they have more than 775,000 human lives on their conscience, by executions and murders alone. The inhabitants of whole villages and towns were literally butchered, while their benevolent patrons, the humanitarian apostles of Western European and American democracy, remained silent."

Hitler further stated.... *"Mr. Roosevelt declared that he had already appealed to me on a former occasion for a peaceful settlement of political, economic and social problems without force of arms. I myself have always been an exponent of this view and as history proves, have settled necessary political, economic and social problems without force of arms, without even resorting to arms.*

Unfortunately, however, this peaceful settlement has been made more difficult by the agitation of politicians, statesmen and newspaper representatives who were neither directly concerned nor even effected by the problems in question."

Does this sound to you like a crazy, power-mad dictator, ready to launch his legions of death upon a defenceless world? Or, is this the voice of a reasonable man, still ready to negotiate for real and lasting peace? If you are still undecided, read on further...

"If the cry of 'Never another Munich' is raised in the world today, this simply confirms the fact that the peaceful solution of the problem appeared to be the most awkward thing that ever happened in the eyes of those warmongers. They are sorry no blood was shed, not their

blood, to be sure for those agitators are, of course, never to be found where shots are being fired, but only where money is being made. No, it is the blood of many nameless soldiers!

They hate us Germans and would prefer to eradicate us completely. What do the Czechs mean to them? They are nothing but a means to an end. And what do they care for the fate of a small and valiant nation? Why should they worry about the lives of hundreds of thousands of brave soldiers who would have been sacrificed for their policy? These Western Peace-mongers were not concerned to work for peace but to cause bloodshed, so in this way to set the nations against one another and to thus cause still more blood to flow. For this reason, they invented the story of German mobilisation.

Moreover, there would have been no necessity for the Munich Conference, for that conference was only made possible by the fact that the countries which had at first incited those concerned to resist at all costs, were compelled later on, when the situation pressed for a solution on one way of another, to try to secure for themselves a more or less respectable retreat; for without Munich that is to say, without the interference of the countries of Western Europe, a solution of the entire problem if it had grown so acute at all would likely have been the easiest thing in the world.

Mr. Roosevelt declared finally that three nations in Europe and one in Africa have seen their existence terminated. I do not know which three nations in Europe are meant. Should it be a question of the provinces reincorporated in the German Reich, I must draw the attention of Mr. Roosevelt to a mistake of history on his part.

It was not now that these nations sacrificed their independent existence in Europe, but rather in 1918. At that time, in violation of solemn promises, their logical ties were torn asunder and they were made into nations they never wished to be and never had been. They were forced into an independence which was no independence but at most could only mean dependence upon an international foreign world which they detested.

Moreover, as to the allegation that one nation in Africa has lost its freedom, that too, is erroneous. On the contrary, practically all the original inhabitants of this continent have lost their freedom through being made subject to the sovereignty of other nations by bloodshed and force. Moroccans, Berbers, Arabs, Negroes, and the rest have all fallen victim to the swords of foreign might, which however, were not marked 'made in Germany' but 'made by Democracies.'

Ireland charges English, not German oppression. Palestine is occupied by English, not German troops. Arabs appeal against English, not German methods."

And, I here solemnly declare all assertions which have in any way been circulated concerning an impending German attack or invasion on or in American territory are rank frauds and gross untruths, quite apart from the fact that such assertions, as far as military possibilities are concerned, could only be the product of the silliest imagination. Friendship and respect for the British Empire must be mutual.

During the whole of my political activity I have always propounded the idea of a close friendship and collaboration between Germany and England. In my movement I found others of like mind. Perhaps they joined me because of my attitude in this regard. This desire for Anglo-German friendship and co-operations conforms not merely to sentiments based on the racial origins of our two peoples but also to my realisation of the importance of the existence of the British Empire for the whole of mankind.

I have never left room for any doubt of my belief that they existence of this empire is an inestimable factor of value for the whole of human culture and economic life. By whatever means Great Britain has acquired her colonial territories and I know that they were those of force and often brutality, I know full well that no other empire has ever come into being in any other way, and that, in the final analysis, it is not so much the methods that are taken into account in history as success, and not the success of the methods as such, but rather the general good which those methods produce.

Now, there is no doubt that the Anglo-Saxon people have accomplished immense colonising work in the world. For this work, I have sincere admiration.

I regard it as impossible to achieve a lasting friendship between the German and the Anglo-Saxon peoples if the other side does not recognise that there are German as well as British interests, that just as the preservation of the British Empire is the object and life-purpose of Britons, so also the freedom and preservation of the German Reich is the life-purpose of Germans.

A genuine lasting friendship between these two nations is only conceivable on a basis of mutual regard. The English people rule a great empire. They built up this empire at a time when the German people were internally weak.

Germany once had been a great empire. At one time she ruled the Occident. In bloody struggles and religious dissensions, and as a result of internal political disintegration, this empire declined in power and greatness and finally fell into a great sleep.

But as this old empire appeared to have reached its end, the seeds of its rebirth were springing up. From Brandenburg and Prussia there arose a new Germany, the Second Reich, and out of it has finally grown the Reich of the German people.

And I hope that all the English people understand that we do not possess the slightest feeling of inferiority to Britons. The part we have played in history is far too important for that."
Adolf Hitler, in response to FDR's accusations of aggression, April 1939

This was evidently too large a dose of truth for FDR to swallow. He ignored it, as did all the bankster-controlled press. It would never do for the real truth about what was happening in the world, to become common knowledge. In fact Hitler had told the absolute truth and so many despicable secrets of World War II are still highly classified to this day, and for good reasons.

But now, history was unfolding exactly according to the banksters' long-term plan. All wars are plotted decades in advance and orchestrated to achieve the destruction of nations and also depopulation, demoralisation, and of course to enhance the banksters' power-base and profits.

The German Luftwaffe (air force) was created and expanded greatly in the 1930s by a British MI-6 'intelligence officer' named Group Captain Frederick William Winterbotham. Winterbotham supervised every aspect of this new air-arm which would later terrorise Europe with its *Heinkel* and *Junkers* heavy bombers ... and the deadly *Stuka* dive bombers.

Winterbotham spelled this out in his own words in his memoirs, published in 1978 ...

"My activities between 1933 and 1938 were closely connected with the rise of Nazi Germany and the rebirth of her mighty armed forces. Although I may sometimes tell it in a light vein, consistent with the character I assumed for my association with the younger people to match their new-found exuberance, the underlying theme was always in deadly earnest. When the invitation from Rosenberg finally came, I once again discussed the whole matter of this strange adventure with my Chief, who in turn discussed it with Sir Robert Vansittart at the Foreign Office. Both these men throughout the thirties believed in the German menace and permission was therefore granted for me to undertake this somewhat unusual mission." Winterbotham, *'The Nazi Connection,'* p. 44

In 1934, Winterbotham had an interview with General Walther von Reichenau, one of Hitler's senior generals and he laid out the strategy for a *blitzkrieg* invasion of Russia ...

General von Reichenau seemed absolutely certain that they would be able to pull all this off and he now turned to both de Ropp and myself and said, 'You see, the whole war in Russia will be over in the early summer. No doubt it will take a good while to mop up the vast Russian forces which have been split up and surrounded.' Again I didn't want him to stop, so I looked a little sceptical and said, 'well, we've always been taught in our history books that the Russian winter has proved the greatest Russian General.' Reichenau put his fist quietly on the table and with great emphasis said, 'there will be no Russian winter, it will be a German winter, all our troops will be comfortably and warmly housed in the great cities and towns of the Communists." Winterbotham, *'The Nazi Connection,'* p. 44

As you may now begin to fully comprehend, the events of World War II, as all previous wars, were in order to advance the banksters' evil agenda of a one-world dictatorial government, the New World Order.

The so-called 'free city' of Danzig was 95% German in the early twentieth century. Along with the surrounding German region, East Prussia, Danzig was totally isolated from the rest of the German mainland by the Versailles Treaty. This formerly-German territory, as of 1919, belonged to Poland which in its newly-expanded form cut right through the Prussian/Pomeranian region of Germany. As was the case with all the ethnic Germans stranded in Czechoslovakia by the inhuman Treaty, the Germans isolated in Poland, became a persecuted minority.

So when Hitler came to power, he attempted to solve the 'Polish Corridor' issue, peacefully by proposing that the people living in Danzig, and the rest of the 'corridor' be permitted to vote in a referendum to decide their status and if the vote mandated a return to German sovereignty, then Poland will be given a 1 mile wide strip, running through Germany to the Baltic Sea so that it would not be landlocked again.

The Poles considered Hitler's solution, but behind the scenes, Poland was urged by FDR to not make any deals with Germany and when it became apparent to Hitler that Poland would not allow a referendum, he then proposed another solution, the international control of the formerly German regions. This entirely reasonable offer was also ignored.

In fact, the banksters intend to use Poland as the catalyst for the outbreak of World War II and on 25th August 1939, the *Polish-British Common Defence Pact* was signed between the nations, pledging mutual support in the event that either was attacked by another European country. This consolidated the previous agreement of March 1939 between the two countries, and also France, by specifically committing to *military action* in the event of any of the three nations being attacked.

With this agreement, powerful Zionist-bankster interests in the UK effectively trapped the reluctant Prime Minister, Neville Chamberlain, as well as France and Poland and all that then remained was for Polish-Jewish thugs to deliberately provoke Germany into action by attacking Germany's heavily defended borders.

Overestimating their own strength, underestimating German strength, and knowing that France and the UK would now be forced to support them, on 31st August, Polish-Jewish terrorists crossed the border and attacked a German radio station near Gleiwitz, Germany. This was no isolated incident and was in fact merely the latest in a whole string of deliberate Polish border infractions against Germany and was to prove the proverbial, 'straw that broke the camel's back.' It was backed-up by a general call to arms in Poland against Germany and Germans in general, whether Polish residents or not. German security services however, quickly arrived on the scene and resumed control, killing one of the Red terrorists in the process.

In fact the Jewish Red terrorists, their Polish government protectors, and their Globalist-Zionist masters had now set in motion a deadly chain of events.

Establishment historians claimed that the 'Gleiwitz Incident' was staged by Germans deceptively dressed as Polish terrorists but as was the case with the 'Reichstag Fire' conspiracy theory, they offered no evidence whatsoever, beyond a forced 'confession' obtained under torture from a captured SS officer, Alfred Naujocks, to support this theory. Please remember that this was a 'theory' that also ignored the outrageous and repeated pattern of provocations directed at Hitler's Germany ever since 1933, including the previous, numerous border incidents, and also Hitler's sincere attempts to negotiate a fair resolution to the Polish Corridor and Danzig controversies.

Robert H. Jackson, a US Supreme Court Justice from 1941 to 1954, was sent to Europe when the war was ending to ensure that Germany alone would be blamed for the Second World War. Jackson, as leader of the US legal team, helped draft the *London Charter of the International Military Tribunal,* which created the legal basis for the Nuremberg Trials.

After studying some of the documents, Jackson knew well and emphasised that the German declaration of war on the United States was perfectly legal. Therefore, he pointed out, it had to be shown before the court that the war in Europe was, from the beginning, a German aggression contrary to international law (making it a crime Against peace.) Thus, the invasion of Poland had to be shown to be an aggressive move with no justification with no blame attached to Poland. Further study of the files brought Jackson to doubt that a fair trial would support, in any way, the finding of Germany's exclusive responsibility. On the contrary, he said ... *"The Germans will certainly accuse our three European allies of having pursued a policy that has enforced the war. I say this because the seized documents from the German Foreign Office, which I have seen, all come to the same conclusion ... 'We have no escape, we must fight, we are surrounded, we are strangled.' How would a judge react if this is found in the trial? I think he would say ... 'Before I condemn anyone as the aggressor, he ought to describe his motives.'"*

"And that would be catastrophic," Jackson continued, *"... because if this trial leads to a discussion of the political and economic causes of the war, this may cause infinite damage, both in Europe which I do not know well, and in America that I know fairly well."*

As a servant of the US Government and US war policy, Jackson arrived at the only possible solution to the issue. That was to in effect ban any discussion on the *causes* of the war at the Nuremberg tribunal. In other words, *not to have a fair trial.* In the transcripts of the proceedings, there is nothing whatsoever regarding the war policies of the West, Poland, or the USSR since almost all documents and testimonies that would have been relevant in this respect were rejected by the court as 'irrelevant.'

But, affidavits such as the one signed by Alfred Naujocks, in which he claimed, without any corroboration, that he participated in a German undercover operation to attack the Gleiwitz radio station, on the very night that Hitler ordered the invasion of Poland, and blame it on the Poles in order to 'justify' Germany's 'crime against peace,' was admitted by the court without question or discussion. Naujocks did not appear in person, only his affidavit was put in evidence and so there was no opportunity for cross-examination of the witness, by the defence.

In reality the real aggressors were Poland, and its guarantors in case of war with Germany, France and Great Britain. Those three nations are the only ones truly guilty of 'crimes against peace.'

By 1st September 1939, Germany had had enough of Poland's open aggression and invaded Poland. As the German army advanced eastwards, the Polish forces, no match for Hitler's legions withdrew rapidly. But in the meantime, cowardly Red-Jewish terrorists characteristically raped, tortured and massacred 3000+ ethnic German Polish civilians in the town of Bromberg, Poland. The massacre was known as 'Bloody Sunday.'

But of course, the Zionist-controlled world press threw-up its hands in mock-horror over Germany's 'aggression' whilst studiously ignoring the Bromberg Massacre as Britain and France simultaneously declared war on Germany.

Then, later in the month and with the Polish army being routed by the advancing Germans in the west, Stalin decided to break the *Soviet-Polish Non-Aggression Pact* of 1932. Poland was stabbed in the back as Soviet, Bolshevik forces rushed-in from the east. The advancing Reds carried-out several massacres, the most infamous being, as mentioned earlier, the Katyn Forest massacre, in which up to 20,000 Polish Army officers were murdered in cold-blood.

Unlike the pre-Versailles Treaty, historical ethnic-German areas which Germany reclaimed, the Soviets conquered *all* of Poland. Exhibiting shocking double-standards, the anti-German Zionist-bankster press, the US, France and the UK remained totally silent regarding this brutal Soviet aggression.

As it came under severe threat from the advancing Red hordes, Poland appealed to Britain for help, citing the Poland-British *Common Defence Pact* that had been signed a mere few weeks previously. Even the Polish ambassador in London contacted the British Foreign Office to point- out that clause 1(b) of the agreement which concerned an 'aggression by a European power' on Poland, should apply to the Soviet invasion. However, the British Foreign Secretary responded with hostility, stating that it was Britain's decision alone as to whether or not to declare war on the Soviet Union.

The truth is that the Allies cared nothing at all about Poland and its helpless citizens. They simply used its ultra-nationalist leaders to provoke Hitler, so that they could have their sought-for war and therefore, the horrors that Poland was to suffer under Soviet invasion and occupation was to be Poland's problem alone, and not Britain's.

Meanwhile, the German-Polish War ended quite abruptly with German forces completely devastating the weaker Polish army and there was now nothing that the Allies could do to help their Polish puppet.

The period between October 1939 and May 1940, was dubbed by a US Senator as 'The Phony War,' as neither side seemed prepared to make the first moves, instead waiting for the other to show their own hand. Also, during this period, Hitler pleaded for the Allies to withdraw their war declarations. To France, he declared . . .

"I have always expressed to France my desire to bury forever our ancient enmity and bring together these two nations, both of which have such glorious pasts."

Whilst to the British, Hitler stated that . . .

"I have devoted no less effort to the achievement of Anglo-German understanding, no, more than that, of an Anglo-German friendship. At no time and in no place have I ever acted contrary to British interests . . . Why should this war in the West be fought?"

However, his pleas for peace and common sense to prevail, fell on deaf ears as the Allies amassed 600,000 troops in Northern France. They were in fact planning to advance eastward upon Germany through Belgium and Holland, as well as establishing bases in neutral Norway and Denmark, with or without the consent of their respective governments.

The *Neutrality Acts* prohibited the United States from selling arms to warring nations, the purpose being to prevent the US from again becoming involved in European wars. But throughout the 1930s, FDR and his bankster-handler, Bernard Baruch (who had also been the handler of Woodrow Wilson), anticipating the proposed new war against Germany, had unsuccessfully tried to amend the previous Neutrality Acts. Soon after the war commenced though, FDR again urged Congress to repeal the Neutrality Acts as per the banksters' wishes, a new Neutrality Act was quickly passed, making the sale of arms to the UK, totally legal under US law.

Thus had the scheming FDR on behalf of his puppet-masters, taken a large step towards involving the US in a war for which the bankers had long been agitating. At the end of November 1939, just two months after the subjugation of Poland, Stalin launched an invasion of Finland. As he had with Poland, Stalin again broke a 1932 non-aggression pact to which he had agreed with the Finnish government, the *Soviet-Finnish Non-Aggression Pact of 1932.*

The invasion was all-powerful, with 21 Soviet divisions consisting of 450,000 Red Army troops. Stalin expected to overwhelm Finland in a matter of weeks, but the brave and outnumbered Finns staged a heroic defence of their homeland causing acute embarrassment for Stalin. Eventually a peace treaty was signed in March 1940, but the Finns were forced to cede 10% of their territory to the mighty USSR.

Stalin had by this time broken two non-aggression treaties and annexed territories from both betrayed parties (Poland and Finland) and so the 'International Community' verbally condemned the Soviet actions, but there were no calls for boycotts or sanctions, nor any declaration of war against the USSR, as there had been against Germany for far less a transgression.

In April 1940, one the Allied plans of attack was to disrupt Germany's iron-ore imports from Sweden by illegally mining Norwegian waters, and then occupying the important Norwegian port of Narvik. Plans were also put in place to impose a base of operations in Denmark, Germany's neutral neighbour to its north.

A Norwegian politician named Vidkun Quisling confirmed the existence of these Allied schemes (Operation Wilfred and Plan R4.) Sympathetic to Germany, and not wishing his country to become a battlefield, Quisling informed Hitler of the Anglo-French plot to wage-war from the two Scandinavian countries. So Germany moved quickly to secure the port of Narvik before the British could deploy their mines, and also to occupy Denmark whilst German diplomats assured the leaders of both nations that Germany sought neither conquest nor interference in their internal politics and so life under limited German occupation went on uneventfully for the Scandinavians during the war. Quisling's name appears today as a word in English dictionaries, synonymous with 'traitor,' a totally unfair characterisation as all Quisling wanted was peace and to avoid bloodshed in his country.

On the 10th of May 1940, the British violation of Iceland's neutrality began with British troops disembarking in the Capital City of Rejkjavik. The British quickly moved inland, disabling communications networks and securing landing locations whilst the government of Iceland vociferously protested the illegal incursion into their territory which was of course, to no avail. This occupation force was then subsequently augmented, to a final strength of 25,000 and this, combined with the recently thwarted, attempted British occupations of neutral Denmark and Norway, clearly demonstrated that bankster-Britain and France were the true aggressors of the war.

Although FDR, up until December 1941, promised that America would remain neutral, 30,000 US troops actually relieved the British and occupied Iceland in the spring of 1941, totally contrary to what we are told and despite America's supposed neutrality.

One of Churchill's first acts upon becoming Britain's un-elected Prime Minister was to suspend all intelligence surveillance on Soviet suspects. This led to the massive infiltration of MI-5/ MI-6 by the communists throughout the 1940s, as previously related.

Churchill, and his wealthy, Zionist backers, had been advocating for war with Germany for the previous five years. His warmongering had made him a virtual outcast in British politics, but now, with the Zionist press of Britain totally misrepresenting the facts surrounding the German-Polish War, Churchill was portrayed as some sort saviour of Western civilisation.

But Hitler well-knew exactly who Churchill was, and what he represented. He even referred to Churchill in his speeches, prior to Churchill's metamorphosis as PM, as part of Britain's 'government of tomorrow,' and once Chamberlain had gone, consigned to the Orwellian 'memory hole' and with Churchill now in power, Hitler knew *for absolute certain* that the 'phony war' was about to transform itself, almost overnight into a very real one.

Hitler's plaintive cries for peace had been repeatedly ignored as approximately 600,000 British and French troops massed in northern France. The massive attack against Germany was planned to be routed through the countries of Belgium and Holland, whose governments were subjected to intense Allied pressure to allow the safe passage of the Allied invasion forces. And thus, again, Hitler's hand was forced and he soon realised that the best form of defence would be attack and so on the very same day that Churchill became PM, and as an act of national self-defence, Germany advanced upon the Allies before they had a chance to realise what was happening.

The stunning advance westward and surprise attack, the German *Blitzkrieg 'lightning war,'* quickly over-ran the smaller nations, and also pushed the Allied armies into a full retreat towards the beaches of northern France, from where they were hoping to scurry back across the English Channel to the relative safety of England, in order to re-group.

The Zionist-banksters' press, as well as today's history books, portray the Blitzkrieg as *'the Nazi conquest of Holland, Belgium, and France,'* but the menacing presence of the 600,000 Allied troops is always conveniently ignored. In fact, Hitler had no designs whatsoever on Holland or indeed Belgium and the German advance through those territories was simply an expedient, direct way of reaching the Allied forces massing in France in preparation for *their* attack on Germany.

But with the eyes of the world focussed firmly on events in Western Europe, Stalin continued to expand his 'Evil Empire,' almost un-noticed, certainly un-reported and definitely un-condemned for his despicable actions. The Zionist-Reds annexed the tiny, virtually defenceless Baltic states of Latvia, Lithuania and Estonia and also parts of eastern Romania. In fact the Soviet Union had violently invaded six countries in just nine months, yet the banksters remained obsessed with demonising and attacking only Germany, a nation whose leader constantly pleaded for peace. Of course, Stalin knew that he was free to act with absolute impunity, safe in the knowledge that his fellow-Zionist sponsors, the western banksters would take secret delight in his quest for global domination. It could be argued that he was actually doing their job for them, which of course—he was.

In order to bring about the defeat of France, Lieutenant-General Erich von Mannstein and his colleague Major Henning von Tresckow, had devised a very sophisticated battle plan. The French army, relying on their experiences of the First World War had dug-in behind an eighty mile long series of fortifications built along the French-German border known as the Maginot line and to the south, always-neutral Switzerland (the banksters monetary safe-haven, of course) provided a natural bulwark against Germany, whilst to the north lay the hilly Ardennes, in which the French believed tank units would find it nigh-on impossible to function. So this natural frontier was ignored by the French high command in all defensive planning but was in fact the strategic weak-point that the Germans exploited to their full advantage.

The western offensive began with von Mannstein confusing the French with a decoy strategy. The Luftwaffe attacked the airfields of Luxembourg, Belgium and Holland, gaining complete air superiority and thereby allowing German paratroopers and ground-troops landed in gliders, to attack and overcome the defenders of the Belgian fort of Eben-Emael, one of the lynch pins of the Allies defence strategy.

The capture of this fort allowed the German forces to cross the Albert Canal, another natural defence barrier and then overrun the Belgian defensive lines causing the Belgians to retreat, but also drawing into a trap the main British and French forces advancing northwards to reinforce the Belgians. Further north, the German advance into Holland was also successful and despite fierce resistance, the Dutch were subdued within five days, surrendering on 15th May.

Having responded to the German attack, some twenty divisions, the best units of the British and French armies were sent north to support Belgium and Holland, with the aim of preventing German troops advancing any further southwards into France. The Allied High Command were totally unaware, that the largest tank squadron ever assembled, and concealed within the dense forests was already rolling ominously through the Eifel mountains and the Ardennes, heading for the River Meuse. Indeed, fifteen-hundred German armoured vehicles reached the river on 12th May, encountering minimal resistance in the process.

On the opposite bank, the French defensive forces had entrenched and were waiting apprehensively for the German invaders and soon found themselves under intense aerial attack from twelve Stuka dive-bomber squadrons, forcing the French heavy artillery to withdraw and inflicting serious casualties upon them. General Heinz Wilhelm

Guderian seized his opportunity and concentrated all his tanks along a one mile-wide section of the Meuse just west of Sedan, and sent across a guards division in inflatable boats. These were quickly followed by light armoured vehicles which secured a 'beachhead' on the French side. Lacking any armoured support whatsoever, the French units quickly found themselves overrun and began to retreat. Eight hours later it was virtually all over and the German bridgehead stretched five miles into French territory, allowing the pioneer units to construct a temporary bridge in order to allow the heavy tanks to successfully cross the Meuse.

This laid wide-open the route to Paris for the Germans, and realising that they now risked being cut-off and encircled, the bulk of the Allied forces in Belgium began to withdraw on the 16th May. Luckily for the Allies the German High Command, at this point became concerned that the Panzer (tank) divisions had become over-extended, and so ordered the advance to halt, in order to allow the bulk of their infantry units to catch-up from the rear. Meanwhile, Guderian was ordered to reconnoitre the area, but interpreted this order extremely freely, allowing his tank squadrons to advance another fifty miles to the west.

This unexpected appearance of German tanks caused French morale and resistance to completely crumble, as they had assumed that the Germans would consolidate and then wait for reinforcements before continuing their advance. On the 20th May 1940, just ten days after the German invasion of France had begun, Guderian's tank divisions had already reached the English Channel at the town of Abbeville. The Germans had now encircled the elite of the British and French armies, forcing them into a desperate retreat, whilst to the north, Holland had already surrendered, Luxembourg had been overrun and Belgium was also on the brink of collapse.

By the 22nd of May, German tank divisions had advanced rapidly north isolating the ports of Boulogne and Calais and therefore only the Belgian port of Dunkirk remained as an option for the retreat back to Britain of the British Expeditionary Force and the remnants of the French Army.

It also appeared that the Allies were in a desperate race against time and it was looking increasingly likely that they would all be captured or worse, when quite suddenly and unexpectedly, a miracle happened, and the inexorable German advance towards them, ground to a halt. Field Marshall von Rundstedt commander of *Army Group A* had become concerned about the wear and tear that his armoured divisions were suffering and the following day Hitler sanctioned the halting of the German armoured advance. However, Boulogne still fell to *Army Group B* on the 25th with Calais falling a day later on the 26th. Now only Dunkirk remained in French hands, so the remaining British and French troops, about 330,000 of them began to congregate there.

When he heard the grave news, Winston Churchill ordered the implementation of *Operation Dynamo*, a plan to evacuate troops and equipment from the French port of Dunkirk, that had been drawn-up by General John Gort, the Commander in Chief of the British Expeditionary Force (BEF.)

The Allied armies had been 'painted into a corner' on the beaches at Dunkirk, France, surrounded by the sea on one side and the massing German forces, seemingly waiting to simply pick them off at will, on the other. Indeed, the entire force could easily have been captured or worse, but Hitler issued a 'halt' command, allowing the Allies to be evacuated, in the very mistaken belief that a show of 'good faith' and generosity towards his tormentors, would be more likely to stop the war, if they were to escape with their dignity remaining intact. .

So, seizing the opportunity that had been unexpectedly allowed them, the British and French High Commands began to implement 'Operation Dynamo.' Using literally any vessel of any size that they could procure, including many civilian volunteers to man them, the evacuation of the encircled armies began on the night of 28th May. Possibly blissfully unaware of how desperate the situation was, a motley flotilla of some 693 ships and boats, consisting of 39 destroyers, 36 Minesweepers, torpedo boats, ferries, 77 trawlers, and even 26 yachts, and a variety of other small craft, set-off from Britain to Dunkirk where they ferried the waiting and exhausted troops from the beaches to larger transport ships lying further offshore. This continued day and night for nearly a week under consistent, yet sporadic attacks from the Luftwaffe, until Dunkirk finally surrendered to German forces on 4th June 1940. Almost all the equipment of the British expeditionary force had been destroyed or fallen into the hands of the Germans, but most importantly, some 338,226 troops had been rescued. Of that number 140,000 were members of the French Army but all heavy equipment was abandoned and left in France.

The Dunkirk evacuation, was the largest evacuation the world had ever seen. But left behind in France were 2,472 guns, almost 65,000 vehicles and 20,000 motorcycles, 377,000 tonnes of stores, more than 68,000 tonnes of ammunition and 147,000 tonnes of fuel. 30,000-40,000 French troops were captured in the Dunkirk pocket.

In addition, six British and three French destroyers were sunk, along with nine other ships, nineteen destroyers were damaged and over 200 of the 'little ships' were sunk, with an equal number damaged.

Prior to the successful evacuation, Churchill gave a warning the House of Commons to expect *"hard and heavy tidings,"* and subsequently, Churchill referred to the outcome as a 'miracle,' and the British press fêted the evacuation as a 'disaster turned to triumph.' However the real reason for the 'miracle' was that Hitler was still desperately trying to end the war and in his, as it turned-out, mistaken view, this was one of the ways he could achieve it . . . a sort of naïve attempt to prove to the Zionist warmongers that he meant no harm and merely wanted to serve his country's best interests geo-politically, without impinging on the sovereign rights of any other nation.

"...he (Hitler) then astonished us by speaking with admiration of the British Empire, of the necessity for its existence, and of the civilisation that Britain had brought into the world...He compared the British Empire with the Catholic Church, saying they were both essential elements of stability in the world. He said that all he wanted from Britain was that she should acknowledge Germany's position on the Continent. The return of Germany's

colonies would be desirable but not essential, and he would even offer to support Britain with troops if she should be involved in difficulties anywhere." German General von Blumentritt, speaking later of Hitler's astonishing 'Halt Order'

How different could the world have been today, but for this totally unavoidable catastrophe, known as the 'Second World War' and the vaulting ambitions of a powerful group of psychopathic Zionist parasites?'

As the fleeing French government collapsed, the Germans entered Paris unopposed on the 14th June 1940 and the new 'loyal' government was headed by the World War I hero Marshal Philippe Petain who had agreed to make peace with Germany. Unlike the brutality of The Versailles Treaty, the terms of this Armistice are generous, insisting only that Germany be allowed to continue its occupation of northern France as a defensive measure against a British invasion of the continent whilst the new French government had its administrative offices in the southern city of Vichy. Other than this strategic occupation of the north, France remained a sovereign nation. And life in occupied France went-on virtually unchanged. The German soldiers established a reputation for their courtesy and consideration and charmed the French ladies, despite the lies we have been told about the ongoing atrocities and oppression under German rule.

Meanwhile, back in England, Churchill and French General Charles De Gaulle, were angered by Marshal Petain's unwillingness to continue fighting. Hitler expressed a desire that Petain ally his country with Germany, but Mussolini's aggressive declaration of war on France left such a bitter taste in the mouths of the French, that it became impossible for them to join any German-Italian alliance.

And with British ground troops now having been forcibly expelled from the European mainland, Churchill and his London/New York bankster-controllers could only continue the fight in the air and on the seas. The Royal Air Force was ordered by the bloodthirsty sadist Churchill, to bomb the Germans into submission by concentrating their efforts on civilian areas. Churchill of course achieved his objective of provoking a like-for-like retaliation from Hitler so that he and FDR could score points as to the *"German bombing of British civilians."*

Professor A.J.P. Taylor wrote that the war of 1939 was... *"...less wanted by nearly everybody than almost any other war in history."*

And on the 15th February 1940, PM Neville Chamberlain in the House of Commons affirmed...

"Whatever the length to which others may go, H.M. Government will never resort to deliberate attacks on women and children, and other civilians, for the purpose of mere terrorism," and in a reply to Captain Ramsey This reaffirmed his position given on 14th September. *"City bombing,"* he emphasised, *"...was absolutely contrary to international law."*

But contrarily in a July 1940 memo to the Minister of UK Aircraft production, the despicable warmonger Churchill, recently voted in several contemporary polls as the 'greatest ever Englishman,' wrote that...

"When I look around to see how we can win the war, I see that there is only one sure path. We have no Continental army which can defeat the German military power ... but there is one thing that will bring him (Hitler) down, and that is an absolutely devastating, exterminating attack by very heavy bombers from this country upon the Nazi homeland. We must be able to overwhelm them by this means, without which I do not see a way through."

If Churchill was indeed the greatest-ever Englishman, what does that say about the rest of us? The implications sadden and absolutely disgust me to be frank. There is little doubt that Churchill's hero-status has been artificially exaggerated and deliberately enhanced in the minds of the British populace throughout the decades. It speaks volumes to me that this 'hero,' this magnificent specimen of humanity, this demi-god was immediately voted-out of office in the greatest landslide ever seen in the entire history of British politics, at the very first opportunity by the British public in the aftermath of the war. Maybe 'the people' are not so 'dumb' as we may think after all, eh?

Indeed Churchill carpet-bombed German civilian areas on a regular basis, killing thousands of innocents including children, in the process. Many Berlin residential neighbourhoods were razed but at first Hitler categorically refused to retaliate in kind and indeed German bombers were under strict orders to limit their attacks to military/industrial targets only. In July 1940 the Luftwaffe began its mass-bombing attacks on British radar stations, aircraft factories and fighter airfields and during the next three months, the Royal Air Force lost 792 planes and over 500 pilots were killed. This period became popularly known as the 'Battle of Britain.'

Finally, on the 4th of September 1940, Hitler was forced to openly declare that any more British bombings of civilian areas would be met reciprocally and right on cue, as expected, when the Luftwaffe dropped its first bombs on British civilian areas, the banksters' world press immediately declared that, *"Germany Bombs Civilians."*

'The Blitz' on London in 1940 and 1941 was a direct response by Germany to the initiation of civilian bombing by Churchill some months earlier but very few are aware of this rudimentary fact, which was central to Britain's role in instigating World War II.

The Blitz is nowadays another element, held-up as proof-positive of Hitler being evil personified and the cause-and-effect connection is never, ever alluded-to or even acknowledged. Winston Churchill and the War Department in fact engineered a situation whereby they knew that London residential suburbs would be bombed mercilessly, whilst neglecting to inform 'the people' that it was in fact Britain that had set the process in motion, several months earlier. This had the double effect of simultaneously traumatising the population and also, more importantly, engendering in them an overwhelming desire for revenge, which gave Churchill and his ilk the licence to fight their sordid, manufactured conflict without recourse to normal conventions of war. These restraints had hitherto established and long-proclaimed that civilians would not be deliberately targeted.

In 1936, RAF 'Bomber Command' was formed and long-range bomber planes were designed and constructed. Its purpose was candidly described by J.M. Spaight of the Air Ministry as . . .

"The whole 'raison d'être' of Bomber Command was to bomb Germany, should she become our enemy."

What a giveaway. So, those who espoused war had already started planning for it in 1936. Germany and France had nothing resembling these sophisticated, state-of-the-art bombers and their development in those countries lagged many years behind that of Britain, despite what we are deceptive told about Hitler's long-term war planning strategy.

In fact, the highly punitive Treaty of Versailles had forbidden war-shattered Germany from ever developing an 'active defence,' alluding to such things as searchlights, flak guns etc. So not only was Britain preparing for a future offensive war, but by the terms of the treaty, had also cunningly attempted to prevent Germany from fighting a defensive one.

Hitler repeatedly sought to secure a truce in city bombing, and to gain agreement that in any future conflicts bombing should be strictly confined to the zone of military operations. Existing conventions and laws of war did not specifically allude to air bombardment, and therefore he repeatedly made offers to restrict the conduct of war by 'confining the action of war to the battle zones.'

But Churchill's first civilian bombing raid on Germany on the 11th May 1940, although in itself, trivial, was an extremely significant event since it was the first deliberate breach of the fundamental rule of civilised warfare; that which exhorted that hostilities must only be waged against enemy combatant forces. On the following day, the War Cabinet minutes noted on 'Bombing Policy,' that the Prime Minister was 'no longer bound by our previously-held scruples as to initiating unrestricted air warfare.'

The Battle of Britain was the largest and most famous air battle in history. By day and night the combatants from Britain (along with pilots from other allied nations) and their enemies from Germany with some limited support from Italy, fought in the skies over south east England, between the 10th July and 31st October 1940. France had fallen to the might of the German Blitzkrieg earlier that year and the Luftwaffe commanded by Hermann Goering now planned to render the Royal Air Force impotent, in preparation for the proposed German invasion of Britain, '*Operation Sea Lion*,' an amphibious and airborne invasion.

The Germans were unable to destroy the majority of British radar stations—the ineffectiveness of the slower-flying Stuka dive bomber against RAF fighter attacks meant that the Germans had nothing capable of conducting accurate strikes on the radar stations and this put them at a distinct disadvantage. But by August 1940, despite the heroic efforts of British pilots, the continuous bombing of airfields, ports and shipping was starting to take its toll on the Royal Air Force. During the early stages of the campaign, under strict orders from Hitler, London had been virtually ignored as a target by the Luftwaffe, however on the 24th August, it was reported that a group of 'lost' German bombers 'accidentally' bombed the capital which resulted in a whole series retaliatory bombing raids by Churchill on Berlin.

However, the Royal Air Force still actually had about 1,000 operational aircraft available and by mid-September 1940, the switch in Luftwaffe tactics to bombing civilian targets, gave the Royal Air Force some 'breathing-space' to repair airfields and radar installations and build more aircraft. Although the RAF fighter pilots were exhausted, the risk of defeat at the hands of the Germans had now lessened for Britain. Now, large formations of Spitfires and Hurricanes could be deployed to attack the German bombers which were concentrated mainly over London. The RAF had the advantage of being close to their bases, ammunition and fuel-supplies allowing them to land and return to the air in a relatively short time-scale, whilst for the Luftwaffe far from 'home,' the losses eventually became unsustainable.

The primary German fighter in the Battle of Britain was the Messerschmitt Bf-109. Although it was a great combat aircraft and could compete equally with the British Spitfires and Hurricanes, its disadvantage was that it lacked sufficient range to provide adequate long-range escort duties for the German bombers and the bombing targets in south-eastern England were at its maximum operational range. The ME-109s could remain to protect the bombers for a short period of time only, before needing to head-back to their bases in France, thus leaving the German bombers highly vulnerable to fighter attacks. The longer-range fighter-plane of the Luftwaffe was the twin-engined Messerschmitt Bf-110 but, this was totally ineffective against the more nimble and faster British fighters. The Luftwaffe had originally been developed as a tactical air-arm to provide air-support to the German ground forces, rather than a strategic, long-range air force and this factor was taking its toll on the otherwise highly-skilled German aircrews.

At the start of the battle, Britain had a strength of 640 fighters and Germany had 2600 bombers and fighters. Although it is difficult to obtain accurate figures on aircraft losses due to exaggerations by both sides during the war, by the end of the battle, it is estimated (according to the BBC and RAF websites) that Britain had lost over 1000 aircraft (the majority were Hurricane fighters) and Germany lost nearly 1900 aircraft, mostly bombers and the ME-109s. During the period of the battle, British factories produced new aircraft at more than double the number of Royal Air Force losses, whilst Germany could only produce enough aircraft to cover half the Luftwaffe's losses, this fact highlights why the Luftwaffe could not continue the battle due to the losses sustained.

In reluctant response to Churchill's bombing of German civilians, the Luftwaffe replied in kind, but only after six such surprise attacks on civilians in Berlin in the previous weeks. Thus Germany justifiably referred to it as a reprisal.

"The British people were not permitted to find out that the Government could have stopped the German raids at any time, merely by stopping the raids on Germany." Professor Arthur Butz

Indeed they are still generally unaware of this fact. Winston Churchill never receives the blame he deserves for instigating the Blitz, although he was never actually popular, even during the war. His 'morale-boosting' personal visits to London's Blitz-devastated East-end had to be curtailed after he was booed and verbally abused on more than one occasion by some angry residents. The German bombs took some one-tenth of the lives of civilians as compared to the British offensive, and Britons do not seem very aware of this ten-to-one ratio.

On the first day of the Blitz, 430 citizens died and around 1,600 were injured. The German bombers returned again the next day and a further 412 died. In all, between September 1940 and May 1941, the Luftwaffe made 127 large-scale night raids. Of these, 71 were targeted on London and other targets outside the capital were Liverpool, Birmingham, Plymouth, Bristol, Glasgow, Southampton, Coventry, Hull, Portsmouth, Manchester, Belfast, Sheffield, Newcastle, Nottingham and Cardiff.

In addition to these raids, and following the disgraceful British bombing of the historical town of Lübeck, the Germans instigated what were known as the 'Baedeker raids,' named after a famous German tourist guide-book of Britain. These raids concentrated upon places of cultural and historic significance and unfortunately for Germany, the outrage invoked by this retaliatory yet petulant, unnecessary action only resulted in a further escalation of the attacks upon their own civilians. During these attacks the non-strategic, historic towns and cities of Norwich, York, Exeter, Bath, Canterbury, Ipswich, Weston-Super-Mare, Kings Lynn and Deal were all targeted, resulting in the destruction of many historic buildings and several hundred civilian deaths. But overall, in comparison to the British raids on Germany, these casualty numbers were tiny—as we shall see later.

Also, during the Blitz, in total, some two million houses were destroyed and 60,000 civilians were killed and 87,000 were seriously injured. Of those killed, the majority were in London and indeed until half-way through the Second World War, more civilians had been killed in Britain, than serving soldiers.

Incidentally, in 1919-1920, it was the British that first developed the technique of bombing towns and villages, bombing Kabul, Afghanistan, and rebellious tribal groups along the border areas of India. And in the 1920s, the British intentionally bombed 'rebel' villages in Somalia and Yemen and instigated an extended bombardment campaign against civilian populations in rebel areas in British-controlled Iraq for several years.

Now that the war was seriously escalating, America and more specifically, the American banksters and their puppet, FDR were becoming impatient for a slice of the 'action.' Understandably, Germany and Japan were equally suspicious of FDR's true, but as yet publicly undisclosed intentions and therefore in order to discourage American military involvement in either Germany's war with Britain, or Japan's unrelated war with China, Germany, Japan and Italy signed the 'Tripartite Pact,' in which they all agreed to assist one another by all political, economic and military means, should one of the signatory nations be attacked by a nation not involved in the European War or in the Japanese-Chinese conflict.

Germany, Italy and Japan hoped that this pact would help to discourage America from joining-in the war but ironically, as it turned-out, it actually facilitated FDR's dastardly scheme to draw America in. Whilst publicly insisting that 'our American boys,' *"...will not be going to foreign wars,"* FDR continued to secretly prepare for US entry into the banksters' Second World War and as a prelude, instituted the peacetime *'Selective Service Act'* which required all males aged 26-35 to register for an upcoming draft, 'just in case.' The actual draft begin in October 1940 and the unlucky draftees were told that they would be compelled to serve a 12-month term, based in either the Western Hemisphere, or a US territory.

Roosevelt signed the Burke-Wadsworth conscription bill in the presence of Secretary of War Henry L. Stimson, Congressman Andrew J. May, chairman of the House Military Affairs Committee, General George C. Marshall and Senator Morris Sheppard, chairman of the Senate Military Affairs Committee, on the 16th September 1940.

By the summer of 1941, the deceitful FDR, who was of course planning to trick America into the war by way of a Japanese provocation, decreed that the draftee's service-periods be lengthened. The outraged draftees protested FDR's broken promise, and threatened to desert when their 12 months were complete, but most of them reluctantly obeyed the new order and continued to serve past the promised October 1941 release date, right up until the 'surprise attack' upon Pearl Harbor by the Japanese in December 1941. This was the first, and only ever, peacetime draft in US history.

It is now well-known that Roosevelt, under pressure from US bankster industrial and financial interests and Churchill, desperate for the US to enter the war to aid a floundering British war effort, conspired together and with others to set in motion events to create a situation which would turn public opinion and generate the outcry that would make war inevitable.

Despite the fact that FDR had won a second term as President largely due to his oft-repeated promise that American soldiers would not become embroiled in the 'European war,' he knew only too well that that is exactly what had been planned.

"'But our boys are not going to be sent abroad,' says the President. Nonsense, Mr. Chairman; even now, their berths are being built in our transport ships. Even now, the tags for identification of the dead and wounded are being printed by the firm of William C. Ballantyne and Co, in Washington DC." Representative Philip Bennett, Missouri, 1939

Also in 1939, Senator Nye of North Dakota, quoted words in the Senate from a volume named 'The Next War', printed in London some years previously. In it was detailed the plan to drag America into WWII by whatever means it could muster, and it said...

"To persuade the US to take our part will be much more difficult, so difficult as to be unlikely to succeed. It will need a definite threat to America, a threat moreover, which will

have to be brought home by propaganda, to every citizen, before the Republic will again take arms in an external quarrel…

… The position will naturally be considerably eased if Japan was involved and this might and probably would bring America in without further ado. At any rate, it would be a natural and obvious effect of our propagandists to achieve this, just as in the Great War they succeeded in embroiling the United States against Germany."

Throughout the US election year of 1940, nationalist Republicans warned that FDR was plotting to drag the US, 'kicking and screaming' into the war. Because the public was strongly opposed to entry in another European war, FDR reassured voters that the 'isolationists' (those who oppose proactive military action) were misrepresenting his intentions. During the campaign, FDR gave his famous 'again and again' speech … *"I say to you mothers and fathers and I shall say it again and again and again. Your boys will not be sent into any foreign wars."*

Then true to form, the Globalists hijacked the nominating process and put forward an unknown patsy, an 'ex-Democrat' named Wendell Willkie, to run against FDR. Many Republicans were shocked when the Republicans (supported by the media's hype of Willkie) sanctioned the appointment of an unknown New York lawyer who had never held *any* public office—of any kind.

"The vast majority of Americans were firmly against intervention in the war, but a covert British propaganda and 'dirty tricks' campaign, employing almost 1,000 people in New York had hijacked democracy with the full co-operation of the FDR administration. In fact more than propaganda was involved, the organiser of the Republican convention, Ralph Williams, an 'isolationist' 'conveniently' died (maybe not too conveniently for him though) on the 16th May and was replaced by a lifelong British agent, Sam Pryor who packed the convention with Willkie delegates and supporters chanting, 'we want Willkie, we want Willkie.'

But historian Thomas Mahl claimed that the British mandate included murder and he implied strongly that this indeed took place. Later, Heinrich Muller, the head of the Gestapo who worked for the CIA during the Truman administration after the war, confirmed that the British had killed many Americans who got in the way." Gregory Douglas, *'The CIA Covenant, Nazis in Washington'*

"Willkie's nomination exempted President Franklin Roosevelt from the normal pressures of an election campaign," Mahl wrote in 1998 in his explosive book *'Desperate Deception: British Covert Operations in the US, 1939-44'*

Had a Republican nationalist such as Robert Taft, won the nomination, Churchill had privately expressed that he was prepared to make peace with Hitler and abandon Stalin to his fate. But that scenario was not to be, unfortunately. Willkie ran a very poor campaign, unsurprisingly to some and was heavily defeated and lo and behold, FDR was elected for an unprecedented 3rd term. Afterwards, FDR appointed Willkie as an Ambassador!

In February 1941, the first units of the German *Afrika Korps* arrived in North Africa to rescue the collapsing Italian forces. General Erwin Rommel, the master tactician known as the 'Desert Fox,' commanded the German forces to some stunning successes, but this diversion of manpower and resources to Africa, eventually proved to be costly for Germany.

Britain meanwhile, was running short of arms and supplies as Germany continued to offer peace on terms favourable to Britain, but of course, Churchill was not interested because, behind the scenes, FDR was reassuring him that the US would shortly enter the war, as soon as they could conjure up a valid reason, of course. But, with his successful re-election campaign of 1940 now behind him, FDR became more voluble and antagonistic in his approach to the anti-war 'isolationists.'

The Lend-Lease programme placed the massive industrial might of the US at the disposal of the UK, and later the Soviet Union. The US was to become 'the Arsenal of Democracy,' according to FDR and Britain would eventually receive $31 billion worth of war supplies *(about $600 billion at 2015 prices.)*

Between mid-1940 and late 1941, Congress appropriated the staggering sum for peacetime of $23bn for the War Department. That was more than the entire total budget of the entire First World War. But remember, the Second World War offered riches far in excess of any bankster's wildest dreams. Indeed, more than 50% of Britain's Conservative Members of Parliament had shares in armaments factories and stood to become very rich in the event of war.

The Comptroller General of the Unites States, Lindsay C. Warren, testified before the House of Representatives in 1943 and 1944, revealing that... *"more than $150bn of 'slush' had already been skimmed off some war contracts, and extensive lobbying on the part of war production firms was ongoing, mainly conducted by ex-military officers after leaving the armed forces."*

US Congressmen were desperate to become involved in the securing of war contracts and sub-contracts to constituent entrepreneurs, for which in return they received lavish 'campaign contributions,' votes and other benefits. Many British and American companies became international conglomerates as a direct result of scrambling for the potential profits of war. Non-descript politicians emerged from the war with absolute fortunes, made from investments in the arms industry, paid for of course with the expendable blood of their nation's youth. Democracy at its finest, of course. In fact Democracy is by far the best political system that money can buy.

Britain, now alone against Germany, which was being armed and fuelled by *Standard Oil (Exxon-Mobil), General Motors, Texaco, DuPont, Alcoa, Ford, IT&T, IBM* et al, appealed to Roosevelt for armaments. Churchill in return, offered the secrets to some of the most important scientific developments of the twentieth century including radar, sonar, antibiotics, the jet engine and much of the original research on atomic power and the atomic bomb.

Ultimately, the US transferred around $21bn worth of war materials to Britain and in addition to providing the US scientific secrets, which had incalculable value to the American bankster-owned multinational corporations, Britain repaid the entire cost of the armaments over the course of the following sixty five years, making the final payment in 2006.

Using the research data provided by Britain and a host of European physicists, the US launched the Manhattan Project in order to develop an atomic bomb. Interestingly, one of the major corporate contributors to the Manhattan Project was none other than Nazi financier and eugenics proponent, Irenee du Pont's *DuPont Chemical*. *DuPont*'s partner-in-crime *IG Farben*, was meanwhile also busily at work in Germany, developing an atomic bomb of their own.

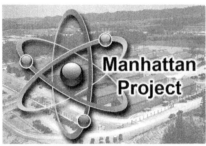

Even after they had converted their military vehicle plant in Russelsheim, Germany to engine production for German bombers, *General Motors* executives informed dissenting shareholders in the US that it was impossible to convert GM assembly lines in the US in order to manufacture airplane engines for the US and Britain.

At around this same time (March 1941,) British intelligence orchestrated a coup in Yugoslavia whereby the new Yugoslavian regime became an anti-German, British puppet-state, which immediately signed a 'Treaty of Friendship' with the USSR. Significantly, Yugoslavia actually shared a border with Germany in its Austrian region.

Long before the German-Polish conflict, FDR had waged a silent war against Germany and with Germany now in control of the European theatre, FDR was even more desperate to drag America into the banksters' war. He baited Hitler relentlessly with such tactics as impounding German ships, clandestinely sinking German U-Boats, freezing German, Italian, and Japanese financial assets in the US, assisting the British Navy in tracing and sinking *The Bismarck*, killing 2200 German sailors, and shipping large quantities of arms to Britain. Hitler bore these humiliating provocations quietly, being fully aware that US entry into the war would be disastrous for Germany.

On the 22nd of June 1941, as Germany and Britain fought each other in the air, at sea and also in North Africa, Stalin's Red Army arrived at Germany's eastern frontier, near the Romanian oil fields that supplied the German war machine. Hitler recalled how Stalin had broken the non-aggression pact and attacked Poland while the Poles were pre-occupied with Germany. Another non-aggression pact was broken when Stalin attacked Finland and Soviet invasions of the Baltic States, and eastern Romania offered even further proof that Stalin could not be trusted. And so, with Germany and Britain distracted, Stalin threatened *all* of Europe. Hitler had hoped to remove the Soviet threat in April, but invasion plans were delayed by Mussolini's misadventures in Africa and Greece but when 'Operation Barbarossa' was launched by Hitler, the Red Army was taken completely unawares and decimated by the German forces.

Millions of Soviet troops were taken prisoner and the devastating loss of weaponry and equipment left the Red Army neutralised. Around 65% of all Soviet tanks, field guns, machine guns, and anti-tank guns were either destroyed or captured and the Germans chased the Reds all the way back to Moscow, liberating the cheering Ukrainian and other Baltic peoples along the way. It was only the onset of the brutal Russian winter that forced the Germans to pause their stunning offensive and it was only the unfortunate two-month delay, due to Mussolini's folly in Greece, requiring German intervention that saved the Red regime from total annihilation in 1941.

But with Stalin's evil Empire on the brink of extinction, Roosevelt moved quickly to rescue the murderous Soviet regime. He released Soviet assets that had been frozen after Stalin's attack on Finland in 1939, enabling the Soviets to immediately purchase more arms and weapons of war. The glorious US of A, bastion of democracy, had now been transformed into the saviour of Communism—exactly as the banksters had hoped, and the tide had now turned distinctly in their favour.

By 1945, the staggering amount of US-provided armaments to Stalin included 11,000 aircraft, 4,000 bombers, 400,000 trucks, 12,000 tanks and combat vehicles, 32,000 motorcycles, 13,000 locomotives and railway cars, 8,000 anti-aircraft cannons, 135,000 submachine guns, 300,000 tons of explosives, 40,000 field radios, 400 radar systems, 400,000 metal cutting machine tools, several million tons of food, steel, other metals, oil and gasoline, chemicals etc. Without this enormous infusion of US aid, there is absolutely no doubt that the German forces would easily have obliterated 'Stalin's Empire' after the spring thaw of 1942.

But back for now to 1941. In late June, the Communist Party of the USSR called upon Party, Soviet, and Trade Union organisations to form 'partisan divisions and diversion groups' and to 'pursue and destroy the invaders in a merciless struggle.' In violation of commonly accepted rules of warfare, many of the Partisans wore no uniforms and nor did they recognise international laws governing warfare. In order to swell the ranks of the Red Partisans and prevent the Germans from winning the 'hearts and minds' of the civilian population of the newly German-occupied areas, Soviet commandoes donned German uniforms and carried out 'false-flag' atrocities against their own people, thereby inciting hatred against the Germans. Communist Jewish partisans, aided by the American OSS (the forerunner to the CIA,) also utilised the same false-flag tactics which meant that the German troops were unable to tell enemy from innocent civilian.

Massive Jewish participation in non-uniform-wearing Partisan groups, including women and children, was one of the reasons for Hitler's decision to intern Europe's Jews in work camps as a wartime security precaution. In much the same way as Britain's ethic German (even 2nd and 3rd generation) population had been interred in Britain and the US-Japanese citizens suffered the same fate in the US.

Volunteers from every nation in Europe including anti-Red Jewish, as well as many from Asia, joined the Germans to fight the Soviet-Communist threat. They were welcomed into Germany's *Waffen SS*, elite fighting force in action on the eastern front. The rabidly anti-Communist *Waffen SS* were strongly motivated by a vision of a greater European family and were tired of the European petty jealousies, border disputes, and economic rivalries. They fought for Europe itself, not for any one country and indeed the *Waffen SS* was a true international army of the European peoples. One million men fought in the *SS*, of which, 600,000 were non-German. During and after the brutal winter of 1941-42, it was the *Waffen SS* who stood their ground and delayed the massive, US-sponsored Soviet counter-offensive. By the war's end 40% of its members were listed as killed or 'missing in action.'

Just as his father before him had, the true American patriot, the famous aviator Charles Lindbergh spoke-out against the banksters' insidious plans. He could clearly see that FDR was manoeuvring towards American involvement in the 'European war.' Lindbergh was a leading figure in the 'America First' movement, or what Zionist-Globalist propaganda disingenuously referred to as 'isolationism.'

Lindbergh was obviously absolutely aware of the truth of what was happening behind the scenes when he warned, "*. . . the leaders of the British and the Jewish races, for reasons which are as understandable from their viewpoint as they are inadvisable from ours, for reasons which are not American, wish to involve us in the war.*"

US relations with Japan had been strained for some time and significantly, Roosevelt was fully aware of Japan's dependence on imports. He had already provocatively, unilaterally terminated America's long-standing commercial treaty with her, resulting in Japan having to ask permission on a case-by-case basis whenever she wished to import anything at all from the United States. In July 1940 the administration had further prohibited exports to Japan by requiring her to obtain a 'licence' to purchase aircraft engines and other strategic materials. In fact, Roosevelt was tightening an economic noose around Japan's neck by stealth, thereby forcing her to source from elsewhere, the supplies and materials she had been accustomed to buying from the United States.

The Japanese had considerable commercial interests in Southeast Asia, especially in French Indochina (now Vietnam, Laos, and Cambodia.) After the fall of France in June 1940, Japan had negotiated with the Vichy government of 'un-occupied France' for permission to occupy French Indochina, so as to take-over military bases there, and to maintain order. The helpless Vichy government had agreed and so as trade with the United States became more difficult, Japan's interests in Indochina gained in importance and she turned more and more towards that source for the foods and raw materials she desperately needed. Trade pacts later concluded with Indochina assured Japan of uninterrupted supplies of rice, rubber and other vital raw materials.

In February 1941, Sir Robert Craigie, the British ambassador in Tokyo, cabled his Foreign Office in London that Japan was about to invade British-held Singapore, which was then a vital commercial and communications link between Britain and her overseas dominions and colonies. Anthony Eden, British Foreign Secretary, summoned

Mamoru Shigemitsu, the Japanese ambassador in London, and strongly berated him regarding the intelligence emanating from the British embassy in Tokyo.

When Eugene Dooman, counsellor at the US Embassy in Tokyo, called on Japan's vice minister for foreign affairs, he was assured that *"there was no truth whatever in Sir Robert's statement."* In fact he said that he had *"repeatedly told Sir Robert that Japan would not move on Singapore or the Dutch East Indies, unless we (the Japanese) are pressed by the imposition of American embargoes."* However, he also said that, *" . . . if disorders beyond the power of the French to control were to arise in Indochina . . . we would be obliged to step in to suppress the disorders."* His assertion was an overt indication of the danger inherent in imposing embargoes on Japan.

But by the end of July 1941, the United States had frozen all Japanese assets in the US, and the Dutch East Indies. All oil deals were cancelled and these moves had the drastic effect of bringing 75% of Japan's foreign trade to a standstill. An intolerable situation for them, of course as the US administration knew well and as was the intent all along.

The US Ambassador in Japan had kept Roosevelt fully informed of her precarious economic situation and urgent need for imports and the US Chief of Naval Operations had also warned the President of the danger of imposing an oil embargo on Japan. He had in fact made it known to the State Department, in no uncertain terms, that in his opinion if Japan's oil were shut off, she would declare war. A fact now well-known to FDR and also part of the cunning entrapment of the Japanese.

In the closing months of 1941, FDR's provocations of Japan had escalated virtually to the level of acts of war,' and FDR further inflamed the situation by denying Japanese ships access to the 'neutral' Panama Canal, and ordering US battleships to undertake 'routine patrols' through Japanese territorial waters. Then on the 26th November 1941, FDR sent an ultimatum to Japan, implying a military threat, demanding that Japan withdraw all of its troops from China and Indochina as a pre-condition for lifting the trade embargo.

On the day before the highly provocative communication was sent, Secretary of War Henry Stimson (a bankster-controlled CFR member) recorded, in his personal diary, the topic of a meeting with FDR as follows, *"The question was how we should manoeuvre them (Japan) into the position of firing the first shot."*

And the answer was . . . to temptingly dangle the bait for the Japanese fish to bite. The tasty bait that the bankster-controlled FDR and his equally traitorous military supremo, George Marshall dangled, was the American Pacific fleet, or at least the 'surplus-to-requirements,' expendable portion of it, which was deliberately left vulnerable and unprotected at the naval base of Pearl Harbor, in the US territory of Hawaii on 7th December 1941.

Occasionally, a bankster-owned puppet does actually speak the truth . . .

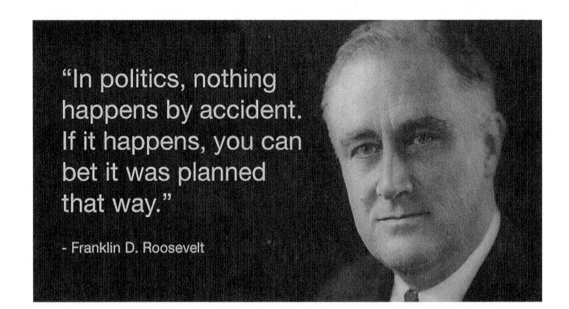

Chapter 10
World War Two – The Reaction

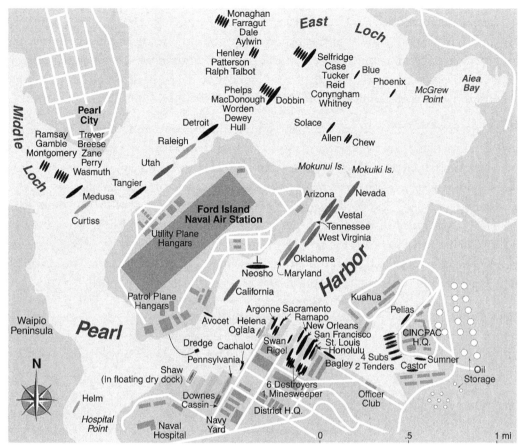

Sunday, 7th December 1941 – Pearl Harbor, Hawaii

Pearl Harbor

"December 7th [the attack on Pearl Harbor] was ... far from the shock it proved to the country in general. We had expected something of the sort for a long time." Eleanor Roosevelt, NY Times Magazine, 8th October 1944

"Yes, the Japanese attacked Pearl Harbor, but we [the US] pulled off an international sting operation to trick them into doing it. Roosevelt actually moved the shipping lanes so that the Japanese fleet would not be discovered and reported by some uninvolved ship's captain. Our own early attempts at radar picked up the incoming Zeros but that was explained as just a flock of birds, which given the unknown capabilities of radar at the time was believable. The fact remains that Roosevelt knew that Pearl Harbor was to be attacked because we had broken the Japanese code. Pearl Harbor was not warned because we wanted to get rid of the WWI ships and be forced to buy new ones and because that war, like all the others was never about nation-states, it was always about the money that every nation needed just to fight in these contrived wars. It has ALWAYS been about the money. And those who died in

the attack on Pearl Harbor were just the price of doing business." Jim Kirwan, Researcher November 2010

On the evening of 5th December 1941, Franklin Delano Roosevelt, the President of the United States, received a message intercepted by the US Navy. Sent from Tokyo to the Japanese embassy in Washington, the message was encrypted in the top-level Japanese 'purple code,' but that was no problem, the Americans had cracked the code long before that. It was imperative that the President should see the message immediately because it revealed that the Japanese, under the heavy pressure of US economic sanctions, were terminating relations with the United States.

Roosevelt read the thirteen-part transmission, looked up and announced, *"This means war."* He then did a very strange thing for a President in his situation...absolutely nothing. On 6th December 1941, at a Cabinet meeting, Secretary of the Navy Frank Knox said, *"Well, you know Mr. President, we know where the Japanese fleet is."* *"Yes, I know,"* replied FDR, *"I think we ought to tell everybody just how ticklish this situation is. We have information... Well, you tell them what it is, Frank,"* said FDR. Knox became very excited and said, *"Well, we have very secret information that the Japanese fleet is out at sea. Our information is..."* and then the scowling FDR cut him short. The very next day, Pearl Harbor was attacked and the rest, as they say, 'is history.' Well, maybe.

Pearl Harbor

At the time of the attack on Pearl Harbor, the US was decrypting a thousand pages per day of coded Japanese communication. Following the attack, the US government maintained that there was no indication of an impending attack but the government however, still classified much of it as secret and denied access to many of the intercepted messages, to the string of enquiries which was attempting to investigate the truth behind the Pearl Harbor incident, over the years. Much of the decrypted traffic is still classified, more than seventy years after the event.

During a naval inquiry in 1944, Captain Laurence Safford, the leading cryptologist responsible for decoding intercepted Japanese messages, testified that on 1st December 1941, the US had... *"...definite information from three independent sources that Japan was going to attack Britain and the United States"* and that, on the 4th December, the US received... *"...definite information from two more independent sources that Japan would attack the United States and Britain, but would maintain peace with Russia."* Early on 6th December, the cryptologist further testified that... *"...we received positive information that Japan would declare war against the United States, at a time to be specified thereafter.*

This information was positive and unmistakable and was made available to Military (US Army) Intelligence at this same time." Further testimony revealed that at 5am Hawaiian time on 7th December, the U.S. received... *"...positive information...that the Japanese declaration of war would be presented to the Secretary of State at 1pm Washington time."*

The larger vessels on 'Battleship Row' in Pearl Harbor could not have been located more conveniently for the Japanese pilots, if they had arranged them themselves. Ignorance was no excuse. The US Navy was very much aware of the devastating success of carrier-borne aircraft against battleships in harbour. A few months earlier the British had destroyed almost the entire Italian battle fleet in a single action in Taranto harbour, Italy, using planes carrying torpedoes modified for shallow water and bombs from aircraft carriers, two hundred miles away.

In view of this and the obvious lessons to be learned from it, and the fact that war with Japan was already being provoked, it is difficult to draw any conclusion other than that the American ships in Pearl Harbor were deliberately arranged as 'sitting ducks' in order to ensure that the Japanese attack became the stunning success it certainly was. At the time of the attack, the ships were left completely vulnerable, with watertight doors and ammunition lockers open and the three more modern aircraft carriers based at Pearl Harbor, the real power and future of the Pacific fleet, were safely away at sea.

The ships sunk at Pearl Harbor were, for the most part, obsolete World War One-era types and of greatly diminished military value. Only one of the battleships, the *Nevada*, was capable of moving under its own power.

In spite of all the warnings and the great likelihood of an attack, anti-aircraft weapons were unmanned, ammunition was locked-away, anti-submarine measures were not implemented, combat air patrols were not flying and scouting aircraft were nowhere to be seen. Newly available, long-range patrol aircraft were not supplied to Pearl Harbor and aircraft were lined up on the ground in convenient, neat, adjacent rows, almost impossible for the Japanese to miss. Does any of this sound even vaguely familiar, perchance, in relation to a slightly more recent 'attack' on the US?

Japan began planning the attack on Pearl Harbor as early as January 1941 as a precaution in the event of the political situation escalating to a war footing and finally, on 26th November 1941 a fleet including 6 aircraft carriers with 423 aircraft aboard, 17 other war ships, 8 oilers, 30 submarines, and 5 midget submarines left Hitokappu Bay in the Kuril Islands of Northern Japan, for Oahu. The sneak attack was pre-planned to occur early on Sunday morning, 7th December 1941, with the main intent of knocking out the US Pacific fleet. However, history has proven that this apparently successful attack was in reality the undoing of the Japanese Empire's desire for Pacific and Asian dominance.

The Commander of the task-force, Admiral Nagumo's mission was to... *"...advance into Hawaiian waters, and at the very opening of hostilities, attack the main force of the US Fleet in Hawaii."* After leaving Japan, the Japanese attack fleet headed eastward until directly north of Hawaii on 3rd December where they turned south, taking them to 230 miles north of Oahu by the early morning of the 7th December and it was from there that the 'surprise' attack began…

Japan's first wave of 183 aircraft, both fighters and bombers, was launched from six aircraft carriers 230 miles north of Oahu at 6.20 am. The plan was obviously to disable the US ability to get fighters in the air, in response to the aggression and the first wave included a destructive collection of aircraft, including 40 torpedo bombers, 51 dive bombers, 50 high altitude bombers and 43 Zero fighters.

A warning of the coming attack occurred as the *USS Ward* destroyed an incoming Japanese midget submarine and a second warning came at 7.02 am when Army radar operators at Kahuku Point detected a large formation of planes coming from the north on their radar screen, but mistakenly believed it to be American B-17 bombers heading-in from California.

The second wave involved an additional 167 fighters and bombers, which delivered another heavy bombardment to all of the same targets, striking ships, aircraft, buildings and personnel whilst they were still desperately trying to recover from the first round of bombings.

At 7.40 am, at this time over Kahuku Point, Japanese Commanding Pilot Lt. Commander Mitsuo Fuchida, the leader of the first wave, signalled the attack to begin and as pre-arranged, the 183 planes of the first wave broke formation. Dive bombers headed upwards to 12,000ft, horizontal bombers to 3,500ft and torpedo bombers plunged to sea level then into mountain passes to avoid detection as they headed for their targets.

Fuchida then radioed his carriers the now famous command, *"Tora! Tora! Tora!"* as his aircraft rounded Barbers Point and headed towards Pearl Harbor. Their primary target was Battleship Row.

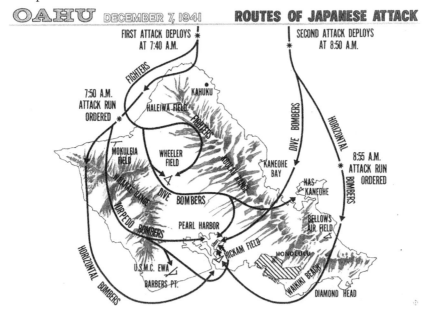

The Air Stations of Oahu were also bombed and strafed simultaneously at the outset of the Japanese raid. This included Air Stations at Ford Island, Kaneohe, Wheeler Field, Ewa, and Hickam plus Bellows Army Air Field and the Marine Air Base at Ewa. This almost eliminated US air response capabilities for the entire duration of the attack on Pearl Harbor.

USS Nevada attempted to escape to the open Ocean but her Captain had to beach her to prevent her sinking in the harbour channel and blocking it. The vessel had been struck by one torpedo at mooring and five 250kg bombs along the way. Tugs helped her across the channel where she was beached off the Waipio Peninsula and one year later the repaired ship re-joined the Fleet, and went on to take part in the Normandy invasion, the invasion of Southern France, and the Battle of Okinawa.

Within minutes of the first wave attack, the battleships, *Arizona, Utah, California, Oklahoma, West Virginia,* and *Nevada* were essentially sunk, and *Maryland, Tennessee* and *Pennsylvania* were badly damaged by torpedoes and bombs.

USS Arizona was the most badly damaged of all of the ships attacked. A 1756lb bomb detonated near the forward munitions magazine, resulting in an incredible explosion that destroyed the front half of the ship, and caused it to sink in nine minutes, resulting in 1177 deaths and only 377 survivors. The unsalvageable ship was left on the bottom of the harbour and remains there to this day as a ghoulish tourist attraction and more importantly, the tomb of all the sadly-deceased crewmen.

USS Arizona destroyed

As the second wave's attack was completed, Commander Fuchida signalled a return to the carriers. 21 vessels had been damaged or destroyed, and most of the aircraft on Oahu's airfields were destroyed. By noon, all but 29 of the Japanese aircraft had returned to their carriers and Japanese commander, Admiral Chiuchi Nagumo, felt the mission was now successfully accomplished. Fearing reprisals from American aircraft carriers, now suspiciously out at sea somewhere, the planned third wave attack was cancelled and thus despite US claims to the contrary, Japanese naval and air forces had actually failed to destroy America's Pacific Fleet.

Personnel casualties included 218 US Army personnel killed in action, and 364 wounded. The Navy lost 2,008 servicemen killed, and 710 wounded and the US Marines lost 109 killed in action, and 69 were wounded. Civilians were also impacted by the attack, including 68 killed and 35 wounded. The total casualty-count was 3581 killed and wounded.

Japan lost 29 aircraft and five midget submarines, and suffered 65 killed and wounded.

Of course, the intelligence regarding the Japanese intent to attack Hawaii, never reached the people who really needed to hear it the most, Admiral Husband Kimmel, Commander in Chief of the United States Pacific Fleet at Pearl Harbor Hawaii, and the unit's commanding general, Walter Short. It was common military knowledge that Pearl Harbor was where the Japanese would strike, if anywhere and the 'surprise' attack was just that, a complete surprise to Kimmel and Short and all the American servicemen and civilians who died. It was however, not a surprise to FDR, Generals George C. Marshall, Leonard T. Gerow, Admirals Harold R. Stark and Richmond Kelly Turner. They were the military's 'top brass' in Washington and the only officers authorised to forward such sensitive intelligence to outlying commanders. But the decoded war declaration was deliberately prevented from reaching Kimmel and Short until after the attack.

Internal army and navy inquiries in 1944, found Stark and Marshall in dereliction of duty for keeping the Hawaiian commanders in the dark, but the military successfully buried those findings.

As far as the public knew, the final truth was uncovered by the Roberts Commission, headed by Justice Owen Roberts of the Supreme Court, and convened eleven days after the attack. As did the Warren Commission, headed by a Supreme Court justice on a different topic more than twenty years later, the Roberts Commission appeared to have identified its culprits in advance and manipulated the facts to make the suspects appear guilty. The scapegoats were Kimmel and Short, who were both publicly crucified, forced to retire, and denied the open hearings they desired. One of the Roberts Commission panellists, Admiral William Standley, referred to Roberts' performance as, *"crooked as a snake."*

There were altogether, eight investigations of the Pearl Harbor incident. The most spectacular was a joint House-Senate probe that reiterated the Roberts Commission findings. At those hearings, Marshall and Stark testified, incredibly, that they 'could not remember' where they were the night the war declaration was received but a close friend of Frank Knox, the secretary of the Navy, later revealed that Knox, Stark, and Marshall spent most of that night in the White House with Roosevelt, awaiting the bombing of Pearl Harbor and relishing the chance for America to join World War II.

From there, a further, widespread cover-up ensued. A few days after Pearl Harbor, historian John Toland reported that Marshall informed his senior officers, *"Gentlemen, this goes to the grave with us."* General Short had once considered Marshall his friend, only to learn that the Chief of Staff was the one who had 'framed' him. Short later remarked that he pitied his former friend because Marshall was the only general who would not be able to write an autobiography.

Indeed, of the multiplicity of warnings of the attack concealed from the commanders at Pearl Harbor, the 'Winds Code' was perhaps the most shocking. This was an earlier transmission, in a fake weather report broadcast on a Japanese short-wave station. It was simply *"east wind, rain."* The Americans already knew that this was the Japanese code for war with the United States but the response of the senior US military was to deny that the message existed and to destroy all records of its being received. But it did in fact exist and it **was** received.

US cryptography apart, the Australian intelligence service had also located the Japanese fleet heading for Hawaii, three days prior to the attack. A warning was immediately sent to Washington where the spin by Roosevelt was that it was a politically motivated rumour circulated by the Republicans. Also, a British double-agent, Dusko Popov, learned of the Japanese intentions and desperately tried to warn Washington too, to no avail. And there were several others.

So why would Roosevelt and the senior military commanders sacrifice the US Pacific Fleet, not to mention thousands of servicemen's lives – which of course was a deliberate act of treason, not to mention mass-murder? As previously related at length, they had concluded long before Pearl Harbor that they wanted to join in the war against the Axis powers and a 'surprise,' and 'unprovoked' attack (of which it was neither) on Pearl Harbor would surely convince American public opinion to accept a war they would have otherwise rejected. In addition Roosevelt would have a strong 'get-out' clause for reneging on his 'no European war,' empty promise.

Roosevelt believed also, that provoking Japan into an attack on Hawaii was the only way that he could overcome the powerful 'America First,' non-interventionist movement led by aviation hero Charles Lindbergh. These anti-war views were shared by 80 percent of the American public from 1940 to 1941. Thus a small group of men, revered and held to be most honourable by millions, had convinced themselves that it was necessary to act dishonourably, commit treason, in effect murder in cold blood, thousands of fellow-Americans and incite a war that Japan had tried to avoid. All at the behest of that their ultimate masters – the Zionist banksters.

Immediately after the Japanese attack, the government of Britain and the Netherlands government-in-exile in Britain declared war on Japan – even before the US itself had done so. The US, shortly afterwards, duly declared war on Japan but, contrary to popular myth in the US, not on Germany or Italy. Even the isolationists could not resist the war fever caused by what FDR referred-to as *"an unprovoked attack."*

"Yesterday, December 7th, 1941 – a date which will live in infamy – the United States of America was suddenly and deliberately attacked by naval and air forces of the Empire of Japan." FDR, 8th December 1941.

Tens of thousands of patriotic American men, oblivious as to how these events were engineered by the banksters, blinded by patriotic fervour and propaganda and overcome by a sense of 'duty,' flocked to volunteer for military service. A few days after the attack on Pearl Harbor, Hitler allowed his personal dislike of Roosevelt to overcome his better judgement and made one of his greatest tactical errors and declared war on the United States, thus saving Roosevelt the time and trouble to do the same.

When Germany and Italy fulfil their Tripartite Treaty obligation to Japan, by announcing that a state of war now existed between the Axis nations and the US, (though in reality, neither country had any way of actually attacking the US mainland) Congress then followed suit with additional war declarations upon Germany and Italy.

Then on the 19th February 1942—FDR's Executive Order 9066 condemned 110,000 Americans of Japanese ancestry to serve the rest of the war years in prison camps. Of those interned, 62% were actual American citizens. One hundred percent of all the Japanese-Americans in the state of California were interred, as well as many in Oregon, Washington, Arizona yet only about 1% of those in Hawaii.

Two-thirds of the total, were American citizens and yet despite that, they unjustly lost their freedom and most of their property, all without due process of law and without having actually done anything wrong other than to be born of the wrong ethnicity.

However, the FBI, unlike the President, the generals, the newspaper editors and the Supreme Court, were against the internment. They had already rounded up all the Japanese-Americans who may possibly present a threat, just as they had rounded up all the German and Italian-Americans who might be a threat too. The FBI knew that apart from a few, isolated extremists, Japanese-Americans were not a danger.

Pearl Harbor will always be remembered in the history books, the TV documentaries, as well as the majority of bankster-influenced and / or controlled websites, such as *Wikipedia*™, as the Japanese 'surprise attack' on the United States that resulted in America being dragged unwillingly and unavoidably into WWII. The idea and the documented fact that it was really engineered by the banksters, aided and abetted by the treasonous Zionists and covert Communist-sympathisers within the US and British governments as part of their long-term global plan still, more than seventy years later, has still not yet resulted in the public 'waking-up' to that very fact.

Even with both the declassification and leakage of WWII secrets, it still has taken a very long time for historians to re-examine Pearl Harbor and, what really adds ironic insult to all the treasonous betrayal and unnecessary, horrific death and injury in all this, is that the Japanese Navy could not have done the deed, without the prior help of the British Royal Navy.

In 1918 the Japanese approached the Royal Navy with a view to obtaining information regarding the new British aircraft carriers. At the time Japan was a close ally of Britain, but nevertheless, the Admiralty refused. They wanted to keep their plans for this new technology secret. However, unfortunately for the Admiralty, the Air Ministry and the Foreign Office had different ideas and believed that here was a potential for large sums of money to be made. And so it was that William Forbes-Sempill was sent to Japan in 1920 to lead a civilian delegation to assist the Japanese with their aircraft carrier ambitions.

This was successful and a huge boost for Japan, who's military now had a potential worldwide capability. This alarmed the US even at this point in history, and they voiced their concerns at the Washington Conference of 1922, eventually leading to the termination of the Anglo-Japanese alliance.

However, the damage had now already been done and all Japan now needed was for their pilots to be trained in aircraft carrier techniques and tactics. Luckily enough for them, one Frederick Rutland made himself available. He had risen through the ranks to become a Squadron Leader and was one of the best carrier pilots in Britain. But, as recorded in an MI5 statement two decades later, Rutland believed in the hype that WWI had been the 'war to end all wars' and believing that war was a thing of the past, left the military and moved to Japan where he began work for the Japanese government, designing planes and training pilots.

So, thanks to the help received from both Sempill and Rutland, Japan made rapid developments in naval aviation and by the 1930s had a carrier fleet equal to the Royal Navy. This in effect gave Japan the capability to wage war virtually anywhere and indeed in 1931 Japan's war began when they invaded Chinese Manchuria. Britain's response to this worrying development in the Pacific was to spend £50 million on turning her Pacific base of Singapore into the largest and most fortified naval base in the world. However, unfortunately for the British, it was discovered a year later that one of the Japanese spies operating in the area purchased plans of the new base from a British serviceman named Roberts, totally compromising British security in the region.

The Fall of Singapore

British Singapore fell to Japanese forces on 15th February 1942. 100,000 British troops were taken prisoner and in Britain, during a secret session, MPs demanded an enquiry to explain how this had happened. Churchill refused. Rutland was eventually deported to Britain, where he ended-up committing suicide whilst Sempill continued to work for the Admiralty until his death in 1965. Despite the mountain of incriminating evidence against him, he was never charged.

British Malaya had been considered a strategic stronghold within the eastern Empire, and the island of Singapore, 273 square miles, on the southern tip of Malaya, was known as the 'Gibraltar of the East.' Acquired by Sir Stamford Raffles for Britain's East India Company in 1819, Singapore became a full British possession five years later, in 1824. Rumours of a Japanese attack were dismissed as nonsense; these 'Japs' with their notoriously poor eyesight could hardly shoot straight, let alone pose a threat to the might of the British Empire – or so it was popularly believed by the arrogant British ruling classes.

An impressive naval defensive system consisting of huge guns had been built at great cost during the 1920s, facing south out to sea. To the north of the island, on the mainland, lay hundreds of miles of dense Malayan jungle and rubber plantations considered by the British to be impenetrable. Stationed on the island, there were almost 100,000 British, Canadian, Australian, Indian and a few local Malay troops.

Without the benefit of air support, the British ships were easily torpedoed and sunk with the loss of 840 lives. 1,285 survivors were taken prisoner but the Japanese, by contrast, lost only four planes. Years later, Winston Churchill wrote, *"In all the war, I never received a more direct shock."*

The Japanese simply executed their invasion plan with ruthless efficiency and were already ashore before any orders to counter the attack were able to be issued. All elements of British strategy, command of the sea and air and an occupation of important ground, had failed to be executed.

The Japanese had advanced south from Kota Bahru with their infantry soldiers on bicycles, and using tanks which the British had thought totally impractical within the dense jungle, and all ably supported by fighter planes. Their aim was to conquer Malaya and capture the island of Singapore on the southern tip of the mainland, 620 miles to the south. They found themselves hundreds of miles north of Singapore and Allied troops, consisting mostly of Indians, Australians and British, stood between them and Singapore but the Japanese quickly dominated the obsolete Allied aircraft and gained air superiority. The Japanese also conducted just enough landings behind Allied lines to tie-up opposing troops and by the end of December, the invaders were halfway to Singapore.

After a brief rally by the British, the Japanese retained the initiative in January 1942. The Allies inflicted some casualties through ambushes and fought delaying actions to enable comrades to escape capture, but the Japanese never faced a serious counterattack, let alone a counter-offensive. Additional Allied troops had arrived, but not enough to stop the onslaught and so, within six weeks of landing in Malaya the Japanese, with total air superiority, were within striking distance of Singapore.

With the loss of only 2,000 of his men, the commander, Yamashita had conquered Malaya in little more than seven weeks. Now there was just the small matter of Singapore, but Yamashita was worried – his supply lines were stretched, he was lacking ammunition and with only 20,000 men, his forces were outnumbered.

Responding to pleas from Australia and New Zealand that Singapore be better defended, Churchill sent reinforcements. These included the 18th British Infantry Division and 44th Indian Brigade, the latter only partially trained, as well as nearly 50 Hurricane fighter planes. Then on 10th February, the hero Churchill, from safely behind his desk in London, ordered... *"The battle must be fought to the bitter end at all costs... Commanders and senior officers should die with their troops. The honour of the British Empire and the British Army is at stake."*

General Arthur Percival, the British commander in Singapore reiterated the Prime Minister's order the following day... *"In some units the troops have not shown the fighting spirit expected of men of the British Empire . . . It will be a lasting disgrace if we are defeated by an army of clever gangsters many times inferior in numbers to our men."*

I find it genuinely staggering that people of this ilk, those who willingly send men to die for virtually nothing (unless you count the banksters' dreams of even more power and wealth,) can simultaneously berate them for not dying quickly enough for their masters' cause and yet have this regarded as 'normal' behaviour by the uncomprehending majority. Either the world is completely insane or I am – and I am genuinely not sure which. But should it turn out to be me after all, then to be frank, I much prefer insanity.

The Allies fought to hold on to the high ground at Bukit Timah, the location of their food and fuel depots, but lost the position on the 11th. With the Japanese threatening Singapore city, the Allies withdrew their troops from the eastern section of the island on the 12th, a move that left Singapore's water reservoirs in Japanese hands.

The British, although running short of food and water, were well equipped with ammunition, unlike the Japanese who were quickly running short. And with 80,000 men at his disposal, Percival's position seemed favourable. But despite Churchill's severe, yet totally characteristic orders, British discipline broke and panic ensued as the Japanese bombed the island and Singapore city was flattened.

His subordinates urged Percival to surrender to save further loss of life. He refused. But the last ships had gone and there was no escape as the Japanese army ran riot, showing no mercy to either soldier or civilian, bayoneting and killing civilians, women, children and hospital patients, alike. The worst atrocity occurred at the Alexandra Hospital, where the Japanese first bayoneted to death a British officer carrying a white flag, then proceeded to massacre 320 staff, nurses and patients.

By 12th February, eighty per cent of the island lay in Japanese hands but Percival did not realise that the Japanese were down to their last few hours' worth of ammunition. At this point, now seeing further resistance as futile, on 14th February, Churchill reluctantly reversed his stance and authorised the surrender of Singapore. Now even Percival had to seek surrender terms but the Japanese commander, Lt. Gen. Tomoyuki Yamashita, told him that any surrender would be unconditional. Percival agreed and reports of the number of troops surrendered to the Japanese ranged from 60,000 to 100,000 men.

The final fall of Singapore was, in Churchill's words, the . . . *". . . worst disaster and largest capitulation in British history."* What Churchill omitted to say however, was that Singapore was not about humiliating and murderous defeat, but betrayal. Although of course, Churchill and his Zionist bankster-masters were experts in the art of betrayal.

Surrender did not bring an end to the suffering, which simply entered a new phase. The Japanese executed, tortured, and killed thousands of prisoners. Other prisoners of war were worked to death and even civilians fared no better. Any amazement or joy of the Japanese victory over their English colonial masters was quickly forgotten under Japanese rule and citizens starved as the Japanese exported their food supplies elsewhere to feed their troops. Japan's post-war estimate of civilian deaths was 5,000, but other sources placed it as high as 50,000.

The myth of the invincibility of the European soldier was shattered and over 80,000 British and Commonwealth troops were forced to spend the rest of the war in captivity, suffering appalling hardship. Indeed more than half of them would never return home.

Yamashita later said of the surrender meeting with Percival... *"I realise now that the British Army had about 100,000 men against my three divisions of 30,000 men. They also had many more bullets and other munitions than I had. I did not know how long we could carry on with our munitions very low. I was preparing for an all-out last attack when their surrender offer came, it was a great surprise. In my heart, I was afraid that they would discover that our forces were much less than theirs and that was why I decided I must use all means to make them surrender without terms."*

That surely is the real irony of what Churchill considered to be the British's *'greatest defeat in history.'* However the shattering defeat of Malaya and Singapore was even more crushing and humiliating for the British because their superiority had been smashed by a weaker, inferior, Asiatic army one third the size of the defending armed forces.

The Battle of Midway

On the 4th to 7th June 1942, the Battle of Midway, the most important naval battle of the Pacific campaign, was fought. The US Navy, under the command of Admiral Chester W. Nimitz, decisively defeated the Japanese, inflicting irreparable damage upon the Japanese fleet. Indeed after Midway, Japan's Pacific defence perimeter of islands steadily shrunk as Japan could not replace its lost ships and aircraft as quickly as could the US navy.

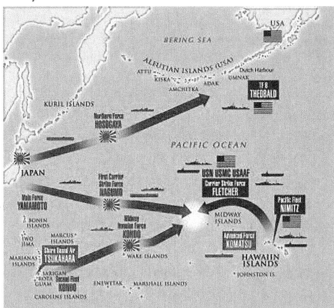

Soon after Pearl Harbor, the armed forces of Japan made various incursions in the Pacific and Southeast Asia, such as the invasions of Guam, the Philippines, Wake,

Corregidor and other strategic island strongholds. These hostile movements all stemmed from the growing need for raw materials in Japan, especially oil. After signing the Tripartite Pact with Germany and Italy, which as Charles Mercer states, *"...promised to enter into war if any of the three was attacked by a new enemy,"* Roosevelt, feeling threatened by Japanese involvement in the war, had suspended all oil sales to Japan, and also convinced France and Britain to do likewise. By doing so, Roosevelt had taken away almost all of the crude oil that Japan was importing, which in turn halted the Japanese imperialistic ambitions in Asia. Oil, after food, is the most important resource available to modern armed forces, as without it, any heavy equipment such as tanks and ships will not run.

In an effort to prevent Japanese advances towards New Guinea, the US Navy sent a carrier task force under the command of Vice Admiral Fletcher, who would later participate in the Battle of Midway. They were to harass the enemy invasion forces and to deal out as much damage and punishment as possible to the marauding Japanese. Although the invasion force provided no significant resistance, a Japanese carrier force that lurked behind the transports attacked the American carriers, and the resulting battle, known as the *Battle of Coral Sea*, became the first engagement between two carrier forces.

Each side lost one carrier and had another damaged. Although considered a stalemate, the battle effectively prevented the invasion of New Guinea and demonstrated to the Japanese high command the potentially lethal threat that the American carrier groups posed. Stung by his setbacks at Coral Sea, Admiral Yamamoto, fleet Admiral of the Japanese Navy and mastermind of the Pearl Harbor raid, decided to lure the American forces into a trap and crush them once and for all.

Thus was the plan set for Midway. Yamamoto had chosen Midway as his intended battleground because of its distance from the US, and believed that with Midway fully-occupying the US naval forces, the Japanese could stage further raids on Pearl Harbor and even the continental US. As in the original Pearl Harbor raid, Vice Admiral Nagumo's First Air Fleet would be the striking arm of the operation and although without two of his veteran carriers, Nagumo's force was nevertheless a formidable one.

The *Battle of Midway*, was more than just a military legend, it was a major feat of intelligence. This operation was almost kept top secret, and would have remained unknown to the Americans, had it not been for the code-breakers at *'Hypo,'* the intelligence installation in Hawaii. Led by one of America's most talented code-breakers, Commander Joseph Rochefort, the intelligence team was able to deduce the location of the Japanese invasion by the letters 'AF.' Because most of the US island bases had closed wire communications, Rochefort assumed that AF was Midway, and told them to send a 'trap' message back to Hawaii, un-encoded saying that Midway was running low on fresh water. Shortly afterwards, *Hypo* intercepted a Japanese message re-iterating that AF was running low on fresh water, thus confirming the intended location of the proposed Japanese assault.

On 4th June, the Japanese carrier aircraft began their attacks on Midway. Although they were relatively successful in shooting down American fighters, they inflicted only insignificant damage to the island installations themselves. After the first wave of Japanese fighters returned to their carriers to re-arm, the Midway defenders launched several attacks of their own against the Japanese. Although these attacks did nothing to damage the Japanese ships, they did tie up the Japanese fighters and forced them to land to refuel.

The fateful decision to have all the carrier-based planes land and refuel at the same time was suggested by one of Yamamoto's most highly regarded subordinates, and was enacted by Admiral Nagumo. This left the carriers vulnerable and without fighters to fend off attackers and by sheer luck, the American carriers had launched their dive bombers just as the Japanese were refuelling, catching them unawares, and setting fire to three of the four carriers. And so with this incredible piece of luck, the Americans now had the upper hand in the battle.

The Japanese force had been dealt a crippling blow. Of the three carriers that were set ablaze, two sank without further intervention, whilst the third was scuttled by its crew to prevent it falling into American hands. And as for the remaining Japanese carrier, the planes of *USS Enterprise* and *USS Hornet* attacked, thereby ending the Japanese resistance.

This one battle that lasted for three days, in effect had decided the fate of Japan in the war. With their carrier air-power completely negated, they could no longer compete on equal terms with the three remaining US Pacific carriers and even with the Pearl Harbor battleships out of commission, the Japanese Navy were no match for US carriers.

The psychological effect upon the Japanese Navy was immense and Yamamoto sunk into a deep, depression in which he lost much of his former ingenuity and bravado. The battle had little negative effect upon Japanese public morale, however, because of the cover-up, propaganda campaign by the government. Indeed, most of the Japanese nation believed that the battle was a great victory.

As far as the Americans were concerned though, Midway was the huge climax to a series of morale-boosting events, from the Doolittle Raids, to Coral Sea and finally Midway. The uplift in morale also resulted in an increase in production of the materials of war and of course, Midway was the turning-point in the Pacific war. It destroyed the Japanese dominance of the Pacific, and it also badly affected the confidence of the Japanese high command.

But although Midway marked a significant turning point in the Pacific war, the US was to sustain many more casualties as the Japanese tenaciously defended their Pacific strongholds, often to the last man, for many months to come.

The Battle of Stalingrad

In July 1942, the Battle of Stalingrad, between the Germans and the Soviets was fought for control of the strategically vital Russian city that Stalin had named after himself and which is today known as Volgograd. The battle was one of the bloodiest battles ever fought in the entire history of warfare, with combined deaths on both sides of almost 2 million.

Hitler had amassed a massive army consisting of tanks and infantry, known as 'Army Group South,' whose purpose was to attack southwest Russia and procure the oil fields. Army Group South consisted of the 6th and 17th armies, and the 1st and 4th Panzer armies. However, Hitler's problem was that his forces were spread too thinly to successfully subdue all of South Western Russia.

The Germans utilised the successful tactic of *Blitzkrieg* once again, in their attack on Stalingrad of which the first phase consisted of the Luftwaffe's bombing of the city for several days, almost reducing it to rubble. Over 10,000 tons of bombs were dropped on the city and this was followed by an artillery bombardment and the storming of the city by the 4th Panzer army and the 6th army. It took several months for the Germans to take the majority of the city, but they never quite managed to break the last Soviet defensive line on the west bank of the Volga River and this was to prove crucial in the final analysis.

Following the initial German offensive which had managed to capture most of the city, the US bankster-supported and Lend Lease-equipped Red Army eventually wore-down the Germans down with bloody house-to-house fighting.

The city's civilian population also fiercely resisted the Germans. Stalin's commandos had dressed in captured German uniforms and committed atrocities against his own people and as intended, this 'false flag' terrorism inflamed the civilian population and made them even more determined to annihilate the Germans.

Unfortunately for the German army, its flanks were also poorly defended, leaving them vulnerable to Russian counter-attacks. Once the Soviets realised this fact, they quickly 'out-flanked' and surrounded the German troops within the city, and completely destroyed them all to the last man, showing no mercy whatsoever. The enormous losses sustained by the Germans, rendered victory in Russia totally impossible as one of the most powerful armies in the world had just been destroyed. A complete army group was lost at Stalingrad and 91,000 Germans were taken as prisoners.

Time magazine named Joseph Stalin Man of the Year in 1939 and 1942.

STALIN - A HERO IN THE WEST

With the Soviet success at Stalingrad, it now looked as if Joseph Stalin might be able to lead the USSR to victory, and he was increasingly portrayed as a hero in the West.

In the United States, the bankster controlled and run, *Time* magazine announced the genocidal maniac Josef Stalin as 1942's 'man of the year.' The accompanying citation concluded, *"Stalin's methods were tough—but they paid off."* A few months later, *Life* magazine described Stalin's secret police, the NKVD as *"a national police similar to the FBI."* Of course most Americans knew nothing about Stalin's genocidal purges or the deportations of hundreds of thousands of Soviet citizens, an ignorance that the banksters were of course keen to maintain. After all, the Soviet Union was bearing the brunt of the war, and Stalin was one of their most important allies.

"It was necessary for the American leadership, the government, the President, to have a sense of realism about the Soviet Union and the public at large, it was not really essential for the public at large to know that. We've got to win the war. That's what counted." George Elsey, Naval Intelligence Officer, the White House

The Dieppe Raid

Like Dunkirk, the Dieppe Raid on 19th August 1942, known as *Operation Jubilee* was a military disaster promoted by the propaganda-masters as a victory. In total there were six thousand troops involved including 5,000 Canadians, the rest consisting of British Commandos, a few Frenchmen, and a token force from the US Ranger battalion. In fact their raid on Dieppe was a bloody massacre and humiliation for the allied forces.

The operation was spearheaded by Churchill's new Chief of Combined Operations, the incompetent, bisexual paedophile, Lord Louis Mountbatten, who chose the Canadian 2nd Division to lead the attack. The objective was to seize and hold a major French Channel-port, test new amphibious equipment, gather intelligence from prisoners and to gauge the Germans' reaction to a sea-based invading force.

Churchill also hoped that the use of Canadian troops would satisfy the Canadian commanders following the long inactivity of Canadian forces in England. General Andrew McNaughton, who commanded the First Canadian Army and General H.D.G. Crerar, commander of the Canadian troops, conscienceless warmongers all, eagerly embraced this chance for Canadian soldiers to get some combat experience. They had been stationed in England for two years without having ever engaged the enemy in a major operation. Canadian public opinion, no doubt stoked by the controlled government and media, was starting to question this inactivity.

Churchill also needed some good news to counter the defeats in Africa earlier in the year. The British press, were also clamouring for further action, the Soviets were pushing Roosevelt to open a second front in Europe, and the overconfident Americans in turn were pressurising Churchill to mount some kind of high-profile operation. The British Prime Minister, was reluctant to agree to a full-scale assault with a poor chance of success, but he nevertheless sanctioned Mountbatten's sheer folly.

So on the evening of 18th August, almost 240 ships left British ports but as they approached the French coast the next morning, things began to go wrong. The ships carrying No.3 Commando ran into a German convoy, which alerted coastal defences at Berneval and Puys, thus meaning that there would be even less chance of success. The vessels carrying No. 3 Commando were scattered and most of the unit never reached shore and those who actually did were quickly overwhelmed. One small party of twenty commandos got within 180 metres of the German shore battery and their accurate sniping prevented the guns from firing on the assault ships for two-and-a-half vital hours, before they were safely evacuated.

At 05.00 am, 2 km east of Dieppe, the Royal Regiment of Canada made their approach to the narrow beach at Puys, a small seaside village. They were behind schedule and had lost the advantages of surprise and darkness and as the sun rose, the well-entrenched German defenders opened fire on the landing craft that were still ten metres from the beaches. At 05.07 am, the first craft lowered its ramp and exiting Canadian soldiers were met with an intense storm of machine-gun and mortar fire, and fell in great numbers, mowed down by bullets and shrapnel. Indeed, those few who made it to the heavily barb-wired seawall were taken prisoner after a short, but ultimately useless resistance.

A total of 200 were killed and 20 died later of their wounds; only 33 made it back to England; the rest were taken prisoner. It was the heaviest toll suffered by a Canadian battalion in a single day throughout the entire war.

The failure to clear the eastern headland enabled the Germans to liberally strafe the Dieppe beaches which condemned the main frontal attack to abject failure from the start. The main attack took place at 05.30 am, thirty minutes after the flanking assaults, the tanks being deployed in the centre with the Essex Scots to the east and the Royal Hamilton Light Infantry to the west.

The western assault gained a brief foothold on the shore-front but few soldiers made it across the bullet-swept boulevard and into the town. When the twenty-seven tanks of the Calgary Regiment were landed, only fifteen managed to climb the shingle banks under intense fire. The six that reached the esplanade were then completely stopped by anti-tank traps and destroyed. Unable to leave the beach, all the remaining tanks could do was provide fire support and cover the inevitable retreat.

Then at around 07.00 am, the disaster was compounded as the Canadian reserve troops – 600 men of Les Fusiliers Mont-Royal – were deployed to the beach due to a mistaken signal that the advance troops had gained a foothold in the town. The Canadians came under intense bombardment and machine-gun fire and only 125 men made it back to England. On White Beach, 369 men of No. 40 Commando, Royal Marines landed under intense fire, and none of those few who actually got ashore, achieved more than a matter of yards. At 10.50 am a general order to retreat was issued and as the tide rose, the sea was stained with red, and many helpless wounded were also carried away by the waves with the dead.

Despite all of this, British archive papers released in 1972 showed that Mountbatten, had informed the War Cabinet that the raid had gone *"very satisfactorily."* This statement begs the question, 'for whom exactly?' Certainly not for those unfortunates who lost their lives in this utterly unnecessary folly and neither, one presumes, for their wives, sweethearts, mothers and fathers or children.

Not unexpectedly, the American Press went even further by giving the impression that the Americans had spearheaded the raid on Dieppe and opened up Europe for the Allies. *"We Land in France,"* gloated the *New York Times* whilst the *New York World-Telegram* declared, *"Tanks and US Troops Smash to the French Coast."* But perhaps the most accurate summary of 'Dieppe,' was actually written by a German, who when visiting a nearby Luftwaffe station afterwards wrote... *"As executed, the venture mocked all the rules of military logic and strategy."*

In fact, 907 Allied troops were killed, 2,460 were wounded, and 1,874 were taken prisoner. Of the 2,210 who did make it back to England only 36 were unhurt despite the fact that 200 had not even made it to the French shore. During the raid, Allied air power suffered its biggest single day loss of the war when 106 aircraft were destroyed. Without a single exception, every tank crew member was a casualty and overall, 60% of the invading force became casualties whereas the plan had estimated just 10%. In his report, the deluded warmonger Mountbatten wrote that the *"...planning was excellent, air support faultless and naval losses extremely light."* He added that *"...of the 6,000 men involved, two-thirds had returned to Britain."*

German losses were 500 dead and there were very few prisoners of war taken. That so few were taken prisoner may have had something to do with the Allied propensity for casually shooting prisoners. A Canadian observer had personally witnessed one such incident when Canadian troops shot eight German prisoners-of-war.

During the raid on Dieppe the local population assisted the Germans in fighting off the attacking British and Canadian (and a few American) troops. The port's German defenders were bolstered by locals braving the fighting to bring them water, food, and in some cases, ammunition. Indeed, such was the German appreciation of the townfolk's actions during the raid that Hitler later approved the repatriation of French POWs to the region soon afterwards. An act of generosity he had never felt previously obliged to offer.

Dieppe was a pathetic failure and even now, more than seventy years later, it seems obvious that it was a bizarre operation with no chance of success whatsoever and likely to result in a huge number of casualties.

Adolf Hitler personally ordered that members of British raiding parties be summarily shot whether they had surrendered or not. This is true enough but as usual, only half the story. The order was only given after a British Commando raid on the Channel Island of Sark went wrong and a number of German prisoners had been taken but the attacking force had to withdraw in a hurry under heavy German fire. The bodies of four German prisoners were later found with their hands still bound – and their throats slit from ear to ear and it was only after this horrendous event and in reprisal, that the German leader issued his order.

The Casablanca Conference

In January 1943, FDR, Churchill and the exiled 'Free French' Generals, Henri Giraud and Charles de Gaulle met in Morocco. At this event, FDR announced a proposal of 'unconditional surrender' for Germany, Italy, and Japan and the others readily agreed to this without question. 'Unconditional surrender' in effect meant that the Allies expected the Axis nations to not only stop fighting, but to also hand over complete political control and subjugate themselves fully to the invading Allied armies.

However, in the following years, this hard-line policy of complete conquest had the (possibly intentional) effect of inspiring the Japanese and Germans to fight on, long after all hope of victory had gone.

The opening months of 1943 marked a significant turning-point in the war. The combination of America's awesome naval, air, and land power, a Jewish/Red partisan guerrilla war, merciless air bombardment of German civilians, and the massive Red Army, armed by the might of America's manufacturing capabilities, all combined to inflict a heavy toll on Germany.

In February, the Germans finally surrendered at Stalingrad, 200,000 German troops having been killed or died of starvation or cold since Stalingrad was first besieged and many more, later died in Siberian labour camps. Then in May, the campaign in North Africa ended as German troops evacuated. That same month, Admiral Donitz withdrew all remaining German U-boats from the Atlantic after 41 of them were destroyed in just 3 weeks.

This was in fact the beginning of the end for the sworn enemies of the banksters and from this point on, Germany was now limited to defensive operations only, as the US, UK, and USSR slowly tightened their oppressive Globalist noose around the neck of Hitler's 'Thousand Year Reich.'

'The Dambusters' Raid

In May 1943, the 'Dambusters Raid,' was one of the most blatant examples of wartime spin and propaganda. RAF Wing Commander Guy Gibson and his pilots of 617 Squadron were carefully selected to carry out a 'daring and innovative' bombing raid on five major dams in the Ruhr Valley, Germany's manufacturing heartland. The dams were widely publicised by the Allies as being '*essential to that country's defensive capabilities.*'

Using a specially-designed 'water skipping bomb' invented by Barnes Wallace, two of the dams, the Moehne and the Eder, were actually breached to their foundations and as the news broke, Britain's joy was almost orgasmic. *"Floods roar down the Ruhr Valley,"* gloated the *Daily Express* headlines. The *Daily Mirror*, not to be outdone also enhanced the story…*"Hundreds of square miles of devastation have spread through the Ruhr, Germany's most densely populated industrial area, by the RAF's staggering attack on the Moehne and Eder dams."* It was also gleefully and sadistically reported that 10,000 Germans had died.

The make-up of 617 squadron consisted of airmen from the RAF, RCAF (Royal Canadian Air Force,) RNZAF (Royal New Zealand Air Force,) and the RAAF (Royal Australian Air Force) and the targets chosen were located in the Ruhr Valley, which was also the Ruhr Industrial Region, the primary site of Germany's mining and steel production. The main targets were the Moehne and Sorpe Dams with the Eder Dam being regarded as a secondary target.

Attacking these targets was anticipated to inflict catastrophic damage upon Germany's industrial output, and cause devastating flooding to the region. It was also determined that the Lancaster bombers would attack from an altitude of 60 ft. and at an air speed of 240 mph, the attacks being conducted at night, to ensure less vulnerability to the German defences.

And so the attack was carried out by 19 Lancaster's, divided into three groups to attack the Moehne, Eder, and Sorpe Dams respectively and on the 16th May the bombers departed at intervals, flying on three different routes in order to evade German flak concentration along the coast and the inland areas, but also flying low to avoid radar detection. They made landfall on the Dutch coast and skirted around Eindhoven and several Dutch cities, before heading east into Germany.

The attacks on the Eder and the Moehne were successful in breaching the dams, while the attack on the Sorpe resulted in only minor damage. The breaching of the Eder and the Moehne caused the destruction of two hydroelectric plants and the destruction or damaging of several factories and mines. However the Germans were able to return to normal levels of production in as little as four months, and by September of 1943. The British lost eight aircraft, and 53 airmen whilst the Germans suffered approximately 1,600 deaths as a result of flooding from the breaching of the two dams.

In 1972, upon examining newly-released Second World War documents, the author and journalist Bruce Page wrote... " ...*the truth about the raid was that it was a conjuring trick, virtually devoid of any military significance, the 'skipping bomb' just a gimmick. The real story of the raid was of sloppy planning, narrow-minded enthusiasm, and misdirected courage... apart from the aircrews, the only people to emerge from the story with real credit are a handful of people in the Ministry of Economic Warfare who tried to calculate in advance whether the raid would damage the German war economy. They calculated accurately that it would not, but they were ignored.*"

The only dam whose damage could potentially have seriously damaged the German war effort was the Sorpe Dam, yet only a token force had attacked it and the resultant damage was minimal.

Certainly the breaching of the Moehne and Eder dams caused flooding, but this mainly affected agricultural land, the one asset that Germany had in abundance. After World War I, 800,000 civilians had died of starvation during the 1919 Royal Naval blockade of war-ravaged Germany and the new German government had seen to it that the nation would be self-sufficient; in fact Germany was one of the few nations in Europe capable of feeding itself. But contrary to Allied propaganda, the raid did not affect hydro-electricity production because the Moehne Dam had negligible electrical capacity and the Eder had none.

The actual loss of life was 1,600 mainly working-class civilians, the majority of whom were non-Germans; the displaced Ukrainian civilians, mostly women and children who were housed in camps downstream of the Moehne Dam.

However, it was a huge propaganda victory, the stuff that encourages and perpetuates the seemingly never-ending supply of young men volunteering and clamouring to die for the banksters.

Hamburg Fire-Storms

In July 1943, the firebombing of Hamburg created a tornado of flames so intense that it actually 'sucked' hundreds of people from the streets and deposited them into the fire. Those who were not burned to death suffocated by their thousands in underground shelters as the intense firestorm above them consumed all the oxygen from the air. Hundreds of US and UK aircraft added to the raging inferno with wave after wave of incendiary bombings. The evil planners of this genocidal, ethnic-cleansing actually had the callous and brazen audacity to code-name the arson attack 'Operation Gomorrah,' after the biblical city destroyed by fire and brimstone.

The Allies mercilessly bombed Hamburg with high explosive, incendiary, phosphorous and napalm bombs and the resulting firestorm was so powerful that "... *with hurricane force, 150 mph winds were sucked into the oxygen vacuum created by the fire, ripping trees out by their roots, collapsing buildings, pulling children out of their mothers' arms. Twenty square miles of the city centre burned in an inferno that would rage for nine full days. ...*" The temperature in the firestorm reached 1,400 degrees Fahrenheit and everything that was flammable, including human flesh, burst spontaneously into flame.

The Royal Air Force alone, dispatched 3,000 bombers in four separate raids on Hamburg during that one night, dropping 9,000 tons of bombs. This affected 22 square kilometres or 8.5 square miles of the city, killing an estimated 60,000-100,000 people, according to the US bomber survey.

The results of this night of infamy were that at least half the city lay in ruins whilst two-thirds of the remaining population were evacuated, leaving almost 1 million homeless.

But of course the bombing of Hamburg was promoted as a huge success by the British ... "*None of our other attacks had produced effects that were a tenth as destructive as the effects of a firestorm.*"

Air Vice-Marshall, Sir Arthur 'Bomber' Harris stated ... "*In spite of all that happened at Hamburg, bombing proved a relatively humane method ... there is no proof that most casualties were women and children.*" German records indicated however, that approximately 65% of those killed were women and children.

When people think of the Allied bombing of Germany, Dresden automatically springs to mind, not Wesel, Nuremberg or Würzburg or the hundreds of other obliterated German towns and cities. While people debate the death toll at Dresden, attention is diverted from the 45,000 to 50,000 civilians murdered in the bombing of Hamburg, the 10,000 people intentionally burned alive in Kassel, the fact that 20% of

Nordhausen's civilian population was killed in a mere fifteen minute attack or that one out of every three people in Pforzheim was murdered and thousands more hideously injured from an unnecessary bombing campaign based purely on a rumour.

We were led to believe that a campaign which dropped environmentally catastrophic bombs with the force of major earthquakes, bombs which actually changed weather patterns, endangered whole species of birds and insects and altered the shape of the map were all within the normal range of warfare and implemented for the 'greater good' and carried out only in cases of sheer necessity to 'shorten the war' and gladly accepted the faulty premise that the carefully planned incineration of thousands of innocent women and children was justified. We accepted the preposterous notion that there was only one villain in this conflict, one supreme face of evil which absolved all others of any wrongdoing and were led in this direction by a relentless effort (still being carried-out) to both conceal activities prejudicial to the saintly image of our 'heroes' and to excuse their own criminal behaviour.

Until recently, no-one understood fully that the terror-bombing of German civilians was not a 'friendly-fire' mistake, or the result of a bomber missing its mark. We believed the lies that schools, churches, cathedrals and castles were attacked only when 'enemy soldiers were firing from them' or because some fanatical Nazi, small town mayor 'refused to surrender.' Until the Internet provided us with uncensored, unfiltered information, most of the truth, the grim images and graphic accounts of the horror which befell Germany were hidden away and free from scrutiny, judgement or condemnation. However, mortality figures from Allied bombing, kept top-secret for many years, have now become publicly available, as have photos, personal accounts and old newspaper clippings.

We were also led to believe that the Allied bombings of Germany were a legitimate response to an equal number of bombings Germany was delivering on Britain, and that the only images of wartime bombings we were (and are) exposed to, were those carried out by Germany, mainly of the Blitz. In reality, Germany bombed Britain with a mere five percent of the tonnage that Britain inflicted upon Germany, and more British bombs fell upon the city of Berlin alone than German bombs fell on the whole of Britain during the entire war. The targeting of residential Hamburg was a calculated, well-planned mass murder of civilians, and British and US bombers killed over a hundred times as many civilians in that one event as Britons died from the German raid on the heavily defended, major industrial centre of Coventry, England, which resulted in the loss of around 400 civilian lives.

Initial RAF bombing of military targets was largely unsuccessful. Only one out of five bombs fell within five miles of its intended target and nearly half of British bombers were being shot down. Therefore, the British leadership was already coldly studying the idea of terror-bombing city centres instead. Contrary to public denials, in September 1941, deputy chief of the Air Staff Norman Bottomley urged *"saturation by incendiaries to break the morale of the population."* His superior, Charles Portal, boasted to Winston Churchill in late 1941 that if Bomber Command was provided with a force of 4,000 planes, huge damage could be inflicted on Germany, including the destruction of six million homes and *"civilian casualties estimated at 900,000."*

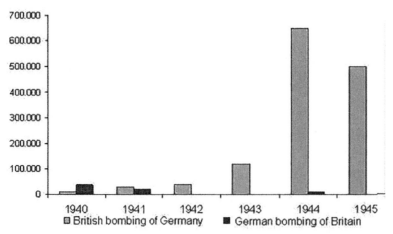

A bit short of his mark in 1941, Portal wrote... *"We have caused death and injury to 93,000 civilians. The result was achieved with a fraction of the bomb-load we hope to employ in 1943."* By early 1942, there were open suggestions that bombing be directed against German working-class houses, leaving factories and military objectives alone. This policy was implemented in full in 1942 when, upon his taking over the entire UK Bomber Command, Arthur Harris issued the following directive... *"It has been decided that the primary objective of your operations should now be focused on the morale of the enemy civil population and in particular, of industrial workers."* Harris prepared a list of 60 German cities he intended to destroy first...

"The aim is the destruction of German cities, the killing of German workers and the disruption of civilised community life through-out Germany. It should be emphasised that the destruction of houses, public utilities, transport and lives; the creation of a refugee problem on an unprecedented scale; and the breakdown of morale both at home and at the battle fronts by fear of extended and intensified bombing are accepted and intended aims of our bombing policy, they are not by-products of attempts to hit factories."

The first, intentional cultural attack of a historic city was the RAF bombing attack on Lübeck on 28th March 1942. This attack by over 200 heavy bombers was ordered by Harris, not to destroy military targets in Germany, but as an experiment to test whether bombing timber-framed buildings could start an inferno large enough to be used as an easy aiming-point for later waves of bombers. In his own words... *"I wanted my crews to be well-blooded, as they say in fox hunting, to have a taste of success for a change."* It destroyed 80% of the city's historic timber-framed core.

The destruction of Hamburg came on the night of 27th July 1943 and followed a smaller bombing campaign three days earlier. In this second attack, a mix of munitions was used which had a higher proportion of incendiaries, including deadly phosphorus. It was here, not Dresden that the term 'firestorm,' was first used, and at least 45,000 to 55,000 civilians were intentionally murdered in a deliberately engendered firestorm that trapped the population within the city, leaving them no possible escape route.

The horrific, ten day-long firebombing not only murdered thousands, it left a million people homeless and the historic ancient city almost entirely obliterated. An astounding 30,000 of those killed in Hamburg were women and children and 1.2 million refugees fled the city in the immediate aftermath, many of them with mental and physical injuries. The choreographed inferno circled the city and spread inward, creating a swirling column of super-heated air which generated ferocious 150 mile per hour tornado-like winds capable of hurling helpless people into the raging fires. Many people were literally melted on to the pavements or slowly choked by poison gases or lack of oxygen in cellars. At the same time the US military denied to the American public that any terror-bombing was taking place, they were supplying the British with the napalm-like phosphorous to burn German civilians alive. The chemical cannot be extinguished once ablaze, and these bombs sprayed their contents on people in such a way that a horrible death was the inevitable outcome.

Beginning with Hamburg, the Allied media, turned the mass murder of German civilian populations into an 'acceptable' and 'legitimate' method of warfare, and aside from the normal terror-bombings, cities incinerated by these manufactured firestorms included Dresden, Wuppertal, Hamburg, Remscheid, Kassel, Braunschweig, Kaiserslautern, Saarbrücken, Darmstadt, Stuttgart, Heilbronn, Ulm, Pforzheim, Mainz, Würzburg and Hildesheim, all of which suffered horrendous civilian casualties. 10,000 died in Kassel's firestorm. Darmstadt, a harmless classic centre of German culture, produced less than two-tenths of one percent of Germany's total war production, yet, a minimum of ten percent of Darmstadt's population died as a result of the intentional firestorm inflicted upon them. Pforzheim lost one-third of its people. Würzburg was 89% destroyed with 90,000 people left homeless and 5,000 civilian deaths with women and children making up 81 percent of that figure. From July 1944 to January 1945, a low average of 14,000 German civilians, not including countless undocumented refugees, were killed from bombings every month in just the western German areas.

In February, 1945, the Yalta Conference created the blueprint for the deaths and relocation of millions of German civilians in the east. Even in January 1945, when German defeat was clearly imminent, Harris and Portal further advocated even more destruction being visited upon Leipzig, Magdeburg, Chemnitz, Dresden, Breslau, Posen, Halle, Erfurt, Gotha, Weimar, Eisenach, and the rest of Berlin, in other words, all the cities to which refugees were fleeing.

When ordering the bombing of Chemnitz following the destruction of Dresden, the Allied commander stated the motive to his pilots... *"The reason you are going there tonight is to finish off the refugees who managed to escape Dresden."* Women, children and the elderly were now to be shot at and incinerated under the approved guidelines which both the British and Americans had set in place and implemented to eliminate the future 'refugee problem' for their Soviet allies. City after city was destroyed well after Germany's defeat was obvious, and under 'Operation Clarion' smaller towns and cities were incinerated under the flimsiest of pretexts. Nuremberg was attacked because it was an 'ideological' centre, and likewise, Bayreuth and other small, ancient cities.

"We have got to be tough with Germany and I mean the German people, not just the Nazis. You either have to castrate the German people or you have got to treat them in such a manner so they can't just go on reproducing people who want to continue the way they have in the past." US President, Franklin D. Roosevelt

This was echoed by Winston Churchill... *"You must understand that this war is not against Hitler or National Socialism, but against the strength of the German people, which is to be smashed once and for all, regardless of whether it is in the hands of Hitler or a Jesuit priest."*

Centuries old castles, cathedrals and medieval villages were needlessly destroyed at this late stage of the war. The birth houses of Bach, Durer and Goethe, Martin Luther landmarks, Leipzig's ancient book district, libraries and universities were all targets. Allied bombing destroyed well over one third of all German books as its universities and libraries and museums were unnecessarily obliterated. Towns with no military significance and having little or nothing to do with the war effort were simply blown away at this point in devastating attacks on vulnerable civilian populations. The mounting devastation of European heritage had already been raised in vain in British parliament by the Bishop of Chichester on 9th February 1944. The Bishop begged for a more humane approach... *"In the fifth year of the war it must be apparent to any but the most complacent and reckless how far the destruction of European culture has already gone. We ought to think once, twice and three times before destroying the rest."* His words fell on deaf ears and he was ruthlessly vilified.

In March 1945, after the smoke had cleared and hundreds of German cities and towns lay in bloody ruins, Churchill, disingenuously distanced himself from the homicidal bombing campaign after the destruction of Dresden and which had generated some unfavourable publicity. He wrote that... *"...the destruction of Dresden remains a serious query against the conduct of Allied Bombing."* Even though he had personally sanctioned it. And even with the German military/industrial complexes already in ruins, the British and Americans compiled new 'hit lists' which included immoral attacks on undefended, mainly small, rural towns that had not yet been assaulted and whose populations were praying for peace.

US General Frederick Anderson explained that these late-stage terror-bombings were NOT carried out to shorten the war but rather to teach the Germans a lesson... *"...if Germany was struck all over it will be passed on, from father to son, thence to grandson, as a deterrent for the initiation of future wars."*

The most intense bombing destruction occurred in the months of February and March 1945, just weeks prior to German surrender when German defences were minimal or absent and the war was all but over. Over 80 million incendiary bombs were dropped on German cities between this time and the end of the war. The full human death toll may never be known, but to this day continues, inexplicably and unforgivably, to be intentionally lowered to an unbelievable and unrealistic level by whichever current formula is popular among conformist social scientists and easily digested by a public unwilling to either learn or accept the real truth.

"The aim of Bomber Command should be . . . publicly stated: the destruction of German cities and the killing of Germans." Sir Arthur Harris, head of Bomber Command of the Royal Air Force, October 1943

'Bomber,' or should that be 'butcher?' Harris served as the head of RAF's Bomber Command from February 1942 until the end of the war when he became chief of the RAF. Through his loyal, blind and utterly ruthless devotion to his so-called 'duty,' he had served Churchill and his Zionist-bankster masters well. But there was even 'some criticism' of his ruthless methods in Britain, and after the war, when he requested that Bomber Command crew receive a campaign medal for their efforts, this was refused. 'Some criticism . . . ?' A truly British understatement if ever there was one, and I will return to Harris and his crimes against humanity, later.

The Allied Invasion of Southern Europe

Upon the successful conclusion of the Allied North Africa campaign and the retreat of Germany from the continent, the Allied invasion of the southern Italian island of Sicily commenced using much the same British personnel as those involved in North Africa plus the addition of the large American contingent. It was another stunning success for Generals Patton and Montgomery and German and Italian resistance was once again overwhelmed. Within four weeks of the initial air and sea assault, Axis troops had to be evacuated to the Italian mainland.

The Italian leader Benito Mussolini was, soon after this, removed from power by his own Grand Council, was arrested by the new government who promptly made peace with and surrendered to the Allies. This left Germany with the sole task of halting Patton's advance northwards up the Italian peninsula and with Italy now under Allied control, Hitler was rightly worried that the Allies would invade Yugoslavia and the Balkan nations, cut off Germany's oil supply, and advance north upon Germany from the *"soft underbelly of Europe,"* as it was referred-to as by Churchill. Then in August of 1943, the British Royal Air Force, departing from bases in southern Italy, began the systematic heavy bombardment of the Ploesti oil fields in German-allied Romania.

However, inexplicably, Allied Commander Eisenhower and Army Chief of Staff George Marshall (who had promoted Eisenhower over scores of his senior officers) insisted upon making preparations for an invasion of heavily fortified Northern France the following year. Well I say 'inexplicably,' but maybe not, if you are in tune with the ongoing agenda. This decision, deliberately or not, had the effect of prolonging the war whilst buying the Soviets **much-needed time to move westwards, and eventually enabling Stalin to occupy and annex all of Eastern Europe.** 'Blunders' such as this, make for extremely happy banksters and enhance their despicable agenda.

The Bari Raid – A Chemical Warfare Cover-Up

On the 2nd of December 1943, the *SS John Harvey* was one of the 2,710 American 'Liberty Ships' built during WWII and had been assigned to deliver a shipment during the invasion of Italy. On her final voyage (as it turned-out to be,) she was carrying a secret cache of chemical weapons. All the combatants in WWII had implicitly agreed not to use chemical weapons, but nevertheless FDR had chemical weapons shipped to the Mediterranean theatre 'just in case they were needed,' and so the *John Harvey* found itself in the seaport of Bari, Italy with a hold containing more than 2,000, 100lb mustard gas shells.

As Bari was one of the principal ports supplying the Allies during the invasion of the Italian mainland, the ship was waiting for its cargo to be offloaded for quite a while and unfortunately this never happened, as on the 2nd December the port was subjected to a major German air raid, with 105 Stuka dive-bombers, complete of course, with their *General Motors* engines. The twenty-minute raid was so massive that it put the port out of commission for more than two months and seventeen of the thirty ships attacked were sunk. The *John Harvey* was not hit directly, but it was showered with flaming debris and soon caught fire and exploded, unleashing its deadly cargo on its crew and indeed the unsuspecting town.

Every member of the *Harvey*'s complement and who knew what was in the hold was killed, so rescuers dealing with the casualties had no idea with what they were dealing. Mustard gas needs to be countered *before* contact with a very specific treatment or, preferably, the entire area needs to be washed down with bleach or a mixture of substances named DS2. Not realising that this was required (of course,) many rescuers succumbed to the attack whilst trying to save the victims. For example, *HMS Bicester* took thirty casualties out of the water but, being damaged itself, was towed to nearby Taranto for repairs. By the time it got there many of its crew, were suffering from chemical burns and blindness.

By the time that the symptoms of mustard gas manifest themselves, it is too late to do anything, but even at that point the medical personnel could not understand what was going on, partly due to the secrecy of the cargo and partly because very few doctors had seen the consequences of mustard gas on the human body. An expert on chemical warfare, Lieutenant-Colonel Stewart Alexander, was sent by the Deputy Surgeon General of the US Army to discover what was going on. Lt.-Col. Alexander ran every test he could think of and eventually pinned down mustard gas as the culprit; he also used the technique pioneered by Dr. John Snow, of mapping the location of Cholera casualties in order to pinpoint the source of the problem and determined that the *John Harvey* was the culprit.

War-time secrecy gagged the official accident reports, but too many had witnessed the tragic event to make for a permanent cover-up operation and the US Army eventually had no option but to admit, a few months later, that the *John Harvey* had indeed been carrying that deadly cargo. Nevertheless, the incident remained lost in the chaos of 1944 and documents pertaining to it were not declassified until 1959.

In all there were 628 known casualties, including 86 deaths, but there were probably many more. As well as the port, the town itself had also been affected by the cloud of vapourised mustard gas that had drifted almost unnoticed across the landscape, in all the smoke and mayhem. The civilian population of Bari had scattered into the countryside during the raid and presumably would have had to deal with the effects of the slow-burning chemical alone, far away from where anyone could either offer assistance or take official notice.

Although US records did mention mustard gas, Winston Churchill insisted that all British Medical records were expunged and that mustard gas deaths and injuries were merely listed as the result of, 'burns due to enemy action.'

The Bari raid was a disaster on two fronts for the Allies. Firstly it was dubbed the 'Second Pearl Harbor,' with 17 ships totalling 75,936 tons sunk, and another 7 ships with a total of 27,289 tons, heavily damaged by the German aircraft. This was the only known poison gas incident associated with WWII, rendered far worse by the inherent secrecy involved.

But the deadly, dirty secrets of World War II did not end there…

The Slapton Sands Debacle

On the 27th / 28th April 1944, more American soldiers died in a D-Day rehearsal, than on the 6th of June at Utah Beach. Attacks by German torpedo boats and 'friendly fire' cost as many as 1500 American servicemen's lives, and yet the incident was kept secret for almost fifty years.

During the months leading up to the D-Day landings in France on June 6, 1944, the Allies secretly trained for the invasion, code-named *Operation Overlord*. Slapton Sands beach in Lyme Bay on the southern coast of England was chosen for its resemblance to Utah beach, where, along with Omaha beach, the Americans would be invading. In the autumn of 1943, approximately 3,000 villagers in the area were evacuated -- many against their will -- so that the beach landings could be held in total secrecy.

As 'D-Day' approached, the training became more vigorous and involved more and more ships and men. 'Exercise Tiger,' planned for 22nd- 30th April 1944 was a full dress-rehearsal for 'D Day,' involving 30,000 men and many ships, including nine large tank landing-ships known as LSTs, fully loaded with men, tanks, fuel and other military equipment. LSTs were designed to run-up onto the beach and open their front cargo doors, allowing its cargo of tanks and vehicles to exit onto the sand.

The Royal Navy patrolled the entrance to Lyme Bay with two destroyers and five smaller boats, whilst across the Channel, they had motor torpedo boats (MTBs) patrolling the waters around Cherbourg, France, to keep watch for marauding German E-boats.

E-boats were large, 100-foot-long, fast torpedo boats which could reach speeds of 40 knots (around 47 mph) and had been intercepting ships in the English Channel. The German designation was S-boot, for 'Schnellboot,' literally 'fast boat.' Their home-base in Cherbourg had noticed the increased radio traffic emanating from the area around Slapton and sent nine E-boats to investigate after having managed to evade the British torpedo boats patrolling Cherbourg.

In the early hours of 28th April, as the eight LSTs were returning to Slapton Sands in a column, the nine German E-boats discovered what they thought was a convoy, prepared to attack and at about 2.00am, LST-507 was torpedoed and burst into flames. It's surviving crew abandoned ship but a few minutes later, LST-531 was torpedoed and sank in only six minutes, trapping most of its occupants below decks. The other LSTs and the two British destroyers opened fire on the German E-boats, but without success, following which, LST-289 was then torpedoed and badly damaged. At least one other LST was struck by a torpedo, but it managed to somehow survive.

By 4.00 am it was all over and the E-boats escaped back to France. Two LSTs had been sunk and at least one was one badly damaged, managing to limp back to port. Flaming oil covered the waters, burning to death many who had abandoned ship, while many who escaped the flames perished from hypothermia in the cold waters of the English Channel. All other ships were ordered to continue the exercise, leaving the dead and dying to their fate, but the captain of LST-515 disobeyed these orders and lowered boats and threw cargo nets over the side to pick up survivors, saving more than 100 men. When it was all over, 749 soldiers and sailors had been killed. No figures have ever been published for the number of men wounded in the attack.

In his CIA interrogation following the end of the war, Heinrich Mueller, Chief of the Gestapo, claimed that an agent had alerted them to a massive exercise involving many men at Slapton Sands and also that the Germans had returned to base with the invasion plans taken from the corpse of a US army officer. "*…this information which indicated that Normandy was the main target was sent on to higher commands but was not* *acted upon."* '*Gestapo Chief: The 1948 Interrogation of Heinrich Mueller,*' ed. Gregory Douglas, p. 142

On the Allied side, the disaster was compounded by a long list of highly conspicuous 'failures.'

1. US naval commanders did not establish liaison with counterparts in the Royal Navy.
2. Royal Navy radar picked up movement of the Nazi E-Boats but did nothing.
3. Escort Corvette *HMS Azalea* knew about the E-Boats but did not inform the LSTs
4. Radio frequencies given to Americans were changed without notice.
5. The one-sided battle had been watched by Royal Artillerymen at Blacknor Fort, high on Portland's western cliffs. The men had the E-boats in their sights, within range, but were ordered not to fire by an American officer, because of the number of Allied personnel fighting for their lives in the water.
6. There was no emergency training so life jackets were not worn correctly. They flipped the wearer upside-down with his head in the water.

Whilst the military, down the years, has acknowledged the aforementioned facts, there are additional allegations that revolved around the order from Supreme Allied Commander General Eisenhower, that real ammunition be used during the exercise in order to acclimatise the men to actual battlefield conditions. It is alleged that later, as the exercise continued, *HMS Hawkins*, a British cruiser, fired live shells while the surviving American soldiers stormed the beach. The soldiers were meant to proceed no further than a white taped line that had been set up, but, in the confusion, many soldiers went straight-on through it resulting in a further 200 to 300 men being killed by friendly fire.

The accounts of those present that day indicate that, as thousands of GIs swarmed ashore from the landing craft, they were cut down by bullets fired by comrades playing the role of German defenders, who had for some reason been given live ammunition, but not informed of this fact. Letters revealed how Lieutenant-Colonel Edwin Wolf, from Baltimore, heard several shots *"zinging"* past his ear as he observed the exercise from a vantage point nearby, and also saw *"infantrymen on the beach, fall down and remain motionless."* Under a hail of fire, Wolf quickly retreated.

Live bullets also whizzed past Hank Aaron from West Virginia, driver to a general who was observing the exercises. Aaron scrambled away from the line of fire, then looked-up and saw five men, dead. Generals Omar Bradley and Eisenhower watched *"the murderous chaos"* and *"were horrified and determined that details of their own mistakes would be buried with their men."* Royal Engineer, Jim Cory watched dumbfounded from an observation post as soldiers streaming from landing craft were *"mown down like ninepins."*

Yet there is not a single, official mention in Army records of any bodies being found on

Slapton Sands and nor has the Pentagon ever mentioned any 'friendly-fire' disaster in Devon that spring. What happened to the bodies provides another twist to the secret of Slapton Sands. Witness statements suggest they were interred, at least temporarily, in a mass grave nearby, despite the fact that there was no shortage of potential burial sites in the remote fields behind the beach. Suspicion that US troops dumped bodies in hastily built graves around nearby Blackawton was first aroused 20 years ago, when Dorothy Seekings, a baker's daughter who supplied bread to the troops during the exercises, said she had seen large numbers of GI bodies being buried near the village.

Seekings was ridiculed at the time, yet her description and the location now seems to match closely that of farmer Francis Burden, who sold the Americans fresh milk. One morning in April 1944, Burden stopped short as he crossed a narrow lane leading out of Blackawton. A huge pit, up to two acres in size, had been dug by US troops and large enough to take hundreds of coffins. Boxes big enough to hold a man were stacked nearby. Today, a discernible mound marks the location.

After the war, the field belonged to farmer Nolan Tope and just before he died, Tope was asked if US troops had ever been buried on his land. He replied enigmatically, that Seekings *"knew only a small part of it,"* but nevertheless vowed to take his secret to the grave. What more was he hiding and why was he so reluctant to tell, I wonder? I would say that there is a strong chance he was threatened that if he ever told what he knew, then it would be the last thing he would ever do, and maybe his family, too.

Detailed records kept by the stationmaster at Kingsbridge railway station, five miles away, revealed that three trains were secretly loaded with the bodies of GIs under military guard between July and August 1944. The trains, each able to carry at least 100 corpses, were *"crammed with men dug from mass graves,"* said local rail historian Ken Williams. The historian's father, George, who served in the Royal Navy during the war, soon realised he also saw the bodies of dozens of men washed ashore on the sands. *"He told me how the sea turned red,"* Ken said. The families however were told that their loved ones had died in the Normandy landings, six weeks later.

Local author Ken Small, whose book *'The Forgotten Dead'* broke the story of the E-boat attack, dismissed the rumours until just before he died. He then told the historian Williams that Seekings had been right. *"I was stunned,"* said Williams.

Even so, many people still refuse to accept that hundreds of US soldiers may have been interred in the sleepy Devon countryside 70+ years ago. Such scepticism fails to explain the account of former land girl, Joyce Newby, who helped to make hundreds of coffin lids at a nearby timber yard in spring 1944. She said they were for victims of *"friendly fire at Slapton."* Or indeed that of former US serviceman Harold McAulley, who told of dragging dead soldiers off the sands and later helping to bury corpses – their faces black with oil and burnt – in a mass inland grave.

In any case, everyone involved, including the doctors, nurses and other personnel in nearby military hospitals filling-up with wounded and burned men, were sworn to secrecy on pain of court martial. The invasion was almost called-off because ten officers who knew the locations of the actual invasion beaches, were missing and it could not be certain whether any of them had been captured by the enemy. However, the invasion was soon back on schedule, after all ten of their bodies were found. As a postscript to the sorry affair, when the survivors of 'Exercise Tiger' stormed Utah Beach on D-Day, 200 were killed or wounded.

Admiral Donald Moon was made the scapegoat and he paid the ultimate price three months later, on 5th August 1944, when he shot himself. Close friends said that he never recovered from the disaster at Slapton Sands.

To this day, the only memorial to the incident is in the village of Torcross, Devon where locals erected a plaque commemorating the dead, along with a Sherman tank that was raised from the waters. Although the military eventually erected another memorial thanking the villagers for evacuating their homes during this period, there is no 'official' memorial to those killed during *Exercise Tiger*. Survivors of the horror of that night still make pilgrimages to Torcross, but their numbers are now drastically dwindling as 'Father Time,' little by little, continues the job started inadvertently by their comrades on that now long-gone-night in April 1944.

D-Day, 6th June 1944

Otherwise known as '*Operation Overlord*,' D-Day was the day that the Allied forces based in England, successfully crossed the English Channel to begin the final advance towards Berlin which would culminate in the total German defeat eleven months later. The cost of the operation in manpower was very high, as nearly 10,000 men were killed storming the fortified beaches of Normandy, but the invasion established an initial beachhead consisting of 100,000 troops. It was from this 'foothold' in Normandy that the Allies would be reinforced for the push eastwards towards Germany.

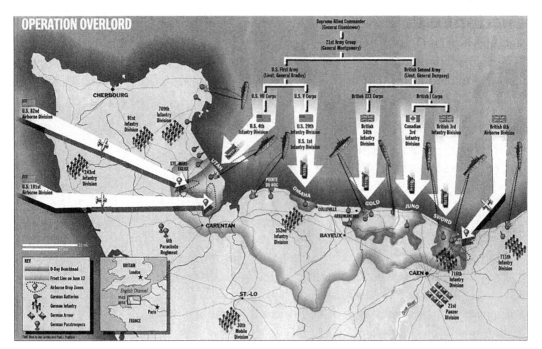

Churchill was not convinced by the idea of a Normandy invasion, instead preferring to supplement the ongoing attack northwards from the 'soft underbelly of Europe,' where Allied troops had already firmly established themselves and were relentlessly pushing the Germans back towards home. Indeed the Normandy landings plan made no kind of logical or tactical sense, but when has that ever stopped the bankster-warmongers from wreaking their bloody havoc upon humanity?

Germans along the coast of France were already aware of the huge build-up of American troops, ships and equipment in southern England in April-June 1944, and knew that an invasion was imminent at some point. The only question being 'where and when?' As a defensive measure, they had begun building the Atlantic Wall, an elaborate system of heavy cement fortifications that spanned the entire French coastline along the English Channel, but as the spring of 1944 gave way to summer and the invasion appeared imminent, it was only around half-finished. To compensate for this, the Germans planted a million mines, laid mile upon mile of barbed-wire, and installed thousands of jagged underwater obstructions designed to rip holes in the hulls of landing craft.

Field Marshals Gerd von Rundstedt and Erwin Rommel, in charge of staving-off any attempted invasion, thought that the Allies would probably land at Calais, the narrowest distance between southern England and the coast of France, a distance of only 20 miles. Their assumption was confirmed by the deceptive, heavy build-up of Allied troops in the seaports directly opposite Calais. In truth, these were fake manoeuvres, cleverly combined with false intelligence leaked by the Allies to convince the Germans they had guessed correctly. Rommel and von Rundstedt therefore positioned the bulk of their troops, fifteen infantry divisions, around Calais, while a smaller number was stationed about 200 miles to the west near the Normandy beaches, which they considered a far less likely landing point.

Even the Allies plans faltered slightly when on the chosen invasion day, Monday, 5th June, the seas were far too rough. The American, British and Canadian landing troops may have ended-up at the bottom of the Channel, or land on the beaches too stricken with sea-sickness if they even survived the crossing. But the problem was, should the invasion be postponed by more than a day or two? The entire force had to stand-down, the next possible date may perhaps be mid-July, or even later, due to the immense amount of logistical coordination involved.

Eisenhower was desperate for a break in the inclement weather. Even in summer in northern Europe, the weather is very unpredictable and sometimes even summer days can be cold, windy or wet – or all three. Checking and rechecking the weather maps, his chief meteorologist calculated that a window of opportunity was emerging for Tuesday morning, 6th June, although conditions would still not be absolutely ideal. After receiving this update, and upon consulting with his landing force commanders, Field Marshal Montgomery and General Bradley, Eisenhower made the decision to go.

And so, in the pre-dawn hours of 6th June, American paratroopers of the 82nd and 101st Airborne Divisions along with the British 6th Division parachuted into Normandy, attacking rear positions of the German 7th Army, while British glider troops seized key bridges. Additionally, BBC radio broadcasts included short declarative sentences which were special encoded messages to the French resistance, encouraging them to sabotage German communications throughout France.

Then at dawn on D-Day, the greatest seaborne invasion force ever assembled, approached the Normandy Coast, taking the German defenders there by surprise. Four thousand assault vessels ferried the troops, whilst over 2,000 American and British warships bombarded the landing zones, five beaches stretching along a sixty-mile front. The British 2nd Army landed toward the east at beaches code-named Gold, Juno and Sword and the American 1st Army landed toward the west at beaches named Utah and Omaha.

At Omaha Beach, the Americans were confronted with absolute carnage. This was by far the best defended of the five landing-points. A soldier of the 116th Infantry Division recalled… *"I got out in water up to the top of my boots. People were yelling, screaming, dying, running on the beach, equipment was flying everywhere, men were bleeding to death, crawling, lying everywhere, firing coming from all directions. We dropped down behind anything that was the size of a golf ball. Colonel Canham, Lieutenant Cooper, and Sergeant Crawford were screaming at us to get off the beach. I turned to say to Gino Ferrari, 'Let's move up, Gino,' but before I could finish the sentence, something spattered all over the side of my face. He'd been hit in the face and his brains splattered all over my face and my stuff. I moved forward and the tide came on so fast it covered him and I no longer could see him."*

The immediate question for the Germans was whether or not the Normandy landings, and earlier attacks by parachutists, were all part of an elaborate Allied ruse to draw their attention away from Calais. No one could say for sure and the result was indecision by Hitler and the High Command. This bought precious time for the Allied landing troops now inching themselves forward in the sand.

At Gold, Juno and Sword beaches, British and Canadian troops under Montgomery met less initial resistance and rapidly advanced a mile or so inland. Meanwhile, German field commanders on the scene waited for authorisation to utilise their reserves and counter-attack. Field Marshal Rommel, the man who was supposed to command the entire coastal defence, was completely out of touch at the moment, rushing back by car from his home, in a 400-mile journey that would take most of the day. Flying was out of the question due to the risk posed by Allied fighters which now enjoyed total air supremacy.

As the hours passed and Calais remained completely quiet, German field commanders phoned High Command for permission to rush all available reinforcements including two nearby Panzer divisions to Normandy, but Hitler said to wait until the overall situation became clearer. In the meantime, British and Canadian troops continued to advance inland while the Americans broke-free of Omaha and moved inland too. Late in the afternoon, with still no action at Calais, Hitler finally gave the go-ahead to deploy reinforcements, but it was too late.

By nightfall, over 150,000 Americans, British and Canadians had landed in France against all odds, suffering 9,000 casualties in the process and within a week, a half-million men had arrived and the five landing beaches were joined in a unified frontline. With the beachhead now secured, two floating seaports were assembled offshore to enable the importing of a gigantic arsenal of American-made weaponry including thousands of Sherman tanks that would be used by the armoured divisions to advance inland.

Field Marshals von Rundstedt and Rommel, met with Hitler on Saturday, 17th June 1944, hoping to thrash out some positive tactics to repel the invading forces. Initially Rommel asked to withdraw his troops from the Normandy coast so they could regroup for an inland counter-offensive, out of range of the Allied warships. Hitler refused but tried to pacify Rommel with promises of newly developed super-weapons including jet-powered planes that would sweep the Allies from the sky and self-propelled flying-bombs that would spell the demise of Britain.

By late June, American troops under General Bradley had liberated Cherbourg at the tip of the Normandy peninsula, whilst taking 25,000 German prisoners. This was followed by intense fighting during the Battle of the Hedgerows throughout July in which American tanks pierced the German southward defences and broke-free of the peninsula entirely. Meanwhile, British and Canadians under Montgomery overcame stiff opposition to capture the city of Caen to the east, following an air raid by two thousand Allied bombers. Soon afterwards, the Americans reached Avranches, in the south of Normandy, then circled eastward to meet up with Montgomery at Falaise, trapping the remnants of the German 7th Army inside a narrow pocket, resulting in 50,000 more prisoners.

At the same time, the Soviet Red Army, fully-armed with state-of-the-art American weaponry, inexorably advanced upon Germany from the east. With Italy also under Allied occupation, Germany was defending three fronts as its cities, railways, dams, factories and civilian population also endured relentless bombardment and Partisan sabotage.

But then with the Allied advance towards Germany from the east, progressing ahead of schedule, and in order to allow Stalin more time to conquer Eastern Europe (which of course was the plan all along,) Generals Eisenhower and Marshall *repeatedly* delayed the advance of General Patton's 3rd army, even resorting to the ceasing of vital shipments of fuel to Patton's army. Patton was incandescent with rage at this action. He knew what the 'game-plan' was and had long-since reached the conclusion that the Allies were fighting the 'wrong' enemy.

But to backtrack in time slightly, under temporary, wartime German occupation (1940-1944), life in Northern France was peaceful for French civilians. The conduct of the German occupiers was impeccable and many French women fell in love with German soldiers. But, with the Normandy invasion, the peace and security of France was completely shattered. To support the cross-channel invasion, and push the Germans eastwards, the Allies unleashed a ferocious aerial bombardment campaign. Entire towns were mercilessly carpet-bombed and destroyed, as were cultural icons and precious, historical works of art, 65,000 French civilians were killed and 150,000 were injured, and at least 500,000 left homeless. Incredibly, twice as many French civilians were killed during only a few months in mid-1944, than the total amount of British civilians killed during the entire war. (But of course, these numbers paled in comparison to the 1 million+ German civilians who were killed by Allied bombings.)

The Allied/bankster invasion of France was largely an American operation with a strong British and other allies supporting cast. In the US, the enraptured public was given the strong impression by the media that their sons, brothers and husbands were a band of liberating angels welcomed by a grateful population, but of course this was very far from the truth.

Covering these events much later, the legendary NBC anchor-man Tom Brokaw for once spoke the real truth and belied the general myths of the invasion when he said… *"The bloodied landscape of France (and) Belgium was American-made. The crimes committed by individual American soldiers – rape, thievery and murder – surpassed the crimes of the 'Nazis' in every respect. Even American generals were stealing from French civilians. During one period over 500 rapes a month were being reported and it got so bad that General Eisenhower threatened hangings, but it was an empty threat."*

Before the invasion, the Allies had dropped over 590,000 tons of bombs on France, equal to almost half the amount of bombs dropped on Germany during the entire course of the war. Over 1 million French homes were destroyed by Allied bombing attacks and some cities such as Caen, Saint-Lo, Carentan, Montbourg and Valgnes, virtually ceased to exist. For every German soldier who lost his life resisting the American invasion of Europe, the lives of four Frenchmen were lost also. Whereas German troops had wandered at will during their occupation of France, the British and the Americans were repeatedly confined to barracks or had their movements restricted because of the French antagonism to their presence on French soil.

Even newly commissioned, Second Lieutenant John Eisenhower, son of the Supreme Commander, commented... "*The attitude of the French was sobering, indeed. Instead of bursting with enthusiasm they seemed not only indifferent but also sullen. There was considerable cause for concern whether these people wished to be liberated.*"

There is indeed evidence to suggest that many of the films and photographs of joyful French citizens greeting the British and American 'liberators,' were in fact, staged for propaganda purposes. Most of the French population were seething with indignation, if not downright hatred for the Allied troops in the aftermath of the utter carnage inflicted upon their country by their so-called 'allies.'

Meanwhile, in the east, Stalin's plot to conquer all of Eastern Europe was greatly facilitated by Eisenhower and Marshall's curious obsession with invading Europe from England, instead of simply incrementing the advance from southern Europe. Stalin also wanted the Soviet hordes to crush Berlin and by July 1944, the murdering and raping Reds had reached Poland, seriously threatening Germany's eastern borders. Terrified German civilians now began a mass exodus away from the marauding Red savages, fleeing westward by land and also via the Baltic Sea.

The Banksters' Bretton Woods Conference

Also in July 1944, the chaos wrought by WWII presented a great opportunity for the Globalist-banksters to restructure the world's monetary system towards a 'global economy.' And so from 1st to 22nd July, at the Mount Washington Hotel in New Hampshire, the 'Bretton Woods Conference,' took place, hosting 730 delegates from 44 nations in order to instigate new rules for commercial and financial relations.

The US was represented by the Zionist, Assistant Treasury Secretary, Harry Dexter-White (originally Weiss.) He was the son of Jewish immigrants from the Russian Empire and several years after 'Bretton Woods,' Dexter-White was exposed as a Soviet spy. The senior British delegate was the legendary Fabian Socialist (secret Communist,) economist, the abusive life-long sexual deviant and paedophile, John Maynard Keynes. The Fabian homosexual circle was incredibly successful in gaining influence in a wide area of activities, mainly because they as a whole and especially Keynes, were very easy for the banksters to control, due to their lifestyles.

Keynes, a 'legend' of economics, was characterised by his male 'sweetheart,' Lytton Strachey, as "*A liberal and a sodomite, an atheist and a statistician.*" His particular depravity was the sexual abuse of little boys and in communications to his homosexual friends, Keynes advised that they should go to Tunis, "*...where bed and boy, were also not expensive.*" As a paedophile-sodomite, he often travelled throughout the Mediterranean area in search of boys for himself and his fellow socialist/communists.

Just before the Bolshevik Revolution, Keynes had made a hurried trip to the United States for the British Government. Here, he made contact with the American Fabians who were similarly entrenched, via the Frankfurter-Lippmann group, in key positions of the Wilson Administration.

At Bretton Woods, Keynes suggested the creation of a World Currency, to be issued by a Global Central Bank, but at the time the conditions were not ready for such a radical step towards The New World Order and so instead of a global currency, it was agreed as a first step toward that ultimate goal, that each nation would link its currency to the US Dollar. Both the *International Monetary Fund* (IMF) and the *World Bank*, were conceived at Bretton Woods.

So, the Bretton Woods Agreement established the dollar as the world's 'reserve currency,' which meant that international commodities were priced in dollars. The agreement, which gave the United States a distinct financial advantage, was made under the condition that those dollars would remain redeemable for gold at a consistent rate of $35 per ounce. The fixed dollar to gold convertibility rate established a stable platform for global economic growth and as the issuer of the world's reserve currency, the United States promised to print dollars in direct proportion to its gold reserves. However, this promise was based on 'honour' since the Federal Reserve refused to allow any audits or supervision of its printing presses.

The 'Liberation' of Paris

After the German surrender of Paris on the 25th August 1944, there was another kind of invasion of France; on this occasion by the vengeful and humiliated, ill-disciplined forces led by Charles De Gaulle. As soon as the American forces had made it safe for the ousted French general and his followers, these brigands – for that is precisely what they were – sought revenge for their earlier humiliation at the hands of the Germans.

The most appalling massacres of civilians began, whilst American and British troops stood idly by. Generally the British media ignored these awful events but one English journalist among others of various nationalities, recorded these sad, desperate events . . .

"There has never been, in the history of France, a bloodier period than that which followed the liberation of 1944-1945. The massacres of 1944 were no less savage than the massacres of Jacquerie, of St. Bartholomew, of the revolutionary terror, of the Commune, and they were certainly more numerous and on a wider scale . . . The American services put the figures of 'summary executions' in France in the first months of the liberation at 80,000 and a former French Minister, Adrien Tixier, later placed the figure at 105,000."

With the collapse of the Vichy French regime, de Gaulle and the bankster-sponsored, Communist sympathising French, imposed a new 'Reign of Terror.' Cruel punishments were meted-out against those labelled as 'Nazi collaborators,' whose only crime was in making peace with Germany, or to have fought against the Soviets on the eastern front as foreign members of the German SS units. The 'Gaullists' murdered as many as 40,000, and imprisoned 100,000 of their countrymen and French women who dated German soldiers during the occupation were humiliated by having their heads shaved.

Less than one-quarter of 1% of the French people wanted anything to do with the 'Resistance.' The Resistance movement had a total membership of 100,000 at its height, whilst France had a population at that time of over 40 million. From this we can deduce that 99%+ accepted or supported the German occupation, which in any case was confined only to those territories that would facilitate an Allied invasion.

Throughout the war, American prisons held 16,000 conscientious objectors. This 'conscientious objection' was widely publicised and denounced, presumably to deter others from taking the same decision and yet, there was no publicity given to the 20,000 or so American servicemen who went AWOL as soon as they landed on the French beaches. Many lived rough and subsisted by occasional sorties back to their encampments and stealing their own Army's supplies.

American renegade black-marketeers sold whole trainloads of clothing, food, fuel and other essential commodities. Indeed, the American revisionist author James J. Martin said... *"No army is ever free of looting but it is questionable if any other army ever looted itself on the scale of ours."* He also recounted how... *"US Army trucks were backed up the whole length of the Champs-Elysees with GIs selling gasoline and cigarettes openly to the French populace."*

In total, over 40,000 Americans 'deserted' during WWII, and some 100,000 British. As in all wars, it is a phenomenon only to be expected but the cruel, shameful irony was that the banksters made it a crime to refuse to kill your fellow man or die in the name of their profits and power. Conscripted into a mass-murdering conspiracy of evil, those that refused to take part in it were forever branded 'cowards' or 'traitors.' They were meant to do their 'duty' and obey without question whilst feeling honoured to serve the cause. This is exactly what their fathers had done, and their father before them and so on, ad nauseum, into the past.

The 'liberators' disregard for French social norms led to their having sex in public with prostitutes and sexually assaulting women, openly on the streets. Immediately following D-Day, the conditions for the ensuing tragedy were perfect. The Allied bombing had killed more French than the Germans had and most of the young men of France were in German prisons or in hiding. The country had fallen to the Germans in an embarrassingly short time and suffered occupation for four years. Then finally, the American conquerors arrived, handsome, well-armed, and comparatively speaking, rich. One look at the beautiful French girls, and the GIs thought they were in heaven, but the honeymoon-period did not last very long.

France was by this time, starving. American soldiers possessed an endless supply of food, and especially chocolate and cigarettes, which the deprived natives craved and as a result, almost overnight, sex became the currency and French women quickly realised that offering sex was practically the only way to survive.

As a result, the French came to be regarded as an immoral, subservient people and in the summer of 1944, all the women of France in effect, became prostitutes for the benefits the practice brought, and to stay alive. Americanisation had turned hungry women into nothing more than tarts. The generals 'looked the other way' whilst American military authorities tried their best to ignore both the disastrous effects on French society and the escalating incidence of venereal disease among their troops. The Army privately believed that sex was good for fighting men, but had little regard for the women who were reluctantly providing this 'relief' to their soldiers.

The 'Battle of the Bulge'

The 'Battle of the Bulge' or the 'Ardennes Offensive' was fought over the winter months of 1944 – 1945, and constituted the final, major German offensive against the Allies in WWII. The battle was a last-ditch attempt by Hitler to halt the Allies in their drive towards Germany and destroy their ability to supply themselves

The Battle of the Bulge began on 16th December 1944. Hitler was still convinced that the alliance between Britain, France and America was fragile and that a major attack and defeat would break-up the pact. He therefore ordered a massive attack against what were primarily American forces, which was originally known as the Ardennes Offensive but because the initial attack by the Germans created a bulge in the Allied front line, it became more commonly known as the Battle of the Bulge. In fact it was the largest battle fought by the Americans in WWII with 600,000 American troops involved.

Hitler's plan was to launch a massive attack on the Allies using three armies which would, in his view, destabilise their accord and also capture the port of Antwerp through which a great deal of Allied supplies were being transported. Thick snow and heavy fog prevented the Americans from employing their air-power and the German advance of 250,000 men quickly, initially drove the American line backwards whilst German troops, dressed in captured American uniforms and driving captured US jeeps, caused confusion and within five days the Germans had surrounded almost 20,000 Americans at Bastogne. Their situation was desperate but when the German commander gave his American equivalent, Major-General Anthony McAuliffe, the chance to surrender, McAuliffe answered with just the one word, 'nuts.'

Meanwhile Patton moved reinforcements into Bastogne and relieved its desperate defenders and Montgomery 'did his bit' by preventing the Germans from crossing the River Meuse.

By the 22nd December, the weather had begun to clear, thus allowing the Allies to bring their air-power to bear and on the following day, the Americans initiated a counter-attack against the Germans.

On Christmas Eve, the Allies were subjected to the first ever attack by jet-bombers. Sixteen German Me-262 jets attacked railway yards in an attempt to disrupt the Allies supply-lines. However, without fuel for their armored vehicles, any air successes were almost meaningless. The German offensive had seen them advance 60 miles in two days, but from that point-on, an attritional stalemate ensued with ferocious fighting from both sides. As 1944 became 1945, the Germans attempted to start a second front in Holland but the weather at this time of year in the Ardennes was often brutal and indeed a period of intense cold and rain ensued. The foot soldiers on the ground in particular, faced very difficult conditions and on both sides of the divide, trench foot was a common problem for infantrymen, as was exposure.

The Americans used the lull to re-group and then suddenly counter-attacked; the Germans ran out of fuel and thus the bulge was burst. The Ardennes Offensive delayed the Allied advance by several weeks, but it was merely a postponement of the inevitable. The Germans began their retreat on the 22nd of January and by the 28th the front-line was back to where it had been on the 16th December. But the cost had been high. The US lost over 80,000 men killed or wounded and the Germans lost over 100,000 and, vitally, much of its aircraft and tanks which, at that stage of the war, with the German armaments industry now decimated, were impossible to replace. The march towards Berlin was back on...

The Sinking of the *Wilhelm Gustloff*

On the 30th January 1945, with the murderous, rampaging Red Army bearing down on them, the German civilians of East Prussia, desperate to escape, fled to the Baltic ports hoping to be evacuated by sea. Many of those caught in the maelstrom of the Soviet advance had already been murdered and raped.

Wilhelm Gustloff

The *Wilhelm Gustloff*, along with many other serviceable ships, was pressed into service to aid the evacuation of German civilians from the Eastern zone. With forty-eight hours' notice before departure, there were scenes of chaos and blind panic in the frozen German port of Gotenhafen as people, frantic for a place, fought on the dock and surged aboard the ship.

Wilhelm Gustloff, weighing 25,000 tons and almost 700 feet in length, was an impressive sight, and could carry almost 2,000 passengers and crew. Launched in 1937, it began its life as a luxury cruise liner for the German workers of Hitler's Third Reich. For the first year of the war she had served as a hospital ship before being held in dock in the port of Gotenhafen on the Baltic coast (modern-day Gdynia) where, until early 1945, it had served as barracks for U-boat trainees.

When the Gustloff left the relative protection of the harbour at Gotenhafen on 30th January 1945, the weather was extremely poor with a wind strength of 7, it was snowing, the temperature was minus 10 degrees Celsius, and there were copious amounts of sea-ice. In short, the chances of human survival in water in those conditions were zero, with or without a life-preserver. Once underway, the *Wilhelm Gustloff* began to battle its way through the choppy, blustery Baltic Sea, un-escorted and with its only protection being the few anti-aircraft guns it had on-board. However, against a submarine attack the Gustloff was powerless.

According to the ships own records, the list of passengers on the 30th included 918 Naval officers and men, 173 crew, 373 members of the Woman's Naval Auxiliary units, 162 wounded, and 4,424 refugees, an 'official' total of 6,050 people. This however fails to take into account the many hundreds of other people that one way or another were able to make their way onto the seemingly safe haven of the Gustloff. In fact, new research has now shown that the total number of people on the Gustloff at the time was actually 10,582 souls (40% of whom were children.) In their blind panic, they had crammed themselves onto a ship designed for less than 2,000 passengers.

When the captains (there were four on board) were informed of a German mine-sweeper convoy coming towards them, they decided, after much argument, to switch on the navigation lights to avoid colliding into the convoy, but by doing so the ship also became visible to a Soviet submarine lurking nearby.

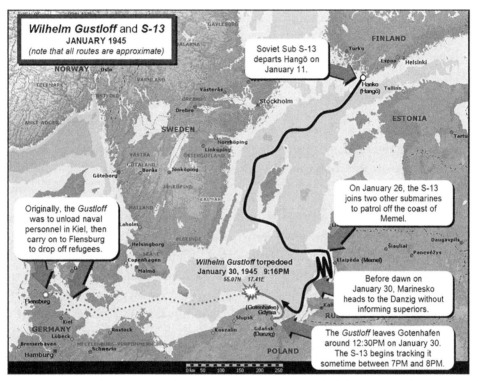

Then, at 9.08pm, the Soviet submarine S-13, commanded by Alexander Marinesko, hit the Gustloff with three torpedoes. She immediately listed to starboard, righted herself, and then listed once again, launched rescue flares and broadcast an SOS message. Less than 50 minutes later she was gone, sunk beneath the icy black waters of the Baltic, along with 9,343 men, women and children. Amazingly, 1,239 people were saved by the heroic and selfless work of a number of smaller German ships in the area but the losses were **six-times greater than those of the *Titanic*.**

When the Gustloff sank, it was an event unlike any in naval history, if for no other reason, because of the sheer scale of the tragedy. Many ships have sunk with terrible loss of life, but never before or since have so many lives been lost on a single ship. As with all maritime tragedies, the scene was one of absolute and complete horror. The suffering of those on board the Gustloff was unspeakable and whether these people were 'enemies' or not is irrelevant, they were fellow human beings, the vast majority of them 'innocents,' i.e. non-combatants. It was such a horrific loss of human life, and one of which even today, few people are aware.

Indeed, Marinesko deserves the epithet 'war criminal,' more than many other recipients of that label. He knew very well that the Gustloff was an innocent refugee ship and this in my view typifies the disgraceful, inhumanity shown by the Soviets as a nation, despite their being portrayed as the 'good guys,' by the bankster-controlled media at the time.

The sinking of the *Wilhelm Gustloff* remains the greatest maritime disaster in history. So why is hardly anyone aware of it and why has bankster-controlled and run Hollywood never made a movie of it? This is of course a rhetorical question. The answer is obvious and that is that Hollywood is run by the same group of people today as it was at that time and anything that hints at sympathy for Germans or paints its adversaries in a bad light, is always 'brushed under the carpet,' whilst anything to the opposite of those is constantly promoted and presented in a positive light.

The Yalta Conference

This was held in the Black Sea resort of Yalta, at the Livadia Palace. At the conference, FDR and Churchill at the banksters' behest, made massive concessions to Stalin as they began the re-organisation of the World's political landscape to fall in-line with the banksters' ambitions.

With the Zionist-Red spies Alger Hiss and Harry Hopkins influencing the now ailing Roosevelt, it was decided that *after* Germany's defeat, that the Soviets would occupy Eastern Europe until 'free elections' could be held. The Soviets would also join the war against Japan and would be supplied with US arms to facilitate their efforts. After Japan was defeated, the Soviets would occupy northern Korea (without Korea's approval,) and Manchuria in China (also without China's approval.) Millions of Russian POWs captured by the Germans, as well as Russian refugees fleeing Stalin, would be forcefully returned to Stalin and Germany would be divided in two, as would Berlin.

The main objective of both Winston Churchill and Stalin was the capture of Berlin, the capital of Germany. However, coached by his bankster bosses, Roosevelt did not agree and this translated itself into a decision by the US military commander, General Eisenhower, to head south-east to Dresden, thereby ensuring that Soviet forces would be the first to reach Berlin.

Dresden – An appalling War Crime

On the night of 12/13th February 1945, over 1000 allied bombers attacked a non-military, civilian target in Germany, the town of Dresden. Dresden was (and is still) famous for its china pottery industry and at that time towards the end of the war, was the adopted home of several hundred thousand refugees from the far east of Germany, who were attempting to flee the marauding Russian hordes, rapidly advancing westwards towards Berlin.

There were no military installations in Dresden, no military headquarters or camps, no munitions factories and no heavy engineering of any kind that could have been linked to Germany's by this time seriously crippled war efforts. In short, Dresden was a medium-large sized, rural, historical town with no strategic importance whatsoever.

By February 1945, the outcome of the war in Europe was already determined. Germany was effectively defeated and would formally surrender within three months. The murderous firebombing of the beautiful city of Dresden, the 'Florence of the North,' was as cruel as it was unnecessary and in an apparent gesture, mocking the mainly Christian Germans, the Zionist-banksters chose the day of 'Ash Wednesday' to turn Dresden into ashes. And what happened in the space of those twelve terrifying hours should live forever in the annals of the shame of the human race. It is thought by many credible commentators that as many as 4 to 500,000 innocent people died that night. Far more than double the two atomic attacks on Hiroshima and Nagasaki combined. In many cases, theirs was not a quick death but a slow agonising death through being 'eaten alive' by the phosphorus and subsequent firestorms generated by the half-million+ incendiary bombs dropped by the Allies.

More than 12,000 houses in the centre of the city were reduced to dust, not rubble, dust during the hellish firestorm. In view of the fact that, in addition to the 600,000 inhabitants of Dresden, another 5-600,000 people, all refugees, had found shelter in the overcrowded city, one can safely assume that each of these 12,000 houses contained no fewer than 20 people. But of these houses virtually nothing remained and the people who had been sheltering in them were transformed into ashes due to a heat of greater than 1600 degrees Celsius being generated by the fire-bombs.

The 'official' figure of 35,000 dead only represents the small part of the victims who could be fully identified. Erhard Mundra, a member of the 'Bautzen committee' wrote in the daily German newspaper *'Die Welt'* on 12th February 1995...

"According to the former general staff officer of the military district of Dresden and retired lieutenant colonel of the Bundeswehr, D. Matthes, 35,000 victims were fully and another 50,000 partly identified, whereas a further 168,000 could not be identified at all."

It also goes without saying that the hapless children, women, invalids and old people whom the firestorm had transformed into nothing more or less than ashes, could not be identified either.

At the time of the attack, Dresden had no anti-aircraft guns and no military defence. It possessed no military industry at all and served as a shelter for refugees from the East, many of them ill, starving, emaciated and disabled. Indeed, many roofs of buildings where they were housed were marked with huge red crosses.

On that terrible night from 12th to 13th February 1945, one of the greatest war criminals of all time, Winston Churchill, was complicit, indeed instrumental in the senseless, pointless mass-murder of around half a million unarmed, helpless citizens, mostly women, children, the disabled and the aged.

"It cannot be disputed that the principles of international law forbade total carpeting bombing…..The historians considered the indiscriminate bombing as an abomination, but refused to lay the whole guilt on Air Marshall Sir Arthur Harris or the Bomber Command. According to them, the entire staff of the RAF, but even more the political leaders, especially Churchill and Roosevelt, plus the majority of their peoples shared the burden of guilt." The joint conclusions of military historians from five countries at a conference in Freiburg, 1988

On the 13th February 1990, exactly forty-five years after the destruction of Dresden, the British historian David Irving, spoke in Dresden. In his speech, Irving quoted the banksters' stooge and war criminal, Churchill, thus… *"I don't want any suggestions how to destroy militarily important targets around Dresden. I want suggestions as to how we can roast the 600,000 refugees from Breslau in Dresden."*

But for Churchill, simply 'roasting' Germans was nothing like enough. On the morning after the firebombing of Dresden, he personally gave the order for low-flying planes to machine-gun the survivors on the banks of the river Elbe where they had dragged themselves to try and find shelter from the suffocating heat by water immersion.

However, to backtrack slightly, as the morning of the 12th February 1945 dawned in Dresden, the streets and squares were filled with refugees and the meadows and parks had been transformed into huge camps. When the fatal hour approached, about 1,130,000 people were living in Dresden.

Dresden's citizens barely had time to reach their bomb shelters, but as it would turn-out, these shelters became death traps anyway. The first bomb fell at 10.09pm and the attack lasted 24 minutes, leaving the inner city a raging sea of fire. Precision saturation bombing had created the desired firestorm.

A firestorm is engendered when hundreds of smaller fires join together and become one vast conflagration. Huge volumes of oxygen are drawn-in to feed the inferno, causing an artificial tornado. Those persons unlucky enough to be caught in the rush of wind can be hurled down the entire length of a street into the flames. Those who seek refuge underground often suffocate as oxygen is extracted from the air to feed the blaze or they perish in a blast of white heat, intense enough to melt human flesh and bone, leaving no visible trace. Indeed, such was the power of the conflagration that night that air was sucked from basements and sewers where the populace hid in large numbers, suffocating many hundreds or even thousands, to death.

Another eyewitness who survived told of seeing, *"young women carrying babies running up and down the streets, their dresses and hair on fire, screaming until they fell down, or the collapsing buildings fell on top of them."*

There was a three-hour pause between the first and second raids. The lull had been calculated to lure civilians from their shelters into the open again. To escape the flames, tens of thousands of civilians had crowded into the 'Grosser Garten,' a beautiful area of parkland nearly one and a half miles square in area.

The second raid came at 1.22 am with no warning as the early warning sirens had been destroyed in the first attack, probably along with their operators. Twice as many bombers returned with another massive payload of incendiary bombs. The second wave was intended to spread the raging firestorm into the Grosser Garten and it was a complete success. Within a few minutes a sheet of flame ripped across the grass, uprooting trees and littering the branches of others with everything from bicycles to human limbs. For days afterward, they remained bizarrely strewn about as grim reminders of Allied sadism.

At the start of the second air assault, many were still huddled in tunnels and cellars, waiting for the fires of the first attack to die down. At 1.30 am an ominous rumble reached the ears of the commander of a Labour Service convoy sent into the city on a rescue mission. He described it this way . . .

"The detonation shook the cellar walls. The sound of the explosions mingled with a new, stranger sound which seemed to come closer and closer, the sound of a thundering waterfall; it was the sound of a mighty tornado howling in the inner city."

Others hiding below ground died, but they died painlessly—they simply glowed bright orange and blue in the darkness and as the heat intensified, they either disintegrated into ashes or melted into a thick liquid, three to four feet deep in places. Shortly after 10.30 am on the morning of the 14th of February, the last raid swept over the city. American fighter-bombers pounded the rubble that had been Dresden for a full forty minutes, but this attack was not nearly as heavy as the first two.

However, what distinguished this raid was the cold-blooded ruthlessness with which it was carried out. US Mustangs appeared low over the city, strafing anything that moved with machine gun fire, including a column of rescue vehicles rushing to the city to evacuate survivors. One assault was aimed at the banks of the Elbe River, where refugees had huddled together during this terrible night.

In the last year of the war, Dresden had become a hospital town. During the previous night's massacre, heroic uninjured individuals had dragged thousands of the devastatingly injured to the banks of the Elbe to escape the worst ravages of the firestorm. The low-flying American Mustangs machine-gunned those people and their helpless charges, as well as thousands of elderly and children who had escaped the city and when the last plane had departed, Dresden was a scorched ruin, its blackened streets filled with corpses. The city was not even spared further horror. A flock of vultures that had escaped from the ruins of the zoo, fed on the carnage and rats also swarmed over the piles of corpses.

In Dresden, the Allied airmen under the orders of the Elite butchers fronted by the sadistic Churchill, murdered several hundreds of thousands people in one single, hellish night and destroyed countless cultural treasures. Women who were giving birth to children in the delivery rooms of the burning hospitals jumped out of the windows, but within minutes, these mothers and their children, who were still hanging at the umbilical cords, were reduced to ashes too. Thousands of people whom the incendiary bombs had transformed into living torches, jumped into the ponds, lakes and rivers, but phosphorus continues to burn even in the water and is indeed 'fed' by water. Even the animals from the zoo, elephants, lions and others, desperately headed for the water, together with the humans. But all of them, the new-born children, the mothers, the old men, the wounded soldiers and the innocent animals from the zoo and the stables, horribly perished in the name of 'liberation'.

What justification is there for this utterly repugnant behaviour? Is it revenge, hatred, blood-lust or ritual sacrifice? I believe it is a mixture of all of these, but I do know one thing for sure and that is that no sane, balanced, rational human being behaves in this disgraceful, cowardly fashion. The people who order these grotesque atrocities are undoubtedly clinical psychopaths with no empathy for the plight of their fellow man, whatsoever.

All German towns and cities with a population greater than 50,000 were from 50% to 80% destroyed. Cologne with a population greater than Glasgow's was turned into a moonscape. Hamburg was totally destroyed and as any as 50,000 civilians died in the most appalling circumstances. As Hamburg burned, the winds feeding the three-mile high flames reached twice hurricane speed to exceed 200 miles per hour. On the outskirts of the city, trees three feet in diameter were sucked from the ground by the unnatural forces of these winds and hurled miles into the city-inferno, as were vehicles, men, women and children.

The Zionist-German émigré Professor Frederick Lindemann, Churchill's friend and scientific advisor had by the closing period of the war, become Lord Cherwell. He submitted a plan to the War Cabinet on 30th March 1942, urging that German working-class houses, being closer together yielded a 'greater flesh-incineration-per-bomb,' so they should be targeted in preference to military objectives, the latter being more difficult to hit. Middle-class homes had too much space around them, he explained. He was of course, not prosecuted for this ghastly new war-crime, hitherto undreamt-of. Lindemann enthusiastically supported the infamous Morgenthau Plan, which Churchill subsequently enthusiastically endorsed.

Lindemann met with Churchill almost daily during the war and wielded more influence than any other civilian adviser. Whilst Lindemann and Churchill agreed on most matters, however, when they did not, Lindemann reportedly worked unceasingly to change Churchill's mind. He was no lover of humanity, as illustrated by the following quotes... "*To consolidate the rule of supermen –to perpetuate the British Empire [i.e. the NWO] – one need only remove the ability of slaves to see themselves as slaves.*" Lindemann suggested that science create a race of humans with "*the mental make-up of the worker bee...*" that would do all of the menial work while not being concerned about individual rights. "*...placid content rules in the bee-hive or ant-heap.*"

One of Roosevelt's first great feats as President had been the gigantic gold swindle (otherwise known as the *Gold Trading Act* of 1934,) which officially committed the US government to support the Zionist banksters in their manipulation of the price of gold. It was FDR and his openly Zionist Secretary of the Treasury, Henry Morgenthau Jr., who were instrumental in bringing this plot to fruition, after a tussle with the Supreme Court. Morgenthau later said... "*If the Supreme Court had decided against us, we had legislation ready to push through Congress which would have given us the same result.*" This Morgenthau was the son of the Henry Morgenthau who paid Woodrow Wilson's way into the White House in 1912 so that Wilson could appoint him as US Ambassador to Turkey, where world Zionists were completing the details of the Communist Revolution in Russia.

Morgenthau was also the author of the infamous Morgenthau Plan which proposed wiping-out the German race in 1944, and which was also broadcast to the German army and caused the lives of thousands of British and Americans to be sacrificed, because the Germans were forewarned as to what would happen after they surrendered. This Plan, so determined in its ruthlessness that it aroused the horror of the entire non-bankster civilised world, was absolutely typical of Jewish/Communist efforts to slaughter whole nations.

Churchill, the unspeakable monster who ordered the Dresden slaughter, was knighted, and the rest is 'history.' The cold-blooded sadism of the massacre, however, was brushed aside by his many biographers, who still can never quite bring themselves to inform the world how the desire of one madman to 'impress' a group of even madder-men, led to the genocide of up to a half million men, women and children in one truly appalling night.

The Fire Bombing of Tokyo

Tokyo after the incendiary raids

On the 10th March 1945, 334 American B-29s rained incendiary bombs on Tokyo, sparking a firestorm that killed upwards of 100,000 people, burned a quarter of the city to the ground, and left a million homeless.

Although it would later be overshadowed by the atomic attacks on Hiroshima and Nagasaki, the firebombing of Tokyo was just as deadly in its initial death toll. This terror-bombing utilised the same incendiary type explosives dropped on Dresden one month earlier, and yielded similar, horrific results. The raid also represented a tactical shift, as the Americans switched from high-altitude precision bombing to low-altitude incendiary raids.

Tokyo was the first of five incendiary raids launched in quick succession against the largest Japanese cities. Nagoya, Osaka and Kobe were also targeted, with Nagoya being hit twice within a week and by the end of the war, more than 60 Japanese cities had been laid waste by firebombing.

The Tokyo raid, codenamed *Operation Meetinghouse*, was part of an aerial onslaught so effective that the American air command concluded by July 1945 that no further, viable targets remained on the Japanese mainland. But if the American objective was to shorten the war by demoralising the Japanese population and breaking its will to resist, it certainly did not work. What had proven true in Germany proved equally true in Japan. Morale was shaken by bombing, but once the shock had passed, the war effort continued.

The Americans began increasingly looking towards the use of incendiaries as their stockpiles of those weapons increased, and also because the typically cloudy weather conditions that prevailed over Japan made precision bombing difficult at best. Major General Curtis LeMay, who had been appointed commander of the 21st Bomber Command in the Pacific in January 1945, became the primary architect of this new policy. He was a strategic innovator, and the most quotable spokesman for the US policy of callously burning enemy cities to the ground, just as was his RAF counterpart, Sir Arthur 'Bomber' Harris.

The intention of the Tokyo mission was to reduce the city to rubble, kill as many of its citizens as possible and instil abject terror into the survivors and this relentless attack on an area that the US Strategic Bombing Survey estimated to be 84.7 percent residential, succeeded beyond the planners' wildest dreams. Whipped by fierce winds, the flames rapidly spread across a fifteen-square-mile area of Tokyo, once again generating immense firestorms.

LeMay, unleashed 496,000 incendiaries in a single raid, and argued that incendiary bombing would be particularly effective, because Japanese cities contained a lot of tightly-packed, wooden structures that would burn easily when set alight. And so, in preparation, the B-29 bombers for the Tokyo raid were stripped of their defensive weapons and packed with various incendiary explosives, including white phosphorus and napalm, a new gasoline-based, fuel-gel mixture developed at Harvard University of all places. Isn't education a wonderful thing?

As opposed to the high-altitude precision bombing, which the Allies practiced with only mixed success over both Germany and Japan, incendiary raids were carried out at low altitudes between 5,000 and 9,000 feet. The attackers were helped by the fact that Japanese air defences were almost non-existent by that point in the war and in fact, only 14 B-29s were lost in the Tokyo raid. As was the case in Europe, pathfinder planes flying ahead of the bombers marked the target with a flaming X, guiding-in the attackers. Tokyo was bombarded constantly for a period of three hours by three bomber streams that dropped roughly 2,000 tons of incendiaries near the docklands and in the industrial heart of the Japanese capital.

Tokyo, almost immediately burst into flames. The combination of incendiaries, the windy weather conditions and lack of co-ordinated firefighting on the ground, resulted in a firestorm similar to the one two years previously in Hamburg, and only a month before in Dresden. Temperatures on the ground in Tokyo reached 1,800 degrees in some places. The human carnage was appalling. Bomber crews arriving towards the end of the raid, reported smelling the stench of charred flesh as they passed over the burning capital.

Sixty-three percent of Tokyo's commercial area, and 18 percent of its industry, was destroyed in that one raid and an estimated 267,000 buildings burned to the ground. The charred bodies of 100,000 dead Japanese citizens littered the streets, and 250,000 buildings and homes were destroyed. One million more were injured, and a further one million more, made homeless. Given a near total inability to fight fires of the magnitude and speed produced by the bombs, casualties may have been several times higher than the estimate of 100,000 deaths.

Then, following the Tokyo raid, the US extended fire-bombing nationwide and in the ten-day period beginning on 9th March, 9,373 tons of bombs destroyed 31 square miles of Tokyo, Nagoya, Osaka and Kobe. Overall, bombing strikes razed to the ground, 40 percent of the 66 Japanese cities targeted.

The bombing was driven not only by a belief that it could end the war but also by the attempt by the Air Force to claim credit for the US victory, and to justify the enormous costs of developing and producing thousands of B-29 bombers and the costs of the hundreds of thousands of bombs used.

The most important way in which WWII shaped the morality of mass destruction was in the elimination of the stigma associated with the targeting of civilian populations from the air. If area bombing remained controversial throughout much of the war, something to be concealed or denied by its practitioners, by the end of the war, with the enormous increase in the destructive power of bombing, it had become a primary war tactic of war, and therefore the international norm. This approach to the destruction of cities, which was perfected in 1944-45, wedded technological predominance with the minimisation of casualties to produce overwhelming 'kill ratios.'

And indeed... Those kill ratios for the banksters as you will soon see, would go on to become even greater than ever imagined. Not just simply through their never-ending and contrived wars and conflicts, but in man-made diseases and epidemics, staged terrorism, and even the food we eat and the air we breathe.

The banksters work in very complex and often seemingly contradictory ways. FDR was certainly, as already shown, a bankster-controlled President. His infamy at Pearl Harbor, his Zionist/Communist handlers, his war-criminal record and so forth, was ample proof of that. But always remember that Churchill and Stalin were also banksters'-men, through and through.

Once the British had declared war on Germany in 1939, it was ironic that Churchill had to turn to Roosevelt and Stalin in order to make sure of saving Britain. Indeed, Churchill and Roosevelt had never been friends. Roosevelt had disliked Churchill from the very first time they met, two decades earlier.

It is also significant that Churchill sent William Stephenson also known as 'Intrepid' of MI-6, to head the British Security Coordination (BSC) a covert organization set up at 30, Rockefeller Center in New York City in May 1940. Its purpose was to investigate enemy activities, prevent sabotage against British interests in the Americas, and mobilise pro-British opinion in the Americas. Churchill has always been fêted as the great leader of the alliance against Germany and Japan. This is just another fantasy engendered by the bankster-elite. Churchill certainly spun some apt and catchy phrases during the war, but they were probably written for him and he had virtually nothing to do with achieving the final victory.

Meanwhile, FDR was doing all he could to reassure Stalin of America's good intentions, and his plans to work with the Soviet Union after the war to bring lasting peace to the world. Roosevelt went out of his way to appease Stalin at every opportunity, again probably at the behest of his bankster 'handlers.' For example, when security officials at the 1943 Tehran Conference told him that he was not safe at the American Embassy, which was located a good distance from the centre of Tehran, he chose to accept Stalin's offer to stay at the Soviet Embassy, rather than Churchill's offer of the British Embassy. Roosevelt also took Stalin's 'side' time after time with regard to substantive issues, and he joined Stalin in ribbing Churchill on numerous occasions. Finally, Stalin did come to trust Roosevelt, but he continued to be wary of Churchill.

Soon after the Stalingrad victory, Churchill enlisted the US bankster-corporate elite in behind-the-scenes talks with German Nazis. Allen Dulles, the OSS man in Switzerland became deeply involved in covert operations, without Roosevelt's knowledge. Treason? Dulles indeed also helped to negotiate the terms of the secret, *Operation Sunrise*, later to become *Operation Paperclip*, under which thousands of high-ranking Germans, most them drawn from the ranks of the (apparently despised) Nazi party, became employees of the government of the United States.

Another important aspect of Dulles' plotting was to substitute Harry Truman as running-mate in 1944 for Henry Wallace, who was even further to the left than Roosevelt. (This is known inside US government inner-circles as the 'Vice President Trick,' and was later used on Eisenhower and Kennedy and with somewhat less success on Ronald Reagan.

The banksters knew Truman well enough to know that he would, as President, allow them to create the first era of peacetime militarism in the United States 150 years of existence and so the planning for the assassination of FDR began at the 1944 Democratic National Convention, in Chicago, Illinois, in July. Roosevelt was running for an unprecedented 4th term and his popular Vice President was Henry A. Wallace.

After his victory, FDR gave his acceptance speech via radio from San Diego, California. He was under pressure to dump Wallace, and replace him with James Byrnes, so he stayed away from the Convention. The President's wife, Eleanor despised Byrnes and so the 'tug of war' was putting tremendous stress on the President.

Vice President Henry Wallace was a plain-speaking farmer's son from Iowa . . . and he was just too honest to engage in the conspiracy and he fully expected to be re-nominated for Vice President at the Convention. The MI-6 agent and children's author Roald Dahl, became a close 'friend' of Henry Wallace but unknown to Wallace, Dahl was spying on him and sending his private papers to Sir William Stephenson at 30, Rockefeller Plaza.

"Marsh had given him a draft of a pamphlet written by his close friend Henry Wallace. Entitled 'Our Job in the Pacific,' it summarised the vice president's post-war goals, among them international control of the airways, economic assistance for the industrial development of Asia, and the demilitarisation of Japan. Wallace was also in favour of 'the emancipation of colonial subjects' in the British Empire, including India, Burma, and Malaya. Dahl could feel his 'hair stand on end' and immediately realised the document's importance, and knowing that his superiors would want to see it, he excused himself saying that he was going to finish reading it downstairs.

He quickly phoned his BSC contact, explained the urgency of the situation, and convinced him to meet him on the corner as soon as possible. The agent knew something was up and materialised on the street in front of Marsh's house in a matter of minutes.

Dahl sneaked out of the house and handed the document through his car window, warning his partner in crime to be back in half an hour or there would be hell to pay. 'He flashed off,' recalled Dahl, 'and I'm around downstairs, near the lavatory door, and if the chap upstairs had come down looking for me saying, 'have you finished reading it,' then I'd have been in the lavatory you see, saying 'I'm sorry I'm caught short.' As it turned out, the agent went straight to the BSC's Washington offices to make copies and made it back within the allotted time. Dahl nipped back out, collected the paper, and no one was the wiser." Conant *'The Irregulars: Roald Dahl and the British Spy Ring in Wartime Washington'*

And so it was that the British spy ring, led by Dahl, made sure that Wallace was not re-nominated for Vice President. A ferocious fight broke out in Chicago between the supporters of Vice President Wallace and the supporters of James Byrnes. Everyone seemed to somehow know that Roosevelt would not survive his 4th term, so his Vice President would then become President.

Byrnes was determined to reach the White House no matter what the cost and the refusal of FDR to make him his VP was a staggering blow to his pride, so he tried to 'sneak in though the back door,' via the position of Secretary of State. He arrived at the convention on the morning of 20th July, absolutely confident that he would be the next Vice President, and therefore by default the next President of the United States.

Byrnes was to face a big disappointment however, as nothing could persuade the absent Roosevelt to name him as his heir apparent. Jimmy Byrnes was one of the few people at the Convention who 'knew' that a new deadly weapon called the atomic bomb was under development. This weapon could be a complete 'game-changer' and its sole possessor could rule the world, completely unchallenged.

Roosevelt would not pledge his support to either Vice President Wallace or to James Byrnes and so a compromise candidate was 'chosen,' named Harry Truman. By whom he was chosen, remains a moot point, but I am sure that we all have our suspicions, eh, dear reader? Truman came to the Convention as an ardent Byrnes supporter and he had no real Presidential ambitions, FDR could not or as is more likely, would not, make a decision and so Truman was nominated 'by default.'

The banksters recruited Bob Hannegan, a crooked political operator from Missouri, to secure the Truman nomination by covertly getting the necessary commitments months in advance from big-city organised-crime groups and their political machines in the North and from conservative Southerners, who made up a substantial block of the Democratic Party. After he was chosen, the banksters' massive propaganda machine went into overdrive, peddling lies about how Truman would strengthen the Democratic cause etc. etc.

None of this was true – at all. Before the convention, Truman was the choice of only 2% of the voters, but Wallace was extremely popular all over the country, and especially so with farmers, who otherwise might have voted Republican. In those now far-off days, small farmers constituted 20% of the population, and they loved Wallace for what he had done for them during the 1930s when he was Secretary of Agriculture.

But FDR would soon be disposed-of anyway and the US, the UK would soon turn full circle with regard to the Soviets and on the surface at least, 'oppose' the evil of Communism. But suddenly something went wrong. Stalin's spies in Switzerland discovered the Dulles operation and Stalin sent a telegram of complaint to Roosevelt. Of course, FDR knew nothing of the Dulles plot, and so in his response he expressed surprise to

Stalin that he (Stalin) would distrust him. But unfortunately for FDR, that was the last action he ever undertook. Realising that they were in danger of being exposed, the conspirators decided to dispense with FDR immediately.

In fact, the conspirators had started to poison FDR with intermittent doses of arsenic tri-oxide and to add insult to injury they started the rumours about FDR being a dying man. The first dosage was apparently given to FDR at the Tehran Conference in 1943. With each subsequent dose, FDR would show the typical symptoms of such poisoning, such as respiratory difficulty and heart trouble, but then he would recover, only to take another turn for the worse when the next dose was administered. Unfortunately for him, either Roosevelt's physicians did not suspect poisoning, or they were 'in' on the whole plot – most probably the latter.

In April 1944, President Roosevelt was assigned a new doctor, a young Navy lieutenant named Dr. Howard Bruenn at Bethesda Naval Hospital. It was very unusual that the President would be attended-to by such a low ranking officer, but obviously, skill in the use of poison was all that was necessary for Dr. Bruenn to possess in terms of medical prowess.

But once the plotters had made the final decision to kill FDR, they would have to use a poison that would act much more quickly than arsenic, so they settled on cyanide. Roosevelt ate around noon each day, usually a bowl of gruel and a drink to stimulate his appetite.

On 30th March 1945, President Roosevelt arrived at his hideaway home in Warm Springs, Georgia, for a 2-week break. It was the place where his security was most lax. Dr. Ross T. McIntire was the White House physician in charge of Roosevelt's health and Dr. McIntire predicted confidently that the President would be a 'different man' when he returned to Washington. When Dr. Bruenn telephoned on Thursday, 12th April, his report to him was most optimistic . . .

"The President had gained back eight of his lost pounds and was feeling so fit that he planned to attend an old-fashioned Georgia barbecue in the afternoon and a minstrel show that evening for the Foundation's patients. Every cause for anxiety seemed to have lifted, and given another lazy, restful week, there was no reason why he should not return to Washington on 20th April to greet the Regent of Iraq." 'McIntire, White House Physician,' p. 240

Admiral McIntire was in Washington DC at that time, but the President's personal physician, Dr. Bruenn, was with the President in Warm Springs. Nicholas Robbins (real name Nicholas Kotzubisky) was the driver and photographer for Elizabeth Shoumatoff, a Russian-born artist. FDR was having his portrait painted by her, when he took a break for lunch.

At twenty minutes to one, Arthur Prettyman, the valet, entered and placed a cup of gruel, a pitcher of cream, and a glass with a green fluid beside the president. FDR grimaced and without lifting his eyes from his reading, downed the latter, a vile concoction that was supposed to increase his appetite. FDR then absently took a few mouthfuls of gruel, still absorbed in his papers and then almost immediately complained of a terrible headache. The MI-6 agent Shoumatoff had resumed painting Roosevelt's portrait when he collapsed. MI-6 agent Lucy Mercer, a long-time mistress of the President, was also present.

Shoumatoff immediately called his physician, Howard Bruenn but doctors can be deadly and a medical assassination is a lot easier to hide than a bullet in the back of the head. Bruenn had prepared the deadly cocktail or 'cup of succession' for the President and Dr. James Paullin, an Atlanta internist, arrived soon after the poisoning and helped Bruenn make sure that the President did not undergo a 'miraculous recovery.' At 3.35 pm, on the 12th April 1945, President Franklin D. Roosevelt was pronounced dead.

Bruenn acted surprised that Roosevelt's lungs had failed. He had said that the President would die from heart trouble, but his heart kept beating for five minutes after his breathing stopped. Lung failure and FDR's other dying symptoms are definitely those indicative of cyanide poisoning, so once again the banksters had discarded another one of their 'useful idiots' and made ready to replace him with another.

Shoumatoff, and Mercer were quickly hustled out of the house by the US Secret Service. Shoumatoff returned to New York whilst Mercer went to find her priest to obtain 'absolution' for her complicity in the assassination of the President of the United States. Totally violating Georgia state law, no autopsy was performed on the President, as his body was rushed back to Washington DC for an indecently hasty funeral. 'Twas ever thus! After death by poisoning, a human body soon begins to emit a terrible odour and burial must be done rapidly but of course, the official cause of death was a cerebral haemorrhage. In fact, FDR was buried at the Roosevelt estate in Hyde Park, New York and from death to burial took less than three days.

And so, Harry S. Truman was sworn in as the 33rd President, immediately after the assassination of Roosevelt and James Byrnes was appointed Truman's Secretary of State. This position put Byrnes just one small step from the Presidency.

Truman soon realised that he could be the next Presidential victim of the poison cup, so he called on Congress to immediately change the law back to the original, 1792 order of succession...

1. President.
2. Vice-President.
3. President pro tempore of Senate.
4. Speaker of the House.

Byrnes totally dominated Truman who knew absolutely nothing about the top-secret atomic bomb project, as Roosevelt had deliberately failed to keep him informed.

And so, the stage was now set for the next phase of the banksters' long-term plan for world domination...

On the same day of FDR's funeral, General Montgomery reasoned that there was now nothing to prevent the Allies from entering Berlin from the west, thus securing the

German capital before the advancing Soviet army could get there. However, Eisenhower had other ideas. As he had done time and time again, Eisenhower employed his stalling tactics in order to delay the Allied advance and thus buying time for Stalin's advance from the east. He issued a 'Halt' order on the 15th April, forbidding all allied forces in the west from crossing the Elbe River.

On 28th March, Eisenhower had already sent a message to Stalin, confirming that the US/UK advance would focus on western Germany, allowing him a free rein in the east…including Berlin. But what was Eisenhower's motivation for these seemingly bizarre actions, you may well ask? Well, we shall see, very soon! Stalin immediately ordered an immediate all-out assault on Berlin with absolutely no consideration for the casualties involved, resulting in a further 80,000 Russians being killed, and 275,000 wounded, plus innumerable German soldiers and civilians. Berlin was finally entered by the Russians on 2nd May 1945.

As previously stated, Eisenhower's two subordinates, the Generals Montgomery and Patton were deeply puzzled and angered by this sudden order to halt the Allied advance, thus condemning Berlin, and all of Eastern Europe, to Soviet barbarism.

The *Goya*

Before the final fall of Berlin, as was the *Wilhelm Gustloff*, the *Goya* was a German transport ship carrying more than 7,000 wounded soldiers, but mainly terrified refugees, westwards in the vain hope of escaping the Red Terror. However, the Soviet submarine Captain, Vladimir Konovalov discovered the *Goya* and ordered it to be sunk by torpedoes. The *Goya* foundered extremely quickly, plunging its passengers into the icy Baltic Sea and less than 200 survived, the final death toll being about the equivalent of 5 *Titanics*.

For this murderous 'war crime,' Konovalov was awarded the Soviet Union's highest military decoration, Hero of the Soviet Union. This must be some rare definition of the word 'hero,' of which I was not previously aware.

Mussolini

With total defeat looming in Europe, Mussolini attempted to escape to neutral Switzerland. However, he was quickly captured and summarily executed near Lake Como on the 28th April 1945, by Italian Partisans (Communists).

Mussolini's 1922 takeover of Italy had probably saved Italy from Communism and to be fair, there were positive economic and social developments during his rule. But in the end, 'Il Duce' and his rampant ego had caused many disastrous problems for the Italian and German military campaigns. His reckless decisions and actions made Italy a huge encumbrance to German strategy.

After death, Mussolini's body and that of his mistress, Clara Petacci and several close companions were transported to Milan, where they were hung upside-down in public in order to both posthumously humiliate them and also to provide confirmation of their deaths.

Hitler

With the situation in Berlin hopeless, it was reported that Hitler married his long-time mistress Eva Braun on 30th April 1945. The two then committed suicide, Eva by poison, Hitler by gunshot. Hitler's dog, Blondie was also poisoned. The staff were then ordered to burn the bodies and escape Berlin before the Soviets captured them ... or so the 'official' story goes.

But one thing is certainly true and that is that the day before 'committing suicide,' Hitler dictated his final Political Testament, in which he truthfully denied any responsibility for instigating the war.

"It is untrue that I or anyone else in Germany wanted war in 1939. It was wanted and provoked solely by international statesmen either of Jewish origin or working for Jewish interests ... Nor have I ever wished that, after the appalling First World War, there would ever be a second against either England or America. Centuries will go by, but from the ruins of our towns and monuments the hatred of those ultimately responsible will always grow anew against the people whom we have to thank for all this: international Jewry and its henchmen."

But, the above, apocryphal story about Hitler and his wife Eva Braun's 'suicides' and subsequent home-made cremations with a can of petrol in the grounds adjoining the 'fuhrerbunker' at the end of April 1945 is simply Soviet Russian propaganda in collusion with British and American wartime High Command and the banksters – and nothing more.

Even the mainstream, politically correct, bankster-controlled *History Channel*'s own investigation in the early 2000s proved beyond reasonable doubt that the skull portion and dental fragments in the possession of the Russians, retrieved from the burial of the burnt corpse of 'Hitler' could not have belonged to him. And this was after an extensive forensic investigation lasting more than a year, during which his authenticated dental records were meticulously compared with the burnt tooth and bone fragments.

At the time, the Russians did not wish to admit that Hitler had evaded capture as they believed it would reflect extremely badly on them and so their propaganda machinery went into overdrive and concocted a credible story to deflect criticism from them, over the sorry affair. As time went on, the propaganda as always, came to be regarded as 'fact' and the real story died, along with the propaganda's perpetrators. In fact, the usual bankster modus operandus.

It is well known that Hitler had more than one 'double,' just as in more recent times there have been several Saddam Husseins and Osama bin Ladens and thus how easy would it have been to surreptitiously execute one of them and burn his body in a pit? I personally find it beyond incredible to seriously suggest that in the last months of the war when the Russians were rampaging through eastern Germany towards Berlin that no arrangements had been made either through his own efforts or on his behalf by third parties, to evacuate him and Eva Braun to safety. Are we really supposed to believe that he just remained there in the bunker awaiting his ultimate and inevitable fate? All the other major Nazi figures (with the possible exception of Josef Goebbels and family – and even that is by no means certain) made good their escapes whilst there was still time enough to do so, albeit that several of them were 'captured' in the following weeks and months.

In accordance with my research, I firmly believe that Hitler and Braun were secretly flown via Hamburg to Vigo on the west coast of Spain, where they were transported to South America (probably Argentina) by U-boat. According to contemporary *Pravda* (the Soviet newspaper) reports, several U-boats full of German high-ranking officials left Spain for Argentina during the period from the end of April to early May 1945.

Hitler aged 90 in 1979

So, the five German U-boats reached Argentina with no less than 50 officials on board including Hitler and Braun. During the trip they even sank a US battleship and the Brazilian cruiser Bahia with a death toll of more than 400, including many US naval personnel.

The co-operative Argentinians established a 'freedom zone' to allow the Germans to disembark without being worried by customs officials, but was Adolf Hitler definitely a passenger on one of these U-boats? It is believed by several respected researchers that Hitler, Eva Braun, her sister Gretel Braun and Martin Bormann escaped via this clandestine operation, however it does still remain unclear whether Hitler specifically landed in Argentina or not.

The Gestapo chief Heinrich Mueller told his US CIA interrogators in 1948 that he personally arranged Hitler's escape from Berlin and that Hitler together with Eva Braun flew to Spain on the 26th April 1945.

"We know for sure that Hitler fled either to Spain or to Argentina." Josef Stalin in conversation with the US Secretary of State, James Byrnes in late 1945

"We have not been unable to unearth one bit of tangible evidence of Hitler's death. Many people believe that Hitler escaped from Berlin." General Dwight D. Eisenhower, 1946

"Russia must accept much of the blame that Hitler did not die in May 1945." Michael Mussmano, presiding judge at the Nuremburg trials, 1946

Colonel W.J. Heimlich, former Chief of United States Intelligence, stated for publication that he was in charge of determining what had happened to Hitler and after a thorough investigation his report was that... *"There was no evidence beyond that of hearsay to support the theory of Hitler's suicide ... On the basis of present evidence, no insurance company in America would pay a claim on Adolf Hitler."*

"We did not identify the body of Hitler. I can say nothing definite about his fate. He could have flown away from Berlin at the very last moment." Marshall Zhukov, Commander in Chief of the Soviet army, 1945

And Zhukov would certainly have known the truth and would have had no motive whatsoever for lying as it would have reflected very badly on him indeed, in the eyes of Stalin.

Do not those quotations alone tell us everything that we need to know? If these people genuinely believed he had escaped, how does this reconcile with the popular myth of his death in the bunker? The simple answer is that it does not. These claims of suicide and cremation on waste land are provably false and were no doubt spread as deliberate disinformation in the aftermath of the war to prevent the truth from reaching the masses. This of course is more compelling evidence of the systematic falsification of history at work, by the banksters and their stooges.

Chicago Times 16th July 1945

Apparently Hitler, once he had reached his final destination, Argentina went into seclusion. He spent the rest of his long life in Mendoza in the northwest of Argentina, protected by the indigenous Jewish community (how ironic, but how appropriate.) Hitler reportedly died in December 1985 at the age of 96 and his remains were buried in a public cemetery in Palmero, thirty miles southeast of Mendoza. The fate of his wife, Eva Braun is unknown.

On the 8th May 1945, jubilant crowds throughout the UK and the US celebrated *Victory in Europe Day* upon the news that Germany had surrendered unconditionally, the previous day. Admiral Karl Donitz, named in Hitler's final testament as the new 'Fuehrer' (leader) of Germany, signed the surrender agreement and remarked that... *"With this signature, the German people and armed forces are for better or for worse, delivered into the victor's hands."*

But there was to be no mercy for the German people, whose government had dared to defy the New World Order, and, for a while, had actually come close to defeating the bankster-sponsored forces of evil. Indeed, Germany's nightmare was only just beginning as the spiteful, vengeful Globalist-Communist-Zionist alliance-of-Evil imposed a collective punishment upon Germany that completely eclipsed the severity of the post-WWI Versailles Treaty, in all but monetary considerations.

The United Nations

At the San Francisco Conference that established the banksters' next One-World-Government attempt, the 'United Nations,' the American official serving as Secretary General of the conference was the Zionist-Communist Alger Hiss.

Hiss was a 'rising star' in US politics. The Harvard graduate was a talented lawyer and negotiator who had been closely identified with FDR's Communist-Socialist 'New Deal' in the 1930s. Experience in international diplomacy brought him the honour of temporary Secretary-General of the United Nations, and he had just become president of the Carnegie Endowment for International Peace.

Then suddenly, it was claimed that this talented and hitherto respected man was a spy, sending the Russians, sensitive information from the highest levels of American politics. The allegations emanated directly from Whittaker Chambers, a senior editor of *Time* magazine, and an ex-communist eager to expose his former compadres. Chambers was testifying before Senator Joseph McCarthy's *House Un-American Activities Committee*, the Republican anti-communist witch-hunting committee which (accurately) claimed that numerous actors, politicians and officials were secretly communist agitators. These damaging allegations were often extracted from colleagues under investigation who found it expedient to name names in order to divert the spotlight away from themselves.

Chambers' version of events was that Hiss and several other named people were members of a communist group during the 1930s. This was a particularly damaging allegation to someone in Hiss' position, and so the lawyer sued the journalist for libel.

Chambers then expanded his claims by saying that Hiss had acted as a spy for the Russians. According to him, Hiss had brought State Department documents home, had them re-typed by his wife, and passed these copies to Chambers while the originals were returned. Chambers had photographed the papers and sent them to a Russian agent. Further evidence was then produced by Chambers after a visit to his Maryland farm, when he returned to the *HUAC* with 35mm film stored, he claimed, in a hollowed-out pumpkin. On the film were various State Department documents and so both men were called before a grand jury investigating these claims of espionage.

If Hiss was a spy, the negative implications were endless. He had attended the post-war Yalta Conference in 1945, rubbing shoulders with Roosevelt, Stalin and Churchill and the same year he was made director of the *Office of Special Political Affairs*, responsible for formulating plans for the United Nations and other aspects of the peace settlement. The Russians would have benefited enormously from his information about American strategy at this time, and from the other inside information that passed across Hiss's desk. Now the Cold War had set in, and America's fears were now firmly directed at their former 'ally,' the Soviet communists and yet here was an 'Ivy League' man who was assisting the new enemy. If this was true, it was a major scandal.

A key piece of evidence was the typewriter on which his wife was said to have typed the documents. The prosecution produced forensic evidence showing it indeed was the machine on which the copies produced by Chambers were typed but nevertheless, the jury at the first trial failed to reach a verdict. However, a second trial found Hiss guilty on 21st January 1950 and he received a five-year jail sentence. He was released on 27th November 1954, and protested his innocence up until his death in 1996. If he was guilty, which appears likely from the evidence, then he paid a very low price for someone who had given state secrets to an enemy foreign power, the usual penalty for high treason, being death.

So in October 1945, the United Nations was instituted, replacing the League of Nations as the foundation-stone of the banksters' New World Order. Its purpose ostensibly, is to 'prevent another world war,' but this is pure hyperbole and propaganda in order to justify its existence.

The huge propaganda campaign surrounding the UN's establishment was pervasive and intense. It was argued that 'isolationist' America's refusal to join the League of Nations after World War I was the tragic mistake that led to World War II. That mistake 'must not be repeated.' So, within 30 days, the US Senate approved the UN treaty by a vote of 89 to 2. The embryonic World Government was to be based in New York, on 18 acres of prime real estate donated by the Rockefellers, no less. What more needs to be said?

The Manhattan Project

The Manhattan Project, led by the US and with participation from the UK, which resulted in the first atomic bomb. The project grew out of the Einstein-Szilard letter to FDR in 1939.

The great 'scientific genius,' Albert Einstein had achieved world fame in the previous decades for his still unproven 'Theory of Relativity,' which itself is now highly suspected to be plagiarised from the work of an Italian physicist. Einstein was a vociferous advocate of world government and was also linked to numerous Communist front groups in Germany. He had always sought fame and fortune, in fact he was a pathological attention-seeker, woman abuser and a fraud. The great satirist H. L. Mencken referred to him as "*...that fiend for publicity.*" Einstein had fled Germany in 1933 not because he was Jewish, but because he was a politically active Marxist, holding membership of several Communist front-groups. An apparent 'pacifist,' in the 1930s, he suddenly became a fierce advocate for total war against Germany. The famous Einstein-Szilard letter, in which the two Zionist scientists urged the Zionist bankster-owned Roosevelt to develop an atomic weapon, was actually written during peacetime in the August of 1939 and falsely accused Germany of developing an atomic bomb and urged FDR to beat the Germans in a race to develop a nuclear military capability.

Ironically, and very significantly, Einstein was not given clearance to be part of the Manhattan Project, as he was deemed by the FBI and military, as being 'too great a security risk.'

The effort to build an atomic bomb, began on a small scale later that year, and between 1942 and 1946, the US, Great Britain, and Canada spent the equivalent of $26bn and employed 130,000 people in the 'race' to create the very first atomic weapon. The first ever test detonation of a nuclear device was conducted at the Alamogordo Range in New Mexico on the 16th July 1945.

From the beginning, there were concerns about the Project's security. Physicist Gregory Breit, an important researcher, left the project team in 1942 because of 'lax security procedures' and the Zionist-Communist physicist, J. Robert Oppenheimer firstly assumed Breit's role and was then appointed to head the secret weapons laboratory at Los Alamos, New Mexico. Under his leadership, many Soviet spies and Communist sympathisers infiltrated the project, Enrico Fermi and Klaus Fuchs, to name the two most prominent.

As Oppenheimer convenient turned a blind-eye, Red spies liberally passed America's nuclear secrets to the Soviets resulting in 1954, in Oppenheimer's security clearance being revoked. But by that time, the Soviets already had everything they needed to build their own nuclear weapons.

On the 26th July 1945, the Pacific war was reaching its bloody climax and on this day, President Truman issued the *Potsdam Declaration*, which called for Japan's unconditional surrender. He had already been informed of the successful detonation of the first atomic bomb at Alamogordo, New Mexico, ten days earlier and the Japanese were warned of the consequences of continued resistance by the terms of the Potsdam Declaration, signed by President Truman and by Prime Minister Attlee of the United Kingdom and with the concurrence of Chiang Kai-Shek, President of the National Government of China. However it was not specified to Japan exactly what form the promised 'prompt and utter destruction' would take in the event of their not agreeing terms.

When Japan rejected the ultimatum, hoping instead for a conditional surrender, Truman immediately authorised use of the bomb. Secretary of War Stimson felt that the decision to deploy the atomic bomb against Japan would be the 'least abhorrent choice.' This would be weighed against sacrificing the lives of thousands of soldiers. Military advisers had told Truman that a potential loss of about 500,000 American soldiers was at stake. This was however, purely propaganda, the big 'official lie,' to justify the dropping of 'Little Boy' and 'Fat Man' on the innocent, unsuspecting civilians of Hiroshima and Nagasaki.

It is a popular, albeit cynically engendered misconception that credits the dropping of the two atomic devices on the Japanese cities of Hiroshima and Nagasaki on the 6th and 9th August 1945, respectively, with ending the war months early and thereby saving the lives of millions.

With WWII rapidly coming to a close, the banksters needed an excuse to move into the next phase of their 'great work of ages,' the 'Cold War.' The attack on Hiroshima and Nagasaki sent a clear message to the Soviets and indeed the rest of the world and it was known by the American branch of the banksters that the Soviets would not sit idly by and let American military technology intimidate them. The Soviets had already begun work on their own version of the terror weapon, helped enormously and probably intentionally by the wholesale leaking of atomic secrets by double agents within the Manhattan Project. Within a year or so of the end of the war, the Russians had their own atomic devices and thus was born the 'Cold War' and the great 'Arms Race' of the second half of the twentieth century, designed solely to terrify and as an excuse to suppress the populations of the whole world in much the same way as the contemporary, bogus 'war on terror' works today.

The Americans and British blatantly and repeatedly ignored desperate Japanese attempts to surrender, because firstly they wanted to drag-out the war for as long as possible and also they needed an actual demonstration to the world, of the devastating effects of the atomic bomb, otherwise the planned, coming 'Cold War' could not have generated the same terror in people's minds, had they not seen for themselves, the deadly weapon's capabilities.

"Our entire post-war programme depends on terrifying the world with the atomic bomb. We are hoping for a tally of a million dead in Japan. But if they surrender, we won't have anything." US Secretary of State, Edward Stettinius Jr., the son of a JP Morgan partner, early 1945

According to the historian Eustace Mullins, President Truman, whose only real job before Senator had been a Masonic 'organiser' in Missouri, did not make the fatal decision alone. A committee led by James Byrnes, the bankster, Bernard Baruch's puppet, instructed him. Baruch was the Rothschild's principal agent in the US and a Presidential 'advisor' spanning the era from Woodrow Wilson to John F. Kennedy.

Baruch, who was also chairman of the Atomic Energy Commission, spearheaded the 'Manhattan Project' named after Baruch's home town. He chose life-long Communist, Robert Oppenheimer to be Research Director. It was very much the 'banksters' bomb.'

On 6th August 1945, a Uranium bomb (isotope U-235) of 20 kilotons was exploded 1850 feet in the air above Hiroshima, for maximum explosive effect. It devastated four square miles of the ancient, historical city and killed outright 140,000 of the 255,000 inhabitants. This figure does not account, however, for the many thousands seriously injured and the many thousands more that would die in agony from radiation in the succeeding months and years.

In the United States the news of the bombing of Hiroshima was greeted with a mixture of relief, pride and shock, but mainly joy. Apparently it was reported that Oppenheimer himself walked around like a prize-fighter, clasping his hands together above his head in triumph when he heard the 'good' news.

But this was not the end. Another bomb was assembled at Tinian Island on the 6th

August and two days later, the order issued from the 20th Air Force Headquarters on Guam, called for its use the following day on either Kokura, the primary target, or Nagasaki, the secondary target.

On the 9th August, three days after Hiroshima, the B-29 bomber, 'Bockscar' piloted by Major Charles W. Sweeney, reached Kokura, but abandoned the primary target because of smoke cover and changed course for Nagasaki, an industrial city with a natural harbour. At 11.02 am, the atomic bomb, 'Fat Man' exploded at 1,800 feet above the city in order to achieve maximum destructive effect. Buildings collapsed, electrical systems were shorted and the city was enveloped in flames.

Energy released by the explosion of the type of atomic bomb used at Nagasaki was roughly equivalent to the power generated by exploding 40 million pounds of TNT, or the quantity that would fill two large cargo ships.

In the early stages of the explosion, temperatures of tens of millions of degrees were produced and emitted light that was around ten times the brightness of the sun. During the explosion, various types of radiation such as gamma rays and alpha and beta particles emanated from the explosion. These radioactive particles may last years or even centuries in those dangerous amounts, causing thousands of cases of radiation sickness in Japan. Firstly the blood of the victim was affected, and then the blood-making organs were impaired including the bone marrow, the spleen and the lymph nodes. Then finally, the organs of the body became necrotic within a few days, causing certain death within a very short period of time.

The total death toll of the two bombs was greater than two hundred thousand, almost all of whom were civilians. In addition to this being a 'war-crime,' although they are obviously not counted as a war-crime when 'we,' the 'good guys' commit them, the atomic bombings of Hiroshima and Nagasaki were also an experiment to determine the differences in yield and effect between the two types of nuclear bomb which had been developed … the uranium 235 bomb dropped on Hiroshima versus the plutonium type dropped on Nagasaki. The deceptively-named US 'Department of Energy,' still lists the nuclear annihilation of the people of Hiroshima and Nagasaki as 'tests.'

Now facing what Truman called a 'rain of ruin,' Japan, like Germany before her, had to make a choice between unrestrained civilian genocide at Allied hands, or unconditional surrender and occupation. And so adopting the lesser of the two evils, Japan surrendered on 15th August 1945, henceforth to be known as 'VJ Day.'

It should also be noted that General Macarthur felt that the atomic bombing was unnecessary, Macarthur later stated … *"My staff was unanimous in believing that Japan was already on the point of collapse and surrender."*

But for the banksters, the atomic bombings served a strategic purpose. The threat of nuclear war would, in the years to come, do much to terrify and then consolidate, the nations of the world into political, economic, and military alliances. The Global fear of 'the bomb' was very good business for the evil banksters.

American Concentration Camps 1945-47

We have been conditioned over the years to believe that during the Second World War the Germans and Japanese were the only ones capable of atrocities whilst 'our boys' were good, moral upstanding people who would never dream of committing immoral and repugnant acts or serious crimes against humanity and our 'illustrious' and heroic leaders especially, even more so. The problem with this view is that it does not stand up to even cursory scrutiny. The number of Germans, civilian and military, murdered, starved and tortured to death in the two-year period following VE day, far exceeded the worst excesses of Nazi brutality including the so-called 'holocaust.' War is horrific and the atrocities committed on both sides in every conflict are inexcusable but at the same time are inevitable consequences of the hatred engendered by propaganda from the banksters and their puppet politicians, fear of the enemy, and also the misguided desire for retribution.

Unfortunately, Germany's defeat in May 1945 and the end of World War II in Europe did not bring an end to the death and suffering for the already vanquished German people. Instead the victorious Allies ushered in a terrible new era of destruction, looting, starvation, rape, 'ethnic cleansing' and mass killing.

A contemporary edition of *Time* magazine referred to this period as *"...history's most terrifying peace."*

Even though this unknown 'holocaust' is ignored in our motion pictures, documentaries, literature and education and by our political leaders, the facts are nevertheless well established. Most historians are in basic agreement about the scale of this unspoken human catastrophe. For example, American historian Alfred de Zayas, along with other scholars, has established that in the years 1945 to 1950, more than 14 million Germans were expelled or forced to flee from large regions of eastern and central Europe, of whom more than four million were deliberately or negligently killed or otherwise lost their lives.

British historian Giles MacDonough details in his book, *'After the Reich: The Brutal History of the Allied Occupation,'* how the ruined and prostrate German Reich (including Austria) was systematically raped and robbed and how many Germans who survived the war were either killed in cold-blood or deliberately left to die of disease, cold, malnutrition or starvation. He explains how some three million Germans died unnecessarily after the official end of hostilities—about two million civilians, mostly women, children and elderly and about one million prisoners of war.

Some may take the view that, given the (alleged) wartime record of the Nazis, some degree of vengeful violence against the defeated Germans was inevitable and perhaps justified. A common response to reports of Allied atrocities is to say that the Germans 'deserved it' but however valid or otherwise that argument may be, the appalling cruelties inflicted upon the totally helpless German people went far beyond any 'understandable' retribution.

It is also worth noting that they were not the only victims of post-war Allied brutality. Across central and eastern Europe, the brutality of Soviet suppression continued to take lives of Poles, Hungarians, Czechs, Ukrainians and many other nationalities in great numbers. As Soviet troops advanced into central and eastern Europe during the war's final months, they imposed a reign of terror, pillage, rape and killing without comparison in modern history. The horrors were summarised thus;

"The disaster that befell this area with the entry of the Soviet forces has no parallel in modern European experience. There were considerable sections of it where, to judge by all existing evidence, scarcely a man, woman or child of the indigenous population was left alive after the initial passage of Soviet forces; and one cannot believe that they all succeeded in fleeing to the West ... The Russians ... swept the native population clean in a manner that had no parallel since the days of the Asiatic hordes." George F. Kennan, historian and former US ambassador to the Soviet Union

In a report that appeared in August 1945 in the Washington DC *Times-Herald*, an American journalist wrote of what he described as *"... the state of terror in which women in Russian-occupied eastern Germany were living. All these women, Germans, Polish, Jewish and even Russian girls 'freed' from Nazi slave camps, were dominated by one desperate desire – to escape from the Red zone. In the district around our internment camp ... Red soldiers during the first weeks of their occupation raped every woman and girl between the ages of 12 and 70. That sounds exaggerated, but it is the simple truth. The only exceptions were girls who managed to remain in hiding in the woods or who had the presence of mind to feign illness – typhoid, diphtheria or some other infectious disease ... Husbands and fathers who attempted to protect their womenfolk were shot down and girls offering extreme resistance were murdered."*

In October 1945, a New York *Daily News* report from occupied Berlin told readers ...

"In the windswept courtyard of the Stettiner Bahnhof, a cohort of German refugees, part of 12 to 19 million dispossessed in East Prussia and Silesia, sat in groups under a driving rain and told the story of their miserable pilgrimage, during which more than 25 percent died by the roadside and the remainder were so starved they scarcely had strength to walk.

A nurse from Stettin, a young, good-looking blonde, told how her father had been stabbed to death by Russian soldiers who, after raping her mother and sister, tried to break into her own room. She escaped and hid in a haystack with four other women for four days ... On the train to Berlin she was raped once by Russian troops and twice by Poles. Women who resisted were shot dead, she said and on one occasion she saw a guard take an infant by the legs and crush its skull against a post because the child cried while the guard was raping its mother. An old peasant from Silesia said ... victims were robbed of everything they had, even their shoes. Infants were robbed of their swaddling clothes so that they froze to death. All the healthy girls and women, even those 65 years of age, were raped in the train and then robbed, the peasant said."

In November 1945 an item in the *Chicago Tribune* told readers ...

"Nine hundred and nine men, women and children dragged themselves and their luggage

from a Russian railway train at Lehrter station in Berlin today, after eleven days travelling in boxcars from Poland. Red Army soldiers lifted 91 corpses from the train, while relatives shrieked and sobbed as their bodies were piled in American lend-lease trucks and driven off for internment in a pit near a concentration camp. The refugee train was a like a macabre Noah's ark. Every car was packed with Germans … the families carry all their earthly belongings in sacks, bags and tin trunks … Nursing infants suffer the most, as their mothers are unable to feed them and frequently go insane as they watch offspring slowly die before their eyes. Today four screaming, violently insane mothers were bound with rope to prevent them from clawing other passengers."

Although most of the millions of German girls and women who were ravished by Allied soldiers, were raped by Red Army troops, Soviet soldiers were not the only perpetrators. During the French occupation of Stuttgart, a large city in southwest Germany, police records show that 1,198 women and eight men were raped, mostly by French troops from Morocco, although the prelate of the Lutheran Evangelical church estimated the number at 5,000.

During WWII, the United States, Britain and Germany all broadly complied with the international regulations on the treatment of prisoners of war, as required by the Geneva Convention of 1929 even though Germany did not formally recognise it. But at the end of the fighting in Europe, the US and British authorities unilaterally scrapped the Geneva Convention. In violation of solemn international obligations and Red Cross rules, the American and British authorities stripped millions of captured German soldiers of their status and their rights as prisoners of war by strategically reclassifying them in true Orwellian fashion as so-called 'disarmed enemy forces' or 'surrendered enemy personnel.'

Accordingly, British and American authorities denied International Red Cross representatives access to camps holding German prisoners of war. Moreover, any attempt by German civilians to feed the prisoners was punishable by death. Many thousands of German POWs died in American custody, most infamously in the so-called 'Rhine meadow camps,' where prisoners were held under appalling conditions, with no shelter or sanitation and inadequate food.

Both during and after the war, the Allies extensively tortured German prisoners. In one British centre in England, 'the London Cage,' German prisoners were subjected to systematic ill-treatment, including starvation and beatings. The brutality continued for several years after the end of the war and treatment of German prisoners by the British was even harsher in the British occupation zone of Germany. At the US internment centre at Schwäbisch Hall in Southwest Germany, prisoners awaiting trial by American military courts were subjected to severe and systematic torture, including long stretches in solitary confinement, extremes of heat and cold, deprivation of sleep and food and severe beatings, including the crushing of testicles and kicks to the groin.

Most of the German prisoners of war who died in Allied captivity were held by the Soviets and a much higher proportion of German POWs died in Soviet custody than perished in British and American captivity. (For example, of the 90,000 Germans who surrendered at Stalingrad, only 5,000 ever returned to their homeland.) Up to ten years after the end of the war, hundreds of thousands of German prisoners were still being held in the Soviet Union. Other German prisoners perished after the end of the war in Yugoslavia, Poland and other countries. In Yugoslavia alone, authorities of the Communist regime killed as many as 80,000 Germans. German prisoners toiled as slave labourers in other Allied countries, often for many years. There is no doubt in my mind that all these acts were a not-so-subtle attempt to 'ethnically cleanse' the German nation.

At the Yalta conference in early 1945, the Allied leaders had agreed that the Soviets could take Germans as forced labourers, or 'slave labour,' contrary to common human decency and morality. It is estimated that a further 874,000 German civilians were forcibly abducted to the Soviet Union. These were in addition to the millions of prisoners of war who were held by the Soviets as forced labourers. Of these so-called 'reparations deportees,' 45% perished.

For two years after the end of the fighting, the Germans were victims of a cruel and vindictive occupation policy, one that meant slow starvation of the defeated population. To sustain healthy life, a normal adult needs a minimum of about 1800 calories per day. But in March and February 1946, the daily intake per person in the British and American occupation zones of Germany was between one thousand and fifteen hundred calories.

In the winter of 1945-46, the Allies forbade anyone outside the country to send food parcels to the starving Germans. The Allied authorities also rejected requests by the International Red Cross to bring in provisions to alleviate the suffering.

Very few persons in Britain or the United States spoke out against the Allied policy. Victor Gollancz, an English-Jewish writer and publisher, toured the British occupation zone of northern Germany for six weeks in late 1946. He publicised the death and malnutrition he found there, which he said was a consequence of Allied policy. He wrote:

"The plain fact is ... we are starving the Germans and we are starving them, not deliberately in the sense that we definitely want them to die, but wilfully, in the sense that we prefer their death to our own inconvenience."

Another person who protested was Bertrand Russell, the noted philosopher and Nobel Prize recipient. In a letter published in a London newspaper in October 1945, he wrote:

"In Eastern Europe now, mass deportations are being carried-out by our allies on an unprecedented scale and an apparently deliberate attempt is being made to exterminate many millions of Germans by depriving them of their homes and of food, leaving them to die by slow and agonising starvation. This is not done as an act of war, but as a part of a deliberate policy of peace."

As the war was ending in what is now the Czech Republic, hysterical mobs brutally assaulted ethnic Germans, members of a minority group whose ancestors had lived there for centuries. In Prague, German soldiers were rounded up, disarmed, tied to stakes, doused with petroleum, and set on fire as living torches. In some cities and towns, every German over the age of six was forced to wear on his clothing, sewn on his left breast, a large white circle six inches in diameter with the black letter N, which is the first letter of the Czech word for German. Germans were also banned from all parks, places of public entertainment and public transportation and not allowed to leave their homes after eight in the evening. Later all these people were expelled, along with the entire ethnic German population. In the Czech Republic alone, a quarter of a million ethnic Germans were killed.

In Poland, the so-called 'Office of State Security,' an agency of the country's new Soviet-controlled government, imposed its own brutal form of 'de-Nazification.' Its agents raided German homes, rounding up some 200,000 men, women, children and infants, 99% of them non-combatant, innocent civilians. They were incarcerated in cellars, prisons, and 1,255 concentration camps where typhus was rampant and torture was commonplace. Between 60,000 and 80,000 Germans perished at the hands of the 'Office of State Security.'

We are ceaselessly and unremittingly reminded, by the thousands of books and documentaries still being produced, of the Third Reich's wartime concentration camps, but few are aware that such infamous camps as Dachau, Buchenwald, Sachsenhausen and Auschwitz were kept in operation after the end of the war, only now packed with German citizens, many of whom also perished miserably.

Justice, as opposed to vengeance, is a standard that is assumed to be applied impartially but in the aftermath of World War II, the victorious powers imposed standards of justice that applied only to the vanquished. The governments of the United States, Britain and the Soviet Union and other member states of the so-called 'United Nations,' held Germans to a standard that they categorically refused to respect themselves.

Robert Jackson, the chief US prosecutor at the Nuremberg Tribunal of 1945-46, privately acknowledged in a letter to President Truman, that the Allies *"... have done or are doing some of the very things we are prosecuting the Germans for. The French are so violating the Geneva Convention in the treatment of German prisoners of war that our command is taking back prisoners sent to them for forced labour in France. We are prosecuting plunder and our Allies are practicing it. We say aggressive war is a crime and one of our allies asserts sovereignty over the Baltic States based on no title except conquest."*

Germans were executed or imprisoned for policies that the Allies themselves were carrying out, sometimes on a far greater scale. German military and political leaders were put to death on the basis of a hypocritical double standard, which meant that these executions were essentially acts of judicial murder dressed up with the trappings and forms of legality. If the standards of the Nuremberg Tribunal had been applied impartially, most American, Soviet and other Allied military and political leaders would also have been hanged.

An awareness of how the defeated Germans were treated by the victors helps in understanding why Germans continued to fight during the final months of the war with a determination, tenacity and willingness to sacrifice that has few parallels in history, even as their cities were being smashed into ruins under relentless bombing (Dresden for example,) and even as defeat against numerically superior enemy forces seemed inevitable.

But two years after the end of the war, American and British policy toward the defeated Germans began to change. The US and British governments began to treat the Germans as potential allies, rather than as vanquished enemy subjects and to appeal for their support. This shift in policy was not prompted by an awakening of humanitarian spirit. Instead, it was motivated by American and British fear of Soviet Russian expansion and by the realisation that the economic recovery of Europe as a whole required a prosperous and productive Germany.

Oswald Spenger, the German historian and philosopher, once observed that how a people learn history is via its form of political education. In every society, including our own, how people learn and understand history is determined by those who control political and cultural life, including the educational system and the mass media. How people understand the past and how they view the world and themselves as members of society, is set by the agenda of those who hold ultimate power, the Elite. This is the reason why, in our society, death and suffering during and after World War II of non-Jews, Poles, Russians and others, and especially Germans is all but ignored and why, instead, more than six decades after the end of the war, Jewish death and suffering above all, what is known as the 'Holocaust™' is given such prominent attention, year after year, in our classrooms, documentaries and motion pictures and by our manipulated and controlled political leaders.

The 'unknown holocaust' of non-Jews is essentially ignored, not because the facts are disputed or unknown, but rather because this reality does not fit well with the Zionist bankster, Judeo-centric view of history that is all but obligatory in our society; a view of the past that reflects the banksters' Jewish-Zionist hold on our cultural and educational life.

This means that it is not enough simply to 'establish the facts.' It is important to understand, identify and counter the power that controls what we see, hear and read in our classrooms, our periodicals and in our motion pictures and which determines how we view history, our world and ourselves, not just the history of what is called the 'Holocaust,' but the history and background of World War II, the Israel-Palestine conflict, the Middle East turmoil and much, much more.

History, as the old saying goes, is written by the victors. In our society the victors, that is, the most important single group that sets our perspective on the past through its grip on the media, and on our cultural life, is the organised bankster community.

An awareness of 'real history' is in itself not enough. It is important to understand the 'how and why' of the systematic falsification of history in our society and the power behind that distortion. Understanding and countering that power is a critically important task, not merely for the sake of historical truth in the abstract, but for the sake of and the future wellbeing of all humankind.

The true facts regarding the events at the end of WWII, are never mentioned in either contemporary or present-day literature and are not taught in schools or memorialised in countless films and documentaries or even museums endlessly, unlike the so-called Jewish 'holocaust.' The question should be asked as to why this and many other similar events are conveniently air-brushed from history, whilst others are continually alluded to, dramatised and sensationalised.

According to the testimony of a former American GI, in late March or early April 1945 he was sent to guard a camp full of German military and civilian prisoners near Andernach on the River Rhine, one of the infamous 'Rhine meadows' camps. He had studied German in high school for four years and so was able to talk to the prisoners, although this was actually strictly forbidden. Eventually however, he was used as an interpreter and asked to try to discover those who had been members of the SS.

In Andernach about 50,000 prisoners of all ages were held in an open field surrounded by barbed wire. The women were kept in a separate enclosure. The men had no shelter and no blankets and most had no coats. They slept in the mud, wet and cold, with inadequate slit trenches for use as toilets. It was a cold, wet spring and their misery from exposure alone was evident.

Even more shocking was to see the prisoners throwing grass and weeds into a tin can containing a thin soup. They did this to help ease their hunger pains but they soon grew very emaciated. Dysentery was rife and soon they were sleeping in their own excrement, too weak and crowded to reach the slit trenches. Many were begging for food, sickening and dying before the eyes of their captors who had ample food and supplies, but did nothing to help them, even refusing them medical assistance.

Outraged, he protested to the officers and was met with hostility or bland indifference. When pressed, they explained they were under strict orders from 'higher up.' No officer would dare do this to 50,000 men if he felt that it was 'out of line,' leaving himself open to charges. Realising that his protestations were useless, he asked a friend working in the kitchen if he could smuggle out any extra food for the prisoners. He too said they were under strict orders to severely ration the prisoners' food and that these orders came from 'above.' But he said they had more food than they knew what to do with and would see what he could do.

When he threw this food over the barbed wire to the prisoners, he was caught and threatened with imprisonment. After repeating the offence, one officer angrily threatened to shoot him but he assumed this was a bluff, until he encountered a captain on a hill above the camp shooting down at a group of German civilian women with his .45 calibre handgun.

When asked why, he mumbled 'target practice' and fired until his pistol was empty. The women ran for cover, but at that distance it was not possible to see if any had been hit. He soon realised he was dealing with cold-blooded killers filled with moralistic hatred that considered the Germans subhuman and worthy only of extermination.

These German prisoners were mostly farmers and working men, as simple and ignorant as many of the US troops. As time went by, more of them lapsed into a zombie-like state of listlessness, while others tried to escape in a demented or suicidal fashion, running through open fields in broad daylight towards the Rhine to quench their thirst. They were mowed down by machine gun fire.

On the 8th May 1945, VE Day, he decided to celebrate with some prisoners he was guarding who were baking the bread the other prisoners occasionally received. This group had all the bread they could eat and shared the jovial mood engendered by the cessation of hostilities. Everyone thought that they would be going home soon, which as it turned out was far from the truth. At this point in time however, they were in what was to become the French zone of occupation, where he soon would witness the brutality of the French soldiers when the prisoners were transferred to them for their slave labour camps. On this day, however, all were happy.

"...it is hard to escape the conclusion that Dwight Eisenhower was a war criminal of epic proportions. His policy killed more Germans in peace than were killed in the European Theatre." Peter Worthington, the '*Ottawa Sun,*' 12th September 1989

'So what', some may say? The enemy's atrocities were worse than 'ours.' It is true that he experienced only the end of the war, when the Allies were already the victors. The German opportunity for atrocities had ended, but two wrongs do not make a right. Rather than mimicking an enemy's crimes, in some form of misguided revenge, should we not aim to break the cycle of hatred and vengeance that has always plagued and distorted human history? In any case it is well worth bearing in mind that the alleged atrocities of the Germans were hyped-up far beyond what was the actual truth. It is not my intention to claim that the Germans were not guilty of any atrocities whatsoever, but we must always apply the accurate maxim, 'history is always written by the victor,' in order to inject reality into any such claims.

We can reject government propaganda that depicts our enemies as subhuman and encourages the kind of outrages that the GI witnessed. We can protest the bombing of civilian targets, which still goes on today in places like Iraq, Pakistan, Palestine, Afghanistan, Syria and Libya and we can refuse ever to condone our government's murder and torture of unarmed and defeated prisoners of war and helpless civilians.

The abuses committed by the forces of the occupation in Germany reached such bestial extremes that various people in the Allied command structure opposed it, or tried to. Charles Lindbergh mentioned how the American soldiers burned the leftovers of their meals to keep them from being scavenged by the starving Germans who hung around the rubbish bins.

Lindbergh also wrote:

"In our homeland the public press publishes articles on how we 'liberated' the oppressed

peoples. Here, our soldiers use the word 'liberate' to describe how they get their hands on loot. Everything they grab from a German house, everything they take off a German is 'liberated' in the lingo of our troops. Leica cameras are liberated, food, works of art, clothes are liberated. A soldier who rapes a German girl is 'liberating' her.

There are German children who gaze at us as we eat ... our cursed regulations forbid us to give them anything to eat. I remember the soldier Barnes, who was arrested for having given a chocolate bar to a tattered little girl. It's hard to look these children in the face. I feel ashamed. Ashamed of myself and my people as I eat and look at those children. How can we have gotten so inhumane?"

Colonel Charles Lindbergh was regarded as a national hero of the United States and was proposed as a candidate for the presidency of his country. He served in the USAF and was no Nazi or Nazi sympathiser, but simply recognised the injustices committed by man against his fellow man, supposed enemy or not.

The Nuremburg Trials

The Nuremberg Trials were created by the banksters in order to prosecute the German general-staff and thereby eliminate anyone in authority that was aware of the pact signed between the Zionists and Hitler in 1933. The end of the German resistance in WWII was only the end of the first stage of the political ploy by the Zionists to illegally found the new home for themselves inside Palestine.

That the trials were a fair and impartial hearing seems very unlikely. That the evidence used against the defendants was very dubious and obtained by even more dubious methods is however, very clear. An example of the techniques employed is described by the distinguished English historian, David Irving in his book, *'Nuremberg: The Last Battle'* ...

"Garnering usable documentary evidence became a mounting nightmare for Jackson [the chief prosecuting attorney.] He had become disenchanted with the productivity and intelligence of General Donovan's OSS. They had promised much but delivered little. What Donovan regarded as evidence, he certainly would not. 'I never had any feeling that anybody had trapped me into the thing,' Jackson commented later. 'But I was in the trap!'"

It soon became clear that the OSS (CIA) had intended all along to stage-manage the whole trial along the lines of a Soviet NKVD show-trial, with Jackson engaged as little more than a professional actor. As part of the stage-management they proposed to run a pre-trial propaganda campaign in the United States with *'increasing emphasis on the publication of atrocity stories to keep the public in the proper frame of mind.'* To this end the OSS devised and scripted for the education of the American public a two-reel film on 'war crimes,' called *'Crime and Punishment,'* it was designed to put the case against the leading Nazis. Jackson declined to participate. He refused even to read the speech that the OSS had scripted for him to read into the cameras. 'As you know,' he wrote to the OSS officer concerned, 'the British are particularly sensitive about lawyers trying their cases in the newspapers and other vehicles of communication.'

The film proposal was followed by an explicit OSS suggestion for launching 'black propaganda' during the course of the trial, with agents in selected foreign countries starting rumours designed to influence public opinion in favour of the trial and against the defendants. This would be far more effective, they pointed out, than mounting a straightforward public relations campaign which would obviously be seen as emanating from the powers conducting the trials. One of Jackson's staff secretly notified him that the suggestion was *"...fantastic, if not entirely dangerous,"* and Jackson himself pencilled a pithy comment on the letter... *"The scheme is cock-eyed. Give them no encouragement."*

Vestiges of the unsavoury methods of the OSS can still be seen among the earlier Nuremberg records. For instance, at the pre-trial interrogations the defendants were not accompanied by lawyers and were frequently persuaded by trickery or intimidation to subscribe to testimonies incriminating others which we now know to have been false. The files are full of obvious chicanery of various kinds, for example anonymous, typed extracts of documents instead of the originals and sworn statements by witnesses like Höss, commandant of Auschwitz, in which all the 'witnesses to his signature' have signed, but not Höss himself. Indeed it is well known that Höss's confessions were all obtained by torture. The Americans also submitted as exhibit '1553-PS' a file of invoices for substantial consignments of Zyklon B (hydrogen cyanide pellets) supplied to the pest-control office at Auschwitz but they concealed the fact that the same file contained invoices for identical quantities of Zyklon B delivered to the camp at Oranienberg near Berlin, where it was never alleged there had been any 'gas chambers.'

These examples are of course only a very brief overview of the innumerable deficiencies of the 'evidence' presented at Nuremberg. The overwhelming Zionist-Jewish presence behind the scenes as prosecutors, judges, interrogators, jailers and torturers is covered elsewhere in Irving's excellent, but far from complete, study but the examination of techniques employed however, is more than sufficient to demonstrate that truth was never the objective of the orchestrators of the trial. The key point in evaluating Nuremberg is that all the evidence, real and faked at the trial, was evidence in pursuit of a pre-determined verdict. It was regarded desirable to demonstrate that the Germans were uniquely evil, that the Germans alone had waged aggressive, illegal war, that the Germans had committed great 'crimes against humanity' and that the greatest of these alleged crimes was the alleged, yet absolutely unprovable, systematic extermination of six million Jews. To reach these pre-determined verdicts, the court manipulated and distorted evidence on a massive scale. Therefore, any honest assessment of the German National Socialist government built on Nuremberg conclusions is inherently flawed. It is another supreme example of the art of writing history based on the propaganda of the victor.

The Summary

World War II was the product of the desire of the Zionist-banksters to achieve several goals...

The primary one was the elimination of Germany and especially Hitler, who openly opposed their plans for the financial and political conquest of the world and had desperately tried in vain to inform the world of the dangers posed by this murderous group. To this end, Hitler had severely clamped-down upon and restricted the Jewish Communist sympathisers within his own borders, who in return had cajoled and rallied world Jewry into the open declaration of war on Germany in March 1933, thereby instigating and subsequently escalating the conflict.

This was also a convenient basis for the justification, exacerbated by the alleged 'holocaust,' of the so-called, 'Jewish homeland' of Israel which had been promised more than twenty years earlier but which promise had remained unfulfilled. Subsequently the expropriation of Palestine for this cause, was completed in 1947 amongst much intrigue and further bloodshed, through the engendering of a huge outpouring of sympathy for 'Jewish suffering.'

In addition, the vast, unimaginable profits generated for the bankster-military-industrial complex during the period 1939-45 at the expense of the lives of almost 75 million people, in the funding of both sides of the conflict, cannot be discounted as a key by-product.

As always, we are constantly drip-fed outright lies and propaganda about the causes of the war and even the individual elements of it are bent and distorted to fit the official story. I refer to such distortions as:

Germany attacked itself to generate an excuse to provoke the outbreak of the war.

German brutality and genocide was endemic but the Allies always played by the rules.

Hitler was hell-bent on conquering the world.

The Germans wished to totally eradicate the Jews from the face of the Earth.

The Japanese categorically refused to surrender and it was only the use of the atomic bombs that ended their resistance.

All these 'facts' and many more inaccuracies, have become embedded in our psyches as the absolute truth after decades of bombardment with them by the lapdogs of the bankster-controlled media in all its forms.

In truth, WWII was no different to all the other wars of the last five hundred years in that there was the same two-fold, underlying agenda. Firstly, the furtherance of the grand master plan, the great work of ages, and secondly to further concentrate even more wealth and power into the hands of the banksters.

The deployment of the atomic bombs upon the Japanese civilian population further served to enable the next phase of the master plan; the atomic arms race, leading to the almost half-century stand-off now known as the 'cold war,' designed to further subjugate and keep the world's unsuspecting populace in a constant state of fear and trepidation.

The exact number of people killed or seriously injured over the course of the war will never be known for sure. Relatively good records were kept for the Allied and Axis servicemen, but civilian deaths and injuries were so widespread and so frequently unreported that they were nearly impossible to tabulate with any accuracy. Tens of thousands of people in all the major theatres remain missing and unaccounted-for to this day.

Germany lost an estimated 3.25 million military personnel plus an estimated further 4 million civilians, over the course of the war. Italy lost 300,000, and Japan, more than 1.5 million from 1937 to 1945.

And then, there is that certain, particular figure of '6 million' Jews ...

Chapter 11
World War Two – The (Final) Solution

Of all that you have been presented with so far, all the death and suffering from all the wars and strife that the banksters have caused and from which they greatly profited, a less well-known, but almost equally insidious tactic has been the using of Jewish people in promoting the evil bankster agenda known as Zionism.

The plight of the so-called '6,000,000' Jews in Germany's concentration camps, has become the very cornerstone of the Zionists' cause, enabling them to continually get away with even more mass murders and despicable crimes. And all the while, the sacred figure of 6,000,000 has become a perverted symbol of human suffering, to be exploited and used to silence any criticism of those that oppose the actions of the Zionists' bankster masters.

The obsessive invocation of the '6,000,000 dead or dying Jews,' dates back at least four decades prior to the events of WWII, and directly undermines and betrays the notion that 6,000,000 Jews perished in Europe between 1939-1945, as the Zionists have claimed. It was a lie the first time around and indeed all the subsequent times it was used, and is still a lie today.

The entire world, for decades, has been inundated and inculcated with an endless onslaught of holocaust-themed Hollywood movies, television shows, 'docudramas,' books and memoirs, in conjunction with the mandatory 'holocaust education' in schools across North America and Europe. The primary function of this insidious global propaganda campaign is to quite simply, brainwash the world into a state of complete, 'sympathetic' paralysis whilst we are ideologically, economically and physically enslaved by the bankster-Zionists. The campaign is also designed to de-legitimise all criticism of Jews and the Zionist State of Israel and to ensnare non-Jews into adopting a pro-Jewish, pro-Zionist worldview. With their hateful, holocaust lies, Zionist myth-makers are systematically indoctrinating all school children to hate all Germans, and European whites for their appalling treatment of the Jews during WWII.

Unfortunately, these children, (and indeed their brainwashed teachers) not knowing any better and unable to think for themselves, blindly believe this deliberate falsification of history and never question what they have been told when they become adults, by which time it is often impossible to undo the effects. The indoctrination of our children with Zionist 'holocaust' fiction is permanently damaging the minds of young people. Force-feeding young children and teenagers, distortions and outright falsehoods about World War II, so that they sympathise with treacherous Zionist causes such as Zionism and Communism, is immoral, destructive, harmful and abhorrent as well as criminal.

I assume that like me, when this information first came to my notice, that your mind is now absolutely rejecting this entire premise as either utterly impossible, deluded garbage or the views of some crazy, 'neo-Nazi apologist?' If so, I do not blame you at all, it is extremely difficult and traumatic to dispense with our learned 'norms,' without a struggle, but please remember the expression from the very beginning of this book... 'Cognitive Dissonance.' If you have never been confronted with this concept before, then actually believing that the whole scenario is a complete invention, is an extremely difficult task. I urge you to strongly resist the temptation to throw this book into the garbage and labelling me as an inhuman monster of some kind, and read on...

A pertinent question that you might ask is, '...what is the significance of the 'six million' figure and where did it originate?'

The totally mythical 'six million™' figure has intriguing origins indeed. Jews have staunchly emphasised the 6,000,000 figure in atrocity propaganda from 1890 through to the present day. World War II ended in 1945, and since that time the apocryphal 6,000,000 figure has now reached sacrosanct status. This has been achieved through a sleazy and deceptive campaign of repetitive propaganda in the news and entertainment media, centred in Zionist Hollywood. As the Jewish-Communist, mass murderer, Vladimir Lenin, once said... "...*a lie told often enough becomes the truth.*" This campaign of Zionist deceit has steadily intensified over the years.

World leaders, Presidents, Prime Ministers, ceremonial Kings and Queens, Popes, Priests and Holy Men of all faiths, genuflect in grovelling reverence to the myth of the six million, who certainly did not perish in 'Nazi gas chambers,' as such entities did not exist and are easily provably to have been an impossibility.

Research has shown that the reason for this bizarre Jewish fixation on the number 6,000,000 primarily stems from an ancient religious prophecy in the Torah, the Jewish holy book. Within its pages, the prophecy clearly states that before the Jewish homeland called 'Israel,' can be established, 6,000,000 Jews would first have to perish in a fiery burnt offering, i.e. the 'Holocaust,' as a sacrifice to their bloodthirsty tribal deity, YHWH (Yahweh – or God.)

Jewish prophecies in the Torah require that six million Jews must 'vanish,' before the state of Israel can be created. *"You shall return minus six million,"* it states and this is the reason that Tom Segev, an Israeli historian, declared that the 'six million' is an attempt to transform the Holocaust story into the official state religion. Those six million, according to prophecy, had to disappear in *"burning ovens,"* which the judicial version of the Holocaust now authenticates. As a matter of fact, Robert B. Goldmann writes, *"...without the Holocaust, there would be no Jewish State."* But as history has now been 'adjusted' to claim that six million Jews were gassed in WWII and ended-up in the 'burning ovens' then the prophecies have now been 'fulfilled' and Israel can therefore be regarded as a 'legitimate state.' In addition, the American Zionist leader, Rabbi Stephen S. Wise, accidently let it slip that the Zionist agenda behind the holocaust fabrication was to promote public sympathy for Zionism (the Jewish takeover of Palestine.)

It is also noteworthy that the authors of the vast majority of the following propaganda articles were the richest of Wall Street's Jewish banksters as well as leaders of Zionist pressure groups...

1902. Under its entry on 'anti-Semitism,' the tenth edition of the *Encyclopaedia Britannica* refers to 'six million Jews' of Rumania and Russia being 'systematically degraded.'

1905. A Jewish preacher declared that if the (Jewish-led) Communist uprising in Russia succeeded in its long-time goal of overthrowing the Tsarist government, Zionism would be obsolete. The figure of 'six million Jews' is also mentioned.

1906. A Jewish publicist addressed an audience in Germany where he claimed that the *Russian* Government had a 'solution to the Jewish Question' and that this solution entailed the 'murderous extermination' of 'six million Jews.' Of course, the Russians never had any such plans.

1910. In the American Jewish Committee's annual report it was claimed that since 1890 Russia has had a policy to 'expel or exterminate 'six million Jews.' Source, the *American Jewish Yearbook* pg. 15

1911. Max Nordau, co-founder of the *World Zionist Organization* together with Theodore Herzl, made an astonishing pronouncement at the tenth Zionist Congress in Basle, Switzerland. He claimed that 'six million Jews would be annihilated.' This was twenty-two years before Hitler came to power and three years before World War I began.

1915. The Jewish leader, Louis Marshall proclaimed... *"In the world today there are about 13,000,000 Jews, of whom more than six million are in the heart of the war zone: Jews whose lives are at stake and who today are subjected to every manner of suffering and sorrow..."*

1919. Shortly after the end of World War I, Zionists claimed a 'holocaust' of 'six million Jews' is imminent in Europe in a deceitful campaign to raise money for Jewish charities and also to distract public attention from the Jewish origins of Communism, the Bolshevik atrocities in Russia and the Armenian Genocide.

1921. Russian patriots gained ground on the Jewish-Bolshevik usurpers of their nation. In a vain attempt to hide their heavy involvement in the brutal Bolshevist atrocities being committed in Russia, Jews reeled-off the 'six million' myth once again.

1922. The Zionist leader, Nahum Sokolow, boasted about organised Jewry's globalist ambitions when, at a Zionist conference in Carlsbad, California, he proclaimed … *"The League of Nations is a Jewish idea, and Jerusalem someday, will become the capital of the world's peace."*

1931. Zionist-Bolshevik Jews demand that Gentiles hand over their food to the poor, innocent, starving 'six million Jews' whilst they simultaneously murder millions of Christians, and ship millions more off to Gulag slave camps in Communist Zionist-controlled Russia.

1936. Zionists who originally coined the phrase '*Final Solution of The Jewish Question*,' somehow already knew that exactly 6,000,000 Jews had *"neither hope nor future."*

1940. Jewish leader Nahum Goldmann, predicted *"six million"* Jewish victims *before* Nazi concentration camps had even been constructed.

1944. In September, eight months *before* the end of WWII, US Communist-Jewish Union leaders proclaimed that... *"... nearly 'six million Jews have been killed,"* long before that could have been known or calculated. And at least three newspapers printed stories informing their readership of the deaths of *"six million Jews."* All of these propaganda articles were based on the lies of Ilya Ehrenburg, a Jewish propagandist in the USSR.

1945. In January, still many months prior to the end of the war, before any official body-counts for any group could have reasonably been calculated or ascertained, the Zionist, Ilya Ehrenburg, a notorious Jewish propagandist in the USSR who agitated for genocide against Germans and incited the mass-rape of German women by the Red Army, prematurely proclaimed that... *"... the world now knows that Germany has killed six million Jews,"* before anyone could have known that was the number (even had it been remotely true.)

So could it possibly be just 'coincidental' that the flimsy and farcical story of 'six million Jews' being murdered in gas chambers and burned in 'ovens,' gave the Zionists the impetus and PR ammunition they needed to make their return to the 'promised land' at the end of the war and establish the racist/apartheid 'Jewish state' of 'Israel' in 1948? And this all just happens to fit the previously cited ancient Torah prophecy to the letter? Not yet convinced? Please do not write it all off as an unconvincing fantasy at this point, I am not even out of the proverbial 'starting blocks' yet.

Zionism is a major strand of the Elite control structure imposed upon this entire planet. It is an undeniable fact that most large organisations are controlled and run by the Zionist banksters, primarily Jews. Zionist Jews have an almost absolute monopoly in the media in all its forms and also in the entertainment industry, from Hollywood to the major recording labels etc. as well as finance and banking.

"Every time we do something you tell me America will do this and will do that... I want to tell you something very clear: Don't worry about American pressure on Israel. We, the Jewish people, control America, and the Americans know it." Ariel Sharon, Prime Minister of Israel, 3rd October 2001.

"You know very well and the stupid Americans know equally well, that we control their government, irrespective of who sits in the White House. You see, I know it and you know it that no American president can be in a position to challenge us even if we do the unthinkable. What can they [Americans] do to us? We control Congress, we control the media, we control showbiz and we control everything in America. In America you can criticise God, but you can't criticise Israel..." Israeli spokeswoman, Tzipora Menache.

"These are the facts of Jewish media control in America. Anyone willing to spend several hours in a large library can verify their accuracy. I hope that these facts are disturbing to you, to say the least. Should any minority be allowed to wield such awesome power? Certainly not and allowing a people with beliefs such as expressed in the Talmud, to determine what

we get to read or watch in effect gives this small minority the power to mould our minds to suit their own Talmudic interests. Interests, which as we have demonstrated are diametrically opposed to the interests of our people. By permitting the Jews to control our news and entertainment media, we are doing more than merely giving them a decisive influence on our political system and virtual control of our government; we also are giving them control of the minds and souls of our children, whose attitudes and ideas are shaped more by Jewish television and Jewish films than by their parents, their schools, or any other influence." Pakalert Press, 2011.

"In off-the-record comment to journalists, embassy spokeswoman Adi Farjon, said that Israel had no interest in full normalization of relations with Germany. A spokeswoman for the Israeli embassy in Berlin recently told Israeli journalists it was in the country's interest to maintain German guilt about the Holocaust, and that it isn't seeking full normalization of relations between the governments. Embassy spokeswoman Adi Farjon made the comments in a closed briefing session with journalists at the embassy. 'We were all in shock,' said a female journalist present at the briefing. 'The spokeswoman clearly said it was in Israeli interests to maintain German guilt feelings. She even said that without them, we'd be just another country as far as they're concerned.' Others present at the event confirmed the journalist's account. Some added that the Israeli ambassador himself, Yakov Hadas-Handelsman, was present for some of the briefing, as were other embassy workers who don't speak Hebrew. Another journalist commented, 'It was so awkward. We couldn't believe our ears. We're sitting there eating peanuts, and behind the spokeswoman there are two German women sitting there who don't understand a word of Hebrew – and the embassy staff is telling us they're working to preserve the German guilt feelings and that Israel has no interest in normalization of relations between the two countries.' The Israeli foreign ministry denied the allegations and said the diplomats were falsely accused of saying these things. This year is a special one for the German and Israeli governments, with Berlin and Jerusalem marking 50 years since the start of diplomatic relations between the two countries. German support for Israel also appears to be at an all-time high – particularly in light of Israel's ongoing battles with the European Union over labelling of products from West Bank settlements and its troubled diplomatic standing in the world." davidduke.com, October 2015

"Goebbels was somewhat of a prophet pariah, he understood organized Jewry like few Americans do today, he understood that their collective calls of anti-Semitism directed at the Nazi leadership and indeed the German people themselves was a technique they had successfully used, even perfected, in order to advance their interests while at the same time suppressing any dissent from the gentile majority. We see this same technique at work today, all around the world, anytime anyone honestly divulges the actions of a Jew in some crime; they are immediately smeared with the label of 'anti-Semitism.'" Curt Maynard, researcher.

This 'label' of 'anti-Semitism' is actually utterly meaningless, yet it has been hijacked by a small group of people to inhibit you (and indeed everyone) from criticising their actions. To fully comprehend this point, it is firstly necessary for me to define three commonly misunderstood or even possibly unfamiliar terms.

Judaism – The Jewish *religion*. Jews can be split into two distinct main sub-groups,

Ashkenazi (Khazarian) Jews who comprise by far the majority (over 90%) and Sephardic Jews. These two sub-groups are racially as different as chalk and cheese and so, despite what you may believe or more accurately have been urged to believe; Judaism is a 'religion' and not a 'race.' In fact many people of Jewish background and parentage are not even religious and so their being described as 'Jews' is actually erroneous.

Zionism – a *political* movement that was originally established to lobby for a Jewish homeland and now exists to promote the superiority of Israel above all other countries, with the ultimate goal of a one-world government based in Tel Aviv. Zionism is comprised primarily of Jewish people, but many non-Jews are Zionists and indeed many Jews are anti-Zionist.

Semitism – Not the state of being Jewish as is generally believed and promoted by Zionism for its own ends but simply the racial group to which inhabitants of a small area of the Middle East belong. Semites may be Sephardic Jews or they may be Arabs, there is no *racial* difference between the two. However Ashkenazi Jews, despite their loud and raucous protestations to the contrary are definitely not Semitic.

"…it is important that you understand what Zionism really is. Zionist propaganda has led the American people to believe that Zionism and Judaism are one and the same and that they are religious in nature. This is a blatant lie." Jack Bernstein, assassinated by the Mossad (the Israeli Secret Service.)

"The meaning of the term 'anti-Semite' has significantly changed in recent years. There was a time when this term referred to those who despised Jews. Later, the term referred to those who promoted myths about a global Jewish conspiracy to rule the world. Today the term 'anti-Semite' is used by the ruling elite to lambast human rights activists who advocate equal rights between Jews, Christians and Muslims, the right of return of Palestinian refugees to their homeland and the vision of a common, democratic state for both Palestinians and Israelis. The word 'anti-Semite,' which initially conveyed a negative and even sinister meaning, refers now to positive and highly commendable attitudes that can be carried with honour. One may lament this change of meaning, but one should remember that a word does not carry any particular meaning. It is merely a conventional symbol that refers to external contents. By convention, society could agree to name animosity towards Jews 'xakaculca', democracy 'zbzb' and elephants 'democracy.' Inasmuch as the term 'anti-Semite' now refers to human rights advocates and radical democrats, I declare myself a radical anti-Semite." Elias Davidsson, June 2011.

"Zionists from the beginning welcomed anti-Semitism as a means of undermining what Zionists believed was the sense of false security of Jews in western, liberal societies, and as the means by which Jews would be kept in a permanent state of neurosis. Large and powerful organizations such as the US-based Anti-Defamation League of B'nai B'rith exist mainly for the purpose of exaggerating the extent of anti-Semitism in order to keep Jews under the Zionist heel and keep Israeli coffers filled." Rabbi Silverstein, 'The Lies of Zionism'

"Anti-Semites will become our surest friends, anti-Semitic countries our allies." Theodor Herzl, founder of Zionism in the 19th century.

It is important here to make the point that Zionists are not the friends of the Jews in any way despite what many Jews believe. Jews worldwide have been and continue to be used, often unknowingly in the Zionists plotting and scheming for world domination.

Ashkenazi Jews originated from the plains of South-Eastern Europe / Western Asia and were originally a large nomadic tribe, the Khazars, who inhabited these regions in the Dark and early Middle Ages. They converted en-masse to Judaism, not through faith but simply in order to bring respectability to their previously god-less reputations when integration with other societies became necessary, more than a thousand years ago. This was the group of 'Jews' who were discriminated against for centuries and expelled from many European nations for their usury, anti-social practices and their own discriminatory practices against non-Jews. I repeat that these people had no racial or genetic ties to the 'Holy Land' whatsoever and so the oft-repeated cries for a Jewish state in their ancestral 'homeland' in the early to mid-twentieth century, was simply Zionist propaganda and deception. Sephardic Jews however, are native to the Holy Land or Palestine and were the original 'biblical Jews.'

So, in effect the Zionists have deliberately blurred the boundaries, between race, religion and politics to prevent criticism of their actions. They have hi-jacked the term 'anti-Semitism,' strictly speaking an accusation of racism and managed over time to associate this with discrimination against Jews in general by deceitful social engineering, whilst also turning the distinction between 'Jewish' and 'Zionist' into a grey area, to the same effect. How have they achieved this? Their almost total control of banking, industry, media and the entertainment industries makes this task fairly straightforward via their vast propaganda machine. Many Hollywood movies subtly promote the superiority of the Jews and the weakness and immorality of non-Jews. Anyone who criticises or stands up to them in any way is subtly and sometimes unfortunately, not so subtly, destroyed. At the very least their detractors are accused of being, (shock-horror,) 'anti-Semitic' with all the attendant stigma this terminology carries. Anti-Semitism is closely related and linked to Nazism in the minds of most people today. The immense power of propaganda, social engineering and mind control should be underestimated only at one's peril.

"We must distinguish between political and racial anti-Semitism. It's obvious that organized Jewry has a political program synonymous with the Rothschild satanic world government agenda." Henry Makow, Jewish-born researcher and author of 'A Cruel Hoax.'

Think about this for a moment. Political criticism is valid today (at least for now anyway) whilst racial criticism (racism) is totally frowned upon and even legislated against. In making their cause a racial rather than a political one by rendering the two distinctly separate terms 'Jewish' and 'Zionist' interchangeable, they have succeeded in duping the world and protecting their own insidious views and actions from any form of censure on pain of being branded by them as an anti-Semite and therefore by implication, a 'Nazi sympathiser.'

So, an 'anti-Semite' strictly speaking, by definition is someone who discriminates against people of the area known as the 'Holy Land,' Palestinian Arabs and Sephardic

Jew alike and not simply someone who is a 'Jew-hater' as it has been engineered to be construed.

Personally speaking, I am not anti-Semitic (or anti-Jewish, to be clear.) Jews have been duped and suffered at the hands of these wolves in sheep's clothing more than any other group and in many ways still are. I believe strongly in the freedom of all to do as they choose as long as it harms no-one, but I am definitely anti-Zionist politically, as their actions and beliefs are calculated to cause maximum harm to those who do not share their insidious views and visions for the world. However, the views expounded herein will no doubt have me labelled as anti-Semitic by the Zionist attack-dogs. If anti-Semitism did not exist, the Zionists would have to invent it. Actually, they already have done so.

Of course there are anti-Jewish people in the world (anti-Semites if you will?) To deny that fact would be ridiculous. But there are also anti-British, anti-American, anti-Muslim and anti-almost-anything-you-can-name elements abounding throughout the world today, too. However, in my view it is highly significant that to be 'anti-anything-else,' does not carry the same stigma as being 'anti-Semitic.' This has been successfully inured into our culture to become a heinous act far more serious than any other form of prejudice, primarily thanks to the impact of Holocaust propaganda.

But the Zionists are not content with merely *labelling* you or I as a 'Nazi' for any criticism, overt or implied, of their actions and policies. No, by using their enormous influence over western societies and governments alike it has now actually become illegal not just to deny that the holocaust of WWII took place but to even question their sacred number of 6 million dead. Yes you did read that correctly, it is *illegal* in many countries in the Zionist-bankster-controlled EU where communitarian European law now trumps that of each individual nation. It is also illegal in Canada, Australia and New Zealand (amongst other places) to merely question the myths and legends of the holocaust on pain of a mandatory prison sentence. Although you could not actually be prosecuted in the UK or the US, yet, for the thought-crime of holocaust denial, a UK citizen can certainly be extradited to Germany to face charges *even if the 'offence' was committed for example, in England.*

Please now think a moment on this extremely important point . . . Why does the truth need to be protected by law? If something, anything is the truth then it is surely a simple matter to prove it, is it not? If this is not the case, then the question needs to be asked why this course of action is not taken rather than passing laws to protect a point of view.

Is it illegal to question or criticise any aspect of Christianity or Muslim culture? Is it illegal to stand in the streets and state that that Christianity is just a made-up fantasy? Is it illegal to question the numbers of American dead in Vietnam or the numbers of British soldiers killed in Afghanistan or even the victims of 9/11 for example? Is it actually specifically illegal to simply *question* anything else at all? You may well be unjustly criticised by your masters and even your peers for having the sheer audacity to question

Government-approved figures, but illegal? The spirit of '1984' and the 'thought-police' *is* alive and well.

"You can tell if something's the truth or not by this one criterion. If they pass a law that says you have to believe a certain story in a certain way, you can be certain that that certain story they're trying to get you to believe is a lie." John Kaminski, researcher, 'A Certain Truth,' 28th January 2011.

"What sort of truth is it that crushes the freedom to seek the truth?" John Swinton, editor New York Times, 1863.

"What they did with their holocaust laws was to make the questioning of their version of what happened during 'the war' sacrosanct and undeniable. What this means is that it doesn't matter how many irrefutable facts you may have, the law says you can't question, period. This fact escapes many people. You are not allowed to mount a defence and it is inadmissible in any and all cases." Les Visible, researcher, April 2011.

Stifling open discussion and debate on the 'holocaust' also does a gross injustice to the other, many non-Jewish victims of the concentration camps; the Romany people, black people, Polish and Russian soldiers and citizens, Jehovah's Witnesses, assorted political prisoners, homosexuals and the mentally and physically disabled. Ask yourself why the Jews are the sole recipients of all the outpourings of sympathy and none of the other groups?

The real threat to the Zionists posed by 'deniers' is that others might be influenced to undertake further in-depth study and thereby uncover embarrassing facts that would refute Israel's 'victim' status. This would threaten Israel's moral legitimacy to exist, currently underpinned by the world's supposed, collective shame for 'looking the other way,' while six million Jews were murdered in cold blood. It is highly significant that all it takes to invoke that shame is the term 'anti-Semite,' either stated or implied.

The previously well-respected British historian, David Irving was first labelled a Neo-Nazi and then jailed for 3 years in the last decade for daring to question 'official' holocaust dogma – all at the behest of the bankster-Zionist thought-police through their corrupt and controlled legal and courts systems. In fact, most such 'revisionist' historians are of the opinion that Irving does not go far enough with his questions regarding the validity of the Zionist's claims. Irving merely publicly queried the six million number, not the event itself.

"If the Holocaust undoubtedly occurred as alleged, then why are laws needed to support said allegations? Why not simply confront deniers with facts instead? Recent court cases in Germany have shown that judges are unwilling (unable?) to present facts; they hide behind 'Offenkundigkeit' (obviousness). Their claim: The Holocaust obviously happened, so there's no need to substantiate it any further. In any other legal trial, 'obviousness' would not stand up in court; the defendant is always allowed to present his/her evidence. One has to also wonder why, if all is 'obvious,' this book had to be written? If the Holocaust has been investigated and evidence exists proving without any doubt that mass murder was committed,

then why not present this evidence — why the laws?" Inconvenient History, 18th February, 2011

On 13th May 1988 the respected historian, Professor Ernst Zündel was sentenced by Judge Ronald Thomas of the District Court of Ontario, in Toronto, to nine months in prison for having distributed a revisionist booklet entitled, 'Did Six Million Really Die?'

"No-one in the USA was more knowledgeable about the functioning of [penitentiary] gas chambers than Fred A. Leuchter, an engineer from Boston. I went to visit Leuchter on February 3 and 4, 1988 and found that he had never asked himself any questions about the 'gas chambers' in the German camps. He had simply believed in their existence. After I began to show him my files, he became aware of the chemical and physical impossibility of the German 'gassings' and he agreed to examine our documents in Toronto.

After that, at Zündel's expense, he left for Poland with a secretary (his wife), a draftsman, a video-cameraman and an interpreter. He came back and drew up a 192-page report (including appendices). He also brought back 32 samples taken, on the one hand, from the crematories of Auschwitz and Birkenau at the site of the homicidal 'gassings' and, on the other hand, in a disinfection gas chamber at Birkenau. His conclusion was simple: there had never been any homicidal gassings at Auschwitz, Birkenau, or Majdanek." Robert Faurisson, historian

"After reviewing all of the material and inspecting all of the sites at Auschwitz, Birkenau and Majdanek, your author finds the evidence as overwhelming. There were no execution gas chambers at any of these locations. It is the best engineering opinion of this author that the alleged gas chambers at the inspected sites could not have then been, or now, be utilized or seriously considered to function as execution gas chambers." Fred Leuchter 1988, p.33; Leuchter et al 2005, p.57

Dr. Fredrick Töben, an Australian scholar and educator, was taken into custody in Mannheim, Germany on 8th April 1999 and detained without bail, for having disputed holocaust extermination allegations. Töben is a leading holocaust revisionist writer and publicist in Australia, where he founded and directed the Adelaide Institute, a prominent revisionist research and publishing centre.

At the conclusion of his three-day trial on 10th November 1999, a Mannheim district court found Töben guilty on charges of incitement to racial hatred, insulting the memory of the dead and public denial of genocide, because he had disputed holocaust extermination claims in writings sent to persons in Germany. Presiding Judge Klaus Kern said that there is no doubt that Töben is guilty of 'denying the holocaust' and that because there is no sign that he would relent his views and activities, a prison sentence was required. The court then sentenced him to ten months imprisonment.

Taking into consideration the seven months he had already served in custody, Judge Kern ruled that Töben could be released on payment of a fine of DM6000 (about US$3500 or £2200) in lieu of the three months remaining of his prison sentence. German sympathisers raised this money and he was freed within 24 hours of the verdict.

A really disturbing neo-Orwellian by-product of Töben's imprisonment was that his defence lawyer was also indicted for the same 'offence' merely for having the audacity to attempt to defend him. So, to be clear, apparently not only is it a crime to merely question the supposed 'truth' and put forward an opposing viewpoint, it is also by implication now a crime to attempt to legally defend someone who has committed this so-called crime. Would we condemn the legal defender of a murderer or other criminal in this way as being complicit in their crimes? Absolutely not. Truly outrageous, I am sure you will agree.

How can a political opinion, especially when backed by factual evidence be treated as a crime in the civilised society in which we are supposed to live? Sadly, the answer is that we do not live in a civilised society any longer, if indeed we ever have done so. We exist in a quasi-police state, governed by dupes and shills whose sole aims are to fulfil the whims and orders of their bankster masters whilst totally subjugating its own citizens and eliminating all forms of dissent in any way deemed necessary either within or if necessary, outside the laws of the land. Even if all these 'dissenters' are genuinely mistaken, after rationally considering all the evidence, surely prison is not the answer to so-called 'thought-crimes' and differences of opinion.

Step by step, this is how we are being slowly but surely condemned ultimately to a life of slavery under the banksters' agenda. Amazing is it not how the people who dare to question or speak out against their blatant lies, deceptions, statements, proclamations and motives have somehow become the 'Nazis,' the 'terrorists' or whatever other label they wish to pin on them, thus enabling the guilt to be deflected from themselves onto their detractors and by so doing give them an inside track through to their ultimate goals, virtually unchallenged? I would suggest that the holocaust, playing the role it was originally designed to play, has been another major leap down the route of fulfilling their sadistic agenda.

However, for the biggest 'shock to the system' and de-bunk of all the propaganda and lies disseminated by the Zionists, it is necessary to backtrack a little once again, to the mid-1930s.

The simple truth is that the Zionists in their quest to set-up a Jewish homeland in Palestine were funded covertly by the Nazis. Yes, you did read that correctly. Captured SS records after the war documented an agreement between the SS and the Haganah, the forerunner of the Israeli Defence Force (IDF.) Under this arrangement the Haganah was permitted to run training camps for Jewish youths inside Germany. These young people, as well as many other Jews were financially encouraged to immigrate to Palestine.

Haganah, in return, agreed to provide the SS with intelligence about British activities in Palestine. Captured German records claimed that Haganah's view was that by wild exaggeration of the Nazi persecution of the Jews, this could be turned to Zionist advantage, at least temporarily, by compelling Jewish immigration to Palestine and that the Haganah commander's sole source of income was by way of secret funds from the SS.

Thus, German brutality against and repression of the Jews was *openly encouraged and embraced* by Zionists.

It is also known that the Nazi regime actually offered all of Europe's Jews to the Zionist leadership, unharmed on condition that they were re-settled somewhere outside Europe. For instance, Madagascar was proposed at one stage but this was turned down out of hand by the Zionists on the basis that six million dead Jews would be more likely to fulfil their twisted agenda than several million merely displaced ones.

European Jews were in fact betrayed by the Zionist leadership. Zionists collaborated with the Nazis to victimise and expel Jews and conspired to manipulate the facts of the holocaust in order to strengthen the case for a Jewish homeland through sympathy for 'Jewish suffering.' Furthermore, Zionists in effect were responsible for the creation of Hitler as a 'bogeyman' to fulfil the role of the persecutor of the Jews, simply in order to build up a strong case for a Jewish homeland.

The vast majority of German Jews vehemently rejected Zionism as an enemy from within as they saw themselves as Germans, first and foremost. 80,000 German Jews had fought in the trenches of WWI and 12,000 died. *"Nowhere was the opposition of Jews to Zionism so widespread, principled and fierce as in Germany."* a Zionist historian wrote.

In order to manipulate Jews into leaving for Palestine, Germans had to be painted with a racist nationalist ideology just like Zionism and in fact, Julius Streicher and other Nazis admitted that their 'Master Race' ideology was modelled on Zionism. Through their bogus, contrived 'conflict,' Zionism and Nazism were subsequently able to advance the banksters' goal of establishing a private army, secret service and nuclear arsenal in Israel.

Past Jewish suffering at the hands of these Elite-controlled Zionists, exhibits parallels with today. Their leadership was usurped by Freemasons (ie. Zionism is a Masonic order) bent on sacrificing them to advance the banksters' grand plan and now we are all in the same situation. The banksters today are using debt to disinherit and enslave us. Bush, Clinton, Obama, Blair, Brown, Cameron, Sarkozy et al, are all 33rd degree Freemasons who agreed to assume trillions of dollars of 'debt' on behalf of us all, from the Zionist-masonic banksters who are in reality all working towards the same ends.

If our so-called leaders represented the interests of the ordinary people, they would let the banks fail as they did in Iceland and default on all the debt created by banksters out of 'thin air.' This is a warning to us all and we will continue to be permanently enslaved (and much worse) as long as we continue to elect and accept leaders who are 100% in league with the Elite-Zionists.

The Holocaust – the real truth

As long as most of us can remember, we have had this almost *sacred* figure of six million dead Jews constantly force-fed to us until it has become indelibly imprinted in our psyche and woven deeply within the very fabric of our culture to such an extent that it has become unthinkable that it may be a fabrication.

"The Western World has been inundated with Holocaust documentaries, Holocaust movies, Holocaust museums, Holocaust books, and Holocaust curriculums. The aim? To immunise Jewry and Israel from valid criticism and most conveniently, to obscure the Allied war crimes perpetrated against millions of German civilians. Perhaps the 'Holocaust fatigue' now infecting German youth will create a thirst for what REALLY happened during World War II and an appreciation of their own, factually-substantiated, Holocaust. And that, ironically to say, will be a very 'inconvenient' history lesson for world Jewry." Nathanael Kapner, October 2011.

The six million figure is quite easily proven as false and this is not just mere supposition or statistical juggling on my part. Consider this for a moment…

In the 1950s, a plaque was placed at the entrance to the so-called 'death camp' at Auschwitz. Firstly, it categorically stated that 4.1 million Jews died there. Then some time later it was surreptitiously replaced with one denoting a figure of 2.6 million. Now, the plaque has been changed again to claim that 'about 1.5 million, mainly Jews' died in Auschwitz and discussions are already being mooted to decide whether or not this figure should be further lowered to around 700,000. Is it not strange indeed then that these reductions never seem to be deducted from the sacrosanct six million total still quoted and treated as indisputable today? Meticulously administered, independently audited Red Cross figures after the war had ended, stated that around 280,000 European Jews actually perished from all causes including 'old age' during the war whilst noting the fact that the Jewish population of Europe actually increased by around half a million between 1939 and 1945. How strange. However in the mid-1990s the Red Cross, of course by this time now totally infiltrated and controlled by the Zionists anyway, 'apologised' for this previous statement.

My research has led me to conclude that approximately 65-75 million people in total, lost their lives in WWII, so it seems incredibly strange to me that we are meant to honour and laud one tiny percentage of that figure and ignore the other 60 or 70 million that died the most futile of deaths in a war waged to secure a Jewish homeland amongst other reasons. Perhaps all those other people's lives were not as important? Yes, that must be the reason.

For more than seven decades now, the world has been held under political blackmail with the story of the slaughter of millions of Jews in the gas chambers of the Third Reich and this has received the full treatment of the Zionist propaganda machine, primarily via Hollywood and the media, which still continues to this day in the form of the seemingly endless and innumerable 'holocaust' and WWII movies and documentaries emphasising the suffering of the 'six million' and the brutality of the Germans, still being relentlessly churned-out. Apparently, there are around one million Jewish survivors of the death camps still living today 70+ years after the event and still claiming reparations payments from Germany whilst Germany's own Zionist leadership happily continues to fund them.

From whence did all these 'millions' originate when it is known for certain and recorded by several independent and impartial sources that there were only 500,000 Jews in Germany prior to the war and only approximately two million in total in the countries bordering Germany?

As related already, this was not the first time that similar 'holocaust' stories had been propagated by these people. There are literally dozens of other examples. In the Talmud (a Jewish holy book,) Gittin 57b claims that four million Jews were killed by the Romans in the city of Bethar. Gittin 57b also claims that 16 million Jewish children were wrapped in scrolls and burned alive by the Romans. Thirdly and more recently, the precise figure of six million saw light of day for the first time shortly after WWI. *"Six million [Jewish] men and women are dying"* in the Ukraine, announced *The American Hebrew* periodical on the 31st October 1919, the very same claim that the Zionists made twenty-odd years later. It would appear that the tendency for extreme exaggeration, if not downright lies, remains alive and well in certain quarters.

"Three of the best known works on the Second World War are General Eisenhower's Crusade in Europe (New York: Doubleday [Country Life Press], 1948), Winston Churchill's 'The Second World War' (London: Cassell, 6 vols., 1948-1954) and the Mémoires de Guerre de General de Gaulle (Paris: Plon, 3 vols., 1954-1959). In these three works not the least mention of Nazi gas chambers is to be found. Eisenhower's Crusade in Europe is a book of 559 pages; the six volumes of Churchill's Second World War total 4,448 pages; and de Gaulle's three-volume Mémoires de Guerre is 2,054 pages. In this mass of writing, which altogether totals 7,061 pages (not including the introductory parts), published from 1948 to 1959, one will find no mention either of Nazi 'gas chambers,' a 'genocide' of the Jews, or of 'six million' Jewish victims of the war." Dr. Robert Faurisson, historian and historical document expert

"It is certain that if there had been 'killing factories' in Europe murdering millions of

civilians, then the Red Cross, the Pope, humanitarian agencies, the Allied governments, neutral governments and prominent figures such as Roosevelt, Truman, Churchill, Eisenhower and many others would have known about it and would have often and unambiguously mentioned it and condemned it. They didn't. Winston Churchill wrote the six volumes of his monumental work, 'The Second World War,' without mentioning a program of mass-murder and genocide. Maybe it slipped his mind? Dwight D. Eisenhower, in his memoir 'Crusade in Europe,' also failed to mention gas chambers. Was the weapon used to murder millions of Jews unworthy of a passing reference? Was the future President being insensitive to Jews?" Unknown source

Moreover, there are apparently no media references to any 'holocaust' of any kind nor radio, film newsreel or newspaper stories until towards the end of the war when the myth had been propagated and was just beginning to gain momentum. Is it really credible that this supposed heinous act was taking place so openly without the knowledge of the Allies and their vast intelligence network in Europe at that time? I believe not. Had it really been happening, the Allied propaganda machine against the Germans would have been cranked-up into overdrive and stories of the atrocities would have been widespread. Why would the Allies need false stories of German atrocities if there were real ones to be had? The railway lines to and from the 'death camps' would also have been destroyed, especially in the latter stages of the war when the Allies were attacking targets both military and civilian all over Germany and Eastern Europe with impunity and with little danger of retaliatory attacks due to German defences being in total disarray or non-existent. In fact the transport trains themselves, rather than the tracks specifically, were often the victims of Allied attacks and many Jews in transit died as a result of these.

Auschwitz has become synonymous with the holocaust, as ***the*** place of methodical extermination of the Jews. Such is the power of propaganda that if anything, true or false, is repeated often enough and forcefully enough, it becomes accepted without any real attempt to verify the facts. Surely 'they' would not lie to us on this scale would they? Err, yes they would, actually and 'they' have done so many, many times over the millennia and will no doubt continue to do so.

Could such an alleged house-of-horrors as Auschwitz is popularly depicted have been equipped with (for the use of the inmates) a post office, a library, a theatre complete with its own resident orchestra, a hospital staffed by 20 Jewish doctors and 300 nurses complete with an intensive care unit and operating theatre? There was also a swimming pool where inmate swimming galas were known to have been regularly organised in the summer months and the camp also staged regular soccer matches complete with its own mini-leagues? There was also a fully-equipped court room for the trial of prisoners accused of misdemeanours. Strange is it not that the Germans would actually bother with trials when they were supposedly randomly murdering millions of people indiscriminately and without need of a trial? How about brothels too? Auschwitz is known to have had a brothel for the inmates staffed by female Jews and as it was illegal and punishable by death for a non-Jewish German to have sexual relations with a Jew, this could hardly have been a facility for the use of the SS guards. Indeed, they had their own similar 'facility' in any event, populated by 'good Aryan stock.'

Are we also supposed to believe that the thousands of babies and children survivors from Auschwitz and other 'death camps,' would not have immediately been selected for extermination upon arrival at the camp, as we are told over and over in Zionist propaganda that the only ones to survive the 'selection' process were ones who were able to contribute to the Nazi war effort? They could hardly have been used as work-horses for the Nazi war machine as were the other survivors, yet many survived. For example, take the case of Anne Frank of 'diary' fame. She was sent to Bergen-Belsen a so-called 'death camp' in late 1944 where she lived for at least two months before finally succumbing to Typhus along with many thousands of others. As a (by this time) very sickly fifteen year old girl, surely she should not have survived the alleged 'selection' process?

Indeed, all the evidence shows that, in fact, a very high percentage of the Jewish inmates were not able to work but nevertheless were not killed. For example, an internal German telex message dated 4th September 1943, from the chief of the Labour Allocation department of the SS Economic and Administrative Main Office (WVHA,) reported that of approximately 25,000 Jewish inmates in Auschwitz, only 3,581 were able to work and that all of the remaining Jewish inmates, some 21,000+ or about 85 percent, were **unable to work.**

In response to the deaths of many inmates due to disease, especially typhus, the German authorities responsible for the camps ordered firm counter-measures. The head of the SS camp administration office sent a directive dated 28th December 1942, to Auschwitz and the other concentration camps. It sharply criticised the high death rate of inmates due to disease and ordered that "*... camp physicians must use all means at their disposal to significantly reduce the death rate in the various camps.*" Furthermore, it ordered ... "*The camp doctors must supervise more often than in the past, the nutrition of the prisoners and, in cooperation with the administration, submit improvement recommendations to the camp commandants ... The camp doctors are to see to it that the working conditions at the various labour places are improved as much as possible ... The Reichsfuehrer SS [Himmler] has ordered that the death rate absolutely must be reduced.*"

Official camp regulations also made it abundantly clear that Auschwitz was not an extermination centre. They stated ...

"New arrivals are to be given a thorough medical examination and if there is any doubt about their health, they must be sent to quarantine for observation.

Prisoners who report sick must be examined that same day by the camp physician. If necessary, the physician must transfer the prisoners to a hospital for professional treatment.

The camp physician must regularly inspect the kitchen regarding the preparation of the food and the quality of the food supply. Any deficiencies that may arise must be reported to the camp commandant.

Special care should be given in the treatment of accidents, in order not to impair the full productivity of the prisoners.

Prisoners who are to be released or transferred must first be brought before the camp physician for medical examination."

Not exactly what one would expect of a 'death camp' is it? The truth is that Auschwitz-Birkenau was in fact **a labour camp** (the preserved sign over the entrance is somewhat of a clue, the almost Orwellian, 'Arbeit Macht Frei,' (work will make you free) and included many different races, religions and political persuasions. There is no dispute that many thousands of people died miserably in Auschwitz and all the other so-called 'death camps' before, during and after the war, but the simple fact is that no-one died in gas chambers.

A problem that always faces any group of people living in unsanitary conditions, severe privation or close confinement is lice and the multitude of diseases they cause. Auschwitz and the neighbouring camp at Birkenau had a serious outbreak of typhus in the summer of 1942, during which many people died, both inmates and guards. To contain the outbreak, the only 'gas chambers' in existence were used for disinfection of the inmates' clothes using the 'Zyklon B' disinfectant. And towards the end of the war when the German nation was on the point of collapse, the fact that the transportation system was in disarray, as a result incidentally of the Allies indiscriminate carpet-bombing of civilian road and rail transport links, totally contrary to the Geneva Convention, and that no supplies of any kind, neither food nor medical assistance were getting through, only exacerbated the situation. Hundreds, if not thousands of innocents subsequently died of starvation and hunger-related diseases (on both sides of the divide.)

"Mike's real name was Olitsky and he was a Lithuanian Jew who'd fled into Germany to escape Stalin's Red Army. He wound up in Dachau for four years. He inadvertently introduced me to Holocaust 'revisionism' when I ventured to ask him about his experience. He shrugged and said, 'It was a factory. We worked during the day and stayed in a dormitory at night.' 'But what about the, uh, the . . . ?' 'The what?' 'You know, the killings.' 'I never saw any of that.' Four years in Dachau, and never saw any of that? OK, he did see the US Army 'liberate' the camp in April 1945. The SS and Alpine troops recuperating there had negotiated surrender to the Americans, who entered the camp and started shooting the guys who thought they were surrendering. Then the Americans marched the surviving soldiers (all the prison guards had fled days earlier) up to a wall near the hospital and set up a machine gun. Three hundred and forty-six German soldiers on R&R [rest and recuperation] were slaughtered in a few minutes, five hundred and twenty in all, that morning." J. Bruce Campbell, 'Veterans Today'

Yes, I am afraid it is all an elaborate hoax. We have all been 'propagandised' and duped over the decades into believing that six million Jews were systematically and brutally exterminated by a Jew-hating race (the Germans) for no other reason than their religion (race.)

"Were the Holocaust shown to be a hoax, the number one weapon in Israel's propaganda armoury would disappear." Professor William Rubinstein, Melbourne University.

The enormity of this utter lie and the abundant evidence available to counter the physical practicality of it, is so overwhelmingly huge that I barely know where to start. However, here are a few simple facts to consider (in no particular order)...

Many detailed aerial reconnaissance photographs taken of Auschwitz-Birkenau on several random days in 1944 (during the height of the alleged extermination period there) were made public by the CIA in 1979. These photos show no trace of piles of corpses, smoking crematoria chimneys or masses of Jews awaiting death, things that have been repeatedly alleged and all of which would have been clearly visible if Auschwitz had been the busy extermination centre it is alleged to have been, despatching thousands of Jews daily.

The Germans were known as an efficient race and indeed still are. They were the kind of people who meticulously and methodically documented every single action they took. Why then amongst the hundreds of *tonnes* of official Nazi documents recovered after the end of the war is there not a single document in existence that even alludes to the 'final solution' being a genocide of the Jews? Could it have been because the Germans destroyed them all before they could fall into Allied hands? This I believe is highly unlikely. Surely at least one or two would have evaded destruction as with many other incriminating policy documents that were painstakingly unearthed by the Allies.

Then could it have been because the Germans did not document their policy of genocidal gassings for fear of it being discovered after the war? Also unlikely in the extreme. At the time the 'final solution' was allegedly proposed at the Wannsee conference in January 1941, the Germans were comfortably winning the war and it is simply unrealistic to assume that they considered that they would ever end-up, let alone forward plan for being, on the losing side. Indeed, war crimes trials were the last thing they would ever consider as there was no such concept until 1946. War crimes trials had never been utilised to deal with the losers in past wars. The Nazis had no reason to try to create an illusion for posterity because they thought they were going to *be* posterity. They never, ever imagined that they would need to answer to anyone for anything they did and yet are we now supposed to believe that even in 1941 they were planning ahead to a post-war era in which it would become necessary to cover up their actions?

"The 'Final Solution' spoken of in the German documents, was a program of evacuation, resettlement, and deportation of Jews with the ultimate objective of expulsion from Europe. During the war, Jews of various nationalities were being moved east, as one stage in this Final Solution. The legend claims that the movements were mainly for extermination purposes." Arthur Butz, 'The Hoax of the Twentieth Century.'

"If there were documents covering the whole sequence of events, then there would be no such thing as revisionism. The problem is that the documents one would expect to find do not exist. We have documents relating to every aspect of the war, including every aspect of the holocaust, except for the gassing of the Jews. It is not possible to gas six million people,

or to do anything else involving millions of people, without leaving a paper trail. If the gassing happened, there would be thousands of documents to verify it, starting with the planning stages and continuing throughout the course of events. But no such paper trail exists." geniebusters.org

On the contrary in fact, a paper-trail making the whole scenario impossible *does* exist, and more of that shortly.

If there were photographs of the entire sequence of events, including photographs of piles of corpses in gas chambers, then the question would be a non-issue and revisionism would not even be an issue. That would absolutely and definitively settle the matter immediately. The problem is that no such pictures exist. We have photographs of every aspect of World War II, including every aspect of the 'holocaust,' *except* for the gassing of the Jews. There are photographs of Jews being coerced on to the trains, disembarking from the trains, photographs of Jews in the camps and photographs of bodies in mass graves and piled in heaps on the ground (many of which incidentally are the remains of German soldiers and civilians murdered by starvation by the Allies after the war), but there are no photographs at all of anyone being gassed, thus rendering all the other evidence merely circumstantial. We already know that the Nazis transported thousands of Jews (and others) in cattle wagons and we already know that there were piles of bodies at camps after outbreaks of disease and extreme food shortages. We also know that Jews were taken to de-lousing facilities and made to undress en-masse, so what exactly do these photographs prove, I would venture to ask?

In 2011, I sat through the full ten hours of the 'epic' 1970s, supposedly definitive, but in my view frankly risible, Hollywood docudrama-cum-Zionist propaganda-piece *'Holocaust,'* for research purposes – not in a single-sitting I may add, I value my sanity a little more than that. This abject piece of over-sentimentalised, corny, nonsensical, melodramatic drivel actually 'won' no less than eight 'Emmys' (TV's equivalent of 'Oscars') – hardly surprising really when we take into account who runs the TV and film industry, I suppose. Its historical inaccuracies are numerous, but that does not really matter as it serves its purpose extremely well in aiding the re-writing of modern history and the propagandising of the masses. Indeed, I would argue that it was this series that was responsible almost single-handedly for the propagandisation of my entire generation, the so-called 'baby-boomers,' into all things 'holocaust,' such was the impact that the programme made upon western society.

In one of the last scenes, at or near the end of the war, the fictional character, SS Major Erik Dorf played by the American actor Michael Moriarty, is confronted by his American captors who show him a sequence of photographs depicting the various stages of the supposed extermination process. Dorf is shown photographs of the Jews being rounded-up, deported on the trains, being 'selected' for gassing, being led to the 'gas chambers' and undressing, all of which are shown 'on camera' and then... whilst his American interrogator is saying 'being gassed,' the camera immediately cuts from the series of photographs to the horrified face of the Dorf character and then immediately resumes the photographic sequence... bodies being moved to the crematoria etc. etc.

Obviously and unfortunately for them, the Zionist/Jewish producers of this slick piece of propaganda, unsurprisingly as there are none, could not find one single appropriate photograph for this particular part of the alleged event.

What about the thousands (millions?) of eye-witnesses though? Not only were six million Jews supposedly exterminated but there also, even in the second decade of the twenty first century, more than 70 years after the event, seems to be many millions more 'survivors' still alive. Incredible really when there were only probably a maximum of 4 million Jews in the entire continent of Europe in 1939 according to official, audited Red Cross figures.

'Holocaust' historian Lucy Dawidowicz similarly noted that… *"…the survivor's memory is often distorted by hate, sentimentality, and the passage of time. His perspective on external events is often skewed by the limits of his personal experience."*

Jewish historian Samuel Gringauz, who was himself interned in the ghetto of Kaunas in Lithuania during the war, criticised what he called the 'hyper-historical' nature of most Jewish 'survivor testimony.' He wrote that… *"…most of the memoirs and reports are full of preposterous verbosity, grapho-manic exaggeration, dramatic effects, overestimated self-inflation, dilettante philosophising, would-be lyricism, unchecked rumours, bias, partisan attacks and apologies."*

And Shmuel Krakowski, archives director of the Israeli government's Holocaust centre, *Yad Vashem*, confirmed in 1986 that more than half of the 'testimonies' of Jewish 'survivors' on file there are *"unreliable."* Many survivors, wanting *"…to be part of history, may have let their imaginations run away with them,"* Krakowski said. *"Many were never in the places where they claimed to have witnessed atrocities, while others relied on second-hand information given them by friends or passing strangers."* He confirmed that many of the testimonies on file at Yad Vashem were later proved to be inaccurate when locations and dates could not pass an historian's expert appraisal.

There are also six other important points that need to be made about so-called witnesses to the events.

1. The witnesses are far from consistent in their allegations. Some witnesses said nothing at all about gas chambers. For example, Jan Karski wrote a report in the autumn of 1942 in which he stated that he visited the camp at Belzec to investigate rumours of extermination. He said that Jews were being killed by electrical shocks in a room with a metallic floor and in 1944, he published a book in which he said that the Jews were being loaded into wagons filled with quicklime and left to die outside the camp. Neither the article nor the book says anything about gas chambers. And of course, the 'official' history of Belzec now says nothing about electrical shocks or wagons filled with quicklime. We are now supposed to believe that the Jews at Belzec were killed in gas chambers but Jan Karski, who was there at the time (so he said,) said nothing at all about gas chambers.

2. Many witness testimonies about gas chambers do not stand up to close examination. For example, one of the most well-known witnesses quoted as an authoritative source is Dr. Miklos Nyiszli, the supposed author of *'Auschwitz, a Doctor's Eyewitness Account.'* Dr. Nyiszli did actually exist. He was a Hungarian doctor who was sent to Birkenau (not Auschwitz,) where he worked in the pathology laboratory under the command of the infamous Dr. Josef Mengele. After the war, he testified at the Nuremburg trials and he died in 1949, 'his' book being published in 1951. Throughout the book, the author says he was in Auschwitz and that there were four crematoria at Auschwitz. In fact, there was one crematorium at Auschwitz, and four at Birkenau. Obviously anyone who was there would know that and also they would doubtless know which camp was which. At the end of the book (page 206,) in the section describing the evacuation of Auschwitz in the January of 1945, the author says:

"We left, filled with the feverish sensation of liberation. Direction: the Birkenau KZ, two kilometres from the crematoriums."

Dr. Nyiszli certainly did not leave Auschwitz and go in the direction of Birkenau as he was already in Birkenau. This is one of the most glaring impossibilities in a book full of much impossibility and as a result of this I would strongly suggest that this book was not written by Dr. Nyiszli at all. It certainly could not have been written by anyone who was there and yet this book is cited by apologists as one of the most authoritative of all witness statements.

3. Witness testimony alone proves nothing. Suppose a hundred thousand witnesses claim that something happened, does that constitute absolute proof that it happened? There are probably more than one hundred thousand people who claim to have 'seen a UFO' at one time or another in the last fifty years. Does that prove that flying saucers exist? Our bankster-controlled media would say 'definitely not,' in that example, yet there are thousands of people who say they have not only seen UFOs, they have been abducted into them. They will tell you in vivid detail about their experiences and these people have no obvious motive for lying, unlike holocaust 'survivors.'

4. Witnesses can easily be 'bought' and influenced by the promise of large amounts of money in the form of 'holocaust reparations' and it is my firm view that this is exactly what enticed most of them. It is also fairly easy to convince someone that an event happened in a certain way and encourage them to link these fictional events to their own experiences. This will then have the effect of creating a false memory which over time becomes more and more embellished until that person actually believes those events really happened.

5. To the contrary, many former inmates have confirmed that they saw no evidence of extermination at Auschwitz at all. For example, an Austrian woman, Maria Vanherwaarden, testified about her camp experiences in a Toronto District Court in March 1988. She was interned in Auschwitz-Birkenau in 1942 for having sexual relations with a Polish forced labourer. Upon arrival, Maria and the other women were ordered to undress and go into

a large concrete room without windows to take a shower. But instead of gas, it was only water that came out of the shower heads.

Auschwitz was certainly no holiday-camp, Maria confirmed. She witnessed the death of many fellow inmates by hunger and disease, particularly typhus and more than a few committed suicide. But she saw no evidence at all of mass killings, gassings or of any extermination programme.

A Jewish woman named Marika Frank arrived at Auschwitz-Birkenau from Hungary in July 1944, when 25,000 Jews were supposedly being gassed and cremated daily. She likewise testified after the war that she heard and saw nothing of 'gas chambers,' during the time she was interned there. She heard the gassing stories only later, after the war had ended.

Some Auschwitz internees who had served their sentences were even released and returned to their home countries. If Auschwitz had actually been a top-secret extermination camp, the Germans would certainly not have released inmates who 'knew' what was happening in the complex.

6. Elie Wiesel is one of the most celebrated eye-witnesses to the alleged Holocaust, yet in his supposedly autobiographical book *Night*, he makes absolutely no mention of gas chambers at all. He claims instead to have witnessed Jews being burned alive, a story now dismissed by *all* historians. Wiesel gives credence to the most absurd stories of other 'eyewitnesses' and he spreads fantastic tales of 10,000 Jews sent to their deaths each day in two flaming pits in Buchenwald – one for the adults and another for the children.

Conventional historians account for the lack of photographs and documents by claiming that the holocaust was so secret that no photographs were ever taken, and no incriminating documents were allowed to exist. This is supposed to have been true even when the 'Final Solution' was alleged to be in the planning stages, as far back as 1941. However, Hitler talked about exterminating or annihilating the Jews on many occasions. For example, here is a sentence from *Mein Kampf*. Hitler wrote...

"The nationalisation of our masses will succeed only when, aside from all the positive struggles for the soul of our people, their international poisoners are exterminated."

So we are supposed to believe that Hitler announced to the world that he would have liked the Jews to be exterminated and yet at the same time went to great lengths to maintain the pretence that they were not being systematically exterminated? The intention was declared openly, but the action itself was so secret that the Nazis never even discussed it among themselves? This is abject nonsense akin to clutching at straws I am afraid.

He also said this:

"If at the beginning of the War and during the War twelve or fifteen thousand of these Hebrew corrupters of the people had been held under poison gas, as happened to hundreds of thousands of our very best German workers in the field, the sacrifice of millions at the front

would not have been in vain. On the contrary, twelve thousand scoundrels eliminated in time might have saved the lives of millions of Germans, valuable for the future."

At this point the 'secret' was now out. Having alluded to the idea of gassing the Jews in *Mein Kampf,* it would make no sense for Hitler to pretend it was not happening, if he was actually doing it, but there is no other reference to gassing in anything else he ever said or wrote.

There are voluminous records of everything Hitler, Himmler, and the other senior Nazis said in public and much of what they said in private and there is no mention of gassing anywhere, even on occasions when they were talking about getting rid of the Jews. For example, when Himmler addressed a private meeting of the senior officers of the SS (the Poznan speech,) even if he wished to refrain from mentioning gassing publicly, he would have felt free to speak plainly at a private meeting of the SS. But the fact is that nothing was said about gassing, even though he was discussing the transportation of the Jews to concentration camps.

The Nazis were certainly not coy about killing people. There are pictures of Nazi soldiers shooting Jews (and other prisoners) in cold blood and laughing about it and these pictures were not taken surreptitiously by someone else, they were taken by the Nazis themselves, but we are supposed to believe that the gas chambers were so secret that no photographs were ever taken. Are we also supposed to believe that it would be *possible* to cover up an action involving six million people or that they would not openly flaunt the fact that the killings were taking place? Really?

The mechanics of the extermination process are alleged to have been . . .

A train-load of Jews arrives at Auschwitz railway station or indeed any other alleged 'death camp.' They are then immediately separated into two groups, the so-called 'selection' of those who are fit for labour and those who are not. The latter group is led directly to the gas chambers immediately. Firstly they enter the changing room, where under protest they are told to remove their clothes and leave behind their possessions. They are then led into another room, which is 'mocked-up' to resemble a shower room or a delousing room. Once in this room, they are locked-in and gassed using Zyklon B granules poured through an open hatch or window in the roof or the top of the wall, the deadly fumes supposedly emanating from the fake shower-heads or even just simply being poured-in directly. A few moments later the guards enter, hose down the bodies (the last act of any victim of asphyxiation/gassing is to involuntarily defecate and urinate) and then drag the bodies out and take the *saturated* bodies to the ovens on handcarts to be cremated and immediately make the gas chambers ready for the next batch of victims to keep the 'conveyer belt' rolling.

Firstly the commonly described and widely accepted, casual approach to the manual 'pouring-in' of Zyklon B granules is utterly risible. As will be demonstrated later, this dangerous substance, a) once it is stimulated to produce cyanide gas is absolutely and totally deadly and could not safely be handled by anyone using such a casual approach, even whilst wearing a gas mask and b) in order to make the substance unstable enough to begin vapourising, it has to first of all reach the relatively high temperature of *at least* 26 degrees Celsius (Centigrade) again unachievable by the simple act of pouring directly from a can by hand.

So, if six million Jews were gassed, this scenario must have been repeated thousands of times. Even being generous, if on average 100 at a time were gassed (a much higher average figure than claimed), this scene must have played-out *sixty thousand* times at all the different camps, over a period of several years.

Zyklon B granules

Assuming for purposes of illustration of the point that these were split equally over 10 'death' camps, that is six thousand events per camp and over a time period of 3 years (1942-45.) This means that on average at each camp there were 2000 gassings per year of 100 people at a time. Break these figures down even further and this produces an average figure of 550 people per day, every day, gassed and cremated for 3 years at every single camp. I submit that this is totally ludicrous in the extreme and such figures if presented as evidence in any impartial court of law would quite rightly be rejected as nonsensical. In addition, please consider that these figures only take account of the alleged six million Jews and not all the hundreds and thousands, if not millions of non-Jews said to have suffered the same fate but obviously not emphasised to the same extent.

In 1998 Frederick Töben the historian, visited all the major death camps still in existence in order to inspect the facilities and gather information. He was not alone. He also took with him, several independent scientists and engineers in order to elicit their opinions about the practicalities of the Zionists' claims. In conjunction with his many years of intensive study of documents and eye-witness testimonies he had already concluded that the collaboration between the Zionist leaders and the Nazis had led to the establishment of the camps in the first place as evacuation or emigration would not produce the Zionists desired results i.e. the inception of a Jewish homeland.

Concentration camps were not unique to the Nazis, neither were they their invention. In the Boer War in South Africa, another manufactured conflict at the behest of the Elite banksters, the British occupiers constructed several camps resulting in the deaths of several hundred thousand Boer men, women and children through disease and malnutrition. Even in WWII, the Americans herded thousands of Japanese-American citizens into camps as did the Australians with their Japanese residents. The Swiss also had such camps for refugees from Nazi-occupied Europe.

Worse still, in the aftermath of WWI, Poland built several dozen camps to house the ethnic German residents of the formerly German territories they 'acquired' as a result of the Treaty of Versailles in 1919, many of whom suffered terribly from disease and starvation, resulting in hundreds of thousands of preventable deaths of innocents.

However back to the subject in hand, the prisoners of Auschwitz and all its 'sister' camps scattered through eastern Germany and eastern Europe, were given rations of 1300-1700 calories per day, according to captured documents and whilst this is nowhere near the standard, modern diet of today especially for those partaking in gruelling physical labour, it is considerably better than the average German citizen received in the last two years of the war. They were lucky to receive 1000 calories per day and often had to make do with much less.

Töben's conclusions about the gas chamber scenario may be summarised as follows:

The rooms and buildings named as being those which were used for the executions of millions of people, firstly were easily provable as fakes. Giveaways such as non-airtight doors, the lack of holes or shafts down which to administer the Zyklon B granules, the lack of any kind of heating equipment to stimulate the emission of the gas, ventilation or extraction systems to deal with the deadly fumes are but a few of the improbabilities, if not downright impossibilities noted by Töben in his research.

For example, are we also expected to believe that the gas chamber, open to the public at Auschwitz which is a mere *twenty metres* from the Commandant's quarters and the SS dining hall was actually used in anger? The dangers of this particular arrangement should be apparent to anyone who understands the way hydrogen cyanide gas kills. Every time the doors were opened, hundreds of cubic metres of deadly fumes would have leaked outside, instantly killing anyone and any other living thing in its path. There were provably no filtration units to automatically safely disperse or neutralise the 'used' gas, either then or now.

The real gas chambers used at Auschwitz, Töben believes, were nothing more or less than fumigation chambers for the delousing of clothes and bed sheets. These are also available for inspection by the public and are placed well away from the inhabited areas of the camp and are fitted, as one would sensibly expect, with all the necessary heating (for the raw granules,) pumping and filtration equipment. However as stated previously, the alleged 'human' gas chambers contain no evidence whatsoever of any of this equipment.

Zyklon B was used worldwide in the 1920s, 30s and 40s as a pesticide against rats, fleas and lice. Its primary reason for being in situ at the camps was to **save** human lives and not to kill.

After Zyklon B has been used, according to the manufacturer's own instructions, which still survive intact, the room or chamber must be thoroughly aerated for at least **ten hours** before entering and gas masks would have been effective for *10 minutes* only, before the poison saturated the filters, killing the wearer. It is also known however, having had access to all supply requisitions, invoices and manifests that there were no gas masks of any kind present at Auschwitz. Another telling argument against the practicality of its large scale use is that the granules only begin to emit the deadly cyanide gas at a temperature sustained at over 26° Celsius, equivalent to a very hot summer day. There is no evidence whatsoever that the rooms named as human gas chambers were ever even heated at all and Central Europe experiences some bitterly cold winters with temperatures often in double-figures below zero.

Dr. Töben interviewed on film, an Australian expert on crematoria and the disposal of human bodies without actually explaining to him the background reasons for his questions to avoid possibly compromising the answers with pre-existing prejudices of any kind. The expert maintained several opinions and divulged facts that proved absolutely fatal to the gas chamber myths and legends.

Modern, present day crematoria ovens burn at 800-1000° Celsius (whereas the Auschwitz ovens were probably able to manage around half that temperature with the available technology of 70+ years ago).

One single corpse takes around two hours to burn to ash at this temperature (1000°) and even then it does not fully incinerate the bones. The bones have to be powdered as a further separate exercise. If the corpse is excessively cold or wet it would take almost twice as long to incinerate. If two or more corpses were burned together then these times would be increased in ratio. (Remember that according to the myth, all the bodies were thoroughly hosed-down immediately prior to transportation to the crematoria.)

Regarding the oft-cited by so-called eye-witnesses 'body-burning pits,' simply pouring copious amounts of fuel on a pile of bodies and setting them alight is just simply fiction. Living and recently deceased bodies contain at least 75% water and this severely impacts on their flammability meaning that witnesses (and there are many, including one of the most fêted, Elie Wiesel) who blithely state that they saw the Germans pile thousands of bodies in large pits, liberally dose them with petrol (gasoline) and burn them to ashes in a few hours (some have said 20 minutes!) are nothing less than outright liars and charlatans.

Auschwitz KZ was constructed on extremely wet, marshy land, sited as it was at the confluence of three rivers and with an unusually high water-table, making it impossible to bury bodies in the ground due to the extreme danger of polluting the drinking water, which was extracted from small reservoirs in the surrounding land. It is this wetland environment that encouraged the proliferation of diseases and the vermin that cause them. Over 74,000 people, both friend and foe were officially recorded as Typhus victims alone, at Auschwitz.

It is a well-known scientific principle that a fire needs free oxygen (i.e. not oxygen mixed with hydrogen in the form of water) in order to burn and that is one major ingredient that would be completely missing once we go further down than the top-most layer of bodies. The amount of fuel that would be needed to incinerate one small pit of bodies would probably be considerably more than the entire German army would use in one day, one suspects. Petrol (gasoline) or indeed any other fuel will always burn itself out long before it has had time to cause combustion in predominantly water-based substances such as human bodies. And this of course all pre-supposes that the pits themselves were dry which is of course impossible due to the presence of the aforementioned, abnormally high water-table. Indeed the whole scenario would be truly laughable were it not so serious a subject.

The crematoria expert also made the point that even in the most fiercely-burning house fires and for example, after a plane crash, bodies are only superficially charred and not reduced to ash, even after being subjected to direct flames for many hours.

In addition, Ivan Lagace, manager of a large crematorium in Calgary, Canada, testified in court in April 1988 that the Auschwitz cremations story is technically impossible. The allegation that 10,000 or even 20,000 corpses were burned every day at Auschwitz in the summer of 1944 in crematoria and open pits is 'simply preposterous' and 'beyond the realms of reality,' he declared under oath.

However, another issue fatal to the credibility of this huge improbability is the absolute impossibility of the disposal of all the bodies in crematoria in the time allowed and by the methods deemed to be used. A single body according to our expert, requires 40kg (90 lbs) of coke to incinerate it whilst still leaving the bones to be disposed of separately. Put another way, one tonne of coke could incinerate 25 bodies. If the body was damp or wet then it would require as much as double this amount, so the following facts and figures are all ***absolutely, exceptionally generous***, best-case scenarios.

We know how many tonnes of coke were ordered by the quartermasters at Auschwitz because all the invoices and delivery manifests are all still in existence. The period of greatest consumption of coke was an 8 month period including the winter of 1942-43, where 641 tonnes of coke were ordered and consumed. 641 tonnes of coke is the equivalent of 16,025 cremations, erring **grossly** on the generous side. 16,000+ cremations in 8 months and this is the busiest period at by far the largest, most prolific camp? The numbers simply do not stack-up. These figures, extrapolated over the three years that the alleged gassings took place, would produce a grand total of 72,000 cremations only. Furthermore, it is known for a fact that the camp's heating system and food ovens were coke-fired. These figures account for no coke being set-aside for use in the heating boilers and the food ovens.

Also, generously assuming that the Zionist-quoted death figures are correct, how were the literally millions of unburned bones destroyed? There is no evidence whatsoever at Auschwitz, or any other camp, of any machinery designed to perform this task nor is there any evidence of the requisitioning or delivery of such a machine.

Furthermore, as proof of the reluctance of even bone-dry substances to burn freely and easily, Dr. Töben enlisted the services of a skilled pyrotechnic expert in order to try to replicate, albeit on a much smaller scale, the body-burning pits alleged to have been in use at Auschwitz. A small ***dry*** pit was dug – around 0.5 cubic metres in size and in it were placed four dry, normal size telephone books one on top of the other. A fire was then set using a liberal amount of a mixture of methylated spirits and highly flammable oil. The fire burned quite strongly for about 10 minutes then slowly petered-out. When the pit contents were then examined it could be seen that the top 10% only of the top book had burned, but even then only around the very edges. When the pages were fully opened, the middle portions were entirely untouched by fire. So, another attempt was made, this time the proportional equivalent of 1500 litres (totally impossible at Auschwitz) was used and the fire indeed became a raging inferno, albeit a relatively small one. Twenty minutes passed and again the fire burned itself out. Even with the air able to circulate freely, less than half of the top book was burned and again the bottom three books remained virtually untouched apart from the exposed edges which were slightly scorched – and all this please remember, was dry paper under totally dry conditions. Wet bodies upon wet bodies in wet earth would have no chance whatsoever of burning to ashes.

Töben also set-up another experiment, again on film, whereby two volunteers were locked in a tiny room about the size of a small garden shed, complete with a stone surface, upon which a generous amount of hydrogen cyanide (exactly like Zyklon B,) granules were manually poured – mere inches from their exposed faces. They wore no protective clothing, no gas masks of any kind and were locked in the room for a total of two hours. The room was then unlocked and they casually walked out, laughing and talking as normal. How is this possible? It is easily possible when the ambient room temperature is maintained at less than 26^0 Centigrade.

The granules are only stimulated to produce the deadly gas once this critical temperature is attained. Until that specific point, the granules are entirely harmless and as the volunteers knew that this temperature would not be reached, they were perfectly happy to take part.

However, let the last words on the subject be these, from P. Samuel Foner in '*The Spotlight*,' Volume XIX No. 2, 31st May 2004 . . .

"In a dramatic and unprecedented videotaped interview, Dr. Franciszek Piper, senior curator and director of archives of the Auschwitz State Museum admitted on camera that 'Krema 1,' the alleged 'homicidal gas chamber' shown off to hundreds of thousands of tourists every year at the Auschwitz main camp, was, in fact, fabricated after the war by the Soviet Union – apparently on the direct orders of Josef Stalin.

What Piper said—in effect and on camera—was that the explosive 1988 Leuchter Report was correct; no homicidal gassings took place in the buildings designated as 'homicidal gas chambers' at Auschwitz.

With this admission by none other than the respected head of the Auschwitz State Museum, one of the most sacred 'facts' of history has been destroyed. This 'gas chamber' is the major historical 'fact' on which much of the foreign and domestic policies of all Western nations since WWII is based.

It is the basis for the $100+ billion in foreign aid the United States has poured into the state of Israel since its inception in 1948 – amounting to $16,500 for every man, woman and child in the Jewish state and billions more paid by Germany in 'reparations' – not to *mention the constructing of Israel's national telephone, electrical and rail systems ... all gifts of the German people. It is the basis for the $10 billion 'loan' (read 'gift') made to Israel for housing its immigrants in the occupied territories ... while Americans sleep on the streets and businesses are bankrupted by the thousands. As of 2004, not a single 'loan' of US tax money made to the state of Israel by Washington has ever been paid back.*

Germany is paying 'reparations' – the United States is making major contributions – to atone for the 'gassings at Auschwitz' and elsewhere. If the 'homicidal gas chambers' were post-war creations of the Soviets, in which no one was gassed regardless of race, creed, colour or country of national origin, then these 'reparations' were unnecessary, and were based on fraud.

The videotape on which Dr. Piper makes his revelations was made in mid-1992 by a young Jewish investigator, David Cole and follows twelve years of intensive investigation by dozens of historians, journalists and scientists who have tried to get to the bottom of what really happened at Auschwitz.

Like most Americans, since his youth, Cole had been instructed in the 'irrefutable fact' that mass homicidal gassings had taken place at Auschwitz. The number of those executed – also declared irrefutable – was 4.1 million.

Then came the Leuchter Report in 1988 which was followed with an official, 're-evaluation' of the total deaths at Auschwitz (down to 1.5 million.) As a budding historian – and a Jew – Cole was intrigued.

Previous to 1992, anyone who publicly doubted or questioned the official 4.1 million 'gassing' deaths at Auschwitz was labelled an anti-Semite or neo-Nazi at the very least. Quietly, because of revisionist findings, the official figure was lowered to 1.5 million. No mention was made of the missing 2.6 million.

The Cole videotape interview proves that the people who run the Auschwitz State Museum had made a practice of fabricating 'proofs' of homicidal gassings. Keep in mind that over the years, millions of tourists have been told that 'Krema 1' is in its original state, while officials knew that 'original state' is a lie.

The political, religious, financial and historical ramifications of this proof of no homicidal gas chambers at Auschwitz cannot be measured. Coupled with the Leuchter Report, the Cole interview with Dr. Piper on videotape proves that what Western governments have taught about the Auschwitz gas chambers since WWII is a lie. It proves that what televangelists such as Jerry Falwell and Pat Robertson have been telling their flocks is simply not true.

No one, regardless of race, creed, colour or country of national origin was gassed to death in any building so designated at Auschwitz. And without 'homicidal gas chambers' at Auschwitz, where is the reasoning for the special treatment of the state of Israel?"

Suffice to say that David Cole has been in hiding, in fear of his life for the past, almost 20 years, labelled by the Zionists, as is their custom in these circumstances as a 'self-hating Jew.'

The Zionist, Ilya Ehrenburg, a notorious Jewish propagandist in the USSR who agitated for genocide against Germans and incited the mass-rape of German women by the Red Army, along with another Communist-Jewish propagandist Vasily Grossman, are considered by many revisionists, to be the brains behind the Holocaust hoax. Together they penned '*The Black Book*,' a work of pure fiction dressed-up as fact, inundated with unconscionable, anti-German hate and propaganda horror stories that are physically impossible, and have since been thoroughly discredited.

The one, significant and yet obvious question that the Zionist banksters will NEVER answer, is that if they care so much for the Jewish people, why did they finance the rise of the very same 'evil Nazis,' they constantly vilify and who they claim have gassed 'six million' of their fellow Jews? The simple answer really is that the banksters do not care at all about any race, religion or political belief, the poor masses, be they Jewish or otherwise, are just there to be exploited in whatever way they see fit.

And as for the real 'holocausts,' they were perpetrated by the Zionists, on the civilian populations of Hamburg, Dresden, Berlin, Nagasaki, Hiroshima and Tokyo, to name just a few cities totally annihilated by 'fire.' There are also their non-fiery 'holocausts,' such as the mass butchery of the Communist Soviets against 80 million Russian Christians and all those that opposed communism, Katyn, the Holodomor and the many other atrocities and genocides, that we are definitely not meant to know about and indeed are never discussed openly.

But as regards the alleged 'holocaust' of the Jews, merely writing or saying that you do not believe it happened, questioning the sacred 'six million' number, or even just wishing to debate the facts, can get you arrested and thrown in jail in many 'civilised' countries.

The Zionist-Jews, who created the 'thought-crime,' of racism and are always preaching 'tolerance,' certainly do not tolerate any debate on the 'holocaust.' They created the so-called 'hate speech' laws, as the perfect shield for their evil lies. Questioning them or their motives, will at best bring you an accusation of anti-Semitism, but possibly far worse than that.

Whereas I, enthusiastically encourage you to follow-up with your own research on anything and everything presented to you within this book... The real TRUTH should always be pursued but when it becomes a crime to seek it out, then that is the time to step-up your pursuit of it.

When one thinks of the Holocaust, almost invariably, images come to mind of helpless Jews, languishing in despair within the confines of a German concentration camp. Such compelling imagery, thanks to decades of media brainwashing and subtle indoctrination, has become so deeply ingrained in the psyche of the average person, that not only will any attempt to question the veracity of this narrative be met with strong suspicion, any suggestion that there may have been other 'holocausts' in the past far more horrific than that involving the Jews during WWII, would be quickly dismissed by many as 'anti-Semitic' or a mere 'conspiracy theory.'

Responsible media coverage of past human tragedies can often serve as a very useful and effective tool to convince an otherwise lethargic public to show more compassion for the oppressed and become more aggressively intolerant of all forms of inhumanity wherever and whenever they occur in our world. However, when the plight of the Jews during the 'holocaust' of WWII garners the lion's share of media coverage to the exclusion of comparable tragedies that have affected other peoples, it indicates a chilling double-standard that puts forward the view that the only episode of human suffering worthy of public attention is that which was visited upon the Jews within Nazi Germany.

It goes virtually without saying that most of what has been written and published about Nazi Germany has been negative. Germany, under the leadership of Adolf Hitler, has been demonised in every 'mainstream' history book to such a degree that WWII Germany became and continues to be the veritable poster-child for the denunciation of every form of tyranny and oppression imaginable. It is true that all governments have their dark side, irrespective of what political system they adopt for their people, but often the details that shape the real course of human events lay buried beneath the weight of unscrupulous political ambition of special interests.

During WWII, Germany conducted a pre-emptive round-up millions of civilians, both Jews and non-Jews, in an effort to protect the country from the threat of potential spies, secret combatants, saboteurs and subversives. However this was also true of Britain and the USA too. They also imprisoned their dissidents although we never get to hear about the conditions that they had to endure, do we? Germany placed *their* dissidents in internment camps for the duration of the war and had plans to move them to places like Madagascar at the war's end. There was never a secret plan to exterminate the Jews of Europe. The so-called, 'final solution' was intended to move the Jews out of Germany, not to annihilate them.

However, large numbers of the Jewish population placed in those camps were indeed saboteurs, owing to their extreme leftist political affiliations. A significant number of them were bona fide Marxists and Communists and therefore, most of them were sympathetic to Soviet Russia, a bastion of Judaic-Zionist power and Germany's main adversary. Their ultimate objective was to engineer the total collapse of Germany as a world power and for those reasons, as well as the Germans' fear of the powerful Zionist banksters' attempt to bankrupt the German economy, they had to be detained at in camps as potential subversives and collaborators with the enemies of the State. This was absolutely no different to what happened in the US and Britain, other than the fact that the bulk of British and US detainees, were not actively working to bring those states down from within.

The question that this engenders is maybe, 'but what justified all the deaths that occurred in the camps?' First of all, it should be understood that the vast majority of those placed in the camps died during the closing months of the war. The estimated death toll was probably, less than 600,000 as opposed to that recurring Zionist figure of 'six million' quoted ad nauseum in the history books and elsewhere.

And as previously related, to explain the deaths in the camps, please recall the fact that from late 1944 to early 1945, Allied forces were engaged in a relentless campaign of genocidal bombardment of civilian and military targets that left Germany in an utter shambles. Roads, bridges, rail systems and the entire industrial infrastructure, needed to remain intact in order to guarantee an uninterrupted flow of supplies to both the civilian communities and the camps, but these were mostly destroyed. Consequently, Germany suddenly found itself unable to provide sufficient food, water and medical supplies to its own civilian population, let alone those placed in the internment camps. Ultimately, many people died of starvation throughout the German civilian population, as well as those living in the concentration camps.

There is one survey of the Jewish question in Europe during World War Two and the conditions of Germany's concentration camps which is almost unique in its honesty and objectivity; the three-volume Report of the International Committee of the Red Cross (ICRC) on its activities during the Second World War, Geneva, 1948, which I will refer to as, 'the Report.' This comprehensive account from an entirely neutral and impartial source incorporated and expanded the findings of two previous works, *'Documents sur l'activité du CICR en faveur des civils detenus dans les camps de concentration en Allemagne 1939-1945'* Geneva, 1946, and *'Inter Arma Caritas: the Work of the ICRC during the Second World War'* Geneva, 1947.

The team of authors, headed by Frédéric Siordet, explained in the opening pages of the Report that their object, in the tradition of the Red Cross, had been strict political neutrality, and herein lies its great value. The ICRC successfully applied the 1929 Geneva military convention in order to gain access to civilian internees held in Central and Western Europe by the Germany authorities. But by contrast, the ICRC was unable to gain any access to the Soviet Union, which had failed to ratify the Convention. The millions of civilian and military internees held in the USSR, whose conditions were known to be by far the worst, were completely cut off from any international contact or supervision.

The Red Cross Report is of value in that it firstly clarifies the legitimate circumstances under which Jews were detained in concentration camps, (i.e. as enemy aliens.) In describing the two categories of civilian internees, the Report distinguishes the second type as *"civilians deported on administrative grounds who were arrested for political or racial motives because their presence was considered a danger to the State or the occupation forces"* Vol. 111, p. 73. These persons, it continues, *"were placed on the same footing as persons arrested or imprisoned under common law for security reasons."* P.74. The Report confirms that the Germans were at first reluctant to permit supervision by the Red Cross of people detained on grounds relating to security, but by the latter part of 1942, the ICRC obtained important concessions from Germany.

They were permitted to distribute food parcels to major concentration camps in Germany from August 1942, and *"from February 1943 onwards this concession was extended to all other camps and prisons"* Vol. 111, p. 78. The ICRC soon established contact with camp commandants and launched a food relief program which continued to function until the last months of 1945 – letters of thanks for which, came pouring in from Jewish internees.

The Report further states that *"... as many as 9,000 parcels were packed daily. From the autumn of 1943 until May 1945, about 1,112,000 parcels with a total weight of 4,500 tons were sent off to the concentration camps"* Vol. III, p. 80. In addition to food, these contained clothing and pharmaceutical supplies. *"Parcels were sent to Dachau, Buchenwald, Sangerhausen, Sachsenhausen, Oranienburg, Flossenburg, Landsberg-am-Lech, Flöha, Ravensbrück, Hamburg-Neuengamme, Mauthausen, Theresienstadt, Auschwitz, Bergen-Belsen and to camps near Vienna and in Central and Southern Germany. The principal recipients were Belgians, Dutch, French, Greeks, Italians, Norwegians, Poles and stateless Jews"* Vol. III, p. 83.

During the course of the war, *"The Committee was in a position to transfer and distribute in the form of relief supplies over twenty million Swiss francs collected by Jewish welfare organizations throughout the world, in particular by the American Joint Distribution Committee of New York"* Vol. I, p. 644. This latter organisation was permitted by the German Government to maintain offices in Berlin until the American entry into the war. In fact, the ICRC complained that the obstruction of their vast relief operation for Jewish internees came not from the Germans but from the tight Allied blockade of Europe. Most of their purchases of relief food were made in Rumania, Hungary and Slovakia.

The ICRC also had special praise for the liberal conditions which prevailed at Theresienstadt up to the time of their last visits there in April 1945. This camp, *"where there were about 40,000 Jews deported from various countries was a relatively privileged ghetto"* Vol. III, p. 75. According to the Report ... *"The Committee's delegates were able to visit the camp at Theresienstadt which was used exclusively for Jews and was governed by special conditions."*

From information gathered by the Committee, this camp had been started as an experiment by certain leaders of the Reich ... These men wished to give the Jews the means of setting up a communal life in a town under their own administration and possessing almost complete autonomy ... two delegates were able to visit the camp on 6th April 1945 and they confirmed the favourable impression gained on the first visit." Vol. I, p. 642.

The ICRC received a voluminous flow of mail from Auschwitz until the period of the Soviet occupation, when many of the internees were evacuated westward. But the efforts of the Red Cross to send relief to internees remaining at Auschwitz under Soviet control were futile. However, food parcels continued to be sent to former Auschwitz inmates transferred west to such camps as Buchenwald and Oranienburg.

One of the most important aspects of the Red Cross Report is that it clarifies the true cause of those deaths that undoubtedly occurred in the camps toward the end of the war. The Report states that ... *"In the chaotic condition of Germany after the invasion during the final months of the war, the camps received no food supplies at all and starvation claimed an increasing number of victims. Itself alarmed by this situation, the German Government informed the ICRC on 1st February 1945 ... In March 1945, discussions between the President of the ICRC and General of the SS Kaltenbrunner gave even more decisive results. Relief could henceforth be distributed by the ICRC, and one delegate was authorised to stay in each camp ... "* Vol. III, p. 83.

Clearly, the German authorities were at pains to relieve the dire situation as far as they were able. The Red Cross is quite explicit in stating that food supplies ceased at this time due to the Allied bombing of German transportation, and in the interests of interned Jews they had protested strongly on 15th March 1944 against *"the barbarous aerial warfare of the Allies."* Inter Arma Caritas, p. 78.

By the 2nd October 1944, the ICRC warned the German Foreign Office of the impending collapse of the German transportation system, declaring that starvation conditions for people throughout Germany were becoming inevitable.

In dealing with this comprehensive, three-volume Report, it is important to stress that the delegates of the International Red Cross found no evidence whatever at the camps in Axis-occupied Europe of a deliberate policy to exterminate the Jews. In all its 1,600 pages the Report does not even mention such a thing as a gas chamber. It admits that Jews, like many other wartime nationalities, suffered rigours and privations, but its complete silence on the subject of planned extermination is ample refutation of the 'six million' legend.

Like the Vatican representatives with whom they worked, the Red Cross found itself unable to indulge in the irresponsible charges of genocide which had become the order of the day. So far as the genuine mortality rate was concerned, the Report pointed out that *"... most of the Jewish doctors from the camps were being used to combat typhus on the eastern front, so that they were unavailable when the typhus epidemics of 1945 broke out in the camps."* Vol. I, p. 204.

Typhus was common in prisons and in crowded conditions where lice spread easily, where it was known as *Jail fever* and often occurs when prisoners are frequently huddled together in dark, filthy rooms. Typhus was a real problem in the concentration camps and in the typhus epidemic in the summer of 1942 in the Auschwitz-Birkenau camp from 1st to 19th August, 4,113 deaths were registered, on average 216 per day. This was the main cause of the deaths in Belsen (also Typhoid from contaminated water, and diarrhoea). Typhus victims were stripped after death in order to burn the clothing and destroy the typhus-bearing lice.

All photographs of heaps of corpses were taken in Western camps around the end of the war, such as Dachau, Bergen-Belsen, and Buchenwald, where historians now agree no mass murders took place and significantly, there are no such photographs taken at the camps in which mass murder is alleged to have occurred (Auschwitz, Treblinka, Belzec, Sobibor, Chelmno, Majdanek.)

These eastern camps were all in areas which came under Soviet control at the end of the war and it is extremely significant that the Soviets released no pictures of mass graves or heaps of corpses and allowed no journalists, medical professionals, or other experts to examine the camps.

Incidentally, it is frequently claimed that mass executions were carried out in gas chambers cunningly disguised as shower facilities. Again, the Report makes nonsense of this allegation... *"Not only were the washing places, but installations for baths, showers, and laundry were inspected by the delegates. They had often to take action to have fixtures made less primitive, and to get them repaired or enlarged."* Vol III, p. 594.

Concerning the gas chambers, they did exist but, contrary to mainstream historical accounts, were used to disinfect the prisoners so as to control the spread of typhus. Zyklon B was the principle chemical agent used to achieve this purpose. It was the standard disinfecting chemical agent commonly used throughout Europe at that time and there is absolutely no basis for any suspicion as regards to what use it was put. For example, there is only one large gas chamber found at the infamous Auschwitz camp and it is now openly admitted that it was built after the war by the Russians for propaganda purposes. This fact was acknowledged by the Polish government and do not forget that Auschwitz is located in Poland, not Germany.

There is no blue staining or concentrations of hydrogen cyanide residue as would be expected as a result of repeated exposure to hydrogen cyanide gas in some of the facilities said to have been used for mass extermination, yet there is significant and clearly visible blue staining, as well as high levels of hydrogen cyanide residue, in the facilities where Zyklon B was used for delousing. This blue staining is resilient and penetrating enough that it can be abundantly clear even on the exterior walls of an enclosure that has been exposed to weather for 70+ years.

The alleged washing of the gas chambers, as mentioned in the prior point, is used to explain the lack of blue staining on the walls and the hydrogen cyanide by-products found in test samples in the alleged gas chambers. However, those making this claim are apparently not aware that 1) water apparently has the opposite effect, making the cyanide residue penetrate deeper into the wall, and 2) the humidity as a result of evaporation from the washing would have greatly reduced the rate at which the hydrogen cyanide gas evaporated from the Zyklon B pellets, thereby making subsequent gassing operations dramatically less efficient.

Furthermore, if we put aside the science that indicates otherwise and assume that water would have washed away the cyanide residue and the blue staining with it, then why is there significant blue staining present in the gas chamber at Majdanek, which is known to have been a gas chamber, but not at Auschwitz, which is alleged to be a homicidal gas chamber? If the gas chamber at Majdanek were used for homicidal purposes as alleged, would not it too have been washed down after the gassings?

Volume III of the Red Cross Report, Chapter 3 deals with the *"aid given to the Jewish section of the free population,"* and this chapter makes it quite plain that by no means all of the European Jews were placed in internment camps, but remained, subject to certain restrictions, as part of the free civilian population. This conflicts directly with the 'thoroughness' of the alleged 'extermination programme,' and with the claim in the forged Höss memoirs that Eichmann was obsessed with seizing *"every single Jew he could lay his hands on."*

Not only did large numbers of the three million or so European Jews avoid internment altogether, but the emigration of Jews continued throughout the war, generally by way of Hungary, Romania and Turkey. Ironically, post-war Jewish emigration from German-occupied territories was also facilitated by the Reich, as in the case of the Polish Jews who had escaped to France before its occupation.

"The Jews from Poland who, whilst in France, had obtained entrance permits to the United States were held to be American citizens by the German occupying authorities, who further agreed to recognise the validity of about three thousand passports issued to Jews by the consulates of South American countries" Vol. I, p. 645. As future US citizens, these Jews were held at the Vittel camp in southern France for American aliens and the emigration of European Jews from Hungary in particular proceeded during the war unhindered by the German authorities.

"Until March 1944," says the Red Cross Report, *"Jews who had the privilege of visas for Palestine were free to leave Hungary."* Vol. I, p. 64. As for the so-called Eastern Front, it is true that many Jews were killed there as well. However, it is important to realise that after their invasion of the USSR in 1941, Germany was confronted with not only Soviet troops but tens of thousands of partisan fighters, most of whom were Jewish and thus loyal to the cause of the Soviets. In response to their attacks the German fighters were successful in capturing and killing most of them. So, to allege that these partisans were 'innocent victims' is totally absurd. Those Jews were Soviet assets who actively engaged in guerrilla warfare against the German troops. It was only natural that Germany should defend itself against its enemies.

The lesson to be learned here is that the Zionists have exaggerated the truth about the Jewish death toll and suffering under the Nazis. They have used the 'six million' figure solely as an effective marketing tool and source of propaganda to sell to the world the notion of Jewish victim-hood. As a consequence, Jews in general, worldwide have garnered an incredible amount of sympathy that has always worked to their political advantage. The reason for this being because once a nation's people are viewed as helpless victims, unsuspecting communities of nations who buy into the propaganda tend to become blind to the moral excesses of that group and, in the case of Israeli Jews, be supportive of any human rights violations they may commit against whoever represents their opposition.

Indeed, the cold, hard truth is that the Allies probably killed more Jews from their cruel, relentless targeted bombing of civilians, and the bombing of the Red Cross relief supply trains to the concentration camps that caused prisoners to starve, than the Germans ever did.

So what proof exists that the Nazis killed six million Jews?

None at all. All we have is post-war testimony, mostly of individual 'survivors.' This testimony is extremely contradictory, and very few claim to have actually witnessed any 'gassings.' There are no contemporaneous documents or hard evidence, no mounds of ashes, no crematories capable of disposing of millions of corpses, no 'human soap,' no lamp shades made of human skin, and no credible demographic statistics.

But what evidence exists that six million Jews were *not* killed by the Nazis?

Extensive forensic, demographic, analytical and comparative evidence demonstrates the impossibility of such a figure.

Did Simon Wiesenthal state in writing that *"there were no extermination camps on German soil?"* Yes. The famous 'Nazi hunter' wrote this in *Stars and Stripes*, 24th January 1993. He also claimed that 'gassings' of Jews took place only in Poland.

If Dachau is in Germany, and even famed Nazi hunter Simon Wiesenthal says that it was not an extermination camp, why do many American veterans say it was an extermination camp?

After the Allies captured Dachau, many GIs and others were led through the camp and shown a room alleged to have been a 'gas chamber.' The mass media widely, but falsely, continues to assert that Dachau was a 'death' camp.

What about Auschwitz? Is there any proof that gas chambers were used to kill people there?

No. Auschwitz, captured by the Soviets, was modified *after the war*, and a room was reconstructed to look like a large gas chamber.

If Auschwitz was not a 'death camp,' what was its true purpose?

It was an internment centre and part of a large-scale manufacturing complex. Synthetic fuel was produced there, and its inmates were used as a workforce.

How did German concentration camps differ from American and British internment camps in which Japanese-American and German-British citizens were interned during WW II?

The main, significant difference was that whereas the Germans only interned persons on the basis of being real or suspected security threats to the war effort, the US and British governments interned persons on the basis of ethnicity alone.

Why did the German government intern Jews in camps? It considered Jews a threat to national security. (Jews were overwhelmingly represented in Communist subversion.) However, all suspected security risks, not just Jews, were in danger of internment.

If the Jews of Europe were not exterminated by the Nazis, what happened to them?

After the war, millions of Jews were still living in Europe, and 2,000 were still living normal lives in Hamburg. Hundreds of thousands (perhaps as many as one and a half million) had died of all causes during the war. Others had emigrated to Palestine, the United States, and other countries. Still more Jews left Europe, after the war.

How many Jews fled or were evacuated to the Soviet Union?

More than two million fled or were evacuated by the Soviets in 1941-1942, and thus never came under German control.

How many Jews emigrated from Europe prior to the war, thus putting them outside of German reach?

Perhaps a million (not including those absorbed by the USSR).

If Auschwitz was not an extermination camp, why did the commandant, Rudolf Höss, confess that it was?

He was tortured by British military police, as one of his interrogators later admitted.

Is there any evidence of American, British and Soviet policy to torture German prisoners to extract 'confessions' for use at the trials at Nuremberg and elsewhere?

Yes. Torture was used to produce fraudulent 'evidence' for the infamous Nuremberg trials, and in other post-war 'war-crimes' trials.

How does the Holocaust story benefit Jews today?

It helps protect Jews as a group from criticism. As a kind of secular religion, it provides an emotional bond between Jews and the Zionist leaders. It is a powerful tool in Jewish money-raising campaigns, and is used to justify billions of dollars of foreign aid to Israel.

How does it benefit the State of Israel?

It justifies the billions of dollars in 'reparations' Germany has paid to Israel and many individual 'survivors.' It is used by the Zionist/Israeli lobby to dictate a pro-Israel American foreign policy in the Middle East, and to force American taxpayer aid to Israel, totalling billions of dollars per year.

How did it benefit the Communists?

It completely diverted attention from Soviet war mongering and atrocities before, during and after the Second World War.

Is there any evidence that Hitler ordered the extermination of Europe's Jews?

No, none whatsoever.

For what purpose was 'Zyklon B' manufactured?

It was a pesticide used to fumigate clothing and buildings to kill typhus-bearing lice and other pests.

Was this product suitable for mass extermination?

No. If the Nazis had intended to use poison gas to exterminate people, far more efficient products were available. Zyklon is a slow-acting, high temperature-only fumigation agent.

How long does it take to ventilate an area after fumigation with Zyklon B?

Normally up to 20 hours. The whole procedure is very complicated and dangerous. Gas masks must be used, and only trained personnel are employed.

Auschwitz commandant Höss said that men would enter the 'gas chambers' to remove bodies ten minutes after the victims had died. How do you explain this?

It cannot be explained because had they done so they would have suffered the same fate as the victims. Höss's statements and confession were obtained through extreme duress and torture.

Höss said in his 'confession' that men would smoke cigarettes as they pulled bodies out of gas chambers, ten minutes after gassing. Isn't hydrocyanic gas explosive?

Yes. The Höss confession is provably false.

How could a mass extermination programme have been kept secret from those who were scheduled to be killed?

It could not have been kept secret. The extermination stories originated as wartime atrocity propaganda.

About how many Jews died in the concentration camps?

The International Red Cross audit to January 16, 1984 records a total 282,077 registered deaths of all internees (of whom Jews were very much the minority) in all German Concentration Camps from all causes.

How did they die?

Mainly from recurring typhus epidemics that ravaged war-torn Europe during the war, as well as from starvation and lack of medical attention during the final months of the conflict, when virtually all road and rail transportation had been bombed out by the Allies.

Holocaust historians claim that the Nazis were able to cremate bodies in about ten minutes. How long does it take to incinerate one body, according to professional crematory operators?

About an hour and a half, although the larger bones still remain intact.

Why did the German concentration camps have crematory ovens?

To dispose efficiently and sanitarily of the corpses of those who had died.

Given a 100-percent duty cycle of all the crematories in all the camps in German-controlled territory, what is the maximum number of corpses it would have been possible to incinerate during the entire period such crematories were in operation? About 430,600.

Can a crematory oven be operated 24/7?

No. Fifty percent of the time is a generous estimate (12 hours per day.) Crematory ovens have to be cleaned thoroughly and regularly when in heavy operation.

How much ash is left from a cremated corpse?

After the bone is all ground down, about a shoe box full.

If six million people had been incinerated by the Nazis, what happened to the ashes?

That has never been explained. Six million bodies would have produced many tons of ashes, yet there is no evidence of any large ash depositories at or around any of the camps.

Do Allied wartime aerial reconnaissance photos of Auschwitz (taken during the period when the 'gas chambers' and crematoria were supposedly in full operation) show evidence of extermination?

No. In fact, these photographs do not reveal even a trace of the enormous amount of smoke that supposedly was constantly over the camp, nor do they show evidence of the 'open pits' in which bodies were allegedly burned.

What was the main provision of the German 'Nuremberg Laws' of 1935? They forbade marriage and sexual relations between Germans and Jews, similar to laws existing in Israel today.

Were there any American precedents for the Nuremberg Laws?

In the nineteenth and early twentieth centuries, many US states had enacted laws prohibiting marriage between persons of different races.

What was the role of the Vatican during the time six million Jews were allegedly being exterminated?

If there had been an extermination programme, the Vatican would most certainly have been in a position to know about it. But because there was none, the Vatican had no reason to speak out against it, and indeed it did not.

What evidence is there that Hitler knew of an on-going Jewish extermination program?

None at all.

Did the Nazis and the Zionists collaborate?

As early as 1933, Hitler's government signed an agreement with the Zionists permitting Jews to emigrate from Germany to Palestine, taking large amounts of capital with them. And remember, it was the Zionist banksters that financed the Nazis.

What about the familiar photographs and film footage taken in the liberated German camps showing piles of emaciated corpses? Are these all faked?

Photographs can easily be faked, even 70 years ago, but it is much easier merely to add a misleading caption to a photo or commentary to a piece of footage. Piles of emaciated corpses do not necessarily mean that these people were gassed or deliberately starved to death. Actually, these were tragic victims of raging epidemics or of starvation due to a lack of food in the camps toward the end of the war.

Are films such as *'Schindler's List'* or *'The Winds of War'* accurate?

No. Such films are fictional dramatisations very loosely based on history. Unfortunately, many people accept them as accurate historical representations. Oskar Schindler's widow repeatedly stated that the movie *'Schindler's List'* was untruthful.

What about the charge that those who question the Holocaust story are merely anti-Semitic or neo-Nazi?

This is a smear designed to draw attention away from facts and honest arguments. Scholars who refute the Holocaust story claims are of all political persuasions and ethnic-religious backgrounds (including Jewish.) There is no correlation between Holocaust revisionism and anti-Semitism or neo-Nazism. A number of Jewish scholars openly admit the lack of evidence for key Holocaust claims. They are usually referred to by the rabid Zionists as 'self-hating Jews,' as is their practice.

At the end of the war in 1945 it was said that exterminations occurred regularly at 22 camps throughout Germany and Poland using methods which included electrocution, carbon monoxide, hydrogen cyanide, steam and even boiling water. A mere five years later that figure was officially reduced to just 6 camps, all of which were located in Poland where they could not be properly examined because of their location behind the 'Iron Curtain' and which were controlled by the Soviets.

It is a well-known and acknowledged fact that the allies faked hundreds of photo images after the war, for the purposes of psychological warfare against the German people. These images were part of the 're-education programme,' which also included such ridiculous hoaxes as the Nazis using Jewish-skin for lampshades and their fat for soap – stories that are now thoroughly discredited – even by the mainstream.

The American Lieutenant in charge of documenting Buchenwald (where the infamous 'shrunken heads' story originated) was an operative of the *Psychological Warfare Division* of the Allied Forces. Albert G. Rosenberg was German-Jewish, born and raised in Germany and had only recently become an American. *'Psychological Warfare Division'* is quite a giveaway for a department that was to historically document a concentration camp for future generations, is it not?

Rosenberg was given the go-ahead to confiscate the villa belonging to Baldur Von Schirach, who had been the wartime mayor of Vienna and used the villa, along with several former Buchenwald inmates as a base, to document the 'history' of the camp. The former inmates were all Jewish Communists, except for one non-communist, an Austrian Catholic named Eugen Kogon. Kogon compiled the report whilst Rosenberg supervised the overall project. One could say that the documentation of Buchenwald, is largely a story of liberated communists working under the supervision of a German-Jewish, *Psychological Warfare Division* Lieutenant. In other words, complete objectivity was assured, of course!

The Soviets were in fact already faking pictures during the war, for the purpose of propagandising their own people.

An original, ordinary photo can very easily become a vile piece of propaganda

The fakery was later exposed, but still, the perception of the truth, lingers on regardless

For example, the idea that Nazi Germany made soap out of Jewish body-fat was largely engineered by the legendary Nazi hunter and Mossad agent, Simon Wiesenthal, co-founder of the *Jewish Historical Documentation Centre* in Austria, and founder of the *Simon Wiesenthal Center* in Los Angeles, California. The idea was so popular then that it was later uncritically accepted as fact in popular history books such as *'The Rise and Fall of the Third Reich'* by William L. Shirer.

Even before that, the most famous Jewish propagandist of that era, Ilya Ehrenburg, stated in his book *'The Complete Black Book of Russian Jewry,'* that *"…in another section of the Belzec camp was an enormous soap factory. The Germans picked out the fattest people, murdered them, and boiled them down for soap. The Gestapo thugs never denied the existence of a 'production process' of this kind. Whenever they wanted to intimidate a Jew, they would say to him, 'We'll make soap out of you.'"*

Wiesenthal, according to the secular '*Standard*,' is a 'Nazi Holocaust hero.' He was nominated four times for the Nobel Peace Prize. Yet, until 2009 no one was able to decipher the complete hoaxes and frauds fabricated by Wiesenthal. As the noted British writer, Guy Walters documented . . .

"His reputation is built on sand. He was a liar — and a bad one at that. From the end of the Second World War to the end of his life in 2005, he would lie repeatedly about his supposed hunt for Eichmann as well as his other Nazi-hunting exploits. He would also concoct outrageous stories about his war years and make false claims about his academic career. There are so many inconsistencies between his three main memoirs and between those memoirs and contemporaneous documents, that it is impossible to establish a reliable narrative from them. Wiesenthal's scant regard for the truth makes it possible to doubt everything he ever wrote or said. For his untruths are not the only shocking discoveries I have made researching the escape of Nazi war criminals. I found a lack of political will for hunting them. Many could have been brought to justice had governments allocated even comparatively meagre resources to their pursuit."

When Norman Finkelstein wrote '*The Holocaust Industry: Reflections on the Exploitation of Jewish Suffering*,' in 2000, he argued that Holocaust 'hoaxers' namely Jewish organisations, have exploited what happened in Nazi Germany in order to obtain millions of dollars from Swiss banks. Finkelstein calls those Jewish leaders a *"repellent gang of plutocrats, hoodlums, and hucksters."*

Amazingly, the German government ended up settling claims with 400,000 'survivors,' shortly after WWII, and then in 1965 over 3 million more Jews claimed to be 'survivors,' in order to receive the payments. These were all settled without question as to have not done so would have brought severe criticism upon a country trying desperately to rebuild its world standing, from the international community. For 'international community,' read the 'Zionist international community.'

As the Zionists extorted and enslaved the world, created and profited from all the wars, depressions and famines . . . Their next step was to create the mythology of the so-called holocaust, to foist upon us, to make us believe in it without question, just as we have been conditioned to believe and accept that for example, paying taxes is legal, and that genocide is justified (but only when they indulge in it.)

The Zionists have been engaged in a *psychological war* against us from the very beginning, but most of us are not even aware of it. It is this monumental ignorance and blind faith that has allowed them to control generation after generation of we, the 'sheeple.'

Without the holocaust, there would be no Israel. Without Israel, there would be peace in the Middle-east. Without the Zionist-bankster control of our governments, our laws, education and media, there would be peace and prosperity everywhere in fact. And without the holocaust there would be no 'guilt' to use as a lever for the extraction of money and to gain sympathy. For as much as the Zionist-banksters use, divide and manipulate all of us, they continue to use the ordinary, hardworking, peace-loving Jewish people most of all.

As I have clearly shown, the Zionist-banksters set-up Germany for two World Wars, simply to vilify and tear them down again, in order to reap enormous financial gain and reshape the world to their own model. It also allowed them to create the state of Israel, the instigator of so much strife and mayhem in the Middle-east and indeed worldwide, thus enabling the further and on-going profits that permanent war brings.

As the banksters already control what we see, hear and read about, is it any wonder that they would like to dominate what we think as well? The fabricated idea that 'six million Jews' in Europe were being exterminated by the Germans and others, was regularly promoted by Jewish propagandists and their allies in the West beginning in 1915 during WWI. This slanderous, entirely false accusation had been and continues to be endlessly promoted to the often gullible and susceptible Western public, resulting in extremely negative anti-German sentiment. Many people still 'hate' the German nation for its alleged transgressions in the two wars.

During and immediately following WWII, deceitful propagandists continued to level this 'atrocity propaganda' against the Germans in order to demonise them and prepare the Western world for the institutionalisation of the myth of 'six million Jews' murdered by the Nazis.

Zionist-bankster-controlled Western and Soviet propagandists, including psychological warfare specialists in the United States Army and individuals connected to Hollywood, were heavily involved in manufacturing 'evidence,' including the construction of fake gas chambers, altered or otherwise misrepresented photographs and videos, 'human lampshades,' 'shrunken heads' and other absurd props – all of which were used to demonstrate to the world that the Germans did in fact commit outrageous atrocities during the war, particularly at the various concentration camps and industrial facilities under their administration.

The propaganda used to sell the idea of a 'Jewish Holocaust' is extremely emotionally and psychologically exploitative, resulting in psychological trauma and an inability of the masses to objectively evaluate the information they are being presented with. This will be discussed in more detail shortly.

This photo (above,) depicts Captain Alfred de Grazia, who was the Commanding Officer of the *Psychological Warfare and Propaganda* team attached to the US Seventh Army during World War II. He is standing in front of a pile of bodies outside the

'Baracke X' building at Dachau on 1st May 1945. The men in America's *Psychological Warfare and Propaganda* military unit were mostly Jewish immigrants from Germany, who had been trained at Camp Ritchie in Maryland; they were also known as the 'Ritchie Boys.'

Propaganda, as a weapon of psychological warfare is in even wider use today but Communists were absolute masters of the art. Often they used a direct approach, just as often they employed distraction tactics to focus the eyes and ears of the world in directions other than where the real conflict was being waged. For many years, through propaganda alone, the *non-existent* threat of Hitler and Nazism had been constantly held before the public in a diversionary tactic which kept attention from being directed towards the *actual* threat of Stalin, Khrushchev and Communism in general.

The Diary of Anne Frank

The story contained within Anne Frank's diary, that world famous testimony to the sufferings of a Jewish family during World War II, may well be a true story as far as it goes, but it is one hundred percent certain that what was published and subsequently became a worldwide best seller was not written by Anne Frank herself.

Now, I would be the last to admit to being a handwriting analyst but there can surely be no doubt that those two samples (below) were written by two completely different individuals. I do not believe it possible that one's handwriting could change that much over an entire lifetime let only in someone of poor Anne's tender years. And just to further prove the point, it is strange is it not that the latter example purporting to be her original diary is written in ballpoint pen? Ballpoint pens were invented by a Hungarian by the name of Laszlo Biro in the mid-1940s and did not become commercially available until 1951, well after Anne's death at Bergen-Belsen concentration camp from typhus at the age of fifteen in 1945.

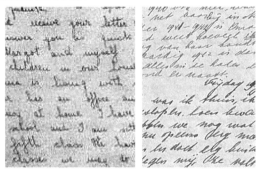

Anne's letter to an American 'penpal'   Anne's diary

Of the above examples of Anne's handwriting, the first example was written to an American pen-friend who introduced the letter to the world after Anne had become posthumously famous and recognised the name – and the other is supposedly taken from the pages of Anne's diary, purportedly written shortly after the first sample.

'The Diary of Anne Frank' was first published in 1952 and immediately became a bestseller. It has been re-published in paperback, with over forty re-printings and it

is impossible to estimate how many people over the last sixty-plus years have been touched and moved in some way by the subject matter.

An interesting question to consider is, why the trial involving the father of Anne Frank, bearing directly on the authenticity of this book has never been officially reported by the overwhelmingly Zionist media? In royalties alone, Otto Frank profited greatly from the sale of this book, purporting to depict events in the tragic life of his family, but is it fact, fiction or propaganda or a combination of all of these? It certainly claims to be the truth but to what degree does it appeal to the emotions through misrepresentation? It was certainly convenient for Otto Frank that he was the only family member to survive the war – and I mean that in the sense of there being no-one left alive to corroborate or deny the story and in no way to diminish the anguish he must have suffered at the loss of his entire family.

School-book publishers have promoted this book for young people for many years, presenting it as the actual work of Anne Frank. Advertising in advance of the release of the movie certainly promoted the drama as being factual but do not writers of such editorials and promoters of such advertising in this way, keep alive the prejudices and hatred they profess to deplore and could this in fact, be the actual objective?

The Franks were upper-class German Jews, both parents emanating from wealthy families. As children, Otto and his siblings lived on the exclusive Meronstrasse in Frankfurt and Otto attended a private preparatory school and also the Lessing Gymnasium, the most expensive school in Frankfurt. Upon leaving school, Otto attended Heidelberg University from whence he eventually graduated.

In 1925 Anne's parents married and settled in Frankfurt, Germany where Anne was born in 1929. The Frank's family business included banking, management of the springs at Bad Soden a famous spa and the manufacture of cough sweets. Anne's mother, born Edith Holländer, was the daughter of a wealthy manufacturing family and in 1934 Otto and family moved to Amsterdam where he bought a spice business, Opekta, which manufactured pectin, a form of gelatine used in the making of household jellies.

In May 1940, after the Germans occupied Amsterdam, Otto remained in the city where his company did business with the German Wehrmacht, whilst his mother and brother moved to Switzerland to escape the German occupation. From 1939 to 1944, Otto sold pectin to the German army to be used as a food preservative, a disinfectant balm for wounds, a thickener for increasing blood volume in blood transfusions and also as an emulsifier of petroleum to be used in the manufacture of fire bombs and flame-throwers. However, by supplying the Wehrmacht, Otto Frank became, in the eyes of many of his Dutch friends and neighbours, a Nazi collaborator. None of this aspect of the official story of course is ever mentioned or even alluded-to.

And also, perhaps significantly, the very fact that the Nazi occupiers were happy to conduct business with a well-known, prominent member of the Jewish community tends to belie the accepted mythology of the definitive persecution of the Jews by the Nazis.

On the 6th July 1942, Otto moved the entire Frank family along with two family friends into the so-called 'secret annex.' The annex was within a three storey townhouse that shared a garden park with fifty other apartments facing inwards to form an approximate square, but was not visible from the street. Whilst allegedly still in hiding, Otto Frank continued to manage his business, venturing downstairs to his office at night and at weekends. Anne and the others would also periodically go to Otto's office and listen to radio broadcasts from England.

The purported diary begins on 12th June, 1942 continuing through to the 5th December 1942. In addition to this first diary, Anne also supplemented it with personal letters. Otto said that Anne heard Gerrit Bolkestein, a Dutch broadcaster, in a wireless programme, ask his listeners to keep a diary and he would publish it after the war and that is why, Otto claimed, she rewrote her diaries for the second time in 1944. In this second edition, the new writer, Anne or whoever it was, changed, rearranged and occasionally combined entries of various dates.

When Anne allegedly rewrote the diaries, she apparently used a ball-point pen (confirmed in Otto Frank's court hearing) which was extremely enterprising of her, since such a device did not exist in 1944 and also the diary was written with literary standards far surpassing those of which even the brightest of fourteen year old children would be capable, reading more like a professionally written documentary than a child's diary.

In 1944, the German authorities in occupied Holland determined that Otto Frank's company had been defrauding them via his extensive and very lucrative Wehrmacht contracts and subsequently the police then raided his offices where during a thorough search the annex was discovered and the eight occupants were sent initially to the *Westerbork* transit camp and forced to perform manual labour. Otto was later sent to Auschwitz and Anne, her sister Margo and her mother subsequently died in one of the frequent outbreaks of typhus in Bergen-Belsen two weeks before liberation by the Allies.

In 1945, after being liberated from German custody, Otto returned to Amsterdam, where he claimed he found Anne's diary cleverly hidden in the rafters of the annex. However, another version of the story tells of a Dutch friend, Meip Geis finding Anne's diary whilst caretaking the building in the Franks' enforced absence, which she then gave to Otto Frank upon his return. Otto took what he claimed were Anne's letters and notes, edited them into a book, which he then gave to his secretary, Isa Cauvern to review. Isa Cauvern and her husband Albert Cauvern, a writer, subsequently authored the first version of the diary.

Upon submitting the diary for publication, questions were raised by some potential publishers as to whether Isa and Albert Cauvern, who assisted Otto in typing out the work, used the original diaries or whether they took it directly from Mr. Frank's personal transcription, but it is known for certain now that the American author, Meyer Levin wrote the third and final edition which became the finished end-product. Meyer Levin was a Jewish author and journalist, who lived for many years in France, where he met Otto Frank around 1949.

If ever file number 2241-1956 in the New York County Clerk's office is opened to public view and its contents widely publicised, then the true nature of this work will be exposed for all to witness. Misrepresentation, exaggeration and falsification has too often coloured the judgment of otherwise decent people and if Frank used the work of Meyer Levin to present to the world what we have been led to believe is the literary work of his daughter, wholly or in part, then the truth should be exposed. To label fiction as fact can never be justified nor should it be condoned.

Otto sued two Germans, Ernst Romer and Edgar Geiss in 1980 for distributing literature denouncing the diary as a forgery. The subsequent court case produced a study by official German handwriting experts that determined that everything in the diary was written by the same person but noted that this person (whoever it was) had used a ballpoint pen throughout! Unfortunately for Frank, as stated previously, the ballpoint pen was not available commercially until 1951 whereas Anne was known to have died of typhus in Bergen-Belsen in February 1945.

Because of this lawsuit in a German court, the German state forensic bureau, the Bundes Kriminal Amt (BKA) forensically examined the manuscript (which at that point in time consisted of three hardbound notebooks and 324 loose pages bound in a fourth notebook) with specialised forensic equipment. The results of these tests, performed at the BKA laboratories, showed that 'significant portions' of the work, including the entire fourth volume, were written with a ballpoint pen and since ballpoint pens were not available before 1951, the BKA concluded those sections must have been added subsequently and fraudulently.

More importantly perhaps, the BKA investigation *clearly* determined that none of the diary handwriting matched known examples of Anne's handwriting. The German magazine, *'Der Spiegel'* published an account of this report alleging that some editing post-dated 1951 and an earlier expert had determined that all the writing in the journal was by the same hand and thus that the entire diary was a post-war fake.

This BKA exposé, as a result of the frantic lobbying of Jewish/Zionist interests was immediately retracted but later 'inadvertently' released to researchers in the United States. I invite the reader to draw his / her own conclusions from this fact.

For what reasons could this fraud have been perpetrated? Were the reasons simply for financial gain or was there a more sinister motive underlying its execution? Could it be part of the overall conspiracy to gain sympathy for the Zionist cause by exaggerating Jewish suffering and casting further aspersions on Nazi activities or is this proposition too unrealistic to contemplate seriously? You decide, but whatever the reason for it, the end result is that the memory of an innocent child-victim has been sullied by being blatantly used either for personal, monetary gain or on behalf of a minority but widely influential group, Zionism in order to surreptitiously benefit certain vested interests. However, perhaps more importantly, this shameful episode further demonstrates how simple is the process by which it is possible to deceive huge numbers of people on virtually any subject one could name by the simple expedient of powerful and persistent propaganda techniques and the constant, incessant repetition of statements designed to create a lasting impression.

But still, the world refuses to believe the truth about the holocaust.

And speaking of 'holocausts,' there *was* actually a 'holocaust' of sorts during and shortly after WWII, but of course we never hear about this particular one…

The 'Rhine Meadows death camps'

To date, the only fully-documented intentional mass-extermination programme in the concentration camps of WWII was actually targeted at Germans. From April, 1945, five million Germans were rounded-up after surrendering, and deliberately mistreated until well over one million had died, in the French and American-run Rhine Meadows concentration camps.

Again, this is the kind of history, the dirty secret that you were not taught in school.

One month before the end of WWII, General Eisenhower issued special orders concerning the treatment of German Prisoners and specific within the language of those orders was this statement, *"Prison enclosures are to provide NO shelter or other comforts."*

Eisenhower's biographer *Stephen Ambrose*, who was given access to the his personal letters, stated that he proposed to exterminate the entire German General Staff, thousands of people, after the war. It is clear from Eisenhower's personal letters, that he did not merely hate the Nazi Regime, and the few who imposed its will down from the top, but that he hated the German race, period and it was his *personal* intent to destroy as many of them as he could, and one way to achieve this was to exterminate as many prisoners of war as possible.

Of course, that was illegal under International law, so he issued an order on 10th March 1945 and verified by his initials on a cable of that date, that German Prisoners of War be re-designated as *"Disarmed Enemy Forces"* referred-to in reports as DEFs. He ordered that as these Germans were now not officially 'prisoners of war' and therefore did not fall under the Geneva Rules, that they were *"not to be fed, nor given any water* or *medical attention."* The Swiss Red Cross was *"not to inspect the camps,"* as under the DEF classification, they had no such authority or jurisdiction. Many months after the war was officially over, Eisenhower's special German DEF camps were still in operation forcing the men into confinement, but still denying that they were 'prisoners.'

The book, *'Other Losses,'* by James Bacque, found its way into the hands of a Canadian news reporter, Peter Worthington of the *Toronto Sun*. He did his own research through contacts he had in Canada, and reported in his column on the 12th September 1989, the following... *"...it is hard to escape the conclusion that Dwight Eisenhower was a war criminal of epic proportions. His (DEF) policy killed more Germans in peace than were killed in the European Theater. For years we have blamed the 1.7 million missing German POWs on the Russians. Until now, no one dug too deeply... Witnesses and survivors have been interviewed by the author; one Allied officer compared the American camps to Buchenwald."*

It is known, that the Allies had sufficient stockpiles of food and medicine to care for these German soldiers but that these were deliberately and intentionally denied them. Many men died of gangrene from frostbite due to *deliberate* exposure.

Colonel James Mason and Colonel Charles Beasley who were in the US Army Medical Corps, published a paper on the Eisenhower death camps in 1950, in which they stated... *"Huddled close together for warmth, behind the barbed wire was a most awesome sight; nearly 100,000 haggard, apathetic, dirty, gaunt, blank-staring men clad in dirty gray uniforms, and standing ankle deep in mud... water was a major problem, yet only 200 yards away the River Rhine was running bank-full."*

In 1945, Martin Brech was an 18 year old, Private First Class in Company C of the 14th Infantry, assigned as a guard and interpreter at the Eisenhower camp at Andernach, along the Rhine River. He stated for *Spotlight*, in February 1990, that... *"My protests regarding treatment of the German DEFs were met with hostility or indifference, and when I threw our ample rations to them over the barbed wire. I was threatened, making it clear that it was our deliberate policy not to adequately feed them. When they caught me throwing C- Rations over the fence, they threatened me with imprisonment. One Captain told me that he would shoot me if he saw me again tossing food to the Germans... Some of the 'men' were really only boys 13 years of age... Some of the prisoners were old men drafted by Hitler in his last ditch stand... I understand that average weight of the prisoners at Andernach was 90 pounds... I have received threats... Nevertheless, this... has liberated me, for I may now be heard when I relate the horrible atrocity I witnessed as a prison guard for one of 'Ike's death camps' along the Rhine."*

Imagine for a moment that you are a young German soldier who survived through the battles of World II. You were not really politically-minded and your parents were also indifferent to politics, but suddenly your education was interrupted and you were drafted into the German army and ordered to fight. Then, in the Spring of 1945, you see that your country and your home-town has been destroyed by the Allies, all the other cities of your country lie in ruins, and half of your family has been killed or is missing. Now, your unit is surrounded, and it is finally time to surrender. The fact is, there is no other choice.

It has been a long, cold winter and army rations have not been all that good, but you managed to survive. Spring came late that year, with weeks of cold rainy weather in Europe. Your boots are shredded, your uniform is falling apart, but they are all the clothes that you have. The stress of surrender and the confusion and uncertainty of what is to come is terrifying you, but now, your war is over and you must surrender or be shot.

So, you are taken as a German PoW along with women civilians too, into American hands. You are marched to a compound surrounded with barbed wire fences as far as the eye can see. Thousands upon thousands of your fellow German soldiers are already in this make-shift corral. You see no evidence of a latrine and after three hours of marching through the mud of the spring rain, the comfort of a latrine is upper-most in your mind. You are driven through the heavily guarded gate and find yourself free to move about, and you begin the futile search for the latrine. Finally, you ask for directions, and are informed that no such luxury exists.

Hundreds more German prisoners are behind you, pushing you on, jamming you together and every one of them searching for the latrine as soon as they could do so. Now, late in the day, there is no space to even squat, much less sit down to rest your weary legs and worse still, none of the prisoners, you quickly learn, have had any food that day. In fact there has been no food at all that any surviving prisoner can testify to. No one has eaten any food for weeks, and they are slowly starving and dying. But, you protest, they can't do this to us! There are rules for the treatment of prisoners of war. There must be some mistake! Hope continues through that first night, with no shelter from the cold, biting rain.

Your uniform is sopping wet, and once-brave fighting men are weeping all around you, as friends begin to die from the lack of food, water, sleep and shelter from the weather. After weeks of this, your own hope turns into despair, and finally you actually begin to envy those who, having surrendered first their dignity, now also surrender life itself. More hopeless weeks go by and finally, the last thing you experience is falling, being unable to get up, and lying face down in the mud mixed with the excrement of those who have gone before.

Your body will be picked up long after it is cold, and taken to a special tent where your clothing is stripped off. So that you will be quickly forgotten, and never identified, your identity dog-tag is cut in half and your body along with those of your fellow soldiers are covered with chemicals for rapid decomposition and buried. You were no exception, for more than one million seven hundred thousand German prisoners of war died in this cruel, inhuman fashion from this deliberate policy of extermination by starvation, exposure, and disease, under direct orders of General Dwight David Eisenhower, future president of the United States.

FDR as you may recall, was controlled by Rothschild Zionist-bankster Bernard Baruch, as was Churchill, so undoubtedly it was he who gave Eisenhower his orders. Baruch had the power to set in motion, as he indeed did, a rapid succession of promotions for Eisenhower, which by-passed many officers who outranked him and who were much more competent and qualified for the posts he occupied. He quickly rose to his ultimate position as Supreme Commander, Allied Expeditionary Force for the invasion of Europe.

It was also Eisenhower, whose open hatred of everything German caused him to promulgate *Operation Keelhaul*, at the end of the war, when thousands of anti-Communist fighters, who had surrendered to American forces, were forced at bayonet point, back to Russia and to the tender mercies of Stalin. Hundreds of thousands of them were subsequently murdered outright, or disappeared forever into the Gulags of Russia.

In 1945, during the post-WW II period, American foreign policy was largely already in the hands of a small group of very powerful Zionists based in Washington DC, ultimately controlled by the Rothschilds. This secret, invisible government, which has been the power in America all along, was headed then by Herbert Lehman, Supreme Court Justice Felix Frankfurter, and Secretary of the Treasury, Henry Morgenthau. They drew up the blueprint for a plan, which bankster-puppet Eisenhower enthusiastically carried-out in Europe, which was the most monstrous policy of hate and vengeance known in the annals of 'civilised' history.

In order to keep a much closer 'watch' on Eisenhower, Winston Churchill and his MI-6 friends, made sure he fell for a beautiful 'honey-trap,' a British agent by the name of Kay Summersby. She was assigned as his military chauffeur and soon became his mistress, all the time that he was in London, North Africa and Europe. Although Summersby secretly despised Eisenhower, she was a loyal British subject, and she successfully carried-off the deception.

The amount of time that Eisenhower had to devote to his career, plus the loss of their first son, had driven him and his wife apart and once the war was underway and he was stationed in Europe, their relationship became even more strained and indeed downright bitter. After the war was over, Eisenhower wrote to his friend and superior, General George Marshall, asking that he be relieved of duty so that he could divorce his wife and marry Kay. But Marshall would not agree and told him bluntly that if he attempted to do so, he would, *"bust him out of the army and make his life hell."*

Besides, the banksters had far more important plans for Eisenhower, but firstly, his fiercest, most vocal opponent had to be dealt with...

The Murder of General Patton

General Patton, perhaps the most popular of the WWII American generals had no qualms about killing enemy soldiers in combat but he absolutely 'drew a line' at the wholesale murder and starvation of helpless prisoners and civilians in his sector of occupation, as advocated by his superiors. However because of this, he came into serious conflict with his superior, Eisenhower and from then on his fate was sealed. It is well-known that the two had on-going, extremely animated debates about how the civilian population of Germany were being treated and Patton was in effect sentenced to death by the directors of this very scenario.

Patton's car was in collision with a military truck in what was regarded as a very 'strange' accident, by its witnesses. The General was taken by ambulance to a hospital, where he was observed to have serious, but not life-threatening injuries. However, despite this, just as he was recovering some days later, he died of a 'heart attack.'

His death was extremely opportune for Eisenhower. Patton had announced that upon his return to the United States, he was going to denounce publicly what was taking place in Germany . . .

"I have a little black book in my pocket and when I get back home I'm going to blow the hell out of everything." General George Patton, August 1945

Unfortunately though, his views had conflicted with too many important people and so Eisenhower ordered that he be silenced, probably under orders himself from the very highest level. Patton's 'black book' was never found.

At the Yalta conference earlier that year (1945) the banksters had agreed via their lackeys, Roosevelt, Churchill and Stalin that the Soviets would be the first to enter the German capital. They needed a strong Soviet presence in Eastern Europe after the war, to maintain the on-going conflict that is their life-blood, in the form of the Cold War and a Western Europe devoid of a Soviet presence would have severely weakened that strategy. Peace was not a desirable state of affairs at all. In fact, as previously related, Patton's troops could quite easily have entered both Berlin and even Prague before the Russians, but were prevented from doing so by an order from Eisenhower.

Patton made no secret of his wish to prevent the entrance of the Red Army into Berlin and in so doing made an enemy of the 'controlled' Eisenhower. He was furious to be informed by his superiors that he was to refrain from taking Berlin. He, as did they, knew that it would have been simple for the Americans to reach Berlin before the Russians and thus gain control of the entire country but that would have been contrary to the Elite's plan for the instigation of the Cold War in the succeeding years which partly hinged upon the division of Germany into the two separate states of 'East' and 'West.' The American progress eastwards through Western Europe had been much swifter than the Russians westward march. In the main this was due to the Germans' readiness to surrender to the British and Americans as they knew that surrendering to the Russians was probably a death sentence. Hence many German units on the eastern front fought to the death of the last man in their futile bid to stop the advancing Russian juggernaut.

Patton's difficulties with the bankster-controlled 'powers that be' over the occupation of Germany were so great that Eisenhower stripped him of his position as Commander of the Third Army and gave him command of a secondary, lesser unit. In fact Patton suspected that his life was in danger and confided as much to his family and close friends. He was feared because of his prestige, popularity and influence on public opinion and was undoubtedly the most renowned American combat General, whilst Eisenhower was nothing more than a 'political soldier,' and Patton's words, if not curbed in some way, would alert the public to the true realities of what was happening in Germany.

Thus the aforementioned accident was arranged and carried-out, but it was not by any means the first. On the 21st April 1945, the plane on which he was being transported to General Headquarters of the Third Army in England was attacked by what was assumed to be a German fighter, but it turned out to be a Spitfire piloted by a Polish RAF pilot. Patton's plane was shot at and badly hit, but was miraculously able to land safely. Then on the 3rd May, some days before the end of the war, the General's jeep was charged by an ox-drawn cart, leaving Patton with light injuries.

The collision with the truck occurred on the 13th October 1945, but just as Patton appeared to be recovering after the accident, the so-called 'heart attack' occurred. The fact is, that after the 13th October only doctors were allowed to see Patton, with all other visitors forbidden. From the hospital, Patton contacted his wife in America in a vain attempt to get her to have him moved from the hospital because, he said, quite accurately, "*They're going to kill me here.*"

For many years it was only speculation that Patton had been assassinated. But now it is known for a fact to be the truth, for one very simple reason. An agent of the OSS (the forerunner of the CIA) an American military spy, Douglas Bazata, a Jew of alleged Lebanese origin, announced before 450 invited guests; high ranking, ex-members of the OSS and CIA, in the Hilton Hotel in Washington, DC on the 25th September, 1979...

"For diverse political reasons, many extremely high-ranking persons hated Patton. I know who killed him because it was I. I am the one who was hired to do it. I was paid ten thousand dollars and General William Donovan himself, director of the OSS, entrusted me with the mission. I also set up the accident but since he didn't die in the accident, he was kept in isolation in the hospital, where he was killed by me with a cyanide injection."

Apparently, Donovan had told Bazata, *"We've got a terrible situation with this great patriot, he's out of control and we must save him from himself and from ruining everything the allies have done."*

The tragic fate of Patton convinced many others of his loyal colleagues and their honourable compatriots of the uselessness of fighting against the bankster-controlled war powers.

The plot to dispose of Patton was undertaken simply because the banksters wished to prolong the conflict following the end of WWII, not merely to garner more profits from arms sales and to increase the debts of fighting nations, to them, but also to allow for the emergence of the Soviet Union, as a major global power. That would guarantee future conflict for many years to come in the shape of the Cold War and a repetition of the same cycle of war through the 'communism versus democracy' dialectic.

In fact many reputable writers even go as far as saying that Donovan was a British agent. Bazata also believed so. In fact it was the British envoy to the US, Sir William Stephenson, himself an intelligence operative carrying the codename *Intrepid*, who worked towards convincing the US President, of the need for setting-up an intelligence organisation, which was then named OSS, which was the previous incarnation of the CIA. He subsequently manoeuvred to have Donovan appointed as Chief of the OSS and triumphantly reported to Stewart Menzies, the British intelligence chief… "*You can imagine how relieved I am after three months of battle and jockeying for position that our man [Donovan] is in a position of such importance to our efforts.*"

Of course, the banksters control all national intelligence agencies, deliberately engineered the two World Wars, the Bolshevik Revolution and controlled the Bolshevik leadership and also funded the Nazis. The collaboration between the OSS and NKVD during WWII, was therefore hardly surprising.

The Nuremberg 'Trials' – A Travesty of Justice

World War II in Europe may have *officially* ended in May 1945, but the period of chaos that followed, lasted for at least five more years. All across Europe, landscapes had been ravaged, entire cities ruined, and millions of people had been killed or displaced in the war. Institutions such as the police, the media, transport and local and national governments were either gone or virtually non-existent. As a result of this, crime rates soared, economies collapsed, hungry women and girls turned to prostitution as the European population hovers on the brink of starvation, and a kind of general anarchy prevails.

Communists, liberals and Jews now used this utter anarchy to impose a cruel vengeance upon their helpless prey. German civilians and their anti-Communist allies everywhere were rounded up, raped, sodomised, drowned in cesspools, tortured, mutilated, burned alive, and executed.

Further massacres and civil wars followed in Greece, Yugoslavia and Poland, as well as parts of Italy and France. In some of the worst acts of ethnic-cleansing the world has ever seen, tens of millions were expelled from their ancestral homelands, as Eisenhower's Allied occupiers 'looked the other way.' The 2012 book *Savage Continent* by Keith Lowe, documented much of this disturbing story in gruesome detail.

But amidst all this death and destruction, the Allies somehow found time to stage the Nuremberg Trials. They were only really show trials of course, of which Stalin and Hitler themselves would have been proud. Pre-determined and as predictable as a TV legal drama, only in this case, the real perpetrators of the worst excesses of war, were not even questioned, let alone indicted. And of course, the worst of them all Joseph Stalin, perhaps the mass-murderer of the Millennium if not of all-time, was not even mentioned.

Roosevelt's eulogists likewise avoided the subject of Stalin, for whom FDR had the highest regard, referring to him as 'a Christian gentleman' during the Yalta conference. He had befriended Stalin from the first year of his administration, when he extended diplomatic recognition to the murderous pariah state of the USSR and time and again, chose to help Stalin when he did not have to, appeasing him from a position of strength. Then when FDR asked Pope Pius XII to condemn Hitler, Pius sent back word that if he did so he would also have to condemn Stalin and so Roosevelt withdrew his request.

And as for Churchill, we are assured that he had no illusions about Stalin, which only makes his wartime indulgence of the tyrant harder to excuse. His 1946 complaint (in a famous speech in Fulton, Missouri) about the *'Iron Curtain'* falling on Eastern Europe after World War II is treated as prophetic, when it was just the opposite, a totally hypocritical gesture. Anyone who did not know what to expect of Stalin by 1946, or who could believe his 'guarantees' at Yalta in 1945, was a moron, but Churchill was no moron, merely a cynic feigning alarm at the obvious.

Stalin had shown his true colours long before Roosevelt and Churchill took him on as their ally. Had they never heard of the Holodomor in Ukraine, the NKVD mass arrests, the Gulag camps, the purges and show trials, the murder of Trotsky, the invasions of Poland and most of the rest of eastern Europe, the Katyn Forest massacre of 15,000 Polish officers not to mention the tens of millions of his own citizens ethnically cleansed for the heinous crime of being anti-Communist or simply Christians?

All these things, and more, revealed not only the brutality of Stalin but the logic of Communism itself, which had begun its reign in Russia with the mass murder of Orthodox priests under Lenin. Communism was in essence a reversion to the principles of primitive warfare, directed not only against external enemies but against its own subjects if they resisted or were even suspected of a disposition to resist its tyranny.

The alliance with the Soviet Union was a permanent bloodstain on the Western democracies and was part of what F.J.P. Veale, a British jurist, called the Allies' *"advance to barbarism"* in his mercilessly trenchant book of that title. But Veale was not as well-informed as you are now, about the role of the banksters in all of this intrigue and chicanery.

The exaltation of the 'Stalin-lovers' as the heroes of the century, and 'saviours of civilisation,' is an almost incomprehensible paradox. It is almost as though we were being asked to believe that the greatest peace-advocates of the Middle Ages, say, Innocent III, Dante and St. Francis of Assisi had been friends and admirers of Genghis Khan.

Veale ranked the Allies' policies of terror-bombing and 'war-crimes' trials with 'Hitler's genocide' as the distinguishing features of the *"retrograde movement of civilisation"* that culminated in World War II. However Veale was almost certainly unaware that

Hitler's so-called 'genocide' was in fact non-existent and completely invented, in order to render him and his regime a byword for evil, for evermore.

The readiness with which Churchill and Roosevelt embraced Stalin as an ally after Hitler attacked Russia in 1941 was only one indication of the new 'morality' of warfare that they were prepared to adopt. They unconditionally forgave Stalin's part in the rape and destruction of Poland that began in 1939 and even entrusted him, at the war's end in 1945, with absolute control of Poland and indeed the rest of Eastern Europe. Of course at the time it suited their own (the banksters') agenda perfectly and was a classic example of the double-standards in politics that not only persist, but flourish, even to this day.

When the trials began at Nuremberg, there were a few 'irregularities.' For example, the accusers (including Soviet judges with long experience in Stalinist methods of the dispensation of 'justice') doubled as jurors and the court was as a result, never impartial from the outset. The accused were in fact judged guilty before the proceedings began and the evidence presented was completely one-sided, its intention being solely to provide 'proof' of guilt. The rules of evidence totally limited the defence in as much as the defendants were not permitted to argue that the Allies had committed the same acts of which they were being accused.

Even so, the Germans were never tried for bombing civilian areas, because the Allies did not want to risk drawing attention to the fact that they themselves had initiated this particular 'crime against humanity.' And the creative charge of 'waging a war of aggression' was never defined either, because no definition could be found that would cover the German invasion of Poland without also covering the Soviet invasions of Poland and several other countries also.

Such treatment of prisoners of war was also a departure from the previous rules, which the Allies justified by arbitrarily declaring the captured German military officers to be civilians. This made them eligible to be tried as criminals under the inchoate new rules. The purpose of the trials was not to do justice or to determine guilt according to normal standards of law (which forbade ex post-facto trials,) but to give the Allies a propaganda victory in addition to their military triumph.

In essence, the Germans were convicted of losing the war. The only real 'war crime,' was being defeated. The honourable German admiral Erich Raeder, for example, was convicted for invading Norway, though he had simply arrived slightly in advance of the British, on the eve of their own planned invasion.

The whole thing was a shameful, contrived farce which set its own precedents for the pursuit of aging 'war criminals' that still continued until recently. The only reason that this incessant pursuit has now been wound-down is that seventy plus years after the event, most of the protagonists are now long-dead. When similar trials were held in Tokyo two years later, an Indian jurist who participated decried the proceedings, thus … *"The farce of a trial of vanquished leaders by the victors was itself an offence against humanity."* No Western jurist had ever found the courage to say as much at Nuremberg.

The Allied crimes have never been acknowledged, except maybe as wartime necessities justified by noble ends and the Allied criminals have never been brought to justice. Instead, they are still honoured as the 'heroes' of the twentieth century. Even the memory of the odious 'Bomber' Harris, long ostracised with distaste and moral embarrassment by the British Establishment for his rather unseemly enthusiasm for killing civilians, was honoured by the erection of a statue in London.

The first and most well-known of the show trials was the 'Trial of the Major War Criminals before the International Military Tribunal.' This was the show trial of the twenty-four most important, captured leaders of Germany. It was held from the 20th November 1945 to the 1st October 1946. There were prosecutors and judges from the United States, Great Britain, France and the Soviet Union. 100,000 documents were accepted into evidence and the transcript of the trial filled 42 volumes with more than 5 million words. According to the US *Holocaust Memorial Museum*, Allied prosecutors submitted some 3,000 tons of documents but the defence was not allowed access to any except the ones that were actually 'used' by the prosecution.

The entire Nuremberg International Military Tribunal trial was captured on film and shown to the world on TV and newsreels which showed the city as a pile of rubble, which had not yet been cleared when the trial started. In fact, the bodies of 20,000 German civilians were still buried under the destroyed buildings as the German 'war criminals' were ushered into the courtroom of the Palace of Justice. The Palace of Justice itself had suffered some damage in the Allied bombing of Nuremberg, but it had been restored by the forced labour of the conquered Germans before the trial began.

It was at these trials that the whole world learned for the first time about the 'German atrocities,' including all the gory details of the 'shrunken heads,' the 'soap made from human fat,' the leather goods 'made from the skin' of concentration camp prisoners, and the gas chambers which accounted for the majority of the deaths at Auschwitz and Majdanek, where the Russians testified that not less than 4 million people had died in the Auschwitz complex and another 1.5 million had died at the Majdanek camp. Today, the 'official' figures given for these camps, are 1.1 million deaths at Auschwitz and 78,000 at Majdanek, including 59,000 Jews. And as demonstrated previously, most of the Nazi 'horrors' were fabricated for Soviet and Allied propaganda, indeed for the banksters' evil propaganda. A starved and diseased body looks just as wretched, just as heart-wrenching, as one presented as 'gassed.' But then, the trials were never about seeking the truth.

The selection of photos below, taken when the concentration camps were liberated and showing the majority of prisoners as they really were, certainly were not entered into evidence for the defence.

Liberation of Dachau | Liberation of Mauthausen | Liberation of Auschwitz

The Nuremberg proceedings violated almost all ancient and fundamental principles of justice. The victorious Allies acted as prosecutor, judge and executioner of the German leaders and the violations were created especially for the occasion and were applied only to the vanquished. Defeated, starving, prostrate Germany was however, in no position to oppose whatever the Allied occupation powers demanded.

As even some leading Allied figures privately acknowledged at the time, the Nuremberg trials were organised not to dispense impartial justice, but for political purposes. Sir Norman Birkett, a British judge at the Nuremberg Tribunal, explained in a private letter in April 1946 that ... " ... *the trial is only in form a judicial process and its main importance is political.*"

Robert Jackson, the chief US prosecutor and a former US Attorney General, declared that the Nuremberg Tribunal ... "... *is a continuation of the war effort of the Allied nations*" against Germany. He added that the Tribunal ... "... *is not bound by the procedural and substantive refinements of our respective judicial or constitutional system ...*"

Judge Iola T. Nikitchenko, who presided at the Tribunal's solemn opening session, was a vice-chairman of the supreme court of the USSR before and after his service at Nuremberg. In August 1936 he had been a judge at the infamous Moscow show trial of Zinoviev and Kamenev. At a joint planning conference shortly before the Nuremberg Tribunal convened, Nikitchenko bluntly explained the Soviet view of the enterprise, thus:

"*We are dealing here with the chief war criminals who have already been convicted and whose conviction has been already announced by both the Moscow and Crimea [Yalta] declarations by the heads of the [Allied] governments ... The whole idea is to secure quick and just punishment for the crime ... The fact that the Nazi leaders are criminals has already been established. The task of the Tribunal is only to determine the measure of guilt of each particular person and mete out the necessary punishment – the sentences.*"

Indicative of the largely political nature of the Nuremberg process was the important Jewish role in organising these trials. Nahum Goldmann, one-time president of both the *World Jewish Congress* and the *World Zionist Organization*, reported in his memoirs that the Nuremberg Tribunal was the brain-child of *World Jewish Congress* officials. Only after persistent effort, were WJC officials able to persuade Allied leaders to accept the idea, he added. The *World Jewish Congress* also played an important but less obvious role in the day to day proceedings. Above all, the powerful but secretive organisation made sure that Germany's 'persecution of the Jews,' was a primary focus of the trials, and that the defendants were punished for their involvement in that process.

Two Jewish officers in the US Army, Lieutenant-Colonel Murray Bernays and Colonel David 'Mickey' Marcus, played key roles in the Nuremberg sham. In the words of historian, Robert Conot, Bernays was *"the guiding spirit leading the way to Nuremberg."* Indeed it was Bernays, a successful New York attorney, who personally persuaded US War Secretary Henry Stimson and others to accept the idea of putting the defeated German leaders on trial.

Marcus, a fervent Zionist, became the 'number three man in making American policy,' in occupied Germany and as chief of the US government's *War Crimes Branch* in 1946 and 1947, he selected almost all of the judges, prosecutors and lawyers for the Nuremberg NMT Trials. (He later became a commander of the Zionist 'Haganah' military forces in Palestine, whose despicable, bloody exploits paved the way for the theft of that country and which eventually became Israel.

Some of the Americans who participated in the Nuremberg trials became disillusioned with the entire business. One of the few to make public his feelings was Charles F. Wennerstrum, an Iowa Supreme Court justice who served as presiding judge in the Nuremberg trial of German generals, and also at some of the twelve subsequent Nuremberg Trials, and was even the presiding judge in the Hostages Trial, where twelve Germans were tried, but the severest sentence handed-down was life imprisonment.

"If I had known seven months ago what I know today, I would never have come here," he declared immediately after sentences were pronounced. *"The high ideals announced as the motives for creating these tribunals have not been evident,"* he added.

After eight months at Nuremberg, Wennerstrum gave an interview to Hal Foust, a journalist for the Chicago Daily Tribune, who was in Nuremberg covering the trials. Wennerstrum expressed his disgust about how the trials had been conducted, cautiously referring to the extensive Jewish involvement in the Nuremberg process…

"The entire atmosphere here is unwholesome… Lawyers, clerks, interpreters and researchers were employed who became Americans only in recent years, whose backgrounds were embedded in Europe's hatreds and prejudices. Most of the evidence in the trials was documentary, selected from the large tonnage of captured records. The selection was made by the prosecution and the defence had access only to those documents which the prosecution considered material to their case… The trials were to have convinced the Germans of the guilt of their leaders. They convinced the Germans merely that their leaders lost the war to tough conquerors." He left Nuremberg, *"…with a feeling that justice has been denied."*

The journalist Hal Foust also complained that the US military had intercepted his article being transmitted back to America and how he was given a rebuttal of Judge Wennerstrum's comments, before they had even been published. Foust also stated that it was not the first time that the US Military had incepted his articles being transmitted back to America. After sending a tele-ticker of his exposé of the corruption at the

Military Government's Rest and Recreation Centre in Garmisch, in the Bavarian Alps, he had been picked-up and interrogated by the American Military only hours later.

US Supreme Court Chief Justice Harlan Fiske Stone, also remarked with irritation... *"Jackson is away conducting his high-grade lynching party in Nuremberg. I don't mind what he does to the Nazis, but I hate to see the pretence that he is running a court and proceeding according to common law. This is a little too sanctimonious a fraud to meet my old-fashioned ideas."* In a private letter he also wrote... *"...I wonder how some of those who preside at the trials would justify some of the acts of their own governments if they were placed in the status of the accused?"*

On another occasion Stone specifically wondered, *"...whether, under this new [Nuremberg] doctrine of international law, if we had been defeated, the victors could plausibly assert that our supplying Britain with fifty destroyers in 1940, was an act of aggression..."*

In Congress, US Representative Lawrence H. Smith of Wisconsin declared... *"The Nuremberg trials are so repugnant to the Anglo-Saxon principles of justice that we must forever be ashamed of that page in our history... The Nuremberg farce represents a revenge policy at its worst."*

Another Congressman, John Rankin of Mississippi, stated... *"As a representative of the American people I desire to say that what is taking place in Nuremberg, Germany, is a disgrace to the United States... A racial minority, two and a half years after the war closed, are in Nuremberg not only hanging German soldiers but trying German businessmen in the name of the United States."*

But probably the most courageous condemnation was by US Senator Robert A. Taft, widely regarded as the 'conscience of the Republican party.' At considerable risk to his political career, he denounced the Nuremberg enterprise in an October 1946 speech, thus...

"The trial of the vanquished by the victors cannot be impartial no matter how it is hedged about with the forms of justice. About this whole judgment there is the spirit of vengeance, and vengeance is seldom justice. The hanging of the eleven men convicted will be a blot on the American record which we will long regret. In these trials we have accepted the Russian idea of the purpose of trials – government policy and not justice – with little relation to Anglo-Saxon heritage. By clothing policy in the forms of legal procedure, we may discredit the whole idea of justice in Europe for years to come."

Milton R. Konvitz, a Jewish specialist of law and public administration who lectured at New York University, warned at the time that the Nuremberg Tribunal... *"...defies many of the most basic assumptions of the judicial process. Our policy with respect to the Nazis is consistent with neither international law nor our own State Department's policy... The Nuremberg trial constitutes a real threat to the basic conceptions of justice which it has taken mankind thousands of years to establish."*

In the years since, distinguished figures in both the United States and other countries have expressed similar views. US Supreme Court Justice William O. Douglas wrote, *"I thought at the time and still think that the Nuremberg trials were unprincipled. Law was created ex post-facto to suit the passion and clamour of the time."*

While the Nuremberg trials were underway, and for some time afterwards, there was much talk about the universal validity of the new legal code established there. A new age of international justice had begun, it was claimed. Many sincerely believed that the four Allied powers would themselves abide by the Tribunal's standards. As it happened, none of the four powers that participated in the Tribunal ever made the slightest effort to apply the principles so solemnly and self-righteously proclaimed at Nuremberg either to their own leaders or to those of any other country.

In conducting the Nuremberg trials, the Allied governments themselves violated international law. For one thing, their treatment of the German defendants and the military prisoners who testified violated articles 56, 58 and others of the Geneva Convention of July 1929. Justice – as opposed to vengeance – is a standard that should be applied equally and impartially. Chief US prosecutor Robert Jackson privately acknowledged in a letter to President Truman that the Allies … *"… have done or are doing some of the very things we are prosecuting the Germans for. The French are so violating the Geneva Convention in the treatment of German prisoners of war that our command is taking back prisoners sent to them. We are prosecuting plunder and our Allies are practicing it. We say aggressive war is a crime and one of our allies asserts sovereignty over the Baltic States based on no title except conquest."*

In violation of the Nuremberg accusation of Germany's, *"planning, preparation, initiating or waging a war of aggression,"* the Soviet Union had attacked Finland in December 1939 and was expelled from the League of Nations as a result. A few months later, the Red Army invaded Lithuania, Latvia and Estonia, and ruthlessly incorporated them into the Soviet Union. The post-war French government violated international law and the Nuremberg charge of *"maltreatment of prisoners of war,"* by employing large numbers of German prisoners of war as forced labourers in France. In 1945 the United States, Britain and the Soviet Union jointly agreed to the brutal deportation of more than ten million Germans from their ancient homelands in eastern and central Europe, a violation of the Nuremberg count of, *"deportation, and other inhumane acts committed against any civilian population."*

While Allied prosecutors charged the defendants with a 'crime against peace' in planning the German invasion of Norway in 1940, the British government eventually had to admit that Britain and France were themselves guilty of the same 'crime' in preparing a military invasion of Norway, code-named 'Stratford,' before the German move. And in August 1941, Britain and the Soviet Union jointly invaded and occupied Iran, a neutral nation. Given this record, it is hardly surprising that the four governments that organised the Nuremberg trial of 1945-1946 included no definition of 'aggression' in the Tribunal's Charter.

Indeed, the Soviet role in the proceedings, which the United States fully supported, moved American diplomat and historian George F. Kennan to condemn the entire Nuremberg enterprise as a 'horror' and a 'mockery.'

Perhaps nothing better illustrates the essential character of the Nuremberg proceedings than the appalling treatment of Rudolf Hess, Hitler's deputy. Hess was sentenced to life imprisonment, dying in Spandau prison in 1987 where he had been kept in solitary confinement for **forty years**, even though he alone of leading figures of the countries involved in the Second World War risked his life in a dangerous, but ultimately fruitless effort to conclude peace between two of the warring nations. The highly-respected British historian, A.J.P. Taylor succinctly summed-up the injustice of the Hess case and, by implication, of the entire Nuremberg enterprise...

"Hess came to this country in 1941 as an ambassador of peace. He came with the intention of restoring peace between Great Britain and Germany. He acted in good faith. He fell into our hands and was quite unjustly treated as a prisoner of war. After the war, we should have released him. Instead, the British government of the time delivered him for sentencing to the International Tribunal at Nuremberg... No crime has ever been proved against Hess... As far as the records show, he was never at even one of the secret discussions at which Hitler explained his war plans."

Officially Hess died by suicide on the 17th August 1987 aged 93, the last of the prisoners to be tried at Nuremberg and was one of the oldest prisoners in the world, having spent 46 years of his life locked-up. He was found in a summer house in the garden located in a secure area of the prison with an electrical cord wrapped around his neck. His death was ruled a suicide by self-asphyxiation, accomplished by tying the cord to a window latch in the summer house.

However marks on his neck found by later autopsies corresponded to strangulation or throttling rather than hanging. In the final years of his life, Hess was a weak and frail old man, blind in one eye and only able to walk stooped forward with a cane. He lived in virtually total isolation according to a strictly regulated daily routine. Regulations stipulated that prison officials could not ever call Hess by name. He was addressed only as 'prisoner No. 7.' Prison guards who knew him in his last years said that he was so crippled by arthritis that he could not lift his arms above his shoulders and therefore there was no way that this crippled old man could have strangled himself.

The sheer quantity of paper seized by the Allies was staggering. For example, the records of the German Foreign Office confiscated by US officials amounted to some 485 *tonnes* of paper. And yet, out of this great mass of paper, not a single document has ever been found that confirms or even refers to an 'extermination programme' of the Jews. A number of historians have commented on this remarkable 'gap' in the evidence. French-Jewish historian Leon Poliakov, for example, noted in his best-known Holocaust work... "...*only the campaign to exterminate the Jews, as regards its conception as well as many other essential aspects, remains shrouded in darkness.*" No documents of a plan for exterminating the Jews have ever been found, he added, because "...*none ever existed.*"

After the Nuremberg Tribunal pronounced its sentence, Foreign Minister von Ribbentrop pointed out some of the obstacles erected in his own case... *"The defence had no fair chance to defend German foreign policy. Our prepared application for the submission of evidence was not allowed ... Without good cause being shown, half of the 300 documents which the defence prepared were not admitted. Witnesses and affidavits were only admitted after the prosecution had been heard; most of them were rejected ... Correspondence between Hitler and Chamberlain, reports by ambassadors and diplomatic minutes, etc., were rejected. Only the prosecution, not the defence, had access to German and foreign archives. The prosecution only searched for incriminating documents and their use was biased. It knowingly concealed exonerating documents and withheld them from the defence."*

It is often claimed that the evidence presented by the prosecution to the Nuremberg Tribunal was so incontrovertible that none of the defence attorneys ever disputed the authenticity or accuracy of even a single prosecution document. This is categorically untrue. Not only did defence lawyers protest against the prosecution use of spurious documents, but some of the most important Nuremberg documents are now generally acknowledged to be fraudulent. For example, defence attorney Dr. Boehm protested to the Tribunal that Nuremberg document 1721-PS, which purportedly confirms attacks by storm-troopers against Jewish synagogues in November 1938, is a clumsy forgery.

Almost forty years after the Tribunal handed down its verdicts, Nuremberg document USSR-378 was definitively exposed as a fraud. It is a purported record of numerous private conversations with Hitler by Hermann Rauschning, a former National Socialist official in Danzig. In brutal language, Hitler supposedly revealed his most intimate thoughts and secret plans for world conquest. Rauschning's 'memoir' was published in 1939 in Britain under the title '*Hitler Speaks*,' and in the United States in 1940, melodramatically as '*The Voice of Destruction*.' It was this US edition that was accepted in evidence at Nuremberg as proof of the *"guiding principles of the Nazi regime."*

Another fraudulent Nuremberg document was the so-called 'Hossbach protocol' (document 386-PS), a purported record of a high-level 1937 conference at which Hitler supposedly revealed his secret plans for aggressive conquest of the world. US Nuremberg prosecutor Sidney Alderman referred to it as ... *"... one of the most striking and revealing of all the captured documents,"* and told the Tribunal that it removed any remaining doubts about the guilt of the Germans leaders for their crimes against peace. It was largely on the basis of this document that Göring was condemned to death.

Along with the millions of people around the world who avidly followed the Nuremberg proceedings by radio and newspaper, the defendants themselves were shocked by the evidence presented to substantiate the extermination charge. Above all, the testimonies of Auschwitz commandant, Rudolf Höss and Einsatzgruppen commander Otto Ohlendorf, made a deep impression. Contrary to what is often claimed or insinuated, however, the Nuremberg Tribunal defendants declared that they were absolutely unaware of any extermination programme during the war and indeed protested vehemently that if there had been such a policy of extermination that they would certainly have known of it. These men were, in a sense, the first 'Holocaust revisionists.'

The principal Nuremberg defendant, Hermann Göring, who had been Hitler's second-in-command and designated successor during most of the Third Reich years, vehemently denied knowledge of any extermination program during the war. *"The first time I learned of these terrible exterminations, was right here in Nuremberg,"* he exclaimed at one point. The German policy had been to expel the Jews, not kill them, he explained, and added that, to the best of his knowledge, Hitler was unaware of any extermination policy either.

Hans Frank, the wartime governor of German-ruled Poland, testified that during the war he had heard only rumours and foreign reports of mass killings of Jews. He had asked other officials, including Hitler, about these stories and was repeatedly assured that they were false.

Frank's testimony is particularly noteworthy because if millions of Jews had actually been exterminated in German-occupied Poland, as alleged, hardly anyone would have been in a better position to know about it. During the course of the trial, Frank was overcome by a deep sense of Christian repentance. His psychological state was such that if he had known about an extermination programme, he would have said so.

The case of Albert Speer, one-time Hitler confidant and wartime Armaments Minister, deserves special mention. That millions of Jews could have been transported across Europe and killed at a wartime industrial centre as important as Auschwitz, and elsewhere, without Speer's knowledge simply defies belief. Such testimony by the men who were most familiar with Germany's overall Jewish policy is routinely dismissed as brazen lying. But the categorical and self-consistent nature of this testimony, sometimes by men, who knew that death soon awaited them, suggests a core of truth. On the other hand, to accept the Holocaust extermination story means giving greater credibility to the most fantastic and often demonstrably false testimonies by very questionable witnesses.

During the decades since Nuremberg, many individuals have been tried in Germany and other countries for alleged wartime participation in the extermination of the Jews. Rarely, if ever, has a defendant ever substantially challenged the Holocaust story. The accused invariably adopted the defence strategy successfully used by Speer at Nuremberg. He accepted the extermination story but denied or minimised his own personal involvement. To deny an extermination programme in trials that were organised on the working assumption that such a programme existed would have been judicial suicide.

Of the accused from the infamous first Nuremberg tribunal, the 'war criminals,' eleven were hanged and seven more received lengthy, or life prison terms. Hermann Goering, head of the Luftwaffe cheated his executioners by taking poison in his jail cell. It is likely that a sympathetic American guard helped Goering by smuggling the poison into his cell.

Operation Paperclip

This is the largely untold story of the Nazis that the banksters did not want to punish, as they were too valuable to them and is of course, yet another example of blatant, political double-standards in action.

So, throughout the time that the Nuremberg Trials were proceeding in Germany, supposedly to bring the 'evil Nazis' to justice, allegedly in order to demonstrate to the world that no one can escape the law, a large group of German rocket scientists arrived at Fort Bliss, Texas in 1946, including Wernher von Braun, Ludwig Roth and Arthur Rudolph. The group had been subdivided into two sections; a smaller one at White Sands Proving Grounds for test launches and the larger one based at Fort Bliss for research purposes. Many of these had previously worked in the development of the V-2 Rocket at Peenemünde, Germany and were brought to the US en masse, after WWII, subsequently working on various rocket projects including the Explorer 1 and Saturn rockets at NASA.

At the end of WWII, over 1,500 Nazis escaped prosecution for their war crimes and instead of a trial at Nuremberg the top German scientists were smuggled into the United States through Boston and West Palm, Florida in a top-secret programme known as Operation Paperclip. Some ended-up working for the CIA in projects such as *'MK Ultra'* and the LSD drug experiments of the 1960s, whilst others were assigned to *Wright Air Force Base* in Ohio, where they were placed in charge of the US *Military Flight Medicine Program*. Also, around one hundred of the German scientists were sent to Huntsville, Alabama to start the US rocket programme along with captured V-2 rockets; the rocket formerly used to terrorise South-eastern England during later stages of the war. Thus began America's secret space programme, headed by Wernher von Braun, who subsequently became the first director of NASA.

Of particular interest to the US government, were scientists specialising in aerodynamics and rocketry, such as those involved in the V-1 and V-2 projects, chemical weapons, chemical reaction technology, and medicine. These scientists and their families were secretly brought to the United States, without State Department review and approval and their previous service for Hitler's Third Reich, NSDAP and SS memberships, as well as the classification of many as war criminals or security threats were deliberately ignored.

Immediately after WWII ended, the United States and Russia started searching for German military and scientific secrets. They were not only looking for designs of new aircraft, weapons and rockets, but for the men and women that designed them, as well as the scientists who worked in the fields of chemistry medicine and physics. When the first batch of rounded-up scientists arrived in the United States, it was blatantly obvious that they knew more, much more than they had been given credit for. The original idea had been to interview them, debrief them and then send them back to Germany, but on discovering the full extent of their knowledge, the plans were immediately changed as they were quite simply, far too valuable to let go.

The War Department decided they would keep these men and women in the United States and learn from them in order to update and perfect techniques hitherto unknown or unsuccessful. This was a problem because US law expressly forbade official members of the Nazi party to live and work in the United States and most of the people in the group were Nazis. The President, Harry Truman, was convinced these scientists could not only help the United States get back on its feet after the war, but that they would put the US on a path that would enable it to become a technological and scientific superpower.

And so in September 1946, Project Paperclip was sanctioned by President Truman. This allowed selected scientists to be brought into the US and although Truman ordered that none of them should be Nazi Party members, all of those in authority knew that it would be impossible to find scientists with the knowledge that the United States coveted, and yet were not members of the party. As a paper exercise, all of the dossiers on those scientists that the *Joint Intelligence Agency* wanted to keep were sent to the Department of Justice, who predictably refused visas on the grounds that they were 'ardent Nazis.' However the director of the Intelligence agency, Captain Bosquet Wev, argued that they were more of a security risk if they were sent back than they would be if they stayed and so with the full knowledge of the CIA director and bankster puppet, Allen Dulles, the files of the scientists were re-written with no mention of their Nazi Party affiliation.

By 1955, more than 750 former-German scientists had obtained US citizenship most of whom held high status within the American scientific community. Not only had these people held Nazi Party membership, but some were former members of the Gestapo.

Allen Dulles went on to open a lab at McGill University in Montreal, Canada. The operation was headed by Dr. Ewan Cameron, a psychiatrist who had served at the Nuremberg Trials and who had full knowledge of what many of the German scientists had been involved in. Cameron conducted experiments that were directly from the notes made by the Nazi scientists. Electro-therapy was used, as was sleep deprivation, memory-implantation, memory-eradication and drug-induced thought-modification. Psychotropic drugs were administered to men and women in the armed forces and experiments conducted to test radiation thresholds of unsuspecting individuals.

It was at this point, having concluded that many of the techniques worked, that MK-ULTRA was born, closely followed by MK-DELTA, MK-SEARCH, MK-OFTEN and MK-NAOMI.

These projects continued unabated into the 1970s before being allegedly closed down, although there is much evidence suggesting that they continue to this day.

And then, just as all the bloodshed, intrigue and destruction wrought by the banksters' second world war, began to abate slightly, the world was about to be plunged into more abject terror, albeit of the psychological kind, in the shape of the 45-year, so called 'Cold War.' Between the two former 'allies,' the USA and the USSR...

And thus the stage was now set for a 'new and improved' bankster agenda of fear...

This concludes volume 1 of 'Behind the Curtain.' To learn how the banksters continued and even tightened their domination of the world's finances (and just about everything else) Please purchase Volume 2.

Printed in Great Britain
by Amazon